U.S. Forces Travel & Transfer Guide
EUROPE
and Near East Areas

by

William "Roy" Crawford, Ph.D.

and

Lela Ann Crawford

Editor: Bryce D. Thompson
Associate Editor: Pamela Greer
Assistant Editor: Bond A. Williams
Editorial Assistant: Richard O'Boyle
Cover Design: James Bullock
Interior Graphic Design: Bryce D. Thompson
Pamela Greer, James Bullock
Layout Artists: James Bullock, June Douglas

Marketing Manager: William R. Crawford, Jr.
Office Staff: Eula Mae Brownlee, Anna Belle Causey
Helen Henderson, Irene Kearney

Military Living Publications
P. O. Box 2347
Falls Church, Virginia 22042-0347
(703) 237-0203
FAX (703) 237-2233

NOTICE

The information in this book has been compiled and edited from the activity/facility listed, its superior headquarters or from other sources that may or may not be noted by the authors. Information about the facilities listed, including contact phone numbers, could change. This book should be used as a guide to the listed facilities with this understanding. Please forward any corrections or additions to: **Military Living Publications, P. O. Box 2347, Falls Church, Virginia 22042-0347.**

This directory is published by Military Marketing Services, Inc., a private business in no way connected with the U.S. Federal or any other government. This book is copyrighted by William Roy and Lela Ann Crawford. Opinions expressed by the publisher and authors of this book are their own and are not to be considered an official expression by any government agency or official.

The information and statements contained in this directory have been compiled from sources believed to be reliable and to represent the best current opinion on the subject. No warranty, guarantee or representation is made by Military Marketing Services, Inc., as to the absolute correctness or sufficiency of any representation contained in this or other publications and we can assume no responsibility.

**Copyright © 1989
William Roy Crawford and Lela Ann Crawford
First Printing May 1989**

**MILITARY MARKETING SERVICES, INC.
(MILITARY LIVING PUBLICATIONS)**

All rights reserved under international and Pan-American copyright conventions. No part of this book may be reproduced in any form without permission in writing from the publisher except by a reviewer who wishes to quote briefly from listings in connection with a review written for inclusion in a magazine or newspaper, with source credit to *MILITARY LIVING'S U.S. FORCES TRAVEL AND TRANSFER GUIDE EUROPE AND NEAR EAST AREAS.* A copy of the review, when published, should be sent to Military Marketing Services, Inc., P. O. Box 2347, Falls Church, Virginia 22042-0347.

Library of Congress Cataloging-in-Publication Data

```
Crawford, William Roy, 1932-
     U.S. forces travel & transfer guide.  Europe and Near East areas /
by William "Roy" Crawford and Lela Ann Crawford ; editor, Bryce D.
Thompson, associate editor, Pamela Greer, assistant editor, Bond A.
Williams.
     p.   cm.
     Includes index.
     ISBN 0-914862-21-9 : $13.95
     1. Military bases, American--Directories.  2. United States--Armed
Forces--Transportation.  3. Soldiers--United States--Recreation.
4. Military dependents--United States--Recreation.  5. United
States--Armed Forces--Recreation.   I. Crawford, Ann Caddell.
II. Thompson, Bryce D.  III. Title.  IV. Title: U.S. forces travel
and transfer guide.  V. Title: US forces travel & transfer guide.
UA26.A24  1989
355.7'025'73--dc20                                           89-9349
                                                                CIP
```

HOW TO USE THIS DIRECTORY

NAME OF INSTALLATION
City/APO/FPO, ZIP Code

Location Identifier: Example: GE01R7. The first two characters (letters) are country abbreviations used in **Military Living's** books (see Appendix M). The next two-character set is a random number (00-99) assigned to a specific location. The fifth character, an R, stands for Region. The sixth character indicates the location of the region. The location identifiers for each of the more than 140 listings in this book are keyed to country maps located at the beginning of each section devoted to a specific country.

Telephone Information: Civ: This is the installation's main or information/operator assistance telephone number accessed via the civilian/commercial telephone system. **ETS:** This is the installation's main or information/operator assistance telephone number accessed via the European Telephone System (ETS). **ATVN:** This is the Department of Defense worldwide Automatic Voice Network (ATVN) telephone number. The number given is, in most cases, for information/operator assistance. When dialing into the following geographic areas using the ATVN system, the following prefixes must be used: 312 (CONUS); 314 (Europe); 313 (Caribbean); 315 (Pacific); 317 (Alaska).

The **Telephone Information** section for many of the listings in this book, especially those in Germany, contains detailed information about civilian and military phone systems and prefixes and instructions for dialing from a civilian telephone to a military extension (where this capability exists). By way of example, the **Telephone Information** section for Ramstein Air Base in Germany looks like this:

Telephone Information: Main installation numbers: Civ: 49-06371-47-1110. ATVN/ETS: 480-1110. Civ prefix: 06371-_____. ATVN/ETS prefix: 480-XXXX. Civ to mil prefix: 06371-47-XXXX.

All Telephone Information sections for Germany and for certain installations in other countries with civilian to military dialing capabilities follow this same basic pattern. The main civilian number breaks down as follows: the first number (49 in this case) is the country code; the second number (06371 in this case) is the local area code; the next number (47 in this case) is the civilian to military conversion number; and the last number (1110 in this case) is the extension. **IMPORTANT: All local area codes in Germany (and several in other countries) begin with a "0". The zero is only used in country. If you are dialing from outside the country, drop the zero.** So, if you wanted to dial Ramstein from the U.S.A., you would dial 011 (the international access code from the U.S.A.)-49-6371-47-1110.

In Germany, if you are within the boundaries of the local area code, you will not need to dial the local area code when dialing a civilian number or a military number. To reach a civilian number, just dial the extension. To reach a military number, dial the military conversion number and the military extension.

IMPORTANT: Throughout this book, the extensions listed are **military numbers** unless preceded by a "C", in which case the extension is a civilian number and therefore does not require the military to civilian conversion number.

Newcomers to Europe should keep in mind that phone systems in the United

— iii —

HOW TO USE THIS DIRECTORY, continued

States are the best and most reliable in the world. They are also the easiest to use. Don't expect your knowledge of American phone systems, especially civilian phone systems, to be of much use to you in Europe. European phone systems can be quite baffling when first encountered. For instance, in the U.K., when dialing a particular location, the number you dial is determined not only by the location you are dialing to, but by the location you are dialing from. When calling someone from within the U.K., we recommend that you consult the local telephone directory or use operator assistance.

General Installation Information: This section contains information about host and tenant unit(s) stationed at the installation and their major missions. This section may also contain a list of abbreviations that are used in that particular listing only.

General City/Regional Information: This section frequently contains information about the history of the city/region in which the installation is located. It may also contain information about important historical sites in the area, museums, festivals, beaches, skiing opportunities and more.

The rest of the listing is divided into **Administrative Support, Logistical Support, Health and Welfare** and **Rest and Recreation** sections. Building numbers and locations, telephone numbers and days of operation (all of which are subject to change) are listed.

The **Appendices** contain information of interest and use to military personnel traveling through or transferring to Europe and the Near East. Appendices D and E, for example, contain information about support authorized active duty and retired personnel in European and Near Eastern countries and thus answer many of the questions most frequently asked by active duty and retired personnel. Appendix H is devoted to driving in Europe and the Near East. Appendix I, about Germany, contains information about gaining access to Berlin via all means of transportation. See the last two pages of the Table of Contents for the names of all the appendices.

A BRIEF WORD ABOUT TIPPING IN EUROPE: Tipping practices vary from country to country in Europe; however, the following categories of service personnel in the following countries expect to be tipped. Inquire locally about customary amounts. AUSTRIA, EGYPT, FRANCE, WEST GERMANY, GREAT BRITAIN, GREECE, ITALY, PORTUGAL and SPAIN—Waiters, Chambermaids, Bellhops and Baggage Porters, Doorman, Concierge, Taxicab Driver, Airport and Station Porter, Ladies' and Men's Room Attendant, Hairdresser, Theater Usher.

STANDARD EMERGENCY & SERVICE NUMBERS
FROM ALL ARMY DIAL TELEPHONES IN WEST GERMANY/BERLIN

EMERGENCY	DDD	ETS
Engineer	91	115
Fire	95	117
Ambulance/Hospital/Clinic	97	116
Military Police	98	114
SERVICE		
Operator	0	0 or 1110
European AUTOVON		314 or thru 112
CONUS AUTOVON		112
Booking	90	112
Information	92	113
Telephone Repair	96	119
Civilian Access	99	99

— iv —

CONTENTS

BAHRAIN

BA01R9 Bahrain Naval Support Unit 2

BELGIUM

BE03R7 Florennes Air Base 4
BE01R7 NATO/SHAPE Support Group and Chièvres Air Base 5

CYPRUS

CY01R9 Akrotiri Airport 10
CY02R9 Larnaca Airport 10

EGYPT

EG01R9 Cairo East Air Base Community 12

GERMANY (WEST) AND WEST BERLIN

GE59R7 Amberg Sub-Community 19
GE60R7 Ansbach Community 21
GE61R7 Aschaffenburg Community 25
GE39R7 Augsburg Community 28
GE90R7 Babenhausen Sub-Community 32
GE91R7 Bad Aibling Sub-Community 35
GE92R7 Bad Hersfeld Sub-Community 37
GE49R7 Bad Kissingen Sub-Community 39
GE01R7 Bad Kreuznach Community 41
GE02R7 Bad Tölz Community 45
GE34R7 Bamberg Community 47
GE03R7 Baumholder Community 50
GE07R7 Berchtesgaden Armed Forces Recreation Center 55
GE26R7 Berlin Community 58
GE50R7 Bindlach/Bayreuth Sub-Community 61
GE04R7 Bitburg Air Base 63
GE63R7 Böblingen/Sindelfingen Sub-Community 66
GE32R7 Bremerhaven Community 69
GE51R7 Butzbach Sub-Community 72
GE08R7 Chiemsee Armed Forces Recreation Center 74
GE64R7 Crailsheim Sub-Community 76
GE37R7 Darmstadt Community 78
GE65R7 Dexheim Sub-Community 82
GE66R7 Erlangen Sub-Community 84
GE05R7 Frankfurt Community 86
GE68R7 Friedberg/Bad Nauheim Sub-Community 92
GE35R7 Fulda Community 95
GE93R7 Garlstedt Sub-Community 98
GE10R7 Garmisch Armed Forces Recreation Center 100
GE46R7 Geilenkirchen Air Base 103
GE69R7 Germersheim Sub-Community 104
GE97R7 Giebelstadt Sub-Community 106

— v —

GERMANY (WEST) AND WEST BERLIN (Continued)

GE23R7 Giessen Community 108
GE06R7 Göppingen Community 110
GE11R7 Grafenwöhr Community (7th Army Training Command) 113
GE12R7 Hahn Air Base 116
GE13R7 Hanau Community 118
GE33R7 Heidelberg/Schwetzingen Community (CENTAG) 123
GE38R7 Heilbronn Community 128
GE70R7 Herzo Base Sub-Community 132
GE45R7 Hessisch-Oldendorf Air Station 134
GE71R7 Hohenfels Sub-Community 136
GE72R7 Illesheim Sub-Community 138
GE30R7 Kaiserslautern Community 140
GE14R7 Karlsruhe Community 145
GE75R7 Kitzingen Sub-Community 149
GE76R7 Lindsey Air Station 152
GE77R7 Ludwigsburg/Kornwestheim Sub-Community 154
GE41R7 Mainz Community 158
GE43R7 Mannheim Community 162
GE15R7 Munich Community 166
GE79R7 Nellingen Sub-Community 169
GE28R7 Neu-Ulm Community 172
GE44R7 Nürnberg/Fürth Community 175
GE42R7 Pirmasens Community 181
GE95R7 Prüm Air Station 184
GE24R7 Ramstein Air Base 185
GE96R7 Regensburg Sub-Community 189
GE80R7 Rheinberg Community 190
GE16R7 Rhein-Main Air Base 193
GE81R7 Schwabach Sub-Community 196
GE82R7 Schwäbisch Gmünd Sub-Community 198
GE17R7 Schwäbisch Hall Sub-Community 201
GE48R7 Schweinfurt Community 204
GE18R7 Sembach Air Base 208
GE19R7 Spangdahlem Air Base 211
GE20R7 Stuttgart Community 213
GE25R7 Tempelhof Central Airport 220
GE85R7 Vilseck Sub-Community 223
GE52R7 Wertheim Sub-Community 225
GE27R7 Wiesbaden Community 228
GE86R7 Wildflecken Community 232
GE31R7 Worms/Northpoint/Weierhof Community 234
GE21R7 Würzburg Community 237
GE87R7 Wüschheim Air Station 241
GE88R7 Zweibrücken Air Base 242
GE29R7 Zweibrücken Community 244

GREECE

GR01R9 Hellenikon Air Base 250
GR02R9 Iraklion Air Station 253
GR04R9 Nea Makri Naval Communication Station 257
GR05R9 Souda Bay Naval Air Facility (Crete) 259

— vi —

ICELAND

IC01R7 Keflavik Naval Station 261

ITALY

IT04R7 Aviano Air Base 265
IT11R7 Comiso Air Station (Sicily) 268
IT12R7 Decimomannu Air Base 270
IT16R7 Gaeta Naval Support Activity Detachment 273
IT13R7 La Maddalena Navy Support Office 275
IT10R7 Livorno (Camp Darby) Community 278
IT05R7 Naples Naval Support Activity 280
IT07R7 San Vito dei Normanni Air Station 282
IT01R7 Sigonella Naval Air Station (Sicily) 285
IT14R7 Vicenza Community 287

THE NETHERLANDS

NT02R7 Schinnen Community (AFCENT HQ) 291
NT01R7 Soesterberg Air Base 293

NORWAY

NO01R7 Oslo (Fornebu/Gardermoen) Community 297

PORTUGAL (AÇORES)

PO01R7 Lajes Field 299

SAUDI ARABIA

SA01R9 Dhahran Community 303
SA02R9 Jeddah Community 304
SA03R9 Riyadh Community 305

SPAIN

SP01R7 Moron Air Base 309
SP02R7 Rota Naval Station 310
SP03R7 Torrejón Air Base 313
SP04R7 Zaragoza Air Base 316

TURKEY

TU01R9 Ankara Air Station 320
TU06R9 Diyarbakir Airport 322
TU03R9 Incirlik Air Base (Adana) 323
TU09R9 Istanbul Support Group (Çakmakli Army Post) 326
TU04R9 Izmir Air Station 328
TU02R9 Sinop Army Field Station 331

UNITED KINGDOM

UK01R7 RAF Alconbury 334

UNITED KINGDOM (Continued)

UK12R7 RAF Bentwaters/Woodbridge 337
UK02R7 Brawdy Wales Naval Facility (Wales) 339
UK03R7 Burtonwood Community 341
UK04R7 RAF Chicksands 343
UK06R7 Edzell Naval Security Group Activity (Scotland) 345
UK11R7 RAF Fairford 347
UK05R7 RAF Greenham Common/Welford 350
UK18R7 High Wycombe Air Station 353
UK19R7 Holy Loch Naval Support Activity (Scotland) 355
UK07R7 RAF Lakenheath 357
UK21R7 London Naval Activity 360
UK29R7 RAF Machrihanish (Scotland) 361
UK22R7 Menwith Hill Station 362
UK08R7 RAF Mildenhall 363
UK24R7 Prestwick Airport (Scotland) 366
UK25R7 RAF St. Mawgan 367
UK26R7 RAF Sculthorpe 369
UK27R7 Thurso Naval Communication Station (Scotland) 370
UK09R7 RAF Upper Heyford/Croughton 371
UK28R7 West Ruislip Air Station 374
UK10R7 RAF Wethersfield 375

APPENDICES

Appendix A Before You Go...Travel Aids 377
Appendix B United States Embassies (E) and Consulates (C) in Selected Countries 380
Appendix C United Services Organization (USO) Europe and Near East Area Locations 384
Appendix D Support Authorized U.S. Military Active Duty Personnel and Their Families 386
Appendix E Support Authorized U.S. Military Retired Personnel and Their Families 387
Appendix F APO/FPO and Mail Information 388
Appendix G United States Military Cemeteries in Europe 390
Appendix H Driving in Europe and the Near East 390
  •Automobile Clubs in Selected European/Near East Countries 390
  •International Driving Permits (IDP) 393
  •International Insurance Card (IIC) ("Green Card") 393
  •International Traffic Signs 394
  •Border, Insurance and License Requirements 395
  •U.S. Forces Gas Coupon Sales 395
  •Gasoline Coupons on the Autobahn 396
  •Allgemeiner Deutscher Automobile-Club (ADAC) 396
  •Who Can Drive Your Vehicle? 396
  •Tunnels and Toll Roads 397
  •Automobile Terms for Travelers 397
  •European Traffic and Safety Regulations 398
  •AAFES Garages Near the Autobahns in Germany 399
  •AAFES/Germany Autobahn Gas Station Map 400
  •Italy Gas Station Map 402
  •The Netherlands Gas Station Map 403
  •Tunnel Routes to Southern Europe 404

— viii —

Appendices (continued)

- •Ferry Route Maps 405
  - —Main Ferry Routes Crossing the Channel 405
  - —Main Ferry Routes to the North 405
  - —Main Ferry Routes Crossing the Eastern Mediterranean . 406
  - —Main Ferry Routes Crossing the Western Mediterranean . 406

Appendix I Germany 407
- •Access to Berlin 407
- •Bremerhaven—Getting There and Picking Up Your Car ... 408
- •Rail Travel in Germany 408
- •Update on German Traffic Laws 409
- •Canadian, French and United Kingdom Exchanges 409

Appendix J Radio and Television Service 411
- •American Forces Network (AFN) Locations and Radio Frequencies 411
- •AFN Radio Trouble Numbers 412
- •AFN TV Network Channel Information 413
- •AFN Television Trouble Numbers 414
- •Southern European Broadcasting Service in Italy 415

Appendix K Conversions of Weights, Measures, Temperatures and Clothing Sizes 416
Appendix L Electric Current/Service Connections in Selected Countries .. 418
Appendix M State, Country and General Abbreviations 420
Appendix N Articles From Military Living's *R&R Space-A Report* 423

Central Order Coupons 425, 429, 431
Moving to Washington Coupon 427

— ix —

DEDICATION

U.S. FORCES TRAVEL and TRANSFER GUIDE EUROPE and Near East Areas is dedicated to the hundreds of military personnel who responded to our requests for information needed to compile this morale boosting book. Without their cooperation, this book would not have been possible.

The list is long and includes the Public Affairs Offices of Headquarters (Hq.), Department of the Army; Hq., Department of the Navy; and Hq., Department of the Air Force in Washington.

In addition, we thank the Public Affairs Offices of Hq., U.S. Army Europe; Hq., U.S. Navy Europe; and Hq., U.S. Air Force Europe.

On the local level, we thank the Community Leader's Offices, Public Affairs Offices, the staff and volunteers of Army Community Services, Navy Family Services and Air Force Family Services offices in Europe and the Near East.

Other organizations which were most helpful were the Army and Air Force Exchange Service, the Navy Resale System, The American Forces Network Europe and the Southern European Broadcasting System. Also, we thank the United Services Organization (USO), the U.S. Battle Monuments Commission, the USAREUR Class VI Agency and Stars and Stripes, Europe.

Especially helpful were the Allgemeiner Deutscher Automobile Club (ADAC) (German Automobile Club), and numerous other country automobile clubs.

NOTICE

There are hundreds of thousands of data points in this book. Please let us know if we left out any military community. Also, please report any changes in phone or building numbers and information about openings or closures of facilities on military installations to Military Living Publications, P.O. Box 2347, Falls Church, VA 22042-0347. Information sent to us will be verified and published in new editions of this helpful guide. We thank you in advance for this courtesy!

U.S. Forces Travel & Transfer Guide Europe — 1

BAHRAIN /BA
State of Bahrain
Manama

Copyright © 1989 Military Living Publications

Bahrain, a group of 33 islands (only five of which are inhabited), is located in the Persian Gulf, northeast of Saudi Arabia. It is about four times the size of Washington, D.C. The population of 417,000 Bahrainis live in six cities and towns, are predominately Arab and speak Arabic. In 1971, after severing relations with the British government, a constitutional emirate assumed power. There are neither political parties nor suffrage. The late 1970s oil boom benefited Bahrain. It was one of the first Arab gulf states to discover oil and it had the first refinery. Sixty percent of its revenues and its exports are derived from petroleum and natural gas. Imports of machinery, industrial equipments, foodstuffs and clothing are received primarily from Japan, the U.K. and the U.S. The Bahraini work force is chiefly involved in industry, commerce and services. The infrastructure received considerable attention from oil boom profits and the airport is served by major international carriers. Bahrain is eight hours ahead of U.S. Eastern Standard Time (EST). Bahraini currency is the *Bahraini dinar*. Climate dictates summer clothing from May to mid-October and fall clothing otherwise. ALWAYS DRESS CONSERVATIVELY. A 25-kilometer causeway opened in 1986 links Bahrain with Saudi Arabia. Bahrain has English-language TV. Traditionally, relations with Bahrain have been excellent.
ENTRY REQUIREMENTS: Passport—yes. No tourist visas issued at this time. Transit visa available at Bahrain International Airport for temporary stay up to 72 hours, must have return/onward ticket. Check with the

BAHRAIN

Embassy of Bahrain, Washington, D.C. 20008, Tel: 202-342-0741/2, for further requirements. Immunizations—AF.

BAHRAIN NAVAL SUPPORT UNIT (BA01R9)
APO New York 09526-2800

TELEPHONE INFORMATION: Main installation numbers: Civ: 973-243-277. ATVN: 237-1110.

LOCATION: An island off the coast of Saudi Arabia in the Persian Gulf. NMC: Dhahran, SA, 30 miles northwest.

GENERAL INSTALLATION INFORMATION: General administrative and support unit for U.S. Navy ships in the Persian Gulf.

GENERAL CITY/REGIONAL INFORMATION: Bahrain is an island state off the coast of Saudia Arabia.

LOGISTICAL SUPPORT

FACILITY/ACTIVITY	BLDG NO/LOC	PHONE	DAYS/COMMENTS
Credit Union	On Base	1067	M-Sa
Education Center	On Base	727-828	Sa-W
Food(Caf/Rest)	On Base	1051	Daily
Food(Snack/Fast)			
Pizza Parlor	On Base	1030	Daily
Package Store	On Base	1050	M-Sa
Space-A Air Ops	Dhahran IAP 5 mi W of Dhahran	C-966-3-891-5678	Daily
Flights to:	Athinai Arpt GR; Jeddah Airfield SA; Ramstein AB GE; Rhein-Main AB GE.		

REST AND RECREATION

FACILITY/ACTIVITY	BLDG NO/LOC	PHONE	DAYS/COMMENTS
NCO Club	On Base	1053	Daily
O'Club	On Base	1051	Daily
Recreation Center	On Base	1066	Daily

BELGIUM
Kingdom of Belgium
Brussels

Copyright © 1989 Military Living Publications

Bordered on the northwest by the North Sea and wedged in between France and the Netherlands, Belgium is about the size of Maryland. With a high population density of 9.9 million, Belgians are principally divided between the Dutch-speakers (Flemish), and the French-speakers (Walloons), historically causing a significant political rivalry. Government is based on parliamentary democracy under a constitutional monarch. Voting is compulsory for those over 18 years of age. Coal resources have resulted in a highly industrialized economy based on exports of machinery, iron and steel, food, livestock and chemicals. Major imports are raw materials and components. The work force is primarily employed in service and transportation, industry and commerce and public service. Currency is *Belgian francs*. Public transportation, telecommunications and the highway system are excellent. Belgium is five hours ahead of the U.S. (EST). The climate approximates our Pacific northwest. Well known for its lace, chocolates, diamonds, tapestries and 300 varieties of beer, Belgium also entices visitors with several North Sea resorts (try mussels and gray shrimp), the Ardennes Forest and museums abounding with masters' works dating from the Middle Ages. Law requires pharmacy service availability at all times—locations are published in the newspaper. Belgium hosts both The North Atlantic Treaty Organization (NATO), located in Brussels, and the Supreme Headquarters Allied Powers Europe (SHAPE), located in Mons, and enjoys excellent relations with the United States.

4 — *U.S. Forces Travel & Transfer Guide Europe*

BELGIUM

ENTRY REQUIREMENTS: Passport—yes. Visa—not required for business or tourist stay up to 90 days. Check with the Embassy of Belgium, Washington, D.C. 20008, Tel: 202-333-6900, for other requirements. Immunizations—EUR.

FLORENNES AIR BASE (BE03R7)
APO New York 09188-5000

TELEPHONE INFORMATION: 32-71-655560. ATVN: 791-3255/3244/3266.

LOCATION: Go east on BE-36 from Phillpeville in the direction of Dinant. Base entrance is ten miles ahead on the left. HE: p-36, F/3. NMC: Brussels, 50 miles north.

GENERAL INSTALLATION INFORMATION: The 485th Tactical Missile Wing of the U.S. Air Force is located at Florennes, a Belgian air base. The wing provides tactical missile support to NATO forces. Note: all services are located at or in the vicinity of the Air Base. Services not provided by the U.S. are provided by the Belgian Air Force.

GENERAL CITY/REGIONAL INFORMATION: Florennes is located near the French border amidst rolling countryside with good high-speed roads and railway service.

ADMINISTRATIVE SUPPORT

FACILITY/ACTIVITY	BLDG NO/LOC	PHONE	DAYS/COMMENTS
Personnel Spt	On Base	C-6552434	M-F
Public Affairs	On Base	C-689961	M-F

LOGISTICAL SUPPORT

FACILITY/ACTIVITY	BLDG NO/LOC	PHONE	DAYS/COMMENTS
Barber Shop(s)	Dorm 3	C-655490	N/A
Beauty Shop(s)	Dorm 3	C-655490	N/A
Bookstore	G-123	C-655442	M-Sa
Exchange(Main)	On Base	C-655442	Daily
Finance(Mil)	On Base	C-65537	M-F
Food(Snack/Fast)	AAFES	C-655442	M-F
Pizza Parlor	On Base	C-655363	Daily
Laundry(Self-Svc)	On Base	N/A	M-F
Postal Svcs(Mil)	G-4	C-655220	M-F
SATO-OS	Base J, Offenburg	C-687125 ext. 410	M-F
Travel Agents	G-128	C-655411	M-F

HEALTH AND WELFARE

FACILITY/ACTIVITY	BLDG NO/LOC	PHONE	DAYS/COMMENTS
Chaplain	Chapel	C-655207	M-F
Medical Emergency	On base	3244/3245	Daily

Florennes Air Base, continued

BELGIUM

REST AND RECREATION

FACILITY/ACTIVITY	BLDG NO/LOC	PHONE	DAYS/COMMENTS
Enlisted Club	On Base	C-655506	Daily

NATO/SHAPE SUPPORT GROUP AND CHIÈVRES AIR BASE (BE01R7)
APO New York 09088-5000 (SHAPE)
APO New York 09088-5000 (Chièvres Air Base)

TELEPHONE INFORMATION: Main installation numbers: Civ: 32-065-44-5500 (SHAPE); 32-068-28-3171 (Chièvres Air Base). ETS: 423-5500 (SHAPE); 431-3171 (Chièvres Air Base). Civ prefix: 065-XXXX (SHAPE); 068-XXXX (Chièvres Air Base). ETS prefix: 423-XXXX (SHAPE); 431-XXXX (Chièvres Air Base). Civ to mil prefix: 065-44-XXXX (SHAPE); 068-28-XXXX (Chièvres Air Base).

LOCATION: The air base is located off BE-56 in the village of Chièvres. To reach NATO/SHAPE Headquarters, take the E-10 north from Paris to the Mons exit and follow signs. HE: p-35, E/3. NMC: Mons, 4 miles southeast of SHAPE and 20 miles southeast of the air base.

GENERAL INSTALLATION INFORMATION: Chièvres Air Base is located about 10 miles from SHAPE Headquarters. Chièvres is a small U.S.-operated air base where military members are assigned to the following: Det 1, 52nd Tactical Fighter Wing (TFW); Headquarters Command; Flight Detachment, Det 1, 55th Aeromedical Flight Airlift Squadron (SACEUR Flight Section); Provost Marshal (U.S.) (NSSG); and Det C, 527th Military Intelligence Battalion.

NATO/SHAPE's (North Atlantic Treaty Organization/Supreme Headquarters Allied Powers Europe) primary mission is to provide personnel, administrative and logistical support to its various commands and to support a wide variety of U.S. organizations located within its jurisdictional boundaries. Note: the following abbreviations are used in this listing only: CH (Chièvres); CD (Caserne Daumerie located at the air base); AB (Chièvres Air Base); SH (NATO/SHAPE Hq).

GENERAL CITY/REGIONAL INFORMATION: Mons is the capital of the industrial province of Hainaut, yet it still maintains its original charm. The 15th-century Gothic architecture of the church of St. Waudru and the 17th-century architecture of the Belfry Tower are of great interest as is the interior of the 15th-century town hall. Don't forget to kiss or stroke the famous "Monkey of the Grand-Garde" at the hall's main entrance—it brings good luck!

The museum of the Chanoine Puissant with its lovely art collection and the Centenaire Museum with its fine examples of glass and pottery are both well worth a visit as are the other museums, churches, open-air markets, parks and gardens in the city.

Although Belgium itself offers numerous sightseeing opportunities, it is also

6 — U.S. Forces Travel & Transfer Guide Europe

BELGIUM
NATO/SHAPE Support Group, continued

ideally located for trips to other European countries. From SHAPE and Chièvres Air Base, you can reach Paris in two and a half hours, Amsterdam in three hours and Frankfurt in five. A journey to England by car and ferryboat takes only five hours.

ADMINISTRATIVE SUPPORT

FACILITY/ACTIVITY	BLDG NO/LOC	PHONE	DAYS/COMMENTS
Advocate	318/SH	4910	M-F
Customs/Duty	220/SH	4217	M-F
Duty Officer	30/CD	5410	Daily
Fire(Mil)	SHAPE	3333	24 hours daily
Fire(Civ)	Mons	100	24 hours daily
Info(Insta)	318/SH	4332	Daily
	30/CH,CD	5419	Daily
Inspector Gen'l	30/CH,CD	5280	M-F
Legal Assist	318/SH	4910	M-F
Locator(Mil)	208/SH	5155(Army)	Daily
	208/SH	4880(AF)	Daily
	208/SH	4818(Navy)	Daily
Locator(Civ)	Mons	C-346087	M-F
Personnel Spt	208/SH	5343	M-F
Police(Mil)	SHAPE	3333	Daily
	CH	5511	Daily
Police(Civ)	Mons	101	24 hours daily
Public Affairs	30/CH,CD	5419	N/A

LOGISTICAL SUPPORT

FACILITY/ACTIVITY	BLDG NO/LOC	PHONE	DAYS/COMMENTS
Auto Drivers Testing	220/SH	4571	M-F
Auto Parts(Exch)	304/SH	C-311402	Daily
	AB	7575	M-F
Auto Registration	210/SH	5147	M-F
Auto Rent(Other)	330/SH	C-348593	Daily
Auto Repairs	304/SH	C-311402	Daily
Auto Sales	330/SH	C-348593	Daily
Auto Ship(Gov)	208/SH	4313	M-F
Auto Wash	304/SH	C-311402	Daily
Bank	506/SH	C-311706	Tu-Sa
	102/SH	5463	M-F
Barber Shop(s)	102/SH	5498	M-F
	504/SH	C-311720	Tu-Sa
Beauty Shop(s)	504/SH	C-311720	Tu-Sa
Bookstore	102/SH	C-311002	M-F
	504/SH	C-311774	Tu-Sa
Bus	220/SH	4514	M-F
Child Care/Dev Ctr	602/SH	4810	Daily
Clothing Sales	PX/AB	5466	M-F
Commissary(Main)	AB	5344	Tu-Sa
Dry Clean(Exch)	AB	8230	Tu-Su
	506/SH	C-354729	Tu-Su
Education Center	212/SH	5173	M-F
Learning Center	SH	3309	M-F
Elec Repair(Civ)	AB	5305	M-F

U.S. Forces Travel & Transfer Guide Europe — 7

BELGIUM

NATO/SHAPE Support Group, continued

Exchange(Main)	15/AB	5305	Tu-Sa
Exchange(Concess)	AB	C-658247	N/A
Finance(Mil)	212/SH	5397	M-F
Food(Snack/Fast)	550/SH	5402	Daily
Pizza Parlor	502/SH	4998	Daily
Laundry(Exch)	AB	N/A	Tu-Sa
Laundry(Self-Svc)	505/SH	C-354729	M-F
Motor Pool	220/SH	4514	M-F
	Hangar 6/AB	5442	M-F
Package Store	506/SH	5368	M-Sa
Parking	SH and AB	N/A	Daily. Long term.
Photo Laboratory	102/SH	4389	M-F
	12/CD	5470	N/A
Postal Svcs(Mil)	102,504/SH	N/A	Tu-Sa
	58/AB	N/A	Tu-Sa
Postal Svcs(Civ)	102,504/SH	N/A	Tu-Sa
SATO-OS	208/SH	4313	M-F
Schools(DOD Dep)			
Elementary	703/SH	5284	M-F
High School	706/SH	5277	M-F
Svc Stn(Insta)	304/SH	C-311402	Daily
Svc Stn(Autobahn)	Many in area		
Space-A Air Ops	Base Ops/AB	2234	Daily
		C-223171	
Protocol Svc	Base Ops/AB	2234	Daily
		C-223171	
Flights to:	Ramstein AB GE.		
Tailor Shop	AB,CH	N/A	M-F
Tel Booking Oper	SH	7111	N/A
	CH	C-283171	N/A
Tel Repair(Gov)	SH	4567	N/A
Thrift Shop	207/SH	4945	M-F
TML			
Guest House	Hotel Raymond/ Mons	C-311131/32	Daily. Across from train station.
Travel Agents	102/SH	5524	M-F. BBL Travel
	506/SH	C-340671	M-F. BBL Travel
	506/SH	5354	M-F. ITT.

===
HEALTH AND WELFARE
===

FACILITY/ACTIVITY	BLDG NO/LOC	PHONE	DAYS/COMMENTS
Ambulance	SH	C-445868	Daily. Duty hours.
	SH	C-445820	Daily. After hours.
	SH	C-445822	Daily. After hours.
Army Comm Svcs	318/SH	C-444332	M-F
Army Emerg Relief	318/SH	C-4887	Daily
Central Appts	401/SH	C-445831	M-F
CHAMPUS Office	401/SH	5853	M-F
Chaplain	601/SH	4430	Daily
	CD	5381	Daily
Chapel	East Chapel/SH	4630	Daily
	13/CD	N/A	Daily
Comm Drug/Alc Ctr	24/CD	5486	M-F
Dental Clinic	SH	C-445806	M-F
	AB	5506	M-F

Belgium
NATO/SHAPE Support Group, continued

Medical Emergency	401/SH	C-445820	24 hours daily
Mental Health	401/SH	5803	M-F
Poison Control	Emerg Rm/SH	C-445820	24 hours daily
Red Cross	318/SH	4008/5131	M-F
Veterinary Svcs	30/AB	5253	M,Tu,Th

REST AND RECREATION

FACILITY/ACTIVITY	BLDG NO/LOC	PHONE	DAYS/COMMENTS
Aero/Flying Club	SH	4509	N/A
Amer Forces Ntwk	318/SH	4121	N/A
Bowling Lanes	502/SH	4998	Daily
Craftshops			
Automotive	314/SH	4693	Tu-Su
Ceramics	209/SH	4680	Sa-Th
Leather	209/SH	4680	Sa-Th
Multi-crafts	209/SH	4680	Sa-Th
Photography	209/SH	4680	Sa-Th
Wood	209/SH	4680	Sa-Th
Enlisted Club	303/SH	4954	N/A
Golf Course	SH	3499	N/A
Gymnasium	SH	4405	Daily
Info Tour & Travel	3/CD	5300	N/A
Library	509/SH	4674	Tu-Su
	3/CD	5300	Tu-Su
NCO Club	307/SH	5313	N/A
O'Club	903/SH	5451	N/A
Picnic/Park Area	Behind 602/SH	None	Daily
Racket Courts	Behind 602/SH	4405	Daily
Riding Club	SH	4917	Daily
Special Services	3/CD	5300	N/A
Sport Field	SH	None	Daily
Swimming Pool	Gym/SH	4405	Daily
Tennis Courts	Gym/SH	4405	Daily
Theater	207/SH	4257	Daily
	501/SH	5385	Daily
Video Rental	102/SH	5318	M-Sa
	505/SH	5352	M-Sa
Youth Center	503/SH	4213	Daily

CYPRUS
Republic of Cyprus
Nicosia

Copyright © 1989 Military Living Publications

Approximately the size of Connecticut, Cyprus is an island located in the eastern Mediterranean, configured of a central plain and north/south mountain ranges. Greeks comprise 77% of the Cypriot population of 617,000 which is rounded out by Turks and Armenians. Greek and Turkish are the official languages. Cyprus, long a site of Greek and Turkish conflict, is an independent, recognized republic, but its power extends only to the Greek Cypriot-controlled southern areas. The head of state is a Greek Orthodox archbishop. Suffrage is universal over age 21. In 1983, the Turkish Cypriots declared a separate republic and they control the north. Travel on the island is difficult, policies and procedures often change. Resources include minerals and lumber; exports consist of food, beverages, cement, clothing, shoes and cigarettes. Petroleum, consumer and agricultural products are imported. The work force is divided among services, industry, commerce, agriculture and public administration. Nearly half of the industry is based on tourism and services. Currency is the *Cyprus pound*. The climate approximates our southern Atlantic states and clothing needs are similar to those in Washington, D.C. Taxi and bus transportation is available, but country-wide travel is limited. Ferry service to Egypt, Lebanon, Syria, the Greek islands and Israel is available. Worldwide communication is excellent, but north to south telephone communications are non-existent. Cyprus is seven hours ahead of U.S. EST. Historic sights include three Crusader castles and the oldest ship ever raised from the sea, at Kyrenia Castle. The U.S. supports the Greek/Turk negotiation settlement and has made significant financial contributions, especially in the relief and rehabilitation areas.

10 — *U.S. Forces Travel & Transfer Guide Europe*

CYPRUS

ENTRY REQUIREMENTS: Passport—yes. Visa—no. Check with the Embassy of Cyprus, Washington, D.C. 20008, Tel: 202-462-5772, for further requirements. Immunizations—EUR.

AKROTIRI AIRPORT (CY01R9)
MAC Representative, Akrotiri, Cyprus

TELEPHONE INFORMATION: Main installation numbers: Civ: 357-51-Ask for MAC Representative or USDAO at Civ: 357-21-65151. ATVN: none.

LOCATION: On Cape Gata, Southern Coast, Island of Cyprus. At a UK RAF Base. HE: p-85, G/4. NMC: Limassol, 5 miles northeast.

GENERAL INSTALLATION INFORMATION: The U.S. military presence at Akrotiri is limited to a MAC representative at the airport. The airport serves as an RAF (UK) base.

GENERAL CITY/REGIONAL INFORMATION: Akrotiri is located on the southern coast of the island of Cyprus. Ferry service from the island is available to all neighboring countries

==
LOGISTICAL SUPPORT
==
FACILITY/ACTIVITY	BLDG NO/LOC	PHONE	DAYS/COMMENTS
Space-A Air Ops	At the airport. Dial the main number and ask for the MAC representative.		
Flights to:	Athinai Arpt GR; Iraklion AS GR.		
==

LARNACA AIRPORT (CY02R9)
MAC Representative, Larnaca, Cyprus

TELEPHONE INFORMATION: Main installation numbers: Civ: 357-41-ask for MAC representative or USDAO at Civ: 357-2-65151. ATVN: none.

LOCATION: On the south coast of the island of Cyprus. HE: p-85, G/3. NMC: Nicosia, 15 miles north.

GENERAL INSTALLATION INFORMATION: The U.S. military presence at Larnaca is limited to a MAC representative at the airport. The airport serves as an RAF (UK) base.

GENERAL CITY/REGIONAL INFORMATION: Larnaca is located directly south of the capital city Nicosia. Ferry service from the island is available to all neighboring countries.

==
LOGISTICAL SUPPORT
==
FACILITY/ACTIVITY	BLDG NO/LOC	PHONE	DAYS/COMMENTS
Space-A Air Ops	At the airport. Dial the main number and ask for the MAC representative.		
Flights to:	Sigonella Arpt IT.		
==

EGYPT
Arab Republic of Egypt
Cairo

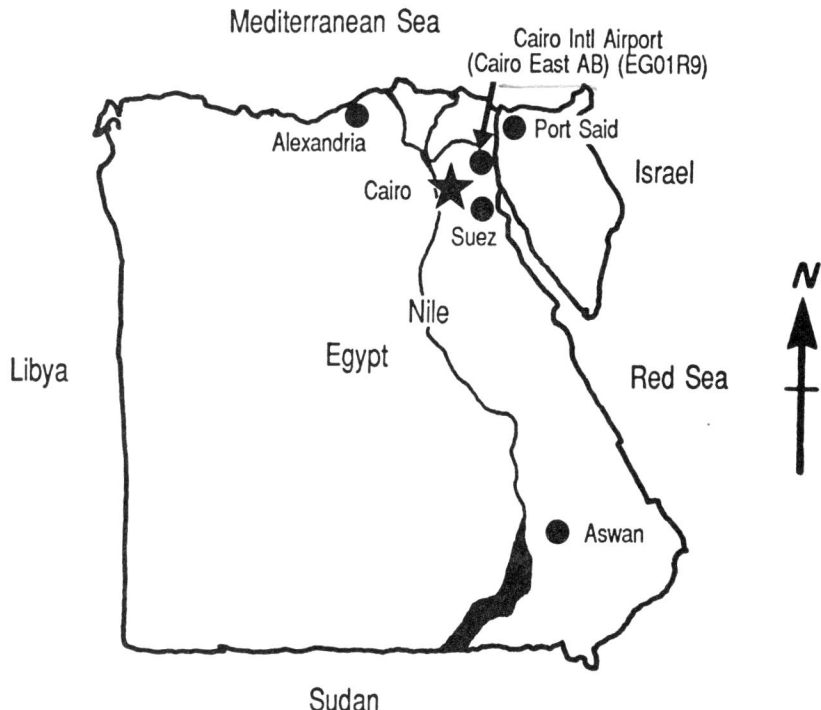

Copyright © 1989 Military Living Publications

Egypt, located in the northeast corner of Africa, is about 400,000 miles square—roughly the size of Texas, Oklahoma and Arkansas combined. It is the most highly populated Arab state with 50.5 million people, ninety-nine percent of whom live along the Nile Valley and Delta. Egyptians, Bedouin Arabs and Nubians comprise the population. Arabic is the official language. Egypt has been a unified state for 5,000 years and declared its independence from its last invader, the British, in 1922. It is a republic with universal suffrage over age 18. Natural resources include petroleum, natural gas and minerals with a strong agricultural base due to the Nile Valley products of cotton, rice, vegetables and citrus. Exports focus on petroleum products, cotton and manufactured goods. Imports are food, machinery and transportation equipment. The currency is the *Egyptian pound.* Over 60 percent of the work force is employed in agriculture and services. Transportation routes follow the Nile Valley pattern; the 2,800-mile rail network runs from Alexandria to Aswan. Adequate roads and a canal system provide interior transportation. Civilian airports are located in most major cities. Newspaper and broadcasting communication is well-developed, but telephone service is

12 — U.S. Forces Travel & Transfer Guide Europe

EGYPT

erratic. Egypt is seven hours ahead of U.S. EST. Clothing for hot summers and moderate winters is advised, and should be MODEST. Rabies and malaria hazards exist in outlying areas. Since the 1952 revolution, Egyptian-U.S. relations have fluctuated, but current president Mubarek has supported strong relations. U.S. economic aid has helped develop the economy and defense system.

ENTRY REQUIREMENTS: Passport and visa—yes. Tourist visa valid three months. Check with Embassy of Egypt, Washington, D.C. 20008, Tel: 202-234-3903, for other requirements. Immunizations—AF.

CAIRO EAST AIR BASE COMMUNITY (EG01R9)
FPO New York 09527-5000

TELEPHONE INFORMATION: American Embassy numbers: Civ: 202-355-7371. ATVN: 895-1456.

LOCATION: Located at the Cairo East International Airport opposite from the airport terminal. The host nation (Egyptian) air base is on the east side of the Nile River and is approximately 75 miles west of the Gulf of Suez. NMC: Cairo, 9 miles southwest.

GENERAL INSTALLATION INFORMATION: The American military community in Cairo is comprised of the Military Airlift Command, OL-W 322 ALD; the American Embassy; and the Office of Military Cooperation (OMC) located at the Embassy. The Embassy's address is 5 Sharia Latin America, Garden City, Cairo, Egypt. Or write to the Embassy at FPO New York 09527.

Be advised that all visitors must have a passport and a visa. A tourist visa is valid for three months and is available at the Cairo IAP. Expect a one to two hour delay when applying for your visa. All tourists need to have an in-country sponsor prior to arrival. A spokesperson for the Egyptian Embassy in Washington says that simply having a hotal reservation amounts to having an in-country sponsor. All persons wishing to visit Egypt are advised to coordinate their arrival with the OMC at the Embassy on extension 3635 since access to Cairo East AB can only be accomplished with the OMC's involvement or with the involvement of the Chief, OL-W, 322 ALD at Cairo AB on extension 3212.

GENERAL CITY/REGIONAL INFORMATION: Cairo is a large metropolitan city with a population in excess of 18 million people. The famous Pyramids are a short drive from the city. Many museums containing relics from Egypt's long history are in and around the city, as are many bazaars, shops, restaurants, and cafés.

LOGISTICAL SUPPORT

FACILITY/ACTIVITY	BLDG NO/LOC	PHONE	DAYS/COMMENTS
Bank	Embassy	7371	N/A
Commissary(Main)	Zahra Bldg	C-00202-983459	N/A
	Embassy	2592/2582	Th-M
Credit Union	Embassy	7371	N/A
Package Store	Embassy	7371	N/A
Postal Svcs(Mil)	Embassy	7371	N/A
Space-A Air Ops	Pax Term	3212	N/A

Cairo East Air Base Community, continued   EGYPT

Pax Lounges(Gen'l)	Pax Term	As above	Sa-Th
Flights to:	Ramstein AB GE.		
Taxi(Comm)	Cairo IAP	Approximately $5 to Cairo	

HEALTH AND WELFARE

FACILITY/ACTIVITY	BLDG NO/LOC	PHONE	DAYS/COMMENTS
Dental Clinic	Embassy	7371	N/A
Medical Emergency	Embassy	7371	24 hours daily

REST AND RECREATION

FACILITY/ACTIVITY	BLDG NO/LOC	PHONE	DAYS/COMMENTS
Consolidated Club	Embassy	7371	N/A

Note: Space available travel for authorized individuals who are not stationed in, or TDY to, Egypt is limited to those individuals with in-country sponsorship by a U.S. agency or official U.S. individual assigned to Egypt. All personnel requesting Space-A transport to Cairo, who are not assigned or TDY to Cairo, will require a sponsor letter. Passengers will not be allowed to sign up for Cairo without all border clearance documentation.

Military personnel on leave traveling on MAC aircraft must have written permission from the Deputy Chief—Office of Military Cooperation (OMC), Cairo, prior to travel. Requests should include names, passport numbers, types of passport, expiration dates or visas, proposed arrival/departure dates and local sponsor's name, address and telephone number. Requests for permission should be addressed to: Office of Military Cooperation, c/o American Embassy Cairo, Box 29, FPO New York 09527-5000. Questions should be directed to the OMC at ATVN: 895-1456 ext. 3157/3566. Sponsor's must be present at Cairo East Air Base when the sponsored traveler arrives and departs.

Passengers arriving without visas will be required to purchase them at the airport for $12.00 (subject to change). Travelers must register their passports with the police if their stay exceeds six days. Uniforms must not be worn for Space-A travel to/from Eqypt in accordance with the Foreign Clearance Guide.

GERMANY (WEST) AND WEST BERLIN
Federal Republic of Germany
Bonn

Copyright © 1989 Military Living Publications

U.S. Forces Travel & Transfer Guide Europe — 15

GERMANY

Locations of military communities and air bases in the German States of Hessen, Rheinland-Phalz, Baden and Bavaria are pinpointed on the following maps.

HESSEN

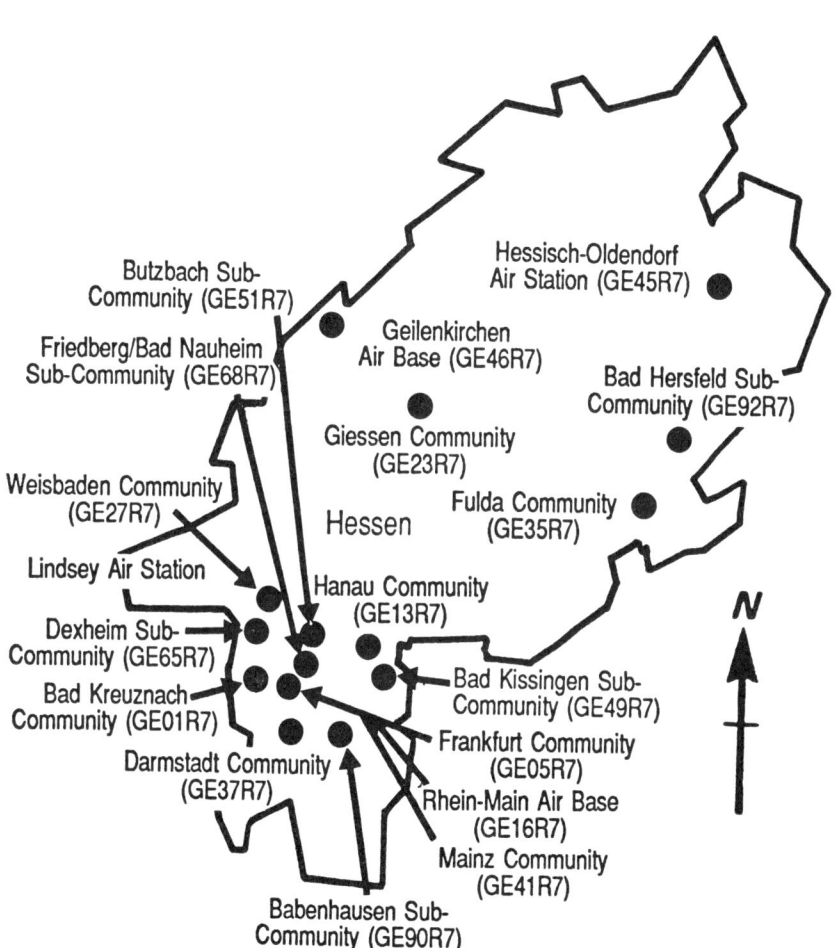

Copyright © 1989 Military Living Publications

16 — U.S. Forces Travel & Transfer Guide Europe

GERMANY

RHEINLAND-PHALZ

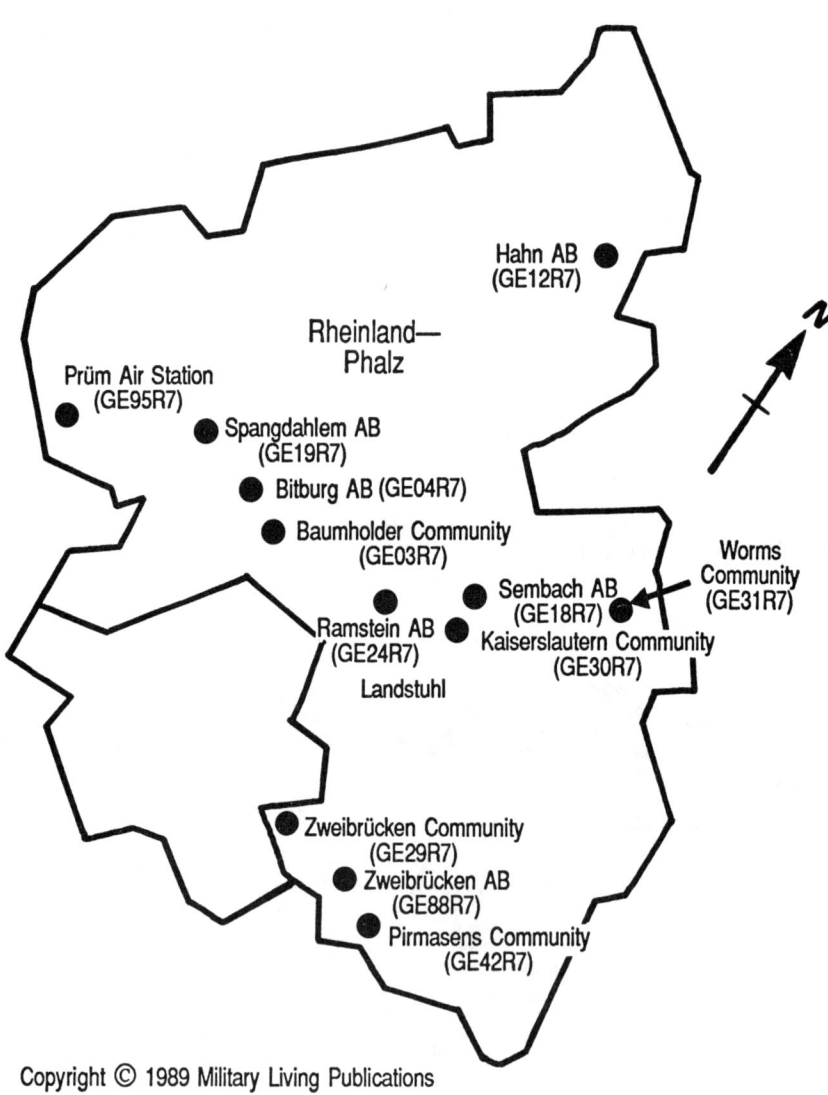

U.S. Forces Travel & Transfer Guide Europe — 17

GERMANY

BADEN

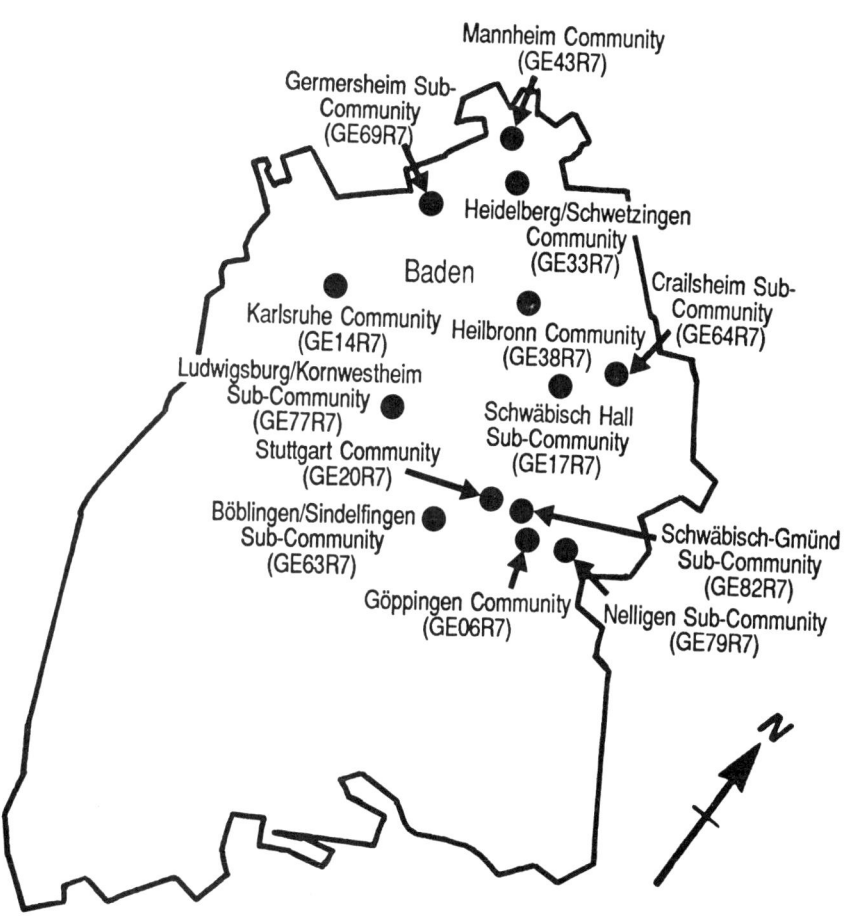

Copyright © 1989 Military Living Publications

GERMANY

BAVARIA

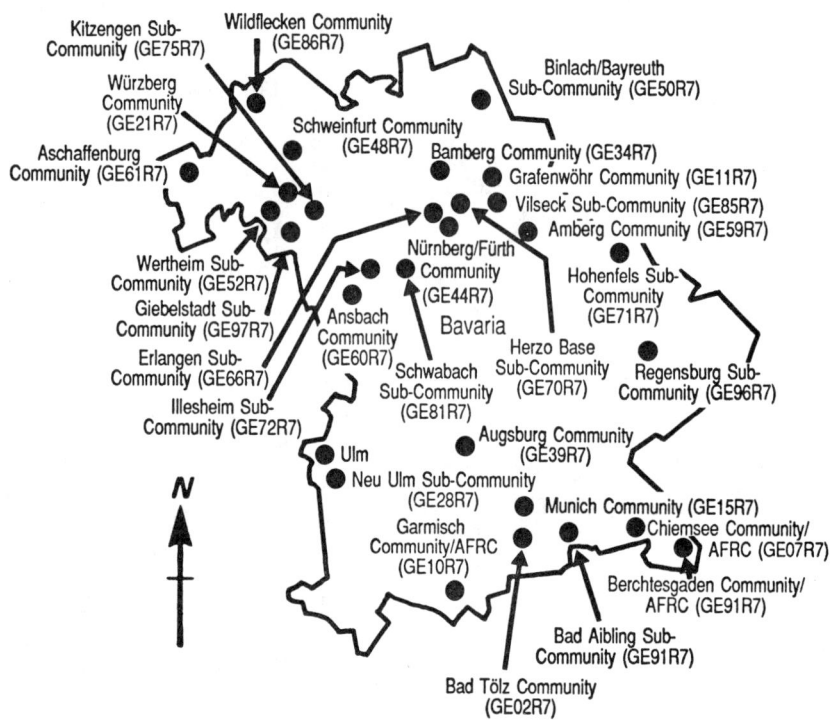

Copyright © 1989 Military Living Publications

About the size of Wyoming, West Germany borders Denmark and the North Sea on the north. Belgium, the Netherlands, Luxembourg, Switzerland and Austria surround its west side and Czechoslavakia and East Germany border it on the east. It also includes West Berlin, which is totally surrounded by East Germany. West Berlin is a vibrant commercial and industrial hub with an exciting nightlife, excellent shopping and dining, and many world-renowned theaters and museums. Please see appendices for Berlin access information. The population of 61 million includes over four million guest workers, mostly from the Middle East. The national language is German. After World War II, the Allies' differences eventually resulted in the establishment of two separate German entities, the Federal Republic of Germany (West Germany/F.R.G.), and the German Democratic Republic (East Germany/G.D.R). In 1949, the F.R.G. was established as a parliamentary federal republic based on a democratic constitution. There is universal suffrage over age 18. Natural resources of iron, hard coal and natural gas have resulted in a heavily export-oriented economy of chemicals, vehicles, iron and steel production and clothing. Imports include food, petroleum,

GERMANY

manufactured and electrical products and clothing. Over 40 percent of the workforce is employed in commerce and industry with the remainder in services, government and agriculture. The currency is the *Deutsche mark*. Both domestic and international transportation and communication systems are excellent and the road system, famous for its high-speed autobahns, is extensive. Germany is five hours ahead of U.S. EST. The climate is temperate but generally cool, especially in summer. Germany is famous for its beer, food, cuckoo clocks, breathtaking scenery, high-tech automobiles and wine. Germany and the U.S. maintain close ties based on economics, politics, and defense.
ENTRY REQUIREMENTS: Passport—yes. Visa—Tourist/business visa not required for stay up to three months including West Berlin if stay is temporary. Check with the Embassy of West Germany, Washington, D.C. 20007, Tel: 202-298-4000 for further requirements. Immunizations—EUR.

AMBERG SUB-COMMUNITY (GE59R7)
APO New York 09452-5000

TELEPHONE INFORMATION: Main installation numbers: Civ: 49-09621-700-780/838. ETS: 476-5780/838. ATVN: 460-1110 (ask for Amberg). Civ prefix: 09621-____. ETS prefix: 476-5XXX. Civ to mil prefix: 09621-700-XXX.

LOCATION: Take the A-6 Autobahn east from Nürnberg, exit to E-12 northeast for six miles to Amberg, follow U.S. Forces signs to Pond Barracks. HE: p-40, G/2. NMC: Nürnberg, 38 miles southwest.

GENERAL INSTALLATION INFORMATION: Amberg is a sub-community of the 7th Army Training Command headquartered in Grafenwöhr.

GENERAL CITY/REGIONAL INFORMATION: Amberg lies on the Vils River in the eastern area of the Upper-Pfalz Jura Mountains. Amberg was first mentioned in the historical record in 1034. In 1242 it was mentioned as having city status. Since the Middle Ages, iron and coal mining have determined the city's economic development.

Sites to see include the Late Gothic Church of St. Martin and the enclosing city wall; the 11th century Church of St. George with its baroque ornamentation; the Late Gothic Town Hall; the local museum; the 15th-century Elector's Castle, now the office of the state council. The city is well known throughout the region because of the festival it hosts during the first week of July.

ADMINISTRATIVE SUPPORT

FACILITY/ACTIVITY	BLDG NO/LOC	PHONE	DAYS/COMMENTS
Fire(Mil)		117	24 hours daily
Housing			
Family	6	766	M-F
Unaccompanied	6	850	M-F
Referral	6	C-72757	M-F
Info(Insta)	6	780/838	N/A
Legal Assist	8	752	M-F
Police(Mil)	5	837	24 hours daily
Emergency		114	24 hours daily
Police(Civ)	N/A	C-890-0	24 hours daily
Public Affairs	8	752/801	M-F

20 — U.S. Forces Travel & Transfer Guide Europe

GERMANY
Amberg Sub-Community, continued

Tax Relief	26	878	M-F

LOGISTICAL SUPPORT

FACILITY/ACTIVITY	BLDG NO/LOC	PHONE	DAYS/COMMENTS
Auto Drivers Testing	N/A	749	M-F
Auto Registration	5	811	M-F
Bank	16B	741	N/A
		C-83140	
Bookstore	40	772	N/A
Child Care/Dev Ctr	6A	786/873	N/A
Commissary(Main)	16A	829/729	Daily
		C-71562	
Dining Facility	7	748	Daily
Education Center	6	812/779	M-F
Elec Repair(Gov)	N/A	115	N/A
Eng'r/Publ Works	14	819/743	N/A
Exchange(Main)	16A	800/791	N/A
		C-72824	
Food(Snack/Fast)	17	C-72823	Daily
McDonald's	N/A	C-12236	Daily
Laundry(Exch)	16A	841	N/A
Motor Pool	N/A	745/827	N/A
Pick-up Point	18	C-72752	N/A
Postal Svcs(Mil)	6	750	N/A
Schools(DOD Dep)			
Elementary	35	809/789	M-F
Space-A Air Ops	Airfield	744	Daily
Tailor Shop	N/A	C-72752	N/A
Tel Booking Oper	N/A	112	24 hours daily
Tel Repair(Gov)	N/A	119	N/A
TML			
Billeting	See Officers Club		
BOQ	50	783	Daily
Protocol Office	N/A	752	N/A

HEALTH AND WELFARE

FACILITY/ACTIVITY	BLDG NO/LOC	PHONE	DAYS/COMMENTS
Ambulance		116	24 hours daily
Army Comm Svcs	18	790/816	N/A
Central Appts	N/A	758	N/A
CHAMPUS Office	N/A	808	N/A
Chaplain	17	825	N/A
Chapel	N/A	725	N/A
Comm Drug/Alc Ctr	N/A	821	N/A
Dental Clinic	31	775	N/A
Medical Emergency	N/A	C-72825	24 hours daily
Red Cross	N/A	797	N/A

REST AND RECREATION

FACILITY/ACTIVITY	BLDG NO/LOC	PHONE	DAYS/COMMENTS
Amer Forces Ntwk	N/A	818/807	N/A

U.S. Forces Travel & Transfer Guide Europe — 21

GERMANY

Amberg Sub-Community, continued

Bowling Lanes	16	755	Daily
Craftshops			
Automotive	21	777	N/A
Multi-crafts	17	771	N/A
Enlisted Club	15	747	N/A
		C-82682	
Gymnasium	12	787	Daily
Info Tour & Travel	26	742	N/A
		C-72458	
Library	16C	774	N/A
NCO Club	16D	747	N/A
		C-82682	
O'Club	15	785	N/A
		C-72824	
Outdoor Rec Ctr	26	877	N/A
Recreation Center	16C	839	N/A
		C-72758	
Theater	16B	751	Call for schedule.
Youth Center	16A	757	N/A

==

ANSBACH COMMUNITY (GE60R7)
APO New York 09177-5000

TELEPHONE INFORMATION: Main installation numbers: Civ: 49-0981-183-113 (Ansbach); 49-09802-83-113 (Katterbach). ETS: 468-7113 (Bleidorn Kaserne and Barton Barracks); 468-8113 (Hindenburg Kaserne); 467-2113 (Katterbach and Bismark Kasernes). ATVN: 460-1110 (ask for Ansbach). Civ prefix: 0981-____ (Ansbach); 09802-____ (Katterbach). ETS prefix: 468-7XXX (Bleidorn Kaserne and Barton Barracks); 468-8XXX (Hindenburg Kaserne); 467-2XXX (Katterbach and Bismark Kasernes). Civ to military prefix: 0981-183-XXX (Ansbach); 09802-83-XXX (Katterbach).

LOCATION: Exit from Autobahn east or west to GE-14 or 13 north for four miles. Follow U.S. Forces signs to Katterbach Kaserne. HE: p-40, E/2. NMC: Nürnberg, 26 miles northeast.

GENERAL INSTALLATION INFORMATION: The Ansbach Community is home to the First Armored Division. The community's mission is to provide administrative, morale and welfare, security, law enforcement, logistic, and base operation support to authorized personnel of DOD tenant units and U.S. government sponsored activities in the Ansbach geographical area. Note: the following abbreviations are used in this listing only: AC (Ansbach Civilian); BaB (Barton Barracks); BisK (Bismark Kaserne); BlK (Bleidorn Kaserne); HK (Hindenburg Kaserne); KC (Katterbach Civilian); KH (Katterbach Heliport); KK (Katterbach Kaserne).

GENERAL CITY/REGIONAL: Ansbach (population 40,000) was first settled in the eight century and has enjoyed a colorful and interesting history. The city is well known for being the former residence of the Margraves of Brandenburg-Ansbach; their palace, built in the 14th century and remodeled many times, is the most popular sight in the city. Tours of the palace's 27 magnificent state rooms are conducted daily. The adjacent orangery and park are equally lovely. The Court House, City Hall, County and City Museums, and Prince's Mansion are but a few of the other special attractions of

GERMANY
Ansbach Community, continued

Ansbach. The "Bach Week Ansbach" musical festival, held on odd-numbered years and the "Rokokospiele" or Rococo Festival, held on even-numbered years, are both world famous.

Ansbach offers vacationers and residents a variety of sport and recreational activities. In addition, the city's central geographic location makes it an important crossroads of international highways and railroad lines.

ADMINISTRATIVE SUPPORT

FACILITY/ACTIVITY	BLDG NO/LOC	PHONE	DAYS/COMMENTS
Customs/Duty	5843E/BisK	896	M-F
Duty Officer	Community Ctr	811	Daily
Fire(Mil)	KH	795/822	24 hours daily
Fire(Civ)	HK	422	24 hours daily
Housing			
Family	5355/HK	429/779	M-F
Unaccompanied	5908/BisK	812	M-F
Referral	5355/HK	485/779	M-F
Info(Insta)	5510/KH	778/779	M-F
Inspector Gen'l	5402/HK	539/769	M-F
Legal Assist	5365/HK	828/337	M-Th
Locator(Mil)	5386/HK	425	M-Sa
Personnel Spt	5254/BaB	816/817	M-F
Police(Mil)	5378/HK	716/811	
Emergency		114	24 hours daily
Public Affairs	5377/HK	802	M-F
Tax Relief	5845/BisK	KC-8891	M-F

LOGISTICAL SUPPORT

FACILITY/ACTIVITY	BLDG NO/LOC	PHONE	DAYS/COMMENTS
Auto Drivers Testing	5730/HK	472	M-F
Auto Parts(Exch)	5401/HK	499	M-Sa
		AC-87768	
Auto Registration	5378/HK	488	M-F
Auto Rental(Exch)	5823/KH	KC-1621	M-Sa
Auto Repairs	5401/HK	499	M-Sa
Auto Sales	5823/KH	KC-1836	Tu-Sa. Ford.
	5823/KH	KC-8566	Tu-Sa. Chrysler.
Auto Ship(Gov)	5354/HK	800/881	M-F
Auto Ship(Civ)	5354/HK	800/881	M-F
Bank	5824/KH	758	M-Sa
		KC-671/672	
Barber Shop(s)	5257/BaB	KC-7256	M-F
	5204/BlK	KC-7210	M-F
	5373/HK	KC-88361	M-F
	5825/KH	KC-1270	M-Sa
Beauty Shop(s)	5825/KH	KC-8616	Tu-Sa
Bookstore	5204/BlK	N/A	M-F
	5406/HK	AC-88427	M-Sa
	5887/KH	KC-1890	Tu-Sa
Bus	5379/HK	756	M-F
Child Care/Dev Ctr	5090/BlK	648/846	M-F
	5984/KH	2828	M-Sa

Ansbach Community, continued

GERMANY

Clothing Sales	5401/HK	466	Tu-Sa
		AC-88326	
Commissary(Main)	5805/KH	825/840	Daily
Credit Union	5373/HK	763	M-Sa
		AC-88791	
Dining Facility	5392/HK	378	M-F
Education Center	5257/BaB	829/661	M-F
	5814/KH	817/847	M-F
	5401/HK	474/771	M-F
Learning Center	5257/BaB	830	M-F
	5203/BlK	669	M-F
	5843-E/BisK	712	M-F
Elec Repair(Gov)	See Engineers		
Eng'r/Publ Works	5358/HK	825	M-F
	Work Orders	115	24 hours daily
Exchange(Main)	5257/BaB	AC-7256	M-F
	5204/BlK	AC-7210	M-F
	5358/HK	AC-8187/88	Tu-Su
	5825/KH	KC-653	Tu-Su
Finance(Mil)	5254/BaB	684	M-F
Food(Caf/Rest)	5373/HK	AC-87846	Daily
Food(Snack/Fast)	5817/KH	KC-356	M-F
	5262/BaB	AC-7257	M-F
	5204/BlK	AC-7405	Daily
	5509/KH	638	Sa,Su
Baskin Robbins	5817/KH		M-Sa
Burger King	5988/KH	KC-691	Daily
Pizza Parlor	5817/KH	KC-267	Daily
Foodland	5257/BaB	AC-7256	M-F
	HK	AC-8187	M-F
Laundry(Self-Svc)	5299/BaB	AC-3787	Daily
	5387/HK	AC-3787	Daily
	5817/KH	AC-3787	Daily
Motor Pool	5379/HK	756/457	M-F
Package Store	5987/KH	838	Tu-Sa
		KC-1702	
Photo Laboratory	BisK	N/A	M-F
Pick-up Point	5257/BaB	AC-7256	M-F
	5204/BlK	AC-7210	M-F
	5358/HK	AC-87947-0	Tu-Sa
	5825/KK	KC-690	Tu-Sa
Postal Svcs(Mil)	5368/HK	725/425	M-F
	5805/KH	740	M-Sa
Postal Svcs(Civ)	Ansbach	AC-101	M-F
Schools(DOD Dep)			
Elementary	5507/KK	628/629	M-F
	5308/BaB	806/808	M-F
High School	5924/KK	808/809	M-F
Space-A Air Ops	Ansbach/	2758/2848	N/A
	Katterbach AAF		
Svc Stn(Insta)	5401/HK	449	M,F
		AC-87768	
Tailor Shop	5825/KH	KC-1449	Tu-Sa
	5257/BaB	AC-7256	M-F
	5358/HK	AC-8187	Tu-Sa

GERMANY
Ansbach Community, continued

Taxi(Comm)	Ansbach	AC-5005	Daily
Thrift Shop	5911/KH	534	Tu,W,Th
TML			
Billeting	5908/KK	756	Daily
	Deputy Cmdr/HK	437	After duty hours
BOQ	5908/KK	756	Daily

HEALTH AND WELFARE

FACILITY/ACTIVITY	BLDG NO/LOC	PHONE	DAYS/COMMENTS
Ambulance		116	24 hours daily
Army Comm Svcs	5083/BlK	664/840	M-F
	HK	424	M-F
Army Emerg Relief	5510/KH	778/779	M-F
Central Appts	5810/KH	700/619	M-F
CHAMPUS Office	5810/KH	717/879	M-F
Chapel	5819/KH	785/885	M-F
	BaB	646	M-F
	BlK	658	M-F
Comm Drug/Alc Ctr	5843-C/BisK	850/852	M-F
Dental Clinic	5810/KH	806/723	M-F
Medical Emergency	5810/KH	116	24 hours daily
Poison Control	See Medical Emergency		
Red Cross	5083/BlK	666/875	M-F
	HK	432/303	
	Emergency	113	24 hours daily
Veterinary Svcs	See Nürnberg Listing		

REST AND RECREATION

FACILITY/ACTIVITY	BLDG NO/LOC	PHONE	DAYS/COMMENTS
Amer Forces Ntwk	See Nürnberg Community listing.		
Bowling Lanes	5509/KH	638	Daily
	BaB	698	Daily
	HK	496	Daily
Craftshops			
Automotive	5262/BaB	662	Tu-Su
	BaB	698	Tu-Su
Ceramics	5207/BlK	627	Sa-W
Multi-crafts	5207/BlK	627	Sa-W
Photography	5817/KK	818/711	Sa-Th
	Rec Center/HK	502	Sa-Th
Wood	5207/BlK	627	Sa-W
Enlisted Club	BisK	KC-1715	Daily
Gymnasium	5250/BaB	683	Daily
	5200/BlK	617	Daily
	5371/HK	403	Daily
	5805/KK	771	Daily
Info Tour & Travel	5373/HK	747	M-F
		AC-85540	
Library	5083/BlK	601/820	Daily
		AC-183820	
	KK	857	Daily
MARS	5280/BaB	635/869	M-F
Museum	5817/KH	KC-832	M-F. 1st Armored.

U.S. Forces Travel & Transfer Guide Europe — 25

GERMANY

Ansbach Community, continued

NCO Club	5091/BlK	612	Tu-Su
		C-7480	
	BaB	AC-15818	Daily
	5370/HK	475	M-Sa
		AC-87900	
O'Club	5845/BisK	704	Daily
		KC-218	
Outdoor Rec Ctr	5262/BaB	600/889	M-Sa
Recreation Center	5372/HK	502	Daily
	Ansbach	755	Daily
Rod and Gun Club	5805/KH	792	M-Sa
		KC-354	
Theater	5389/HK	471	M-F
Video Rental	5845/BlK	N/A	Tu-Su
Video Club	5823/KH	KC-8566	Tu-Sa
Youth Center	5927/KH	632	Tu-Sa
		KC-7341	
	5110/BlK	N/A	Tu-Sa

===

ASCHAFFENBURG COMMUNITY (GE61R7)
APO New York 09162-5000

TELEPHONE INFORMATION: Main installation numbers: Civ: 49-06021-35-113. ETS: 323-113. ATVN: 320-1110 (ask for Aschaffenburg). Civilian prefix: 06021-____. ETS prefix: 323-XXXX. Civ to mil prefix: 06021-35-XXXX. Note: from a military phone on post, dial 99 and then the number to reach an off-post line.

LOCATION: From Frankfurt, take the A3 toward Würzburg. Take the Aschaffenburg West exit, which brings you on to the B8. Follow B8 into Aschaffenburg.

GENERAL INSTALLATION INFORMATION: The Aschaffenburg military community is comprised of the 3rd Brigade and VII Corps, whose job is to support and protect our NATO allies. The 3rd "Drive On" Brigade is one of the most modern in today's Army. Aschaffenburg is host to six battalions, three separate companies, and many other supporting detachments and activities provided by the division and the corps to include the military community staff. **Note: the following abbreviations are used in this listing only:** FK (Fiori Kaserne); GK (Graves Kaserne); JK (Jaeger Kaserne); RK (Ready Kaserne); SK (Smith Kaserne); SpMH (Spessart Manor Housing).

GENERAL CITY/REGIONAL: Aschaffenburg is a charming and beautiful city located around 30 miles southeast of Frankfurt on the right bank of the Main River at the foothills of the Spessart Mountains. Once a Roman outpost, this city has a proud history of more than 1000 years. The city's best known landmark is the Schloss Johannesburg, a 17th-century castle situated above the Main River. Although it was shelled during World War II, the castle has been painstakingly restored to its original splendor. The castle's museum and the Pompeiianum, a small castle nearby, are favorite attractions for visitors as are the free concerts during spring and summer and the beautiful Schönbusch Park just outside the city.

GERMANY
Aschaffenburg Community, continued

ADMINISTRATIVE SUPPORT

FACILITY/ACTIVITY	BLDG NO/LOC	PHONE	DAYS/COMMENTS
Customs/Duty	26/JK	7058/8905	M-F
Duty Officer	22/JK	7275	Daily
		C-22762	
Fire(Mil)	N/A	117	24 hours daily
		C-93815	
Fire(Civ)	N/A	C-96543	24 hours daily
Housing			
Family	26/JK	7187	M-F
Unaccompanied	26/JK	7187	M-F
Referral	26/JK	7187/8967	M-F
Info(Insta)	N/A	113	N/A
Legal Assist	301/GB	7318/8808	M-F
Locator(Mil)	N/A	7133/8833	24 hours daily
Personnel Spt	26/JK	8865/7359	M-F. Passport.
	26/JK	8928/7368	M-F. ID.
Police(Mil)	RK	8972/7288	24 hours daily
Emergency	RK	C-93815	24 hours daily
Police(Civ)	N/A	8940	24 hours daily
Public Affairs	RK	7252/8855	M-F
Tax Relief	4/JK	7303	M-F

LOGISTICAL SUPPORT

FACILITY/ACTIVITY	BLDG NO/LOC	PHONE	DAYS/COMMENTS
Audio/Photo Ctr	JK	C-96657	Daily
Auto Drivers Testing	2/JK	7262	M-F
Auto Registration	14/JK	7188	M-F
Auto Rental(Exch)	N/A	C-96250	N/A
Auto Rent(Other)	6/JK	C-95096	Budget
Auto Repairs	685	C-92313	M-Sa
Auto Ship(Gov)	26/JK	8061	M-F. Out going.
	26/JK	8187	M-F. In coming.
Bank	1/JK	8851/7125	M-Sa. Merchants.
		C-96349	
	401/RK	7210	M-F. Ltd service.
Barber Shop(s)	FK	None	M-F
	GK	None	M-F
	JK	C-25715	M-F
Beauty Shop(s)	JK	C-97358	M-Sa
Bookstore	12/JK	C-96642/	Tu-Su
		25642	
Child Care/Dev Ctr	17,21/JK	8809	M-F. Full day.
	38/JK	7156	M-F. Drop in.
Clothing Sales	JK	7392	Tu-Sa
Commissary(Main)	688 Rhon St	7171/8971	Daily
Credit Union	Andrews CU	7248	M-F
		C-91383	
Dry Clean(Gov)	202/SK	7005	M-F
Education Center			
Learning Center	FK	7335	M-F
	GK	7113	M-F

GERMANY

Aschaffenburg Community, continued

	BLDG	PHONE	DAYS
	JK	7080	M-F
	RK	7381/7092	M-F
	SK	7012	M-F
Elec Repair(Gov)	11/JK	2317/8800	M-F
Eng'r/Publ Works	11/JK	7386/8886	M-F
		8800	Emergency
Exchange(Main)	6/JK	9070	Daily
		C-25714	
Exchange(Annex)	GK	7304	M-F
		C-25704	
	FK	7378	M-Sa
		C-25978	
Exchange(Concess)			
Finance(Mil)	26/JK	7383/8942	M-F
Food(Caf/Rest)			
Food(Snack/Fast)			
Baskin Robbins	5/JK	N/A	Daily
Burger Bar	5/JK	C-96118	Daily
Burger King	669	C-90746	Daily
Pizza Parlor	FK	C-28902	Daily
Snack Bar	FK	C-91878	M-Sa
Foodland	JK	C-97656	Daily
Laundry(Self-Svc)	25/JK	None	Daily
Motor Pool	14/JK	7069/7193	M-F
Package Store	405/RK	7216	Tu-S
Pick-up Point	JK	7286	M-F
Postal Svcs(Mil)	RK	7133/8833	M-Sa
	2/JK	8833	M-Sa
Postal Svcs(Civ)	25/JK	C-33383	M-F
Schools(DOD Dep)			
Kindergarten	690 Rhon St	7334	M-F
Elementary	690 Rhon St	C-91878	M-F
High School	Hanau	322-8154	M-F
		C-06181-55711	
Svc Stn(Insta)	Rhon St	7169	M-Sa
		C-93214	
Space-A Air Ops	Airfield	7223	Daily
Flights to:	Local German areas		
Tailor Shop	FK	7378	M-F
	GK	8862	M-F
	JK	7286	M-F
Taxi(Comm)		C-23030	Daily
		C-21464	Daily
Tel Booking Oper	N/A	112	24 hours daily
Tel Repair(Gov)	N/A	119	N/A
Thrift Shop	202/SK	7362	M,W,F
TML			
Billeting	16/JK	7273	M-F
BEQ/BEQ	JK near O'Club	7273	Daily

==
HEALTH AND WELFARE
==

FACILITY/ACTIVITY	BLDG NO/LOC	PHONE	DAYS/COMMENTS
Ambulance	N/A	116/8929	24 hours daily
	N/A	C-29082	
Army Comm Svcs	26/JK	7165/8840	M-F

GERMANY
Aschaffenburg Community, continued

Army Emerg Relief	26/JK	8840	M-F
Central Appts	321/GB	7126/8879	M-F
CHAMPUS Office	Dispensary	7290 C-29082	M-F
Chapel	Rhon St/JK	7296/8825	Daily
	SpMH	7265/8845	Daily
Comm Drug/Alc Ctr	N/A	7363/8963	M-F
Dental Clinic	5/JK	7056/8846	Daily
Medical Emergency	Local Hospital	N/A	24 hours daily
Poison Control	N/A	98	Daily
Red Cross	26/JK	8890/7190	M-F
Veterinary Svcs	Beside School Annex	7131	W,F
	After hours see Frankfurt listing		

REST AND RECREATION

FACILITY/ACTIVITY	BLDG NO/LOC	PHONE	DAYS/COMMENTS
Bowling Lanes	317/GB	7226 C-95023	Daily
Consolidated Club	SK	7227	Daily
Craftshops			
Automotive	GB	7036	W-Su
Ceramics	Mainaschaff	None	M-W
Multi-crafts	307/GB	7307/7242	F-Sa
Gymnasium	114/FK	7237	Daily
	318/GK	7207	Daily
	430/RK	7365	Sa,Su
	SK	7238	Daily
	210/SK	8810	Nautilus
Info Tour & Travel	25/JK	7349/7373	M-F
Library	JK	8981	Daily
Marina	N/A	8853/7053	Daily
NCO Club	124 Rhon St	7095 C-25979	Daily
O'Club	Castle Club	7179 C-93210	Daily
Outdoor Rec Ctr	N/A	C-96865	N/A
Recreation Center	FK	7360	Daily
	GK	8987	Daily
	4/JK	7161	24 hour recording
Rod and Gun Club	JK	C-96865	Th
Theater	310/GK	7248	Call for schedule.
	2/JK	7191	After 6 pm
Video Rental	Videotek	94399	M-Sa
Youth Center	N/A	8973	N/A

AUGSBURG COMMUNITY (GE39R7)
APO New York 09178-5000

TELEPHONE INFORMATION: Main installation numbers: Civ: 49-0821-449-113. ETS: 434-113. ATVN: 434-1110. Civilian prefix: 0821-_____. ETS prefix: 434-XXXX. Civ to mil prefix: 0821-449-XXXX.

U.S. Forces Travel & Transfer Guide Europe — 29

Augsburg Community, continued

GERMANY

LOCATION: From Munich-Stuttgart, take Autobahn E-8 and exit at Augsburg West and follow U.S. Military Facilities Augsburg signs to the different kasernes. HE: p-40, F/4-5. NMC: Augsburg, in the city.

GENERAL INSTALLATION INFORMATION: The Augsburg Military Community has five small posts or kasernes (Sheridan, Quartermaster, Flak, Reese, and Gablingen) and four housing areas (Sullivan Heights, Centerville North and South, Cramerton and Fryar Circle), plus four leased housing areas.

Sheridan Kaserne is the home of the Augsburg community commander, and elements of the U.S. Navy and U.S. Army Field Station (USAFS), 1st Battalion, 18th FA; 1st Battalion, 30th FA; and other units. Quartermaster Kaserne houses the supply depots for the community. Reese Kaserne is the hub of the entire community and houses the 1st Battalion, 36th FA; 218th Military Police Company; Headquarters, 17th FA Brigade; 105th Finance Section; and the 569th Personnel Service Company. Flak Kaserne is the home of the 34th General Hospital Augsburg; the 502nd I and S Battalion and Air Force Security Group; and other units. Gablingen Kaserne is the working area for the U.S. Army Field Station. All operational functions are contained here. It is a limited access facility. **Note: the following abbreviations are used in this listing only: FK (Flak Kaserne); QK (Quartermaster Kaserne); RK (Reese Kaserne); SK (Sheridan Kaserne).**

GENERAL CITY/REGIONAL: Towers and gates, churches and mansions, splendid fountains, museums, and monuments make Augsburg a fascinating town to visit. The lovely parks, gardens, picturesque streets and shops are all reasons to carry a camera wherever you go. For evening entertainment, seek out the operas, theaters, concerts, and festivals of the city. Come to Augsburg and see one of Germany's most beautiful cities.

ADMINISTRATIVE SUPPORT

FACILITY/ACTIVITY	BLDG NO/LOC	PHONE	DAYS/COMMENTS
Customs/Duty	N/A	6685/7190	M-F
Duty Officer	130	7414	24 hours daily
Fire(Mil)	37/RK	117	24 hours daily
Fire(Civ)	On Barracks	112 C-402735	24 hours daily
Housing			
Family	29/RK	6525/7228	M-F
Unaccompanied	29/RK	6518	M-F
Info(Insta)	3	113	24 hours daily
Legal Assist	104/SK	6501	M-F
Locator(Mil)	On Barracks	370-7571	M-F
Police(Mil)	On Barracks	7500	24 hours daily
Emergency	On Barracks	114	24 hours daily
Police(Civ)	N/A	323-1	24 hours daily
Public Affairs	101/SK	7171/6472	M-F
Tax Relief	113/SK	6622/6251	M-F

LOGISTICAL SUPPORT

FACILITY/ACTIVITY	BLDG NO/LOC	PHONE	DAYS/COMMENTS
Audio/Photo Ctr	On Barracks	C-403122	M-F

GERMANY
Augsburg Community, continued

Auto Drivers Testing	42/RK	7280	M-F
Auto Parts(Exch)	45/RK	6577	M-Sa
Auto Rental(Exch)	106/SK	C-543232	M-F
Auto Repairs	45/RK	C-403402	M-Sa
Bank	113/SK	6664	M-F
	24/RK	6662	M-Sa
Barber Shop(s)	106/SK	C-523817	M-Sa
	203/FK	None	M-F
	214A/FK	None	M-F
	18/RK	C-409314	M-F
Beauty Shop(s)	63/QK	C-401393	Tu-Sa
Bookstore	214A/FK	None	M-F
	63/QK	C-404672	Daily
	15/SK	C-52697	M-Sa
Child Care/Dev Ctr	134/SK	6112/7442	M-F
Clothing Sales	63/QK	7200	M-F
Commissary(Main)	91/QK	6688	Daily
Credit Union	60/QK	7157	M-Sa
Dining Facility	All locations	N/A	Daily
Dry Clean(Gov)	29, 28/RK	7243/6395	Daily
	209/FK	4551	Daily
Education Center	2054/RK	6452	M-F
	108/SK	6402/7511	M-F
	211/RK	4441/4693	M-F
Eng'r/Publ Works	26/RK	6623	Daily
	37/RK	7539	Emergency
Exchange(Main)	106/SK	C-524307	M-F
	63/QK	C-403122	Daily
Exchange(Annex)	203/FK	C-524307	M-F
	214A/FK	C-524307	M-F
Finance(Mil)	3/RK	6456	M-F
Food(Caf/Rest)	63/QK	C-403368	Daily
Food(Snack/Fast)			
Burger Bar	106/SK	6542	Daily
Burger King	QK	C-520250	Daily
Pizza Parlor	106/SK	6542	Daily
Foodland	64/QK	C-403453	Daily
Laundry(Self-Svc)	136/SK	None	Daily
Package Store	18/RK	6556	Tu-Sa
Photo Laboratory	3/RK	6552	Tu-Sa
Pick-up Point	106/SK	None	M-F
	173/SK	None	M-F
	203/FK	None	M-F
	18/RK	None	M-F
	62/QK	C-409676	Daily
Postal Svcs(Mil)	113/SK	6520	M-F
	214A/FK	None	M,W,F
	17/RK	6320	M-F
Postal Svcs(Civ)	24/RK	C-404062	M-F
SATO-OS	29/RK	C-40988	M-Sa
Schools(DOD Dep)			
Elementary	528	6304	M-F
High School	591	6379	M-F
Svc Stn(Insta)	P-590/RK	C-402521	Daily
Tailor Shop	106/SK	None	M-F

U.S. Forces Travel & Transfer Guide Europe — 31

Augsburg Community, continued **GERMANY**

	BLDG NO/LOC	PHONE	DAYS/COMMENTS
	173/SK	None	M-F
	203/FK	None	M-F
	18/RK	None	M-F
Taxi(Comm)		C-35025	24 hours daily
		C-36333	24 hours daily
Tel Booking Oper		112	24 hours daily
Tel Repair(Gov)		119	N/A
TML			
Billeting	29/RK	6445/6277	Duty days
Guest House	53/RK	7270	24 hours daily
		C-409001	
Guest House	180-182/SK	7270	Daily
		C-409001	
Watch Repair	18/RK	None	Tu,Th

HEALTH AND WELFARE

FACILITY/ACTIVITY	BLDG NO/LOC	PHONE	DAYS/COMMENTS
Ambulance		116	24 hours daily
Army Comm Svcs	24/RK	7213	M-F
Army Emerg Relief	24/RK	7213	Daily
Central Appts	N/A	4405	M-F
CHAMPUS Office	214A/FK	4686	M-F
Chaplain	116/SK	6185/7529	M-F
Chapel	136/SK	6185/7529	Daily
Comm Drug/Alc Ctr	125/SK	6462/6318	M-F
Dental Clinic	103/SK	6453/6653	M-F
	105/SK	7113/6693	M-F
	280/FK	4391	M-F
Medical Emergency	214,215,270/FK	4132/4162	24 hours daily
	216/FK	4405	24 hours daily
Mental Health	201/FK	4501/4644	M-F
Poison Control	FK	4132	24 hours daily
Red Cross	24/RK	7139/7578	Duty days
	On Barracks	113	After duty hours
Veterinary Svcs	57/QK	7501	M-W

REST AND RECREATION

FACILITY/ACTIVITY	BLDG NO/LOC	PHONE	DAYS/COMMENTS
Bowling Lanes	4026/SK	6306	Daily
Consolidated Club	133/SK	6443	M-Sa. All ranks.
	175/SK	6514	Daily. All ranks.
	180/SK	6115	Daily. NCOs/Officers.
Craftshops			
Automotive	107/SK	6250	Daily
Ceramics	33/RK	6114/6543	M-Sa
Multi-crafts	112/SK	6592	Sa-W
Photography	112/SK	6326	Daily
Wood	202/FK	4422	M-F
Enlisted Club	210/FK	4446	Tu-Sa
Golf Course	Bavarian GC	6451	N/A
Gymnasium	135/SK	6667	Daily
	166/SK	6675	Daily
	10/RK	6537	Daily

GERMANY
Augsburg Community, continued

Info Tour & Travel	115/SK	7277	M-F
Library	116/SK	6380	Sa-Tu
Outdoor Rec Ctr	33/RK	7518	Daily
Recreation Center	112/SK	6678	Daily
	33/RK	7518	M-F
Family Fitness Ctr	33/RK	7216	M-Sa
Rod and Gun Club	35/RK	6618	M-Sa
		C-403410	
Skating Rink	8/RK	6305	Th-Su
Theater	34/RK	6416	M-Sa
	222/FK	4375	M-Sa
	163/SK	6417	M-Sa
Video Rental	62/QK	C-406024	Daily
Youth Center	56/RK	7447	M-Sa

BABENHAUSEN SUB-COMMUNITY (GE90R7)
APO New York 09455-5000

TELEPHONE INFORMATION: Main installation numbers: Civ: 49-06073-38-113. ETS: 348-3113. Civ prefix: 06073-____ (Babenhausen); 06151-____ (Darmstadt). ETS prefix: 348-3XXX. Civ to mil prefix: 06073-38-XXX.

LOCATION: Located midway between Darmstadt and Aschaffenburg. HE: p-40, C/1. NMC: Darmstadt, approximately 10 miles southwest.

GENERAL INSTALLATION INFORMATION: Babenhausen is a sub-community of the Darmstadt Military Community. The host unit is the 41st Field Artillery Brigade.

GENERAL CITY/REGIONAL INFORMATION: Babenhausen can trace its history to the year 1236. It is thought, however, that a document located in the monastery in Seligenstadt from the year 945 makes mention of Babenhausen. This document, a will made by a landowner and his wife, grants land holdings known as Babobingen to the monastery, which without a doubt refers to Babenhausen. In 1295 Babenhausen was granted "City Rights" by King Adolf of Nassau. Part of these rights included walling the city for protection, maintaining a market on Wednesday (a custom which is still observed by the majority of the merchants) and building a castle.

Two sieges during the 30 Years War almost destroyed the city and the year of the plague, 1635, claimed over 900 lives and started the downfall of Babenhausen. In 1736 the last Count of Hanau-Lictenberg died and Babenhausen fell to Hesse-Cassel, ending over 400 years of prosperity. From 1736 until the end of the 19th century, Babenhausen ceased to exist. Late in the 19th century, Babenhausen became a crossing point for two major railway lines, which revived the local economy somewhat. The construction of a kaserne further enhanced the area's revival.

Today Babenhausen has a population of over 15,000 and is comprised of the city itself and the villages of Harpertshausen, Sickenhofen, Hergershausen, Landstadt, and Harreshausen. Babenhausen is the largest industrial center within the Dieburg area.

U.S. Forces Travel & Transfer Guide Europe — 33

GERMANY

Babenhausen Sub-Community, continued

ADMINISTRATIVE SUPPORT

FACILITY/ACTIVITY	BLDG NO/LOC	PHONE	DAYS/COMMENTS
Customs/Duty	Darmstadt	348-7170	M-F
Fire(Mil)	Darmstadt	C-6995	24 hours daily
Housing			
Family	T4682	784	M-F
Referral	T4682	874/654	M-F
Info(Insta)	4501	721/621	M-F
Legal Assist	4501	668/872	M-F
Locator(Mil)		0	Daily
Locator(Civ)		0101	24 hours daily
Personnel Spt	4521	616/724	M-F
Police(Mil)	4501	701/832	24 hours daily
Emergency	Darmstadt	C-6998	24 hours daily
Police(Civ)		110	24 hours daily
Public Affairs	N/A	621/834	M-F
Tax Relief	4501	721/621	M-F

LOGISTICAL SUPPORT

FACILITY/ACTIVITY	BLDG NO/LOC	PHONE	DAYS/COMMENTS
Audio/Photo Ctr	Darmstadt	C-64144	Tu-Su
Auto Drivers Testing	T4682	None	Tu,F
Auto Parts(Exch)	Darmstadt	C-60538	Tu-Sa
Auto Registration	4501	701	Tu
Auto Rental(Exch)	Darmstadt	C-64200	M-Sa
Auto Rent(Other)	Babenhausen	C-5888	M-Sa
Auto Repairs	Darmstadt	C-60538	M-Sa
Auto Ship(Gov)	Darmstadt	348-6170	M-F
Bank	4513	769	M-F
Barber Shop(s)	4526	741	M-F
Bookstore	4571	None	M-Sa
Bus	4501	721/621	M-F
Child Care/Dev Ctr	4551	644/824	M-F
Clothing Sales	4610	768	M-F
Commissary(Main)	Darmstadt	348-8413	M-Sa
Commissary(Annex)	4615	747	M-Sa
Dining Facility	4659	689	Daily
Dry Clean(Exch)	See pick-up point.		
Education Center	4554	856/656	M-F
Learning Center	4554	673/774	M-F
Elec Repair(Gov)	See Eng'r/Public Works.		
Eng'r/Publ Works	4679	705/828	M-F
	Emergency	662	
Exchange(Main)	Darmstadt	348-6198	Daily
Exchange(Annex)	4518	889/798	Daily
Finance(Mil)	4521	726	M-F
Food(Snack/Fast)	4571	613	M-Sa
Bowling Center	4553	688	Daily
Burger King	4571	684	Daily
Pizza Parlor	4571	613	Daily
Foodland	4518	678	Daily
		C-3434	

GERMANY
Babenhausen Sub-Community, continued

Laundry(Self-Svc)	4619	None	M-Sa
Package Store	4513	748	Tu-Sa
Photo Laboratory	4612	650	M,W,Sa,Su
Pick-up Point	4526	788 C-2174	M-Sa
Postal Svcs(Mil)	4517	698/868	M-F
Postal Svcs(Civ)	4501	C-3430	M-F
Railroad/RTO	Bahnhof	C-2244	Daily
Schools(DOD Dep)			
Elementary	4572	818	M-F (K-6)
High School	See Hanau Community listing.		
Space-A Air Ops	Frankfurt	C-069-699-7015/7016	Daily
Flights to:	German locations		
Tailor Shop	4526	N/A	Daily
Taxi(Comm)	Babenhausen	C-2500/2200	Daily
Tel Repair(Gov)	4518	710	M-F
Tel Repair(Civ)	N/A	C-01171	M-F
Thrift Shop	4613	667	Th
Travel Agents	Babenhausen	C-61255	M-Sa

HEALTH AND WELFARE

FACILITY/ACTIVITY	BLDG NO/LOC	PHONE	DAYS/COMMENTS
Ambulance	Civilian	C-06071-2754	24 hours daily
		797/871	Duty hours
Army Comm Svcs	4526	847/647	M-F
Army Emerg Relief	4526	847	M-F
Central Appts	4516	797/871	M-F
CHAMPUS Office	See Darmstadt Community listing.		
Chaplain	4527	719/819	Su-F
Chapel	4527	719/819	Su-F
Comm Drug/Alc Ctr	4516	648/815	M-F
Dental Clinic	4585	725/835	M-F
Medical Emergency	See Hanau Community listing.		
Mental Health	See Central Appts/Dispensary.		
Poison Control	See Landstuhl Community listing.		
Red Cross	4526	611/811	M-F
Veterinary Svcs	See Frankfurt Community listing.		

REST AND RECREATION

FACILITY/ACTIVITY	BLDG NO/LOC	PHONE	DAYS/COMMENTS
Aero/Flying Club	Babenhausen	C-2880	Daily
Amer Forces Ntwk	See Frankfurt Community listing.		
Bowling Lanes	4524	688	W-M
Craftshops			
Automotive	4527	744	W-M
Multi-crafts	4612	781/871	M-Th
Photography	4515	650	Sa-Th
Enlisted Club	4517	672	Daily
Gymnasium	4524	762	M-F
	Fitness Center	692	M-F
Info Tour & Travel	4515	850	Tu-F

U.S. Forces Travel & Transfer Guide Europe — 35

GERMANY

Babenhausen Sub-Community, continued

Library	4514	646	Tu-Su
MARS	N/A	863/767	Tu-Sa
NCO Club	4517	672	Daily
O'Club	4509	674	Daily
Outdoor Rec Ctr	4515	651/850	Daily
Racket Courts	4627	762	Daily
Recreation Center	4515	651/850	Tu-Su
Theater	4524	682	F-Su,W
Video Rental	4518	789	M-Sa
Youth Center	4551	745	Tu-Sa

BAD AIBLING SUB-COMMUNITY (GE91R7)
APO New York 09098-5000

TELEPHONE INFORMATION: Main installation numbers: Civ: 49-08061-80-113. ETS: 441-3113. Civ prefix: 08061-____. ETS prefix: 441-3XXX. Civ to mil prefix: 08061-80-XXX.

LOCATION: Bad Aibling is located approximately ten minutes south from the Bad Aibling-Munich-Salzburg E-11 Autobahn exit. HE: p-94, A-3. NMC: Munich, 33 miles northwest.

GENERAL INSTALLATION INFORMATION: Not available at press time.

GENERAL CITY/REGIONAL INFORMATION: Bad Aibling began as a Celtic and Roman settlement. In 804 it appears in the historical record for the first time as "Epilingen." In 1321 it was awarded increased trading rights, and in 1845 the clinical mud baths in Bad Aibling were founded. Since the end of the 19th century, the spa has helped to make the town's name known.

Points of interest include the Church of Maria Himmelfahrt, which was first a court church and was renovated in 1755 as a rococo church; the Church of St. Sebastian (1765); the 16th century Marktschreiberhaus (or house of the market reporter); and the local museum.

ADMINISTRATIVE SUPPORT

FACILITY/ACTIVITY	BLDG NO/LOC	PHONE	DAYS/COMMENTS
Fire(Mil)	On Barracks	835	24 hours daily
Housing	On Barracks	755	M-F
Family	On Barracks	800	M-F
Personnel Spt	On Barracks	719	M-F
Police(Mil)	On Barracks	773	Daily

LOGISTICAL SUPPORT

FACILITY/ACTIVITY	BLDG NO/LOC	PHONE	DAYS/COMMENTS
Audio/Photo Ctr	On Barracks	785	M-F
Auto Drivers Testing	On Barracks	773	M-F
Auto Parts(Exch)	On Barracks	760	Tu-Su
Auto Repairs	On Barracks	760	M-Sa
Bank	On Barracks	763	M-F

36 — U.S. Forces Travel & Transfer Guide Europe

GERMANY
Bad Aibling Sub-Community, continued

Barber Shop(s)	On Barracks	748	Tu-Sa
Beauty Shop(s)	On Barracks	668	Tu-Sa
Bookstore	On Barracks	781	M-Tu,Th-Sa
Child Care/Dev Ctr	On Barracks	722	Daily
Commissary(Main)	326	752/795	Tu-Sa
Credit Union	On Barracks	851	Tu-Sa
Dining Facility	On Barracks	778	Daily
Education Center	On Barracks	753	M-F
Eng'r/Publ Works	On Barracks	836	Daily
Exchange(Main)	On Barracks	761	Tu-Sa
Food(Caf/Rest)	On Barracks	549	Tu-Sa
Foodland	On Barracks	549	Tu-Sa
Package Store	On Barracks	747	Tu-Sa
Pick-up Point	On Barracks	765	Tu-Sa
Postal Svcs(Mil)	On Barracks	789/889	M-Sa
Schools(DOD Dep)			
Elementary	On Barracks	706/884	M-F
Space-A Air Ops	Erding AB	581	Daily
Flights to:	German locations		
Tailor Shop	On Barracks	549	M-Sa
Thrift Shop	On Barracks	766	M-F
TML			
Billeting	On Barracks	868	Daily
Travel Agents	N/A	C-8563/ 3763	N/A

HEALTH AND WELFARE

FACILITY/ACTIVITY	BLDG NO/LOC	PHONE	DAYS/COMMENTS
Army Comm Svcs	On Barracks	887	M-F
Central Appts	On Barracks	791	M-F
Chaplain	On Barracks	898	Daily
Dental Clinic	On Barracks	839	M-F

REST AND RECREATION

FACILITY/ACTIVITY	BLDG NO/LOC	PHONE	DAYS/COMMENTS
Bowling Lanes	On Barracks	747	Daily
Craftshops			
Automotive	On Barracks	746	M-F
Multi-crafts	On Barracks	756	M-F
Photography	On Barracks	738	M-F
Enlisted Club	On Barracks	757	Daily
Gymnasium	On Barracks	886	Daily
Library	On Barracks	738	Daily
NCO Club	On Barracks	757	Daily
O'Club	On Barracks	778	Daily
Recreation Center	On Barracks	887	Daily
Service Club	On Barracks	887	Daily
Theater	On Barracks	740/788	Daily

U.S. Forces Travel & Transfer Guide Europe — 37

GERMANY

BAD HERSFELD SUB-COMMUNITY (GE92R7)
APO New York 09141-5000

TELEPHONE INFORMATION: Main installation numbers: Civ: 49-06621-86-113. ETS: 321-5113. Civ prefix: 06621-____. ETS prefix: 321-5XXX. Civ to mil prefix: 06621-86-XXX.

LOCATION: Bad Hersfeld is located north of the E-70 Autobahn. Take the Bad Hersfeld exit north on Route 27 for 1.25 miles. HE: p-36, F/4. NMC: Fulda, 45 miles south.

GENERAL INSTALLATION INFORMATION: The Third Squadron of the 11th Armored Cavalry Regiment is located at McPheeters Barracks in Bad Hersfeld. The squadron consists of HHT, I Troop, K Troop, L Troop, M Company, the 58th Combat Engineer Company, and one Howitzer Company.

GENERAL CITY/REGIONAL INFORMATION: Bad Hersfeld, peacefully nestled in the Fulda River Valley, is a rising industrial center in Hesse. Today there are over 30,000 inhabitants in Hersfeld. Their chief occupations are cloth weaving, wood working, and the manufacture of industrial machines and computers. Hersfeld suffered little damage during World War II and still retains many of its old, half-timbered buildings embellished with wood carvings. The principle buildings are the Stadtkirche, a beautiful Gothic building erected about 1320 and restored in 1899; the old town hall (Rathaus); and the ruins of Stiftskirch, the largest Romanesque Cathedral in Germany, in which are housed the first molded church bells made in Germany. Hersfeld's spa, famed for its waters since 1604, lies in the southwestern part of the city.

ADMINISTRATIVE SUPPORT

FACILITY/ACTIVITY	BLDG NO/LOC	PHONE	DAYS/COMMENTS
Duty Officer	8016	671	Daily
Fire(Mil)	On Barracks	117	24
Housing			
Referral	5218	646/892	M-F
Personnel Spt	On Barracks	618	M-F
Police(Mil)	8208	825	24 hours daily
Emergency	On Barracks	114	24 hours daily
Tax Relief	8208	70	M-F

LOGISTICAL SUPPORT

FACILITY/ACTIVITY	BLDG NO/LOC	PHONE	DAYS/COMMENTS
Auto Drivers Testing	8208	657	M-Tu,Th,F
Auto Parts(Exch)	On Barracks	C-5642	M-F
Auto Registration	8208	688	Tu-F
Auto Repairs	8021	C-5642	M-F
Bank	8000	660	M-F
Barber Shop(s)	8000	C-995273	M-F
Beauty Shop(s)	8000	C-995273	M-F
Bookstore	8013	None	M-Sa
Child Care/Dev Ctr	8209	813	M-F
Clothing Sales	8002	864	M-F
Commissary(Main)	8014	803/682	M-Sa

GERMANY
Bad Hersfeld Sub-Community, continued

Facility	BLDG NO/LOC	PHONE	DAYS/COMMENTS
Dining Facility	On Barracks	668	Daily
Education Center	On Barracks	696	M-F
Learning Center	On Barracks	862	Tu-Sa
Eng'r/Publ Works	8211	692	Daily
Emergency		115	24 hours daily
Exchange(Main)	8000	624	Tu-Sa
Food(Caf/Rest)	8000	C-12926	Daily
Laundry(Exch)	8013	615	M-F
Laundry(Self-Svc)	8010	663	Daily
Motor Pool	8208	824	M-F
Package Store	8013	684	Tu-Sa
Pick-up Point	8000	C-992822	M-Sa
Postal Svcs(Mil)	8000	855	M-F
Railroad/RTO	On Barracks	804	Daily
Schools(DOD Dep)			
Elementary	8107	817	M-F
High School	See Fulda Community listing.		
Space-A Air Ops	Airfield	811	Daily
Tel Repair(Gov)	On Barracks	119	Daily
Thrift Shop	8002	N/A	Tu-Th
TML			
BOQ	8112	678	Daily

HEALTH AND WELFARE

FACILITY/ACTIVITY	BLDG NO/LOC	PHONE	DAYS/COMMENTS
Ambulance	On Barracks	116	24 hours daily
Army Comm Svcs	208	647	M-F
Central Appts	8113	638/698	M-F
Chaplain	8006	808	M-F
Comm Drug/Alc Ctr	On Barracks	622	M-F
Dental Clinic	8113	829	M-F
Medical Emergency	8113	819	24 hours daily
Red Cross	8208	708	M-F
Veterinary Svcs	Rec Center	N/A	2nd Tu

REST AND RECREATION

FACILITY/ACTIVITY	BLDG NO/LOC	PHONE	DAYS/COMMENTS
Bowling Lanes	8013	629	Daily
Craftshops			
Automotive	8021	616	Tu-Sa
Multi-crafts	8021	700	Tu-Sa
Enlisted Club	On Barracks	622	Daily
Gymnasium	8016	836	Daily
Library	8021	675	M-Sa
NCO Club	8025	633	Tu-Sa
O'Club	On Barracks	614	Tu-Su
Outdoor Rec Ctr	On Barracks	615	Daily
Recreation Center	8006	809	Daily
Riding Club	8010	809	Daily
Rod and Gun Club	8202	622	Th-Tu
Service Club	8005	809	Daily
Theater	8017	640	M-W,F,Sa
Video Rental	8006	702/3	M-Sa

Bad Hersfeld Sub-Community, continued   **GERMANY**

Youth Center	8003	604	M-Sa

BAD KISSINGEN SUB-COMMUNITY (GE49R7)
APO New York 09330-5000

TELEPHONE INFORMATION: Main installation numbers: Civ: 49-0971-86-113. ETS: 354-2113. ATVN: 350-1110 (ask for Bad Kissingen). Civ prefix: 0971-____. ETS prefix: 354-2XXX. Civ to mil prefix: 0971-86-XXX.

LOCATION: From the Kassel-Würzberg E-70 Autobahn, exit Bad Kissingen/Hammelburg to GE-287 northwest for nine miles. U.S. Forces signs indicate directions to the community. HE: p-36, G/6. NMC: Schweinfurt, 12 miles southeast.

GENERAL INSTALLATION INFORMATION: The major units assigned to Bad Kissingen include the 2nd Battalion, 11th Cavalry Regiment; 2nd Battalion, 41st Field Artillery; A Battery, 3rd Battalion, 52nd Air Defense Artillery; and B Company, 10th Engineer Battalion (Combat). All units are first-line combat and combat support organizations.

GENERAL CITY/REGIONAL INFORMATION: Bad Kissingen is located in an area of hills and dark forests and is famous worldwide as a spa and tourist town. During World War II, the Bad Kissingen spa with its hotels, sanatoriums, and nursing homes became a rest center for the German Army. An undefended city, Bad Kissingen never suffered aerial assaults and in 1945 surrendered peacefully.

The town is first mentioned in an 8th-century chronical. It grew in prominence in the 18th century when a pharmacist rediscovered the celebrated Racoczy Spring. From then on the mineral springs have been used by those who sought to cure various ailments. Kings and emperors have visited the spa and even today thousands of visitors flock to Bad Kissingen to "take the cure" or simply to enjoy their vacation.

The 19th century architecture of the town remains unchanged. The beautiful gardens and quiet streets delight visitors of all ages. Pleasant sidewalk cafes and specialty shops line the streets that lead to the Obermarkt or square. The town's nightlife centers around the gambling casino and fine restaurants. For music lovers, concerts are held during the summer in the Kur Gardens and the Opera House. Boat rides on the river, miniature golf, horseback riding, and golf are some of the attractions in the Bad Kissingen area.

ADMINISTRATIVE SUPPORT

FACILITY/ACTIVITY	BLDG NO/LOC	PHONE	DAYS/COMMENTS
Customs/Duty	21	867/780	M-F
Fire(Mil)	11	117	24 hours daily
Fire(Civ)		112	24 hours daily
Housing			
Family	22	721/870	M-F
		C-5567	
Referral	22	631	M-F
Info(Insta)		113	24 hours daily

GERMANY
Bad Kissingen Sub-Community, continued

Legal Assist	1	720/830	M-F
Personnel Spt	1	670/815	M-F
Police(Mil)	79	727	24 hours daily
Emergency		114	24 hours daily
Police(Civ)		110	24 hours daily
Public Affairs	1	666	M-F
Tax Relief	1	625	M-F

===
LOGISTICAL SUPPORT
===

FACILITY/ACTIVITY	BLDG NO/LOC	PHONE	DAYS/COMMENTS
Audio/Photo Ctr	90	C-61998	N/A
Auto Drivers Testing	22	706	M,W, or by appoint
Auto Registration	79	727/657	M-F
Bank	79	887	M-F
		C-2455	
Barber Shop(s)	79	C-67054	Tu-Sa
	58	C-66758	M-F
Beauty Shop(s)	79	C-67054	Tu-Sa
Bookstore	65	630	M-Sa
Bus	N/A	755	N/A
Child Care/Dev Ctr	25	819	M-F
		C-3550	
Clothing Sales	12	722	M-F
Commissary(Main)	93	678/878	Tu-Sa
Dining Facility	5	654	Daily
	1	651	Daily
Dry Clean(Gov)	22	729	M-F
Education Center	59	709/660	M-F
Learning Center	60	659	M-F
Eng'r/Publ Works	10	115	24 hours daily
Exchange(Main)	79	801	Daily
		C-3649	
Finance(Mil)	1	876	M-F
Food(Caf/Rest)	79	C-3743	Daily
Foodland	90	C-65620	Daily
Laundry(Exch)	22	729	M-F
Laundry(Self-Svc)	12	623/739	Daily
Motor Pool	21	867	N/A
Package Store	51	621	Tu-Sa
Photo Laboratory	60	602	M-W
Pick-up Point	12	C-66803	M-F
Postal Svcs(Mil)	22	820	M-F
		C-2620	
Postal Svcs(Civ)	79	C-2158/	M-F
		1361	
Schools(DOD Dep)			
Elementary	94	601	M-F
Middle School	See Schweinfurt Community listing.		
High School	See Würzberg Community listing.		
Svc Stn(Insta)	23	C-3581	Tu-Sa
Space-A Air Ops	Airfield	609	N/A
Flights to:	Various German locations		
Tailor Shop	12	752	Tu-Sa
Tel Repair(Gov)	N/A	810	N/A
Tel Repair(Civ)	N/A	C-1171	N/A

GERMANY

Bad Kissingen Sub-Community, continued

Thrift Shop	82	623	Tu,W,F
TML			
Billeting	Daley	721	Daily
TLF	11 Kurhaus St	890	N/A
Travel Agents	79	C-3965	N/A

HEALTH AND WELFARE

FACILITY/ACTIVITY	BLDG NO/LOC	PHONE	DAYS/COMMENTS
Ambulance		116	24 hours daily
Army Comm Svcs	59	670	M-F
		C-65357	
Army Emerg Relief	59	670	M-F
Central Appts	30	724/865	M-F
CHAMPUS Office	201	N/A	N/A
Chapel	92	718/849	Su-F
Comm Drug/Alc Ctr	61	603/753	M-F
Dental Clinic	192	610	M-F
Red Cross	59	888/707	M-F
Veterinary Svcs	See Würzberg Community listing.		

REST AND RECREATION

FACILITY/ACTIVITY	BLDG NO/LOC	PHONE	DAYS/COMMENTS
Amer Forces Ntwk	N/A	727	N/A
Bowling Lanes	174	737	Daily
Consolidated Club	N/A	C-61648	M-Sa
Craftshops			
Automotive	1	624	Su-Th
Multi-crafts	60	644	Su-Th
Photography	90	692	Su-Th
Enlisted Club	80	645	Daily
		C-4600	
Gymnasium	81	840	Daily
Info Tour & Travel	90	860	M-F
		C-66563	
Library	90	638	Sa-Th
NCO Club	80	645	Daily
		C-4600	
O'Club	192	683	M-F
		C-61648	
Recreation Center	59	613	W-Sa
Theater	78	739	Daily
Video Rental	12	None	M-Sa
	22	620	M-Sa
Youth Center	202	738	Tu-Sa

BAD KREUZNACH COMMUNITY
(GE01R7)
APO New York 09252-5000

TELEPHONE INFORMATION: Main installation numbers: Civ: 49-0671-

42 — U.S. Forces Travel & Transfer Guide Europe

GERMANY
Bad Kreuznach Community, continued

609-113 (Bad Kreuznach); 49-0671-792-113 (Bad Kreuznach Hospital). ETS: 490-6119. ATVN: 490-1110. Civ prefix: 0671-____ (Bad Kreuznach); 0671-____ (Bad Kreuznach Hospital). ETS/ATVN prefix: 490-XXXX (Bad Kreuznach); 490-5XXX (Bad Kreuznach Hospital). Civ to mil prefix: 0671-609-XXXX (Bad Kreuznach); 0671-792-XXX (Bad Kreuznach Hospital).

LOCATION: Approximately 50 miles south from Frankfurt am Main, via Mainz to Bad Kreuznach, Autobahn A-66 & A-60. Take B-41 at the east outskirt of the city, go south on Bosenheimer St, left on Alzeyer St, to Nahe Club on the right. Billeting next to club. HE: p-40, A/1. NMC: Bad Kreuznach, in the city.

GENERAL INSTALLATION INFORMATION: The main mission of Bad Kreuznach Community is to provide base operation support to the 8th Infantry Division. Bad Kreuznach Community consists of the Bad Kreuznach Hospital, Minnick Kaserne and Rose Barracks. Note: the following abbreviations are used in this listing only: BKH (Bad Kreuznach Hospital Kaserne); MnK (Minnick Kaserne); MslK (Marshall Kaserne); RB (Rose Barracks).

GENERAL CITY/REGIONAL: The city of Bad Kreuznach is a health resort with a beautiful park, many interesting shops, and a famous museum with a mosaic floor dating from Roman times. The most renowned attractions in the city are the unique 600-year-old bridge houses on the Nahe River. Bad Kreuznach Community also offers an Army Travel Camp at the nearby Kuhberg Community Park. It is located in a rustic setting with grassy fields and beautiful forested surroundings.

ADMINISTRATIVE SUPPORT

FACILITY/ACTIVITY	BLDG NO/LOC	PHONE	DAYS/COMMENTS
Customs/Duty	5990(MP Sta)	7298/6126	M-F
Duty Officer	5555/MslK	7105	24 hours daily
Fire(Mil)	5214/MnK	7262	24 hours daily
Fire(Civ)	N/A	C-65190	24 hours daily
Housing			
Family	5543/MslK	7102/6175	M-F
Unaccompanied	5543/MslK	7102/6175	M-F
Referral	5543/MslK	7234	M-F
Info(Insta)	5608(Outreach)	6119	M-F
Inspector Gen'l	5300/RB	6409	M-F
Legal Assist	5301/RB	6327	M-F
Locator(Mil)	5312/RB	6274	M-F
Locator(Civ)	5533/MslK	6311	M-F
Personnel Spt	5331/RB	7151	M-F
Police(Mil)	5990	6366	24 hours daily
Emergency		114	24 hours daily
Police(Civ)	N/A	C-110	24 hours daily
Public Affairs	5555/MslK	7373	M-F
Tax Relief	5306/RB	6054	M-F

LOGISTICAL SUPPORT

FACILITY/ACTIVITY	BLDG NO/LOC	PHONE	DAYS/COMMENTS
Audio/Photo Ctr	5306/RB	C-68517	Tu-Su

U.S. Forces Travel & Transfer Guide Europe — 43

GERMANY

Bad Kreuznach Community, continued

Auto Drivers Testing	5325/RB	6255	M-F
Auto Parts(Exch)	Near airfield	C-68897	Tu-Sa
Auto Registration	5990	7431	M-F
Auto Rental(Exch)	Near Bldg 5625	C-72029	M-F
Auto Repairs	Near airfield	C-68897	M-F
Auto Sales	Main PX area	N/A	Daily
Auto Ship(Gov)	5541 MslK	N/A	M-F
Auto Ship(Civ)	5625(Transcar)	C-72029	M-F
Bank	Main PX area	6265	M-Sa
Barber Shop(s)	5325/RB	6488	M-F
Beauty Shop(s)	Main PX area	C-68544	M-Sa
Bookstore	5628	6464	M-F
	RB	None	Daily
Bus	5536/MslK	7346	M-F
Child Care/Dev Ctr	5250/BKH	795	Su-F
Clothing Sales	5312/RB	·7251	M-F,1st and 3rd Sa
Commissary(Main)	Main PX area	6296/8349	Tu-Su
		C-71269	
Credit Union	5305/RB	7190	M-F
Dry Clean(Exch)	Main PX area	C-68260	Tu-Sa
Dining Facility	5306/RB EM Mess	N/A	Daily
	5333/RB EM Mess	N/A	Daily
	5534/MslK	N/A	Daily
Education Center	5309/RB	6167/7266	M-F
Learning Center	5312/RB	6169/7227	M-F
Elec Repair(Gov)	5555/MslK	7202	M-F
Elec Repair(Civ)	Main PX area	C-68260	Tu-Sa
Eng'r/Publ Works	5572/MslK	6470	M-F
Emergency		115	After duty hours
Exchange(Main)	5607/Hsg Area	C-68517	Daily
Exchange(Annex)	5305/RB	C-61080	M-Sa
Finance(Mil)	5305/RB	6148	M-F
Food(Snack/Fast)			
Burger Bar	Main PX area	C-68370	Daily
Burger King	5305/RB	6360	Daily
Foodland	5630/Hsg Area	C-64828	Daily
Laundry(Exch)	Main PX area	C-68260	Tu-Sa
Laundry(Self-Svc)	Main PX area	None	Daily
Motor Pool	5536/MslK	7346	M-F
Package Store	5625/Hsg Area	6201	Tu-Sa
Photo Laboratory	Main PX area	C-68260	Tu-Sa
Pick-up Point	Main PX area	C-68260	Tu-Sa
Postal Svcs(Mil)	5312/RB	7130	M-Th
Postal Svcs(Civ)	3a Schumannst	N/A	M-Sa
Railroad/RTO	5592(Train Sta)	7285	M-F
SATO-OS	5325/RB	6192	M-F
		C-66800	
Schools(DOD Dep)			
Elementary	5621/Hsg Area	6133/7110	M-F
High School	5260/BKH	821	M-F
Svc Stn(Insta)	5630/Hsg Area	6283	Daily
Space-A Air Ops	Airfield	6430	Daily
Flights to:	Local German locations		
Tailor Shop	5225/RB	6488	M-F
Taxi(Comm)	N/A	2333	24 hours daily

GERMANY
Bad Kreuznach Community, continued

Tel Booking Oper	N/A	117	24 hours daily
Tel Repair(Gov)	BKH	119	24 hours daily
Tel Repair(Civ)	In town	C-96522	N/A
Thrift Shop	5608 Hsg Area	6387	Tu,Th
TML			
Billeting	5649 Hsg Area	C-61247	Daily
Guest House	5649 Hsg Area	6175	After hrs call NCO
DV/VIP(06+)	5648 Hsg Area	6466	Daily
Travel Agents	5325 RB	6192	M-F
		C-66800	
Watch Repair	Main PX area	C-68260	Tu-Sa

HEALTH AND WELFARE

FACILITY/ACTIVITY	BLDG NO/LOC	PHONE	DAYS/COMMENTS
Ambulance	5253/BKH	116	24 hours daily
Army Comm Svcs	5610A/Hsg area	6482/7107	M-F
Army Emerg Relief	5610A/Hsg area	6333	M-F
Central Appts	5253/BKH	710/727	Daily
CHAMPUS Office	5253/BKH	717	M-F
Chaplain	5345/Rose Chapel	6458	M-F
Chapel	5345/Rose Chapel	6458	Daily
Comm Drug/Alc Ctr	5329/RB	6341	M-F
Dental Clinic	5253/BKH	815	M-F
Medical Emergency	5253/BKH	116	24 hours daily
Mental Health	5253/BKH	797	M-F
Poison Control	5253/BKH	733	M-F
Red Cross	5306/RB	6260/8380	M-F
Emergency		0	After duty hours
Veterinary Svcs	5250/BKH	732/182	M,Th

REST AND RECREATION

FACILITY/ACTIVITY	BLDG NO/LOC	PHONE	DAYS/COMMENTS
Bowling Lanes	5310 RB	6433	Daily
Camping/RV Area	Kuhberg 2.8 mi SW of RB	6498/6496	Daily
Craftshops			
Automotive	5206/MnK	6392	W-M
Multi-crafts	5325/RB	6420	Tu-Su
Enlisted Club	5351	6156/6266	Daily (E-1 to E-6)
Gymnasium	5326/RB	6468	Daily
Info Tour & Travel	5325/RB	6192	M-F
Library	5325/RB	6448/7122	Daily
NCO/O'Club	5650 (Nahe Club)	6252 C-63582	M-F (E-7+)
Outdoor Rec Ctr	5329/RB	6498	M-Sa
Picnic/Park Area	T5438/Kuhberg	6228	Th-M
Racket Courts	5326/Rose Gym	6488	Call for resv
Recreation Center	5325/RB	7113/6215	Tu-Su
Sport Field	Patton Field	6177	M-F
Tennis Courts	5326/RB	6488	Daily
Theater	5270/BKH	739	M-F
Track	Patton Field	6177	M-F
Trails	T5438/Kuhberg	6228	Th-M

U.S. Forces Travel & Transfer Guide Europe — 45

Bad Kreuznach Community, continued

GERMANY

Video Rental	Main PX area		Su-F
Youth Center	5356/Hsg area	6256	M-Sa
		C-68525	

BAD TÖLZ COMMUNITY (GE02R7)
APO New York 09050-5000

TELEPHONE INFORMATION: Main installation numbers: Civ: 49-08041-30-113. ATVN: 440-1110 (ask for Bad Tölz). ETS: 441-4113. Civ prefix: 08041-___. ETS prefix: 441-4XXX. Civ to mil prefix: 08041-30-XXXX.

LOCATION: Between the Salzburg and Garmisch/Partenkirchen Autobahns on Nat-13. Exit from Autobahn E-11 south at Holzkirchen and travel 22 kilometers southwest on Nat-13. Signs mark Flint Kaserne. HE: p-92, H/2. NMC: Munich, 37 miles northwest.

GENERAL INSTALLATION INFORMATION: Bad Tölz is home to the U.S. Army Combat Support Training Center, the 769th Medical Detachment (Dental), and the 5th General Dispensary. Most facilities are located at Flint Kaserne.

GENERAL CITY/REGIONAL INFORMATION: Bad Tölz a city of 13,000 people located at the foot of the Bavarian Alps on both sides of the Isar River, 2,300 feet above sea level.

ADMINISTRATIVE SUPPORT

FACILITY/ACTIVITY	BLDG NO/LOC	PHONE	DAYS/COMMENTS
Customs/Duty	1-W	838	Daily
Fire(Mil)	On Barracks	117/884	24 hours daily
Housing			
Family	48	722	M-F
Referral	48	780	M-F
Info(Insta)	1-W	113	Daily
Police(Mil)	2	733/813	Daily
Emergency	2	114	24 hours daily
Public Affairs	1-W	847	M-F

LOGISTICAL SUPPORT

FACILITY/ACTIVITY	BLDG NO/LOC	PHONE	DAYS/COMMENTS
Auto Registration	12	838/631	M-F
Auto Repairs	11	C-3297	M-F
Bank	1-S	660	M-F
Barber Shop(s)	1-S	619	Tu,W,Sa
Beauty Shop(s)	1-E	C-3225	Tu,Sa
Bookstore	1309	719	M-F
Child Care/Dev Ctr	1-S	690	Tu-Su
Clothing Sales	1-E	613	M-Sa
Commissary(Main)	15	809/608	Tu-Sa
Dining Facility	1-S	747	Daily
Dry Clean(Exch)	1-S	C-3120	M-F

46 — U.S. Forces Travel & Transfer Guide Europe

GERMANY
Bad Tölz Community, continued

Education Center	1-N	703	M-F
Eng'r/Publ Works	30/31 South	648	M-F
	Emergency	115	24 hours daily
Exchange(Main)	1-E	C-3229	Daily
Food(Snack/Fast)	1-W	C-2583	Daily
Foodland	1-E	C-3229	Daily
Laundry(Self-Svc)	1-E	C-3120	M-F
Motor Pool	12	632	Daily
Package Store	1-S	680	M-Sa
Postal Svcs(Mil)	1-W	823	M-F
Postal Svcs(Civ)	1-S	N/A	M-F
Schools(DOD Dep)			
Elementary	On Barracks	784	M-F
High School	See Munich Community listing.		
Svc Stn(Insta)	13	C-3238	M-Sa
Space-A Air Ops	Airfield	693	M-F
Flights to:	German locations		
Tel Booking Oper	1-E	112	24 hours daily
Tel Repair(Gov)	1-E	119/731	M-F
Tel Repair(Civ)	On Barracks	C-9666/2140	M-F
TML			
Billeting	1-W	890	Duty days
	SDO	800	After hours
BEQ	49	745	M-F
VAQ/VOQ	A-102	890/800	Daily
DV/VIP	1-W	760/790	M-F
Train Station	Bad Tölz	C-08041-4404	Daily

HEALTH AND WELFARE

FACILITY/ACTIVITY	BLDG NO/LOC	PHONE	DAYS/COMMENTS
Ambulance	1-I	116	24 hours daily
Army Comm Svcs	1-S	622/888	M-F
Central Appts	1-I	654/858	M-F
CHAMPUS Office	1-S	650	M-F
Chaplain	10	617	Daily
Chapel	10	617	Sa,Su
Comm Drug/Alc Ctr	1-S	630	M-F
Dental Clinic	1-I	788	M-F
Medical Emergency	1-I	654	24 hours daily

REST AND RECREATION

FACILITY/ACTIVITY	BLDG NO/LOC	PHONE	DAYS/COMMENTS
Bowling Lanes	5	683	F-W
Civ/Contract Club	1-E	616	Daily
Consolidated Club	1-S	619	Daily
Craftshops			
Automotive	On Barracks	655	T-Th,Sa
Multi-crafts	1-S	657	Tu-Sa
Photography	1-S	662	Tu-Sa
Enlisted Club	1-S	619	M-Sa
Gymnasium	5	666	Daily
Info Tour & Travel	1-W	794	M-F

Bad Tölz Community, continued

GERMANY

Library	1-S	697	Daily
NCO Club	1-S	619	M-Sa
O'Club	65	651	Tu-Su
Rod and Gun Club	41	792	Daily
Swimming Pool	5	683	Tu-Su
Theater	1-S	662	Daily
Youth Center	6	724	M,Tu,Th,F

BAMBERG COMMUNITY(GE34R7)
APO NEW YORK 09139-5000

TELEPHONE INFORMATION: Main installation numbers: Civ: 49-0951-400-113. ETS: 469-113. Civ prefix: 0951-____. ETS prefix: 469-XXXX. Civ to mil prefix: 0951-400-XXXX.

LOCATION: On GE-26/505. Warner Barracks, the main installation, is on the E side of the city between Zollner and Pödeldorter Straßes. Follow sign. HE: p-40, E/1. NMC: Nürnberg, 30 miles southeast.

GENERAL INSTALLATION INFORMATION: In 1970, Bamberg was designated a Community with a general officer as the Community Commander. The Bamberg Community is home to more than 6500 soldiers, most of whom are assigned to the nine combat battalions located here: 3rd Brigade, 1st Armor Division; 7/6 Infantry; 1/54 Infantry; 3/35 Armor; 3/1 Field Artillery; 2/2 Armored Cavalry Regiment; 82nd Engineer Battalion; 4/14 Field Artillery; and 2/14 Field Artillery.

GENERAL CITY/REGIONAL INFORMATION: Bamberg offers tourists and residents alike a feast for the senses. Notable sights include the Altes Rathaus, or old city hall, built on an artificial island in the river; the Dom (cathedral) with its Gothic and Romanesque architecture and many art treasures; and the Neue Residenz, the palace of the prince-bishops who used to rule the city. The sounds of the city can be heard during walks through the cobblestone streets and at the many city concerts. Visitors can enjoy the smell and taste of fine German cuisine and the unique local specialty, Rauchbier, or smoked beer. Finally, the feel of the city—its warmth, beauty, and tradition—will beckon you to return.

ADMINISTRATIVE SUPPORT

FACILITY/ACTIVITY	BLDG NO/LOC	PHONE	DAYS/COMMENTS
Customs/Duty	7113	8865/8665	M-F
Duty Officer	7119	8727/8660	24 hours daily
Fire(Mil)	7111	117/8887	24 hours daily
Fire(Civ)	Margaretendamm	112/ C-47288	24 hours daily
Housing			
Family	7114	7654/5	M-F
Unaccompanied	7114	8607	M-F
Referral	7029	8808	M-F
Info(Insta)		113	24 hours daily
Inspector Gen'l	7113	8825	M-F
Legal Assist	7000	8633	M-F

GERMANY
Bamberg Community, continued

Locator(Mil)	7117	7738	M-F
Locator(Civ)	7107	8812	M-F
Personnel Spt	7290	8614	M-F
Police(Mil)	7108	8700	24 hours daily
Emergency		114	24 hours daily
Police(Civ)	Schildstrasse	C-110	24 hours daily
Public Affairs	7114	8835	M-F
Tax Relief	7325	8668	M-F

LOGISTICAL SUPPORT

FACILITY/ACTIVITY	BLDG NO/LOC	PHONE	DAYS/COMMENTS
Audio/Photo Ctr	7120	C-47350/ 32562	Daily
Auto Drivers Testing	7119	8685	M-F
Auto Parts(Exch)	7011	7530 C-32472	M-Sa
Auto Registration	7113	8825	M-F
Auto Rental(Exch)	7123	C-46451	M-Sa
Auto Rent(Other)	Auto Endler Zollner St	C-46012	M-Sa
Auto Repairs	7027	7530	M-F
Auto Sales	7011	C-37695	M-F. Ford.
	N/A	C-32401	M-Sa. AMC.
	N/A	C-33888	M-Sa. Dodge.
	N/A	C-34078	M-Sa. VW.
Auto Ship(Gov)	7113	8825	M-F
Auto Ship(Civ)	7113	8825	M-F
Auto Wash	7038	7546	W-Su
Bakery	7123	C-47060	M-F
Bank	7117	8778	M-Sa
Barber Shop(s)	Exchange	C-32738	M-F
	Panzer	C-32644	M-Sa
	2/2 ACR	C-32120	M-F
Beauty Shop(s)	7120	C-36245	M-Sa
Bookstore	7124	C-32165	Daily
Bus	7102	8698	M-F
Child Care/Dev Ctr	7089	8660/8727	M-F
Clothing Sales	7040	C-47785	M-F
Commissary(Main)	7123	7650/8819	M-Sa
Commissary(Annex)	Foodland	C-35923	Daily
Credit Union	7127	7607 C-32007	M-F
Dining Facility	Each battalion has its own dining facility.		
Dry Clean(Exch)	7039	C-33184	M-F
Education Center	7047	8836	M-F
Learning Center	7116	8883	M-F
Elec Repair(Gov)	7047	C-31845	M-F
Elec Repair(Civ)	7047	C-31845	M-F
Eng'r/Publ Works	7116	7645/115	M-F
Exchange(Main)	7121	C-32551/ C-32563	Daily
Exchange(Concess)	Belows Gift Shop	C-39240	Daily
Finance(Mil)	7290	8638	M-F
Food(Caf/Rest)	7011	C-39883	Daily

Bamberg Community, continued   **GERMANY**

Food(Snack/Fast)
Baskin Robbins	7116	C-32271	Daily
Burger Bar	7116	C-32271	Daily
Burger King	6050	C-34292	Daily
Pizza Parlor	Panzer	C-39883/ 31358	Daily
Foodland	7011	C-35923	Daily
Laundry(Exch)	8631, 8483	C-31845	Daily
Laundry(Self-Svc)	7047, 7119	None	Daily
Motor Pool	7113	8825	M-F
Package Store	7120	7116/7716	Tu-Sa
Photo Laboratory	7047	7436	W-Su
Pick-up Point	Exchange	C-31845	M-Sa
	Panzer	C-33184	M-Sa
	2/2 ACR	C-32114	M-F
Postal Svcs(Mil)	7117	7738/8820	M-F
Postal Svcs(Civ)	German PO	881	M-F
Railroad/RTO	7340	C-46001	M-F
SATO-OS	7113	8844	M-F
Schools(DOD Dep)			
Elementary	7332	8884	M-F
High School	7643	7630	M-F
Svc Stn(Insta)	7027	C-34063	M-F
Svc Stn(Autobahn)	Memmelsdorfer St	N/A	Daily. Shell.
Space-A Air Ops	Airfield Cmdr	8636/8869	Daily
Flights to:	German locations		
Tailor Shop	7039	C-31844	M-Sa
	Panzer	C-31844	M-Sa
	2/2 ACR	C-32114	M-F
Taxi(Comm)	Bamberg City	C-15015	24 hours daily
Tel Booking Oper	7089	111	24 hours daily
Tel Repair(Gov)	7089	119	24 hours daily
Tel Repair(Civ)	7089	C-1171	M-F
Thrift Shop	7118	C-32406/ 32048	W-F,1st Sa
TML			
Billeting	7678	7596	M-F
	7108	8700	After duty hours
Guest House	7070/7678	7596	M-F
Travel Agents	7108	7580	M-F

==
HEALTH AND WELFARE
==

FACILITY/ACTIVITY	BLDG NO/LOC	PHONE	DAYS/COMMENTS
Ambulance	7334	97/116	24 hours daily
Army Comm Svcs	7089	8735/7777	M-F
Army Emerg Relief	7029	8727	M-F
Central Appts	Dispensary	8839/7772	M-F
CHAMPUS Office	7334	8619	M-F
Chaplain	7040	8719	Daily
Chapel	7040	7783/8879	M-F
Comm Drug/Alc Ctr	7486	8779	M-F
Dental Clinic	7334	7485/8895	M-F
Medical Emergency	7334	97/8741	24 hours daily
Mental Health	Bamberg	8795	M-F
Poison Control	7123	7639	M-F

GERMANY
Bamberg Community, continued

Red Cross	7029	8729/8882	24 hours daily
Veterinary Svcs	DYA	7777	Once a month for shots only

REST AND RECREATION

FACILITY/ACTIVITY	BLDG NO/LOC	PHONE	DAYS/COMMENTS
Aero/Flying Club	Bamberg	C-37860	Eves, Wknds
Bowling Lanes	7116	7722	Daily
Craftshops			
Automotive	7038	7546	W-Su
Ceramics	7047	7436/8659	W-Su
Multi-crafts	7047	7436/8659	W-Su
Photography	7047	7436/8659	W-Su
Wood	7047	7436/8659	W-Su
Enlisted Club	7492	7766	Eves
Golf Course	At Rod & Gun C	7583	Daily
Gymnasium	JFK Gym	8890	Daily
	7693 (May Hall)	7597	Daily
	PFC Gym		Daily
Info Tour & Travel	7340	C-46001	M-Sa
Library	7047	8875	Daily
MARS	7117	8610	M-F
NCO Club	7120	7556	Daily
		C-36378	
O'Club	7070	8708/7596	Tu-Su
Outdoor Rec Ctr	7340	7450/7578	M-Sa
Racket Courts	7693	7597	Daily
Recreation Center	7647	8837	Daily
Rod and Gun Club	Zollner St	C-32223	Daily
Service Club	3d Brigade Area	8837	Daily
Sport Field	Pendleton Field	None	Daily
Tennis Courts	Pendleton Field	None	Daily
Theater	7022 (Movie)	7637	Daily
	7119 (Stage)	8647	Weekends
Track	Pendleton Field	None	Daily
Video Rental	7047, 7210	C-32176/ 47350	Daily

BAUMHOLDER COMMUNITY (GE03R7)
APO New York 09034-5000

TELEPHONE INFORMATION: Main installation numbers: Civ: 49-06783-6-113 (Baumholder); 49-06782-13-113 (Neubrücke Kaserne); 49-06781-61-113 (Strassburg Kaserne). ETS/ATVN: 485-113 (Baumholder); 493-113 (Neubrücke Kaserne); 492-113 (Strassburg Kaserne). Civ prefix: 06783-____ (Baumholder); 06782-____ (Neubrücke Kaserne); 06781-____ (Strassburg Kaserne). ETS/ATVN prefix: 485-XXXX (Baumholder); 493-XXXX (Neubrücke Kaserne); 492-XXXX (Strassburg Kaserne). Civ to mil prefix: 06783-6-XXXX (Baumholder); 06782-13-XXXX (Neubrücke Kaserne); 06781-61-XXXX (Strassburg Kaserne).

LOCATION: To reach Baumholder from Kaiserslautern, take Autobahn 62

GERMANY

Baumholder Community, continued

toward Trier and exit north at Freisen and follow signs to Baumholder. HE: p-39, G/1. NMC: Kaiserslautern, 56 kilometers southeast. Neubrücke Kaserne is nine miles southeast of Baumholder on GE-41. Signs are posted. Strassburg Kaserne in Idar-Oberstein is also approximately nine miles from Baumholder on GE-41 northeast of Birkenfeld. It can be reached from the E-6 Mannheim-Saarbrucken Autobahn.

GENERAL INSTALLATION INFORMATION: The Baumholder Military Community's primary function is to support the 8th Infantry Division. The community consists of both Army and Air Force units and has one of the largest concentrations of American combat soldiers outside the U.S. H.D. Smith Barracks and Wetzel Kaserne in Baumholder, Neubrücke Kaserne, and Strassburg Kaserne in Idar-Oberstein comprise the community. Note: the following abbreviations are used in this listing only: BC (Baumholder Community); NK (Neubrücke Kaserne); SK (Strassburg Kaserne in Idar-Oberstein).

GENERAL CITY/REGIONAL INFORMATION: The Baumholder Community is located in a rural, mountainous area with narrow winding roads in the southwest corner of West Germany. Kaiserslautern, the Mosel River, and the French border are within a fifty mile radius of Baumholder. The community's location allows visitors to easily travel to many points of interest in Germany and in several neighboring countries, including France, Belgium, Holland, and Luxemburg. Baumholder is at a higher elevation than the surrounding countryside and the climate is comparable to that of the Pacific Northwest.

Idar-Oberstein is one of the gem-cutting capitals of the world. Semi-precious stones from all over the world are sent to the city to be cut, polished and colored. Visitors can tour gem-cutting shops as well as the local museum speciaizing in jewelry exhibits. The most famous landmark of Idar-Oberstein is the legendary rock church, built 150 feet above the street against a rocky wall.

ADMINISTRATIVE SUPPORT

FACILITY/ACTIVITY	BLDG NO/LOC	PHONE	DAYS/COMMENTS
Customs/Duty	8248/BC	7442	M-F
Duty Officer	BC	8333/6157 C-5344	Daily
Fire(Mil)	All locations	117	24 hours daily
Fire(Civ)	BC	2386	24 hours daily
Housing			
Family	8680/BC	6136/6137	M-F
Unaccompanied	8076/BC	6136/6137	M-F
	9926/NK	8016/7087	Daily
	9032/SK	6713	M-F
Referral	8681/BC	7113/7138	M-F
	9925/NK	8022/7005	M-F
Info(Insta)	All locations	113	Daily
Inspector Gen'l	8698/BC	7180/6277	M-F
Legal Assist	8222/BC	6506	M-F
Locator(Mil)	8667/BC	7551	M-Sa
	9921/NK	7516	M-F
	9008/SK	6720	M-F
Personnel Spt	8745/BC	7368	M-F

GERMANY
Baumholder Community, continued

Police(Mil)	8720/BC	6217/7581	Daily
Emergency	On Barracks	114	24 hours daily
Police(Civ)	BC	C-3111/3112	24 hours daily
Public Affairs	8698/BC	6191	M-F
Tax Relief	8544/BC	7305/6130	M-F

LOGISTICAL SUPPORT

FACILITY/ACTIVITY	BLDG NO/LOC	PHONE	DAYS/COMMENTS
Auto Drivers Testing	8312/BC	7103/6490	M-F
Auto Parts(Exch)	8407/BC	6433	M-F
	8407/BC	4714	M-Sa. AAFES.
Auto Rental(Exch)	8407/BC	C-5446	M-F
Auto Rent(Other)	8407/BC	C-8640	M-F
Auto Repairs	8407/BC	C-4714	M-F
Auto Sales	8402/BC	2618	Daily. AMC.
	8402/BC	C-4157	M-Sa. Chrysler.
	8402/BC	C-2167	M-Sa. Ford.
	8402/BC	C-2157	M-Sa. GM.
Auto Wash	8407/BC	2101	Daily
Bank	8669/BC	6658/7575	M-Sa
	9935/NK	7011/7211	M-F
	9954/SK	6724	M-Th
Barber Shop(s)	8668/BC	C-2434	M-Sa
	8222/BC	None	M-F
	8243/BC	C-3277	M-Sa
	8548/BC	None	M-F
	8125/BC	None	M-F
	9939/NK	1209	M,Tu,Th-Sa
	9008/SK	None	M,Tu,Th,F
Beauty Shop(s)	8669/BC	C-2438/5759	Tu-Sa
	9939/NK	7120	Tu,Sa
	9032/SK	C-42455	Th-Sa
Bookstore	PX/BC	6521	Tu-Su
	9939/NK	7585	M,Tu,Th-Sa
	9026/SK	6805	Th-Tu
Bus	BC	6472	Daily
Child Care/Dev Ctr	8748/BC	7198	M-F
	8099/BC	7203	M-F. Preschool.
	8884/BC	7003	M-F
	9941/NK	7513	M-F
	9040/SK	6861	M-F
	9042/SK	6861	M-F
Clothing Sales	8219/BC	7221	M-Sa
Commissary(Main)	8575/BC	7208/6666	Daily
Commissary(Annex)	9944/NK	7118	M-Sa
	9025/SK	6829/6739	Tu-Sa
Dining Facility	1 Batt, 13 Inf	6343	Daily
	2 Batt, 68 Armor	6302	Daily
	3 Batt, 16 FA	6541	Daily
Dry Clean(Gov)	8544/BC	6120	Daily
	9939/NK	None	Daily
	9025/SK	None	Daily
Education Center	8209/BC	6308	M-F
	9911/NK	7074/8184	M-F
	9035/SK	6853/6756	M-F

U.S. Forces Travel & Transfer Guide Europe — 53

GERMANY

Baumholder Community, continued

Learning Center	8404/BC	6220	M-F
	8508/BC	7173/6669	M-F
	8544/BC	6460	M-F
	8207/BC	6201/8264	M-F
	8317/BC	6595	M-F
	8246/BC	6457	M-F
	8215/BC	6144	M-F
	8118/BC	6550	M-F
	8741/BC	6555	M-F. Dispensary.
	9911/NK	7084	M-F
	9035/SK	6704	M-F
Eng'r/Publ Works	BC	115	Daily
Exchange(Main)	8401/BC	6275	Daily
		C-1071	
Exchange(Annex)	9938/NK	C-5452	Th-Tu
	9026/SK	C-42352	Th-Tu
Finance(Mil)	8670/BC	7293/8336	M-F
Food(Caf/Rest)	8085/BC	5205	Daily

Food(Snack/Fast)	8401/BC	C-5677	Daily
	9026/SK	C-43436	Daily
Baskin Robbins	8219/BC	C-5211	Daily
Burger Bar	8125/BC	C-5025/2844	Daily
	9939/NK	C-6637	Daily
Burger King	8219/BC	C-2390/7941	Daily
Pizza Parlor	8219/BC	C-5211	Daily
Foodland	8881/BC	7128	Daily
	8665/BC	C-4754	Daily
Laundry(Self-Svc)	8255/BC	None	Daily
	9025/NK	C-5031	Daily
Motor Pool	8413/BC	7225/7273	M-F
Package Store	8656/BC	7556	Tu-Sa
	9942/NK	7243	M,Tu,Th-Sa
	9032/SK	6716	Tu-Sa
Photo Laboratory	8666/BC	8337	M-W,Sa,1/3Su
	9940/NK	7022	Tu-Sa
	9035/SK	6762	Sa-W

Pick-up Point	8664/BC	5384	M-F
	8243/BC	6379	Tu-F
	8246/BC	C-4489	M-F
	8741/BC	C-3266	M-F
	8253/BC	None	M-F
	8424/BC	C-5517	M-F
	8547/BC	6648	M-F
	8501/BC	6648	M-F
	8116/BC	None	M-F
	9939/NK	7209	M,Tu,Th-Sa
	9008/SK	C-47337	M,W,F
Postal Svcs(Mil)	8667/BC	8351	M-Sa
	9920/NK	7006/8116	M-F
	9030/SK	6720	M-F
Postal Svcs(Civ)	8667/BC	C-2101	M-F
Schools(DOD Dep)			
Elementary	8035/BC	7589/7587	M-F (K-6)
	8882,8885/BC	6416/7492	M-F (K-6)
Jr/Sr High School	8801/BC	8390/8391	M-F (7-12)

GERMANY
Baumholder Community, continued

Svc Stn(Insta)	8406/BC	7111 C-1583	Daily
Space-A Air Ops Flights to:	Smith Bks Locations in Germany.	7277	Daily
Tailor Shop	9939/NK	1209	M,Tu,Th,F
Taxi(Comm)	BC	6100	24 hours daily
Tel Repair(Gov)	All locations	119	Daily
Thrift Shop	8554/BC	6653	M,W,F
	9919/NK	7260	W,F
	9034/SK	None	N/A
TML			
Billeting	8076/BC	6188	M-F
	SDO/BC	7533	After hours
	Old 98th General Hospital Site	7287/7416	M-F
	Security/BC	7415/7309	After hours
	9032/SK	6713	24 hours daily
Guest House	9961,9963/NK	See billeting	
TLQ	Same as billeting/BC Same as billeting/SK		

HEALTH AND WELFARE

FACILITY/ACTIVITY	BLDG NO/LOC	PHONE	DAYS/COMMENTS
Ambulance	BC	116	24 hours daily
	German/BC	C-2063	24 hours daily
Army Comm Svcs	8746/BC	6468/7196	M-F
	9919/NK	7400	M-F
	9034/SK	6791	M-F
Army Emerg Relief	8746/BC	6344	M-F
		6157/8333	After hours
Central Appts	8740/BC	6205	M-F
CHAMPUS Office	8740/BC	6667/6205	M-F
Chaplain	8308/BC	6355	Su-F
Chapel	8249/BC	7150/6341	Daily
	9936/NK	8038/7438	Daily
Comm Drug/Alc Ctr	BC	6641	M-F
Dental Clinic	8741/BC	6448/7596	M-F
	8744/BC	7484/6319	M-F
	9036/SK	6886/6770	M-F
Medical Emergency	8740/BC	7462	24 hours daily
Red Cross	8125/BC	7508	M-F
		6313	After hours
Veterinary Svcs	8746/BC	6636	By appointment

REST AND RECREATION

FACILITY/ACTIVITY	BLDG NO/LOC	PHONE	DAYS/COMMENTS
Bowling Lanes	8105/BC	6569	Daily
	9955/NK	7292	Daily
	9024/SK	6702	Th-Tu
Consolidated Club	8661/BC	6574	Daily
	9032/SK	6776	Daily
Craftshops	8895/BC	6687	W-M
Automotive	8438/BC	6344	Tu-Su

Baumholder Community, continued
GERMANY

Multi-crafts	8438/BC	6117	W-Su
Photography	8666/BC	7263	M-Th,Sa
Wood	8438/BC	6117	W-Su
Enlisted Club	8125/BC	6607	Daily
Equip/Gear Locker	8896/BC	7182	Daily
Golf Course	8895/BC	7160	W-Su
	Comm Center	6172	Daily
Gymnasium	8895/BC	6156	Daily. Family fitness.
	8105/BC	6615/7164	Daily
	8220/BC	6486	Daily
	9555/NK	7184	Daily
	9021/SK	6495	Daily
Info Tour & Travel	8666/BC	6503	M-F. Tours.
		7206	M-F. Flights.
	9972/NK	7586	M-F
	9035/SK	6771	M-F
Library	8106/BC	7229	Daily
	9972/NK	7570	Sa-Th
	9035/SK	6728	Tu-Th,Sa,Su
MARS	8104/BC	7498/6389	Daily
O'Club	8085/BC	6128	Tu-Su
	9966/NK	7219	Daily
Outdoor Rec Ctr	8895/BC	7182	Daily
Recreation Center	8332/BC	6475	Daily
	9972/NK	7586	Daily
	9035/SK	6814	Daily
Rod and Gun Club	8167/BC	6345	Daily
	9942/NK	7044	M-Sa
Swimming Pool	8895/BC	6575	W-M
Theater	8125/BC	6387	M-F. Weekends as scheduled.
	9938/NK	7096	As scheduled
	9027/SK	6727	As scheduled
Video Rental	9939/NK	None	M,Tu,Th-Sa
Youth Center	8046/BC	7276	Tu-Sa
	8880/BC	7475	Tu-Sa
	9997/NK	7514	Tu-Sa
	9042/SK	6832	Tu-Sa

===

BERCHTESGADEN ARMED FORCES RECREATION CENTER (GE07R7)
APO New York 09029-5000

TELEPHONE INFORMATION: Main installation numbers: Civ: 49-08652-58-113. ETS: 441-5113. ATVN: 440-1110 (ask for Berchtesgaden). For reservations call Civ: 49-08821-750-575 or ETS: 440-2575. Civ prefix: 08652-__. ETS prefix: 441-5XXX. Civ to mil prefix: 08652-58-XXX.

LOCATION: Exit the Munich-Salzburg Autobahn E-11 at Bad Reichenhall, south on GE-20, 18 kilometers to Berchtesgaden. HE: p-94, D/4. NMC: Munich 100 miles northwest.

GENERAL INSTALLATION INFORMATION: There are no military units

GERMANY
Berchtesgaden Armed Forces Recreation Center, continued

permanently stationed at Berchtesgaden AFRC. Note: the following abbreviations are used in this listing only: BHof (Berchtesgaden Hof Hotel); CTO (Central Transportation Office); HB (Hallenbach); HQ (Community Headquarters at Strub Kaserne); SC (Shopping Center); SK (Stanggass Kaserne); SL (Skytop Lodge); WH (Walker Hotel).

GENERAL CITY/REGIONAL INFORMATION: Nestled in the heart of the Bavarian Alps, just eight miles from the Austrian border, Berchtesgaden is a 1,200-year-old storybook village, with church spires framed by scenic mountains rising to nearly 9,000 feet.

Breathtaking scenery and a wide variety of sport and tour opportunities await the visitor to this popular all-season recreation spot. Skiers will love Berchtesgaden! The superbly designed ski facility is a great place to learn or enhance your skills. There are ski packages for beginners, intermediates and experts in downhill and cross-country skiing. The Ski Austria program offers daily skiing on such well-known slopes as Flachau, Maria Alm, Hochkoenig, Zauchensee, Steinplatte, Jenner, and Obertauern. There is mountaineering for individuals and groups, golfing at the Skytop Golf Course, intermediate and advanced tennis programs and kayaking and white-water rafting, to name only some of the sport opportunities available.

Visitors can explore vast open rooms carved out of a salt mountain on the Salt Mine Tour, visit the World War II bunkers in the Obersalzberg Mountain that were designed for Hitler and other ranking Nazis or take the Berchtesgaden Town Tour on which you'll see the Royal Castle and visit a cuckoo clock factory and much more!

ADMINISTRATIVE SUPPORT

FACILITY/ACTIVITY	BLDG NO/LOC	PHONE	DAYS/COMMENTS
Customs/Duty	MP Station	753	Make appointment
Duty Officer	HQ	616	N/A
Fire(Mil)	On Barracks	117	24 hours daily
Housing	HQ	815/771	M-F
Info(Insta)	On Barracks	113	N/A
Police(Mil)	HQ	616	24 hours daily
Emergency	On Barracks	114	24 hours daily
Public Affairs	HQ	795	M-F
Tax Relief	SK	635	W

LOGISTICAL SUPPORT

FACILITY/ACTIVITY	BLDG NO/LOC	PHONE	DAYS/COMMENTS
Auto Registration	HQ	616/826	Tu,W,F
Bank	214/HQ	693	M-F
Barber Shop(s)	BHof	N/A	Tu-F
Beauty Shop(s)	BHof	N/A	Tu-F
Bookstore	Billeting	662	M,W-Sa
Child Care/Dev Ctr	WH	638	M-Sa
Commissary(Main)	211/HQ	662/748	Tu-Sa
Eng'r/Publ Works	HQ	675	M-F
	Emergency	115	24 hours daily
Exchange(Main)	SC	C-2981	Daily
Motor Pool	HQ	616/826	M-F

GERMANY

Berchtesgaden Armed Forces Recreation Center, continued

Package Store	HQ	660	Tu-Sa
Postal Svcs(Mil)	214/HQ	651	M-F
Postal Svcs(Civ)	Next to Bahnhof	N/A	M-Sa
Schools(DOD Dep)			
Elementary	SK	641	M-F
High School	Salzburg International Preparatory School		
Svc Stn(Insta)	Banhhof St	N/A	Daily
Tel Booking Oper	On Barracks	112	24 hours daily
Tel Repair(Gov)	On Barracks	119	M-F
TML			
Reservations	AFRC	08821-750-575	Daily
Hotels	Exec Office	659	Daily
	Alpine Inn	640 C-63044	Daily
	Berchtesgadener Hof	627 C-61071	Daily
	General McNair	627	Daily
	General Walker	657	Daily
	Evergreen Lodge	642	Daily
	Skytop Lodge	645	Daily
	Haus Chancellor	620	Daily
	Haus Watzmann	622	Daily

HEALTH AND WELFARE

FACILITY/ACTIVITY	BLDG NO/LOC	PHONE	DAYS/COMMENTS
Ambulance	Dispensary	116	24 hours daily
Central Appts	220/HQ	807/667	M-F
Chaplain	HQ	601/770	M-F
Medical Emergency	Dispensary	116	24 hours daily
Poison Control	Dispensary	116	24 hours daily

REST AND RECREATION

FACILITY/ACTIVITY	BLDG NO/LOC	PHONE	DAYS/COMMENTS
Bowling Lanes	CTO	680	Daily
Craftshops			
Automotive	SK	678	Tu-Sa
Multi-crafts	Activity Center	684	M,W,F,Sa
Golf Course	SL	690	Seasonal
Info Tour & Travel	CTO	637/802	M-F
Library	SK	635	M-F
Outdoor Rec Ctr	N/A	684/751	N/A
Racket Courts	MP Station	826/616	Make reservation.
Recreation Center	112/HQ	684/751	M-F
	SL	786	M-F
Theater	WH	669/684	W,Th,Sa-M
Youth Center	Activity center	684	M,W,Sa

GERMANY

BERLIN COMMUNITY (GE26R7)
APO New York 09742-5000

TELEPHONE INFORMATION: Main installation numbers: Civ: 49-030-819-113. ETS: 332-113. Civ prefix: 030-____. ETS prefix: 332-XXXX. Civ to mil prefix: 030-819-XXXX.

LOCATION: Can be reached from the E-2, Helmstedt-Berlin Autobahn, by air to Tempelhof AB or via duty train from Frankfurt or Bremerhaven. Note: those traveling to Berlin must follow the strict guidelines outlined in USAREUR Regulation 550-180. Noncompliance with these rules can result in delays or travel denied by the Soviet government. Reservations must be made 42 days in advance. See the personnel officer to get your flag orders. HE: p-63, F/6. NMC: Berlin, in the city.

GENERAL INSTALLATION INFORMATION: The size and structure of the Berlin Brigade has remained relatively stable since 1950. Three infantry battalions form the heart of the Brigade. They are supported by a tank company, an artillery battery, and an engineer company organized since 1980 in a Combat Support Battalion.

The infantry, of course, is not the only branch of the U.S. Army represented in the Berlin Brigade. Artillery, engineers, chemical, signal, military police, armor, ordnance, quartermaster, military intelligence, and service support branches are also present. Working as a team, the Brigade brings together the successors of the soldiers who first entered Berlin more than 40 years ago to establish the Berlin Military Post. Note: the following abbreviations are used in this listing only: AB (Andrews Barracks); LDC (Lucius D. Clay Headquarters); McNB (McNair Barracks); RB (Roosevelt Barracks); TP (Truman Plaza); VS (Von Steuben).

GENERAL CITY/REGIONAL INFORMATION: Berlin is a beautiful city of great historical significance. Tourists can explore numerous world-famous castles and museums; visit the Berlin Wall, zoo, aquarium and botanical gardens; take a boat ride on the Wannsee; spend some time at the unforgettable exhibit at Checkpoint Charlie; attend an opera, concert or ballet; participate in a number of sports; or purchase some souvenirs in one of Berlin's fine shops. A visit to East Berlin is also a very popular and memorable activity for tourists and residents alike. See our special appendix, "Access to Berlin," for more information.

ADMINISTRATIVE SUPPORT

FACILITY/ACTIVITY	BLDG NO/LOC	PHONE	DAYS/COMMENTS
Customs/Duty	935/AB	3522	M-F
Drivers Testing	948/AB	3429	M-F
Duty Officer	LDC	7222	24 hours daily
Fire(Mil)	All locations	117	24 hours daily
Fire(Civ)	All locations	112	24 hours daily
Housing	871A/VS	7325	M-F
Info(Insta)	All locations	113	24 hours daily
Inspector Gen'l	2/LDC	6009	M-F
Legal Assist	5/LDC	6427	M-F
Personnel Spt	11/LDC	6911	M-F
Police(Mil)	901/AB	114	24 hours daily
Police(Civ)	901/AB	110	24 hours daily

U.S. Forces Travel & Transfer Guide Europe — 59

Berlin Community, continued   GERMANY

| Public Affairs | 2/LDC | 6816 | M-F |

LOGISTICAL SUPPORT

FACILITY/ACTIVITY	BLDG NO/LOC	PHONE	DAYS/COMMENTS
Audio/Photo Ctr	McNB	9484	W-M
Auto Parts(Exch)	113/near TP	6417	Daily
Auto Registration	936/AB	6994	M-F
Auto Rental(Exch)	TP	5075/7873	M-Sa
Auto Repairs	113/near TP	6417	M-F
Auto Sales	113/near TP	8773/8684/8847	Tu-Sa
Bank	TP	6943	M-Sa
	906/AB	3209	M,W,Th,F
	1025/McNB	9142	M-F,EOM Payday
Barber Shop(s)	TP	7124	Tu-Sa
	AB	3538	M-F
	McNB	C-817-8191	M-F
Beauty Shop(s)	81/TP	7125	M-Sa
Bookstore	85/TP	6723	Daily
	906/AB	N/A	M-F
	1025/McNB	N/A	M-F
Bus	TP	3410/3418	Daily
Child Care/Dev Ctr	194/near TP	6270	M-F
	Hospital	7273	M-F
Clothing Sales	1017/McNB	9193	M-F
Commissary(Main)	64/TP	6107	Tu-Su
Credit Union	85/TP	6545	Tu-Sa
Dining Facility	1001C/McNB	9761	Daily
	901/AB	3509	Daily
Dry Clean(Exch)	84/TP	6109	Daily
	AB	3719	M-F
	McNB	9114	M-F
Education Center	901/AB	3162	M-F
Learning Center	1001D/McNB	9615/9120	M-F
Eng'r/Publ Works	VS	115	Daily
Exchange(Main)	81/TP	C-813-3082	Daily
Exchange(Annex)	1022C/McNB	9150	Daily
	906/AB	3585	Daily
Finance(Mil)	9/LDC	6710	M-F
Food(Snack/Fast)			
Baskin Robbins	84/TP	6827	Daily
Burger Bar	906/AB	3420	Daily
	1022E/McNB	9462	Daily
Burger King	TP	6834	Daily
Foodland	84/TP	6659	Daily
Laundry(Self-Svc)	84/TP	6323	Daily
	AB	3358	24 hours daily
	McNB	9616	24 hours daily
Package Store	84/TP	6309	Tu-Su
Pick-up Point	TP	None	Tu-Su
	AB	None	M-F
	McNB	None	M-F
Postal Svcs(Mil)	TP	4408/6625	Tu-Su
	AB	3552	M-F
	McNB	9170	M-F

GERMANY
Berlin Community, continued

Postal Svcs(Civ)	McNB	9170	M-F
	TP	6625	Tu-Su
Railroad/RTO	Lichterfelde S-bahn	6916/6917	Daily
SATO-OS	LDC	7184 C-6932082	M-F
	McNB		M-F
Schools			
Elementary	101A/near TP	6361	M-F
High Schools	65/near Turner Barracks	6392	M-F
Svc Stn(Insta)	N/A	6417 C-813-7172	Daily
Space-A Air Ops	See Templehof Central Airport listing.		
Tailor Shop	TP	C-832-4372	M-Sa
	AB	C-833-1576	Tu-Sa
	McNB	9688	M-F
Taxi(Comm)	N/A	C-26-1026	Daily
	N/A	C-21-6060	Daily
Tel Booking Oper	All locations	112	Daily
Tel Repair(Gov)	N/A	C-218-3950	Qtrs tel only
Thrift Shop	26/LDC	C-831-3648	M-Th
TML			
Billeting	Fam Hsg Branch	6654	M-F
Guest Houses			
Dahlem	145/LDC	6425	Daily
Harnack House	605/LDC	6654	Daily
Roosevelt Arms	RB	6654	Daily
Wansee Facility	N/A	6654	Daily
DV/VIP-Protocol Office	1, Rm 2024-2032	6933	06+
Travel Agents	TP	6523	M-F

===
HEALTH AND WELFARE
===

FACILITY/ACTIVITY	BLDG NO/LOC	PHONE	DAYS/COMMENTS
Ambulance	All locations	116	24 hours daily
Army Comm Svcs	TP	6456/6500	M-F
Army Emerg Relief	TP	6984	M-F
Central Appts	Hospital	4211	M-F
CHAMPUS Office	Hospital	4180/4181	M-F
Chaplain(Amer Comm Chapel)		6019/6946	M-F
Chapel	McNB	6761/62	M-F
Comm Drug/Alc Ctr	N/A	9632	M-F
Dental Clinic	AB	3491	M-F
	Hospital	4266	M-F
	McNB	9351/55	M-F
Medical Emergency	Hospital	4131/32/33	24 hours daily
Mental Health	Hospital	4190	M-F
Poison Control	Hospital	4130/31	24 hours daily
Red Cross	1/LDC	4167/6459	M-F
		7222	After hours
Veterinary Svcs	N/A	4242	M-F

===

Berlin Community, continued

GERMANY

REST AND RECREATION

FACILITY/ACTIVITY	BLDG NO/LOC	PHONE	DAYS/COMMENTS
Amer Forces Ntwk	24/LDC	6046/6145	M-F
Bowling Lanes	56/near TP	6581/6775	Daily
	1001A/McNB	9198	Th-M
Craftshops			
Automotive	943/AB	3349/3288	Daily
Ceramics	906/AB	3534	Th-M
Multi-crafts	1001Q/McNB	9180	Sa-W
Photo	McNB	9484	Sa-W
Wood	AB	3544	Th-M
Enlisted Club	910/AB	3557	M-Sa
	1001I,L,M/McNB	9737/9743	Tu-Su
Golf Course	Berlin American	6533	Daily
Gymnasium	920/AB	3521	Daily
	56/near TP	6581	Daily
	1015/McNB	9365	Daily
Info Tour & Travel	Admin Office	7187/85	M-Sa
Library	1001Q/AB	3529	Daily
	Hospital	4265	M-Sa
	906/AB	9175	Daily
	193/nearTP	6559	Daily
MARS	N/A	3567	N/A
Museum	McNB	9165	W-F
NCO Club	Checkpoint	7127/07	Daily
	Eagle's Nest/McNB	9152	
	912 NCO Annex	3667	
O'Club	605 Harnack Hse	6252/6415	Tu-Su
Outdoor Rec Ctr	Near TP	6696/6623	W-M
Recreation Center	AB	3554	Daily
All-American Comm Ctr	AB	9754	Daily
Rod and Gun Club	1025/Clubhouse Store	6121/9566	Tu-Su
Swimming Pool	AB	3521	Th-Tu
	79/near TP	6871/6768	Daily
Tennis Courts	78/near TP	6581	Daily
Theater	AB	3538	Th-Tu
	Music Ctr/AB	3570	Call for schedule.
	1022A,B/McNB	9131	Daily
Water Recreation	Wannsee	6555	Seasonal
Youth Center	86/near TP	6239	M-F
	Admin/Social	6249/6952	M-F
	Social Game Rm		M-Sa

BINDLACH/BAYREUTH SUB-COMMUNITY
(GE50R7)
APO New York 09411-5000

TELEPHONE INFORMATION: Main installation numbers: Civ: 49-09208-83-113. ETS: 462-3113. ATVN: 460-1110 (ask for Bindlach/Bayreuth). Civ prefix: 09208-____. ETS prefix: 462-3XXX. Civ to mil prefix: 09208-83-XXX.

GERMANY
Bindlach/Bayreuth Sub-Community, continued

LOCATION: Bindlach is located north of Bayreuth on Route 2. It can also be reached from the E-6 Autobahn. Take the Bayreuth Nord exit north on Route 2 for three miles. HE: p-40, F/1. NMC: Bayreuth, in the city.

GENERAL INSTALLATION INFORMATION: Bindlach/Bayreuth Sub-Community is the home of Christensen Barracks. The installation's mission is to serve as a support unit for the 7th Army Training Command.

GENERAL CITY/REGIONAL INFORMATION: Bayreuth was founded in the 12th century and is first mentioned in 1194. It became a city with city rights in 1231. Since 1603 it has been the residence of the House of Ansbach-Bayreuth. In 1791 it became a part of Prussia, and in 1805 of Bavaria.

Local attractions include the Municipal Church (1400s); the New Castle (1700s); the Opera House (1744-1748); and Eremitage Castle (1700s). The Richard Wagner Festival Hall (1872-1876) is located north of the city. Bayreuth is near many crystal and porcelain factories. The area is also known for its ski resorts.

ADMINISTRATIVE SUPPORT

FACILITY/ACTIVITY	BLDG NO/LOC	PHONE	DAYS/COMMENTS
Customs/Duty	On Barracks	805	M-F
Fire(Mil)	On Barracks	117	24 hours daily
Housing	On Barracks	658	M-F
Personnel Spt	On Barracks	811	M-F
Police(Mil)	On Barracks	812	Daily
Emergency		114	24 hours daily
Public Affairs	On Barracks	825	M-F

LOGISTICAL SUPPORT

FACILITY/ACTIVITY	BLDG NO/LOC	PHONE	DAYS/COMMENTS
Auto Drivers Testing	On Barracks	685	M-F
Bank	On Barracks	651	Tu-Sa
Bookstore	9288	653	Tu-Sa
Commissary(Main)	9270	814/655	Tu-Sa
Dining Facility	On Barracks	842	Daily
Education Center	On Barracks	859	M-F
Eng'r/Publ Works	On Barracks	641	Daily
Motor Pool	On Barracks	855	Daily
Package Store	9270	635	Tu-Sa
Photo Laboratory	On Barracks	648	Daily
Pick-up Point	On Barracks	C-363	Tu-Sa
Postal Svcs(Mil)	On Barracks	866	M-Sa
Schools(DOD Dep)			
Elementary	On Barracks	809	M-F
Space-A Air Ops	Airfield	827	Daily
Flights to:	Locations in Germany		
Tailor Shop	On Barracks	C-366	Tu-Sa
Tel Repair(Gov)	On Barracks	119	Daily

U.S. Forces Travel & Transfer Guide Europe — 63

Bindlach/Bayreuth Sub-Community, continued

GERMANY

HEALTH AND WELFARE

FACILITY/ACTIVITY	BLDG NO/LOC	PHONE	DAYS/COMMENTS
Ambulance	On Barracks	116	24 hours daily
Army Comm Svcs	On Barracks	819	M-F
Central Appts	9232	656/822	Daily
Chaplain	9220	833/634	Daily
Comm Drug/Alc Ctr	9232	819	M-F
Dental Clinic	9232	839	M-F

REST AND RECREATION

FACILITY/ACTIVITY	BLDG NO/LOC	PHONE	DAYS/COMMENTS
Bowling Lanes	9220	650	Daily
Craftshops			
Multi-crafts	On Barracks	648	Daily
Enlisted Club	9231	634	Daily
Gymnasium	On Barracks	659	Daily
Library	On Barracks	648	Daily
NCO Club	9230	635	Daily
Outdoor Rec Ctr	On Barracks	648	Daily
Service Club	9220	648	Daily
Theater	8220	644	Call for schedule.
Youth Center	On Barracks	844	Daily

BITBURG AIR BASE (GE04R7)
APO New York 09132-5000

TELEPHONE INFORMATION: Main installation numbers: Civ: 49-6561-61-1110. ETS/ATVN: 453-1110. Civ prefix: 06561-____. ETS/ATVN prefix: 453-XXXX. Civ to mil prefix: 06561-61-XXXX.

LOCATION: From Trier, take Hwy B-51 N to Bitburg or Prüm, turn R at the "Bitburg Flugplatz" sign. HE: p-39, F/1. NMC: Trier, 17 mi S.

GENERAL INSTALLATION INFORMATION: The primary unit is the 36th Tactical Fighter Wing. The mission is to prepare and conduct air defense operations as directed; provide administrative and logistical support for assigned, attached and tenant units; and operate and maintain the Bitburg Air Base complex and such other stations and facilities as directed.

GENERAL CITY/REGIONAL INFORMATION: Bitburg began as a stopover for Roman troops some 2,000 years ago and, therefore, claims to be almost as old as Trier, the self-proclaimed "oldest city in Germany," located just 25 kilometers to the south. Because of its rich history and central location, the region offers much for the visitor. Attractions include castles and gothic and baroque churches, partly restored ruins in nearby areas of Germany and Luxembourg, museums exhibiting materials dating back 2,000 years, walking trails and wine-tasting events and a number of local festivities.

GERMANY
Bitburg Air Base, continued

ADMINISTRATIVE SUPPORT

FACILITY/ACTIVITY	BLDG NO/LOC	PHONE	DAYS/COMMENTS
Advocate	116	7032	M-F
Customs/Duty	217	7614	M-F
Duty Officer	412	7133	24 hours daily
Fire(Mil)	405,66 (Hsg)	117/7641	24 hours daily
Fire(Civ)	Bitburg	112	24 hours daily
Housing Referral	206	7551	M-F
Info(Insta)	211	113	24 hours daily
Inspector Gen'l	116	7001	M-F
Legal Assist	116	7665	M-F
Locator(Mil)	445	7449/7814	M-F
Locator(Civ)	134	7321	M-F
Personnel Spt	116	7456	M-F
Police(Mil)	On Base	7400	24 hours daily
Emergency	117	114	24 hrs dly
Police(Civ)	Bitburg	5011	24 hrs dly
Emergency	Bitburg	110	24 hrs dly
Public Affairs	107	7717	M-F
Tax Relief	301	7665	M-F

LOGISTICAL SUPPORT

FACILITY/ACTIVITY	BLDG NO/LOC	PHONE	DAYS/COMMENTS
Audio-Photo Ctr	328	C-8951/7477	M-F
Auto Drivers Testing	304/239	7827/7969	M,W,F
Auto Parts(Exch)	83	7818	M-Sa
Auto Registration	132	7404	M-F
Auto Rent(Other)	101(Budget)	C-12392	M-Sa
Auto Repairs	83	7450	M-F
Auto Sales	Beside Bldg 83	C-4600	M-Sa
	At BX	2175/2300	M-Sa
Auto Ship(Gov)	217	7132	M-F
Bank	70	7646/7894	M-Sa
Barber Shop(s)	209	7943	M-Sa
	61 (Hosp)	6256	M-Sa
	70	C-2781	M-Sa
Beauty Shop(s)	70	C-2781	M-Sa
Bookstore	209	C-8536	M-Sa
	70	C-3615	Dly
Child Care/Dev Ctr	84	7012/7813	M-Sa
A new center will open in Jan 1990.
Clothing Sales	70	7322	M-Sa
Commissary(Main)	70	7635	Tu-Sa
A new commissary will open in Oct 1989.
Credit Union	201	7370	M-F
Dining Facility	108	7368/7639	Daily.
Dry Clean(Exch)	209	C-2307	M-Sa
Education Center	304	7602/7676	M-F
Eng'r/Publ Works	206	7957	M-F
Exchange(Main)	70	7221	Daily
Exchange(Annex)	209	2596	M-Sa

Bitburg Air Base, continued GERMANY

Finance(Mil)	115	7339	M-F
Food(Snack/Fast)			
Baskin Robbins	On Base	C-2783	Daily
	300	C-2411/2718	Daily
Burger Bar	70	C-2783	Daily
Foodland	86	C-2411	Daily
Laundry(Exch)	209	C-2307	M-Sa
Laundry(Self-Svc)	208	N/A	24 hours daily
Motor Pool	239	7497	Daily
Package Store	70	7369	Tu-Sa
Photo Laboratory	213	7244	M-F
Pick-up Point	209	C-2307	
Postal Svcs(Mil)	205	7933	M-Sa
Postal Svcs(Civ)	300	C-131	M-F
Railroad/RTO	Erdorf	C-3235	Daily
SATO-OS	217	7624/7625	M-F
Schools(DOD Dep)			
Elementary	87	7215	M-F (K-5)
Middle School	60	7731	M-F (6-8)
High School	98	7937	M-F (9-12)
Svc Stn (Insta)	64	C-4900	Daily
Tailor Shop	209	N/A	M-Sa
Taxi(Comm)	N/A	C-17066	24 hours daily
Tel Booking Oper	N/A	1110	24 hours daily
Tel Repair(Gov)	216	7533	M-F
Tel Repair(Civ)	300	C-131	M-F
Thrift Shop	2001	7120	Call for hrs
TML(All ranks)			
Billeting	101,124	7458	24 hours daily
VAQ(E1-E6)	101	1458	24 hours daily
VOQ(E9 & O6+)	101	7200	24 hours daily
VOQ(O1-O5)	101, 123	8493	24 hours daily
DV/VIP(O6+)	116	7458	24 hours daily
Travel Agents	300	7691	Daily
Watch Repair	70	7221	Daily

HEALTH AND WELFARE

FACILITY/ACTIVITY	BLDG NO/LOC	PHONE	DAYS/COMMENTS
AF Family Svcs	2002	7023	M-F
AF Relief	105	7491	M-F
		7330	After hours
Ambulance	61	116	24 hours daily
Central Appts	61	7821	M-F
CHAMPUS Office	61	6200	M-F
Chaplain	114	7127	Daily
Chapel	114	7748	M-F
	73	7592	Call for hours.
Comm Drug/Alc Ctr	105	7711	M-F
Dental Clinic	62	6222	M-F
Medical Emergency	61	6233/116	24 hours daily
Mental Health	61	6225	M-F
Poison Control	61	116	24 hours daily
Red Cross	2002	7169/7127	24 hours daily
Veterinary Svcs	222	7988	Call for appoint.

GERMANY
Bitburg Air Base, continued

REST AND RECREATION

FACILITY/ACTIVITY	BLDG NO/LOC	PHONE	DAYS/COMMENTS
Amer Forces Ntwk	N/A	483-8602	Days
	N/A	320-6101	Eves/Wknds
Bowling Lanes	503	7158/7787	Daily
Craftshops			
Automotive	328	7450	Daily
Multi-crafts	246	7519	Tu-Su
Enlisted Club	302	7544	Call for hours.
Equip/Gear Locker	308	7377	Daily
Fam Camp	300	7252	Daily
	This camp opened in the summer of 1989.		
Golf Course	See Spangdahlem Air Base listing.		
Gymnasium	308	7377/7710	Daily
Info Tour & Travel	300	7691	Daily
Library	304	7056	Daily
MARS	300	7828	M-F
NCO Club	302	7544	Daily
O'Club	103	7217/7543	Su-F
Outdoor Rec Ctr	300	7252	Daily
Racket Courts	308 (Gym)	7377	Daily
Recreation Center	300/Skyblazer	7252/7691	Daily
Rod and Gun Club	T558	7757	Tu-Sa
Special Services(MWR)	335	7849	M-F
Sport Field	308 (Gym)	7377	Daily
Tennis Courts	308 (Gym)	7377	Daily
Theater	72	7541	Daily
	201	7696	Daily
Track	308 (Gym)	7377	Daily
Trail(s)	308 (Gym)	7377	Daily
Video Rental	70	N/A	Daily
Water Recreation	308 (Gym)	7377	Daily
Youth Center	2005 (Hot Spot)	N/A	F-Sa
	58 (Activities)	7329	M-Sa

BÖBLINGEN/SINDELFINGEN SUB-COMMUNITY (GE63R7)
APO New York 09046-5000

TELEPHONE INFORMATION: Main installation numbers: Civ: 49-07031-15-113. ETS/ATVN: 431-2113. Civ prefix: 07031-____. ETS/ATVN prefix: 431-2XXX. Civ to mil prefix: 07031-15-XXX.

LOCATION: Located off the E-70 Autobahn south of Stuttgart. HE: p-40, C/4. NMC: Stuttgart, 10 miles north.

GENERAL INSTALLATION INFORMATION: The Böblingen/Sindelfingen Military Community, which includes Panzer Kaserne, is headquarters for the 2nd Battalion, 37th Armor; 1st Battalion, 16th Infantry; and the 1st Maintenance Battalion. The primary mission of the community is to support the 1st Infantry Division and VII Corps.

Böblingen/Sindelfingen Sub-Community, continued

GERMANY

GENERAL CITY/REGIONAL: Böblingen is located on a site that has been settled since the Stone Age. In the 1800s, the city became a prosperous industrial center. Although the town suffered heavy damage during World War II, after the war the old city was reconstructed, the Market Square enlarged, and the city church rebuilt. The city continues to grow today and has a population of over 42,000.

Visitors strolling through the city will see spacious boulevards, thriving industry, and bits of parkland that make up the cityscape. As in many parts of Germany, the ancient and the modern blend easily. For example, the Christopher Fountain, built in 1526, stands in contrast to the modern City Hall, built in 1952. The city has a new shopping mall where many of the stores cater to the prosperous clientele from nearby Sindelfingen, home to the Mercedes-Benz factory and an IBM Complex. For summer fun, one of the lakes close to the city rents paddleboats, rowboats, and sailboats.

ADMINISTRATIVE SUPPORT

FACILITY/ACTIVITY	BLDG NO/LOC	PHONE	DAYS/COMMENTS
Duty Officer	On Barracks	606	Daily
		C-226806	
Fire(Mil)	On Barracks	117	24 hours daily
Housing	See Stuttgart Community listing.		
Legal Assist	On Barracks	750/430	M-F
Police(Mil)	2900	824	24 hours daily
Emergency		114	24 hours daily
Police(Civ)	Böblingen	117	24 hours daily
Public Affairs	On Barracks	612	M-F

LOGISTICAL SUPPORT

FACILITY/ACTIVITY	BLDG NO/LOC	PHONE	DAYS/COMMENTS
Bank	2953	436	M-F
		C-223012	
Barber Shop(s)	2948	622	M-Sa
		C-25139	
Beauty Shop(s)	3948	C-25139	M-F
Bookstore	2981	566	Daily
		C-225694	
Bus	On Barracks	321/391	Daily
Child Care/Dev Ctr	3162	619	Daily
		C-25392	
Dining Facility	On Barracks	407/602/420	Daily
Education Center	2962	344/506	Daily
Elec Repair(Gov)	2931	322/606	After duty hours
Eng'r/Publ Works	2931	115/478	M-F
Exchange(Main)	2961	585	Daily
		C-25451	
Food(Caf/Rest)	2949	585	Daily
Food(Snack/Fast)			
Pizza Parlor	2900	535/413	Daily
Snack Bar	2949	429	Daily
		C-223062	
Foodland	2952	585	M-Sa
		C-25511	

GERMANY
Böblingen/Sindelfingen Sub-Community, continued

Laundry(Self-Svc)	Besdie S&S	None	24 hours daily
Package Store	2961	440	Tu-Sa
Pick-up Point	2948	636 C-26832	Tu-Sa
Postal Svcs(Mil)	2961	563	M-F
Schools(DOD Dep)			
Elementary	2915	715/528	M-F
High School	See Stuttgart Community listing.		
Svc Stn(Insta)	2972	469	Daily
Tailor Shop	2948	None	M-F
Taxi(Comm)	On Barracks	C-26066	Daily
Tel Booking Oper	On Barracks	112	24 hours daily
Tel Repair(Gov)	On Barracks	731	Daily
Thrift Shop	2948	603	W-F
TML	On Barracks	680	Daily
BEQ	On Barracks	455	Daily
	Also, see Stuttgart Community listing.		
Travel Agents	2948	316 C-25016	M-F

HEALTH AND WELFARE

FACILITY/ACTIVITY	BLDG NO/LOC	PHONE	DAYS/COMMENTS
Army Comm Svcs	2948	524/706	M-F
Army Emerg Relief	2948	524/695	M-F
Central Appts	Patch Bks	430-7102/ 5204/7130	Daily
CHAMPUS Office	5th General Hosp	422-2845	M-F
	Patch Bks	430-5227	M-F
Chaplain	2940	819/447	Tu-Th
Chapel	2940	819/447	Daily
Comm Drug/Alc Ctr	N/A	530	M-F
Dental Clinic	2948	410/310	M-F
Medical Emergency	2951	491/850 C-25279	24 hours daily
Red Cross	2948	818	M-F

REST AND RECREATION

FACILITY/ACTIVITY	BLDG NO/LOC	PHONE	DAYS/COMMENTS
Bowling Lanes	2931	459	Daily
Craftshops			
Automotive	2926	555	Sa-Th
Multi-crafts	2948/9	479	Daily
Photography	2948/9	479	Daily
Enlisted Club	2961	635	Tu-Sa
Golf Course	See Ludwigsburg-Kornwestheim listing.		
Gymnasium	2990	724	Daily
Library	2914	553	Su-F
MARS	On Barracks	713	Daily
NCO Club	2916	635	Tu-Su
O'Club	3180	301 C-25432	M-Sa
Recreation Center	2949	760/540	Daily
Sport Field	Near Schools	None	Seasonal

U.S. Forces Travel & Transfer Guide Europe — 69

GERMANY

Böblingen/Sindelfingen Sub-Community, continued

Swimming Pool	Schönaicher	C-669411	Seasonal
	Galgenberg	C-669345	Seasonal
Theater	2947	469	Daily
Youth Center	Pre-teen Ctr	495	M-F
		C-25460	
	Activity Ctr	568	Tu-Sa

==

BREMERHAVEN COMMUNITY (GE32R7)
APO NY 09069-5000

TELEPHONE INFORMATION: Main installation numbers: Civ: 49-0471-891-1110. ETS/ATVN: 342-1110. Civ prefix: 0471-____. ETS/ATVN prefix: 342-XXXX. Civ to mil prefix: 0471-891-XXXX (Bremerhaven Military extensions that begin with 8); 0471-893-XXXX (Bremerhaven Hospital extensions that begin with 7).

LOCATION: Exit from the E-3 Autobahn north or south at Bremen, N E-71 for 60 kilometers. Follow American Forces signs to facilities. HE: p-33, D/4 NMC: in the city.

GENERAL INSTALLATION INFORMATION: U.S. Forces in Bremerhaven are stationed at Carl Schurz Kaserne and are composed of Army, Navy, and Air Force personnel. Major Units in Bremerhaven include the 1st Movements Region, 39th Signal Battalion, 69th Transportation Company, 176th Personnel Service Company, MEDDAC, Navy Military Sealift Command, 606th Tactical Control Squadron, and 626th/636th Tactical Control Flights. The 2nd Armored Division (Fwd) is at the Lucius D. Clay Kaserne in Garlstedt along with a large housing complex at Osterholz-Scharmbeck, 13 miles south of Bremerhaven. (See Garlstedt listing.) The outlying areas of the community are the 294th Artillery Group at Flensburg (E-3 Autobahn 3-4 hours north), 552nd Artillery Group at Soegel (2-3 hours drive south), and Helmstedt Support Detachment (E-8 Autobahn at East German border).

GENERAL CITY/REGIONAL INFORMATION: The land mass of Norddeutschland is widely varied, ranging from coastal beaches, flat plains and rolling hills to the Harz Mountains, a winter skiing area. Bremerhaven is the largest city on Germany's North Sea coast with population of approximately 130,000. It is the second largest German seaport and an international trade and transportation center. Bremerhaven offers a zoo, the German Maritime Museum, and the North Sea Aquarium. Parks, open-air markets and fine seafood and ethnic restaurants are plentiful in this Norddeutschland area. **Note: Bremerhaven is a departure point for the duty train to Berlin. It also has a Frankfurt-bound duty bus.** Contact RTO or travel agent for details.

==
ADMINISTRATIVE SUPPORT

FACILITY/ACTIVITY	BLDG NO/LOC	PHONE	DAYS/COMMENTS
Customs/Duty	108	8246	Daily
Duty Officer	1	8515	Daily
Fire(Mil)	On Barracks	117	24 hours daily
Fire(Civ)	BHN	112	24 hours daily

70 — U.S. Forces Travel & Transfer Guide Europe

GERMANY
Bremerhaven Community, continued

Housing
Family	103	8686	M-F
Unaccompanied	103	8686	M-F
Referral	103	8686	M-F
Info(Insta)	332	113	24 hours daily
Inspector Gen'l	321	8536	M-F
Legal Assist	229	8672	M-F
Locator(Mil)	2	8247	Daily
Locator(Civ)	2	8785	Daily
Personnel Spt	332	8705	M-F
Police(Mil)	3	8252	24 hours daily
Emergency	3	114	24 hours daily
Police(Civ)	BHN	110	24 hours daily
Public Affairs	2	8786	M-F
Tax Relief	108	8045/8554	M-F

LOGISTICAL SUPPORT

FACILITY/ACTIVITY	BLDG NO/LOC	PHONE	DAYS/COMMENTS
Audio/Photo Ctr	253	C-82000	Daily
Auto Drivers Testing	251	8282	M-F
Auto Parts(Exch)	128	8231	M-Sa
Auto Registration	10	8174/8124	M-F
Processing Center	101	8684	M-Sa
Auto Rental(Exch)	129	C-81044	M-Sa
Auto Rent(Other)	129	C-81044	M-Sa
Auto Repairs	128	8231	M-F
Auto Sales	129	C-81984	Tu-Sa
Auto Ship(Gov)	101	8187	Outgoing
	101	8061	Incoming
Auto Wash	Perimeter Rd		
Bank	109	8239	M-F,1st Sa
	Hospital	7618	M-F,payday
Barber Shop(s)	229	8014	Tu-Sa
	Hospital	7692	Tu-Sa
Beauty Shop(s)	Hospital	7733	M-Sa
Bookstore	253	8021	Tu-Su
	Hospital	7672	M-F
Child Care/Dev Ctr	228	8349	M-F
	Hospital area	7877	M-F
Clothing Sales	229	8732	M-F,1st Sa
Commissary(Main)	107	8228/8302	Tu-Su
Credit Union	250	8204/8345	M-F
		C-82131	
Dining Facility	205,206	N/A	Daily
Education Center	251	8068/8274	N/A
Eng'r/Publ Works	228	115	Daily
Exchange(Main)	253	8361	Daily
Finance(Mil)	2	8009	M-F
Food(Snack/Fast)			
Burger Bar	105	8069	Daily
Burger King	105	8069	Daily
Foodland	105	8354	Daily
Laundry(Self-Svc)	631	8205	Daily
	Hospital area	7733	Daily
Package Store	100	8122	Tu-Sa

GERMANY

Bremerhaven Community, continued

Photo Laboratory	13	8238	Su-Tu-Th-Sa
Pick-up Point	250	8033	Daily
Postal Svcs(Mil)	109	8753	M-Sa
Railroad/RTO	Hospital area	7869	M-F
Schools(DOD Dep)			
Elementary	754 Hospital area	7656	M-F
High School	See Garlstedt Community listing.		
Svc Stn(Insta)	128	8231/8298	M-Sa
Tailor Shop	229	8444	M-F
Tel Booking Oper	17	112	24 hrs
Tel Repair(Gov)	17	119	Daily
Thrift Shop	Hospital area	7733	Tu,Th
TML	Harbor House Hotel		
Billeting	602-604	7604/7878	24 hours daily
Guest House	602-604	8094	24 hours daily
DV/VIP(06+)	602-604	8094	24 hours daily
Travel Agents	AMEX	8237	M-F
Watch Repair	253	8081	Tu-Sa

HEALTH AND WELFARE

FACILITY/ACTIVITY	BLDG NO/LOC	PHONE	DAYS/COMMENTS
Ambulance	Hospital	116/7694	24 hours daily
Army Comm Svcs	662	7617/7640	M-F
Army Emerg Relief	662	7617	M-F
Central Appts	Hospital	7696/7710	M-F
CHAMPUS Office	Hospital	7876 C-83813	M-F
Chaplain	228	8063	N/A
Chapel	228	8063/8201	N/A
Comm Drug/Alc Ctr	250	8545/8165	M-F
Dental Clinic	Hospital	7606/7858	M-F
Medical Emergency	Hospital	7858	24 hours daily
Poison Control	Hospital	7858/7676 C-040-638-5346	24 hours daily
Red Cross	228	8265 93	M-F After hours
Veterinary Svcs	14	7654	Call for appointment.

REST AND RECREATION

FACILITY/ACTIVITY	BLDG NO/LOC	PHONE	DAYS/COMMENTS
Amer Forces Ntwk	1	8108	Daily
Bowling Lanes	105	8310	Daily
Craftshops			
Automotive	113	8219	M-W, Sa-Su
Multi-crafts	105	8424/8238	
Enlisted Club	4	8290/8272	Daily
Golf Course	176	8674/6435	May-Oct
Gymnasium	103	8320/8418	Daily
Info Tour & Travel	105	8397/8798	M-F
Library	229	8277	Daily
NCO Club	4	8290/8272	Daily
O'Club	On Barracks	7600	Daily

GERMANY
Bremerhaven Community, continued

Outdoor Rec Ctr	103	6435	May-Oct
Recreation Center	105	8397/8277	Sa-W
Rod and Gun Club	On Barracks	8100	Tu-Sa
Service Club	105	8397	M-W, Sa-Su
Theater	105	8370/8378	M-Sa,Hol
Video Rental	253	8361	Tu-Su
Youth Center	Hospital area	8474	M-W, Sa-Su

BUTZBACH SUB-COMMUNITY (GE51R7)
APO New York 09077-5000

TELEPHONE INFORMATION: Main installation numbers: Civ: 49-06033-82-113 (Butzbach); 49-06033-81-113 (Kirch-Göns). ATVN: 320-1110 (ask for Butzbach or Kirch-Göns). ETS: 343-2113 (Butzbach); 343-113 (Kirch-Göns). Civ prefix: 06033-_____ (both locations). ETS prefix: 343-2XXX (Butzbach); 343-XXXX (Kirch-Göns). Civ to mil prefix: 06033-82-XXX (Butzbach); 06033-81-XXXX (Kirch-Göns).

LOCATION: Located on GE-3, 12 miles south of Giessen. May be reached from the Frankfurt-Giessen E-3 Autobahn. HE: p-36, E/5. NMC: Giessen, 12 miles north.

GENERAL INSTALLATION INFORMATION: The mission of the units at the Butzbach Sub-community is to provide community command support to Ayers Kaserne in Kirch-Goens, Schloss Kaserne in Butzbach, and the Roman Way Housing Area. The major combat unit is the 1st Brigade, 3rd Armored Division at Ayers Kaserne. Note: the following abbreviations are used in this listing only: AK (Ayers Kaserne); RW (Roman Way in Butzbach); SK (Schloss Kaserne).

GENERAL CITY/REGIONAL INFORMATION: Located on the eastern slope of the Taunus mountains, Butzbach is a city of 20,000, including its suburbs. Once occupied by Roman troops, Butzbach became a city in 1321. The city hall was built in 1560, the church of St. Mark in 1320. The city's historic guesthouse, the "Zum Löwen," should also be included in any tour of the city.

ADMINISTRATIVE SUPPORT

FACILITY/ACTIVITY	BLDG NO/LOC	PHONE	DAYS/COMMENTS
Customs/Duty	AK	7158	Daily
Duty Officer	AK	8111/8116	Daily
Fire(Mil)	AK	8150	24 hours daily
Housing			
Referral	SK	434	M-F
Info(Insta)	SK	715	M-F
Legal Assist	SK	707/850	M-F
Personnel Spt	AK	7176	M-F
	SK	360	M-F
Police(Mil)	AK	8120	24 hours daily
	SK	829	24 hours daily

U.S. Forces Travel & Transfer Guide Europe — 73

GERMANY

Butzbach Sub-Community, continued

LOGISTICAL SUPPORT

FACILITY/ACTIVITY	BLDG NO/LOC	PHONE	DAYS/COMMENTS
Auto Parts(Exch)	AK	C-60994	Tu-Sa
Auto Registration	SK	750	M-F
Bank	AK	7250	M-Sa
		C-60966	
	SK	770	M-Sa
		C-64908	
Barber Shop(s)	AK	C-60915	M-Sa
	SK	730	M-Sa
Bookstore	SK	691	M-F
Child Care/Dev Ctr	RM	C-67922	Daily
	SK	751/754	Daily
Dining Facility	AK	7215	Daily
Education Center	AK	7152	M-F
	SK	721	M-F
Elec Repair(Gov)	AK	8113	24 hours daily
Eng'r/Publ Works	AK	7108	Daily
	SK	921	Daily
Exchange(Main)	SK	706	Tu-Sa
Food(Caf/Rest)	AK	201	Daily
		C-60977	
Food(Snack/Fast)	AK	C-60977	Daily
	SK	C-64966	Daily
Foodland	AK	C-60977	Daily
	RM	927	Daily
	SK	C-64977	Daily
Package Store	AK	7280	Tu-Sa
Pick-up Point	SK	C-65630	Tu-Sa
Postal Svcs(Mil)	AK	7219	M-Sa
	SK	747	M-Sa
Schools(DOD Dep)			
Elementary	RM	688	M-F
Svc Stn(Insta)	AK	7211	Daily
Tel Repair(Gov)	SK	869	Daily
Tel Repair(Civ)	Butzbach	C-60971	Daily
TML			
Billeting	SK	727	Daily
BEQ	SK	739	Daily
BOQ	AK	7116	Daily
	SK	776	Daily

HEALTH AND WELFARE

FACILITY/ACTIVITY	BLDG NO/LOC	PHONE	DAYS/COMMENTS
Army Comm Svcs	6532/RM	809	M-F
Chaplain	AK	7269	Daily
Comm Drug/Alc Ctr	AK	6163	M-F
	Butzbach	745	M-F
Dental Clinic	AK	7190	M-F
	Butzbach	717	M-F
	RM	839	M-F
Medical Emergency	AK	7126	24 hours daily

GERMANY
Butzbach Sub-Community, continued

Red Cross	Butzbach	824	24 hours daily
	RM	724	24 hours daily
	AK	7107	M-F
	SK	783	M-F

REST AND RECREATION

FACILITY/ACTIVITY	BLDG NO/LOC	PHONE	DAYS/COMMENTS
Bowling Lanes	AK	7170	Daily
	SK	760	Daily
Civ/Contract Club	AK	8090	Daily
Craftshops			
Automotive	SK	700	Tu-Sa
Multi-crafts	SK	777	Tu-Sa
Enlisted Club	AK	7193	Daily
Gymnasium	AK	7200	Daily
	SK	769	Daily
NCO Club	AK	7169	Daily
	SK	705	Daily
Recreation Center	AK	7105	Daily
	SK	843	Daily
Rod and Gun Club	AK	7234	Tu-Sa
Service Club	SK	809	Tu-Sa
Theater	SK	706	Daily
Youth Center	SK	859	Tu-Sa

CHIEMSEE ARMED FORCES RECREATION CENTER (GE08R7)
APO New York 09029-5000

TELEPHONE INFORMATION: Main installation numbers: Civ: 49-08051-803172. ETS: 441-2355. ATVN: 440-1110. Civ prefix: 08051. ETS prefix: 441-2XXX. Civ to mil prefix: 08061-802-XXX. For reservations: Civ: 49-08051-803172. ETS: 440-2575.

LOCATION: Located directly off the Munich-Salzburg Autobahn (E-11) southeast of Munich. Buses use Felden exit; automobiles continue for 800 meters and exit at the sign for AFRC Chiemsee. HE: p-94, B/3. NMC: Munich, 50 miles northwest.

GENERAL INSTALLATION INFORMATION: There are no military units permanently stationed at Chiemsee AFRC.

GENERAL CITY/REGIONAL INFORMATION: The AFRC Chiemsee is situated along the shores of Germany's largest lake—Chiemsee. Visitors can enjoy a variety of water sports such as canoeing, paddleboating, scuba diving, sailing, windsurfing, or swimming. Or take advantage of the nearby Chiemgauer Alps, which offer opportunities for hiking, hang gliding and scenic panoramas of Chiemsee and the Alps. For a ski vacation, AFRC Chiemsee is near Austrian resorts such as Kitzbühel and St. Johann. There are ski programs for beginners to experts.

Night life at AFRC Chiemsee can include an evening with a gourmet meal in

GERMANY
Chiemsee Armed Forces Recreation Center, continued

the Lake Hotel Bavarian Restaurant, dancing in the lake-front lounge, free movies, ice skating and swimming. Evening tours are offered to Munich and Salzburg, where you can go disco-hopping, visit charming restaurants, beer cellars, wine parlors, or just enjoy either of these beautiful cities after dark.

AFRC Chiemsee has the Chiemsee Park Hotel and Chiemsee Lake Hotel with accommodations for more than 250 guests. A modern travel camp offering shower and camp store facilities is also available. There are 110 camp sites with 220 volt electrical hook-ups and nearby laundromats, bathhouses with hot showers, and campstores.

ADMINISTRATIVE SUPPORT

FACILITY/ACTIVITY	BLDG NO/LOC	PHONE	DAYS/COMMENTS
Fire(Civ)		08051-112	24 hours daily
Info(Insta)	701 Lake Hotel	355	Daily
Police(Mil)			
Emergency	On Center	114	24 hours daily

LOGISTICAL SUPPORT

FACILITY/ACTIVITY	BLDG NO/LOC	PHONE	DAYS/COMMENTS
Child Care/Dev Ctr	Park Hotel	488	Summer/Winter only
Dining Facility	701 Lake Hotel	N/A	Daily
Food(Caf/Rest)	701 Lake Hotel	N/A	Daily
Food(Snack/Fast)	701 Lake Hotel	N/A	Daily
Laundry(Self-Svc)	Annex Park Hotel	N/A	Daily
Parking	Lake/Park Hotels	N/A	Daily
Postal Svcs(Mil)	701 Lake Hotel		Front Desk Postings
Tel Booking Oper	Munich	0	24 hours daily
TML			
Billeting	Park Hotel	355	Daily
	Lake Hotel	355	Daily
Travel Agents	Lake Hotel	728	Tours Office

HEALTH AND WELFARE

FACILITY/ACTIVITY	BLDG NO/LOC	PHONE	DAYS/COMMENTS
Ambulance	On Center	116	24 hours daily
Medical Emergency	Civilian hospital only		

REST AND RECREATION

FACILITY/ACTIVITY	BLDG NO/LOC	PHONE	DAYS/COMMENTS
Beach(es)	Lake Hotel	None	Seasonal
Camping/RV Area	AFRC Travel Camp	719	Seasonal
Enlisted Club	Lake Hotel	N/A	Windjammer Bar
Gymnasium	On Center	724	Daily
Info Tour & Travel	Lake Hotel	570	Tours Office
Picnic/Park Area	Lake Hotel	719	Daily
Recreation Center	Lake Hotel	630	Daily
Tennis Courts	Lake Hotel	301	Daily

GERMANY
Chiemsee Armed Forces Recreation Center, continued

Trails	Many in area
Water Recreation	Plentiful

CRAILSHEIM SUB-COMMUNITY (GE64R7)
APO New York 09751-5000

TELEPHONE INFORMATION: Main installation numbers: Civ: 49-07951-35-113. ETS: 420-3113. Civ prefix: 07951-____. ETS prefix: 420-3XXX. Civ to mil prefix: 07951-35-XXX.

LOCATION: Take the Crailsheim exit off the A-6 Autobahn between Heilbronn and Nürnberg. HE: p-40, D/3. NMC: Nürnberg, 59 miles northeast.

GENERAL INSTALLATION INFORMATION: Crailsheim is home to the 7th Support Group, the 4/12 Field Artillery and other smaller units.

GENERAL CITY/REGIONAL INFORMATION: Over 1,000 years ago, Crailsheim existed as a small settlement on the Jagst River. Since then, the area has had many different rulers and did not become a part of the state of Württemberg, as it is today, until 1810. Little is remaining from the time when Crailsheim was a strong fortification. Along the Jagst River, you will still find some parts of the city wall with its small towers. Near the old cemetery on the road to Bad Mergentheim is the old Thieves Tower (the oldest remaining fortification).

The tall St. John's Church, which stands high above the river on the road to Dinkelsbuhl, is almost 600 years old. The church has a valuable high altar and a beautiful tabernacle. Another very old church is the Chapel of Our Dear Lady behind the city hall. The local museum is located in the so-called Hospital Chapel on the road to Dinkelsbuhl.

ADMINISTRATIVE SUPPORT

FACILITY/ACTIVITY	BLDG NO/LOC	PHONE	DAYS/COMMENTS
Fire(Mil)	On Barracks	117	24 hours daily
Housing			
Family	41	760/655	M-F
Referral	41	606	M-F
Personnel Spt	53	514	M-F
Police(Mil)	12	527	24 hours daily
Emergency	12	114	24 hours daily
Police(Civ)	Crailsheim	625	24 hours daily
Public Affairs	9	535/700	M-F
Tax Relief	9	609/833	M-F

LOGISTICAL SUPPORT

FACILITY/ACTIVITY	BLDG NO/LOC	PHONE	DAYS/COMMENTS
Audio/Photo Ctr	21	507	Sa-Th
Auto Drivers Testing	39	521	Tu,Th
Auto Parts(Exch)	55	800	M-F
Auto Registration	12	529	M-F

GERMANY

Crailsheim Sub-Community, continued

Bank	39	598	M-F
Barber Shop(s)	55	509	M-F
Beauty Shop(s)	55	509	M-F
Bookstore	23	517	Tu-Sa
Child Care/Dev Ctr	21	578/832	M-Sa
Clothing Sales	13	513 C-24186	M-F
Commissary(Main)	105	814 C-21942	Tu-Sa
Dining Facility	51, 62	510	Daily
Education Center	59	500	Daily
Eng'r/Publ Works	100	635/831	M-F
Exchange(Main)	23	800	Tu-Sa
Food(Caf/Rest)	23	C-23695	Daily
Food(Snack/Fast)	23	C-23695	Daily
Foodland	23	621	Daily
Laundry(Self-Svc)	104	None	Daily
Motor Pool	85	613	Daily
Package Store	104	533	Tu-Sa
Pick-up Point	55	C-23276	M-F
Postal Svcs(Mil)	13	555/761	M-F
Schools(DOD Dep)			
Elementary	207	559/741	M-F (K-9)
Middle School	207	559/741	M-F (K-9)
High School	See Ansbach/Katterbach Community listing.		
Tailor Shop	23	None	M-F
TML			
BOQ	3-6	590/523/ 629/528	Daily
Thrift Shop	54	650	Tu,Th

HEALTH AND WELFARE

FACILITY/ACTIVITY	BLDG NO/LOC	PHONE	DAYS/COMMENTS
Ambulance	24	116	24 hours daily
Army Comm Svcs	54	534	M-F
Army Emerg Relief	54	534	M-F
Central Appts	24	826/538	M-F
Chaplain	11	819/631	M-F
Comm Drug/Alc Ctr	44	544/780	M-F
Dental Clinic	24	573	M-F
Red Cross	75	830	M-F

REST AND RECREATION

FACILITY/ACTIVITY	BLDG NO/LOC	PHONE	DAYS/COMMENTS
Bowling Lanes	40	549	Tu-Su
Craftshops			
Automotive	113	524	Tu-Sa
Multi-crafts	21	537	M,W,Sa,Su
Photography	21	537	M,W,Sa,Su
Enlisted Club	37	658/735	M,Th-Sa
Gymnasium	38	556	Daily
Info Tour & Travel	21	661	Tu-F
Library	21	550	Sa-Th

GERMANY
Crailsheim Sub-Community, continued

NCO Club	37	535/658	M,Th-Sa
O'Club	7	680/780	Tu-Sa
Recreation Center	21	737	Daily
Rod and Gun Club	37	585	Tu,Th-Sa
Theater	22	574/474	Daily
Youth Center	104	568/711	Tu,Th,Sa

==

DARMSTADT COMMUNITY (GE37R7)
APO New York 09175-5000

TELEPHONE INFORMATION: Main installation numbers: Civ: 49-06151-69-7158/6469 (all locations except Münster Kaserne); 49-06071-84-113 (Münster). ETS: 348-7158/6469 (all locations except Münster Kaserne); 348-4113 (Münster Kaserne). ETS (Oper): 348-6300. ATVN: 394-1110 (ask for Darmstadt). Civ prefix: 06151-_____ (all locations except Münster Kaserne); 06071-_____ (Münster Kaserne). ETS prefix: 348-XXXX (all locations except Münster Kaserne); 348-4XXX (Münster Kaserne). Civ to mil prefix: 06151-69-XXXX (all locations except Münster Kaserne); 06071-84-XXX (Münster Kaserne).

LOCATION: Accessible from the E-5 and E-67 Autobahns. One mile south of downtown Darmstadt. Follow signs to Jefferson Village. HE: p-40, B/1. NMC: Darmstadt, 1 mile north.

GENERAL INSTALLATION INFORMATION: The mission of the Darmstadt Military Community is to provide for the health, welfare, safety, morale, and discipline of all military and civilian personnel and their families living and working in the geographical boundaries of the community. Tenant units include the 32nd Air Defense Command, the 10th Air Defense Artillery Brigade, the 11th Air Defense Signal Battalion, the 440th Signal Battalion, the 94th Engineer Battalion, the 547th Engineer Battalion, the 15th Ordnance Battalion, and the 165th Military Intelligence Battalion. **Note: the following abbreviations are used in this listing only: CFK (Cambrai Fritsch Kaserne); KB (Kelly Barracks); LV (Lincoln Village); MK (Münster Kaserne); NHD (Nathan Hale Depot).**

GENERAL CITY/REGIONAL INFORMATION: In the early Middle Ages, Darmstadt was given the name of one of Charlemagne's gamekeepers, a certain Darmunde. Throughout the following centuries, Darmstadt had a number of different rulers. Finally, in 1567, Darmstadt became the residence of George I. The importance of Darmstadt grew in measure as the residence acquired a greater reputation. The modest castle, surrounded by a moat, gave way to a splendid castle where the Landgraves kept court modeled after the French court.

In 1820, the town received municipal self-government for which the citizens showed their appreciation by building a monument in honor of their sovereign, Ludwig I, in the middle of town. The monument is known as "Langer Ludwig". The early construction of the railroad and the industrialization that followed helped Darmstadt gain in prosperity in the 19th century. In 1944, the town was almost completely destroyed by Allied air attacks.

Darmstadt's economy is made up of chemical plants, and many other

GERMANY
Darmstadt Community, continued

companies of worldwide reputation that produce machinery and special equipment. In addition, there are many publishing houses, printing plants and bookbinders. In addition to the "Ludwig Langer" monument on Luisenplatz, visitors to Darmstadt can visit a variety of castles, museums, churches, galleries, parks and gardens. Those with transportation are sure to enjoy an excursion to the Bergstraße or Hill Road. The 33-mile-long road leads to the ruins of the Frankenstein Castle and offers lovely panoramas of the Rhine Plain. **For Newcomers:** Sign up for the "Discover Darmstadt" orientation tour by calling ETS: 348-7411.

The headquarters of Stars and Stripes Europe is located at a former Luftwaffe training field in Griesheim, a small town on the outskirts of Darmstadt. The plant's number is 348-5741 or 348-5823.

ADMINISTRATIVE SUPPORT

FACILITY/ACTIVITY	BLDG NO/LOC	PHONE	DAYS/COMMENTS
Advocate	4005/CFK	7358	M-F
Customs/Duty	CFK	7350	M-F
Duty Officer	Emergency	6557	Daily
	MK	N/A	24 hours daily
Fire(Mil)	N/A	7400/117	M-F
Fire(Civ)	N/A	117	Daily
Housing			
Family	4106/NHD	7112/6184	M-F
Unaccompanied	Contact billeting.		
Referral	4107/NHD	6102/7101	M-F
Info(Insta)	4027/CFK	6544/118	M-F
Inspector Gen'l	4005/CFK	6538	M-F
Legal Assist	4006/CFK	7145	M-Th
Locator(Mil)	Post Locator	6229	M-F
Locator(Civ)	Post Locator	6229	M-F
Personnel Spt	4027/CFK	7410	M-F
Police(Mil)	4025/CFK	7350/8351	Daily
	MK	812	Daily
Public Affairs	4027/CFK	7158	M-F
Tax Relief	4037/CFK	6121	M-F

LOGISTICAL SUPPORT

FACILITY/ACTIVITY	BLDG NO/LOC	PHONE	DAYS/COMMENTS
Audio/Photo Ctr	4038/CFK	C-64144	Tu-Su
Auto Drivers Testing	4025/CFK	6190	M,W,Th,F
Auto Parts(Exch)	4442/LV	C-60538	Tu-Sa
Auto Registration	4025B/CFK	6386	M-F
Auto Rental(Exch)	4032/CFK	C-64200	M-Th,Sa
Auto Rent(Other)	In city	C-64161	M-F. Avis.
	In city	C-24686	M-Sa. Hertz.
Auto Repairs	4442/LV	C-60531	M-Sa
Auto Sales	4033/CFK	N/A	Tu-Su
Auto Ship(Gov)	4025B/CFK	6386	M-F
Auto Ship(Civ)	Frankfurt PX	C-069-567162	Tu-Sa
Bakery	4032/CFK	N/A	Daily
Bank	4037/CFK	6195	M-Sa

GERMANY
Darmstadt Community, continued

	MK	753	N/A
Barber Shop(s)	4004/CFK	C-64181	M-Sa
	4233/ELK	6204	M-F
	Next to O'Club	6363	M-F
	MK	None	M,W
Beauty Shop(s)	4037/CFK	C-64181	Tu-Sa
Bookstore	4033/CFK	N/A	Daily
	4167/KB	N/A	Daily
Stars and Stripes HQ	4319/Griesheim	5741/5823	N/A
Bus	4009/NHD	7403	M-F
Child Care/Dev Ctr	4039/CFK	7431	M-F
Clothing Sales	4110/NHD	7182	M-F
Commissary(Main)	4132/NHD	8413	M-Sa
		C-64298	
Dining Facility	4103/CFK	6382	Daily
	4232/Ludwig Ksrn	6257	Daily
	4170/KB	6371	Daily
	MK	745	Daily
Dry Clean(Exch)	4038/CFK	C-64198	Tu-Sa
Dry Clean(Gov)	4020/CFK	None	M-F

Education Center	4025/CFK	6116	M-F
	4233/ELK	6118/7189	M-F
	4162/KB	6117/7187	M-F
Learning Center	4025/CFK	6312	M-F
	4196/KB	6218	M-F
	MK	771	M-F
Elec Repair(Civ)	4038/CFK	C-64198	Tu-Sa
Eng'r/Publ Works	4106/NHD	6181	M-F
Exchange(Main)	4033/CFK	C-64168	Daily
Exchange(Annex)	4233/ELK	6210	M-F
	4167/KB	6504	M-F
	MK	C-37237	M-Sa
Finance(Mil)	4162/KB	8435	M,Tu,Th,F
Food(Snack/Fast)	4032/CFK	C-60535	Daily
Pizza Parlor	4032/CFK	C-60535	Daily
Foodland	4032/CFK	C-60528	Daily
Laundry(Exch)	4038/CFK	C-64198	Tu-Sa
Laundry(Self-Svc)	4020/CFK	None	Daily
	4166/KB	None	Daily

Motor Pool	4011/NHD	6464	M-F
Package Store	4044/CFK	6212	Tu-Sa
Photo Laboratory	4038/CFK	C-64198	Tu-Sa
Pick-up Point	4038/CFK	C-64198	Tu-Sa
	4233/ELK	C-64288	M-F
	4167/KB	6211	M-F
	MK	763	M-F
Postal Svcs(Mil)	4034/CFK	7223	M-F
Postal Svcs(Civ)	4025/CFK	C-63030	M-F
Railroad/RTO	Frankfurt/RTO	320-5159	Daily
Schools			
Elementary	LV	6513/8390	M-F (K-5)
Middle	LV	7185	M-F (6-9)
High School	See Frankfurt Community listing.		
Svc Stn(Insta)	4442/LV	C-60531	M-Sa
Svc Stn(Autobahn)	ESSO/BP	N/A	Daily

Darmstadt Community, continued

GERMANY

Space-A Air Ops Flights to:	Army Airfield German locations	5800	Daily
Tailor Shop	4038/CFK	C-64198	Tu-Sa
	4167/KB	6127	Tu-F
Taxi(Comm)	Darmstadt	C-26868	24 hours daily
Tel Booking Oper	On Barracks	112	24 hours daily
Tel Repair(Gov)	On Barrakcs	119	N/A
Thrift Shop	4013/CFK	6454	Tu,Th,1st Sa
TML			
Billeting	4091/Jefferson Village	7111 C-6811	Daily
	Other Hours	6557/7423	Daily
BEQ/BOQ	Available for housing unaccompanied duty personnel		
Guest House	4091/Jefferson Village	7111 C-6811	Daily
	Other Hours	6557/7423	Daily
Protocol Office	4005/Jefferson Village	C-7304	Daily. 06+.
Travel Agents	4038/CFK	7107	M-F
Watch Repair	4038/CFK	C-64198	Tu-Sa

HEALTH AND WELFARE

FACILITY/ACTIVITY	BLDG NO/LOC	PHONE	DAYS/COMMENTS
Ambulance	On Barracks	116	24 hours daily
Army Comm Svcs	4027/CFK	6304	M-F
Army Emerg Relief	4027/CFK	6304/8411	M-F
Central Appts	4087/CFK	6266/6270	M-F
CHAMPUS Office	4087/CFK	8378/6263	M-F
Chaplain	4089/CFK	8419	M-F
	4191/KB	6339	M-F
Chapel	4089/CFK	8419	Sa-M
	MK	N/A	Tu,Su
Comm Drug/Alc Ctr	4004/CFK	6111/7204	M-F
Dental Clinic	4087/CFK	8335	M-F
Medical Emergency	4087/CFK	116	M-Sa
	After hours go to the Darmstadt Staedtische Kliniken or 97th General Hospital in Frankfurt (see the Frankfurt Community listing).		
Mental Health	Frankfurt	325-6311	
Poison Control	Frankfurt	325-6127	Daily
Red Cross	4087/CFK	6541/7425	M-F
Veterinary Svcs	4167/KB	N/A	Every other F

REST AND RECREATION

FACILITY/ACTIVITY	BLDG NO/LOC	PHONE	DAYS/COMMENTS
Aero/Flying Club	Griesheim AF	N/A	Daily
Amer Forces Ntwk	Frankfurt	320-6101	Daily
Bowling Lanes	CFK	6148/7166	Daily
	MK	N/A	Daily
Consolidated Club	MK	N/A	M-Sa
Craftshops			
Automotive	4007/CFK	6471	Daily
Multi-crafts	4020/CFK	6256	Daily

GERMANY
Darmstadt Community, continued

Photo	4176/KB	6255	Daily
Enlisted Club	4020/CFK	6128	M-Sa
	MK	741	N/A
Gymnasium	4070/CFK	6318	Daily
	4249/ELK	6547	Daily
	4169/KB	6361	Daily
	MK	766	N/A
Info Tour & Travel	4038/CFK	6431/7107	M-F
Library	4004/CFK	6272	Daily
MARS	CFK	6178/8401	Daily
NCO Club	4088/CFK	6227	Tu-Su
	MK	741	N/A
O'Club	4037/CFK	7191	Su-F
Outdoor Rec Ctr	4017/CFK	6277/3746	M-F
Press Club	Griesheim	348-5292	N/A
Racket Courts	See Gymnasiums		
Recreation Center	4017/CFK	6277/6226	M-F
	MK	754	Daily
Rod and Gun Club	4017/CFK	6402/6189	Daily
Service Club	4008/CFK	6226	Daily
Special Services	4017/CFK	6277	M-F
Sport Field	4021/CFK	7359	M-F
Swimming Pool	Ludwigshoh St	C-132392	Daily
Tennis Courts	See Gymnasium		
Theater	4021/CFK	6214	Daily
Track	See Gymnasium		
Trails	Odenwald	6277	Daily
Video Rental	4038/CFK	N/A	Tu-Su
Youth Center	4441/LV	6242	Tu-Sa, Hol

===

DEXHEIM SUB-COMMUNITY (GE65R7)
APO New York 09111-5000

TELEPHONE INFORMATION: Main installation numbers: Civ: 49-06133-38-113. ETS: 334-5113. Civ prefix: 06133-____. ETS prefix: 334-5XXX. Civ to mil prefix: 06133-38-XXX.

LOCATION: Dexheim is a very small post which is located on Highway 420 and is two and a half miles west of Nierstein Am Rhein. The road going from Nierstein Am Rhein to Bad Kreuznach passes Anderson Barracks in Dexheim. HE: p-40, A/1. NMC: Mainz, 20 miles north.

GENERAL INSTALLATION INFORMATION: Dexheim is a sub-community of the Bad Kreuznach Community, where most logistical and support facilities are located. The 12th Engineering Battalion is located at Anderson Barracks in Dexheim.

GENERAL CITY/REGIONAL INFORMATION: Many wine festivals occur in the Dexheim area. Nearby Oppenheim has a clothing factory outlet.

U.S. Forces Travel & Transfer Guide Europe — 83

GERMANY

Dexheim Sub-Community, continued

ADMINISTRATIVE SUPPORT

FACILITY/ACTIVITY	BLDG NO/LOC	PHONE	DAYS/COMMENTS
Duty Officer	6309	727/856	Daily
Fire(Mil)	7262	117	24 hours daily
Fire(Civ)	Oppenheim	112	24 hours daily
Housing	6459	710	M-F
Referral	6313	710	M-F
Info(Insta)	N/A	113	24 hours daily
Locator(Mil)	6317	741	M-F
Police(Mil) Emergency	N/A	114	24 hours daily
Police(Civ)	Oppenheim	112 C-2077	M-F

LOGISTICAL SUPPORT

FACILITY/ACTIVITY	BLDG NO/LOC	PHONE	DAYS/COMMENTS
Audio/Photo Ctr	6320	723	M-Sa
Auto Registration	6317	741	M,W
Auto Rent(Other)	6320	C-58327	M-F
Bank	6320	C-58915	M-F
Barber Shop(s)	6320	C-50255	M-F
Beauty Shop(s)	6320	C-59586	Tu-Sa
Bookstore	6320	746	M-Sa
Child Care/Dev Ctr	6317	C-58996	M-F
Commissary(Main)	6302	883	Tu-Sa
Dining Facility	6328	748	Daily
Education Center	6326	886	M-F
Learning Center	6333T	720	M-F
Eng'r/Publ Works	6316	115	M-F
Exchange(Main)	6320	C-50599	Daily
Food(Caf/Rest)	6460	C-58995	Daily
Food(Snack/Fast)	6320	C-58995	Daily
Laundry(Self-Svc)	6330	743	Daily
Package Store	PX area	714	Tu-Sa
Pick-up Point	6331	C-58935	M-F
Postal Svcs(Mil)	6317	745	M-F
Schools(DOD Dep)			
Elementary	6352/6360	876	M-F
Middle School	See Bad Kreuznach Community listing.		
High School	See Bad Kreuznach Community listing.		
Tailor Shop	6331	C-58935	M-F
Taxi(Comm)	N/A	C-5665	M-F
Tel Repair(Gov)	Mainz	119	M-F
Thrift Shop	6459	None	Tu-Th

HEALTH AND WELFARE

FACILITY/ACTIVITY	BLDG NO/LOC	PHONE	DAYS/COMMENTS
Ambulance	N/A	116	24 hours daily
Army Comm Svcs	6454	893	M-F
Army Emerg Relief	6454	893	M-F

GERMANY
Dexheim Sub-Community, continued

Central Appts	Bad Kreuznach	490-5727	M-F
Chaplain	6301	885	Su-F
Comm Drug/Alc Ctr	6331	742	M-F
Dental Clinic	6335	721/877	M-F
Medical Emergency	Bad Kreuznach	116	M-F
Red Cross	6454	893/709	M-F

REST AND RECREATION

FACILITY/ACTIVITY	BLDG NO/LOC	PHONE	DAYS/COMMENTS
Bowling Lanes	6321	743	Daily
Craftshops			
Automotive	6330	717	W-Su
Multi-crafts	6322	879	Tu-Sa
Enlisted Club	6327	739	Daily
Gymnasium	6321	746	Daily
Library	6320	723	Tu-Sa
NCO Club	6327	739	Daily
O'Club	6351	712	M-Sa
Outdoor Rec Ctr	6322	879	M-Sa
Racket Courts	6321	746	Daily
Recreation Center	6322	C-59548	Tu-F
Theater	6319	761	Tu-Th,Sa,Su
Youth Center	6464	740	Tu-Sa

ERLANGEN SUB-COMMUNITY (GE66R7)
APO New York 09066-5000

TELEPHONE INFORMATION: Main installation numbers: Civ: 49-09131-83-113. ETS: 464-3113. Civ prefix: 09131-____. ETS prefix: 464-3XXX. Civ to mil prefix: 09131-83-XXX.

LOCATION: Take Highway 73 north from Nürnberg and follow signs to Erlangen. HE: p-40, F/2. NMC: Nürnberg, 10 miles south.

GENERAL INSTALLATION INFORMATION: Ferris Barracks in Erlangen is home to the 2nd Brigade, 1st Armored Division, which consists of 2nd Battalion, 6th Infantry; 1st Battalion, 35th Armor; 2nd Battalion, 81st Armor; and 3rd Battalion, 34th Armor. The 2nd Forward Support Battalion and C Battery, 1st Battalion, 94th Field Artillery are also located at Ferris.

GENERAL CITY/REGIONAL INFORMATION: Erlangen is a university town just northwest of Nürnberg. The town is made up of two sections: the old city, established in 1367; and the new city, dating from 1636. Friedrich Alexander University in Erlangen is a renowned institute with a fine library that houses a collection of rare editions.

The baroque style of architecture is evident in the ancient residence in the center of the city, as well as the palace garden and botanical garden. Theater goers are sure to enjoy the many performances given here each year by various stage companies; sports enthusiasts will want to take advantage of the tennis, skating, riding, camping and swimming facilities in Erlangen.

Erlangen Sub-Community, continued   **GERMANY**

ADMINISTRATIVE SUPPORT

FACILITY/ACTIVITY	BLDG NO/LOC	PHONE	DAYS/COMMENTS
Fire(Mil)	On Barracks	117	24 hours daily
Fire(Civ)	Erlangen	C-3722	24 hours daily
Housing	4322	684/847	M-F
Inspector Gen'l	4058	666	M-F
Legal Assist	4301	683/860	M-F
Police(Mil)	4072	696/832	24 hours daily
Tax Relief	4023	708/808	M-F

LOGISTICAL SUPPORT

FACILITY/ACTIVITY	BLDG NO/LOC	PHONE	DAYS/COMMENTS
Audio/Photo Ctr	4032	701	M,Tu,Th-Sa
Auto Parts(Exch)	4066	C-56616	M-Sa
Auto Registration	4072	878	M-F
Auto Repairs	4066	C-56616	M-Sa
Bank	4028	735 C-52589	M-F
Barber Shop(s)	4030	707	M-Sa
Beauty Shop(s)	4030	707	Th-Sa
Bookstore	4314	687	M-Sa
Child Care/Dev Ctr	4303	710	M-F
Clothing Sales	4030	C-54957	M,Tu,Th-Sa
Commissary(Main)	4068	729/637	Tu-Sa
Dining Facility	4000,4057,4300	N/A	Daily
Dry Clean(Exch)	Pick-up point	C-51641	M-Sa
Education Center	4022	741/812	M-F
Elec Repair(Gov)	N/A	708/808	N/A
Eng'r/Publ Works	4017	115	M-F
Exchange(Main)	4030	C-501216	Th-Tu
Food(Caf/Rest)	4059	867 C-501185	Daily
Foodland	4030	C-501216	Daily
Laundry(Self-Svc)	4312	None	Daily
Motor Pool	4006/7/11/12	N/A	M-F
Package Store	4031	702	Tu-Sa
Photo Laboratory	4035	681	M-F
Pick-up Point	4040	C-58970	M,Tu,Th-Sa
Postal Svcs(Mil)	4031	851	M-F
Schools(DOD Dep)	43M	747 C-57164	M-F
Tailor Shop	4040	C-58970	Tu-F
Tel Repair(Gov)	N/A	810	N/A
Thrift Shop	4035	785	Tu,Th

HEALTH AND WELFARE

FACILITY/ACTIVITY	BLDG NO/LOC	PHONE	DAYS/COMMENTS
Ambulance	On Barracks	116	24 hours daily
Army Comm Svcs	4033	765/831	M-F
Central Appts	4058	620	M-F

GERMANY
Erlangen Sub-Community, continued

Chapel	4071	824/622	Daily
Comm Drug/Alc Ctr	4023	715/858	M-F
Dental Clinic	4323	820/721	M-F
Medical Emergency	4058	116	24 hours daily
Red Cross	4059	765/831	M-F

REST AND RECREATION

FACILITY/ACTIVITY	BLDG NO/LOC	PHONE	DAYS/COMMENTS
Bowling Lanes	4039	693	Daily
Craftshops			
Automotive	4033	831	F-Tu
Multi-crafts	4035	C-58681	Th-M
Enlisted Club	4021	601	Tu-Su
Gymnasium	4013	740	Daily
Info Tour & Travel	4030	C-57706	M,W,F
Library	4030	690/809	Tu-Sa
NCO Club	4026	720	M-Sa
Outdoor Rec Ctr	4035	C-57706	Tu-Su
Recreation Center	4035	781	Daily
Skating Rink	4029	679	Tu-Su
Theater	4051	724	Daily
Youth Center	2110	872	Tu-Sa

FRANKFURT COMMUNITY (GE05R7)
APO New York 09710-5000

TELEPHONE INFORMATION: Main installation numbers: Civ: 49-069-1549-113 (Drake Kaserne and Edwards Kaserne); 49-06196-705-113 (Camp Eschborn); 49-069-1541-113 (97th Hospital and Gibbs Kaserne); 49-069-151-113 (Frankfurt, including Betts Kaserne, Atterberry Housing and Abrams Complex); 49-069-3101-113 (McNair Kaserne); 49-06171-61-113 (Camp King). ETS: 328-113 or 328-8113 (Drake Kaserne and Edwards Kaserne); 320-2113 (Camp Eschborn); 325-113 (97th Hospital and Gibbs Kaserne); 320-113 (Frankfurt, including Betts Kaserne, Atterberry Kaserne and Abrams Complex); 325-5113 (McNair Kaserne); 325-2113 (Camp King). ATVN: 320-1110 (all locations). Civ prefix: 069-____ (Drake Kaserne, Edwards Kaserne, 97th Hospital, Gibbs Kaserne, Frankfurt, Betts Kaserne, Atterberry Kaserne, Abrams Complex and McNair Kaserne); 06196-____ (Camp Eschborn); 06171-__ (Camp King). ETS prefix: 328-XXXX or 328-8XXX (Drake Kaserne or Edwards Kaserne); 320-2XXX (Camp Eschborn); 325-XXXX (97th Hospital and Gibbs Kaserne); 320-XXXX (Frankfurt, including Betts Kaserne, Atterberry Kaserne and Abrams Complex); 325-5XXX (McNair Kaserne); 325-2XXX (Camp King). Civ to mil prefix: 069-1549-XXX(X) (Drake Kaserne and Edwards Kaserne); 06196-705-XXX (Camp Eschborn); 069-1541-XXXX (97th Hospital and Gibbs Kaserne); 069-151-XXXX (Frankfurt, including Betts Kaserne, Atterberry Kaserne and Abrams Complex); 069-3101-XXX (McNair Kaserne); 06171-61-XXX (Camp King).

LOCATION: The Ambassador Arms Hotel is on the corner of Miguel Allee and Hansa Allee within the General Creighton Abrams Complex in Frankfurt. HE: p-39, B/1. NMC: Frankfurt, in the city.

Frankfurt Community, continued
GERMANY

GENERAL INSTALLATION INFORMATION: Frankfurt is the location of Headquarters, V Corps. Among the 70+ other units assigned to Frankfurt are the 3rd Armored Division, the European Division of Engineers, the Fourth Transportation Command, the 97th General Hospital and Headquarters, Armed Forces Network. Note: the following abbreviations are used in this listing only: AC (Abrams Complex); AK (Atterberry Kaserne); BK (Betts Kaserne); CE (Camp Eschborn); CK (Camp King); DK (Drake Kaserne); ED (Edwards Kaserne); GK (Gibbs Kaserne and 97th General Hospital); HA (Hansa Allee); MK (McNair Kaserne); SC (Shopping Center in Frankfurt)

GENERAL CITY/REGIONAL INFORMATION: Frankfurt is the industrial, commercial, cultural, recreational and entertainment center of West Germany. Although some say that the city was named by Charlemagne in the 8th century, recent geological findings reveal that the area was occupied much before that time—by stone age men as well as Germanic tribes and Romans.

Today Frankfurt is a busy, modern metropolis. Travelers will be interested to know that the city is the location not only of the main terminal station of the German Railway System but also of the largest airport in central Europe. In addition, it is a crossroads where many of the main European highways intersect, and it has a vast, modern public transportation system.

Tourists will find that Frankfurt offers innumerable sights to visit: museums, churches and cathedrals, parks and gardens and historically significant structures and buildings. Shoppers, gourmets, theater-goers, jazz fans, sports lovers—in short, everyone will enjoy their time in Frankfurt.

ADMINISTRATIVE SUPPORT

FACILITY/ACTIVITY	BLDG NO/LOC	PHONE	DAYS/COMMENTS
Advocate	AC	5810/6389	Daily
Customs/Duty	56/AC	5865/6423	M-F
Duty Officer	AC	5810/6389	Daily
Fire(Mil)	All locations	117 C-555555	24 hours daily
Fire(Civ)	All locations	112	24 hours daily
Housing			
Family	73/AC	7094/5565	M-F
Unaccompanied	73/AC	7672	M-F
Referral	73/AC	7246/7118	M-F
Info(Insta)	All locations	113	24 hours daily
Inspector Gen'l	5/AC	8309/5405	M-F
Legal Assist	AC	6490/7129	M-F
Locator(Mil)	AC	5810/0	Daily
Locator(Civ)	AC	5948/0	Daily
Personnel Spt	56/AK	7490/7906	M-F
Police(Mil)	417/GK	7637/6137	24 hours daily
Emergency	AC	114	24 hours daily
Police(Civ)	Frankfurt	110	24 hours daily
Public Affairs	132A/Frankfurt	5257/6419	M-F
Tax Relief	SC	7362	M-F

GERMANY
Frankfurt Community, continued

LOGISTICAL SUPPORT

FACILITY/ACTIVITY	BLDG NO/LOC	PHONE	DAYS/COMMENTS
Audio/Photo Ctr	SC	C-56000360	Daily
Auto Drivers Testing	56/AC	7950/6398	M-F
Auto Parts(Exch)	SC	C-56000346	M-F
Auto Registration	56/AC	7521/7568	M-F
Auto Rent(Other)	SC	C-564887	M-Sa
Auto Repairs	SC	C-56000344	Daily
Auto Sales	SC	C-569328	AMC
	SC	C-569153	Chrysler
	SC	C-567122	Ford
	SC	C-569153	GM
	SC	C-569275	VW
Auto Ship(Gov)	Off Post	C-5487311	M-F
Auto Ship(Civ)	Off Post	C-5487311	M-F
Auto Wash	SC	C-56000346	Daily
Bakery	SC	C-569482	Daily
Bank	AC	5584	M-Sa
	755/CE	828	M,W,F
	1042/CK	825	Tu,F
	518/DK	622	M-F
	Frankfurt	6107	M-F
	SC	C-563061	M-F
Barber Shop(s)	AC	5667	M-F
	Ambassador Arms	5738/9	M-Sa
	CE	658	M-F
	CK	C-702	M-F
	DK	8680	
	Frankfurt	6312	M-F
	GK	6210	M-F
	MK	C-316851	M-F
	SC	C-5601152	M-Sa
Beauty Shop(s)	Terrace Club/AC	C-555064	M-F
	CK	C-702	M-F
	GK	C-5481690	Tu-Sa
	Frankfurt	6312	M-F
	MK	697	M-F
	SC	C-5601152	M-Sa
Bookstore	AC	6595/5860	M-F
	1031/CK	746	M-Sa
	489/ED	C-545980	M-Sa
	1020/GK	C-542267/ 545496	M-F
	332/Hospital	6337	M-F
	883/MK	None	M-F
	SC	C-569412	Daily
Bus	GK	7601	
Child Care/Dev Ctr	33/AC	7333/5154	M-F
	28/AC	8266	M-F. Preschool.
	324/AH	7615	M-F
	984,891/CK	641	M-F
	524/DK	7373	M-F
	330/Frankfurt	7572	M-F
	132B/HQ	5888/7898	M-F

U.S. Forces Travel & Transfer Guide Europe — 89

GERMANY

Frankfurt Community, continued

	MK	809	M-F
Clothing Sales	SC	5889	Daily
Commissary(Main)	1571/SC	8373/6270	Daily
Credit Union	AC	6479	M-F
Dining Facility	35/AC	7592	Daily
	749/CE	661/803	Daily
	1018/CK	682	Daily
	522/DK	7218	Daily
	487/EK	7220	Daily
	GK	6264	Daily
	882/MK	629	Daily
	Hospital	6105/6449	Daily
	MK	694	Daily
	884/MK	715	Daily
Dry Clean(Gov)	AC	6030	M-F
	Hospital	6106	M-F
	MK	5662	M-F

==

Education Center	4/AC	5465	M-F
	274/BK	7006/8351	M-Th
	654/CE	667/705	M-F
	1044/CK	771/749	Th
	524/DK	8675	M-F
	412/GK	7567/6208	M-F
	882/MK	800/693	M-F
Learning Center	4/AC	5335	M-F
	643/CE	2827/2705	M-Th
	524/DK	8675	M-F
	4412/GK	7567/6208	M-F
	882/MK	5800	M-F
Elec Repair(Gov)	Frankfurt	C-8308280	M-F
Elec Repair(Civ)	SC	C-8308280	M-F
Eng'r/Publ Works	Frankfurt	6070/6078	M-F
	After hours	115	
Exchange(Main)	AC	C-592194	M-F
	CE	C-315198	M-Sa
	CK	C-21900	M-Sa
	DK	C-544343	M-Sa
	Hospital	C-556049	M-F
	MK	C-312637	Daily

==

Exchange(Concess)	SC	C-566115	N/A
	SC	C-569659	N/A
Finance(Mil)	44/AC	7084/6205	M-F
Food(Caf/Rest)	SC	C-558138	Daily
Food(Snack/Fast)			
Baskin Robbins	1574/SC	C-5600366	Daily
Burger King	SC	C-56000352	Daily
Pizza Parlor	AC	5394	M-F
	489/EK	C-545980	Daily
	405/GK	C-545496	M-Sa
	MK	C-312601	Daily
	SC	C-561287	Daily
Foodland	1/AC	C-592194	M-F
	BK	1630	M-Sa
	CE	C-48593	Daily
	EK	C-546782	Daily

GERMANY
Frankfurt Community, continued

Laundry(Self-Svc)	SC	C-561452	Daily
	CE	None	M-Sa
	GK	None	Daily
	MK	None	Daily
	5/SC	C-569786	Daily
Package Store	SC	7422	Tu-Sa
Pick-up Point	AC	5525	M-F
	CE	C-346256	M-F
	CK	C-61690	M-F
	EK	C-540995	M-F
	GK	C-542267	M-F
	Hospital	C-556049	M-F
	MK	C-307130	M-F
	SC	C-567869	M-F
Postal Svcs(Mil)	AC	5073	M-F
	CK	602	M,Tu,Th,F
	EK	8234/7206	M-F
	MK	650	M,Tu,Th,F
	SC	5543	M-Sa
Postal Svcs(Civ)	AC	C-590300	M-Sa
	Hospital	C-590800	M-F
Railroad/RTO	Frankfurt	5159/8147	M-F
SATO-OS	56/AC	7005 C-5602700	M-F
Schools(DOD Dep)			
Elementary	251/AH	8371/6242	M-F (1-5)
	2201/Frankfurt	7491/5435 C-566504	M-F (1-5)
Middle School	DK	7364/8297	M-F (6-8)
High School	37/AC	8469/5804 C-5961467	M-F (9-12)
Svc Stn(Insta)	SC	C-56000346	Daily
Svc Stn(Autobahn)	Frankfurt	C-762065	Daily
Space-A Air Ops	See Rhein-Main Air Base listing.		
Tailor Shop	CE	C-346256	Tu-Th
	EK	C-546782	M-F
	GK	C-544358	M-F
	MK	684	W-F
	SC	C-569894	W-Sa
Taxi(Comm)	Frankfurt	C-230001	Daily
Tel Booking Oper	All locations	112	24 hours daily
Tel Repair(Gov)	All locations	119	24 hours daily
Tel Repair(Civ)	Frankfurt	C-1171	Daily
Thrift Shop	132B/HQ	7646/5092	M,Tu,Th,F, 1st Sa,1st W
TML			
Billeting	Ambassador Arms Hotel/AC	7441/5738	24 hours daily
Guest House	2351/52/63/66/71	5738 C-550641	24 hours daily
DV/VIP	COFS,V Corps/AC	7141	07+

==
HEALTH AND WELFARE
==

FACILITY/ACTIVITY	BLDG NO/LOC	PHONE	DAYS/COMMENTS
Ambulance	All locations	116/6292	24 hours daily

GERMANY

Frankfurt Community, continued

Army Comm Svcs	132B/HQ	7428	M-F
Army Emerg Relief	132B/HQ	7080/7443	M-F
Central Appts	Hospital	6311	M-W
	Hospital	6111/6112	24 hours daily. Info.
CHAMPUS Office	Hospital	6313/7505	M-F
Chaplain	Frankfurt	5513/7293	M-F
	Frankfurt	5271/8456	M-F
Chapel	AH	6410	Su
	CE	662/821	Su
	CK	2607/2807	Su
	DK/EK	7309/7256	Su
	Frankfurt	5513/7293	Su
	Frankfurt	5271/8456	Su
	Hospital	8328	Su-Th
	MK	5893	Su
Comm Drug/Alc Ctr	BK	8325	M-F
	T276/BK	7511/6280	M-F
	CE	659	M-F
	DK	7212	M-F
	132A/HQ	7541/6548	M-F
	MK	732	M-F
Dental Clinic	56/AC	5983/5660	M-F
	477/EK	7232/7216	M-F
	Hospital	7586/6323	M-F
Medical Emergency	Hospital	6379/8376	24 hours daily
Mental Health	Hospital	6255/7614	M-F
Red Cross	132B/HQ	5697/5395	M-F
	Hospital	7649/7043	M-F
	Emergency	113	24 hours daily
Veterinary Svcs	274/BK	5658/7490	M-F

REST AND RECREATION

FACILITY/ACTIVITY	BLDG NO/LOC	PHONE	DAYS/COMMENTS
Amer Forces Ntwk	SC	6101 ext. 236	Daily
Bowling Lanes	AC	5735	Daily
	CK	2663	Daily
	DK	7167	
	GK	6253	Daily
	MK	2723	
Camping/RV Area	See Rhein-Main Air Base listing.		
Consolidated Club	1045/CK	2693	M-F
Craftshops			
Automotive	CE	684	M-Sa
	411/GK	6349	M-Sa
	405/GK	6263	Sa-W
	838/MK	719	F-Tu
Multi-crafts	405/GK	6263/6350	Sa-W
	857/MK	720	W-Su
Enlisted Club	286/BK	6256	W-Su
	758/CE	680	W-M
	531/DK	7317	Tu,W,F,Sa
	862/MK	749	Tu-Su
Golf Course	See Wiesbaden Community listing.		
Gymnasium	AC	5178	M-F

GERMANY
Frankfurt Community, continued

	A21/CE	693	M-F
	1031/CK	680	Daily
	273/BK	7561	Daily
	519/DK	7172	Daily
	408A/GK	6157	Daily
	151/HQ	5533	M-F
	856/MK	635	Daily
Info Tour & Travel	AC	C-5970203	M-F
	SC	C-568075	M-Sa

The AFRC opened its first branch reservations office at the Frankfurt shopping center ITT Office in April of 1989. The civilian extensions are 568076, 568077 and 568078.

Library	2401/AC	5678/7194	Daily
	1031/CK	688	M-F
	489/EK	7343	Tu-Su
	857/MK	705	Su-Th
Museum	DK	8163	M-Sa
NCO Club	286/BK	6256	W-Su
	758/CE	680	W-M
	531/DK	7317	Tu,W,F,Sa
	862/MK	749	Tu-Su
	SC	5466	M-Sa
O'Club	2/AC	6357/5002	M-Sa
	CK	2738	M-Sa
	Hospital	6147/6149	M-F
Outdoor Rec Ctr	245/AK	7646/7001	M-Sa
Recreation Center	489/EK	8153/8653	W-Su
	857/MK	888/898	W-Su
	56C/MK	664/710	W-Su
Rod and Gun Club	See Rhein-Main Air Base listing.		
Skating Rink	BK	6267	Daily
Swimming Pool	Ask Recreation Services for list.		
Tennis Courts	BK,CK,ED,GK,MK—reserve through Gym		
Theater	AC	5427	Daily
	CK	2601	Daily
	Frankfurt	5835	M-F
	Hospital	6351	M-F
	MK	5745	M-F
Video Rental	405/GK	None	M-S
	883/MK	None	Daily
	SC	C-568026	Daily
Youth Center	1007/CK	2766	Daily
	2153/EK	8236	Daily
	132B/HQ	7443	Daily
	2436/MK	5809	Daily

==

FRIEDBERG/BAD NAUHEIM SUB-COMMUNITY (GE68R7)
APO New York 09074-5000

TELEPHONE INFORMATION: Main installation numbers: Civ: 49-06031-81-113 (Friedberg); 49-06032-81-113 (Bad Nauheim). ETS: 324-113. Civ prefix: 06031-____ (Friedberg); 06032-____ (Bad Nauheim). ETS prefix: 324-XXXX.

GERMANY

Friedberg/Bad Nauheim Sub-Community, continued

Civ to mil prefix: 06031-81-XXXX (Friedberg); 06032-81-XXXX (Bad Nauheim).

LOCATION: Ray Barracks in Friedberg is 20 miles northeast of Frankfurt off the Frankfurt-Giessen Autobahn. Bad Nauheim is located two and three quarter miles north of Friedberg. HE: p-36, E/6. NMC: Frankfurt, 20 miles southwest.

GENERAL INSTALLATION INFORMATION: Ray Barracks in Friedberg is home to the 3rd Brigade, 3rd Armored Division. Note: the following abbreviations are used in this listing only: BN (Bad Nauheim); FB (Friedberg); RB (Ray Barracks).

GENERAL CITY/REGIONAL INFORMATION: Friedberg is the county seat of Kreis Friedberg. Archaeological findings indicate that the area was inhabited in prehistoric times. Strikingly situated upon the pinnacle of a hill approximately 190 meters above sea level, it dominates the lower surrounding countryside. Its castle, which predates the founding of the town in 1216, can be seen from miles away in most directions.

Situated close to the center of a rich agricultural area, Friedberg is an important trading center. Though modern in most respects, many historic structures still stand. The stone foundation of the Liebfrauenkirche, a church constructed in the French Gothic architectural style, was laid in 1260. The church stands on the former site of a Roman basilica. Also in 1260, work began on the Judische Bad, which extends some 25 meters underground. Jewish women used the Bad, or bath, for centuries. It is a splendid example of medieval architecture and one of only four existing Hebrew baths in all of Germany.

ADMINISTRATIVE SUPPORT

FACILITY/ACTIVITY	BLDG NO/LOC	PHONE	DAYS/COMMENTS
Fire (Mil)	RB	117	24 hours daily
Housing			
Family	RB	3294/3540	M-F
Referral	RB	3109	M-F
Police (Mil)	FB	3547	24 hours daily
	RB	3269	24 hours daily
Emergency	FB,RB	114	24 hours daily
Public Affairs	RB	3263	M-F
Tax Relief	RB	3100	Call for hours.

LOGISTICAL SUPPORT

FACILITY/ACTIVITY	BLDG NO/LOC	PHONE	DAYS/COMMENTS
Auto Registration	FB	3013	W,Th
Bank	5618/BN	3160	M-F
	BN	C-8491	Tu,F
	RB	3282	M-F
Barber Shop(s)	BN	C-84131	M-Sa
	RB	C-13533	M-Sa
Beauty Shop(s)	BN	C-84131	M-Sa
	RB	C-3533	M-Sa
Bookstore	5618/BN	C-81131	Tu-Sa
	FB	C-5254	M-Sa

GERMANY
Friedberg/Bad Nauheim Sub-Community, continued

Child Care/Dev Ctr	BN	C-85511	M-F
	RB	3137	M-F
Clothing Sales	RB	3212	M-Sa
Commissary(Main)	5618/BN	3244/3544	M-Sa
Dining Facility	Canopy Club/RB	3122	Tu-Su
		C-14789	
Education Center	RB	3119/3529	M-F
Elec Repair(Gov)	RB	3480	Daily
Eng'r/Publ Works	RB	3165/3480	M-F
Exchange(Main)	BN	C-81659	Daily
	RB	3196	Daily
Food(Snack/Fast)	RB	C-5254	Daily
Pizza Parlor	RB	3090	Call for hours.
Laundry(Exch)	RB	3217	M-F
Package Store	5618/BN	3136	Tu-Sa
	FB	3222	Tu-Sa
Pick-up Point	BN	C-84880	M-Sa
	RB	C-2275	M-Sa
Postal Svcs(Mil)	RB	3240	M-F
Schools(DOD Dep)			
Elementary	BN	3242/3548	M-F
Middle School	See Frankfurt Community listing.		
High School	See Frankfurt Community listing.		
Svc Stn(Insta)	RB	C-81659	M-Sa
Space-A Air Ops	Airfield	3252	Daily
Flights to:	German locations		
Tailor Shop	RB	None	M-F
Thrift Shop	BN	None	Tu-Th
TML			
Billeting	RB	8140	Daily
BOQ	RB	3272/3	Daily
SBEQ	RB	3137	Daily

HEALTH AND WELFARE

FACILITY/ACTIVITY	BLDG NO/LOC	PHONE	DAYS/COMMENTS
Ambulance	RB	116	24 hours daily
Army Comm Svcs	5618/RB	3465/3587	M-F
Army Emerg Relief	RB	3100	M-F
Central Appts	RB	3204/3187	M-F
Chaplain	RB	3508	Daily
Chapel	RB	3508	Su
Comm Drug/Alc Ctr	RB	3142	M-F
Dental Clinic	RB	3537/3237	M-F
Red Cross	RB	3108/3528	M-F

REST AND RECREATION

FACILITY/ACTIVITY	BLDG NO/LOC	PHONE	DAYS/COMMENTS
Bowling Lanes	RB	3270	Daily
Craftshops			
Automotive	RB	3218	Th-M
Multi-crafts	RB	3266	Sa-W
Photography	RB	3266	Sa-W
Enlisted Club	RB	3120	Daily

Friedberg/Bad Nauheim Sub-Community, continued

GERMANY

Gymnasium	RB	3155/3555	Daily
Library	RB	3283	Daily
NCO Club	RB	3122	Tu-Su
O'Club	RB	3122	Daily
Outdoor Rec Ctr	RB	3143	M,Tu,Th,Sa
Recreation Center	RB	3158/3530	Daily
Theater	RB	3261	Daily
Video Rental	BN	None	Daily
	RB	C-13317	Tu-Su
Youth Center	BN	3195	M-Sa
	RB	3492	N/A

FULDA COMMUNITY (GE35R7)
APO New York 09146-5000

TELEPHONE INFORMATION: Main installation numbers: Civ: 49-0661-86-113. ETS: 321-3113. ATVN: 320-1110 (ask for Fulda). Civ prefix: 0661-____. ETS prefix: 321-3XXX. Civ to mil prefix: 0661-86-XXX.

LOCATION: Take the Fulda Nord exit from E-7 Autobahn to GE-27 south. In Downs Barracks. HE: p-36, F/5. NMC: Frankfurt, 65 miles southwest.

GENERAL INSTALLATION INFORMATION: Fulda is home to the 11th Armored Cavalry Regiment. Its responsibilities include protection and maintenance of the East/West German interzonal border.

GENERAL CITY/REGIONAL INFORMATION: Fulda is one of the oldest cities in Central Germany. Located in the upper Fulda River Valley between the Rhön and Vogelsberg mountain ranges, Fulda was founded in 744 A.D. as a monastery. The cathedral built then, known as the Dom, was considered the center of Christianity in Germany. The Dom and its crypt of St. Boniface are still popular tourist attractions, as are St. Michael's Church, second oldest in Germany; St. Paul's Gate; the baroque Stadtschloss (City Palace); and the Orangery, a part of the palace compound. Art and history lovers will want to see the Gutenberg Bible in the State Library, the famous paintings in Fulda's museums and the treasures from the Fulda Porcelain collection. Other local activities include tours to a ski resort and shooting range and fishing in a nearby stream.

ADMINISTRATIVE SUPPORT

FACILITY/ACTIVITY	BLDG NO/LOC	PHONE	DAYS/COMMENTS
Customs/Duty	Haimbacher St	735/635	M-F
Drivers Testing	Kahrmann Hse I	550	M-F
Duty Officer	8112	583/803	Daily
Fire(Mil)	7101	114	Daily
Fire(Civ)	Fulda	112	Daily
Housing			
Family	Sub-post	844/694	M-F
Referral	Sub-post	575/719	M-F
Info(Insta)	On Barracks	113	Daily
Inspector Gen'l	On Barracks	887	Daily
Legal Assist	7136	519	M-F

GERMANY
Fulda Community, continued

Locator(Mil)	In Giessen	343-6347	Daily
Locator(Civ)	Kurfürsten St	661/645	M-F
Personnel Spt	7216	790	M-F
Police(Mil)	7219	114/827	M-F
Police(Civ)	Fulda	C-110	Daily
Public Affairs	7221	515/851	M-F
Tax Relief	7126	769	M-F

LOGISTICAL SUPPORT

FACILITY/ACTIVITY	BLDG NO/LOC	PHONE	DAYS/COMMENTS
Auto Parts(Exch)	7214	693 / C-73491	Daily
Auto Registration	7219	827	M-F
Auto Rent(Other)	6400 Kreuzberg	C-495030	N/A
Auto Repairs	7214	693 / C-73491	M-Sa
Auto Sales	7133	C-79434	Daily
Auto Ship(Gov)	Kahrmann Hse II	889/576	M-F
Auto Ship(Civ)	Pfandhaus Str	C-68800	M-F
Bank	7102	671 / C-73120	M-Sa
Barber Shop(s)	7133	C-73658 / C-86578	M-Sa
Beauty Shop(s)	7133	C-74908	M-Sa
Bookstore	7136	N/A	Daily
Bus	Call Motor Pool		
Child Care/Dev Ctr	7322	443 / C-73662	M-F
Preschool	7314	C-74552	M-F
Clothing Sales	7103	441 / C-21174	M-Sa
Commissary(Main)	7308	588/778 / C-71105	M-Sa
Dining Facility	7127	642	Daily
Dry Clean(Exch)	7133	C-76116	M-Sa
Dry Clean(Gov)	7215	557	M-F
Education Center	7107	590/781	M-F
Elec Repair(Gov)	Pick-up Point	C-76116	M-F
Eng'r/Publ Works	Sub-post	641	M-F
Exchange(Main)	7133	660 / C-73660	Daily
Finance(Mil)	7407	543/516	M-F
Food(Snack/Fast)			
Burger Bar	7133	C-75566	Daily
Pizza Parlor	7133	C-75566	Daily
Foodland	7133	C-73660	Daily
Laundry(Exch)	7133	C-76116	M-Sa
Laundry(Self-Svc)	7103	644	Daily
Motor Pool	Subpost	850	M-F
Package Store	7174	582	Tu-Sa
Parking	On post	None	Daily
Photo Laboratory	7133	C-76116	M-Sa
Pick-up Point	7133	C-76116	M-Sa
Postal Svcs(Mil)	7302	730	M-Sa

GERMANY

Fulda Community, continued

Postal Svcs(Civ)	7201	C-89607	M-F
Railroad/RTO	Frankfurt	C-069-151-5755	M-F
SATO-OS	See Frankfurt Community listing.		
Schools			
Elementary	7323	853	M-F
High School	7315	523/843	M-F
Svc Stn(Insta)	Beside Commiss	C-73497	Daily
Svc Stn(Autobahn)	ESSO/Fulda-Nord	C-66027	24 hours daily
Space-A Air Ops	Airfield	594	Daily
Tailor Shop	7133	C-78466	M-Sa
Taxi(Comm)	Fulda	C-601010	24 hours daily
Tel Booking Oper	Bundespost	112 C-89607	M-F
Tel Repair(Gov)	N/A	119	N/A
Tel Repair(Civ)	N/A	C-117	N/A
Thrift Shop	7122	407	M-F
TML			
Billeting	7307	632/803	Daily
	8112	583/803	After duty hrs
BOQ(All Ranks)	7307/7309	632	Daily
DV/VIP(06+)	Deputy Cmdr	604/882	Daily
Travel Agents	7133/ITT	647	M-F
Watch Repair	7133 PUP	76116	M-Sa

HEALTH AND WELFARE

FACILITY/ACTIVITY	BLDG NO/LOC	PHONE	DAYS/COMMENTS
Ambulance		114	24 hours daily
Army Comm Svcs	7130	832/672	M-F
Army Emerg Relief	7130	832/672	M-F
Central Appts	7123	677	M-F
CHAMPUS Office	7123	862	M-F
Chaplain	7124	518/618	M-F,Su
Chapel	7124	618/818	M-F
Comm Drug/Alc Ctr	7106	894	M-F
Dental Clinic	7158	636	M-F
Medical Emergency	7123	795/514	Dly
Mental Health	Haimbacher Str	747/542	M-F
Red Cross	7300	687/838	M-F
Veterinary Svcs	7109	607	Every 2nd Tu of month

REST AND RECREATION

FACILITY/ACTIVITY	BLDG NO/LOC	PHONE	DAYS/COMMENTS
Aero/Flying Club	5 Dalbers Str		Glider Club
Bowling Lanes	7317	634	Daily
Camping/RV Area	Call outdoor recreation.		
Consolidated Club	7172	637	Daily
Craftshops			
Automotive	Sorg Bldg	569	Tu-Su
Ceramics	7133	540	Tu-Su
Leather	7133	540	Tu-Su
Gymnasium	7212	870	Daily

GERMANY
Fulda Community, continued

Info Tour & Travel	7133	647 C-73409	M-F
Library	7133	780	Tu-Su
Outdoor Rec Ctr	7166	508	M-F
Racket Courts	7212	870	Daily
Recreation Center	7120	670	Daily
Riding Club		C-41122	
Sport Field	Call Gym	870	Daily
Swimming Pool	Hallenbad Fulda	C-77533	Daily
	Schwimmbad	C-62759	Daily
Tennis Courts	Call Gym	870	
Theater	7117	631	Daily
Track	Call Gym	870	
Video Rental	Blackhorse Store	449	Daily
Water Recreation	Fulda River		
Youth Center	7306	608	M-Sa

GARLSTEDT SUB-COMMUNITY (GE93R7)
APO New York 09069-0027

TELEPHONE INFORMATION: Main installation numbers: Civ: 49-04795-77-113. ETS/ATVN: 342-113. Civ prefix: 04795-_____. ETS prefix: 342-XXXX. Civ to mil prefix: 04795-77-XXXX.

LOCATION: Take Autobahn E-71 north from Bremen to Garlstedt. HE: p-33, D/5. NMC: Bremen, 13 miles south.

GENERAL INSTALLATION INFORMATION: Garlstedt Sub-Community is located near the Bremerhaven Military Community and shares some of the Bremerhaven facilities. Garlstedt is home to the 2nd Armored Division (Forward). The construction of Clay Kaserne was something of a landmark in USAREUR history, in that this facility was the first ever to be completely constructed for use by U.S. Army forces in Germany.

GENERAL CITY/REGIONAL: Osterholz-Scharmbeck, nicknamed O'Beck by U.S. forces, is located ten kilometers southeast of Lucius D. Clay Kaserne in Garlstedt. O'Beck is an attractive community that combines the charm of a small city with the advantages of the nearby metropolitan area of Bremen. A few of the things to see in Osterholz-Scharmbeck include the 16th-century windmill, the water tower, the water wheel, the museum, the park and St. Mary's Church, which has celebrated its 800th anniversary.

ADMINISTRATIVE SUPPORT

FACILITY/ACTIVITY	BLDG NO/LOC	PHONE	DAYS/COMMENTS
Customs/Duty	386	6781	M-F
Duty Officer	321	6274/6801	Daily
Fire(Mil)	On Barracks	117	24 hours daily
Fire(Civ)	N/A	112	24 hours daily
Housing			
Family	332	6428	M-F
Referral	332	6432	M-F
Info(Insta)	On Barracks	113	24 hours daily

GERMANY

Garlstedt Sub-Community, continued

Inspector Gen'l	321	6346/6703	M-F
Legal Assist	321	6827/6438	M-F
Police(Mil)	386	114	24 hours daily
Emergency	386	114	24 hours daily
Public Affairs	321	6351	M-F
Tax Relief	321	8045/8554	M-F

LOGISTICAL SUPPORT

FACILITY/ACTIVITY	BLDG NO/LOC	PHONE	DAYS/COMMENTS
Auto Parts(Exch)	396	8291	M-Sa
		C-58630	
Auto Rent(Other)	396	1234	Tu-Sa
Auto Repairs	372	C-58630	Tu-Sa
Auto Ship(Civ)	Karl Gross	C-48380	M-F
Bakery	396	8298	M-Sa
Bank	396	6766	M,W-F
		C-1373	
Barber Shop(s)	396	6465/6297	M-Sa
Beauty Shop(s)	396	6465	M-Sa
Bookstore	396	6434	Tu-Su
Child Care/Dev Ctr	On Barracks	5485	M-F
Clothing Sales	321	6571	M-F
Commissary(Annex)	O'Beck	8894	Daily
Education Center	392	6449	M-F
Exchange(Main)	396	6752	Tu-Su
Finance(Mil)	396	6787	M-Sa
Food(Snack/Fast)			
Burger King	420	6573	Daily
Foodland	396	6415	Daily
Package Store	396	6487	Tu-Sa
Pick-up Point	396	6439	Tu-F
Postal Svcs(Mil)	396	6422	Tu-Sa
Railroad/RTO	Bahnhof	6792	M-F
Schools(DOD Dep)			
Elementary	O'Beck	7022	M-F
		C-57136	
High School	O'Beck	5025	M-F
		C-57130	
Tailor Shop	T-3	None	N/A
Taxi(Comm)	O'Beck	C-1344/2525	Daily
Tel Repair(Gov)	On Barracks	119	Daily
Tel Repair(Civ)	O'Beck	C-01171	N/A
Thrift Shop	T-1	None	Tu,Th
TML	See Bremerhaven Community listing.		
Travel Agents	396	6496	M-F

HEALTH AND WELFARE

FACILITY/ACTIVITY	BLDG NO/LOC	PHONE	DAYS/COMMENTS
Ambulance	391	116	24 hours daily
Army Comm Svcs	391	8881	M-F
Army Emerg Relief	391	8881	M-F
Central Appts	391	6251/1675	Daily
CHAMPUS Office	391	6474/6734	M-F

GERMANY
Garlstedt Sub-Community, continued

Chaplain	393	6815/6429	M-F
Chapel	393	6429	Daily
Comm Drug/Alc Ctr	391	6366	M-F
Dental Clinic	391	6804/6244	M-F
Poison Control	391	7858/7676	Daily
Red Cross	321	6431	M-F
		0	After hours

REST AND RECREATION

FACILITY/ACTIVITY	BLDG NO/LOC	PHONE	DAYS/COMMENTS
Bowling Lanes	310	6252	Daily
Consolidated Club	397	6858	Tu-Sa
Craftshops			
Automotive	395	6224	W-M
Multi-crafts	395	6339	W-M
Gymnasium	398	6485	Daily
Info Tour & Travel	395	6496	M-F
Library	395	6566	Daily
MARS	Custodian	2443-6402	Daily
Recreation Center	395	6564/6294	Daily
Theater	396	6573/6480	Daily
Youth Center	O'Beck	8882	M-Sa

GARMISCH ARMED FORCES RECREATION CENTER (GE10R7)
APO New York 09053-5000

TELEPHONE INFORMATION: Main installation numbers: Civ: 49-08821-750-712/847. ETS: 440-2712/2847. For reservations: Civ: 49-08821-750-575. ETS: 440-2575. Civ prefix: 08821-_____. ETS prefix: 440-2XXX. Civ to mil prefix: 08821-750-XXX.

LOCATION: Take Autobahn E-6 south from Munich to Garmisch. From Austria take national roads numbered 2 or 187. HE: p-92, F/3. NMC: Munich, 60 miles north.

GENERAL INSTALLATION INFORMATION: The Garmisch-Berchtesgaden area is the home of Headquarters, the Armed Forces Recreation Center (AFRC), the U.S. Army Russian Institute, and the Oberammergau NATO School. The AFRC was established over 35 years ago to enhance the life of American service members and their families living and traveling in Europe. The U.S. Army Russian Institute has been located in Garmisch since 1964; it provides the overseas training phase of the Army's Russian Area Officers' Program. The Oberammergau NATO School is located twelve miles from Garmisch. The mission of the school is to prepare officers and non-commissioned officers and their civilian equivalents for their NATO or NATO-oriented appointments.

GENERAL CITY/REGIONAL INFORMATION: Garmisch is one of the most beautiful resorts in Bavaria. It is located around 60 miles south of Munich at the foot of the world-famous Zugspitze, Germany's tallest mountain. The area was the site of the 1936 Winter Olympics and is still a very popular winter

GERMANY
Garmisch Armed Forces Recreation Center, continued

recreation area. In the summer, visitors enjoy hiking, mountain-climbing and exciting water sports such as kayaking and white-water rafting. The central location of Garmisch makes it an ideal base from which to make short excursions to Innsbruck and Munich and to visit picturesque nearby castles, churches and villages. Garmisch is a popular resort area for Americans and Europeans alike because of the sightseeing opportunities, recreational facilities and beauty of the surrounding countryside. Although the AFRC runs a number of fine hotels and a travel camp in the area, they fill up quickly. See the appendix title "Support Authorized Retired U.S. Military Personnel" for information regarding the use of AFRC facilities by retirees and other non-residents of Germany.

ADMINISTRATIVE SUPPORT

FACILITY/ACTIVITY	BLDG NO/LOC	PHONE	DAYS/COMMENTS
Customs/Duty	PMO	600	M-F
Duty Officer	PMO	801/827	24 hours daily
Fire(Mil)	Comm HQ	789	24 hours daily
Fire(Civ)	Munchener St	112	24 hours daily
Housing	Sheridan Ksrn	604/705	M-F
Referral	Sheridan Ksrn	660	M-F
Info(Insta)	Comm Hq	0	24 hours daily
Inspector Gen'l	Comm HQ	803/503	M-F
Legal Assist	Munich Ksrn	440-8313	M-F
Locator(Mil)	Comm HQ	803/503	M-F
Locator(Civ)	101-CPO	530/794	Daily
Personnel Spt	Comm HQ	803/503	Daily
Police(Mil)	PMO	801/827	24 hours daily
Police(Civ)	Munchener St	110	24 hours daily
Public Affairs	109/Sheridan	712/847	M-F
Tax Relief	501/Comm HQ	711	M-F

LOGISTICAL SUPPORT

FACILITY/ACTIVITY	BLDG NO/LOC	PHONE	DAYS/COMMENTS
Auto Drivers Testing	PX	827/648	M-F
Auto Parts(Exch)	PX	C-3245	Tu-Sa
Auto Registration	PMO	827/648	M-F
Auto Repairs	PX	C-3245	Tu-Sa
Bank	PX	619 C-53872	Tu-Sa
Barber Shop(s)	PX	None	Tu-F
Bookstore	PX	C-55289	Tu-Su
Bus	Field Arty Bks	631	M-F
Child Care/Dev Ctr	Kramer Lodge	684	Daily
Commissary(Main)	PX	587/780	Tu-Sa
Dry Clean(Exch)	PX	C-4425	M-Sa
Education Center	Kramer Lodge	461	Daily
Learning Center	Kramer Lodge	467	Daily
Eng'r/Publ Works	129	615/715	M-F
Exchange(Main)	PX	C-3743	Daily
Exchange(Concess)	PX	C-50310	Daily
Food(Caf/Rest)	Abrams Complex	C-3977	Daily
Food(Snack/Fast)			
Pizza Parlor	Breitenau Hsg	609	Daily

GERMANY
Garmisch Armed Forces Recreation Center, continued

Foodland	PX	C-3743	Daily
Motor Pool	Field Arty Bks	781	M-F
Package Store	PX	673	M-Sa
Photo Laboratory	PX	C-4425	Tu-Sa
Postal Svcs(Mil)	101/Sheridan	535	M-F
Railroad/RTO	Bahnhof	C-52521	Daily
Schools			
Elementary	Breitenau Hsg	611	M-F (K-8)
Svc Stn(Insta)	PX	C-3245	Tu-Sa
Tailor Shop	PX	C-4425	Tu-Sa
Taxi(Comm)	Bahnhofplatz	C-1616	24 hours daily
Tel Booking Oper	Comm Hq	112	24 hours daily
Tel Repair(Gov)	Comm Hq	119/2515	24 hours daily
Tel Repair(Civ)	Bahnhofplatz	C-01171	24 hours daily
Thrift Shop	PX	552	Tu,F,Sa
TML			
Billeting	116/Sheridan	705/575	Daily
Hotels	Abrams	672	Daily
	Haus Flora	584	Daily
	Haus Loisach	832	Daily
	Patton	695	Daily
	Sheridan Plaza	690	Daily
	Von Steuben	691	Daily

Note: Construction began during the Spring of 1989 on a 450-room hotel and recreation complex at Garmisch. The rooms will be more spacious than those currently in use, with private bath, telephone and television. A disco, pub, coffee shop, specialty restaurant and separate game rooms for children and adults will be included in the complex. This new hotel will replace five existing hotels, all of which pre-date World War II. The hotel will be finished in 1992, with partial opening in 1991.

Watch Repair	PX	C-4425	Daily

HEALTH AND WELFARE

FACILITY/ACTIVITY	BLDG NO/LOC	PHONE	DAYS/COMMENTS
Ambulance	Kreiskrankenhaus	C-2222	24 hours daily
Army Comm Svcs	Kramer Lodge	777/809	M-F
Army Emerg Relief	Kramer Lodge	777/809	M-F
CHAMPUS Office	Abrams Complex	816/859	M-F
Chaplain	Sheridan Ksrn	819	M-F
Chapel	Sheridan Ksrn	819/801	M-F
Comm Drug/Alc Ctr	Kramer Lodge	809/755	M-F
Dental Clinic	Abrams Complex	740	M-F
Medical Emergency	Kreiskrankenhaus	C-2222	24 hours daily
Red Cross	Munich	440-6211	24 hours daily
Veterinary Svcs	Marienplatz	C-3752	M-Sa

REST AND RECREATION

FACILITY/ACTIVITY	BLDG NO/LOC	PHONE	DAYS/COMMENTS
Beach(es)	Lake Chiemsee	441-2396	Daily

GERMANY

Garmisch Armed Forces Recreation Center, continued

Craftshops
Auto	Behind Sheridan Hotel		M,Tu,Sa,Su
Multicrafts	Kramer Lodge	752	M-Th
Golf Course	Golf Course	626	Daily
Gymnasium	Sheridan Ksrn	747	Daily
Info Tour & Travel	St. Martin St	546	Daily
Library	Kramer Lodge	467	Daily
Marina	Lake Chiemsee	441-2396	Daily
Outdoor Rec Ctr	AFRC Campgrnd	848	Daily
Racket Courts	Sheridan Gym	747	Daily
Recreation Center	Kramer Lodge	461	Daily
Special Services	Kramer Lodge	777/809	M-F
Swimming Pool	Near Sports Ctr	461	Daily
Tennis Courts	Garmisch Court	675	Daily
Theater	Sports Ctr	606	Daily
Water Recreation	Field Arty Bks	639	Daily
Youth Center	Kramer Lodge	751	Daily

GEILENKIRCHEN AIR BASE (GE46R7)
APO New York 09104-5000

TELEPHONE INFORMATION: Main installation numbers: Civ: 49-02451-63-1110. ATVN: 453-1110 (ask for Geilenkirchen).

LOCATION: Take GE-221 north from Aachen or take the A-44 Autobahn exit to GE-56 northwest for ten miles. HE: p-36, A/4. NMC: Aachen, approximately 10 miles south.

GENERAL INSTALLATION INFORMATION: A U.S. Air Force unit is located on Geilenkirchen, a German Air Base. Major base operations are NATO AEW, E-3A/AWACS. A U.S. Air Force medical clinic is on base, with limited additional U.S. facilities. NATOs first multinational flying unit is based at Geilenkirchen, which makes it unique in military history.

GENERAL CITY/REGIONAL INFORMATION: Geilenkirchen is a medium-sized village near the Netherlands border and HQ Allied Forces Central Europe (AFCENT) at Brunssum. Old watermills, palaces, and castles dot the surrounding countryside.

ADMINISTRATIVE SUPPORT

FACILITY/ACTIVITY	BLDG NO/LOC	PHONE	DAYS/COMMENTS
Personnel Spt	On Base	6229	M-F

LOGISTICAL SUPPORT

FACILITY/ACTIVITY	BLDG NO/LOC	PHONE	DAYS/COMMENTS
Child Care/Dev Ctr	On Base	321	M-F
Dining Facility	108	N/A	Daily
Education Center	89	C-5442	M-F
Schools(DOD Dep)			
Elementary	On Base	N/A	M-F (K-6)

GERMANY
Geilenkirchen Air Base, continued

High School	See Schinnen Community listing.		
Taxi(Comm)	N/A	C-7070	Daily

HEALTH AND WELFARE

FACILITY/ACTIVITY	BLDG NO/LOC	PHONE	DAYS/COMMENTS
Ambulance	211	6221	24 hours daily
Central Appts	211	6221	M-F
Medical Emergency	211	C-68708	24 hours daily

REST AND RECREATION

FACILITY/ACTIVITY	BLDG NO/LOC	PHONE	DAYS/COMMENTS
Library	On Base	C-63224	N/A

GERMERSHEIM SUB-COMMUNITY (GE69R7)
APO New York 09095-5000

TELEPHONE INFORMATION: Main installation numbers: Civ: 49-07274-58-113. ETS: 378-3113. Civ prefix: 07274-____. ETS prefix: 378-3XXX. Civ to mil prefix: 07274-58-XXX.

LOCATION: Germersheim is 35 kilometers north of Karlsruhe and can be reached via the B-9 and B-35 Autobahns. HE: p-40, D/3. NMC: Karlsruhe, 35 kilometers south.

GENERAL INSTALLATION INFORMATION: Germersheim is a sub-community of the Karlsruhe Military Community and is located across the Rhine River in Rheinland-Pfalz. The area population is approximately 2,500. Major activities include General Support Center Germersheim, Reserve Storage Activity Germersheim, 4th Combat Equipment Company (M & S), and smaller units.

GENERAL CITY/REGIONAL INFORMATION: The town of Germersheim was once a weapons arsenal for the Roman army. It was first mentioned in 1090 in the chronicles of Sinsheim. King Rudolph I of Habsburg elevated Germersheim in 1276 to Free Federal City status. In 1674 the town was completely destroyed by General Turenne. Between 1834 and 1855 Germersheim was fortified. The town sustained heavy damage during World War II, but was rebuilt thereafter.

ADMINISTRATIVE SUPPORT

FACILITY/ACTIVITY	BLDG NO/LOC	PHONE	DAYS/COMMENTS
Duty Officer	7856	805	24 hours daily
Fire(Mil)	On Barracks	117	24 hours daily
Housing			
Referral	7809	575	M-F
Legal Assist	7854	715	M-F
Police(Mil)	7856	707	Daily
Emergency	On Barracks	114	24 hours daily

GERMANY

Germersheim Sub-Community, continued

Public Affairs	7856	617	M-F

LOGISTICAL SUPPORT

FACILITY/ACTIVITY	BLDG NO/LOC	PHONE	DAYS/COMMENTS
Auto Drivers Testing	7805	814	M-F
Auto Repairs	7926	588	W-Su
Bank	Nr bowling alley	388/659	M-F
Barber Shop(s)	7846	666/746	M-F
Child Care/Dev Ctr	7842	611/840	M-F
Commissary(Main)	7851	730	Tu-Sa
Dining Facility	7832	661	Daily
Dry Clean(Gov)	7854	705	M-F
Education Center	7853	646	M-F
Elec Repair(Gov)	7856	508	M-F
Eng'r/Publ Works	7855	115	M-F
Exchange(Main)	7846	666/746	M-Sa
Food(Snack/Fast)	7835	C-2737	Daily
Laundry(Self-Svc)	7826	None	M-Sa
Package Store	7846	830	Tu-Sa
Photo Laboratory	7840	568	W-Su
Pick-up Point	7826	627/666	Tu,W,F
Postal Svcs(Mil)	7826	512	M,Th
Schools(DOD Dep)			
Elementary	7906	802	M-F (1-6)
Space-A Air Ops	Airfield	650	
Flights to:	Various German locations		
Tel Repair(Gov)	7842	119	Daily
Watch Repair	See Pick-up Point.		

HEALTH AND WELFARE

FACILITY/ACTIVITY	BLDG NO/LOC	PHONE	DAYS/COMMENTS
Ambulance	7834	116	24 hours daily
Army Comm Svcs	7859	700/546	M-F
Army Emerg Relief	7811	700/546	M-F
Central Appts	7834	524	M-F
Chaplain	7845	810	M-F
Chapel	7845	810	Su-F
Comm Drug/Alc Ctr	7853	705	M-F
Dental Clinic	7834	523	M-F

REST AND RECREATION

FACILITY/ACTIVITY	BLDG NO/LOC	PHONE	DAYS/COMMENTS
Bowling Lanes	7826	601	Daily
Consolidated Club	7811	633/C-2556	Tu-Sa
Craftshops			
Automotive	7926	588	Daily
Multi-crafts	7840	568	Th-M
Photography	7840	568	W-Su
Gymnasium	7840	582/841	Daily
Library	7840	692	M-F
NCO Club	7811	633	Tu-Su

GERMANY
Germersheim Sub-Community, continued

Recreation Center	7840	841	Daily
Rod and Gun Club	7892	623	Daily
Youth Center	7892	593/841	M-Sa

GIEBELSTADT SUB-COMMUNITY
(GE97R7)
APO New York 09182-5000

TELEPHONE INFORMATION: Main installation numbers: Civ: 49-09334-87-113. ETS: 352-7293. Civ prefix: 09334-____. ETS prefix: 352-XXXX. Civ to mil prefix: 09334-87-XXXX.

LOCATION: Take Highway 19 south from Würzburg. HE: p-40, D/2. NMC: Würzburg, 10 miles north.

GENERAL INSTALLATION INFORMATION: Giebelstadt is a sub-community of Würzburg Military Community. Until WWI, Giebelstadt Army Airfield was a secret German airbase. Now it is home to the 3rd Infantry Division's 4th Brigade and Detachment 10, 7th Weather Squadron. The newest arrival is the 8th Battalion, 43rd Air Defense Artillery, with the new Patriot Missile System.

GENERAL CITY/REGIONAL: Giebelstadt traces its history to a small Celtic town established in the early 9th century. Visitors can see evidence of this history by visiting the town's three castles: the Florian Geyer ruins; the Frierenhauer Castle; and the best preserved of the three, the von Zobel Castle, still occupied by the current Baron of Giebelstadt. Modern-day Giebelstadt is a small industrial town with a major boat factory and a bag and net factory. Its population is around 2,000.

ADMINISTRATIVE SUPPORT

FACILITY/ACTIVITY	BLDG NO/LOC	PHONE	DAYS/COMMENTS
Duty Officer	On Barracks	7293	Daily
Fire(Mil)	On Barracks	117/7413	24 hours daily
Fire(Civ)	Giebelstadt	C-99-112	24 hours daily
Housing	On Barracks	7379	M-F
Referral	On Barracks	7282	M-F
Legal Assist	611	7313/7448	M-F
Police(Mil)	On Barracks	114	24 hours daily
Police(Civ)	Giebelstadt	C-99-110	24 hours daily
Public Affairs	351	7408/9	M-F
Tax Relief	609	7234	M-F

LOGISTICAL SUPPORT

FACILITY/ACTIVITY	BLDG NO/LOC	PHONE	DAYS/COMMENTS
Audio/Photo Ctr	On Barracks	7259	M-F
Auto Drivers Testing	612	7330	M-F
Auto Parts(Exch)	Stripping Yard	7225	M-F
Bank	659	7488 C-71081	M-F

GERMANY

Giebelstadt Sub-Community, continued

Barber Shop(s)	611	7367	M-Sa
Bookstore	531	7221	M-F
Child Care/Dev Ctr	34B,645	7265/8 C-1536	Daily
Commissary(Main)	632	7208	Tu-Sa
Dining Facility	On Barracks	7410	Daily
Dry Clean(Gov)	531	7276	M-F
Education Center	531	7434/7291	M-F
Eng'r/Publ Works	On Barracks	115	Daily
Exchange(Main)	612	7423	M-Sa
Food(Snack/Fast)	612	C-1332	Snackbar
Laundry(Self-Svc)	612	N/A	Daily
Package Store	On Barracks	7283	M-Sa
Pick-up Point	524	7260	M-F
Postal Svcs(Mil)	On Barracks	7423	M-Sa
Schools			
Elementary	See Würzberg Community listing.		
High School	See Würzberg Community listing.		
Space-A Air Ops	Airfield	7323/7309	
Flights to:	German locations		
Tailor Shop	612	N/A	M-Sa
Tel Repair(Civ)	On Barracks	119	Daily
TML	See Community Würzburg listing.		

==
HEALTH AND WELFARE
==

FACILITY/ACTIVITY	BLDG NO/LOC	PHONE	DAYS/COMMENTS
Ambulance	On Barracks	116 C-09321-22222	Daily
Army Comm Svcs	531	7424 C-87424	Daily
Army Emerg Relief			
Central Appts	541	7237/7411	
Chaplain	On Barracks	7233/7407	Daily
Chapel	On Barracks	7398/7407	Daily
Comm Drug/Alc Ctr	541	7480	M-F
Red Cross	531	7408/9	Daily

==
REST AND RECREATION
==

FACILITY/ACTIVITY	BLDG NO/LOC	PHONE	DAYS/COMMENTS
Bowling Lanes	530	7224	Daily
Craftshops			
Automotive	On Barracks	7225	Daily
Leather	On Barracks	7226	Daily
Photo	On Barracks	7260	Daily
Wood	On Barracks	7226	Daily
Gymnasium	259	7223	Daily
Library	607	7467	Daily
NCO Club	Giebel People Inn	7231	Daily
O'Club	Beside Health Clinic	7204	Daily
Outdoor Rec Ctr	612	7275	In basement

GERMANY
Giebelstadt Sub-Community, continued

Recreation Center	On Barracks	7266 C-150811	Daily
Swimming Pool	Beside Motor Pool	7273	Open in summer
Theater	On Barracks	7230	Daily
Youth Center	3	7494	Near back gate

GIESSEN COMMUNITY (GE23R7)
APO New York 09169-5000

TELEPHONE INFORMATION: Main installation numbers: Civ: 49-0641-402-113. ETS: 343-113. ATVN: 343-1110. Civ prefix: 0641-____. ETS prefix: 343-XXXX. Civ to mil prefix: 0641-402-XXXX.

LOCATION: Take Autobahn E-5 to Giessener Ring and take the Grunberg exit. Follow signs to Giessen General Depot. HE: p-36, E/5. NMC: Giessen, in the city.

GENERAL INSTALLATION INFORMATION: Note: the following abbreviations are used in this listing only: GN (Giessen North); PB (Pendleton Barracks); RB (Rivers Barracks); SC (Shopping Center).

GENERAL CITY/REGIONAL INFORMATION: In the center of the Lahn Valley, Giessen has become a modern university town with an Old and New Castle, as well as the fortresses of Staufenberg, Gleiberg and Schiffenberg, romantically perched atop the wooded hills in the local area. The interesting Liebig Museum and the City Theater are worth visiting as well.

ADMINISTRATIVE SUPPORT

FACILITY/ACTIVITY	BLDG NO/LOC	PHONE	DAYS/COMMENTS
Customs/Duty	GN	8436	M-F
Duty Officer	GN	6303	24 hours daily
Fire(Mil)	Giessen	117	24 hours daily
Housing	GN	6305/6451	M-F
Referral	GN	6131	M-F
Legal Assist	GN	7220	M-F
Locator(Mil)	GN	1110	M-F
Personnel Spt	GN	7139	ID
	GN	6576	Passports
Police(Mil)	501/PB,GN	6362	24 hours daily
Emergency	GN	114	24 hours daily
Police(Civ)	Giessen	112	24 hours daily
Public Affairs	Giessen	6424	M-F

LOGISTICAL SUPPORT

FACILITY/ACTIVITY	BLDG NO/LOC	PHONE	DAYS/COMMENTS
Auto Drivers Testing	GN	6233	M-F
Auto Parts(Exch)	SC	6235	Daily
Auto Registration	GN	7127	M-F
Auto Rental(Exch)	SC	C-493112	Daily

GERMANY

Giessen Community, continued

Facility	Bldg No/Loc	Phone	Days/Comments
Auto Repairs	SC	C-33697	Daily
Auto Sales	N/A	C-43375	AMC
	N/A	C-43795	Chrysler
	N/A	C-43113	Ford
	N/A	C-43999	GM
Auto Ship(Gov)	N/A	C-46401	M-F
Bank	526/SC	7280/6118	M-Sa
Barber Shop(s)	SC	C-43998	M-Sa
Beauty Shop(s)	SC	C-43998	M-SA
Bookstore	1007/RB	6385	M-F
	526/SC	C-6385	Daily
Child Care/Dev Ctr	140 Grunberger Strasse	6200	Daily
Clothing Sales	SC	6665	Daily
Commissary(Main)	SC	8448	Daily
Dining Facility	GN	6413	Daily
Education Center	GN	6511	M-F
Learning Center	GN	6256	M-F
Eng'r/Publ Works	GN	6471	Daily
Exchange(Main)	GN	7117	Daily
Exchange(Annex)	RB	6143	Daily
Finance(Mil)	SC	8365	M-F
Food(Caf/Rest)	SC	6413	M-Sa
Foodland	SC	C-43996	Daily
Laundry(Exch)	SC	6145	Daily
Laundry(Self-Svc)	79/GN	6431	Daily
Motor Pool	GN	8320	Daily
Package Store	SC	6360/8301	Daily
Pick-up Point	GN	C-43996	Daily
	PB	C-43984	Daily
Postal Svcs(Mil)	PB	6354	M-Sa
Schools(DOD Dep)			
Elementary	PB	6690	M-F
Middle School	PB	6111	M-F
High School	See Frankfurt Community listing.		
Svc Stn(Insta)	PB	6452	Daily
	RB	6243	Daily
Space-A Air Ops	Airfield	6479	Daily
Flights to:	German locations		
Tailor Shop	RB	C-33608	M-Sa
Taxi(Comm)	Giessen	C-34011	Daily
Tel Booking Oper	PB	0/112	Daily
Tel Repair(Gov)	PB	6500	24 hours daily
Thrift Shop	GN	6407	M-F
TML			
Billeting	32	6422	Daily
		C-46215	
	1	8434	SDO. After hours.
Guest House	63	6422	Daily
	4118	6422	Daily
DV/VIP	Commander	8434	Daily

HEALTH AND WELFARE

FACILITY/ACTIVITY	BLDG NO/LOC	PHONE	DAYS/COMMENTS
Ambulance	PB	116	24 hours daily

GERMANY
Giessen Community, continued

Army Comm Svcs	601/GN	7209	M-F
Army Emerg Relief	PB	6533	M-F
Central Appts	504	6236/7102	Daily
Chaplain	5424/RB	6331	Daily
Chapel	RB	6327	Daily
Comm Drug/Alc Ctr	GN	6215	M-F
Dental Clinic	504/PB	6686	M-F
Red Cross	601/GN	6689	M-F
Veterinary Svcs	T42	6539	M-F

REST AND RECREATION

FACILITY/ACTIVITY	BLDG NO/LOC	PHONE	DAYS/COMMENTS
Bowling Lanes	RB	6472	Daily
	Skyline	6172	Daily
Craftshops			
Automotive	506/PB	6142	Daily
Multi-crafts	506/PB	6162	Daily
Photography	N/A	6473	Daily
Enlisted Club	RB	6192	Daily
	Woodland	6183	Daily
Gymnasium	Miller Hall	6497	Daily
	1008/RB	6501	Daily
Library	1007/SC	6140	Daily
	526/PB	6287	Daily
	RB	6537	Daily
NCO Club	67/GN	6113	Daily
O'Club	64/GN	6431	Daily
Recreation Center	1022/RB	6339	Daily
Rod and Gun Club	503/PB	6562	Tu-Sa
Service Club	1022/RB	7497	Daily
Swimming Pool	GN	6135	Daily
Theater	1029/RB	6594	Daily
	PB	6593	Daily
Youth Center	RB	C-42413	Daily

GÖPPINGEN COMMUNITY (GE06R7)
APO New York 09454-5000

TELEPHONE INFORMATION: Main installation numbers: Civ: 49-07161-618-113. ETS: 425-3113. ATVN: 425-1110. Civ prefix: 07161-____. ETS/ATVN prefix: 425-3XXX. Civ to mil prefix: 07161-618-XXX.

LOCATION: Three kilometers northeast of Göppingen off B-10. Follow signs for Cooke Barracks. HE: p-40, C/3. NMC: Stuttgart, 50 kilometers northwest.

GENERAL INSTALLATION INFORMATION: Since 1972, Cooke Barracks at Göppingen has housed the First Infantry Division and its respective battalions and detachments. The division includes the 4/16th Infantry; 198th Personnel Services; 589th Signal Unit; Stinger Detachment; 193rd Aviation; 299th Support; 101st Military Intelligence Unit; and the HHC 1st IDF.

GENERAL CITY/REGIONAL: Göppingen was named for its founder, Geppo,

Göppingen Community, continued

GERMANY

an Alemannian leader who established a settlement here in 261 A.D. Today, that small village has become a bustling city with a population of 53,000. The Town Museum, "Storchen," the Natural History Museum, the Märklin Museum with its displays of model trains, as well as the city's many churches and ancient structures are fascinating to visitors of all ages. The city is a great starting point for motoring excursions into the surrounding countryside.

Those lucky enough to be in Göppingen at the end of May are sure to enjoy the "Maientag," a children's and folklore festival dating back to the mid-17th century.

ADMINISTRATIVE SUPPORT

FACILITY/ACTIVITY	BLDG NO/LOC	PHONE	DAYS/COMMENTS
Advocate	138	797	M-F
Customs/Duty	On Barracks	806	24 hours daily
Fire(Mil)	On Barracks	117	24 hours daily
Fire(Civ)	Göppingen	112	24 hours daily
Housing			
Family	137	633	M-F
Referral	137	582	M-F
Info(Insta)	On Barracks	113	Daily
Inspector Gen'l	225	507/709	M-F
Legal Assist	130	708/724	M-F
Locator(Mil)	120	735	Daily
Locator(Civ)	264	567	M-F
Personnel Spt	160	405	M-F
Police(Mil)	101	593/827	24 hours daily
Emergency	101	114	24 hours daily
Public Affairs	Cooke Bks	545/805	M-F
Tax Relief	138	840	M-F

LOGISTICAL SUPPORT

FACILITY/ACTIVITY	BLDG NO/LOC	PHONE	DAYS/COMMENTS
Auto Drivers Testing	242	530	M-F
Auto Parts(Exch)	PX Complex	C-74838	M-F
Auto Registration	101	827/593	M-F
Auto Rental(Exch)	PX Complex	404	M-F
Auto Repairs	PX Complex	C-74838	M-Sa
Auto Sales	PX Complex	None	M-F
Auto Ship(Gov)	Thru Transportation		
Auto Wash	Thru Gym	427/595	M-F
Bank	138	811 C-72192	M-F
Barber Shop(s)	160	579	Tu-Sa
Beauty Shop(s)	160	539	Tu-Sa
Bookstore	229	515	M-Sa
Bus	242	N/A	Schedule at Transportation Ofc.
Child Care/Dev Ctr	338	763	M-F
Clothing Sales	143	485	Tu-Sa
Commissary(Main)	314/Hsg Area	812 C-74970	Tu-Sa
Commissary(Annex)	117	457	M-F

GERMANY
Göppingen Community, continued

Dry Clean(Exch)	117	C-74875	M-F
Dry Clean(Gov)	Thru Unit Supply		
Education Center	169	511	M-F
Exchange(Main)	108	C-74887	Tu-Sa
Finance(Mil)	165	787	M,Tu,Th,F
Food(Caf/Rest)	110	544	M-F
Food(Snack/Fast)			
Burger Bar	160	C-74919	
Foodland	117	457	Daily
Laundry(Self-Svc)	115	N/A	Daily
Package Store	257	523	Tu-Sa
Photo Laboratory	138	599	W-Su
Pick-up Point	117	C-74875	M-F
Postal Svcs(Mil)	120	735	M-F
SATO-OS	183	437	M-F
Schools(DOD Dep)			
Elementary	Housing Area	474	M-F (K-8)
High School	See Ludwigsburg Community listing.		
Svc Stn(Insta)	PX Complex	C-74811	M-Sa
Space-A Air Ops	Airfield	451	Daily
Flights to:	German locations		
Tailor Shop	160	None	Tu-Sa
Tel Booking Oper	Göppingen	112	24 hours daily
Tel Repair(Gov)	On Barracks	119	24 hours daily
Thrift Shop	117	424	M-F
TML			
Billeting/TLF	304	562	Daily
BEQ	306	560	Daily
BOQ	304	517	Daily
SBEQ	309	572	Daily

HEALTH AND WELFARE

FACILITY/ACTIVITY	BLDG NO/LOC	PHONE	DAYS/COMMENTS
Army Comm Svcs	138	477/828	M-F
Army Emerg Relief	138	797	M-F
Central Appts	239	441/596	Daily
CHAMPUS Office	239	441	M-F
Chapel	136	844	M-F
Comm Drug/Alc Ctr	239	714/514	M-F
Dental Clinic	230	500	M-F
Medical Emergency	239	824	24 hours daily
Red Cross	Schwäbisch	427-5475/ 5861	M-F
	Gmünd	C-07171-15-475/861	
Veterinary Svcs	Stuttgart	420-6038	M-F

REST AND RECREATION

FACILITY/ACTIVITY	BLDG NO/LOC	PHONE	DAYS/COMMENTS
Amer Forces Ntwk	Stuttgart	4206-431	Daily
Bowling Lanes	268	468	Daily
Craftshops			
Automotive	138	407/420	Tu-Sa

Göppingen Community, continued

GERMANY

Facility	Bldg	Phone	Days
Ceramics	138	407/579	W-Su
Photography	138	755	W-Sa
Wood	117	424	W-Su
Enlisted Club	160	568/808	Varies
Equip/Gear Locker	268	468	M-Sa
Golf Course	Behind Gym	468	9-hole
Gymnasium	Across from HQ	427/595	Daily
Info Tour & Travel	738	C-74820	M-F
Library	167	407	M-F
NCO Club	255	552 C-74984	Tu-Su
O'Club	In Housing Area	540 C-74746	Varies
Outdoor Rec Ctr	268	468	M-Sa
Racket Courts	Beside Gym		
Recreation Center	138	755	Varies
Rod and Gun Club	268	468	M-Sa
Service Club	268	468	M-Sa
Sport Field	Contact Gym		
Tennis Courts	Beside Gym		
Theater	160	539	Daily
Trails	Several in area		
Video Rental	Beside O'Club	C-76699	Tu-Su
Youth Center	Off Post	803	Varies

GRAFENWÖHR COMMUNITY
(7th ARMY TRAINING COMMAND) (GE11R7)
APO New York 09114-5000

TELEPHONE INFORMATION: Main installation numbers: Civ: 49-09641-83-113. ATVN: 475-1110. ETS: 475-113. Civ prefix: 09641-____. ETS prefix: 475-XXXX. Civ to mil prefix: 09641-83-XXXX.

LOCATION: From the E-6 Autobahn north from Nürnberg exit west to GE-85/470 to Grafenwöhr. Follow U.S. Forces signs to the training area and community: HE: p-40, G/1. NMC: Nürnberg, 42 miles southwest.

GENERAL INSTALLATION INFORMATION: Units at Grafenwöhr operate in support of the 7th Army Combat Training Command. The 547th General Dispensary and the 87th Dental Detachment are located at Grafenwöhr.

GENERAL CITY/REGIONAL INFORMATION: The 90-square-mile area that the 7th Army Training Command now occupies at Grafenwöhr and Vilseck was first used by Prince Leopold, regent of Bavaria, to train the Bavarian Army just after the turn of the present century. The area was later used as a military training area by German forces during World Wars I and II. U.S. units began using the area in May of 1947.

ADMINISTRATIVE SUPPORT

FACILITY/ACTIVITY	BLDG NO/LOC	PHONE	DAYS/COMMENTS
Advocate	215	7115	M-F
Customs/Duty	507	8359	M-F

GERMANY
Grafenwöhr Community, continued

Duty Officer	621	6332/8324	Daily
Fire(Mil)	On Barracks	117/8303	24 hours daily
Fire(Civ)	Grafenwöhr	112	24 hours daily
Housing			
Family	258	6192/7196	M-F
Referral	258	6245	M-F
Info(Insta)	On Barracks	113/6336	24 hours daily
Legal Assist	216	6170/7114	M-F
Locator(Mil)	621	6128	Daily
Locator(Civ)	536	6247	M-F
Personnel Spt	623	6311	M-F
Police(Mil)	507	8319/6319	24 hours daily
Emergency	507	114	24 hours daily
Public Affairs	621	7113/0287	M-F
Tax Relief	500	8317	M-F

LOGISTICAL SUPPORT

FACILITY/ACTIVITY	BLDG NO/LOC	PHONE	DAYS/COMMENTS
Audio/Photo Ctr	623	6272/8397	Th-Sa
Auto Drivers Testing	301	7214	M-F
Auto Parts(Exch)	442	C-533	M-Sa
Auto Registration	506	6173	M-F
Auto Repairs	442	C-553	M-Sa
Bakery	105	6140	M-Sa
Bank	105/Queen St	6140	Tu-Sa
Barber Shop(s)	209,623	C-470	M-F
Beauty Shop(s)	623	2814	Tu-Sa
Bookstore	148	6248 C-1461	M-S
Child Care/Dev Ctr	122	7238/6232	Su-F
	505,507	7238	M-F
Clothing Sales	1008	7109	M-Sa
Commissary(Main)	150	7141/6418	Tu-Sa
Dry Clean(Gov)	5154	8350	M-F
Education Center	623	6219/7156	M-F
Elec Repair(Gov)	7130	6324	M-F
Elec Repair(Civ)	624	C-574/579	M,W,F
Eng'r/Publ Works	329	6324/115	Daily
Exchange(Main)	141	3761 C-646	M-Sa
Exchange(Concess)	141	C-646	M-Sa
Finance(Mil)	633	6171/8328	M-F
Food(Caf/Rest)	141,622,623	C-515	Daily
Foodland	624	C-1613	Daily
Laundry(Exch)	556	3761	Tu-Sa
Laundry(Self-Svc)	556	1616	Daily
Motor Pool	301	7104	M-F
Package Store	141A	6185	M-Sa
Pick-up Point	623	C-1232	Tu-Sa
Postal Svcs(Mil)	623	6128/7148	M-Sa
Postal Svcs(Civ)	105	C-2041	M-Sa
Schools(DOD Dep)			
Elementary	124	6132/7133	M-F
Middle School	484/Vilseck	476-2554	M-F
High School	Nürnberg	460-6675	M-F

Grafenwöhr Community, continued   **GERMANY**

Svc Stn(Insta)	441	C-606	Daily
Tailor Shop	623	C-470	Tu-Sa
Taxi(Comm)	Gate	2300	Daily
Taxi(Gov)	301	8304	Daily
Tel Booking Oper	Grafenwöhr	112	24 hours daily
Tel Repair(Gov)	On Barracks	119/6310	Daily
Thrift Shop	6134	6181	M-F
TML			
Billeting	214	6182	Daily
	Reservations	7166/6182	Daily
BEQ/BOQ	209	6352	Daily
Guest House	214	6169	Daily

HEALTH AND WELFARE

FACILITY/ACTIVITY	BLDG NO/LOC	PHONE	DAYS/COMMENTS
Ambulance	129	116	24 hours daily
Army Comm Svcs	215	7115/8371	M-F
Army Emerg Relief	521	6138	M-F
Central Appts	129	7102/8393	Daily
CHAMPUS Office	129	7118/7152	M-F
Chaplain	140	6263/7142	M-F
Chapel	140	8372/6269	Daily
Comm Drug/Alc Ctr	206	7207/6109	M-F
Dental Clinic	131	6306/8340	M-Sa
Medical Emergency	131	6256/8307	24 hours daily
Red Cross	215	6141/6320	M-F
		0	After hours
Veterinary Svcs	131	6277	M-F

REST AND RECREATION

FACILITY/ACTIVITY	BLDG NO/LOC	PHONE	DAYS/COMMENTS
Bowling Lanes	600	6177	Daily
Craftshops			
Automotive	311	6239	M-Sa
Multi-crafts	607	6101	M-Sa
Photography	607	6304	M-Sa
Enlisted Club	Pineview	0168	Daily
Field House	547	6426/8361	Daily
Golf Course	On Barracks	6426	Daily
Gymnasium	102,103	6426/6408	Daily
Info Tour & Travel	641	8166	M-F
		C-5271	
Library	107	6231	Daily
NCO Club	445	6144	Daily
O'Club	209	6200	Daily
Outdoor Rec Ctr	641	7186	Daily
Picnic/Park Area	On Barracks	6317	Daily
Recreation Center	641	8313/6282	Daily
Rod and Gun Club	540	6116	Daily
Service Club	Algiers Rec Ctr	6246	Daily
	Open Hearth Ctr	6282	Daily
Special Services	547	6317	M-Sa
Theater	620	6195	Sa,Su

GERMANY
Grafenwöhr Community, continued

Youth Center	508	6161	M-Sa

HAHN AIR BASE (GE12R7)
APO New York 09122-5000

TELEPHONE INFORMATION: Main installation numbers: Civ: 06543-51-113. ETS: 450-1110. Civ prefix: 06453-____. ETS prefix: 450-XXXX. Civ to mil prefix: 06543-51-XXXX.

LOCATION: On Highway 327 between Morbach and Kastellaun, 2 kilometers from Sohren on B-50. HE: p-39, G/1. NMC: Frankfurt, 70 miles southeast.

GENERAL INSTALLATION INFORMATION: The mission of the 50th Tactical Wing at Hahn is to provide tactical aviation support to interdiction, counter-air and air interception missions. Other units at Hahn include the 50th Combat Support Group, the 2184th Communications Squadron, 6911th Electronic Security Squadron, C-Battery 2nd Battalion, and 7451st Tactical Intelligence Squadron.

GENERAL CITY/REGIONAL INFORMATION: Hahn is located in the state of Rhineland-Pfalz, known as the land of vineyards and forests. Seventy per cent of Germany's wine is made here and the nearby Palatine Forest is world famous. Visitors enjoy seeing the lovely castles, churches, and ruins in the area. Archaeology buffs will want to explore the Hunruck region, famous for fossils up to 500 million years old.

ADMINISTRATIVE SUPPORT

FACILITY/ACTIVITY	BLDG NO/LOC	PHONE	DAYS/COMMENTS
Customs/Duty	11	7795	M-F
Duty Officer	134C	7377/8	24 hours daily
Housing	404	7747	M-F
Info(Insta)	1378	C-3949	24 hours daily
Legal Assist	On base	7377/7378	M-F
Locator(Mil)	111	7747/7679	M-F
Personnel Spt	117,102	7747/7679	M-F
Police(Civ)	Polizei	112	24 hours daily
Police(Mil)	301	7795	M-F
Emergency	301	114	24 hours daily
Public Affairs	401	7715,7716	24 hours daily

LOGISTICAL SUPPORT

FACILITY/ACTIVITY	BLDG NO/LOC	PHONE	DAYS/COMMENTS
Audio/Photo Center	105	C-2241	Daily
Auto Registration	620	7466	M-F
Auto Rental(Exch)	105	6705	Daily
Auto Repairs	1401	7603	M-F
Auto Sales	On base	C-4081	M-Sa
Auto Ship(Civ)	318	C-4081	M-F
Bank	107/BX Mall	7604 C-2240	M-Sa

U.S. Forces Travel & Transfer Guide Europe — 117

GERMANY

Hahn Air Base, continued

Beauty Shop(s)	1342	7137	M-S
Bookstore	105	C-2074	Daily
Child Care/Dev Ctr	1381,1344	7470/7472	Daily
Clothing Sales	349	7137	M-Sa
Commissary(Main)	108	7339	Tu-Su. With deli.
Credit Union	308	7747	M-F
Dining Facility	304	7747	Daily
Dry Clean(Exch)	318	7167	M-Sa
Education Center	111	7747	M-F
Elec Repair(Gov)	318	C-3949	M-F
Exchange(Main)	105	2197/8600 C-4081	Daily
Finance(Mil)	401	C-3949	M-F
Food(Caf/Rest)	304-Falcon Inn	7367	Daily
Foodland	105	7712	Daily
Laundry(Exch)	318	7137	M-Sa
Laundry(Self-Svc)	343	8600	Daily
Package Store	1404	7428	Tu-Sa
Photo Laboratory	Basement of gym	C-3949	M-F
Pick-up Point	320	7137	Daily
Postal Svcs(Mil)	317	7679	M-Sa
SATO-OS	501	C-06543 6275	M-Sa
Schools(DOD Dep)			
Elementary	1335,1338	C-3949	M-F
High School	1335,1337	C-3949	M-F
Svc Stn(Insta)	506	7768	Daily
Tailor Shop	BX Mall	7167	M-F
TML			
Billeting	407	7140/7679	24 hours daily
TLF	1380	7140/7679	24 hours daily
VAQ	407	7140/7679	24 hours daily
Protocol Office	401	7221	24 hours daily
Transport	White Swan	N/A	N/A

HEALTH AND WELFARE

FACILITY/ACTIVITY	BLDG NO/LOC	PHONE	DAYS/COMMENTS
AF Family Svcs	1378	3949/7036	M-F
Ambulance	112	116	24 hours daily
Central Appts	112	7616	M-F
CHAMPUS Office	Hahn Hospital	7456/7192	M-F
Chapel	311,1349	7533	Call for hours.
Dental Clinic	113	7652	M-F
Medical Emergency	112	116/7192	M-F
	112	7062	After hours
Red Cross	112	7156	M-F
Veterinary Svcs	110	7118	By appoint

REST AND RECREATION

FACILITY/ACTIVITY	BLDG NO/LOC	PHONE	DAYS/COMMENTS
Bowling Lanes	601	7707	Daily
Craftshops			
Automotive	1003	7466	Tu-Su

GERMANY
Hahn Air Base, continued

Ceramics	330	7725	Tu-Su
Leather	330	7725	Tu-Su
Photography	330	7725	Tu-Su
Wood	123	7725	Tu-Su
Golf Course	644	7229	Daily. W/dr range.
Gymnasium	109	7725	Daily
Library	111	7677	Daily
MARS	112	7176	M-F
NCO Club	403	7566	Daily
O'Club	1402	7481/6333	Daily
Racket Courts	109	7725	Daily
Recreation Center	314	7468	Daily
Rod and Gun Club	626	7402	Daily
Theater	106	7782	Daily
Video Rental	318	7725	Daily
Youth Center	1349	7238	M-Sa

HANAU COMMUNITY (GE13R7)
APO New York 09165-0015

TELEPHONE INFORMATION: Main installation numbers: Civ: 49-06181-88-113 (Hanau); 49-06183-51-113 (Fliegerhorst Kaserne in Hanau); 49-06051-81-113 (Gelnhausen); 49-06042-80-113 (Büdingen). ETS: 322-113 (Hanau, including Fliegerhorst); 321-2113 (Gelnhausen); 321-4113 (Büdingen). Civ prefix: 06181-_____ (Hanau); 06183-_____ (Fliegerhorst); 06051-_____ (Gelnhausen); 06042-_____ (Büdingen). ETS prefix: 322-XXXX (Hanau, including Fliegerhorst); 321-2XXX (Gelnhausen); 321-4XXX (Büdingen). Civ to mil prefix: 06181-88-XXXX (Hanau); 06183-51-XXXX (Fliegerhorst); 06051-81-XXX (Gelnhausen); 06042-80-XXX (Büdingen).

LOCATION: From Autobahn 66 to Highway 8 or 40 to Hanau. Clearly marked. HE: p-36, E/6. NMC: Frankfurt, 15 miles west.

GENERAL INSTALLATION INFORMATION: The Hanau Military Community consists of Pioneer Kaserne, Fliegerhorst Kaserne, Hutier Kaserne, Hessen-Homburg, François Kaserne, Yorkhof Kaserne, Wolfgang Kaserne, Argonner Kaserne, Cardwell Housing and Patriot Kaserne, all located in Hanau; of Armstrong Barracks in Büdingen; and Coleman Kaserne in Gelnhausen. Units that make up the Hanau Community include the 555th Combat Support Company; the 2/43rd Air Defense Battalion; the 567th Engineer Company; 3rd Battalion, 61st Air Defense Artillery; and the 3rd Reconnaissance Squadron, 12th Cavalry. Note: the following abbreviations are used in this listing only: AB (Armstrong Barracks); CH (Cardwell Housing); CK (Colmen Kaserne); FK (Fliegerhorst Kaserne); FrK (François Kaserne); HH (Hessen-Homburg); HK (Hutier Kaserne); NA (New Argonner Housing); OA (Old Argonner Housing); PK (Pioneer Kaserne); WK (Wolfgang Kaserne); YK (Yorkhof Kaserne).

GENERAL CITY/REGIONAL INFORMATION: Although Hanau received status as a city by Albrecht I in 1303, it was not until religious refugees poured into the city in 1597 that it began to flourish. Given religious freedom by the ruling Count, these refugees, mostly Dutchmen and Belgian Walloons, constructed a new city and started new trades, including gold and silversmithing. The refugees also built the Netherland Walloon Double Church

Hanau Community, continued

GERMANY

which stands on Französische Allee as a monument to them. Hanau's Academy of Art was established in 1772 to train young people to work in the city's gold and silver trade. It is the oldest existing school of its kind in Germany. At the beginning of the 20th century, Hanau's Main River Port was constructed. This paved the way for trade of all kinds.

Among Hanau's more notable attractions are the Goldsmith House on Altstädter Market and the Philippsruhe Castle. Built in 1537 and then rebuilt following the last war, the Goldsmith House was once the town hall. It is one of Hanau's prettiest buildings and now displays many works of gold, silver and other precious metals.

ADMINISTRATIVE SUPPORT

FACILITY/ACTIVITY	BLDG NO/LOC	PHONE	DAYS/COMMENTS
Duty Officer	YK	8510	Daily
Fire(Mil)	All locations	117	24 hours daily
Fire(Civ)	All locations	112	24 hours daily
Housing			
Family	Gelnhausen	864/808	M-F
	11/PK	8763	M-F
Referral	2205/AK	794	M-F
		C-1077	
	Gelnhausen	C-4794	
	11/PK	8151/8071	M-F
Info(Insta)	All locations	113	24 hours daily
Inspector Gen'l	YK	8361	M-F
Legal Assist	2204/Büdingen	755/845	Tu,Th
	1604/CK	792/816	M-F
	4/PK	8428/8429	M-F
Locator(Mil)	All locations	113	24 hours daily
Locator(Civ)	YK	8361	M-F
Personnel Spt	2308/Büdingen	860/861	M-F. IDs.
	1604/CK	771/758	M-F. IDs.
	4/PK	8432	M-F. IDs.
Police(Mil)	1357/FK	657/516	24 hours daily
Emergency	11/PK	114	24 hours daily
Public Affairs	1640/CK	862	M-F
	1202/YK	8277	M-F
Tax Relief	4/PK	8418	M-F

LOGISTICAL SUPPORT

FACILITY/ACTIVITY	BLDG NO/LOC	PHONE	DAYS/COMMENTS
Auto Drivers Testing	1632/CK	765	M-F
	45/PK	8769	M-F
Auto Parts(Exch)	Hanau	C-54011	M-Sa
Auto Rental(Exch)	125/PK	8750	M-Sa
		C-54071	
	503/WK	C-571188	M-Sa
Auto Sales	WK	C-56073	Daily. VW.
	WK	C-55602	Daily. Chrysler.
	WK	C-56048	Daily. AMC.
	WK	C-56823	Daily. Ford.
	WK	C-51558	Daily. GM.

GERMANY
Hanau Community, continued

Bank	2205/AB	725	M-F
	1662/CK	711	M-F
	1357/FK	7458	M-F
	916/FrK	8256	M-F
	28/PK	8064/8629	M-Sa
Barber Shop(s)	2205/AB	C-2825	M-Sa
	1663/CK	C-4210	M-Sa
	1357/FK	C-4383	M-Sa
	916/FrK	C-12974	M-F
	5/PK	C-56884	M-F
	WK	C-572787	M-Sa
Beauty Shop(s)	1663/CK	739	Tu-Sa
	WK	C-55171	M-Sa
Bookstore	2207/AB	None	M-F
	1662A/CK	None	M-Sa
	1357/FK	None	M-F,1st Sa
	WK	C-52434	Daily
Child Care/Dev Ctr	2223/AB	746	M-F
	1824A/CK	684	M-F
	1280/CH	8026	M-F
	406/OA	8083	M-F
	514/WK	C-572286	M-F
	1206/YK	C-8458	M-F
Clothing Sales	1604/CK	883	M-F
	29/PK	8363	M-F
Commissary(Main)	2235/AB	726/826	M-Sa
	1357/FK	7408	M-F
	Gelnhausen	788/728	M-Sa
	500/WK	8323/8992	Daily
Credit Union	5/PK	8062	M-F
Education Center	2225/AB	736/812	M-F
	1310/FK	7747/7538	M-F
	903/FrK	8813/8519	M-F
	Gelnhausen	825/744	M-F
	601/GK	8540	M-F
	11/PK	8314/8945	M-F
Learning Center	2209/AB	793	M-F
Elec Repair(Gov)	See pick-up point.		
Eng'r/Publ Works	All locations	115	After hours emerg
Exchange(Main)	2206/AB	C-2828	M-Sa
	1663/CK	870	M-Sa
	1357/FK	7595/8222	M-Sa
	916/FrK	C-12974	M-Sa
	1106/HK	C-12901	M-F
	503/WK	8603	Daily
Finance(Mil)	2205/AB	860	M-F
	1604/CK	943	M-F
	5/PK	8805	M-F
Food(Snack/Fast)	1309/FK	C-2700	M-F
Burger Bar	2205/AB	C-2826	M-Sa
	1662/CK	C-4282	Daily
	1357/FK	C-2700	Daily
	909/FrK	C-12976	M-F
	616/GK	C-53860	M-F
	1106/HK	C-12975	Daily

U.S. Forces Travel & Transfer Guide Europe — 121

GERMANY

Hanau Community, continued

Burger King	30/PK WK	C-55169 N/A	M-Sa Daily
Foodland	2206/AB 1662/CK 1357/FK 1106/HK 30/PK	C-1572 C-4404 7595/8298 C-12901 C-55436	Daily Daily Daily Daily Daily
Laundry(Exch)	2205/AB 1662/CK 1370/FK 903/Frk 1101/HK 67/PK	None None None None None 8352	24 hours daily Daily Daily Daily Daily 24 hours daily
Package Store	2235/AB 1663/CK WK	326 650 8329	Tu-Sa Tu-Sa Tu-Sa
Photo Laboratory	1662/CK	712	Tu-Su

===

Pick-up Point	2204/AK 1663/CK 1372/FK FrK 30/PK	None C-4218 C-2709 C-16557 C-51508	M-F M-Sa M-F M-F M-Sa
Postal Svcs(Mil)	2213/AB 1663/CK 1357/FK 916/FrK 59/PK	870/719 860 7736 8053 8918/8351	M-F M-F M-F M-F M-Sa
Postal Svcs(Civ)	1662/CK 1372/FK 15/PK	C-5021 C-2210 C-55395	M-F M-F M-F
Schools(DOD Dep)			
Elementary	2330/AB 1280/CH 1807/CK 414/OA 360/SH	749 8026 850/688 8819/8374 8600	M-F (K-3) M-F (Pre-school) M-F (K-6) M-F (K-6) M-F (1-6)
High School	Behind BOQ/NA	8165	M-F (7-12)

===

Svc Stn(Insta)	1822/CK Hanau	C-4266 C-56806	M-Sa Daily
Space-A Air Ops	See the Frankfurt Community listing.		
Tailor Shop	2203/AB 1604/CK 1372/FK 30/PK	727 C-4218 C-4300 C-56118	M-F M-Sa M-F Tu-Sa
Taxi(Comm)	Hanau Büdingen Gelnhausen	C-24111 C-3000/3434 C-2200	Daily Daily Daily
Thrift Shop	2255/AB 1604/CK 12/PK	None None C-55801	M,Tu,Th M-W Tu,Th
TML			
Billeting	204/NA 4/PK	8947 8947	M-F After hours
Guest House	203/NA	8947	Daily
VAQ	204/NA	8947	Daily

GERMANY
Hanau Community, continued

HEALTH AND WELFARE

FACILITY/ACTIVITY	BLDG NO/LOC	PHONE	DAYS/COMMENTS
Ambulance	425/NA	116	24 hours daily
Army Comm Svcs	2304/AB	786/804	M-F
	1604/CK	790	M-F
	4/PK	8093/8828	M-F
Army Emerg Relief	4/PK	8093/8828	M-F
Central Appts	425/NA	8630/8640	M-F
CHAMPUS Office	245/NA	8741/8388 Ext. 19	M-F
Chapel	Büdingen	805	W,Su
	FK	7767/7579	Tu-Th,Su
	FrK	8288	Su
	Gelnhausen	819/719	Su-Th
	PK	8119/8924	Daily
Comm Durg/Alc Ctr	425/NA	8801/8808	M-F
Dental Clinic	2204/Büdingen	862/729	M-F
	1373/FK	797	M-F
	1660/Gelnhausen	774	M-F
	245/NA	8343/8327	M-F
Red Cross	4/PK	8731/8205	M-F
		8708	After hours
Veterinary Svcs	Büdingen	C-650	M-F

REST AND RECREATION

FACILITY/ACTIVITY	BLDG NO/LOC	PHONE	DAYS/COMMENTS
Amer Forces Ntwk	See Frankfurt Community listing.		
Bowling Lanes	2214/Büdingen	740	Daily
	1661/Gelnhausen	714	Daily
	22/PK	8060	Daily
Craftshops			
Automotive	2110/AB	None	Sa-W
	1633/CK	667	Tu-Su
	1322/FK	407	W-Su
Multi-crafts	1005A/CK	669	Sa-W
	545/WK	8082/8692	Tu-Su
Enlisted Club	2320/AB	722	Tu-Su
	1282/CH	8518	Tu-Su
	1616/CK	604	M-F
	1985/FK	7309	Daily
	1012/HH	8391	Daily
	41/PK	8565	Daily
Equip/Gear Locker	2318/Büdingen	None	W
	1615/CK	740	Tu-Th
	24/PK	8200	M-F
Gymnasium	2214/Büdingen	737	Daily
	1281/CH	8607	Daily
	1657/CK	721	Daily
	1376/FK	672	Daily
	41/PK	8197	Daily
Info Tour & Travel	2207/AB	770	M-F
	1662/CK	735	M-F

Hanau Community, continued

GERMANY

	1351/FK	735	M-F
	Hanau	C-54048/9	M-F
	125/PK	739	M-Sa
Library	2207/AB	739	Sa-Th
	1662/CK	738	Sa-Th
	1351/FK	7532	M-Sa
	5/PK	8715	Daily
NCO Club	2320/AB	722	Daily
	1666/CK	705	M-F
	909/FrK	8525	M-F
	1012/HH	8391	Daily
	12/PK	8691	M-Sa
O'Club	Büdingen	C-2827	Tu-Su
	1617/CK	708	Su-F
	405/OA	8209	Su-F
Recreation Center	2207/AB	770	Daily
	1662/CK	785	Daily
	1351/FK	7759	Daily
	1116/Hutier	8693	Daily
	38/PK	8088	Daily
Rod and Gun Club	Hanau	8153	Daily
Tennis Courts	Several in the area		
Theater	AB	774	Call for schedule.
	CK	602	Call for schedule.
	FK	440	Call for schedule.
	Hanau	8819	Call for schedule.
	Hanau	8673	Call for schedule.
Video Rental	Büdingen	None	M-Sa
	1354/FK	None	M-Sa
	27/PK	C-52684	Daily
	WK	None	Daily
Youth Center	2205/Büdingen	849	Tu-Su
	1827/CK	671	Tu-Sa
	1333/FK	7445	Tu-Sa

==

HEIDELBERG/SCHWETZINGEN COMMUNITY (CENTAG) (GE33R7)
APO New York 09102-5000

TELEPHONE INFORMATION: Main installation numbers: Civ: 49-06221-57-113 (Heidelberg); 49-06621-172-113 (Heidelberg Hospital); 49-06202-80-113 (Schwetzingen/Rheinau). ETS: 370-113 (Heidelberg); 370-2113 (Heidelberg Hospital); 379-113 (Schwetzingen/Rheinau); 374-0113 (CENTAG). ATVN: 370-1110. Civ prefix: 06221-____ (Heidelberg); 06221-____ (Heidelberg Hospital and CENTAG); 06202-____ (Schwetzingen/Rheinau). ETS prefix: 370-XXXX (Heidelberg); 370-2XXX (Heidelberg Hospital); 379-XXXX (Schwetzingen/Rheinau); 374-0XXX (CENTAG). Civ to mil prefix: 06621-57-XXXX (Heidelberg); 06621-172-XXX (Heidelberg Hospital); 06202-80-XXXX (Schwetzingen/Rheinau); 06221-398-XXX (CENTAG).

LOCATION: Access from the E-5 and E-67 Autobahns. A spur off the E-67 Autobahn terminates in Heidelberg. Follow signs to the community. HE: p-40, B/2. NMC: Heidelberg, in the city.

GERMANY
Heidelberg/Schwetzingen Community, continued

GENERAL INSTALLATION INFORMATION: Heidelberg is the headquarters of the United States Army Europe (USAREUR). 1st Personnel Command (1st PERSCOM) is located in nearby Schwetzingen. There are nine military kasernes in the community spread over a ten mile radius. Central Army Group (CENTAG), a multi-national NATO force, is located at Campbell Barracks. Note: the following abbreviations are used in this listing only: CB (Campbell Barracks—CENTAG); MTV (Mark Twain Village in Heidelberg); PB (Patton Barracks in Heidelberg); PHV (Patrick Henry Village in Heidelberg); SC (Shopping Center in Heidelberg); TB (Tompkins Barracks in Schwetzingen).

GENERAL CITY/REGIONAL INFORMATION: Heidelberg, Germany's oldest university town, is situated on the banks of the Neckar River. Heidelberg Castle and the "Altstadt" (the Old Town), with its historical landmarks, student pubs, and quaint shopping area, attract many tourists. Summertime castle illuminations and the local musical production of *The Student Prince* are special treats for Americans.

The Palatinate Museum offers rich collections of artifacts from prehistoric and Roman times as well as art and china. Königstuhl and Heiligenberg are two nearby mountains affording magnificent panoramas of the surrounding area. The famous Schwetzingen Castle, a 15-minute drive from Heidelberg, dates back to 1350. The castle has been added to and renovated throughout the centuries. Tourists now enjoy the castle's world-renowned fountains and gardens and visit its unique Rococo Theater where Mozart once performed.

ADMINISTRATIVE SUPPORT

FACILITY/ACTIVITY	BLDG NO/LOC	PHONE	DAYS/COMMENTS
Customs/Duty	3850/SC	7180/8136	M-F
Duty Officer	CB	8500	After hours
	3613/Hospital	840	After hours
	PB	7280	After hours
	4241/TB	7888	After hours
Fire(Mil)	All locations	117	24 hours daily
Fire(Civ)	All locations	112	24 hours daily
Housing	3962/DEH Compound	6710/8398	M-F
Family	3980/DEH Compound	6953	M-F
Referral	3850/SC	6576	M-F
Info(Insta)	All locations	113	24 hours daily
Inspector Gen'l	106/PB	7052/8470	M-F
Legal Assist	9/CB	7340	M-F
	107/PB	6421/6410	M-F
Locator(Mil)	128/PB	6832	M-F
Personnel Spt	3850/SC	6876/8502	M-F
	Passport	7514	M-F
Police(Mil)	3850/SC	6400/8800	24 hours daily
Emergency	3850/SC	114	24 hours daily
	4241/TB	6537/8794	24 hours daily
Police(Civ)	3850/SC	8549	M-F
Emergency	3850/SC	110	24 hours daily
Public Affairs	110/PB	7414/8655	M-F
Tax Relief	3850/SC	6576	M-F

Heidelberg/Schwetzingen Community, continued

GERMANY

LOGISTICAL SUPPORT

FACILITY/ACTIVITY	BLDG NO/LOC	PHONE	DAYS/COMMENTS
Audio/Photo Ctr	SC	C-25095	Daily
Auto Drivers Testing	3852/PB	6305/6514	M-F
Auto Parts(Exch)	3801/SC	C-24900	M-Sa
Auto Registration	3980/DEH Compound	7222/8263	M-F
Auto Rental(Exch)	3803/SC	C-14880	M-Sa
Auto Repairs	3801/SC	C-24900	M-F
Auto Sales	Heidelberg	C-20452/ 27637	Chrysler
	Heidelberg	C-160171	Ford
	Heidelberg	C-24961	GM
	Heidelberg	C-160118	VW
Auto Ship(Gov)	PB	6643	M-F
Bank	31N/CB	C-160021/ 160022	M-F
	3619/Hospital	617	Th
	3803/SC	C-10861	Tu-Sa
Barber Shop(s)	31/CB	C-390777	M-F
	3619/Hospital	C-300295	M-F
	4505/PHV	C-761937	Tu,F
	104/PB	None	M-Sa
	TB	C-806367	M-F
Beauty Shop(s)	131/MTV	C-390106	Tu-Sa
	4505/PHV	C-762160	Tu-Sa
Bookstore	3802/SC	6880	Daily
	31/CB	8311	M-F
	4505/PHV	None	M-Sa
	104/PB	6531	M-F
	3619/Hospital	2679	M-F
	4233/TB	None	M-F
Bus	PB	6951/8646	Daily
Child Care/Dev Ctr	3628H/Hospital	697	M-F
	6060/MTV	7548	M-F
	3733/MTV	8738 C-390815	M-F
	4442,4443/PHV	7256/6190	M-F
Clothing Sales	3850/SC	6254 C-23192	M-Sa
Commissary(Main)	3850/SC	8465/6493	Daily
Credit Union	3850/SC	7138/7540 C-14307	M-F
Dining Facility	107/CENTAG	588	Daily
	3617/Hospital	747	Daily
	112/PB	6219	Daily
Dry Clean(Exch)	119/PB	6391	M-F
Education Center	3733/CB	8120/6632	M-F
	3603/Hospital	2778/2595	M-F
	106/PB	6176/8700	M-F
	4235/TB	7696/6220	M-F
Eng'r/Publ Works	All locations	115	24 hours daily
Exchange(Main)	3803/SC	C-27234	Daily
Exchange(Annex)	18/CB	C-390787	M-F

GERMANY
Heidelberg/Schwetzingen Community, continued

	3619/Hospital	C-300203	M-F
	104/PB	C-24594	M-Sa
	4233/TB	C-3165	Daily
Finance(Mil)	31N/CB	8312/7284	M-F
	TB	7634/6363	M-F
Food(Snack/Fast)	201/Airfield	C-700200	Daily
	3619/Hospital	C-300287	Daily
	3803/SC	C-24423	Daily
Burger King	4544/PHV	C-7626861	Daily
Pizza Parlor	104/PB	7252	Daily
		C-25250	
Foodland	3734/MTV	C-390727	Daily
	4505/PHV	C-762164	Daily
Laundry(Self-Svc)	3733/MTV	None	24 hours daily
	4517/PHV	None	24 hours daily
	128/PB	None	24 hours daily
Package Store	4537/PHV	6982	Tu-Sa
	3803/SC	6724	M,W,F,Sa
	4298/TB	6108	M,F

Pick-up Point	18/CB	7494	M-F
	4505/PHV	C-762667	Daily
	3802/SC	C-24513	M-Sa
	4251/TB	6332	M-F
Postal Svcs(Mil)	31N/CB	7254	M-F
	3617/Hospital	676	M-F
	4537/PHV	None	M-Sa
	104/PB	6437	M-F
	3803/SC	6462	Tu-Sa
	4236/TB	6374	M-F
Postal Svcs(Civ)	3850/SC	5379	M-F
		C-25378	
Railroad/RTO	Heidelberg	6481/8651	M-F
		C-21446	
SATO-OS	3850/SC	7495	M-F
		C-26575	
	Hauptbahnhof	C-576949	Daily

Schools(DOD Dep)			
Elementary	MTV	8158/6996	M-F (K-5)
	PHV	7454/8430	M-F (K-5)
Middle School	678/PHV	8796/7372	M-F (6-8)
High School	MTV	8004/7513	M-F (9-12)
Svc Stn(Autobahn)	3956/Autobahn	C-24591	M-Sa
Space-A Air Ops	Heidelberg AAF	6201/7088	Daily
	Also see Ramstein AB and Rhein-Main AB listings.		
Tailor Shop	3802/SC	C-25217	Daily
Taxi(Comm)	Heidelberg	C-37676	Daily
Tel Booking Oper	All locations	112	24 hours daily
Tel Repair(Gov)	All locations	119	24 hours daily
Tel Repair(Civ)	In Heidelberg	1171	24 hours daily
	Outside Heidelberg	0117	24 hours daily
Thrift Shop	PHV	C-767991	Tu-Th,Sa
TML			
Billeting	4527/PHV	7979/6941	24 hours daily
Guest House	4527/PHV	7979/6941	24 hours daily

Heidelberg/Schwetzingen Community, continued   **GERMANY**

| DV/VIP | Hq USAREUR | 8707 | Extended duty hours |

HEALTH AND WELFARE

FACILITY/ACTIVITY	BLDG NO/LOC	PHONE	DAYS/COMMENTS
Ambulance	All locations	116	24 hours daily
Army Comm Svcs	3850/SC	6975/6883	M-F
Army Emerg Relief	3850/SC	8141	M-F
Central Appts	Hospital	622/623	M-F
CHAMPUS Office	Hospital	633/575 C-300061	M-F
Chaplain	101/PB	6250/8675	M-F
Chapel	MTV	8448	M-F
	PHV	8071/6927	M-F
	PB	8043	M-F
	TB	7692	M-F
Comm Drug/Alc Ctr	117/PB	6666	M-F
	426/TB	6226	M-F
Dental Clinic	3613/Hospital	682/571	M-F
	4539/PV	6978/6968	M-F
	4252/TB	6448	M-F
Medical Emergency	All locations	116	24 hours daily
Mental Health	3611/Hospital	607/690	M-F
Poison Control	3613/Hospital	891	24 hours daily
Red Cross	3850/SC	8711/6777	M-F
Veterinary Svcs	4510/PHV	7202	M-F

REST AND RECREATION

FACILITY/ACTIVITY	BLDG NO/LOC	PHONE	DAYS/COMMENTS
Bowling Lanes	PHV	6965	Daily
Craftshops			
Automotive	PB	7473	Daily
	4226/TB	6181	Daily
Multi-crafts	108/PB	7167	M,T,F-Su
Photography	104/PB	6630	Tu-Su
Enlisted Club	3608/Hospital	762	Tu-Su
	4506/PHV	8241 C-762150	Th-Tu
	109/PB	7364 C-24639	M-Sa
Golf Course	Rheinau	6139	Seasonal
Gymnasium	18/CB	6350	Daily
	3618/Hospital	553	Daily
	152/PB	6110	Daily
	4225/TB	6203	Daily
Info Tour & Travel	3850/SC	6543	M-F
Library	3617/Hospital	635	M-F
	3796/MTV	6678/8239	M-F
	4509/PHV	7067	Daily
MARS	128S/PB	8256/6608	N/A
NCO Club	3608/Hospital	762	Tu-Su
	4506/PHV	8241 C-762150	Th-Tu
	109/PB	7364	M-Sa

GERMANY
Heidelberg/Schwetzingen Community, continued

O'Club	4507/PHV	7040	Tu-Sa
Outdoor Rec Ctr	PHV	8737	M-F
Racket Courts	18/CB	6350/8183	Daily
	3618/Hospital	553	Daily
	152/PB	6110	Daily
	4225/TB	6203	Daily
Recreation Center	1104/PB	6258	Daily
	TB	6178	Daily
Rod and Gun Club	Oftersheim	C-51193	N/A
Sport Field	Sports Office	6460	N/A
Tennis Courts	PHV	6386	N/A
	PB	6110	N/A
Theater	3619/Hospital	617	N/A
	4502/PHV	6263	N/A
	109/PB	6670	N/A
Video Rental	N/A	C-22106/ 161870	Daily
Youth Center	Teens/PHV	7131	Daily
	Preteens/PHV	7703	Daily

==

HEILBRONN COMMUNITY (GE38R7)
APO New York 09176-0015

TELEPHONE INFORMATION: Main installation numbers: Civ: 49-07131-58-113 (Heilbronn); 49-07132-15-113 (Neckarsulm); 49-07264-801-113 (Siegelsbach). ETS: 426-2113 (Heilbronn); 426-5113 (Neckarsulm); 426-3113 (Siegelsbach). ATVN: 370-1110 (ask for Heilbronn). Civ prefix: 07131-____ (Heilbronn); 07132-____ (Neckarsulm); 07264-____ (Siegelsbach). ETS prefix: 426-2XXX (Heilbronn); 426-5XXX (Neckarsulm); 426-3XXX (Siegelsbach). Civ to mil prefix: 07131-58-XXX (Heilbronn); 07132-15-XXX (Neckarsulm); 07264-801-XXX (Siegelsbach).

LOCATION: Off Autobahn E-81 south near the intersections of E-81 and E-6. HE: p-40, C/3. NMC: Heidelberg, 30 miles northwest.

GENERAL INSTALLATION INFORMATION: The units that comprise the Heilbronn Community provide combat readiness and Army aviation support to outlying units. Wharton Barracks is the primary support activity for the entire community. Artillery Kaserne is located nine miles away in Neckarsulm. The housing area in Neckargartach is approximately seven miles from Wharton Barracks and approximately 4 miles from Artillery Kaserne. Relatively small installations are found in Siegelsbach, approximately 35 miles away, and in Dallau Tactical Defense Station. **Note: the following abbreviations appear in this listing only: BK (Badenerhof Kaserne in Heilbronn); NAK (Neckarsulm Artillery Kaserne); SAF (Siegelsbach Ammunition Facility); WB (Wharton Barracks in Heilbronn).**

GENERAL CITY/REGIONAL INFORMATION: The Heilbronn Community is situated in the Neckar River Valley in the southwestern German state of Baden-Württemberg. The area abounds with museums, castles, art galleries, parks and forests, all of which offer tourists and residents alike hours of pleasure and adventure.

In addition, the state of Baden-Württemberg observes more holidays than any

U.S. Forces Travel & Transfer Guide Europe — 129

Heilbronn Community, continued   **GERMANY**

other in Germany. From the "Silvester" parties marking the beginning of the new year through Fasching parades, the summer Unterlander Volksfest, fall's Heilbronner Herbst wine festival to the last Christmas celebration, the year is rich in festivities. Theater goers, music-lovers and history buffs will all enjoy their stay in Heilbronn.

ADMINISTRATIVE SUPPORT

FACILITY/ACTIVITY	BLDG NO/LOC	PHONE	DAYS/COMMENTS
Customs/Duty	2/WB	424	M-F
Duty Officer	1/WB	462/400	Daily
Fire(Mil)	816/WB (Non-emergency)	817	24 hours daily
	Emergency	117	24 hours daily
Fire(Civ)	816/WB (Non-emergency	C-162868	24 hours daily
Housing	2/WB	621	M-F
Family	204/WB	485/527	M-F
Unaccompanied	204/WB	523	M-F
Referral	204/WB	402	M-F
		C-53433	
Info(Insta)	1/WB	113	24 hours daily
Inspector Gen'l	5/WB	710/337	Tu-Th by appoint
Legal Assist	10/WB	490/2775	M,Tu,W,F
Locator(Mil)	1/WB	113	24 hours daily
Locator(Civ)	1/WB	544	M-F
Personnel Spt	1/WB	652/575	M-F
	1/WB	416	M-F. ID cards.
		C-2416	Closed every 2nd Tu
Police(Mil)	1/WB	529	24 hours daily
Emergency	1/WB	114	24 hours daily
Police(Civ)			
Public Affairs	26/WB	844	M-F
Tax Relief	6/WB	565/308	M-F
		C-575438	

LOGISTICAL SUPPORT

FACILITY/ACTIVITY	BLDG NO/LOC	PHONE	DAYS/COMMENTS
Auto Drivers Testing	1/WB	470	M-F
Auto Parts(Exch)	223/WB	C-53107	M-Sa
Auto Registration	1/WB	837/547	M-F
Auto Repairs	223/WB	C-53107	M-Sa
Auto Sales	11/WB	C-21484	M-Sa
Auto Wash	80/WB	N/A	Daily
Bank	501/NAK	N/A	M-F
	17/WB	498	M-F
Barber Shop(s)	811/BK	C-72390	M-F
	506/NAK	None	M-F
	PX Mall/WB	C-53123	M-Sa
Beauty Shop(s)	PX Mall/WB	C-53123	Tu-Sa
Bookstore	302/BK	437	M-F
	50/WB	525	Tu-Su
Bus	Call ACS for latest schedule.		
Child Care/Dev Ctr	23/WB	556	M-F

GERMANY
Heilbronn Community, continued

	811/BK	649	M-F
		C-16239	
	WB	C-576933	M-F
Clothing Sales	19/WB	571	Tu-Sa
		C-577324	
Commissary(Main)	217/WB	833/466	Tu-Su
Commissary(Annex)	506/NAK	716	M-F
Dining Facility	702/BK	N/A	Daily
	505/NAK	N/A	Daily
	7/WB	N/A	Daily
Dry Clean(Exch)	Pick-up Points		
Dry Clean(Gov)	307/BK	N/A	M-F
	5/WB	431	M-F
Education Center	302/BK	572	M-F
	523/NAK	767/742	M-F
	5/WB	431	M-F
Learning Center	2039/SAF	290	M-F
	7/WB	413	M-F
Eng'r/Publ Works	BK Emergency	115	24 hours daily
	BK Non-emerg	590	M-F
Exchange(Main)	WB/JFK Housing	C-50090	Daily
Exchange(Annex)	811/BK	C-75514	M-Sa
	506/NAK	C-6174	M-Sa
Finance(Mil)	2/WB	700/840	M-F
Food(Snack/Fast)	811/BK	C-72390	M-F
	513/NAK	C-6494	M-F
	2031/SAF	C-373	Daily
	11/WB	C-53121	Daily
Burger King	PX Mall/WB	C-57719	Daily
Pizza Parlor	10/SAF	C-571041	Daily
Foodland	16/WB	C-54092	Daily
Laundry(Exch)	See Pick-up Point.		
Laundry(Self-Svc)	5/WB	450	Daily
	2001/SAF	N/A	Daily
Motor Pool	WB	521	M-F
Package Store	81/WB	410	Tu-Sa
Pick-up Point	811/BK	C-72390	M-F
	506/NAK	C-6194	M-F
	2001/SAF	C-7313	M,W,F
	41/WB	C-53118	M-Sa
Postal Svcs(Mil)	16/WB	558/720	
SATO-OS	2/WB	793	M-F
		C-576923	
Schools(DOD Dep)			
Elementary/Middle	224	570/866	M-F
		C-575428	
High School	See Ludwigsburg Community listing.		
Svc Stn(Insta)	223/WB	C-53133	Daily
Space-A Air Ops	Airfield/WB	494	Daily
Flights to:	German locations		
Tailor Shop	4351/DB	C-42653	Tu-Sa
	19/WB	N/A	M-F
	507/NAK	N/A	M,W,Th
Tel Repair(Gov)	1/WB	119	Daily
Thrift Shop	204/WB	C-574087	M-F,1st Sa

GERMANY

Heilbronn Community, continued

TML

Billeting	201,204/WB	523/496	M-F
	WB	806	After hours
BOQ	201,204/WB	523/496	M-F. Limited.
Watch Repair	Pick-up Point		

HEALTH AND WELFARE

FACILITY/ACTIVITY	BLDG NO/LOC	PHONE	DAYS/COMMENTS
Ambulance	WB	116	24 hours daily
Army Comm Svcs	12/WB	666/454	M-F
	2034/SAF	233	M-F
Army Emerg Relief	12/WB	666/704	M-F
Central Appts	36,53/WB	433/446	Daily
CHAMPUS Office	3653/WB	433/446	M-Th
Chaplain	2069/SAF	202	M-F
Comm Drug/Alc Ctr	T-182/WB	583/703	M-F
Dental Clinic	53/WB	428	M-F
		C-582428	
Medical Emergency	36,53/WB	116	24 hours daily
Red Cross	12/WB	536/870	M-F
		1110	After hours
Veterinary Svcs	See the Stuttgart Community listing.		

REST AND RECREATION

FACILITY/ACTIVITY	BLDG NO/LOC	PHONE	DAYS/COMMENTS
Amer Forces Ntwk	16/WB	442/670	M-F
Bowling Lanes	42/WB	459	Daily
		C-575441	
Craftshops			
Automotive	6/WB	586	M-F
	810/BK	539	Daily
	NAK	735	Daily
Multi-crafts	6/WB	409/455	M-F
	3/WB	378	Daily
Photography	WB	409	Daily
	505/NAK	757/709	Daily
Wood	810/BK	443/861	Daily
Gymnasium	33/WB	533	Daily
	519/NAK	700	Daily
	306/BK	467	Daily
	2044/SAF	296	Daily
Info Tour & Travel	12A/WB	812	M-F
		C-570098	
	512/NAK	762/833	M-F
Library	29/WB	504	Daily
	521/NAK	736	Tu-Sa
	302/BK	437	M-Sa
NCO Club	216/WB	626	M-F
		C-5312	
O'Club	216/WB	626	M-F
		C-5312	
Outdoor Rec Ctr	5/WB	133	M-Th

132 — U.S. Forces Travel & Transfer Guide Europe

GERMANY
Heilbronn Community, continued

	6/WB	455/113	M-F
Recreation Center	335/DB	712	Daily
	505/NAK	783	Daily
	T2070/SAF	248	M-F
	12A/WB	888	Daily
Rod and Gun Club	5/WB	452	M-F, Sa after pay days
Theater	11A/WB	525	Daily
	NAK	741	Daily
	BK	532	Daily
Video Rental	PX Mall/WB	N/A	Daily
	5/WB	N/A	Daily
Youth Center	202/WB	C-54084	M-Sa

HERZO BASE SUB-COMMUNITY (GE70R7)
APO New York 09352-5000

TELEPHONE INFORMATION: Main installation number: Civ: 09132-83-3648. ETS:465-3648. Civ prefix: 09132-____. ETS prefix: 465-3XXX. Civilian to mil prefix: 09132-83-XXX.

LOCATION: Take Autobahn E-3 west from Nürnberg. IIE: p-40, E/2. NMC: Nürnberg, 10 miles southeast.

GENERAL INSTALLATION INFORMATION: Herzo Artillery Base is a sub-community of Nürnberg Military Community. It was designed by a French architect and constructed in 1936 by the German Air Force. The Post was then used as a training school for gliders. The U.S. Army acquired the base in 1945 and the U.S. Army Security Agency occupied the base until 1971 when the 210th Field Artillery Group took over. Herzo Base is presently Headquarters for the 210th Field Artillery Brigade, 3rd Battalion, 37th Field Artillery and 2nd Battalion, 377th Field Artillery.

GENERAL CITY/REGIONAL: Herzo Base is located near the town of Herzogenaurach. The thickly wooded area between Bamberg and Nürnberg that surrounds the base was settled by farmers as early as the 8th century. The town church was built in honor of St. Martin and given as a present to the Monastery of Kitzingen; in the 14th century a protective wall was built to encompass the church and the town. The wall, however, was no protection against military occupation. During the Thirty Years' War, the town fell into Swedish hands, and Bavarian troops occupied the town near the beginning of the 19th century. Despite the proximity of Herzogenaurach to the air base, a nearby bridge was the only structure destroyed during World War II. Shoppers will enjoy the area's many factory outlet stores, which offer a savings of up to 50% on a variety of items.

ADMINISTRATIVE SUPPORT

FACILITY/ACTIVITY	BLDG NO/LOC	PHONE	DAYS/COMMENTS
Duty Officer	1552	647	Daily
Fire(Mil)	On Base	117	24 hours daily
Fire(Civ)	Herzo	112	24 hours daily

U.S. Forces Travel & Transfer Guide Europe — 133

GERMANY

Herzo Base Sub-Community, continued

Housing
Referral	1605	883/623	M-F
Legal Assist	1552	630	M-F
Police(Mil)	See Erlangen Community listing.		
Police(Civ)	Herzo	C-8025	24 hours daily
Public Affairs	On Base	666	M-F
Tax Relief	1551	685	M-F

LOGISTICAL SUPPORT

FACILITY/ACTIVITY	BLDG NO/LOC	PHONE	DAYS/COMMENTS
Auto Registration	See Erlangen Community listing.		
Bank	1605	C-9244	M-F
Barber Shop(s)	1605	C-5718	Tu-Sa
Beauty Shop(s)	1605	C-5718	M-Sa
Bookstores	1625	627	M-F
Child Care/Dev Ctr	1603	620/801	M-F
Commissary(Annex)	1605	686	Tu-Sa
Dining Facility	1613	881	Daily
Education Center	1610	687	M-F
Learning Center	1610	688	M-F
Elec Repair(Gov)	1611	820	M-F
Engineers	1611	828	Daily
Exchange(Annex)	1605	C-8786	M-Sa
Food(Snack/Fast)			
Burger Bar	1573	C-9219	Daily
Pizza Parlor	1573	C-9219	Daily
Laundry(Self-Svc)	1574	C-705230	Daily
Package Store	1605	689	Tu-Sa
Pick-up Point	1515	C-6712	M-Sa
Postal Svcs(Mil)	1616	659	M,Tu,Th,F
SATO-OS	See Nürnberg Community listing.		
Schools			
Elementary	See Erlangen Community listing.		
High School	See Nürnberg Community listing.		
Tailor Shop	1605	None	M,W,Th,F
Tel Booking Oper	1552	112	24 hours daily
Tel Repair(Gov)	1552	810	Daily
Thrift Shop	1616	663	Tu,W
TML			
Billeting	1566	661	Daily
BOQ	1560	611	24 hours daily

HEALTH AND WELFARE

FACILITY/ACTIVITY	BLDG NO/LOC	PHONE	DAYS/COMMENTS
Ambulance	1562	116/99-2074	24 hours daily
Army Comm Svcs	1605	614 C-83614	M-F
Central Appts	1562	827/617	M-F
Chaplain	1595	667/819	Daily
Comm Drug/Alc Ctr	1616	823/610	M-F
Dental Clinic	1562	624	M-F
Red Cross	See Erlangen Community listing.		
Veterinary Svcs	See Nürnberg Community listing.		

GERMANY
Herzo Base Sub-Community, continued

REST AND RECREATION

FACILITY/ACTIVITY	BLDG NO/LOC	PHONE	DAYS/COMMENTS
Bowling Lanes	1615	639	M-F
Craftshops			
Automotive	1608	615	F-Tu
Photography	1573	692	F-Tu
Enlisted Club	1612	634	Tu-Su
Golf Course	Herzo	628	Daily
Gymnasium	1615	626	Daily
	1611 (annex)	657	Daily
Library	1563	668/846	Su-Th
NCO/O'Club	1612	629	Tu-Su, E7-010
Racket Courts	1615	657	Daily
Recreation Center	1573	882	F-Tu
Tennis Courts	Near dispensary		
Theater	1595	677	W,F,Sa
Video Rental	1605	None	M-Sa
Youth Center	1559	812	M-Sa

HESSISCH-OLDENDORF AIR STATION (GE45R7)
APO New York 09669-5000

TELEPHONE INFORMATION: Main installation numbers: Civ: 49-05152-74-113. ATVN: 781-4745. ETS: 331-1110. Civ prefix: 05152-____. ETS prefix: 331-XXXX. Civ to mil prefix: 05152-74-XXXX.

LOCATION: Take Autobahn 2 from Herford north or Garbsens and exit to GE-83 south to Hessisch-Oldendorf. HE: p-36, E/1-2. NMC: Hannover, 27 miles northeast.

GENERAL INSTALLATION INFORMATION: The 600th Tactical Control Group and the 600th Combat Support Squadron provide control and support to the 2nd Allied Tactical Air Force radar units and logistical support services to the TACS units.

GENERAL CITY/REGIONAL INFORMATION: The community of Hessisch-Oldendorf is in the northern section of the Weserbergland, a land of rolling hills dotted with picturesque villages and green fields. People who live and work in the Weserbergland don't know the meaning of being in a hurry, in contrast to the fast pace of life in much of the United States. Castles are within a short driving distance, as are 1,000 year old communities and many houses and buildings built before the discovery of the New World.

ADMINISTRATIVE SUPPORT

FACILITY/ACTIVITY	BLDG NO/LOC	PHONE	DAYS/COMMENTS
Duty Officer	36	212	M-F
Housing			
Family	3	202	M-F

U.S. Forces Travel & Transfer Guide Europe — 135

GERMANY

Hessich-Oldendorf Air Station, continued

Referral	3	202	M-F
Info(Insta)	3	113	24 hours daily
Legal Assist	3	287	M-F
Locator(Mil)	3	204	Daily
Personnel Spt	12	279	M-F
Police(Mil)	10	204/211	24 hours daily
Emergency	10	114	24 hours daily

LOGISTICAL SUPPORT

FACILITY/ACTIVITY	BLDG NO/LOC	PHONE	DAYS/COMMENTS
Bank	6	C-3894	M-F
Barber Shop(s)	4	330	Tu-Sa
Beauty Shop(s)	4	330	Tu-Sa
Bookstore	4	C-3046/7/8	Tu-Sa
Child Care/Dev Ctr	N/A	285	Daily
Clothing Sales	32	C-1200	Daily
Commissary(Main)	36	222 C-4692	Tu-Sa
Dining Facility	7	350	Daily
Education Center	3	210	M-F
Exchange(Main)	3	230 C-1200	Daily
Finance(Mil)	36	297	M-F
Food(Caf/Rest)	3	629	Daily
Food(Snack/Fast)	3	356/237	Daily
Laundry(Self-Svc)	41	None	24 hours daily
Motor Pool	13	221	24 hours daily
Package Store	5	235	Tu-Sa
Postal Svcs(Mil)	12	284	M-Sa
Schools(DOD Dep)			
Elementary	N/A	215	M-F (K-8)
TML			
Billeting	4	201	24 hours daily

HEALTH AND WELFARE

FACILITY/ACTIVITY	BLDG NO/LOC	PHONE	DAYS/COMMENTS
AF Family Svcs	41	214	M-F
Ambulance	11	116	24 hours daily
Central Appts	11	260/204	M-F
CHAMPUS Office	11	C-34142 ext. 249	M-F
Chaplain	7	218	Su-F
Medical Emergency	11	116	24 hours daily

REST AND RECREATION

FACILITY/ACTIVITY	BLDG NO/LOC	PHONE	DAYS/COMMENTS
Bowling Lanes	30	356	Daily
Consolidated Club	On Base	269	Daily
Craftshops			
Automotive	35	365	Tu-Sa
Enlisted Club	On Base	269	Daily

GERMANY
Hessich-Oldendorf Air Station, continued

Gymnasium	9	254	Daily
NCO Club	7	369	Daily
O'Club	6	351	Call for schedule.
Special Services	41	335	M-F
Video Rental	4	230	Tu-Su

HOHENFELS SUB-COMMUNITY (GE71R7)
APO New York 09173-5000

TELEPHONE INFORMATION: Main installation numbers: Civ: 49-09472-83-113. ATVN: 460-1110 (ask for Hohenfels). ETS: 466-2113. Civ prefix: 09472-____. ETS prefix: 466-2XXX. Civ to mil prefix: 09472-83-XXX.

LOCATION: Take the E-5 Autobahn southeast from Nürnberg and exit at Parsberg then drive seven miles east to Hohenfels. Follow the American installation signs. HE: not listed in Hallwag. NMC: Nürnberg, 35 miles west.

GENERAL INSTALLATION INFORMATION: Hohenfels is a 7th Army Training Command community that operates the Combat Maneuver Training Center (CMTC). A military general dispensary and a dental services unit are located at Hohenfels.

GENERAL CITY/REGIONAL INFORMATION: Hohenfels is located in the mountains on the edge of a U.S. Army Training Area near the confluence of the Vils and Naab rivers.

ADMINISTRATIVE SUPPORT

FACILITY/ACTIVITY	BLDG NO/LOC	PHONE	DAYS/COMMENTS
Advocate	1	082	M-F
Duty Officer	1	801	M-F
Fire(Mil)	Camp Nainhof	858	24 hours daily
Emergency	Camp Nainhof	117	24 hours daily
Housing	1	647/708	M-F
Info(Insta)	1	113	24 hours daily
Police(Mil)	Camp Nainhof	812	24 hours daily
Emergency	Camp Nainhof	114	24 hours daily
Public Affairs	Camp Nainhof	832	M-F

LOGISTICAL SUPPORT

FACILITY/ACTIVITY	BLDG NO/LOC	PHONE	DAYS/COMMENTS
Audio/Photo Ctr	Camp Albertshof	863	M-Sa
Auto Parts(Exch)	Camp Poellnricht	727 C-334	M-Sa
Auto Registration	1/Camp Nainhof	842	M-F
Auto Rent(Other)	Camp Nainhof	840	N/A
Bank	Camp Nainhof	856/888	M-F
Bookstore	168/Camp Albertshof	734	M-Sa
	3/Camp Nainhof	703	M-Sa
Child Care/Dev Ctr	Camp Nainhof	080	M-F

GERMANY

Hohenfels Sub-Community, continued

Clothing Sales	Camp Albertshof	688	M-Sa
Commissary(Main)	Camp Nainhof	830/630	M-Sa
Dining Facility	Camp Nainhof	866	Daily
	On Barracks	942	Daily
Education Center	On Barracks	668/882	M-F
Learning Center	On Barracks	627	M-F
Eng'r/Publ Works	On Barracks	679/752	M-F
	Emergency	115	24 hours daily
Exchange(Main)	Camp Albertshof	671	M-Sa
	Camp Nainhof	828	M-Sa
Exchange(Annex)	Camp Poellnricht	731	M-Sa
Food(Caf/Rest)	Camp Nainhof	C-324	Daily
	Camp Albertshof	734	Daily
Motor Pool	On Barracks	786/808	Daily
Package Store	On Barracks	635	M-Sa
Pick-up Point	On Barracks	862	M-Sa
Postal Svcs(Mil)	Camp Nainhof	887	M-Sa
Schools(DOD Dep)			
Elementary	On Barracks	829/729	M-F
Space-A Air Ops	Army Airfield	614/617/814	Daily
Tel Booking Oper	1	112/805	24 hours daily
Tel Repair(Gov)	1	810	Daily
Emergency	1	119	24 hours daily
TML			
Billeting	On Barracks	574	Daily
	Camp Nainhof	647	Daily
BEQ	Camp Nainhof	667	Daily
BOQ	Camp Nainhof	663	Daily
	6	737	Daily
Guest House	71	498	Daily
SEBQ	20	667	Daily
DV/VIP	176	881	Daily

HEALTH AND WELFARE

FACILITY/ACTIVITY	BLDG NO/LOC	PHONE	DAYS/COMMENTS
Ambulance	On Barracks	116	24 hours daily
Army Comm Svcs	On Barracks	861	M-F
Central Appts	On Barracks	N/A	Daily
Chapel	Camp Nainhof	797/819	Daily
Comm Drug/Alc Ctr	On Barracks	844	M-F
Dental Clinic	On Barracks	803/763	M-F
Medical Emergency	On Barracks	116	24 hours daily
Red Cross	On Barracks	817	M-F

REST AND RECREATION

FACILITY/ACTIVITY	BLDG NO/LOC	PHONE	DAYS/COMMENTS
Bowling Lanes	Camp Nainhof	751	Daily
Consolidated Club	On Barracks	754	Daily
Craftshops			
Automotive	On Barracks	690/537	Daily
Multi-crafts	On Barracks	538	Daily
Photography	On Barracks	537	Daily
Gymnasium	On Barracks	726	Daily

138 — U.S. Forces Travel & Transfer Guide Europe

GERMANY
Hohenfels Sub-Community, continued

	Fieldhouse	631/883	Daily
Info Tour & Travel	On Barracks	840	M-F
Library	Camp Nainhof	627/853	Daily
Outdoor Rec Ctr	On Barracks	060	Daily
Recreation Center	On Barracks	870	Daily
Special Services	On Barracks	146	Daily
Theater	General Parton	687	Daily
Water Recreation	Camp Nainhof	832	Daily
Youth Center	On Barracks	822	M-Sa

ILLESHEIM SUB-COMMUNITY (GE72R7)
APO New York 09140-5000

TELEPHONE INFORMATION: Main installation numbers: Civ: 49-09841-83-113. ATVN: 460-1110 (ask for Illesheim). ETS: 467-4113. Civ prefix: 09841-___. ETS prefix: 467-4XXX. Civ to mil prefix: 09841-83-XXX.

LOCATION: From GE-13 north or south exit to GE-470 northeast in the direction of Bad Windsheim. Follow the U.S. signs marked Storch Barracks. HE: p-40, E/2. NMC: Nürnberg, 38 miles east.

GENERAL INSTALLATION INFORMATION: The installation provides general support to the Ansbach Community, which consists of the 87th Medical Detachment (Dental); the 536rd General Dispensary; 1st Brigade, 1st Armored Division; and a detachment of Military Police and other support units.

GENERAL CITY/REGIONAL INFORMATION: Located on the Aisch River and settled in the 8th century, Illesheim was once the site of four castles, three of which were destroyed during the 15th century. A 14th century castle, however, remains. Primarily a farming village, Illesheim is only 12 miles from the ancient walled city of Rothenburg on the Tauber River.

ADMINISTRATIVE SUPPORT

FACILITY/ACTIVITY	BLDG NO/LOC	PHONE	DAYS/COMMENTS
Duty Officer	On Barracks	515	Daily
Fire(Mil)	On Barracks	835	24 hours daily
Housing			
Family	6546	523/743	M-F
Referral	6546	633	M-F
Info(Insta)	On Barracks	113	24 hours daily
Legal Assist	6502	735/537	M-F
Personnel Spt	On Barracks	559	M-F
Police(Mil)	6518	565/581	24 hours daily
Emergency	6518	114	24 hours daily
Public Affairs	6546	527	M-F
Tax Relief	6546	737	M-F

Illisheim Sub-Community, continued

GERMANY

LOGISTICAL SUPPORT

FACILITY/ACTIVITY	BLDG NO/LOC	PHONE	DAYS/COMMENTS
Auto Drivers Testing	6541	604/732	M,W,Th
Auto Parts(Exch)	6555	C-8880	M-Sa
Auto Registration	6541	732/604	M-F
Auto Repairs	6555	C-8880	M-Sa
Bank	6532	609 C-8907	M-F
Barber Shop(s)	6528	C-8101	Tu-Sa
Beauty Shop(s)	See Ansbach/Katterbach Community listing.		
Bookstore	6651	569	Tu-Su
Child Care/Dev Ctr	6650	821	M-F
Clothing Sales	6509	636	Tu-Sa
Commissary(Main)	6509	517/717	Tu-Sa
Dry Clean(Exch)	6503	628	M-F
Education Center	6508	750/538	M-F
Elec Repair(Gov)	Storck Bks	846/515	Duty hours
		813	After hours
Eng'r/Publ Works	6537	622/722	M-F
Exchange(Main)	6528	551 C-8765	Tu-Su
Finance(Mil)	See Ansbach/Katterbach Community listing.		
Food(Caf/Rest)	6528	674/567	M-F
Foodland	6528	C-8765	Daily
Laundry(Self-Svc)	6525	C-8748	24 hours daily
Motor Pool	6546	604/732	M-F
Package Store	6657	653	Tu-Sa
Photo Laboratory	6510	663	Sa-Th
Pick-up Point	6508	C-8401	M-Sa
Postal Svcs(Mil)	6510	706	M-Sa
Postal Svcs(Civ)	8531	C-8758	M-Sa
Schools(DOD Dep)			
Elementary	6621	631/731 C-8408	M-F (K-8)
High School	See Ansbach/Katterbach Community listing.		
Svc Stn(Insta)	6645	C-8802	M-Sa
Space-A Air Ops	Airfield Ops	734/674	Daily
Tailor Shop	6508	C-8401	Tu-Sa
Taxi(Comm)	Illesheim	C-8827	Daily
Thrift Shop	6510	578	Tu,Th
TML			
BOQ	Beside O'Club	550/650	Daily

HEALTH AND WELFARE

FACILITY/ACTIVITY	BLDG NO/LOC	PHONE	DAYS/COMMENTS
Ambulance	N/A	116	24 hours daily
Army Comm Svcs	6508	555	M-F
	Action line	555	24 hours daily
Central Appts	6620	512/588 C-8181	M-Sa
Chaplain	6043	826/642	Su-F
Chapel	6043	826/642	Su-F

GERMANY
Illesheim Sub-Community, continued

Comm Drug/Alc Ctr	6546	817/566	M-F
Dental Clinic	6652	591/757	M-F
		830	After hours
Medical Emergency	Bad Windsheim Hospital	C-2091	24 hours daily
Red Cross	6508	689/744	M-F
Veterinary Svcs	See Nürnberg Community listing.		

REST AND RECREATION

FACILITY/ACTIVITY	BLDG NO/LOC	PHONE	DAYS/COMMENTS
Bowling Lanes	6508	530	Daily
		C-8697	
Craftshops			
Automotive	6541	608	Tu-Su
Multi-crafts	6510	663	Sa-W
Gymnasium	6504	582	Daily
Info Tour & Travel	6525	570	M-F
		C-5441	
Library	6510	675	Daily
O'Club	6622	587	Daily
		C-8750	
Outdoor Rec Ctr	6504	659	Seasonal
Recreation Center	6510	845/645	Daily
Rod and Gun Club	6529	623	M-Sa
Theater	6641	546	Daily
Video Rental	6508	None	Daily
Youth Center	6504	583/703	M-Sa

KAISERSLAUTERN COMMUNITY (GE30R7)
APO New York 09054-5000

TELEPHONE INFORMATION: Main installation numbers: Civ: 49-0631-411-8119 (Kaiserslautern); 49-06731-86-70 (Landstuhl); 49-0631-536-113 (Vogelweh and Kapaun Air Station). ETS: 483-8119 (Kaiserslautern); 486-113 (Landstuhl); 483-113 (Vogelweh). ATVN: 489-1110 (Kaiserslautern). Civ prefix: 0631-_____ (Kaiserslautern, Vogelweh and Kapaun AS); 06731-_____ (Landstuhl). ETS prefix: 483-XXXX (Kaiserslautern); 486-XXXX (Landstuhl); 489-XXXX (Vogelweh). Civ to mil prefix: 0631-411-XXXX (Kaiserslautern); 06731-86-XXXX (Landstuhl); 0631-536-XXXX (Vogelweh and Kapaun AS).

LOCATION: Take the A-6 Mannheim-Saarbrücken Autobahn to the Kaiserslautern east exit and follow signs to Army kasernes. HE: p-40, A/2. NMC: Kaiserslautern, 3 miles northeast.

GENERAL INSTALLATION INFORMATION: The U.S. Forces Support District Rheinland-Pfalz is headquartered in Kaiserslautern and supports activities in Bad Kreuznach, Baumholder, Kaiserslautern, Mainz, Pirmasens, Worms, and Zweibrücken. The missions of the 29th Area Support Group in Kaiserslautern involve theater war reserve stocks, theater Army repair programs, and direct support/general support maintenance. The 29th has major storage and maintenance facilities in Kaiserslautern (66th Maintenance Battalion), Pirmasens and Luxembourg. **Note: the following abbreviations**

GERMANY
Kaiserslautern Community, continued

are used in this listing only: DK (Dänner Kaserne in Kaiserslautern); KAS (Kapaun Air Station in Vogelweh); KK (Kleber Kaserne in Kaiserslautern); KS (Kaiserslautern); LS (Landstuhl); PK (Panzer Kaserne in Kaiserslautern); PuK (Pulaski Kaserne in Vogelweh); VW (Vogelweh).

GENERAL CITY/REGIONAL INFORMATION: Kaiserslautern earned its name as the favorite hunting retreat of Emperor (Kaiser) Frederick Barbarossa, who ruled the diverse lands of the Holy Roman Empire from 1155 to 1190. The Lauter was then an important river that actually made the old section of Kaiserslautern an island in Medieval times.

Kaiserslautern's history reaches back much further than Barbarossa's time. Since the earliest times, this area has been one of the great East-West passageways of Europe, from France to the Rhine Valley. As early as 800 B.C., a prehistoric settlement was located in the Kaiserslautern area. Kaiserslautern's first castle was built in 622 A.D. by King Dagobert, a Frankish monarch. The population of the village grew, and in 1276 Emperor Rudolf von Habsburg gave the town its charter.

World War II had a major effect on Kaiserslautern with over 60 percent of the city bombed and destroyed by allied aircraft. Of the 20,000 homes, 11,000 were damaged or destroyed. On March 20, 1945, the U.S. 80th Division, 319th Infantry (a part of Patton's 3rd Army) seized Kaiserslautern without resistance.

After the war, the pace of the economy remained slow until a boom of sorts occurred in 1952. At that time, construction on a large scale began for newly established garrisons of American troops. This construction brought a much-needed infusion of money into the area.

Since then the city has been totally rebuilt. Kaiserslautern annexed several surrounding villages in 1969. Population was recently recorded at about 108,000.

ADMINISTRATIVE SUPPORT

FACILITY/ACTIVITY	BLDG NO/LOC	PHONE	DAYS/COMMENTS
Customs/Duty	VW	6066	M-F
Duty Officer	2200/KS	8674	M-F
Fire(Mil)	3083/KS	117	24 hours daily
	LS	7195	24 hours daily
Fire(Civ)	Kaiserslautern	112	24 hours daily
Housing			
Family	1001/VW	6671/6672	M-F
Referral	1001/VW	7627/7642	M-F
	374/LS	N/A	M-F
	1001/VW	6868	M-F
Info(Insta)	VW	113	24 hours daily
Inspector Gen'l	3003/PK	8163/8179	M-F
Legal Assist	3004/PK	7677/8304	M-F
	3792/LS	7345	M-Th
Locator(Mil)	VW	113	24 hours daily
Locator(Civ)	3104/DK	7094/7077	M-F
Personnel Spt	3208/PK	7650	M-F
Police(Mil)			

GERMANY
Kaiserslautern Community, continued

Emergency	2039/VW	114	24 hours daily
Police(Civ)		C-110	24 hours daily
Public Affairs	2200/KS	8279	M-F
Tax Relief	2053/VW	6155	M-F

LOGISTICAL SUPPORT

FACILITY/ACTIVITY	BLDG NO/LOC	PHONE	DAYS/COMMENTS
Audio/Photo Ctr	2013	C-57475	Tu-Sa
Auto Drivers Testing	3226/KK	7276	Tu,Th
	2099/VW	7191	M,W,F
Auto Parts(Exch)	2043/VW	C-57492	Daily
	KS-N of DK	7001	Th-M
Auto Registration	2806/KAS	7542	M-F
Auto Rental(Exch)	2050/VW	C-59881	Daily
Auto Repairs	2043/VW	C-51606	Tu-F
Auto Sales	VW Parking Lot	7244	Daily
Auto Ship(Gov)	2806/KAS	7750	M-F
Auto Ship(Civ)	Einsiedlerhof	C-55106	Daily
Auto Wash	2034/VW	C-55268	Daily
Bakery	Main exch/VW	7244	Daily
Bank	3208/KK	7644	M-F
	2011/VW	6100	M-Sa
	3776/LS	7224	M-F
Barber Shop(s)	3221/KK	C-48659	Daily
	2013/VW	6729	Daily
	2779/LS	C-55452	N/A
Beauty Shop(s)	2013/VW	6729	Daily
		C-54120	
	3774/VW	2648	Tu-Sa
Bookstore	2013/VW	C-56831	Daily
	3005/PK	3681	M-F
	3774/LS	7374	M-Sa
	3231/KK	C-93663	M-Sa
Bus	29th ASG Trans Office/KS	7355/8182	Daily
Child Care/Dev Ctr	3224/KK	8307	M-F
	3812/LS	7350	M-F
	1028/VW	7632	Daily
		C-55471	
Clothing Sales	3225/KK	8487/7754	Tu-Sa
Commissary(Main)	2011/VW	7652	Tu-Su
Commissary(Annex)	3701/LS	7652	Tu-Su
Dry Clean(Exch)	3224/KK	C-48679	M-F
Dry Clean(Gov)	2171/KK	None	M-F
Education Center	3212/KK	7204	M-F
	2782/KAS	6196/7457	M-F
	3701/LS	7182/7393	M-F
Elec Repair(Civ)	3224/KK	C-48679	M-F
Engineers	FEI Workctr/KS	7281/7385	M-F
Exchange(Main)	2013/VW	7244/7394	Daily
		C-53589-0	
	3774/LS	8397	Daily
Exchange(Annex)	3224/KK	C-48677	Daily
Exchange(Concess)	BX area/VW	7244	Daily

GERMANY
Kaiserslautern Community, continued

Finance(Mil)	3208/KK	8196	M-F
Food(Caf/Rest)	3231/KK	C-47436	Daily
	3774/LS	C-2704	Daily
Food(Snack/Fast)	3231/KK	C-47436	M-F
	2200/KK	N/A	M-F
	3005/PK	None	M-F
	2059/VW	7539	Daily
	2779/KAS	C-55452	Daily
Pizza Parlor	1004/KS	C-59852	Daily
Foodland	2769/KAS	6673	Daily
	3774/LS	8373	Daily
Laundry(Exch)	3224/KK	C-48679	M-Sa
Laundry(Self-Svc)	2044/VW	None	Daily
Motor Pool	DK	8192/8301	M-F
Package Store	2011/VW	7400	M-Sa
	3701/LS	N/A	M-Sa
Parking	O'Club/VW	6000	24 hours daily
Photo Laboratory	3224/KK	8418	Daily
Pick-up Point	3224/KK	C-48679	M-F
	2011/VW	C-51166	Daily
	2769/KAS	C-55001	M-Sa
	3774/LS	C-17288	M-F

Postal Svcs(Mil)	3221/KK	7296	M-Sa
	2012/VW	7216	M-Sa
Postal Svcs(Civ)	2011/VW	C-87608	M-F
	3776/LS	C-2183/1271	M-F
Railroad/RTO	2099/VW	7613/7349	M-F
SATO-OS	3224/KK	8628	M-F
		C-47427	
Schools(DOD Dep)			
Elementary	2007/KS	6322	M-F
	3830,3831/LS	7221	M-F
Sr Elem	3810/LS	7190	M-F
Middle School	2000/KS	6517	M-F
Middle School	3803/LS	8108	M-F
High School	2000/KS	7300	M-F
Svc Stn(Insta)	2047/VW	6068	Daily
Space-A Air Ops	See Ramstein Air Base listing.		
Tailor Shop	2013/VW	C-55515	M-F
	3774/LS	8397	M,Tu,W,F
	3224/KK	C-48677	M,W,F

Taxi(Comm)	11 Altenwoog/KS	C-92800	Daily
	LS	C-2794	Daily
Tel Booking Oper	VW	114	24 hours daily
Tel Repair(Gov)	VW	119	Daily
Tel Repair(Civ)	11 Rummel/KS	C-1171	Daily
Thrift Shop	2901/PuK	C-51605	Tu,Th,F,Sa
	3703/LS	7313	Tu-Th
TML			
Billeting	305/LS	7267	Daily
	1002,3,4/VW	7641	Daily
BEQ	3752/LS	7267	Daily
BOQ	3752/LS	7267	Daily
Travel Agents	3187/KS	8110	M-F

GERMANY
Kaiserslautern Community, continued

	3705/LS	8216	M-F
	1036/VW	7279	M-Sa
Watch Repair	3224/KK	C-48679	M-F

HEALTH AND WELFARE

FACILITY/ACTIVITY	BLDG NO/LOC	PHONE	DAYS/COMMENTS
Ambulance	VW	116	24 hours daily
	LS	8160	24 hours daily
Army Comm Svcs	1044/VW	6476/7521	M-F
	3705/LS	7313/7162	M-F
Army Emerg Relief	3208/KK	8247	M-F
	3705/LS	7313	M-F
Central Appts	3765/LS	7131	M-F
	1043/VW	6143	M-F
CHAMPUS Office	See the Ramstein Air Base listing.		
Chaplain	3150/DK	7507/8161	M-F
Chapel	KAS	7062	Daily
	3773/LS	8143	Daily
	KK	7272	Daily
	2063/VW	6859	Daily
Comm Drug/Alc Ctr	3201/KK	7455	M-F
	1044/VW	7377/6492	M-F
	3703/LS	8394/7337	M-F
Dental Clinic	2067/VW	6584	M-F
	3201/KK	7057/8426	By appointment
	LS	8136	M-F
Medical Emergency	LARMC/LS	7280	24 hours daily
Mental Health	3753/LS	8122/8244	By appointment
Poison Control	Hospital/LS	8160	24 hours daily
Red Cross	3224/KK	8702/8722	M-F
	3768,3772/LS	7298/8126	M-F
	2768/VW	6458	M-F
Veterinary Svcs	2067/VW	7592/7068	M-F

REST AND RECREATION

FACILITY/ACTIVITY	BLDG NO/LOC	PHONE	DAYS/COMMENTS
Amer Forces Ntwk	2058/VW	7206	24 hours daily
Bowling Lanes	3231/KK	8646	Daily
	3722/LS	7142	Tu-Sa
	2060/VW	6543	Daily
Consolidated Club	3109/KS	7330	M-F
		C-44818	
	3780/LS	7244	Tu-Sa
Craftshops			
Automotive	3264/KS	7375	Daily
	2806/VW	6875	Daily
	3800/LS	7335	Sa-W
Ceramics	3224/KK	8418/7373	Tu-Sa
Multi-crafts	3224/KK	8418	Tu-Sa
	2059/VW	7692	Daily
	3705/LS	7373	Th-Su
Photography	3224/KK	8418/8675	Tu-Sa
	2059/VW	7692	Daily

GERMANY

Kaiserslautern Community, continued

Wood	3705/LS	7373/8375	Sa-W
Enlisted Club	3115/DK	7286	M-W,Sa,Su
	3109/KS	7330	M-Sa
		C-44818	
	3794/LS	7198	Tu-Su
	2057/VW	7261	M,W-Sa
Golf Course	See the Ramstein Air Base listing.		
Gymnasium	3235/KK	7610	Daily
	2050/VW	7138	Daily
	3720/LS	7172/8330	Daily
Info Tour & Travel	3187/DK	8110	M-F
		C-46225	
	3705/LS	8216	M-F
	2059/VW	7664/7279	M-F
Library	3183/KK	7740/8443	Daily
	3809/LS	7322	Tu-Su
	2059/VW	7665	Daily
NCO Club	2057/VW	7261	M,W-Sa
	3794/LS	7198	Tu-Su
	3109/KS	7330	M-Sa
		C-44818	
O'Club	1036/VW	6000	Tu-Sa
		C-59200	
	3780/LS	7244	M-Sa
Outdoor Rec Ctr	3705/LS	7308	M-Sa
	3083/DK	7060	M-F
	2785/VW	7752	M-F
Recreation Center	3224/KK	7408	Daily
	3705/LS	7278/8375	Daily
	2059/VW	7626	Daily
Rod and Gun Club	2960/VW	7274	M-Su
Skating Rink	See Ramstein Air Base listing.		
Special Services	KK	8198/7115	M-F
Sport Field	KS	7056	Daily
	Sports Fld/VW	None	Daily
Tennis Courts	VW/KAS/DK/LS		
Theater	3718/LS	7286	Call for schedule.
	3232/KK	7108	Call for schedule.
	2062/VW	6167	Call for schedule.
Track	Sports Fld/VW	None	Daily
Video Rental	2785/VW	C-57981	Tu-Sa
Youth Center	1057/VW	6397/7605	M-Sa
	3851/LS	7219	M-Sa
	3718/LS	7286	M-Sa

==

KARLSRUHE COMMUNITY (GE14R7)
APO New York 09164-3876

TELEPHONE INFORMATION: Main installation numbers: Civ: 49-0721-759-7168. ETS: 376-7168. ATVN: 370-1110 (ask for Karlsruhe). Civ prefix: 0721-____. ETS prefix: 376-XXXX. Civ to mil prefix: 0721-759-XXXX.

LOCATION: Take the Karlsruhe exit off Autobahn E-4. Follow signs to the community. HE: p-40, B/3. NMC: Karlsruhe, in the city.

… U.S. Forces Travel & Transfer Guide Europe

GERMANY
Karlsruhe Community, continued

GENERAL INSTALLATION INFORMATION: The mission of the Karlsruhe Community is to provide administrative, logistical and engineering facilities and housing support to all U.S. forces in South Baden, Landkreis, Enzkreis, Germersheim, Kreis Landau-Bergzabern and the city of Landau. This support involves four kasernes and numerous small facilities with a population of 13,000 soldiers, their families, and employees of the U.S. forces. Note: the following abbreviations are used in this listing only: GB (Gerszewski Barracks); NK (Neureut Kaserne); PRV (Paul Revere Village); RK (Rheinland Kaserne); SB (Smiley Barracks).

GENERAL CITY/REGIONAL INFORMATION: Karlsruhe, the fan-shaped city of parks and gardens, was founded by Karl-Wilhelm, the Margrave of Baden Durlach. The baroque castle he built is the base of the fan and a network of nine streets radiates from the palace grounds. Karlsruhe, home of the 1989 World Games, offers a wide variety of museums, art galleries, theaters, tours, concerts, boat rides, and exhibits. Sports enthusiasts will enjoy the city's many swimming pools, tennis courts, and sauna facilities. The city also boasts excellent road and rail facilities that link it to all parts of Germany and Europe.

ADMINISTRATIVE SUPPORT

FACILITY/ACTIVITY	BLDG NO/LOC	PHONE	DAYS/COMMENTS
Customs/Duty	9262/NK	6521/7131	Daily
Duty Officer	SB	6433/6362	24 hours daily
Fire (Mil)	On Barracks	117	24 hours daily
Fire (Civ)	Karlsruhe	112	24 hours daily
Housing			
Family	9259/SB	7120/7114	M-F
Unaccompanied	9259/SB	6010	M-F
Referral	9259/SB	7001	M-F
Inspector Gen'l	9258/SB	6433	M-F
Legal Assist	9650/GB	7481/6351	M-F
Locator (Mil)	NK	6350	M-F
Personnel Spt	9259/SB	7100	M-F
Police (Mil)	9256/SB	6122/6123	24 hours daily
Emergency	9256/SB	114	24 hours daily
Police (Civ)	Emergency	110	24 hours daily
Public Affairs	9258/SB	6578/7377 C-72470	M,Tu,F
Tax Relief	9261/SB	6254	M-F

LOGISTICAL SUPPORT

FACILITY/ACTIVITY	BLDG NO/LOC	PHONE	DAYS/COMMENTS
Audio/Photo Ctr	8125/NK	7107 C-72489	Tu-Sa
Auto Drivers Testing	SB	7151	M-F
Auto Parts (Exch)	PRV	6486	Tu-Su
Auto Registration	9259/SB	6126	M-F
Auto Repairs	9065/PRV	C-72604	N/A
Auto Sales	901/PRV	C-72731/73500	Tu-Sa
Auto Wash	Near Shoppette	6228	24 hours daily
Bank	PRV	6113	M-Sa

U.S. Forces Travel & Transfer Guide Europe — 147

GERMANY

Karlsruhe Community, continued

Barber Shop(s)	PRV	None	Tu-Sa
Beauty Shop(s)	PRV	C-72680	Tu-Sa
Bookstore	9063/SB	C-73966	Daily
	9641H/GB	C-554836	M-F
	9708/RK	C-07243	M-F
	8109/NK	C-73114	M-F
	PRV	751558	Daily
Bus	SB	7166	M-F
Child Care/Dev Ctr	9096/SB	6441	M-F
	9261/SB	6066	M-F
	9264/SB	6141/7142	M-F
Clothing Sales	On Barracks	6158	Tu-Sa
Commissary(Main)	9063/PRV	6443/7220	Tu-Su
Credit Union	See Heidelberg Community listing.		
Dining Facility	NK	6250	Daily
Dry Clean(Gov)	SB	C-755114	M-Sa

==

Education Center	9647/GB	6579/7037	M-F
Elec Repair(Gov)	On Barracks	C-755114	M-Sa
Eng'r/Publ Works	On Barracks	115 7378/6589	24 hours daily
Exchange(Main)	9050/PRV	C-72489	Daily
Exchange(Annex)	9641/GB	C-554828	Tu-Sa
	8109/NK	6134 C-73114	M-F
	702/RK	None	M-F
Finance(Mil)	9259/SB	7448	M-F
Food(Caf/Rest)	PRV	7239	Daily
Food(Snack/Fast)	9266/PRV	7066	Daily
	9733/GB	C-554836	Daily
	8146/NK	C-73114	Daily
	702/RK	C-07243-93172	Daily

==

Foodland	Shoppette/PRV	C-73983	Daily
Laundry(Exch)	9266/SB	C-7066	Daily
	9642/GB	None	Daily
	8110/NK	None	Daily
Laundry(Self-Svc)	GB/NK/SB	7066	Daily
Motor Pool	SB	6127	M-F
Package Store	PRV	7171	Tu-Sa
Photo Laboratory	SB	6392	N/A
Pick-up Point	9641/GB	C-554828	M-F
	2144/NK	C-73349	M-F
	7908/RK	7908	M-F
Postal Svcs(Mil)	On Barracks	6147	M-F
Postal Svcs(Civ)	Bundespost/PRV	C-71055	Tu-F
Schools(DOD Dep)			
Elementary	9250/PRV	7130/6409	M-F (K-6)
High School	9250/PRV	7053	M-F (7-12)
Svc Stn(Insta)	9065/PRV	6115	M-Sa
Tailor Shop	PRV	C-72591	Tu-Sa
	9641/GB	C-558424	M-F
	8144/NK	C-72249	M,W,F
	9704/RK	C-07243-15304	M-F
Taxi(Comm)	Karlsruhe	C-30033	24 hours daily

GERMANY
Karlsruhe Community, continued

Tel Booking Oper	SB	7381/6433	Daily
Tel Repair(Gov)	On Barracks	119	M-F
Thrift Shop	PRV	None	Tu,W,F
	GB	6393	Tu,W,F
	RK	2301	Tu,W,F
TML			
Billeting	9942/SB	6010	24 hours daily
Guest House	9942/SB	6010	24 hours daily
Travel Agents	9050/PRV	C-74668	M-F
Watch Repair	9050/PRV	N/A	Tu-F

HEALTH AND WELFARE

FACILITY/ACTIVITY	BLDG NO/LOC	PHONE	DAYS/COMMENTS
Ambulance	On Barracks	116	24 hours daily
		C-23332	24 hours daily
Army Comm Svcs	PRV	6144	M-F
	9261/SB	6542	M-F
Army Emerg Relief	SB	6066	M-F
Central Appts	On Barracks	6056/6541	M-F
CHAMPUS Office	SB	6035	M-F
Chapel	PRV	6493	Daily
	GB	8393	Daily
Comm Drug/Alc Ctr	9627/GB	6348/6388	M-F
	9261/SB	6003	M-F
	8150/NK	6348/6388	M-F
	9707/RK	2605	M-F
Dental Clinic	8143/NK	7191/7490	M-F
Medical Emergency	See Heidelberg Community listing or go to local hospital: Karlsruhe Stadtkrankenhaus; Karlsruhe Kinder Clinic (children's clinic); or Karlsruhe Stadisches Klinikum.		
Mental Health	NK	7203	M-F
	GB	7203/6302	M-F
Red Cross	9259/SB	6197/7332	M-F
Veterinary Svcs	See Heidelberg Community listing.		

REST AND RECREATION

FACILITY/ACTIVITY	BLDG NO/LOC	PHONE	DAYS/COMMENTS
Amer Forces Ntwk	9621/GB	6394	Daily
	8214/NK	6439	Daily
Bowling Lanes	9622/PRV	6372	Daily
Consolidated Club	9623/GB	6366	Th-Tu
	8108/NK	6285	Daily
	9703/RK	2528	W-M
	9067/PRV	6551	Tu-Su
	9251/PRV	6441	Daily
Craftshops			
Automotive	9639,9640/GB	6486	W-Su,Hol
	9704/RK	2613	W-F,Hol
Ceramics	NK	6030	Sa-W
Multi-crafts	8157/NK	6030	Sa-W
	9261/SB	6333	N/A
	9704/RK	2809	M-W,Sa,Hol

Karlsruhe Community, continued

GERMANY

Photography	8215/NK	None	Tu-Sa
	9266/GB	6253	M-W,Sa,Hol
	9704/RK	2527	Sa-Th
Enlisted Club	Closed for renovation at press time		
Gymnasium	9276/SB	6162	Daily
	9732/RK	2551	Daily
	8126/NK	6457	Su-F,Hol
	9645/GK	6313	M-Sa
Info Tour & Travel	9050/PRV	6546	M-Sa
Library	9262/SB	6202	Daily
	9622/GB	6135	Su-Th
NCO Club	NK	6285	Daily
O'Club	Closed for renovation at press time		
Outdoor Rec Ctr	9286	6535	M-F
Recreation Center	8107/NK	6596/6290	Daily
	9622/GK	6153/8379	M-F
	9703/RK	2720	Tu,Th,Sa,Su
Skating Rink	Downtown		
Swimming Pool	GB	7326	Summer only
Theater	PRV	6128	Daily
Video Rental	See Library		
Youth Center	N/A	7079	M-Sa

===

KITZINGEN SUB-COMMUNITY (GE75R7)
APO New York 09031-5000

TELEPHONE INFORMATION: Main installation numbers: Civ: 49-09321-305-113 (Kitzingen and Harvey Barracks); 49-0932-702-113 (Larson Barracks). ETS: 355-113 (Harvey Barracks); 355-2113 (Larson Barracks). Civ prefix: 09321-____ (Kitzingen and Harvey Barracks); 0932-____ (Larson Barracks). ETS prefix: 355-XXXX (Kitzingen and Harvey Barracks); 355-2XXX (Larson Barracks). Civ to mil prefix: 09321-305-XXXX (Kitzingen and Harvey Barracks); 0932-702-XXX (Larson Barracks).

LOCATION: From Würzburg, take highway B-8 SE about 12 miles to Kitzingen. HE: p-40,D/1. NMC: Würzburg, 10 miles north.

GENERAL INSTALLATION INFORMATION: Harvey Barracks in Kitzingen is home to the 3rd Infantry Division's 2nd Brigade, including 1st Battalion, 15th Infantry; 1st Battalion, 64th Armor; 3rd Battalion, 63th Armor; and other attached units. Larson Barracks houses the headquarters of Division Support Command, 2nd Battalion, 39th Field Artillery; 3rd Battalion, 67th Air Defense Artillery; 2nd Support Battalion; the 10th Engineer 4th Support Battalion (Main); in addition to other company-size support units. **Note: the following abbreviations are used in this listing only: HB (Harvey Barracks); LB (Larson Barracks).**

GENERAL CITY/REGIONAL INFORMATION: The tumultuous history of Kitzingen contrasts markedly with the green, rolling hills, cobblestone streets, and quaint houses and shops seen here today. The city's most outstanding monument is the Falterturm, or Leaning Tower, constructed in the 15th century. Inside the tower is the unique Fasching Museum devoted to the celebration of the annual German feast of fun and frivolity. Other sights include St. John's Church, the Alte Mainbrücke (Old Bridge), and the

GERMANY
Kitzingen Sub-Community, continued

Kreuzkapelle (Chapel of the Cross).

ADMINISTRATIVE SUPPORT

FACILITY/ACTIVITY	BLDG NO/LOC	PHONE	DAYS/COMMENTS
Customs/Duty	1/LB	432	M-F
Duty Officer	142/HB	8620	24 hours daily
Fire(Mil)	141/HB	117	24 hours daily
Housing			
Family	1/LB	455	M-F
Referral	1/LB	412	M-F
Legal Assist	170/HB	8707/8672 C-36443	M-F
Police(Mil)	141/HB	855	24 hours daily
Emergency	141/HB	114	24 hours daily
Public Affairs	143/HB	8607/8807	M-F
Tax Relief	138/HB	8678	M-F
	113/HB	8704	M-F
	122/HB	8808	M-F
	107/HB	8503	M-F
	142/HB	8801	M-F
	27/LB	620	M-F
	46/LB	792/616/	M-F
	46/LB	753	M-F
	44/LB	708	M-F

LOGISTICAL SUPPORT

FACILITY/ACTIVITY	BLDG NO/LOC	PHONE	DAYS/COMMENTS
Audio/Photo Ctr	138/HB	C-4912	Tu-Sa
Auto Drivers Testing	123/HB	8622	M-Th
Auto Parts(Exch)	152/HB	C-32960	M-Sa
Auto Registration	141/HB	8635	M-F
Auto Repairs	152/HB	8571 C-4960	M-Sa
Bank	138/HB	8630 C-33678	M-F
	2/LB	631 C-4962	M-F
Barber Shop(s)	138/HB	None	M-F
	2,6,10/LB	None	M-F
Beauty Shop(s)	313/HB	C-6412	Tu-Sa
Bookstore	139/HB	8679	M-Sa
	23/LB	C-4970	Daily
Child Care/Dev Ctr	349/HB	8616	M-Sa
	T3038/HB	C-4986	M-Sa
Clothing Sales	130/HB	8694	M-F,1st Sa
Commissary(Main)	186/HB	8824/8504 C-35715	Tu-Su
Dining Facility	113/HB	8581	Daily
Dry Clean(Exch)			
Dry Clean(Gov)	2/LB	None	M-F
Education Center	105/HB	8743/8689	M-F
	35/LB	651	M-F
	60/LB	482	M-F

GERMANY

Kitzingen Sub-Community, continued

Facility	Bldg No/Loc	Phone	Days/Comments
Eng'r/Publ Works	144/HB	8555	M-F
Emergency		115	24 hours daily
Exchange(Main)	140/HB	C-32968	Tu-Sa
	23/LB	789	Tu-Sa
		C-4912	
Finance(Mil)	1/LB	691	M-F
Food(Snack/Fast)			
Burger Bar	26/LB	C-5211	Daily
Burger King	138/LB	C-31812	Daily
Foodland	138/LB	C-32968	Su-F
	23/LB	C-4912	M-Sa
Laundry(Self-Svc)	138/HB	None	Daily
	23/LB	None	Daily
Package Store	138/HB	8579	Tu-Sa
Photo Laboratory	138/HB	8648	Sa-Th
	26/LB	659	F-W
Pick-up Point	141/HB	C-35212	M-F
	223/HB	None	M-F
	2/LB	C-4964	M-F
	9/LB	None	M-F
Postal Svcs(Mil)	139/HB	8841	M-F
	4/LB	604	M-F
Postal Svcs(Civ)	138/HB	C-32051	M-F
	1/LB	C-4111	M-F
Schools(DOD Dep)			
Elementary	319,350/HB	8637/8745	M-F (K-8)
High School	Information not available		
Svc Stn(Insta)	152/HB	C-355871	M-F
Taxi(Comm)	28/HB	C-8808	Daily
Thrift Shop	305/HB	C-3893	Tu-Th
TML			
Billeting	1/LB	8540	M-F
		C-3558647	
Travel Agents	105/HB	C-31845	M-F

HEALTH AND WELFARE

FACILITY/ACTIVITY	BLDG NO/LOC	PHONE	DAYS/COMMENTS
Ambulance	N/A	116	24 hours daily
	N/A	C-702790	24 hours daily
Army Comm Svcs	141/HB	8513/8663	M-F
	1/LB	470	M-F
Army Emerg Relief	141/HB	8513	M-F
Central Appts	1/LB	404	M-F
		C-84209	
CHAMPUS Office	146/HB	8763	M-F
Chaplain	105/HB	8669	Daily
Chapel	102/HB	8669/8878	M-F
	31/LB	742	M-F
Comm Drug/Alc Ctr	160/HB	8736/8515	M-F
	T99/LB	2781	M-F
Dental Clinic	9/LB	452/752	M-F
Medical Emergency	146/HB	8811	24 hours daily
Poison Control	146/HB	8811	24 hours daily
Red Cross	1/LB	478/996	M-F

GERMANY
Kitzingen Sub-Community, continued

REST AND RECREATION

FACILITY/ACTIVITY	BLDG NO/LOC	PHONE	DAYS/COMMENTS
Bowling Lanes	Marshall Heights	C-21615	Daily
Civ/Contract Club	170/HB	8558	M-F
Craftshops			
Automotive	15/LB	605	Su-W
Multi-crafts	138/HB	8648	Su-W
	70/LB	659	Su-W
Enlisted Club	105/HB	8509	Daily
	12/LB	609	Daily
Golf Course	LB	C-4956	Tu-Su
Gymnasium	138/HB	8651	Daily
	71/LB	611	Daily
Info Tour & Travel	See Rec Center.		
Library	138/HB	8593	Tu-Su
	26/LB	755	Sa-Th
NCO Club	12/LB	609	Daily
O'Club	HB	8600	Daily
Outdoor Rec Ctr	138/HB	544	M-F
Recreation Center	105/HB	8509	Daily
		C-35647	
	26/LB	755	Daily
		C-4969	
Swimming Pool	LB	611	Daily in summer
Theater	155/HB	8638	Call for schedule.
	70/LB	631	Call for schedule.
Youth Center	341/Marshall Heights	8647 C-4939	M-Sa

LINDSEY AIR STATION (GE76R7)
APO New York 09633-5000

TELEPHONE INFORMATION: Main installation numbers: Civ: 49-06121-82-1110. ETS/ATVN: 339-1110. Civ prefix: 06121-____. ETS/ATVN prefix: 339-XXXX. Civ to mil prefix: 06121-82-XXXX.

LOCATION: Lindsey Air Station is located in the central part of the country in downtown Wiesbaden, 20 miles east of Frankfurt. Take Autobahn 66 from downtown Frankfurt to downtown Wiesbaden (several exits to downtown). NMC: Frankfurt, 20 miles west.

GENERAL INSTALLATION INFORMATION: The primary unit stationed at Lindsey Air Station, a U.S. Air Force non-flying installation, is the 7100th Combat Support Wing, with more than 500 personnel. The mission of the 7100th CSW is to provide logistical and administrative support to the 25 assigned, attached, and tenant Air Force units in the Wiesbaden area, the largest of which is the 7100th Combat Support Wing Medical Center.

GENERAL CITY/REGIONAL INFORMATION: For centuries, Wiesbaden has been known for the curative powers of its 26 thermal springs. Each year Wiesbaden draws a number of visitors, some coming to use the spas, some

GERMANY
Lindsey Air Station, continued

coming to attend the many meetings and conventions held there each year, and others coming to see the various attractions in the city. Among the city's famous sights are the Old City Hall, the Market Well and Schloss Square, City Castle and a great many churches, gardens and parks.

ADMINISTRATIVE SUPPORT

FACILITY/ACTIVITY	BLDG NO/LOC	PHONE	DAYS/COMMENTS
Duty Officer	20015	3814/3333	24 hours daily
Fire(Mil)	20015	3208	M-F
Fire(Civ)	Wiesbaden	117	24 hours daily
Housing	See Wiesbaden Community listing.		
Info(Insta)	20015	3636	M-F
Inspector Gen'l	20015	3059	M-F
Legal Assist	20015	3669	M-F
Locator(Mil)	20015	3811	M-F
Personnel Spt	20013	3526	M-F
Police(Mil)	20004	3333	24 hours daily
Police(Civ)	20004	114	24 hours daily
Public Affairs	20015	3636	M-F
Tax Relief	10011	3650	M-F

LOGISTICAL SUPPORT

FACILITY/ACTIVITY	BLDG NO/LOC	PHONE	DAYS/COMMENTS
Auto Drivers Testing	10001	3355	M-F
Auto Repairs	20035	3006	N/A
Bank	10015	3659	M-F
Barber Shop(s)	10028	3349	M-F
Bookstore	20008	3004	M-F
Child Care/Dev Ctr	10009	6100	M-Sa
Clothing Sales	10009	3304	M-F
Commissary(Main)	N/A	0639	Tu-Su
Dining Facility	20022	2278	M-F
Dry Clean(Exch)	10017	C-843195	M-F
Education Center	10014	3430	M-F
Eng'r/Publ Works	20015	3208	M-F
Exchange(Annex)	20002	C-843551/ 719081	M-Sa
Finance(Mil)	20015	3017	M-F
Motor Pool	10024	3403	M-F
Photo Laboratory	10004	3467	M-F
Pick-up Point	10015	C-843195	N/A
Postal Svcs(Mil)	20010	3640	M-Sa
SATO-OS	101	C-87164	M-F
Schools(DOD Dep)	See Wiesbaden Community listing.		
Svc Stn(Insta)	N/A	3065	Daily
Tailor Shop	10009	C-843195	M-F
Taxi(Comm)	N/A	C-33991	24 hours daily
Tel Booking Oper	Wiesbaden	112	M-F
Tel Repair(Gov)	20023	3828	M-F
TML			
Billeting	Amelia Earhart Hotel	C-8161	24 hours daily

GERMANY
Lindsey Air Station, continued

Guest House	American Arms Hotel	C-8161	24 hours daily
	Amelia Earhart Hotel	C-8161	24 hours daily
DV/VIP	20015, Rm 207	3636	24 hours daily

HEALTH AND WELFARE

FACILITY/ACTIVITY	BLDG NO/LOC	PHONE	DAYS/COMMENTS
Ambulance	Medical Bldg 1	116	24 hours daily
Central Appts	Medical Bldg 1	6268	M-F
CHAMPUS Office	Medical Bldg 1	7351	M-F
Chaplain	20003	3673	M-F
Chapel	20003	3673	Call for schedule.
Comm Drug/Alc Ctr	20014	3001	M-F
Dental Clinic	Medical Bldg 3	3695	M-F
Medical Emergency	Medical Bldg 1	3801/116	24 hours daily
Navy Fam Svcs	30001	6285	N/A
Poison Control	Medical Bldg 1	3801	24 hours daily
Red Cross	Medical Center	7220	M-F
Veterinary Svcs	See Wiesbaden Community listing.		

REST AND RECREATION

FACILITY/ACTIVITY	BLDG NO/LOC	PHONE	DAYS/COMMENTS
Bowling Lanes	10027	3022	Daily
Consolidated Club	10006	6622	Call for hours.
Craftshops			
Automotive	N/A	3881 C-844048	N/A
Golf Course	Rheinblick	N/A	Varies by season
Gymnasium	10006	3456	Daily
Library	10019	6333	Daily
Racket Courts	40006	3459	Daily
Recreation Center	10008	3492	Daily
Service Club	10011	3553	M-F
Sport Field	40006	3459	Daily
Tennis Courts	100032	3275	Daily
Theater	10019	3008	Daily

LUDWIGSBURG/KORNWESTHEIM SUB-COMMUNITY (GE77R7)
APO New York 09279-5000

TELEPHONE INFORMATION: Main installation numbers: Civ: 49-07141-15-113 (all locations except Ludendorff and Wilkin Barracks in Kornwestheim); 49-07154-XXX-113 (Ludendorff and Wilkin Barracks). ETS: 428-2113 (all locations). Civ prefix: 07141-_____ (all locations except Ludendorff and Wilkin Barracks); 07154-_____ (Ludendorff and Wilkin Barracks). ETS prefix: 428-2XXX (all locations). Civ to mil prefix: 07141-15-XXX (all locations except as above); 07154-15-XXX (Ludendorff and Wilkin Barracks).

U.S. Forces Travel & Transfer Guide Europe — 155

GERMANY
Ludwingsburg/Kornwestheim Sub-Community, continued

LOCATION: North of Stuttgart off Highway 27. HE: p-40, C/3. NMC: Stuttgart, 10 miles south.

GENERAL INSTALLATION INFORMATION: Ludendorff Kaserne in Kornwestheim is the home to the 7th Engineer Brigade and Karls Kaserne in Ludwigsburg is home to the 93rd Signal Brigade. Note: the following abbreviations are used in this listing only: CB (Coffey Barracks); FK (Flak Kaserne); KK (Karls Kaserne); KlK (Krabbenloch Kaserne); LK (Ludendorff Kaserne); PT (Pattonville); WB (Wilkin Barracks); VK (Valdez Kaserne).

GENERAL CITY/REGIONAL INFORMATION: The Ludwigsburg-Kornwestheim area is located north of Stuttgart. This historically significant region boasts the Royal Palace, Germany's largest and best-preserved Baroque palace, surrounded by the color "Baroque in Bloom" gardens. Another well-known sight is "Favorite," a summer palace/hunting lodge with a large wildlife park preserve. The lakeside palace, called "Monrepos," is also very popular with tourists. Ludwigsburg offers many fairs, exhibits and special displays throughout the year featuring a variety of subjects—wine, porcelain, gardens, art and horses to name a few.

ADMINISTRATIVE SUPPORT

FACILITY/ACTIVITY	BLDG NO/LOC	PHONE	DAYS/COMMENTS
Customs/Duty	See Stuttgart Community listing.		
Duty Officer	LK	815	Daily
Fire(Mil)	All locations	117	24 hours daily
Housing	See Stuttgart Community listing.		
Legal Assist	604/LK	311/872/775	M-F
Personnel Spt	1700/FK	308	M,Tu,Th,F
Police(Mil)	942/PT	667/347	M-F
Emergency	942/PT	114	24 hours daily
Public Affairs	LK	761	M-F

LOGISTICAL SUPPORT

FACILITY/ACTIVITY	BLDG NO/LOC	PHONE	DAYS/COMMENTS
Auto Drivers Testing	FK	676	M-F
Auto Parts(Exch)	964/PT	C-80353	M-Sa
Auto Registration	942/PT	667/347	M-F
Auto Rent(Other)	Heilbronner St	C-27180	M-Sa
Auto Repairs	PT	C-80352	M-Sa
Auto Sales	Stuttgarter St	C-21697	Mazda
	Teinacher St	C-32011	Volvo
Bakery	PT-German	None	M-Sa
Bank	964/PT	C-84018/19	M-F
Barber Shop(s)	1814/CB	C-41320	M,W,Th
	1722/FK	C-81290	M-F
	1614/KK	None	M-F
	616/LK	C-26687	M-F
	942/PT	C-82350	M-Sa
	406/WB	C-27316	M-F
Beauty Shop(s)	942/PT	C-82350	W-Sa
Bookstore	1804/CB	None	M-F
	1614/KK	None	M-F

GERMANY
Ludwigsburg/Kornwestheim Sub-Community, continued

	603/LK	C-21401	M-F
	942/PT	None	M-F
	706/WB	None	M-F
Child Care/Dev Ctr	Ludwigsburg	C-2895	M-F
	PT	C-82367	M-F
Commissary(Main)	1926/LK	864	Tu-Sa
Education Center	1818/CB	573	M-F
	1722/FK	890	M-F
	1601/KlK	772	M-F
	605/LK	450/608	M-F
	702/WK	695	M-F
Eng'r/Publ Works	1230/KK	494/846	M-F
Exchange(Annex)	1814/CB	C-41320	M-F
	1716/FK	C-89215	M-Sa
	1370/KK	C-20828	M-Sa
	1614/KlK	C-89184	M-Sa
	616/LK	C-7394	M-F
	706/WB	C-7137	M-F
Finance(Mil)	1706/FK	877/471	M,Tu,Th,F
Food(Caf/Rest)	1717/FK	C-80262	Daily
	1614/KlK	C-89226	Daily
Food(Snack/Fast)	1804/CB	C-42616	M-Sa
	1717/FK	C-80262	Daily
	603/LK	C-21401	Daily
Pizza Parlor	943/PT	C-85580	Tu-Sa
Foodland	KlK	C-89226	Daily
	943/PT	C-89130	Daily
Laundry(Self-Svc)	See Pick-up Point.		
Package Store	1373/KK	390	M,W-Sa
	964/PT	C-89130	Daily
Pick-up Point	1814/CB	C-41320	M-F
	1722/FK	C-81290	M-F
	1614/KK	C-871024	M-F
	616/LK	C-27317	M-F
	WB	C-27316	M-F
Postal Svcs(Mil)	1805/CB	None	W,F
	1722/FK	None	M,F
	1601/KlK	None	M-Th
	942/PT	496/512	M-F
Schools(DOD Dep)			
Elementary	926/PT	558/858	M-F (K-4)
Middle School	1002/Ludwigsburg	457/467	M-F (5-8)
High School	See Stuttgart Community listing.		
Svc Stn(Insta)	964/PT	C-80353	M-Sa
Space-A Air Ops	See Stuttgart Community listing.		
Tailor Shop	1722/FK	C-81290	M-F
	616/LK	None	M-F
Thrift Shop	944/PT	681	M-W,F
TML			
Billeting	1/KlK	490	Daily
BEQ	170/FK	420	Daily
	949/PT	507	Daily

U.S. Forces Travel & Transfer Guide Europe — 157

GERMANY

Ludwigsburg/Kornwestheim Sub-Community, continued

HEALTH AND WELFARE

FACILITY/ACTIVITY	BLDG NO/LOC	PHONE	DAYS/COMMENTS
Army Comm Svcs	942/PT	681	M-F
Army Emerg Relief	942/PT	681	M-F
Central Appts	1612/KlK	316/816/300	M-F
CHAMPUS Office	See Stuttgart Community listing.		
Chapel	1806/CB	380	Call for schedule.
	1726/FK	339	Call for schedule.
	1609/KK	357	Call for schedule.
	612/LK	839	Call for scheduel.
	71/LK	712	Call for schedule.
	927/PT	811/320	Call for schedule.
Comm Drug/Alc Ctr	604/LK	455/456/518	M-F
Dental Clinic	1612/KlK	736/421	M-F
Red Cross	604/LK	730	M-F
Veterinary Svcs	See Stuttgart Community listing.		

REST AND RECREATION

FACILITY/ACTIVITY	BLDG NO/LOC	PHONE	DAYS/COMMENTS
Amer Forces Ntwk	See Stuttgart Community listing.		
Bowling Lanes	1004/PT	C-85956	Daily
Consolidated Club	975/PT	484	Tu-Su
Craftshops			
Automotive	715/WB	464	
Multi-crafts	1120-1/Aldingen Housing	C-871204	Daily
Enlisted Club	1817/FK	368	Tu-Su
	CB	C-42641	Tu-Su
	1614/KlK	310	Tu-Su
	706/WB	322	Tu-Su
Golf Course	975/PT	484	Daily
		C-89150	
Gymnasium	1807/CB	588	Daily
	1613/FK	C-4282454	Daily
	1613/KlK	485	Daily
	606/LK	397	Daily
	703/WK	444	Daily
Info Tour & Travel	See Stuttgart Community listing.		
Library	1727/FK	596	M-F
	2948/PT	512	Sa-Th
NCO Club	CB	C-42641	Tu-Su
	LK	414	Tu-Su
	706/WK	322	Tu-Su
Recreation Center	1715/FK	336	Su,M
		C-87071	
	735/WB	C-29244	Su,M
	1600/KlK	553	Su,M
		C-82301	
Theater	See Stuttgart Community listing.		
Video Rental	1711/FK	378	Call for schedule.
	1579/KK	736	Call for schedule.
	PT	None	Daily

GERMANY
Ludwigsburg/Kornwestheim Sub-Community, continued

Youth Center	939/PT	550	M-Sa
		C-89178	
	VK	358	M-Sa

===

MAINZ COMMUNITY (GE41R7)
APO New York 09185-0029

TELEPHONE INFORMATION: Main installation numbers: Civ: 49-06131-48-113 (Mainz, including Dragoone Kaserne, Martin Luther King Village and Lee Barracks); 49-06131-469-113 (Finthen Army Airfield); 49-06132-508-113 (McCully Barracks and Wackernheim). ETS: 334-113 (Mainz); 334-3113 (Finthen Army Airfield); 334-4113 (McCully Barracks and Wackernheim). ATVN: 320-1110 (ask for Mainz). Civ prefix: 06131-____ (Mainz and Finthen Army Airfield); 06132-____ (McCully Barracks and Wackernheim). ETS prefix: 334-XXXX (Mainz); 334-3XXX (Finthen Army Airfield); 334-4XXX (McCully Barracks and Wackernheim). Civ to mil prefix: 06131-48-XXXX (Mainz); 06131-469-XXX (Finthen Army Airfield); 06132-508-XXX (McCully Barracks and Wackernheim).

LOCATION: Take the Mainz exit from the E-61 Autobahn to GE B-9. Follow the signs to the community. HE: p-40, A/1. NMC: Mainz, in the city.

GENERAL INSTALLATION INFORMATION: Lee Barracks at Mainz is headquarters of the 1st Brigade, 8th Infantry Division (Mechanized). Other units assigned there include 4th Brigade, 34th Armored 118th Forward Support Battalion. The 1st Battalion, 59th Air Defense Artillery is at McCully Barracks and the 4th Brigade (Aviation) is at Finthen Army Airfield. Note: the following abbreviations are used in this listing only: DK (Dragoone Kaserne); FAA (Finthen Army Airfield); LB (Lee Barracks); MB (McCully Barracks); MLKV (Martin Luther King Village).

GENERAL CITY/REGIONAL INFORMATION: Mainz, a bustling, two-thousand-year-old city, lies at the junction of the Rhein and Main Rivers. It is the regional capital of Rheinland-Pfalz, an area known for its cultural, historical and industrial importance. Mainz was the birthplace of Johannes Gutenberg; since its founding in 1962, the Gutenberg Museum of Printing has gained international recognition. The wine industry was established here centuries ago, and the city's deep wine cellars are considered an architectural wonder.

At the center of Mainz rises the Dom, an imposing cathedral over one thousand years old. Another landmark is the University of Mainz. Throughout the city, picturesque squares, magnificent palaces, ancient churches and lovely fountains intermingle harmoniously with modern buildings.

Mainz is a tourist's delight since it is the perfect starting point for excursions to the whole middle Rhein region. Some fortunate tourists will be able to join the celebration of the Mainzer Fastnacht, a carnival that begins on the Thursday before Ash Wednesday and is marked by parades, ceremonies, and costume balls. Mainzers happily enjoy life to the fullest and with their good-natured humor, hospitality and sociability, they make the stay of every visitor to their city comfortable and entertaining.

Mainz Community, continued

GERMANY

ADMINISTRATIVE SUPPORT

FACILITY/ACTIVITY	BLDG NO/LOC	PHONE	DAYS/COMMENTS
Customs/Duty	LB	7327	M-F
Fire(Mil)	All locations	117	24 hours daily
Fire(Civ)	All locations	112	24 hours daily
Housing			
Family	6118/LB	7390/8581	M-F
Unaccompanied	6118/LB	7552	M-F
Referral	6118/LB	7490/8514	M-Sa
Info(Insta)	All locations	113	24 hours daily
Legal Assist	6104A/LB	7580/7477	M-F
Personnel Spt	LB	7319/8176	M-F
Police(Mil)	6652/DK	7111	24 hours daily
Emergency	All locations	114	24 hours daily
Police(Civ)	All locations	110	24 hours daily
Public Affairs	DK	7564	M-F
Tax Relief	6111/LB	7393 C-487393	M-F

LOGISTICAL SUPPORT

FACILITY/ACTIVITY	BLDG NO/LOC	PHONE	DAYS/COMMENTS
Audio/Photo Ctr	6726/MKLV	C-383001	Daily
Auto Drivers Testing	LB	7115	M-F
Auto Registration	DK	7112	M-F
Auto Repairs	See Lindsey Air Station listing.		
Auto Ship(Gov)	Mainz	C-41309	M-F
Bank	FAA	836 C-475232	M-F
	6110/LB	7586 C-46098	M-Sa
	6141/MB	897	M-F
	6726/MLKV	C-382404	M-F
Barber Shop(s)	5805/FAA	None	M-F
	6132/LB	C-42959	M-Sa
	6244/MB	None	M-F
	6726/MLKV	C-387170	M-Sa
Beauty Shop(s)	6726/MLKV	C-387590	Tu-Sa
Bookstore	5803/FAA	None	M-F
	6719/LB	None	M,W-Sa
	6752/MLKV	None	Daily
Child Care/Dev Ctr	6719/LB	7611	M-F
	MLKV	8156	M-F
Clothing Sales	6117/LB	8244	M-Sa
Commissary(Main)	MLKV	8577/7342	Daily
Commissary(Annex)	6717/MB	832	Daily
Credit Union	See Wiesbaden Community listing.		
Dining Facility	5826/FAA	N/A	Daily
Education Center	5803/FAA	711/800	M-F
	6106/LB	7538	M-F
	6203/MB	773/865	M-F
Eng'r/Publ Works	6609/LB	7554/7377	M-F
	6609/LB	115	After duty hours

GERMANY
Mainz Community, continued

Exchange(Main)	6726/MKLV	C-383001	Daily
Exchange(Annex)	5805/FAA	C-40629	M-Sa
	6117/LB	C-42204	M-Sa
	6241/MB	C-59229	M-Sa
Finance(Mil)	6121/LB	7493/8300	M-F
Food(Snack/Fast)	5805/FAA	C-40515	Daily
	6106/LB	C-41837	Daily
	6244/MB	C-58985	Daily
	MLKV	C-387644	Daily
Foodland	6726/MLKV	C-383001	Daily
	LB	42204	Daily
Laundry(Self-Svc)	5805/FAA	None	Daily
	6106/LB	None	Daily
	6241/MB	None	Daily
	6751/MLKV	None	Daily
Package Store	6718/MLKV	C-383939	M-F
Photo Laboratory	5844/FAA	816	M-W,Sa,Su
Pick-up Point	5805/FAA	None	M-F
	6117/LB	C-42600	M-F
	6241/MB	None	M-F
	6726/MLKV	C-387746	Daily
Postal Svcs(Mil)	5803/FAA	796	M-F
	6110/LB	8596	M-F
	6244/MB	710	M-F
	6726/MLKV	7274	Tu-Sa
Railroad/RTO	T-6680/Mainz	7398/8530	Daily
Schools(DOD Dep)			
Elementary	6705/MLKV	8496/7182	M-F
Middle School	See Wiesbaden Community listing.		
High School	See Wiesbaden Community listing.		
Space-A Air Ops	FAA	866/794	Daily
Flights to:	Various German locations		
Tailor Shop	5805/FAA	C-42600	M-Sa
	MB	C-5497	M-Sa
Taxi(Comm)	Maine	C-60011	Daily
Tel Booking Oper	All locations	112	24 hours daily
Thrift Shop	6719/MLKV	C-387796	Tu,W,Th
TML			
Billeting	6706/MLKV	7396	Daily
		C-38650	
TLQ	6706/MLKV	7396	Daily
		C-38650	

HEALTH AND WELFARE

FACILITY/ACTIVITY	BLDG NO/LOC	PHONE	DAYS/COMMENTS
Ambulance	All locations	116	24 hours daily
Army Comm Svcs	6121/LB	7619/7553	M-F
Army Emerg Relief	6121/LB	8302	M-F
Central Appts	297th Hospital/Mainz	7436/7404	24 hours daily
Chapel	6659/DK	7604	M-F
	5823/FAA	895	Daily
	6430/LB	7576	Daily
	6210/MB	744	Daily
Comm Drug/Alc Ctr	FAA	783	M-F

Mainz Community, continued   **GERMANY**

	6128/LB	7404	M-F
	6251/MB	828	M-F
Dental Clinic	LB	7146	M-F
	6245/MB	775/718	M-F
Medical Emergency	See Wiesbaden Community listing.		
Mental Health	6128/LB	8755	M-F
Red Cross	6104D/LB	7442	M-F
Veterinary Svcs	See Wiesbaden Community listing.		

==
REST AND RECREATION
==

FACILITY/ACTIVITY	BLDG NO/LOC	PHONE	DAYS/COMMENTS
Bowling Lanes	6114/LB	7137	Daily
	6209/MB	727	Daily
Craftshops			
Automotive	6126/LB	7571	Tu-Su
	6237/MB	776	W-Su
Multi-crafts	6136/LB	7367	Tu-Sa
Photography	FAA	816	Tu-Sa
Wood	6136/LB	7367	Tu-Sa
Enlisted Club	5803/FAA	709	N/A
	6111/LB	8146	Daily
	MB	747	N/A
Golf Course	See Wiesbaden Community listing.		
Gymnasium	5844/FAA	816	Daily
	6125/LB	7205/7239	Daily
	6213/MB	737	Daily
Info Tour & Travel	6170/LB	8470/7258	M-F
	MB	713	M-F
	6726/MLKV	7252 C-382995	Tu-Sa
Library	6102/LB	7186	Daily
	6206/MB	783	Daily
NCO Club	5803/FAA	709	N/A
	6707/MLKV	7246 C-384667	Tu-Su
O'Club	6707/MLKV	7246 C-384667	Tu-Su
Outdoor Rec Ctr	6133/LB	7417	M-F
Recreation Center	5803/FAA	815	M-Sa
	6106/LB	8252/7181	Daily
	6212/MB	815/713	Daily
Theater	6114/LB	7554	Call for schedule.
Video Rental	FAA	None	Daily
	LB	None	Daily
	6241/MB	None	Daily
	6707/MLKV	None	Daily
Youth Center	FAA	816	N/A
	6749/MLKV	8130	Tu-Sa

==

GERMANY

MANNHEIM COMMUNITY (GE43R7)
APO New York 09086-5000

TELEPHONE INFORMATION: Main installations numbers: Civ: 49-0621-730-113 (information); 49-0621-730-1110 (operator). ETS: 380-1110 (Mannheim); 382-1110 (Coleman). ATVN: 380-1110. Civ prefix: 0621-____. ETS prefix: 380-XXXX (Mannheim); 382-XXXX (Coleman). Civilian to mil prefix: 0621-730-XXXX (Mannheim); 0621-779-XXXX (Coleman).

LOCATION: Accessible from the E-5 or E-67 Autobahns. Take the Viernheim exit, follow signs to Benjamin Franklin Housing Area on Fürther Strasse. HE: p-40, B/2. NMC: Mannheim, 8 miles southwest.

GENERAL INSTALLATION INFORMATION: The Mannheim Military Community provides a single point of control for Americans and base operations support for tenant units in the surrounding area. Mannheim supports tenant units from every major command within USAREUR. There are 19 separate installations within the community boundaries. Major tenant units include: 3rd Brigade, 8th Infantry Division; 3rd Squadron, 7th Cavalry, 8th Infantry Division; 7th Signal Brigade; 44th Signal Battalion, a subordinate unit of the 5th Signal Command; 70th Transportation Battalion; 97th Signal Battalion; Armored Battalions assigned to the 3rd Brigade, 8th Infantry Division; 21st SUPCOMs 51st Maintenance Battalion; HQ, Combat Equipment Group, Europe; 181st Transportation Battalion; 7th Signal Brigade NCO Academy; 28th Transportation Battalion of 37th Group, 4th TRANSCOM; and other units. **Note: the following abbreviations are used in this listing only:** BFV (Benjamin Franklin Village); CB (Coleman Barracks); CM (Coleman Military); FB (Funari Barracks); MM (Mannheim Military); SB (Spinelli Barracks); SlB (Sullivan Barracks); TB (Turley Barracks); TyB (Taylor Barracks).

GENERAL CITY/REGIONAL INFORMATION: Mannheim is located fifty miles south of Frankfurt and thirteen miles northwest of Heidelberg in the state of Baden-Württemberg, at the junction of the Neckar and Rhein rivers. Mannheim has a population of approximately 300,000 and is the seventeenth largest city in Germany. It also has one of the larger inland ports on the Rhein river. The climate in the area is comparable to that of the Great Lakes region of the United States. Local attractions include the Mannheim Castle, completed in 1720, the Old Observatory and the Modern National Theater.

ADMINISTRATIVE SUPPORT

FACILITY/ACTIVITY	BLDG NO/LOC	PHONE	DAYS/COMMENTS
Action Line	BFV	MM-7000	24 hours daily
Advocate	TB-Crisis Line	MM-6145	Daily
Customs/Duty	CB	MM-7610	M-F
	333/TyB	MM-6847	Daily
Duty Officer	335/TyB	MM-8168/ 7462/6173	Daily
Housing			
Family	255/BFV	MM-7547	M-F
Unaccompanied	255/BFV	MM-6252	M-F
Referral	255/BFV	MM-7349	M-F
Inspector Gen'l	CB	MM-6869	M-F
Legal Assist	50/CB	CM-7118	M-F
	332/TyB	MM-6792	M-F

U.S. Forces Travel & Transfer Guide Europe — 163

GERMANY

Mannheim Community, continued

Locator(Mil)	49/CB	CM-4336	M-F
Personnel Spt	821/FB	MM-6038/6667	M-F
Passports	821/FB	MM-6044	M-F
Police(Mil)	256/BFV	MM-8359/6378	24 hours daily
Emergency	256/BFV	114	24 hours daily
Public Affairs	335/TyB	MM-6487	M-F
Tax Relief	820/FB	MM-6150	M-F

LOGISTICAL SUPPORT

FACILITY/ACTIVITY	BLDG NO/LOC	PHONE	DAYS/COMMENTS
Audio/Photo Ctr	BFV	C-722646	M-Sa
	50/CB	C-783428	M-Sa
Auto Drivers Testing	253/SB	MM-6875	M-F
Auto Parts(Exch)	351/TB	C-731900	N/A
Auto Registration	255/BFV	MM-7384/6586	M-F
Auto Rent(Other)	351/TB	N/A	Bonanza
Auto Repairs	351/TB	C-731900	M-Sa
Auto Sales	BFV	C-731548	American Motors
	BFV	C-735998	GM
	BFV	C-731695	Chrysler
	BFV	C-732800	Ford
Auto Ship(Gov)	Bremerhaven	342-8168	M-Sa. In-processing
		342-8167	M-Sa. Out-processing
Auto Ship(Civ)	Frankfurt	320-5159	N/A
Bank	255/BFV	MM-6615	M-Sa
	50/CB	CM-6969	M-F
Barber Shop(s)	275/BFV	C-735991	M-Sa
	25/CB	CM-4164	M-Sa
	T819/FB	C-737210	M-Sa
	1583/SB	MM-6210	M-Sa
	250/SlB	C-731030	M-Sa
	331/TyB	MM-6107	M-Sa
Beauty Shop(s)	275/BFV	C-731212	M-Sa
	485/TB	C-3727885	M-Sa
Bookstore	BFV	None	Daily
	BFV	MM-6028	Daily
Bus	BFV	MM-6953/8249	Daily
Child Care/Dev Ctr	737/BFV	MM-7194	M-Sa
		C-731888	
Clothing Sales	238/CB	CM-5187	M-Sa
	38/SlB	MM-7363	M-Sa
		C-722545	
Commissary(Main)	BFV	MM-8265	Daily
Education Center	50/CB	CM-5276	M-F
	1579/SB	MM-6135	M-F
	253/SlB	MM-8361	M-F
	353/TyB	MM-6468	M-F
	493/TB	MM-7618	M-F
Elec Repair(Gov)	BFV	MM-8168	M-Sa
Elec Repair(Civ)	BFV	C-472011	M,Tu,Th
Eng'r/Publ Works	Emergency	MM-115	Daily
	Emergency	C-730115	Daily
Exchange(Main)	BFV	C-735066	Daily

GERMANY
Mannheim Community, continued

Facility	Bldg No/Loc	Phone	Days
		MM-6401	Daily
Exchange(Annex)	25/CB	C-783393	M-F
	1583/SB	C-791791	M-F
	483/TB	C-734952	M-W,F,Sa
Food(Caf/Rest)	BFV	C-735908	Daily
	443/CB	C-783431	Daily
	FB	C-731076	Daily
Food(Snack/Fast)			
Burger King	324/BFV	C-722917	Daily
Hot Dog Kiosk	SB	C-735908	Daily
Hot Dog Stand	BFV	C-783431	Daily
Pizza Parlor	Gate 252/SlB	MM-6593	Daily
Snackbar	487/TB	C-332977	Daily
Foodland	303/BFV	C-732721	With deli
Shoppette	CB	CM-5280	Daily
Laundry(Self-Svc)	BFV	C-733680	Daily
	CB	C-471673	Daily
Package Store	Behind Theater	MM-6460	Tu-Sa
Photo Laboratory	335/TyB	MM-7167	M-Th
Pick-up Point	1443/CB	C-781515	M-Sa
	1581/SB	MM-6210	M-Sa
		C-791156	
	311/SB	MM-6297	M-Sa
	331/TyB	C-735909	M-Sa
	485/TB	C-373193	M-Sa
Postal Svcs(Mil)	277/BFV	MM-6429	M-Sa
	40/CB	CM-4196	M-F
Postal Svcs(Civ)	255/BFV	C-733733/ 736911	M-F
Schools			
Elementary	BFV	MM-7506	M-F (K-5)
Middle School	BFV	MM-7092	M-F (6-8)
High School	BFV	MM-7139	M-F (9-12)
Svc Stn(Insta)	311/BFV	MM-734348	Daily
Space-A Air Ops	Flight Opns/CB	5160/4253	Daily
Flights to:	German locations		
Tailor Shop	277/BFV	C-731713	M-Sa
	49/CB	C-786459	M-Sa
	331/TyB	C-735909	M-Sa
Taxi(Comm)	BFV	C-444044	Daily
Thrift Shop	BFV/879	MM-6028	Tu,Th,EOM Payday
TML			
Billeting	312/BFV	C-738607	Daily
		MM-8118	
BEQ	72,73,81,81/BFV	See Bltg	Daily
BOQ	375,377/BFV	See Bltg	Daily
Guest House	312/BFV	See Bltg	Daily
Protocol Office	335/BFV	C-722578	Daily
		MM-6487/8369	
Watch Repair	See Pick-Up Points.		

HEALTH AND WELFARE

FACILITY/ACTIVITY	BLDG NO/LOC	PHONE	DAYS/COMMENTS
Ambulance	BFV	MM-116	24 hours daily
Army Comm Svcs	255/BFV	MM-8180/	M-F

Mannheim Community, continued GERMANY

		6240/6266	
		MM-6145	Crisis Line
	1474/CB	CM-5270	M-F
Army Emerg Relief	255/BFV	MM-6896	M-F
Central Appts	255/BFV	MM-7095	Daily
CHAMPUS Office	BFV/Dispensary	MM-6062/	M-F
		7341	
Chaplain	342/TB	MM-6530	M-F
	After Hours	MM-8168/	SDNCO
		7462	
Chapel	698/BFV	MM-6448/	Daily
		8219/8379	
	85/CB	CM-5196/	Daily
		4465/5193	
Comm Drug/Alc Ctr	1492/CB	CM-5225	M-F
	214/SB	MM-6377	M-F
Dental Clinic	BFV	MM-6442/	M-F
		7072	
Medical Emergency	BFV	MM-7045	24 hours daily
Mental Health	214/SB	MM-7425	M-F
Red Cross	322/BFV	MM-6671	M-F
	50/CB	CM-4332/	M-F
		5281	
Veterinary Svcs	See Heidelberg Community listing.		

===
REST AND RECREATION
===

FACILITY/ACTIVITY	BLDG NO/LOC	PHONE	DAYS/COMMENTS
Bowling Lanes	BFV	MM-6528	Daily
	25/CB	CM-4329	Daily
	1528/SB	MM-6712	Daily
	514/TB	MM-7114	Daily
Craftshops			
Automotive	801/FB	MM-6812	Daily
Multi-crafts	251/BFV	MM-6863	Daily
	1585/SlB	MM-3920	Daily
Enlisted Club	25/CB	CM-4261	M-F
	46/CB	CM-4410	M-Sa
	TyB	MM-6419	Sa,Su
Golf Course	See Heidelberg Community listing.		
Gymnasium	736/BFV	MM-6054	Daily
	25/CB	CM-4322	Daily
	6166/HB	MM-6166	Daily
	1581/SB	MM-6821	Daily
	487/TB	MM-7151	Daily
Info Tour & Travel	313/BFV	MM-6716	M-F
	25/CB	CM-4261	M-F
Library	25/CB	CM-5213	Daily
	252/SB	MM-7206	Daily
MARS	See Heidelberg Community listing.		
NCO Club	738/BFV	MM-6370	Daily
	86/CB	CM-4410	M-Sa
O'Club	240/BFV	MM-6884	Su-F
		C-731333	
	TB	6419	Sa,Su
Outdoor Rec Ctr	254/BFV	MM-6120	Daily

GERMANY
Mannheim Community, continued

Recreation Center	25/CB	CM-4498	Daily
	1583/SB	CM-6561	Daily
Rod and Gun Club	See Heidelberg Community listing.		
Tennis Courts	BFV	MM-6633	Daily
	CB	CM-4322	Daily
Theater	735/BFV	MM-6534	Daily
	25/CB	CM-4440	Plays
Video Rental	275/CB	C-783428	M-Sa
Youth Center	696/BFV	MM-7012	M-Sa

MUNICH COMMUNITY (GE15R7)
APO New York 09407-5000

TELEPHONE INFORMATION: Main installation numbers: Civ: 49-089-6229-113. ETS: 440-1110. Civ prefix: 089-____. ETS/ATVN prefix: 440-XXXX. Civ to mil prefix: 089-6229-XXXX.

LOCATION: Munich can be reached from Autobahns E-8 or E-9. Follow the Salzburg Autobahn signs on Mittlerer Ring, watch for signs indicating directions to McGraw Kaserne. HE: p-40, G/5. NMC: Munich, in the city.

GENERAL INSTALLATION INFORMATION: McGraw Kaserne is the site of HQ, Army/Air Force Exchange Service, Europe. Von Steuben Hall at Stadelheimer Strasse 4 is the site of HQ, U.S.M.C.A. Munich with 14 directorates. Note: the following abbreviations are used in this listing only: McG (McGraw Kaserne); PF (Perlacher Forst Housing Area); VSH (von Steuben Hall).

GENERAL CITY/REGIONAL INFORMATION: Founded in 1158, Munich is a cultural and industrial center, with a thriving economy and a great variety of fairs, exhibitions, museums, galleries and historic sites. Every years, thousands of tourists visit the grounds of the 1972 Olympics and the world-famous Nymphenberg Castle, the summer residence of the rulers of Bavaria. Theaters, clubs, cabarets and outdoor beer gardens provide exciting nightlife for residents and tourists alike. Although Munich is famous for its annual Oktoberfest, which attracts millions each year, it is a wonderful, friendly city to visit any time of the year.

The Munich campus of the University of Maryland offers undergraduate courses for college credit at the education center, subject to the usual entrance requirements. The University of Maryland also offers a two-year resident program for freshman and sophomore college students who are family members of U.S. personnel. Its "campus" facility, complete with dormitories, is located on McGraw Kaserne.

ADMINISTRATIVE SUPPORT

FACILITY/ACTIVITY	BLDG NO/LOC	PHONE	DAYS/COMMENTS
Advocate	6, Rm 218/McG	6317/6298	M-F
Customs/Duty	16/McG	6285	M-F
Duty Officer	54/VSH	8300	Daily
Fire (Mil)	6/McG	E-117	24 hours daily
Fire (Civ)	Munich Civ	C-112	24 hours daily

Munich Community, continued

GERMANY

Housing	54/VSH	8337/7135	M-F
Referral	54/VSH	6550	M-F
Info(Insta)	6/McG	E-113	24 hours daily
Inspector Gen'l	54/VSH	6137	By appointment
Legal Assist	6, Rm 218/McG	6317	M-F
Locator(Mil)	6/McG	7345	M-F
Locator(Civ)	54, Rm 108/VSH	8311	M-F
Personnel Spt	54, Rm 107/VSH	7218/6368	M-F. ID cards only on M,W.
Police(Mil)	54, Rm 104/VSH	E-114/98	24 hours daily
Police(Civ)	Munich Police	C-110	24 hours daily
Public Affairs	54, Rm 208/VSH	8353	M-F
Tax Relief	22/AMEXCO Bldg	6516	M-F

LOGISTICAL SUPPORT

FACILITY/ACTIVITY	BLDG NO/LOC	PHONE	DAYS/COMMENTS
Audio/Photo Ctr	McG	C-690-0611	N/A
Auto Drivers Testing	19/McG	7149	M,W,Th
Auto Parts(Exch)	19/McG	C-6220-666	M-Sa
Auto Registration	4, Rm 5/McG	7186	M-F
Auto Rental(Exch)	470/PF	C-690-3070	M-Sa
Auto Rent(Other)	Local Economy		
Auto Repairs	10/McG	C-6220-666	M-F
Auto Sales	472/PF	C-690-1150/3128	M-Sa
Auto Ship(Gov)	54/VSH	6319/7319	M-F
Auto Ship(Civ)	4/McG	C-690-3907	M-F
Auto Wash	3/McG	6513	Tu-Su
Bakery	472/PF	None	Daily
Bank	22/McG	C-690-3499	M-F
Barber Shop(s)	12/McG	C-699-0872	M-Sa
Beauty Shop(s)	472/PF	C-690-3313	Tu-Sa
Bookstore	19/McG	C-690-1150	Daily
	472/PF	C-690-1946	Daily
Bus			
Child Care/Dev Ctr	396/PF	6294/8323	M-F
	311/PF	7196/6270	M-F
Clothing Sales	12/McG	7238	M-F
Commissary(Main)	2/McG	7287	M-Sa
Credit Union	See Augsburg Community listing.		
Dining Facility	3/McG	7117/6419	Daily
Dry Clean(Exch)	McG	C-690-1972	M-Sa. Pick-up point.
Dry Clean(Gov)	4/McG	7107	M-F
Education Center	2, Rm 202/McG	6437	M-F
Learning Center	22/AMEXCO Bldg	6334	M-F
Eng'r/Publ Works	16A/McG	6545/6050	M-F
Exchange(Main)	472/PF	C-690-0611	M-Sa
Exchange(Annex)	472/PF	C-690-4409	Daily
Exchange(Concess)	Auto Sales/	C-690-4409	Daily
Finance(Mil)	54, Rm 1/VSH	6288	M-F
Food(Snack/Fast)	7/McG	6171	Daily
Baskin Robbins	472/PF	0106	Daily
Burger King	472/PF	C-699-0166	Daily
Foodland	17/McG	4102	Daily
Laundry(Exch)	1/McG	6213	24 hours daily

GERMANY
Munich Community, continued

Laundry(Self-Svc)	1/McG	6213	24 hours daily
Motor Pool	19/McG	6408/6222	24 hours daily
Package Store	19/McG	7129	Tu-Sa
Parking	McG,PF	7128	Daily
Photo Laboratory	22/AMEXCO Bldg	6524/6516	M-F
Pick-up Point	4/McG	6214/7107	M-F
Postal Svcs(Mil)	1/McG	6409	M-F
	397/PF	6543	M-F
Postal Svcs(Civ)	7/McG	C-691-7960	M-F
	397/PF	6453	M-F
Retirement Svcs	54/McG	6444	M-F
SATO-OS	22/McG	C-6906598	M-F
Schools			
Elementary	459/PF	6571	M-F (K-6)
High School	386/PF	6346	M-F (7-12)
U. of Maryland	McG	6535	M-F
Svc Stn(Insta)	470/PF	C-690-1333	Daily
Tailor Shop	12/McG	C-6220-525	M-Sa
Taxi(Comm)	Taxi Center	C-21611	24 hours daily
Tel Booking Oper	6/McG	E-112	24 hours daily
Tel Repair(Gov)	6/McG	E-119	24 hours daily
Tel Repair(Civ)	City of Munich	C-1171	24 hours daily
Thrift Shop	4/McG	C-690-2975	M,W,F
TML			
Billeting	13/McG	C-6229-6011/7105	24 hours daily
Guest House	13/McG	C-6229-6011	24 hours daily
Protocol Office	54,Rm 218/McG	8300/6244	06+
Travel Agents	22,Rm 106/AMEXCO Bldg	6234/7376	M-F
Watch Repair	472/PF	C-690-1907	W,Sa

HEALTH AND WELFARE

FACILITY/ACTIVITY	BLDG NO/LOC	PHONE	DAYS/COMMENTS
Ambulance	City of Munich	C-222666	24 hours daily
	Health Clinic	C-19222	24 hours daily
Army Comm Svcs	397A/PF	6343/7268	M-F
Army Emerg Relief	Same as ACS		
Central Appts	370/PF	7295/6284	M-F
CHAMPUS Office	370/PF	6338/7295	M-F
Chaplain	311/PF	8312/6005 6006	M-F
Chapel	311/PF	8312/6005	M-F
Comm Drug/Alc Ctr	397A,Rm 110/PF	8327	M-F
		6110	Hotline
Dental Clinic	370/PF	7292	M-F
Medical Emergency	370/PF	7295	24 hours daily
Mental Health	370/PF	7295	M-F
Poison Control	See Augsburg Community listing.		
Red Cross	22/AMEXCO Bldg	6211	M-F
Veterinary Svcs	399/PF	6442/7271	M,W

GERMANY
Munich Community, continued

REST AND RECREATION

FACILITY/ACTIVITY	BLDG NO/LOC	PHONE	DAYS/COMMENTS
Amer Forces Ntwk	45/Kaulbach St	8328/6497	M-F
	Radio Frequency: 1107; TV channel: 22.		
Bowling Lanes	3/McG	6315	Daily
Consolidated Club	7/McG	7286/6370	Daily
Craftshops			
Automotive	3/McG	6513	Tu-Sa
Ceramics	4/McG	6123	Tu-F, by appoint
Multi-crafts	4/McG	6123	Th-M,Tu & W by appointment
Golf Course	In Dachau	C-08131-10879	In season daily Closed 1st M ea mo.
Gymnasium	3/McG	8366	Daily
Info Tour & Travel	22,Rm 106/ AMEXCO Bldg	6234/7376	M-F
Library	3/McG	6533/7140	Daily
MARS	See Augsburg Community listing.		
Outdoor Rec Ctr	4/McG	6237	Th-M
Picnic/Park Area	PF	NOne	Daily
Racket Courts	3/McG	8366	Daily
Recreation Center	54,Rm 411/VSH	6031	M-F
Rod and Gun Club	19/McG	6355	M-Sa
Service Club	19/McG	6355	M-Sa
Skating Rink	PF	N/A	Adjacent to Family Theater
Special Services	54/VSH	6031	M-F
Sport Field	Harlaching Sports Complex	8366	By appointment
	Autobahn/Hosp	6238	By appointment
Tennis Courts	Chiemgau St	8366	Daily
	Hospital	8366	Daily
Theater	402/PF	6221	Daily
Video Rental	472/PF	None	M-Sa
Water Recreation	Isar River	None	Daily
Youth Center	397B/PF	6238	M-F
	398/PF	6259	Tu-Su

NELLINGEN SUB-COMMUNITY (GE79R7)
APO New York 09061-5000

TELEPHONE INFORMATION: Main installation numbers: Civ: 49-0711-3488-113. ETS: 421-113. Civ prefix: 0711-____. ETS prefix: 421-XXXX. Civ to mil prefix: 0711-3488-XXXX. NOTE: See the Stuttgart Community listing for prefix information for Robinson Barracks.

LOCATION: Take the E-52 (8) Autobahn southeast from Stuttgart to Nellingen. HE: p-40, D/4. NMC: Stuttgart, 25 miles northwest.

GENERAL INSTALLATION INFORMATION: Nellingen is a sub-community of the Stuttgart Community. The primary mission of all Stuttgart

170 — U.S. Forces Travel & Transfer Guide Europe

GERMANY
Nellingen Sub-Community, continued

sub-communities is to provide support to Headquarters, VII Corps, located on Kelley Barracks.

GENERAL CITY/REGIONAL INFORMATION: See the Stuttgart Community listing.

ADMINISTRATIVE SUPPORT

FACILITY/ACTIVITY	BLDG NO/LOC	PHONE	DAYS/COMMENTS
Duty Officer	3506	6810/6560	Daily
Fire(Mil)	On Barracks	114/6217	24 hours daily
Housing			
Referral	On Barracks	7002	M-F
Info(Insta)	On Barracks	113	24 hours daily
Locator(Civ)	111/RB	6293	M-F
Personnel Spt	3666	6283/6308	M-F
Police(Mil)	3600	6200/8341	24 hours daily
Emergency	3600	114	24 hours daily
Police(Civ)	Nellingen	C-353066	24 hours daily
Public Affairs	3500	6221/6347	M-F

LOGISTICAL SUPPORT

FACILITY/ACTIVITY	BLDG NO/LOC	PHONE	DAYS/COMMENTS
Auto Drivers Testing	3655	6350	M-F
Inspection	3518	8332	M-F
Auto Registration	3600	6200	M-Th
Auto Rental(Exch)	132/RB	C-852604	M-Sa
Bank	3503	6408/6297	M-F
		C-341849	
Barber Shop(s)	3735	6258	M-F
	3252	C-850273	M-F
Beauty Shop(s)	3735	C-341838	Tu-Sa
Bookstore	3772	6229	M-Sa
Child Care/Dev Ctr	3516	6443	Daily
		C-342788	
Education Center	3633	6441/6291	M-F
	3250	4244	M-F
	3633	6442	M-F
Elec Repair(Gov)	On Barracks	6188	M-F
Elec Repair(Civ)	Nellingen	C-341885	Daily
Eng'r/Publ Works	On Barracks	7109	Daily
		C-341885	
Exchange(Main)	3734	6187	M-Sa
		C-341847	
Finance(Mil)	3693	6115/7119	M-F
Food(Snack/Fast)	Canteen	3734	Daily
		C-342787	
Foodland	3675	C-341856	Daily
Laundry(Self-Svc)	3676	None	Daily
Package Store	3503	6364	Tu-Sa
Pick-up Point	3735	C-341885	M,W-Sa
Postal Svcs(Mil)	3738	6401/7238	M-W
Railroad/RTO	See Stuttgart Community listing.		

GERMANY

Nellingen Sub-Community, continued

Schools(DOD Dep)			
Elementary	N/A	6329/6620	M-F (K-6)
High School	See Stuttgart Community listing.		
Svc Stn(Insta)	3732	6243/5600	Daily
Svc Stn(Autobahn)	N/A	C-342827	Daily
Space-A Air Ops	Echterdingen AAF	2385	Daily
Flights to:	Local German areas		
Tailor Shop	3735	C-341885	Tu-Sa
Taxi(Comm)	Nellingen	C-347516	Daily
Tel Repair(Gov)	On Barracks	119	M-F
Thrift Shop	3730	6346	M-F
TML			
Billeting	On Barracks	6330/6317	Daily

HEALTH AND WELFARE

FACILITY/ACTIVITY	BLDG NO/LOC	PHONE	DAYS/COMMENTS
Ambulance	Nellingen	116	24 hours daily
Army Comm Svcs	3648	6716/6415	M-F
Army Emerg Relief	3648	6415/6716	M-F
Central Appts	HQ Bldg	6323	Daily
CHAMPUS Office	See Stuttgart Community listing.		
Chapel	3649	6379	Daily
Comm Drug/Alc Ctr	3607	6367/6114	M-F
Dental Clinic	3650	6459	M-F
Medical Emergency	3507	116	24 hours daily
Veterinary Svcs	See Stuttgart Community listing.		

REST AND RECREATION

FACILITY/ACTIVITY	BLDG NO/LOC	PHONE	DAYS/COMMENTS
Bowling Lanes	3730	6389	Daily
Craftshops			
Automotive	3518	6590/6284	Tu,F-Su
Multi-crafts	3503	6302/6284	Sa-Th
Photography	3599	6194	Daily
Enlisted Club	3731	6388/6456	M-Sa
Gymnasium	3706	8353	Daily
Info Tour & Travel	3503	6158	M-F
Library	3735	6602/7102	Daily
MARS	3503	6244/7220	Daily
NCO Club	3503	6338	M-Sa
O'Club	3696	6290/6257 C-341820	M-Sa
Recreation Center	3503	7220/6305	Daily
Rod and Gun Club	3766	6416 C-342840	Tu-Su
Theater	3736	6378	Daily
Youth Center	3765	6843/6596	M-Sa

172 — U.S. Forces Travel & Transfer Guide Europe

GERMANY

NEU-ULM COMMUNITY (GE28R7)
APO New York 09035-0509

TELEPHONE INFORMATION: Main installation numbers: Civ: 49-0731-809-113. ETS: 427-113. Civ prefix: 0731-____. ETS prefix: 427-XXXX. Civ to mil prefix: 0731-809-XXXX.

LOCATION: South of the E-8 Munich-Stuttgart Autobahn. Take the Ulm Ost exit south for four miles. HE: p-40, D/4-5. NMC: Stuttgart, 50 miles northwest.

GENERAL INSTALLATION INFORMATION: Neu-Ulm is home to the 2-5 Field Artillery Battalion, as well as the 1-9 Field Artillery Battalion, the 2-4 Infantry Battalion, and the 55th Support Battalion. **Note: the following abbreviations are used in this listing only: NB (Nelson Barracks); OSC (Offenhausen Support Center); VH (Vorfield Housing); WB (Wiley Barracks).**

GENERAL CITY/REGIONAL INFORMATION: The Danube (Donau) River separates Ulm from its younger sister city, Neu-Ulm. This geopolitical division has little meaning for the proud residents of the area. Ulm is home of the cathedral with the world's tallest spire; it is also the site of the renowned "crooked house," an enchanting dwelling whose thick beams have become bent and worn with weight, time, and weather. The location of Neu-Ulm provides quick access to the ski slopes of Germany, Austria, and Switzerland, and to the beaches of the Italian and French coasts. Visitors can enjoy sights, lively festivals, peaceful strolls, and delicious local cuisine and wines. Neu-Ulm is a wonderful blend of old and new.

ADMINISTRATIVE SUPPORT

FACILITY/ACTIVITY	BLDG NO/LOC	PHONE	DAYS/COMMENTS
Customs/Duty	304/NB	6559	M-F
Duty Officer	304/NB	6647	M-F
Fire(Mil)	All locations	117 C-82278	24 hours daily
Fire(Civ)	Neu-Ulm	112	24 hours daily
Housing			
Family	5/Baumgarten St	6212/6538	M-F
Referral	5/Baumgarten St	6317	M-F
Info(Insta)	N/A	113 C-118/1188	24 hours daily
Legal Assist	304/NB	6404/6264	M-F
Personnel Spt	207/WB	6228/6401	M-F
Police(Mil)	304/NB	6648	M-F
Emergency	304/NB	114 C-722818	24 hours daily
Police(Civ)	Neu-Ulm	110	24 hours daily
Public Affairs	131/OSC	6523	M-F
Tax Relief	335/WB	C-722822	M-F

LOGISTICAL SUPPORT

FACILITY/ACTIVITY	BLDG NO/LOC	PHONE	DAYS/COMMENTS
Audio/Photo Ctr	235/WB	6243	M-Sa

GERMANY

Neu-Ulm Community, continued

Auto Drivers Testing	213/WB	6305	M-F
Auto Parts(Exch)	OSC	C-78964	M-Sa
Auto Registration	304/NB	6648	M-F
Auto Rent(Other)	Neu-Ulm	C-84166	M-F
Auto Repairs	OSC	C-78964	M-Sa
Auto Sales	WB	C-82820	N/A
Auto Ship(Gov)	132/OSC	6465	M-F
Bank	335/WB	6488/6188 C-77022	M-Sa
Barber Shop(s)	309/NB	None	M-F
	309/NB	6208	Tu-Sa
	235/WB	C-82344	Tu-Sa
Beauty Shop(s)	235/WB	C-82344	Tu-Sa
Bookstore	272/WB	C-82877	Daily
Bus	132/OSC	6611	M-F
Child Care/Dev Ctr	387/VH	C-78310	M-F
	WB	C-77752	M-F
	250/WB	6265 C-82822	M-F. Nursery.
Clothing Sales	309/NB	C-79597/ 77162	M-Sa
Commissary(Main)	132/OSC	6618 C-73883	M-Sa
Credit Union	335/WB	6310 C-76709	M-F
Dining Facility	WB	6494	Daily
Dry Clean(Gov)	NB	6303	M-F
	213/WB	6285	M-F
Education Center			
Learning Center	213/WB	6409/6589	M-F
Elec Repair(Gov)	131/OSC	6415	M-F
Eng'r/Publ Works	131/OSC	6540/6415	M-F
	208/WB	115	After hours
Exchange(Main)	235/WB	6243 C-82344	M-Sa
Exchange(Annex)	209/NB	C-76624	M-Sa
	309/NB	None	Tu-Sa
Finance(Mil)	207/WB	6514/6251	M-F
Food(Caf/Rest)	WB	C-85799	Daily
Food(Snack/Fast)	309/NB	None	Daily
Baskin Robbins	235/WB	N/A	M-Sa
Burger King	WB	6243	Daily
Foodland	335/WB	C-73401	Daily
Laundry(Self-Svc)	235/WB	None	Daily
Motor Pool	OSC	6405	M-F
Package Store	308/NB	6579	Tu-Sa
Photo Laboratory	235/WB	6217	Daily
Pick-up Point	WB	6285	Tu-Sa
Postal Svcs(Mil)	207/WB	6223/6510	M-F
Postal Svcs(Civ)	235/WB	C-86948	M-F
Railroad/RTO	132/OSC	6546/6465	M-F
SATO-OS	235/WB	C-77975	M-F
Schools(DOD Dep)			
Elementary & HS	359/VH	6294/7144	M-F (K-12)
Elementary	Laupheim	C-07392-6031	M-F (K-6)

GERMANY
Neu-Ulm Community, continued

Elementary	Leipheim	C-08221-7897	M-F (K-6)
Svc Stn(Insta)	N/A	6207	M-Sa
		C-75582	
Svc Stn(Autobahn)	Leipheim	C-08821-7814	Daily
Tailor Shop	235/WB	None	M-Sa
Taxi(Comm)	132/OSC	6611	M-F
Tel Booking Oper	N/A	112	24 hours daily
Tel Repair(Gov)	N/A	119	N/A
		C-117/1171	
Tel Repair(Civ)	208/WB	6457	Tu,F
Thrift Shop	335/WB	6457	Tu,F
TML			
Billeting	Donau Club	C-74071	Daily
BEQ	236/WB	6336	Daily
BOQ	237/WB	6267	Daily
Guest House	Donau Club	C-74071	Daily
Travel Agents	WB	6448	Daily

HEALTH AND WELFARE

FACILITY/ACTIVITY	BLDG NO/LOC	PHONE	DAYS/COMMENTS
Ambulance	German Red Cross	C-77067	24 hours daily
Army Comm Svcs	208/WB	6206/6771	M-F
Army Emerg Relief	WB	6707/6206	N/A
Central Appts	238/WB	6241/6511	M-F
CHAMPUS Office	238/WB	6511	M-F
Chaplain	233/WB	6407	N/A
Chapel	233/WB	6407/6408	M-F
Comm Drug/Alc Ctr	208/WB	6520/6229	M-F
Dental Clinic	237/WB	6322/6633	Tu,F
		6631	Emergency
Medical Emergency	Adults go to the military hospital in Augsburg or the civilian hospital in Neu-Ulm. Take children to the Universitatsklinik in Safranberg.		
	Neu-Ulm	116	24 hours daily
		C-78528	
Mental Health	238/WB	6631/6241	M-F
Poison Control	238/WB	114	24 hours daily
Red Cross	208/WB	6653/6203	M-F
		434-1110	After hours
Veterinary Svcs	214/WB	None	Th

REST AND RECREATION

FACILITY/ACTIVITY	BLDG NO/LOC	PHONE	DAYS/COMMENTS
Bowling Lanes	207/WB	6402	Daily
Craftshops			
Automotive	308/WB	6297	F-Tu
Multi-crafts	235/WB	6312/6323	M-W,Sa,Su
Photography	235/WB	6312/6323	M,Th-Su
Enlisted Club	307/NB	6492	Daily
		C-78188	
	234/WB	6270	M-Sa
		C-82861	
Gymnasium	305/NB	6224	Daily

GERMANY

Neu-Ulm Community, continued

	264/WB	6495	Daily
Info Tour & Travel	235/WB	C-84166/	N/A
		82850/83877	
Library	335/WB	6566	M-Th,Sa,Su
MARS	235/WB	6210	Daily
NCO Club	307/NB	6492	Daily
		C-78188	
	234/WB	6270	M-Sa
		C-82861	
O'Club	Augsburger Stq	C-74071	Tu-Sa
Outdoor Rec Ctr	220/WB	6261	N/A
		C-82649	
Picnic/Park Area	NB/WB	6323	M-F
Racket Courts	NB/WB	6323	M-F
Recreation Center	235/WB	6312	Daily
Rod and Gun Club	220/WB	C-84497	Daily
Sport Field	NB/WB	6323	M-F
Tennis Courts	WB	6323	M-F
Theater	214/WB	6498	Call for hours.
Track	WB	6323	M-F
Video Rental	335/VH	C-73401	M-Sa
Youth Center	210/WB	C-74508	Daily
	Ford	C-56560	M-Sa
	Leipheim	None	M-Sa

===

NÜRNBERG/FÜRTH COMMUNITY (GE44R7)
APO New York 09696-5000

TELEPHONE INFORMATION: Main installation numbers: Civ: 49-0911-700-113 (William O. Darby Kaserne, Nürnberg, Fürth, Johnson Barracks, Dambach Barracks, Kalb Community, Pastorius Housing Area); 49-0911-4509-113 (Merrell Barracks); 49-0911-7380-113 (Monteith Barracks); 49-0911-6999-XXX (Pinder Barracks); 49-0911-653-113 (Hospital). ETS: 460-113 (William O. Darby Kaserne, et. al.); 460-5113 (Merrell Barracks); 460-4113 (Monteith Barracks); 460-3113 (Pinder Barracks); 461-113 (Hospital). Civ prefix: 0911-__ (William O. Darby Kaserne, et. al., and Hospital); 0911-___(Merrell Barracks, Monteith Barracks, and Pinder Barracks). ETS prefix: 460-XXXX (William O. Darby Kaserne, et. al.); 460-5XXX (Merrell Barracks); 460-4XXX (Monteith Barracks); 460-3XXX (Pinder Barracks); 461-XXXX (Hospital). Civ to mil prefix: 0911-700-XXXX (William O. Darby Kaserne, et. al.); 0911-4509-XXX (Merrell Barracks); 0911-7380-XXX (Monteith Barracks); 0911-6999-XXX (Pinder Barracks); 0911-653-XXXX (Hospital).

LOCATION: Access from Autobahns E-3 (East-West), E-6 (East-West), and E-9 (North-South). Also from GE-2 and -4 (North-South) and GE-8 and -14 (East-West). HE: p-40, F/2. NMC: Nürnberg, in the city.

GENERAL INSTALLATION INFORMATION: The Nürnberg Military Community includes four sub-communities and five installations. The headquarters for the community is in the city of Fürth. One of the key functions of the community headquarters is to provide the morale, welfare, and supporting activities to military personnel and family members in the community. The community commander is a brigadier general who is also the 1st Armored Division's Assistant Division Commander. The four sub-

GERMANY
Nürnberg/Fürth Community, continued

communities are located in the cities of Erlangen, Herzogenaurach, Zirndorf, and Schwabach. Erlangen, Herzogenaurach (Herzo Base), and Schwabach are each listed separately elsewhere in this book.

The U.S. Army Hospital, the Bavarian American Hotel transient facility, and Merrell Barracks are located within Nürnberg. William O. Darby Kaserne, the Kalb Community, and Johnson Barracks are located within the adjacent city of Fürth. Pinder Barracks is located in the nearby city of Zirndorf just west of Fürth. The Dambach Housing Area is also located west of Fürth. Monteith Barracks is located a short drive north of Pinder Barracks.

The mission of the Nürnberg-Fürth Community is to provide administrative support to all military units, military and civil agencies, and authorized individuals in or outside the geographical area of jurisdiction as directed, and to perform assigned responsibilities pertaining to the security of installations, non-combatant evacuation and emergency plans. **Note: the following abbreviations are used in this listing only: DK (William O. Darby Kaserne); JB (Johnson Barracks); KC (Kalb Community); MB (Merrell Barracks); MTB (Monteith Barracks); PB (Pinder Barracks); PHA (Pastorius Housing Area).**

GENERAL CITY/REGIONAL INFORMATION: Nürnberg is a lovely combination of ancient and modern culture. Parts of the city resemble a medieval town with its Gothic churches, burghers houses, the Imperial Castle, and the wall that rings the inner city. Outside that wall, however, is a city of glass and concrete buildings, busy streets, and bustling shopping areas. The city offers a number of museums, art galleries, parks, gardens, and markets. The annual "Christkindlesmarkt," Germany's finest Christmas fair, attracts tourists from all over the world from late November through Christmas Eve. The countryside around Nürnberg is equally delightful, with many castles and palaces, woods, valleys, and vineyards.

ADMINISTRATIVE SUPPORT

FACILITY/ACTIVITY	BLDG NO/LOC	PHONE	DAYS/COMMENTS
Customs/Duty	89/DK	6594	M-F
Duty Officer	1/DK	8306	24 hours daily
Fire(Mil)	All locations	117	24 hours daily
Fire(Civ)	All locations	112	24 hours daily
Housing	Nürnberg/Fürth	7067/6572	M-F
Referral	79/DK	6692/6683	M-F
Info(Insta)	All locations	113	24 hours daily
Inspector Gen'l	1/DK	7304	M-F
	564B/MB	813	M-F
	315/MTB	616	457
	352/PB	810	M-F
	457/Hospital	5822	M-F
Legal Assist	14/DK	6496/7420	M-F
Locator(Mil)	942/Fürth	6619	Daily
Locator(Civ)	DK	6554	Daily
Personnel Spt	DK	6804	M-F
Police(Mil)	DK	6600/6647	24 hours daily
Emergency	All locations	114	24 hours daily
Police(Civ)	All locations	110	24 hours daily
Public Affairs	16/DK	6877 C-718848	M-F

Nürnberg/Fürth Community, continued

GERMANY

Tax Relief	905/JB	6848	M-F
	564A/MB	852	M-F
	260/MTB	860	M-F
	352/PB	820	M-F
	Hospital	5998	M-F

LOGISTICAL SUPPORT

FACILITY/ACTIVITY	BLDG NO/LOC	PHONE	DAYS/COMMENTS
Audio/Photo Ctr	Fürth	C-707042/ 708171	M-Sa
Auto Drivers Testing	67/DK	7005/6835	M,Tu,Th
Auto Parts(Exch)	1415/KC	C-712293	Daily
Auto Registration	87/DK	6409	M-F
Auto Rental(Exch)	Fürth	C-711616	M-Sa
Auto Repairs	1415/KC	C-711844	M-F
Auto Sales	Fürth	C-707696	
Auto Ship(Gov)	31/DK	C-711616	M-Sa
Bank	100/Fürth	C-78780	M-Sa
	564/MB	C-441027	M-Sa
	293/MTB	C-735322	M-F
	361/PB	695	M-F
	Hospital	C-612456	M-Sa
Barber Shop(s)	36/DK	N/A	M-F
	100/Fürth	Call Beauty Shop	Tu-Sa
	905/JB	Call PX	M-F
	MB	Call PX	M-Sa
	MTB	681	M-Sa
	354/PB	None	M-F
	Hospital	C-612404	M-Sa
Beauty Shop(s)	Fürth	C-705011	Tu-Sa
Bookstore	36/DK	6830	Su-F
	100/Fürth	C-705180	Daily
	584/MB	666	M,W-Sa
	293/MTB	681	M-F
	361/PB	None	M-F
	457/Hospital	None	M-Sa
Child Care/Dev Ctr	90/DK	6574	M-F
	95/Fürth	7146	M-F
	601/PHA	C-405819	M-F
Clothing Sales	121/Fürth	C-712784	Tu-Sa
	69/DK	6549	M-F
Commissary(Main)	100/Fürth	6670/7243	Daily
Credit Union	F16/DK	6868 C-71635	M-F
Dining Facility	DK	6548	Daily
Dry Clean(Exch)	13/DK	None	M-F
	324/MTB	N/A	M-F
Education Center	43/DK	7183/6851	M-F
	907/JB	6656	M-F
	551A/MB	830/655	M-F
	293/MTB	613/664	M-F
	354/PB	616/862	M-F
	465/Hospital	5948	M-F
Learning Center	43/DK	6633	M-F

GERMANY
Nürnberg/Fürth Community, continued

	907/JB	6656	M-F
	551A/MB	765	M-F
	293/MTB	625	M-F
	354/PB	602	M-F
	465/Hospital	5384	M-F
Eng'r/Publ Works	All locations	115	24 hours daily
Exchange(Main)	100/Fürth	C-78790	Daily
Exchange(Annex)	31/DK	C-711810	M-F
	905/JB	C-713238	M-F
	564/MB	C-441028	M,W,Sa
	361/PB	C-601483	M-Sa
	457G/Hospital	C-613169	M-F
Finance(Mil)	65/DK	7357	M-F
Food(Caf/Rest)	36/DK	C-711877	Daily
	JB	C-713172	Daily
	MB	C-449172	Daily
	MTB	C-757890	Daily
	361/PB	C-606607	Daily

==

Food(Snack/Fast)	457G/Hospital	C-613169	M-F
Baskin Robbins	100/Fürth	C-706058	Daily
Burger Bar	100/Fürth	C-706841	Daily
Foodland	265/KC	C-713383	Daily
	564/MB	C-441028	M,W-Sa
	604/PHA	C-405706	M,W-Sa
Laundry(Self-Svc)	1512/Fürth	C-705230	Daily
	560B/MB	C-705230	24 hours daily
	MTB	C-705230	24 hours daily
	361/PB	C-705230	Daily
Motor Pool	DK	7174/6887	M-Sa
Package Store	101/Fürth	6824	Tu-Sa
Pick-up Point	13/DK	None	M-F
	100/Fürth	C-706590	M-Sa
	905/JB	C-711221	M-F
	561/MB	C-445506	M-F
	293/MTB	681	M-F
	361/PB	C-601483	M-F
	457G/Hospital	C-612404	M-F

==

Postal Svcs(Mil)	Fürth Shop Center	6553	M-F
	MB	777	M-F
	MTB	627	M-F
	954/PB	682	M-F
	Hospital	5695	M-F
Postal Svcs(Civ)	71 Herren St/Fürth	C-7790425	M-F
SATO-OS	79/DK	7705630	M-F
Schools(DOD Dep)			
Elementary	JFK St/KC	7029/6852	M-F
	JFK St/Nürnberg	6500/7034	M-F
	PHA	C-401167	M-F
High School	1444 Fronmüller St/Nürnberg	7055/7075	M-F
Svc Stn(Insta)	1415/KC	C-712874	Daily
	2031/MB	C-712874	Daily
Space-A Air Ops	Nürnberg Airport	N/A	Daily
	Feucht AAF	461-4660/808	Daily

U.S. Forces Travel & Transfer Guide Europe — 179

GERMANY

Nürnberg/Fürth Community, continued

Flights to:	Ramstein AB GE;	Rhein-Main AB GE.	
Tailor Shop	13/DK	N/A	M-F
	905/JB	C-711221	M,Tu,Th,F
	561/MB	C-445503	M-F
	361/PB	None	M-F
	293/MTB	681	M,Tu,Th,F
Taxi(Comm)	All locations	C-777991	Daily
Tel Booking Oper	Nürnberg	112	24 hours daily
Tel Repair(Gov)	Nürnberg	119	M-F
Tel Repair(Civ)	Nürnberg, Fürth	1171	N/A
Thrift Shop	100/Fürth	6880	W,F
TML			
Billeting	3 Bahnhof St/	6632	24 hours daily
	Nürnberg	C-23440	
	DK	6888	Daily
Hotel	Bavarian Ameri-	6632	24 hours daily
	can Hotel	C-23440	
Travel Agents	Main PX/Fürth	C-78156/7	M-Sa

==
HEALTH AND WELFARE
==

FACILITY/ACTIVITY	BLDG NO/LOC	PHONE	DAYS/COMMENTS
Ambulance	All locations	116	24 hours daily
Army Comm Svcs	90/DK	6781/7060	M-F
	551A/MB	756/897	M-F
Army Emerg Relief	90/DK	6468	M-F
Central Appts	Nürnberg	5600/1/2/3	M-F
		C-615477/8	
	36/PB	615/835	M-F
CHAMPUS Office	457/DK	5924	M-F
Chaplain	32/DK	7407/6698	Daily
Chapel	32/DK	7091/6792	Daily
	43/DK	7090	Daily
	MB	841/695	Daily
	MTB	832	Daily
	354/PB	675/812	Daily
Comm Drug/Alc Ctr	21/DK	7344/6530	M-F
	558/MB	648/801	M-F
	306/MTB	841/673	M-F
	360/PB	664/694	M-F
Dental Clinic	1414/Fürth	6406/7162	M-F
	Children's Hospital		
	305/PB	684	M-F
	454/Hospital	5652	M-F
Medical Emergency	Fürth	5951/5952	Daily
Red Cross	67/DK	7141/6555	M-F
	457/Hospital	5656	M-F
Veterinary Svcs	469/DK	5686/5992	M-F

==
REST AND RECREATION
==

FACILITY/ACTIVITY	BLDG NO/LOC	PHONE	DAYS/COMMENTS
Amer Forces Ntwk	All locations	7409/7123	Daily
Bowling Lanes	30/DK	6535	Daily
	558B/MB	603	Daily

GERMANY
Nürnberg/Fürth Community, continued

	257/MTB	624	Daily
	361/PB		
Craftshops			
Automotive	DK	6766	
	351/MB	651	F-Tu
	316/MTB	652	Tu-Su
	359/PB	671	Th-M
Multi-crafts	551/MB	651	F-Tu
	Nürnberg	7114	Daily
Photography	551/MB	651	F-Tu
	361/PB	620	Th-M
Wood	Nürnberg	7114	Daily
Enlisted Club	DK	6668	Tu-Su
	JB	C-713141	Daily
	MB	634	Tu-Su
	MTB	634	Tu-Su
	PB	677	Daily
	Hospital	C-612266	Tu-Su
Golf Course	MTB	621	Daily
Gymnasium	DK	6742	Daily
	MB	688	Daily
	MTB	676	Daily
	384/PB	635	Daily

Info Tour & Travel	Main PX/Fürth	7138	M-Sa
Library	561/MB	649	Su-Th
	293/MTB	880	M-F
	354/PB	696	Su-Th
	457A/Hospital	5657	M-F
NCO Club	KC	6589	Tu-Su
	PHA	640	Tu-Su
O'Club	KC	6589	Daily
	PHA	640	Tu-Su
Racket Courts	47/DK	None	Daily
	For MB and MTB see gymnasium.		
Recreation Center	11/DK	7187	Daily
	905/JB	7425	Daily
	551B/MB	870	Daily
	261/MTB	660	Sa-Th
	361/PB	827	Daily
Rod and Gun Club	54/DK	7169/6626	M,Tu,Th-Su
Sport Field	893/MB	None	M-F
Swimming Pool	DK	None	Seasonal
Tennis Courts	47/MB	None	Daily
	Outside gym/PB	635	Daily
Theater	1416/KC	N/A	Sa-Th
	564A/MB	N/A	Tu-Th,Sa,Su
	259/MTB	N/A	M,W,F-Su
	385/PB	None	W-Su
	1444/Nürnberg	7370	M-F
Video Rental	361/PB	C-601267	Tu-Sa
Youth Center	MB	890	Tu-Sa
	603/PHA	N/A	N/A

U.S. Forces Travel & Transfer Guide Europe — 181

GERMANY
PIRMASENS COMMUNITY (GE42R7)
APO New York 09189-5000

TELEPHONE INFORMATION: Main installation numbers: Civ: 49-06331-86-113. ETS: 495-113. ATVN: 495-1110 (ask for Pirmasens). Civ prefix: 06331-___ (Pirmasens); 06395-___ (Münchweiler); 06393-___ (Fischbach). ETS prefix: 495-XXXX (Pirmasens); 495-3XXX (Münchweiler); 495-4XXX (Fischbach). Civ to mil prefix: 06331-86-XXXX (Pirmasens); 06395-401-XXX (Münchweiler); 06393-801-XXX (Fischbach).

LOCATION: On the triangle of GE-10 from Zweibrücken and GE-270 from Kaiserslautern. HE: p-39, G/2. NMC: Pirmasens, 1 mile southeast.

GENERAL INSTALLATION INFORMATION: The primary mission of Pirmasens Community is to provide general support with emphasis on REFORGER stocks and ordnance operations. In addition to the main community installation, Husterhöh Kaserne, two sub-communities, Münchweiler and Fischbach, are located nearby. The US Army Health Clinic as well as two ordnance battalion headquarters are located on Münchweiler; an ammunition storage facility and a number of other smaller units are located at Fischbach. Note: the following abbreviations are used in this listing only: FB (Fischbach); MW (Münchweiler); PM (Pirmasens, Husterhöh Kaserne).

GENERAL CITY/REGIONAL INFORMATION: Pirmasens is built atop seven hills and affords visitors some spectacular views of surrounding valleys and slopes. Its location near the French border makes it an ideal home base for travels throughout Europe.

The city traces its origins back to the 8th century. Its modern history began in 1720 when the Count Johann Reinhard III built a hunting lodge there. Later his son, Ludwig IX, developed a private army in the town. When Ludwig died, the people of the town found themselves poverty stricken and began to make shoes from old bits of cloth and leather. This was the foundation of the shoe-making industry in Pirmasens. For decades, the city has been known as the shoe-manufacturing capital of Germany and 90 shoe factories are now located within the city limits.

Today Pirmasens is a lovely city with a population of 60,000. It has many fine restaurants, ample recreational facilities, a modern theater and, not surprisingly, a boot and shoe museum.

ADMINISTRATIVE SUPPORT

FACILITY/ACTIVITY	BLDG NO/LOC	PHONE	DAYS/COMMENTS
Customs/Duty	4405/PM	6541	M-F
Duty Officer	4617/PM	6442	24 hours daily
Fire(Mil)	4604/PM	117	24 hours daily
Fire(Civ)	Pirmasens	112	24 hours daily
Housing			
Family	4624/PM	7165/6148	M-F
Unaccompanied	5437/PM	6535/7393	M-F
Referral	4624/PM	6516/7203	M-F
	7132/FB	728/878	M-F
Info(Insta)	On Barracks	113	Daily
Inspector Gen'l	4408/PM	6402/7331	M-F

GERMANY
Pirmasens Community, continued

Legal Assist	4406/PM	7223/6132	M,Tu,Th,F
Personnel Spt	4617/PM	7117	M-F. ID.
	4617/PM	6442/7387	M-F. Visitor passes.
Police(Mil)	4620/PM	7311	24 hours daily
Emergency		114	24 hours daily
Police(Civ)		110	24 hours daily
Public Affairs	4617/PM	6133	M-F
Tax Relief	4617/PM	6110	M-F

LOGISTICAL SUPPORT

FACILITY/ACTIVITY	BLDG NO/LOC	PHONE	DAYS/COMMENTS
Auto Drivers Testing	4624/PM	6365	M-F
Auto Parts(Exch)	4554/PM	C-64895	M-Sa
Auto Registration	4618/PM	7277	M-F
Auto Repairs	4554/PM	C-64895	M-F
Auto Sales	4525/PM	C-64525	M-Sa
		C-64525	
Bank	4602/PM	7142	M-Sa
		C-64884	
Barber Shop(s)	4525/PM	6515	Tu-Sa
	4611/PM	6502	M-F
	7123/FB	None	M-F
	4322/MW	327	M-W,F,Sa
Beauty Shop(s)	4525/PM	6515	Tu-Sa
Bookstore	4611/PM	6050	M-F
		C-99561	
	4525A/PM	6050	Daily
	2123/FB	None	M-W,F,Sa
	PM	6529	Su-F
Child Care/Dev Ctr	4539/PM	6560/6113	M-Sa
		C-63160	
	4624/PM	7202	M-Sa
	4308/MW	621	M-F
		C-8308	
	4320/MW	652	M-F
Clothing Sales	4602/PM	7321/7231	M-F
Commissary(Main)	4525/PM	6241	M-Sa
Commissary(Annex)	7123/FB	716	M-Sa
Credit Union	4602/PM	6566	M-F
Dining Facility	4611/PM	6574	Daily
Dry Clean(Exch)	4602/PM	6254	Tu-Sa
Education Center	4600/PM	7198/6457	M-F
Elec Repair(Gov)	4548/PM	C-99641	Tu-Sa
Eng'r/Publ Works	4656/PM	6295	M-F
	4656/PM	115	After hours
Exchange(Main)	4525/PM	7363	Daily
		C-63006	
Exchange(Annex)	4613/PM	C-65756	M,Th,F
	7113/FB	373	M-W,F,Sa
	4322/MW	327	M,W,F,Sa
Finance(Mil)	4617/PM	7368	M-F
Food(Snack/Fast)	4614/PM	C-65757	Daily
Baskin Robbins	4547/PM	C-64501	Daily
Pizza Parlor	4614/PM	6266	Daily
	4322/MW	327	M-F

Pirmasens Community, continued

GERMANY

Snack Bar	4525/PM	C-65757	M-Sa
	4322/MW	327	M-F
Foodland	4638/PM	C-12592	F-W
Laundry(Exch)	See Pick-up Points		
Laundry(Self-Svc)	4601/PM	None	24 hours daily
	7123/FB	None	24 hours daily
Package Store	4602/PM	6534	Tu-Sa
Photo Laboratory	4612/PM	6128	Tu-Sa
Pick-up Point	4602/PM	None	Tu-Sa
	7123/FB	None	Tu-Sa
Postal Svcs(Mil)	4634/PM	6164	M-F
	7128/FB	None	M,T,Th,F
	4310/MW	None	M,W,F
Schools(DOD Dep)			
Elementary	4528/PM	6440	M-F
High School	See Zweibrücken Air Base listing.		
Space-A Air Ops	See Ramstein Air Base listing.		
Svc Stn(Insta)	4554/PM	C-62863	Daily
Tailor Shop	4602/PM	None	Tu-Sa
Tel Booking Oper	All locations	112	M-F
Tel Repair(Gov)	All locations	119	M-F
Tel Repair(Civ)	PM	C-01171	M-F
Thrift Shop	4624/PM	6119	M,W,F
TML			
Billeting	4537/PM	6535/7393	M-F
	4617/PM SDO	6442	Sa,Su
BEQ	MW	611	Daily
BOQ	4536,4537/PM	6536/6537	Daily
Guest House	4535,4536/PM	6535/7393	Daily
DV/VIP	4617/PM	7383	M-F
Watch Repair	See Pick-up Points		

HEALTH AND WELFARE

FACILITY/ACTIVITY	BLDG NO/LOC	PHONE	DAYS/COMMENTS
Ambulance	All locations	116/620	Duty hours
Army Comm Svcs	4624/PM	6444/6528	M-F
Army Emerg Relief	4624/PM	6444/7172	M-F
Central Appts	821MW	625/821 C-7204	M-F
CHAMPUS Office	Landstuhl Army Reg. Med. Center	480-2223	M-F
Chaplain	4540PM On call through SDNCO.	6107/7491	M-F
Chapel	4540/PM	6107/7491	M-F
	MW	705	M-F
	FB	855	M-F
Comm Drug/Alc Ctr	4624/PM	6422/7176	M-F
Dental Clinic	4616/PM	7217	M-F
	821/MW	701	M-F
Medical Emergency	Pirmasens	C-75021	Daily
For children	Kinder Clinic	C-73071	Daily
Poison Control	4620/Landstuhl	480-8160 C-06395-86-8160	24 hours daily
Red Cross	4624/PM	6380/7360	M-F

GERMANY
Pirmasens Community, continued

	Emergency	6442	After hours

REST AND RECREATION

FACILITY/ACTIVITY	BLDG NO/LOC	PHONE	DAYS/COMMENTS
Bowling Lanes	4400/PM	6533	Daily
	7131/FB	747	Su-F
Craftshops			
Automotive	4647/PM	6558	Tu-Su
	7152/FB	751826	W-Su
Multi-crafts	4614/PM	6552	Tu-Su
	4307/MW	666	W-Su
Photography	4614/PM	6128	Tu-Sa
Gymnasium	4673/PM	6180	Daily
	4672/PM	6372	Daily
	7152/FB	775/751	Daily
Info Tour & Travel	4612/PM	6387	M-F
Library	4612/PM	6237/7387	Tu-Sa
	7122/FB	805/732	M-F
MARS	4611/PM	6226	M-F
NCO/EM Club	4546/PM	6530	Su-F
	7113/FB	702/373	M-F
	4333/MW	613	Daily
O'Club	4538/PM	6520	Tu-Sa
Outdoor Rec Ctr	4405/PM	6483	M-F
Recreation Center	4612/PM	7287	Daily
Theater	4532/PM	6510/6205	Limited
	4673/PM	6205	Daily
	FB	711	Limited
	MW	646	Limited
Video Rental	4548/PM	N/A	Daily
Youth Center	4544A/PM	7210	Tu-Sa
	4343/MW	648	Tu-Sa

PRÜM AIR STATION (GE95R7)
APO New York 09652-5000

TELEPHONE INFORMATION: Main installation numbers: Civ: 49-06552-79-705. ATVN/ETS: 455-1110. Civ prefix: 06552-____. ATVN/ETS prefix: 455-3XXX. Civ to mil prefix: 06552-79-XXX.

LOCATION: Take GE-51 north from Bitburg or exit from the 60 Autobahn to GE-51 north. Follow U.S. Forces signs to the installation. HE: p-36, A/6. NMC: Bonn, 25 miles northeast.

GENERAL INSTALLATION INFORMATION: Prüm Air Station is a communications/radar installation controlled by the Air Force.

GENERAL CITY/REGIONAL INFORMATION: Prüm is located in the Eifel Mountains region, 12 miles east of the French border.

Prüm Air Station, continued

GERMANY

ADMINISTRATIVE SUPPORT

FACILITY/ACTIVITY	BLDG NO/LOC	PHONE	DAYS/COMMENTS
Personnel Spt	See Bitburg Air Base listing.		
Police(Mil)	On the Station	742	24 hours daily
Emergency	On the Station	114	24 hours daily
Public Affairs	2612	749	M-F

LOGISTICAL SUPPORT

FACILITY/ACTIVITY	BLDG NO/LOC	PHONE	DAYS/COMMENTS
Commissary(Annex)	See Bitburg Air Base listing.		
Dining Facility	On the Station	679	Daily
Exchange(Annex)	On the Station	667	N/A
Schools(DOD Dep)	See Bitburg Air Base listing.		

HEALTH AND WELFARE

FACILITY/ACTIVITY	BLDG NO/LOC	PHONE	DAYS/COMMENTS
Ambulance	N/A	116	24 hours daily
Chaplain	On the Station	680	Daily

REST AND RECREATION

FACILITY/ACTIVITY	BLDG NO/LOC	PHONE	DAYS/COMMENTS
Gymnasium	On the Station	605	Daily
Racket Courts	See Gymnasium.		
Youth Center	See Bitburg Air Base listing.		

RAMSTEIN AIR BASE (GE24R7)
APO New York 09094-5000

TELEPHONE INFORMATION: Main installation numbers: Civ: 49-06371-47-1110. ATVN/ETS: 480-1110. Civ prefix: 06371-____. ATVN/ETS prefix: 480-XXXX. Civ to mil prefix: 06371-47-XXXX.

LOCATION: Adjacent to Autobahn 6 (Saarbruken-Mannheim). Take the Flugplatz Ramstein exit. East and west gates are within two miles of exit. HE: p-39, G/2. NMC: Kaiserslautern, 10 miles east.

GENERAL INSTALLATION INFORMATION: The host unit of Ramstein Air Base and the Kaiserslautern Military Community is the 316th Air Division. The 86th Tactical Fighter Wing handles the air division's operational mission: to prepare for and maintain the capability to destroy enemy forces, both air and ground, through use of assigned tactical forces as directed for the support of NATO. The tactical flying units are the 512th and 526th Tactical Fighter Squadrons. Both squadrons are equipped with the F-16C/D Fighting Falcon. The air division's 377th Combat Support Wing provides administrative, security, civil engineering and logistical support for the

GERMANY
Ramstein Air Base, continued

Kaiserslautern Military Community, the only Air Force-run community outside the continental United States. It has more than 50 additional outlying units throughout Europe. Associate units include: SAC's 7th Air Div; MAC's 322nd Airlift Division; AFCC's 1964th Communications Group; HQ AFCOMS-Europe; and ATC's Field Training Detachment 906.

GENERAL CITY/REGIONAL INFORMATION: Kaiserslautern is located in the southwestern German state of Rhein-Pfalz and has a population of 110,000. The countryside is mostly flat or rolling hills. Evergreen forests cover more than one-fourth of the country and strips of cultivated land give the surrounding area a patchwork appearance. World War II changed the face of Kaiserslautern as more than 60 per cent of the city was destroyed. As a result, large portions of the city have been rebuilt and relatively few buildings of historical significance have endured. The Stiftskirche in the center of the city is the oldest church hall and the most important Gothic structure in the area. The Theodore Zink Museum houses a rich collection of folk art and artifacts from the region. The city museum (Pfalzische Landesgewerbeanstalt) exhibits a variety of textiles, porcelain, glass, and sacred art. Landstuhl, a nearby town, offers a number of well preserved old churches, houses, and buildings; particularly popular is the Nanstein Castle, built in the late twelfth century.

ADMINISTRATIVE SUPPORT

FACILITY/ACTIVITY	BLDG NO/LOC	PHONE	DAYS/COMMENTS
Customs/Duty	2202	5809	Daily
Fire(Mil)	1124	117	24 hours daily
Fire(Civ)	N/A	112	24 hours daily
Housing	305	2084	M-F
Inspector Gen'l	2201	2457	M-F
Legal Assist	2137	5911	M-F
Locator(Mil and and Civ)	426 2122	6120 6989	M-F After duty hours
Personnel Spt	2401	5719	M-F
Police(Mil) Emergency	2371	2050 5323	24 hours daily 24 hours daily
Police(Civ)	N/A	110	24 hours daily
Public Affairs	2201	5914	M-F
Tax Relief	2119	5309	M-F

LOGISTICAL SUPPORT

FACILITY/ACTIVITY	BLDG NO/LOC	PHONE	DAYS/COMMENTS
Audio-Photo Center	2113	C-42406 5428	Tu-Sa
Auto Drivers Testing	2406	2394	M-F
Auto Parts(Exch)	2136	5837/5666	M-Sa
Auto Registration	2121	2108	M-F
Auto Rental(Exch)	1202	6281	M-Sa
Auto Repairs	2136	5666	M-Sa
Auto Sales	1101	6879	Call for hours.
Auto Shipping	2406	2163	M-F
Bakery	1101	C-42466	Call for hours.
Bank	1101	6509	M-Sa

U.S. Forces Travel & Transfer Guide Europe — 187

GERMANY

Ramstein Air Base, continued

	2163	2390	M-F
Barber Shop(s)	2411	5638	M-Sa
	2162	5673	M-Sa
	1101	C-42408	M-Sa
Beauty Shop(s)	1101	6040	M-Sa
Bookstore	1100	6878	Daily
	201	N/A	M-F
Bus	1404	5961	24 hours daily
Child Care/Dev Ctr	800	7873/6011	Daily
Clothing Sales	2140	2273	M-F
Commissary(Main)	1200	6195/6712	24 hours daily
Credit Union	2410	5656/5556	M-F
Dining Facility	411	6162	M-F
	2107	5750	Daily
Dry Clean(Exch)	408	C-42750	M-Sa
	723	C-42409	M-Sa
Dry Clean(Gov)	2171	5704	M-F

===

Education Center	2166	5611	M-F
Learning Center	2766/Kapaun AS	489-6339	M-F
Eng'r/Publ Works	520	6540	24 hours daily
Exchange(Main)	1100	7110	Daily
Finance(Mil)	2108	5630	M-F
Food/Caf/Rest)	1101	6061	Daily
Food(Snack/Fast)	2303	6061	Daily
Foodland	404	C-42404	24 hours daily
Laundry(Exch)	2163	N/A	24 hours daily
Laundry(Self-Svc)	403	N/A	24 hours daily
Motor Pool	1404	5961	24 hours daily
Package Store	1101	6264/6364	M-Sa
Photo Laboratory	2204	5533	M-F
Pick-up Point	1101	C-42409	M-Sa
	408	C-42750	M-Sa
	2187C	C-42069	M-F
Postal Svcs(Mil)	426	7857	M-Sa
	2110	2490	M-F

===

Postal Svcs(Civ)	2113	C-42946	M-F
	1004	C-43981	M-F
	412	C-43312	M-F
SATO-OS	2406, Rm 3A	5246	M-F
		C-42003	
Schools			
Elementary	904	6135	M-F
	909	6021	M-F
Middle School	1001	7104	M-F
High School	900	6951	M-F
Svc Stn(Insta)	1202	2940/6281	Daily
	1134	6555	Daily
Space-A Air Ops			
Pax Lounges	2202	5363/5461	Daily
Protocol Svc	201	6854	Daily
(USAFE spon'd)			
Flights to	Aviano AB IT; Cairo Intl EG; Charleston AFB SC; Decimomannu AB IT; Dhahran Intl SA; Dover AFB DE; Goose AB CN; Incirlik Arpt TU; King Abdullah AB JR; McGuire AFB NJ; RAF Mildenhall UK; Oslo		

GERMANY
Ramstein Air Base, continued

	Fornebu NO; Rhein-Main AB GE; Sigonella Arpt IT; Souda Bay NAF GR; Tinker AFB OK; Torrejon AB SP; Travis AFB CA; Zaragoza AB SP.		
Tailor Shop	1101	C-42404	M-F
Taxi(Comm)	2103	C-50510	24 hours daily
Tel Booking Oper	N/A	112	24 hours daily
Tel Repair(Gov)	N/A	119	24 hours daily
Thrift Shop	2140	5492	M,W,F
TML			
Billeting	305	7864/7345	24 hours daily
Crew Qtrs	538,2408	See billeting	Daily
Protocol Office	201	7558	N/A
TAQ	1003,2408,2409	See billeting	Daily
	3752,3756	See billeting	Daily
TLQ	303,1004	See billeting	Daily
VOQ	304-306, 530, 540, 541 1002, 3751, 3754	See billeting	Daily
DV/VIP(06+)	1018	7558	N/A
Travel Agents	412	6330/6279	M-F

HEALTH AND WELFARE

FACILITY/ACTIVITY	BLDG NO/LOC	PHONE	DAYS/COMMENTS
AF Fam Svcs	2140	5900	M-F
AF Relief	2140	5719	M-F
Ambulance	N/A	116	24 hours daily
Central Appts	2114	2037/5291	M-F
CHAMPUS Office	2114	5544	M-F
Chapel	2403/Ramstein S	5753	M-F
	1201/Ramstein N	6148	M-F
Chaplain	2403	2050	24 hours daily
Comm Drug/Alc Ctr	2104	5425	M-F
Hotline		5683	24 hours daily
Dental Clinic	301	6903	M-F
Medical Emergency	2114	5225	M-F
Mental Health Clinic	2114	5505	M-F
Emergency	N/A	2050	Call for hours.
Poison Control	Landstuhl	486-8233	24 hours daily
Red Cross	2122	5464	M-F
		2050	After duty hours
Veterinary Svcs	108	5343	M-Sa

REST AND RECREATION

FACILITY/ACTIVITY	BLDG NO/LOC	PHONE	DAYS/COMMENTS
Aero/Flying Club	Tower	5229	Daily
Amer Forces Ntwk	Vogelweh	6353	M-F
Bowling Lanes	2139	5447/5547	24 hours daily
Craftshops			
Automotive	2477	2324	Daily
Multicrafts	552	6534	Daily
Equip/Gear Locker	2177	5705	M-Sa
Golf Course	553	6240	Daily
Gymnasium	552	6676	Daily

U.S. Forces Travel & Transfer Guide Europe — 189

GERMANY

Ramstein Air Base, continued

	2117	2371	Daily
	Racket and field sports, contact gymnasium.		
Library	409	6667	Daily
NCO Club	2411	5705/2333	Daily
O'Club	302	6065	Daily
Recreation Center	412	6600	Daily
	Picnic/Park Areas-contact Rec Ctr.		
Rod and Gun Club	See Kaiserslautern Community listing.		
Theater	1123	6147	Daily
	2101	5550	Daily
Video Rental	2113	5428	Th-T
Youth Center	428	6444	M-Sa

REGENSBURG SUB-COMMUNITY (GE96R7)
APO New York 09173-5000

TELEPHONE INFORMATION: Main installation numbers: Civ: 49-0941-7801-2805. ATVN: 460-1110 (ask for Regensburg). ETS: 471-3113. Civ prefix: 0941-____. ETS prefix: 471-3XXX. Civ to mil prefix: 0941-7801-XXX.

LOCATION: Located at the intersection of the E-5 Autobahn east from Nürnberg and the E-90 Autobahn north from Munich (not complete). Near the Czech and Austrian borders. HE: p-40, G/3. NMC: Nürnberg, 35 miles northwest.

GENERAL INSTALLATION INFORMATION: Regensburg is a 7th Army Training Command sub-community and is home to the 20th Ordnance Company. **Note: the following abbreviation is used in this listing only: PK (Pioneer Kaserne).**

GENERAL CITY/REGIONAL INFORMATION: Regensburg is the only German city that is almost completely preserved from medieval times, with more than 1,400 historic buildings in its vicinity including the Cathedral, the Old Town Hall, the Stone Bridge, the Praetorian Gate, St. Emmeram's Church, and Scots Kirk.

ADMINISTRATIVE SUPPORT

FACILITY/ACTIVITY	BLDG NO/LOC	PHONE	DAYS/COMMENTS
Duty Officer	5/PK	670/801	24 hours daily
Housing			
Family	5/PK	819	M-F
Info(Insta)	5/PK	113	24 hours daily
Locator(Mil)	5/PK	113	24 hours daily
Locator(Civ)	5/PK	806	M-F
Police(Mil)			
Emergency	5/PK	114	24 hours daily
Police(Civ)	Gate Guards	656	24 hours daily

GERMANY
Regensburg Sub-Community, continued

LOGISTICAL SUPPORT

FACILITY/ACTIVITY	BLDG NO/LOC	PHONE	DAYS/COMMENTS
Bookstore	5/PK	677	M-Sa
Commissary(Annex)	5/PK	653	Tu-Sa
Dining Facility	5/PK	808	Daily
Education Center	5/PK	675	M-F
Elec Repair(Gov)	PK	809/670	Duty hours
	PK	818	After hours
Eng'r/Publ Works	PK	664	M-F
	Emergency	115	24 hours daily
Exchange(Main)	PK	422	M-Sa
Food(Snack/Fast)	PK	422	Daily
Foodland	PK	422	Daily
Motor Pool	PK	829	Daily
Railroad/RTO	PK	812	Daily
Schools(DOD Dep)			
Elementary	PK	682	M-F
Tel Repair(Gov)	PK	466-2800/2610	Daily

HEALTH AND WELFARE

FACILITY/ACTIVITY	BLDG NO/LOC	PHONE	DAYS/COMMENTS
Ambulance	PK	116	24 hours daily
Medical Emergency	PK	801/116	24 hours daily

REST AND RECREATION

FACILITY/ACTIVITY	BLDG NO/LOC	PHONE	DAYS/COMMENTS
Enlisted Club	PK	662	Daily
NCO Club	PK	662	Daily
Special Services	PK	475-6146	Daily

RHEINBERG COMMUNITY (GE80R7)
APO New York 09712-5000

TELEPHONE INFORMATION: Main installation numbers: Civ: 49-02843-70-113. ATVN: 320-1110 (ask for Rheinberg). Civ prefix: 02843-_____ (Rheinberg); 02161-_____ (Mönchengladbach); 0251-_____ (Münster). Civ to mil prefix: 02843-70-XXXX.

LOCATION: Exit Autobahn 57 north or south at Rheinberg/Kamp-Lintfort and drive north one mile to Rheinberg. Also located on GE-57 on the west side of the Rhein River. HE: p-36, B/3. NMC: Essen, 16 miles southeast.

GENERAL INSTALLATION INFORMATION: Rheinberg is home to the 7th TAACOM, the 54th Area Support Group and other support units. Note: the following abbreviations are used in this listing only: MGM (Mönchengladbach); MSR (Münster); RBG (Rheinberg).

GERMANY

Rheinberg Community, continued

GENERAL CITY/REGIONAL INFORMATION: Rheinberg is located on the Rhein River in an industrial/manufacturing area near the Netherlands/German border. It is located up river from Duisburg, Europe's largest inland port.

ADMINISTRATIVE SUPPORT

FACILITY/ACTIVITY	BLDG NO/LOC	PHONE	DAYS/COMMENTS
Advocate	RBG	C-706518	M-F
Housing			
Family	RBG	C-707556	M-F
	MGM	C-88549	M-F
Referral	RBG	C-707554	M-F
Legal Assist	RBG	C-707829	M-F
Personnel Spt	RBG	C-706506	M-F
Police(Mil)	RBG	C-706526	24 hours daily
	MSR	C-329669	24 hours daily
Public Affairs	RBG	C-707798	M-F
Tax Relief	RBG	C-707794	M-F

LOGISTICAL SUPPORT

FACILITY/ACTIVITY	BLDG NO/LOC	PHONE	DAYS/COMMENTS
Audio/Photo Ctr	RBG	C-706772	M-F
Auto Drivers Testing	RBG	C-706572	M-F
	MSR	None	M-Th
Auto Registration	MSR	C-394255	M-F
	RBG	C-706524	M-F
Auto Rent(Other)	RBG	C-60998/9	N/A
Bank	RBG	C-8482	M-F
Barber Shop(s)	RBG	None	M,Tu,F
Beauty Shop(s)	RBG	C-706658	W-Sa
Bookstore	1/RBG	None	M-F
	MSR	None	M-F
Child Care/Dev Ctr	RBG	C-706651	M-F
	MSR	C-328330	M-F
Commissary(Main)	1/RBG	C-706577	Tu-Sa
	MSR	C-324026	Tu-Sa
Credit Union	RBG	C-706672	M-F
Education Center	RBG	C-907789	M-F
	MGM	C-86452	M-F
Exchange(Main)	RBG	C-707602	M-F
	MSR	C-32253	Tu-Sa
	MGM	C-559522	M-Sa
Learning Center	MSR	None	M-F
	MSR	4225 C-328297	M-F
Finance(Mil)	RBG	C-706516	M-F
	MSR	4224	M-F
Food(Snack/Fast)	RBG	None	Daily
	MSR	C-325006	M-F
Motor Pool	RBG	C-707835	M-F
Package Store	RBG	C-8565	N/A
	MGM	C-87038	M-F
	MSR	4255	Tu-Sa

GERMANY
Rheinberg Community, continued

Postal Svcs(Mil)	RBG	C-706655	M-F
	MSR	C-328297	M-F
	MGM	C-328297	M-F
Schools(DOD Dep)			
Elementary	Moers	C-02841-62906	M-F
	Kalkar	C-02824-5881	M-F
	MGM	C-187182	M-F
	MSR	C-278941	M-F
High School	Düsseldorf	N/A	M-F
Tailor Shop	RBG	None	M-F
Taxi(Comm)	MGM	C-10077	24 hours daily
	MSR	C-60011	24 hours daily
	RBG	C-2121	24 hours daily
Tel Repair(Gov)	RBG	C-706545	N/A
	All others	C-01171	N/A

HEALTH AND WELFARE

FACILITY/ACTIVITY	BLDG NO/LOC	PHONE	DAYS/COMMENTS
Ambulance	RBG	C-706601	M-F
Army Comm Svcs	RBG	C-706685/7	M-F
	MGM	C-88239	M-F
	MSR	C-324572	M-F
Army Emerg Relief	RBG	C-706688	M-F
Central Appts	MGM	C-477255	M-F
	MSR	C-20061	M-F
	RBG	C-2055	M-F
CHAMPUS Office	RBG	C-706601	M-F
Chapel	RBG	C-707848	M-F
Comm Drug/Alc Ctr	RBG	C-707690	M-F
	MSR	C-328328	M-F
	MGM	C-894309	M,Tu,Th,F
Medical Emergency	RBG	C-706601	M-F

REST AND RECREATION

FACILITY/ACTIVITY	BLDG NO/LOC	PHONE	DAYS/COMMENTS
Consolidated Club	RBG	C-70698	N/A
	MSR	C-327429	Su-W,F
Craftshops			
Automotive	RBG	C-706603	F-Tu
Multi-crafts	RBG	C-706624	Tu-Sa
Gymnasium	RBG	C-707679	M-Sa
Library	MSR	C-394224	N/A
	RBG	C-70683	M,Tu,Th,F
Recreation Center	RBG	C-706603	N/A
	MSR	C-328382	M-F
Youth Center	RBG	C-706572	M-F

GERMANY
RHEIN-MAIN AIR BASE (GE16R7)
APO New York 09097-5000

TELEPHONE INFORMATION: Main installation numbers: Civ: 49-069-699-1110. ETS/ATVN: 330-1110. Civ prefix: 069-_____. ETS/ATVN prefix: 330-XXXX. Civ to mil prefix: 069-699-XXXX.

LOCATION: Adjacent to Frankfurt IAP 10 miles south of Frankfurt. Take the Rhein-Main exit from Autobahn A-5 which runs north to Frankfurt and Bremerhaven, and south to Darmstadt and the Black Forest area. HE: p-40, B/11. NMC: Frankfurt, 10 miles north.

GENERAL INSTALLATION INFORMATION: Rhein-Main Air Base and the 435th Tactical Airlift Wing are the center for all MAC air transportation in Europe. The C-9A Nightingale aeromedical aircraft and a squadron of C-130 Hercules aircraft are assigned to the base. Also, en route support is provided for several C-5 Galaxy and C-141 Starlifter aircraft each day. Detachments and operating locations of the 435th TAW's parent unit, the 322th Airlift Division at Ramstein Air Base, provide direct support for airlift through Europe and the Middle East. The base supports many tenant organizations, the largest of which is the 1945th Information System Group, which provides long-distance communications service from the English Channel to Austria.

GENERAL CITY/REGIONAL INFORMATION: The Rhein-Main region is the Federal Republic's second heaviest populated area. It is here that the cities of Frankfurt, Darmstadt, Wiesbaden, Offenbach, Hanau, and a dozen smaller cities come together in a complex of industrial, commercial and cultural centers mixed with high-rise apartments and parks. Only the Ruhr industrial area of Northwest Germany is more densely populated.

ADMINISTRATIVE SUPPORT

FACILITY/ACTIVITY	BLDG NO/LOC	PHONE	DAYS/COMMENTS
Customs/Duty	400	6208	M-F
Duty Officer	140	7801	24 hours daily
Fire(Mil)	32	117	24 hours daily
Fire(Civ)	N/A	112	24 hours daily
Housing	345	6095	M-F
Referral	345	7152	M-F
Info(Insta)	107	1110	24 hours daily
Inspector Gen'l	347	7304	M-F
		7777	24 hour hotline
Legal Assist	347	7275	M-F
Locator(Mil)	140	7691	M-F
Locator(Civ)	140	7691	M-F
		6131	After hours
Personnel Spt	347	7441	M-F. Passports, etc.
		4155	M-F. Customer svc.
Police(Mil)	343	7177	24 hours daily
Emergency		114	24 hours daily
Police(Civ)	N/A	112	24 hours daily
Public Affairs	347	7804	M-F
		7801	After hours
Tax Relief	350	7586	M-F

GERMANY
Rhein-Main Air Base, continued

LOGISTICAL SUPPORT

FACILITY/ACTIVITY	BLDG NO/LOC	PHONE	DAYS/COMMENTS
Audio/Photo Ctr	349	C-693212	Tu-Su
Auto Drivers Testing	348	7930	M-F
Auto Parts(Exch)	240	7524	M-F
Auto Registration	347	7003	M-F
Auto Rental(Exch)	110	C-691091	N/A
Auto Repairs	240	7524	M-F
		C-691334	
Auto Sales	167	C-692471	Daily
Auto Ship(Gov)	345	7154	M-F
Auto Ship(Civ)	400	7483	M-F
Auto Wash	240, 248	7467	Daily
Bakery	611	C-691750	M-Sa
Bank	168	7235	M-F
Barber Shop(s)	125	7239	M-F
	100	7214	M-F
	110	C-693272	M-F
Beauty Shop(s)	100	7245	M-Sa
	110	C-693272	M-Sa
	611	C-691442	M-Sa
Bookstore	100	C-693383	Daily
Bus	244	7051	Daily
Child Care/Dev Ctr	117	7017	M-Sa
	110	7775	M-Sa
Clothing Sales	168	6196	M-F
Commissary(Main)	166	7490	Tu-Sa
Commissary(Annex)	166	6027	Daily
Credit Union	168	7380	M-F
Dining Facility	131	7367	Daily
Dry Clean(Exch)	100	1556	M-F
Dry Clean(Gov)	345	6194	M-F
Education Center	140	7484	M-F
Eng'r/Publ Works	205	7789	24 hours daily
Exchange(Main)	100	7261	Daily
		C-694131	
Exchange(Annex)	340	7569	Daily
Exchange(Concess)	N/A	None	Daily
Finance(Mil)	153	7133	M-F
Food(Caf/Rest)	110	C-692679	Daily
	400	C-692107	Daily
Food(Snack/Fast)	345	C-693076	M-F
Baskin Robbins	100	C-69704226	Daily
Burger Bar	110	C-69704210	Daily
Pizza Parlor	110	C-693339	Daily
Foodland	166	6027	Daily
Laundry(Exch)	100	C-691556	Daily
Laundry(Self-Svc)	349	7645	24 hours daily
Motor Pool	244	7051	24 hours daily
Package Store	119	6125	M-Sa
Parking	400	None	Daily
Photo Laboratory	36	7110	M-F
Pick-up Point	100	C-691556	M-Sa
	Gateway Gardens	C-691117	M-Sa

GERMANY
Rhein-Main Air Base, continued

Postal Svcs(Mil)	142	7680	M-F
Postal Svcs(Civ)	110	C-691050	M-Sa
Railroad/RTO	N/A	C-692303	24 hours daily
SATO-OS	400	7021	M-F
		C-6905603	
Schools(DOD Dep)			
Elementary	610	7537	M-F
Middle School	610	7748	M-F
High School	See Frankfurt Community listing.		
Svc Stn(Insta)	127	4172	Daily
Space-A Air Ops	400	7015	24 hours daily
Pax Lounges(Gen'l)	400	7015	24 hours daily
Protocol Svc	N/A	6264	N/A
Flights to:	Andrews AFB MD; Athinai Arpt GR; Aviano AB IT; Brindisi/Casale Arpt IT; Capodichino Arpt IT; Charleston AFB/IAP SC; Cigli TAB TU; Dhahran IAP SA; Dover AFB DE; Esenboga TU; Incirlik Arpt TU; Iraklion AS TU; Lambert-St. Louis IAP MO; Lajes Fld PO; McGuire AFB NJ; RAF Mildenhall UK; Philadelphia IAP PA; Port Sudan Arpt SU; Ramstein AB GE; Rota NAS SP; San Guisto Arpt IT; Sigonella Arpt IT; Tempelhof Arpt GE; Torrejon AB SP; Venezia/Tessera Arpt IT; Zaragoza AB SP.		
Tailor Shop	100	C-691556	M-Sa
Taxi(Comm)	400	7528	24 hours daily
Tel Booking Oper	107	0	24 hours daily
Tel Repair(Gov)	353	7721	M-F
Tel Repair(Civ)		C-01171	24 hours daily
Thrift Shop	340	7095	Tu,F,1st Sa of month
TML			
Billeting	7265-7267	7682/83	M-F
		7266	After hours
Guest House	110	7682/83	Daily
Protocol Office	110	6059	M-F
VAQ	345	7682/83	Daily
Travel Agents	150	C-694094	M-F
Watch Repair	100	C-692204	Daily

HEALTH AND WELFARE

FACILITY/ACTIVITY	BLDG NO/LOC	PHONE	DAYS/COMMENTS
AF Family Svcs	165	6282	M-F
AF Relief	110	7992	M-F
Ambulance	170	116	24 hours daily
Central Appts	170	7307	M-F
CHAMPUS Office	170	6231	M-F
Chaplain	N/A	7801	After hours
Chapel	155	7501	M-F
Comm Drug/Alc Ctr	131	7681	M-F
Dental Clinic	170	7709	M-F
Medical Emergency	170	116	24 hours daily
Mental Health	170	6426	M-F
Poison Control	170	116	24 hours daily
Red Cross	110	7546	M-F
		7801	After hours
	Airport Lounge	C-691581	24 hours daily

GERMANY
Rhein-Main Air Base, continued

Veterinary Svcs	N/A	7294	M

REST AND RECREATION

FACILITY/ACTIVITY	BLDG NO/LOC	PHONE	DAYS/COMMENTS
Amer Forces Ntwk	See Frankfurt Community listing.		
Bowling Lanes	164	7219	Daily
Consolidated Club	125	7120	Daily
Craftshops			
Automotive	248	7467	M-F
Multi-crafts	158	7231	Tu-Su
Enlisted Club	150	7727	Daily
Equip/Gear Locker	165	7274	M-F
Gymnasium	273	6062	Daily
Info Tour & Travel	131, 150	7667	M-Sa
Library	159	7373	Daily
MARS	140	7407	24 hours daily
NCO Club	125	7121	Daily
O'Club	125	7120	Daily
Outdoor Rec Ctr	150	7667	M-F
Picnic/Park Area	N/A	7444	N/A
Racket Courts	273	6062	Daily
Recreation Center	150	7667	Daily
Rod and Gun Club	110	4016	Tu-Su
Skating Rink	270	7228	Seasonal
Special Services	360	7662	M-F
Sport Field	273	6062	Seasonal
Tennis Courts	273	6062	Seasonal
Theater	Gateway Gardens	7232	Daily
	168	7225	Daily
Video Rental	349	7712	Tu-Sa
Youth Center	Gateway Gardens	7125/6250	Daily

SCHWABACH SUB-COMMUNITY (GE81R7)
APO New York 09142-5000

TELEPHONE INFORMATION: Main installation numbers: Civ: 49-09122-83-113. ETS: 463-3113. Civ prefix: 09122-____. ETS prefix: 463-3XXX. Civ to mil prefix: 09122-83-XXX.

LOCATION: Take the B2 or the B466 Autobahn south from Nürnberg to the Schwabach exit. HE: p-40, F/2. NMC: Nürnberg, 16 kilometers north.

GENERAL INSTALLATION INFORMATION: O'Brien Barracks at Schwabach was constructed in 1935-1936 as a training center for the Horse Cavalry, Signal Units, and the German Shepherd (K-9) Corps. Named the Nachrichten Kaserne, it was part of the German Army until the U.S. Army acquired it in 1945. The post was originally named in honor of CPT Thomas F. O'Brien, 7th Field Artillery Battalion. O'Brien Barracks is currently the home of the 1st Squadron, 1st Cavalry, and 2nd Battalion, 59th Air Defense Artillery.

GENERAL CITY/REGIONAL INFORMATION: Schwabach is first

GERMANY

Schwabach Sub-Community, continued

mentioned in the historical record in 1117 and was originally called Suabach. In the 1300s it became an established market town. The Burggrafen from Nürnburg was the city's first legitimate ruler. Later, the Markgrafen, or market count, from Ansbach came to power. From 1791 to 1806 the city was a part of the state of Preußen. Thereafter it was a part of Bayern. Among the many things to see in Schwabach are the market place and courthouse (1528), the Markgrafen water fountain (1716), and the Franconian Church of St. Joseph (1469-1495) with its high altars. The city museum features many cultural displays.

ADMINISTRATIVE SUPPORT

FACILITY/ACTIVITY	BLDG NO/LOC	PHONE	DAYS/COMMENTS
Duty Officer	1002	500	24 hours daily
Fire(Mil)	On Barracks	117	24 hours daily
Housing			
Family	1036	595/711	M-F
Referral	1036	711/595	M-F
Inspector Gen'l	1013	805	M-F
Police(Mil)	1002	550/817	24 hours daily
Emergency		114	24 hours daily
Tax Relief	1002	838	Tu,Th

LOGISTICAL SUPPORT

FACILITY/ACTIVITY	BLDG NO/LOC	PHONE	DAYS/COMMENTS
Bank	1017	5195	M-F
Barber Shop(s)	1017	835	M-F
Bookstore	1036	502	M-F
Child Care/Dev Ctr	1006	541	M-F
Commissary(Annex)	1005	534/734	Tu-Sa
Dining Facility	1073	N/A	Daily
Education Center			
Learning Center	1017	552/735	M-F
Elec Repair(Gov)	On Barracks	C-6698	M-F
Eng'r/Publ Works	On Barracks	115	24 hours daily
Exchange(Annex)	1027	C-16049	M,Tu,Th-Sa
Food(Snack/Fast)	1036	C-705308	Daily
Foodland	1027	C-16049	Daily
Laundry(Self-Svc)	1026	C-705230	Daily
Package Store	1001	568	Tu-Sa
Pick-up Point	1036	508	Daily
Postal Svcs(Mil)	1029	784/584	M-F
Railroad/RTO	Schwabach	C-4085	Daily
Schools(DOD Dep)			
Kindergarten	Schwabach	C-890370	M-F
Nürnberg Elem.	Kalb Housing	460-7034	M-F (K-6)
Nürnberg H S	Kalb Housing	460-6675	M-F (7-12)
Tailor Shop	1017	None	M-F
Taxi(Comm)	Schwabach	2011	Daily
Tel Repair(Gov)	On Barracks	119	M-F
Thrift Shop	1036		M,Tu,Th-Sa
TML			
Billeting	371	530	Daily
Other Times	320 (SDO)	525	After hours

GERMANY
Schwabach Sub-Community, continued

Guest House	371	530	Daily

HEALTH AND WELFARE

FACILITY/ACTIVITY	BLDG NO/LOC	PHONE	DAYS/COMMENTS
Ambulance	On Barracks	116	24 hours daily
Army Comm Svcs	1004	727/560	M-F
Central Appts	1003	556/825	M-F
Chapel	On Barracks	719/587	Daily
Comm Drug/Alc Ctr	1010	729/579	M-F
Dental Clinic	1029	567/709	M-F

REST AND RECREATION

FACILITY/ACTIVITY	BLDG NO/LOC	PHONE	DAYS/COMMENTS
Bowling Lanes	1017	566	Tu-Su
Consolidated Club	1017	586	Tu-Su
Craftshops			
Photography	1036	706/824	Th-M
Enlisted Club	1017	586	W-M
Gymnasium	1007	828/576	Daily
Library	1036	706	Tu-Sa
Racket Courts	In gym		
Recreation Center	1036	824	Tu-F
Tennis Courts	Beside gymnasium		
Theater	1016	580	Th-Su
Youth Center	52A	818/826	M-Sa

SCHWÄBISCH GMÜND SUB-COMMUNITY
(GE82R7)
APO NEW YORK 09281-5000

TELEPHONE INFORMATION: Main installation numbers: Civ: 49-07171-15-113. ETS/ATVN: 427-5113. Civ prefix: 07171-____. ETS/ATVN prefix: 427-5XXX. Civ to mil prefix: 07171-15-XXX.

LOCATION: From Stuttgart follow B-14 to Nürnberg. B-14 will divide at the junction with B-29. Follow B-29 to Aalen and Schwäbisch Gmünd. HE: p-40, D/4. NMC: Stuttgart, 32 miles west.

GENERAL INSTALLATION INFORMATION: Schwäbisch Gmünd is home to the HHB 56th Field Artillery Command, Pershing. It is a sub-community of the Göppingen Military Community. The 56th Field Artillery Command; the 2/9 Field Artillery and four Firing Batteries; and the 38th Signal Battalion with HHC, A, and D Companies, are headquartered in Schwäbisch Gmünd. Note: the following abbreviations are used in this listing only: BK (Bismarck Kaserne); HK (Hardt Kaserne); SGD (Schwäbisch Gmünd).

GENERAL CITY/REGIONAL INFORMATION: Schwäbisch Gmünd, formerly a free city of the Holy Roman Empire, is today a German center of industry and commerce. Founded around 500 A.D., it is located in the Rems River Valley in the state of Baden-Württemberg. By the eighth century,

U.S. Forces Travel & Transfer Guide Europe — 199

GERMANY

Schwäbisch Gmünd Sub-Community, continued

municipal laws were in place. In the 1100s it officially became a town by order of Emperor Frederick I of the Hoherstaufen Dynasty. Since the middle of the 15th Century, the town has been famous for its goldsmiths and silversmiths.

Gmünd is also known for its three magnificent churches: Saint John's Church (1220-50), the Holy Cross Cathedral and Saint Augustine's, the only Protestant church in the town. Many homes built in the Baroque style give the streets a quaint appearance. The streets are mostly narrow and winding and are closely bordered by buildings notable for the many and various architectural styles in which they were constructed.

Also worthy of mention is the spacious market square with its monument to Holy Mary. Many other things that a visitor will enjoy viewing can be found beyond the main part of the town: charming old streets; numerous chapels of all eras, including the Herfottsruh Chapel, upon which a legend is based; and the magnificent views of the surrounding countryside.

ADMINISTRATIVE SUPPORT

FACILITY/ACTIVITY	BLDG NO/LOC	PHONE	DAYS/COMMENTS
Customs/Duty	See Göppingen Community listing.		
Duty Officer	302/BK	810	24 hours daily
Fire(Mil)	BK	117	24 hours daily
Fire(Civ)	SGD	117	24 hours daily
Housing			
Family	502A/BK	854/711	M-F
Referral	502A/BK	770 / C-61701	M-F
Info(Insta)	502B/BK	113	M-F
Inspector Gen'l	508/BK	815/856	M-F
Legal Assist	508/BK	801/842	M-F
Locator(Mil)	437/HK	892	M-F
Locator(Civ)	502B/BK	948	M-F
Personnel Spt	502A/BK	880/891	M-F
Police(Mil)	501/BK	114	24 hours daily
Emergency	501/BK	114	24 hours daily
Police(Civ)	SGD	C-3580	24 hours daily
Public Affairs	505/BK	895/804	M-F
Tax Relief	502A/BK	810 / C-39214	M,Tu,Th,F

LOGISTICAL SUPPORT

FACILITY/ACTIVITY	BLDG NO/LOC	PHONE	DAYS/COMMENTS
Auto Drivers Testing	505/BK	697	M-F
Auto Parts(Exch)	524/BK	644 / C-39285	Tu-Sa
Auto Registration	501/BK	714	M-F
Auto Ship(Gov)	See Göppingen Community listing.		
Bank	407/HK	779 / C-30561	M-F
Barber Shop(s)	516/BK	808	M-F
	416/HK	809	M-F
Beauty Shop(s)	416/HK	809	M-F

GERMANY
Schwäbisch Gmünd Sub-Community, continued

Bookstore	516/BK	N/A	M-F
	416/HK	N/A	M-F
Child Care/Dev Ctr	403/HK	670	M-F
		C-39448	
Clothing Sales	537/BK	C-39161	M-F
Commissary(Main)	708/HK	702	Tu-Sa
		C-61750	
Dining Facility	508/BK	N/A	Daily
	407/HK	N/A	Daily
Dry Clean(Exch)	516/BK	None	M-F
	416/HK	None	M-F
Dry Clean(Gov)	Available through unit supply		
Education Center	516/BK	788/961	M-F
Eng'r/Publ Works	511/BK	726	M-F
Exchange(Main)	416/HK	C-62117	Tu-Sa
Exchange(Annex)	516/BK	C-2146	M-F
Finance(Mil)	502A/BK	764/776	M-F
Food(Snack/Fast)			
Baskin Robbins	BK	516	Daily
Burger Bar	516/BK	C-64120	Daily
	412/HK	C-2152	Daily
Pizza Parlor	516/BK	C-64120	Daily
Foodland	416/HK	C-62117	Tu-Sa
Laundry(Self-Svc)	537L/BK	None	24 hours daily
Motor Pool	502A/BK	848	M-F
Package Store	411/HK	771	M-Sa
Photo Laboratory	519D/BK	719/637	M-Th
Pick-up Point	516/BK	None	M-F
	416/HK	None	Tu-F
Postal Svcs(Mil)	437/HK	892	M-F
Postal Svcs(Civ)	Downtown	C-82572	M-F
SATO-OS	416/HK	826	M-F
Schools(DOD Dep)			
Elementary	709/HK	888/805	M-F
		C-39238	
High School	Bussed to Ludwigsburg		
Space-A Air Ops	Airfield	425-3726	Daily
Tailor Shop	516/BK	N/A	M-F
	416/HK	N/A	M-F
Taxi(Comm)	SGD	C-2900	24 hours daily
Tel Repair(Gov)	502B/BK	731	M-F
Thrift Shop	407/HK	793	M-F
TML	See Göppingen Community listing.		

HEALTH AND WELFARE

FACILITY/ACTIVITY	BLDG NO/LOC	PHONE	DAYS/COMMENTS
Ambulance	BK	116	24 hours daily
Army Comm Svcs	508/BK	851/656	M-F
Army Emerg Relief	508/BK	861/656	M-F
Central Appts	515/BK	724/822	M-F
CHAMPUS Office	515/BK	724	M-F
Chaplain	503/BK	840	M-F
Chapel	503/BK	840	Daily
Comm Drug/Alc Ctr	508/BK	937	M-F
Dental Clinic	434/HK	886	M-F

U.S. Forces Travel & Transfer Guide Europe — 201

GERMANY

Schwäbisch Gmünd Sub-Community, continued

Medical Emergency	5th General Hospital in Bad Cannstatt. See the Bad Cannstatt Community listing.		
Red Cross	508/BK	861	M-F
		800/832	After hours
Veterinary Svcs	See the Stuttgart Community listing.		

REST AND RECREATION

FACILITY/ACTIVITY	BLDG NO/LOC	PHONE	DAYS/COMMENTS
Bowling Lanes	412/HK	774	Daily
Craftshops			
Automotive	409/HK	N/A	N/A
Ceramics	See the Göppingen Community listing.		
Multi-crafts	519D/BK	719	M-Th,Sa
Photography	519D/BK	637	M-Th,Sa
Wood	See multi-crafts above.		
Community Club	523/BK	941/695	M-Sa
Enlisted Club	519E/BK	733	Tu-Sa
	410/HK	773	Tu-Sa
Equip/Gear Locker	524/BK	626	N/A
Golf Course	Nine hole in Göppingen. Eighteen hole in Stuttgart.		
Gymnasium	404/HK	863	Daily
Info Tour & Travel	416/HK	826 C-64761	M-F
Library	516/BK	754	Sa-Th
MARS	See the Stuttgart Community listing.		
NCO Club	523/BK	965	Daily
O'Club	523/BK	965	Daily
Racket Courts	One in BK		
Recreation Center	519D/BK	719	Daily
Rod and Gun Club	See the Göppingen Community listing.		
Sport Field	Baseball and football in HK		
Tennis Courts	Two in HK		
Theater	519G/BK	757 C-5757	Daily
Track	One outdoor track		
Video Rental	516/BK	N/A	M-F
Youth Center	HK	639 C-39233	M-Sa

SCHWÄBISCH HALL
SUB-COMMUNITY (GE17R7)
APO New York 09025-5000

TELEPHONE INFORMATION: Main installation numbers: Civ: 49-0791-45-113. ETS: 426-4113. ATVN: 460-1110 (ask for Schwäbisch Hall). Civ prefix: 0791-___. ETS prefix: 426-4XXX. Civ to mil prefix: 0791-45-XXX.

LOCATION: Take B-14 or B-19 exit from Heilbronn/Nürnberg Autobahn to Schwaebisch Hall. HE: p-40, D/3. NMC: Stuttgart, 33 miles southwest.

GENERAL INSTALLATION INFORMATION: Schwäbisch Hall is a sub-community of Heilbronn Military Community. Dolan Barracks at Schwäbisch

GERMANY
Schwäbisch Hall Sub-Community, continued

Hall is unique in USAREUR. It is the only Army installation in USAREUR devoted entirely to Army aviation or aviation support. The 11th Aviation Group (Combat), 59th Air Traffic Control Battalion and the USAREUR Safety and Standardization Board are headquartered here. Other units located here are the 18th Medical Detachment; 90th Medical Detachment (Dental); a detachment of the 194th Military Police; 180th Aviation Company (ASH); 189th Air Traffic Control Company (Forward); 139th Adjutant General Company (Postal); and an Air Force Detachment, Det 4, 7th Weather Squadron.

GENERAL CITY/REGIONAL INFORMATION: The city of Schwäbisch Hall, located about two miles from Dolan Barracks in the midst of the Hohenlohe-Franken region, is a beautiful city, rich in history. The most striking architectural landmark of the city is the Basilica of St. Michael's, consecrated in 1156. Only the tower remains of the original romanesque structure. The original romanesque hall church was replaced by the present Gothic-style hall between 1427 and 1525. The 53 wide and imposing steps leading to the front entrance were added in 1507. These steps are not only architecturally outstanding but have become a symbol of the city. They form a dramatic and unusual stage on which open air theater performances take place every year from June to August.

Located only a short drive from the downtown area is the fortified Comburg, a former monastery erected in the 11th century. It was used as a monastery from 1078 till 1116 and today is an academy for teachers. Other interesting places to see are the Alt-Stadt or old town; the ruins of the Limburg Castle, which was the ancient home of feuding knights; the Sulfer Tower, a fortification tower and gate built in 1250, and a roofed wooden bridge built in 1728.

ADMINISTRATIVE SUPPORT

FACILITY/ACTIVITY	BLDG NO/LOC	PHONE	DAYS/COMMENTS
Customs/Duty	304	510	M-F
Duty Officer	320	525/827	Daily
Fire(Mil)	On Barracks	832	24 hours daily
	Emergency	117	24 hours daily
Housing	306	702	M-F
Referral	306	580	M-F
Police(Mil)	303	807	24 hours daily
Emergency	303	114	24 hours daily
Public Affairs	320	827	M-F
Tax Relief	335	563	M-F

LOGISTICAL SUPPORT

FACILITY/ACTIVITY	BLDG NO/LOC	PHONE	DAYS/COMMENTS
Auto Drivers Testing	304	679	Tu,Th
Auto Parts(Exch)	428	C-2245	M-Sa
Auto Registration	304	807/507	M,W,F
Auto Repairs	428	C-2245	M-Sa
Bank	334	C-2257	M-F
Barber Shop(s)	374	C-42516	M-Sa
Beauty Shop(s)	374	C-42516	Tu-Sa
Bookstore	335	None	M-Sa

GERMANY

Schwäbisch Hall Sub-Community, continued

Child Care/Dev Ctr	330	600	M-F
		C-2668	
Commissary(Annex)	435	517/547	Tu-Sa
Dining Facility	329	604	Daily
Dry Clean(Exch)	435	C-42653	Tu-Sa
Education Center	320	710	M-F
Eng'r/Publ Works	426	581	M-F
	Emergency	832	24 hours daily
Exchange(Main)	435	C-2697	Tu-Sa
Food(Snack/Fast)	335	C-2269	Daily
Foodland	334	C-2676	Daily
Laundry(Self-Svc)	374	None	Daily
Package Store	423	564	Tu-Sa
Pick-up Point	435	C-42653	Tu-Sa
Postal Svcs(Mil)	435	522	M-F
Schools(DOD Dep)			
Elementary	344	568	M-F (K-6)
Middle School	See Crailsheim Community listing.		
High School	See Ludwigsburg Community listing.		
Svc Stn(Insta)	433	C-2656	M-Sa
Space-A Air Ops	Flt Operations	4508	Daily
Flights to:	German Locations		
Tailor Shop	435	C-42653	Tu-Sa
Taxi(Comm)	N/A	C-2161	Daily
Tel Repair(Gov)	N/A	119	M-F
	Emergency	119	M-F
Thrift Shop	435	None	Tu,Th
TML			
Billeting	371	530/702	Daily
	320	525	After hours
Guest House	371	530	Daily
Watch Repair	Pick-up Point		

HEALTH AND WELFARE

FACILITY/ACTIVITY	BLDG NO/LOC	PHONE	DAYS/COMMENTS
Ambulance	326	116	24 hours daily
Army Comm Svcs	306	560	M-F
Army Emerg Relief	306	560	M-F
Central Appts	326	566	M-F
CHAMPUS Office	326	566/816	M-F
		C-2669	
Chapel	319	819/687	M-F
Comm Drug/Alc Ctr	320, Rm 312	706	M-F
Dental Clinic	316	729	M-F
Medical Emergency	326	116	24 hours daily
Mental Health	See Stuttgart Community listing.		
Poison Control	See Stuttgart Community listing.		
Red Cross	335	623	M-F
Veterinary Svcs	See Stuttgart Community listing.		

REST AND RECREATION

FACILITY/ACTIVITY	BLDG NO/LOC	PHONE	DAYS/COMMENTS
Bowling Lanes	339	548	Daily

GERMANY
Schwäbisch Hall Sub-Community, continued

Craftshops			
Automotive	418	610	Tu,F,Sa,Holidays
Ceramics	335	653	Tu-Su
Multi-crafts	315	653	Tu-Su
Photography	335	653	Tu-Su
Enlisted Club	428	536	Daily
Gymnasium	339	588	Daily
Info Tour & Travel	335	712	W
Library	335	554/563	Sa-Th
NCO Club	336	608	M-F
O'Club	336	608	M-F
Outdoor Rec Ctr	305	500	M-F
Recreation Center	335	712	W-Su
Theater	Thomas Theater	552	F-Su
Video Rental	435	N/A	Tu-Sa
Youth Center	324	575	M-Sa

===

SCHWEINFURT COMMUNITY (GE48R7)
APO New York 09033-5000

TELEPHONE INFORMATION: Main installation numbers: Civ: 49-09721-96-113. ETS: 354-113. ATVN: 350-1110 (ask for Schweinfurt). Civ prefix: 09721-____. ETS prefix: 354-XXXX. Civ to mil prefix: 09721-96-XXXX.

LOCATION: Located nine miles east of Kassel-Würzburg off the E-70 Autobahn. On GE-303, two miles past GE-B19. Follow the U.S. Forces signs. HE: p-40, D/1. NMC: Schweinfurt, in the city.

GENERAL INSTALLATION INFORMATION: As part of the NATO shield that protects Western Europe, the 3rd Infantry Division at Schweinfurt plays a vital role. Schweinfurt is also home to the 1st and 2nd Battalions of the 30th Infantry; the 2nd and 3rd Battalions of the 64th Armor; and two field artillery Battalions, the 1st Battalion 76th and the 1st Battalion 10th. Air defense and helicopter units are also stationed in Schweinfurt. **Note: the following abbreviations are used in this lisitng only: AM (Askren Manors); CB (Conn Barracks); LB (Ledward Barracks).**

GENERAL CITY/REGIONAL INFORMATION: Schweinfurt is located in the state of Northern Bavaria in an area known as Franconia. This city of 60,000 inhabitants, known in the modern industrial world as the "ball bearing capital of the world," lies only 30 kilometers from the East German border.

The history of Schweinfurt can be traced back prior to 714 A.D. when it was little more than a country town of farmers, boatsmen and fishermen. By 1254 Schweinfurt was an Imperial City. In 1309 Emperor Henry VII of Luxembourg pawned the town. The citizens of Schweinfurt raised the means to redeem the town themselves, though centuries would pass before the debt was repaid in full.

During World War II, Schweinfurt, because of its industrial prominence, was largely destroyed by Allied air raids; however, some of the city's finest buildings survived, including the Johanneskirche (1554-1672), the Rathaus or Town Hall (1570-1572), the Altes Gymnasium or boys' school (1582), the Armory (1589-1590), and Erbacher Hof (1563-1575). Other landmarks include

U.S. Forces Travel & Transfer Guide Europe — 205

GERMANY

Schweinfurt Community, continued

the beautiful Stadtpark near the Main River, the Tiergehege or animal park and the 800 seat downtown theater. The city's farmers' market, a centuries-old tradition, is open year round.

ADMINISTRATIVE SUPPORT

FACILITY/ACTIVITY	BLDG NO/LOC	PHONE	DAYS/COMMENTS
Customs/Duty	64/CB	6607	M-F
	296/LB	6273	M-F
Duty Officer	206/LB	6708	24 hours daily
		C-803834	
Fire(Mil)	74/CB	117	24 hours daily
		C-87711	24 hours daily
Fire(Civ)	Schweinfurt	112	24 hours daily
Housing	252/LB	7148/6448	M-Th
Referral	252/LB	6282	M-F
Info(Insta)	Würzburg	0931-889-113	N/A
Inspector Gen'l	206/LB	6666	M-F
Legal Assist	1/CB	6505	M-F
Locator(Mil)	2, 3/CB	6743	M-F
Locator(Civ)	444/LB	6444	M-F
Personnel Spt	215/LB	6463	M-F
Police(Mil)	295/LB	6622/6624	24 hours daily
Emergency		114	24 hours daily
Police(Civ)	Schweinfurt	110	24 hours daily
Public Affairs	206/LB	6492	M-F
		C-802218	
Tax Relief	206/LB	7122	M-F
		C-86798	

LOGISTICAL SUPPORT

FACILITY/ACTIVITY	BLDG NO/LOC	PHONE	DAYS/COMMENTS
Audio/Photo Ctr	64/CB	C-82057	M-F
Auto Drivers Testing	82/CB	6761	M-F
Auto Parts(Exch)	501/AM	C-82539	M-Sa
Auto Registration	295/LB	6755	M-F
Auto Rental(Exch)	22/LB	C-808834	M-F
Auto Repairs	501/AM	C-82539	M-Sa
Auto Sales	228/LB	C-808834	Daily
Auto Ship(Gov)	40/CB	6482	M-F
Auto Ship(Civ)	40/CB	6482	M-F
Bank	64/CB	6269	M-F
	226/LB	7103/6403	M-F
		C-88096	
Barber Shop(s)	64/CB	C-82303	M-F
	226/LB	C-82432	M-Sa
Beauty Shop(s)	226/LB	C-82432	M-Sa
Bookstore	64/CB	6240	M-Sa
	225/LB	6241/6739	Daily
Bus	63/CB	6482	M-F
Child Care/Dev Ctr	500/AM	6281/6279	M-F
		C-82984	
	50/CB	C-87678	M-F

GERMANY
Schweinfurt Community, continued

Clothing Sales	235/CB	C-81131	M-Sa
Commissary(Main)	502/AM	6650	Tu-Su
Credit Union	203/LB	C-87096/ 85843	M-F
Dining Facility	214/LB	6352	Daily
Dry Clean(Exch)	226/LB	C-808834	M-Sa
Dry Clean(Gov)	228/LB	C-89764	M-Sa
Education Center	509/AM	6356	M-F
	20/CB	6661	M-F
	242/LB	6383	M-F
Elec Repair(Gov)	252/LB	6201	M-F
Elec Repair(Civ)	252/LB	C-96201	M-F
Eng'r/Publ Works	251/LB	C-801483	M-F
Exchange(Main)	226/LB	6710 C-80880	Daily
Exchange(Annex)	64/CB	C-85988	M-Sa
Finance(Mil)	215/LB	6729/6716	M-F
Food(Caf/Rest)	226/LB	C-82334	Daily
Food(Snack/Fast)	64/CB	C-82334	Daily
Baskin Robbins	228/LB	C-808834	Daily
Burger King	64/CB	C-82482	Daily
Foodland	225/LB	C-802795	Daily
Laundry(Exch)	274/LB	6489 C-802795	M-F
Laundry(Self-Svc)	19C/CB	None	Daily
	243/LB	None	Daily
Motor Pool	CB	6482	M-F
Package Store	229/LB	6115/6715 C-88136	Tu-Sa
Parking	PX lot	None	Daily. 2 hour limit.
Photo Laboratory	64/CB	6709	M-F
Pick-up Point	64/CB	C-84761	M-Sa
	229/LB	C-802496	M-Sa
Postal Svcs(Mil)	64/CB	6240	M-F
	229/LB	6784	Daily
Postal Svcs(Civ)	242/LB	C-82068/ 540469	M-F
Railroad/RTO	63/CB	6482	M-F
SATO-OS	63/CB	6482	M-F
Schools(DOD Dep)			
Elementary	505/AM	7218/6134 C-81893	M-F (K-6)
Middle School	509/AM	7198/6356 C-81895	M-F (7-8)
High School	See Würzburg Community listing.		
Svc Stn(Insta)	501/AM	6519 C-82539	M-Sa
Svc Stn(Autobahn)	Schweinfurt	C-19211	24 hours daily
Tailor Shop	64/CB	C-84761	M-Sa
	229/LB	C-89764/ 802496	M-Sa
Taxi(Comm)	Schweinfurt	C-16060	24 hours daily
Tel Booking Oper	Würzburg	112	24 hours daily
Tel Repair(Gov)	206/LB	6390	M-F
Thrift Shop	229/LB	6723	Tu-F,1st Sa of mo

GERMANY

Schweinfurt Community, continued

TML

Billeting	89	6245/6248 C-82931	Daily
Guest House	89/Bradley Inn	6245/6248 C-82931	Daily
DV/VIP	1/Housing Chief	C-96448	M-F
Travel Agents	203/LB	C-89743	M-Sa
Watch Repair	226/LB	C-82057	M-F

HEALTH AND WELFARE

FACILITY/ACTIVITY	BLDG NO/LOC	PHONE	DAYS/COMMENTS
Ambulance	201/LB	116/6665 C-82397	24 hours daily
Army Comm Svcs	242/LB	C-802441	M-F
Army Emerg Relief	242/LB	6486	M-F
Central Appts	N/A	6771	M-F
CHAMPUS Office	201/LB	6638	M-F
Chaplain	242/LB	6662	M-F
Chapel	CB	6620	
	242/LB	6662/6250	M-F
Comm Drug/Alc Ctr	54/CB	6633	M-F
	201/LB	6770/6513	M-F
Dental Clinic	201/LB	6376/6642	M-F
Medical Emergency	201/LB	116/6665	24 hours daily
Mental Health	201/LB	6276	M-F
Poison Control	201/LB	6665	Daily
Red Cross	206/LB	6251	M-F
Veterinary Svcs	Würzburg	350-6132 C-0931-284151	M-F

REST AND RECREATION

FACILITY/ACTIVITY	BLDG NO/LOC	PHONE	DAYS/COMMENTS
Amer Forces Ntwk	Würzburg	350-7142	M-F
Bowling Lanes	64/CB	6707	Daily
	224/LB	6332	Daily
Craftshops			
Automotive	36, 37/CB	6224	Tu-Su
Ceramics	64/CB	6709	M-W,Sa,Su
Electronics	228/LB	C-808834	Daily
Multi-crafts	242/LB	6394/6304	Tu-Su
Photography	64/CB	6709	M-W,Sa,Su
Enlisted Club	224/LB	6333 C-87677	Daily
Gymnasium	64/CB	6234	Daily
	241/LB	6216 C-85077	Daily
Info Tour & Travel	203/LB	6326	M-F
Library	64/CB	6365	M-F
	242/LB	6211	Daily
MARS	LB	6498	Daily
NCO Club	444/LB	C-804413	Tu-Su
O'Club	90/CB	6398	Daily

GERMANY
Schweinfurt Community, continued

Outdoor Rec Ctr	289/LB	6232	M-F
Racket Courts	203/LB	C-85077	Call for schedule.
Recreation Center	64/CB	6476	Daily
	206/LB	6216	M-F
Skating Rink	Schweinfurt	C-88283	Daily
Sport Field	451/LB	C-85077	Daily
Swimming Pool	Schweinfurt	C-9311	Daily
Tennis Courts	Schweinfurt	C-33149	Daily
Theater	82/CB	6761	Daily
	238/LB	6238	Tu-F
Video Rental	90/CB	C-83403	Daily
Youth Center	570/AM	6617	Tu-Sa
	LB	C-82181	Tu-Sa

SEMBACH AIR BASE (GE18R7)
APO NY 09136-5000

TELEPHONE INFORMATION: Main installation numbers: Civ: 011-49-06302-67-113. ATVN: 496-7110. Civ prefix: 06302-_____. ATVN prefix: 496-XXXX. Civ to mil prefix: 06302-67-XXXX.

LOCATION: From E-12/A-61, take Exit 1-6 marked Enkenbach-Alsenborn. Follow B-48 in the direction of Bad Kreuznach. Immediately past town of Munchweiller, take right turn off to Sembach AB. HE: p-40,A/2. NMC: Kaiserslautern 9 miles west.

GENERAL INSTALLATION INFORMATION: The 66th Electronic Combat Wing (ECW) is the host unit at Sembach Air Base. Headquartered at Sembach are a number of units including the 17th Air Force, 601st Tactical Control Wing and the 2005th Communications Wing.

GENERAL CITY/REGIONAL INFORMATION: Small villages abound in the Rheinland-Pfalz area of Germany where Sembach AB is located. Sembach Village was founded in the 12th century by the Kolbs of Wartenberg, a noble family. The town offers churches, sports facilities, shops, gasthäusen and hundreds of friendly people. Four miles southwest of Sembach on B-40 is a fishing lake, stocked weekly with trout by its German owners. A fishing license is necessary—inquire at the skeet range or Tiger Sports Shop. Picnic and camping areas are located at the lake as well.

ADMINISTRATIVE SUPPORT

FACILITY/ACTIVITY	BLDG NO/LOC	PHONE	DAYS/COMMENTS
Customs/Duty	143	7965	M-F
Fire(Mil)	322	7524	24 hours daily
Fire(Civ)	Kaiserslautern	C-0631-16014	24 hours daily
Housing			
Family	216	7655	M-F
Unaccompanied	216	7655	M-F
Referral	217	7655	M-F
Info(Insta)	On Base	113	24 hours daily
Inspector Gen'l	112(66 ECW)	7576	M-F

U.S. Forces Travel & Transfer Guide Europe — 209

GERMANY

Sembach Air Base, continued

	203(601 TCW)	6510	M-F
Legal Assist	206	7774	M-F
Locator(Mil)	222	7535	M-F
Locator(Civ)	200	7864	M-F
Police(Mil)	210	7171	24 hours daily
Police(Civ)	Rockenhausen/Kaiserslautern Polizei		
Public Affairs	112	7854	M-F
		7864	After duty hrs/wknds
Tax Relief	105	7419	M-F

LOGISTICAL SUPPORT

FACILITY/ACTIVITY	BLDG NO/LOC	PHONE	DAYS/COMMENTS
Auto Drivers Testing	143	7376	M-F
Auto Parts(Exch)	124	7408	M-Sa
Auto Rent(Other)	85	C-5603	M-Sa. Budget.
Auto Repairs	124	7408	M-Sa
Auto Wash	124	7408	Seasonal hours
Bakery	In commissary		
Bank	149	7406	M-Sa
Barber Shop(s)	216(Main)	7820	M-F
	110(VOQ)	7442	M-Sa
Beauty Shop(s)	50	C-2398	Tu-Sa
Bookstore	148	6235	Tu-Su
Child Care/Dev Ctr	83	7002	F-W
Clothing Sales	84	7332	M-F
Commissary(Main)	88	7240	Tu-Su
Credit Union	231	7444	M-F
Dining Facility	218	7723	Daily
Dry Clean(Exch)	212	6170	M-Sa
Dry Clean(Gov)	216	6140	N/A
Education Center	212	7956	M-F
	17	7040	M-F
Eng'r/Publ Works	390	7860	M-F
Exchange(Main)	147	7198	Tu-Su
Finance(Mil)	214	7461	M-F
Food(Caf/Rest)	201	7741	Daily
Food(Snack/Fast)	201	7696	Daily
Pizza Parlor	201	C-2452	Daily
Foodland	98	7596	Daily
Laundry(Self-Svc)	N/A	None	Daily
Motor Pool	155	7658	M-F
Package Store	262	7811	Tu-Sa
Photo Laboratory	213	7615	M-F
Pick-up Point	212	2541	M-Sa
Postal Svcs(Mil)	222	7748	M-Sa
SATO-OS	143	6585	M-F
		C-2490	
Schools(DOD Dep)			
Elementary & Middle	Housing area	7429	M-F
High School	See Kaiserslautern listing.		
Svc Stn(Insta)	227	C-2170	M-Sa
Space-A Air Ops			
Pax Lounges(Gen'l)	322	7081	M-F
Protocol Svc	111	7606	M-F
Flights to:	Ahlhorn GAFB GE; RAF Bentwaters UK.		

GERMANY
Sembach Air Base, continued

Tailor Shop	84	7432	M-F
Tel Booking Oper	113	1110	Daily
Tel Repair(Gov)	251	6000	24 hours daily
Thrift Shop	74	6196	M-Sa
TML			
Billeting	216	7588/7149	24 hours daily
TAQ(E1-E6)	216/217	7588/7149	24 hours daily
VOQ/DV/VIP(All ranks)	110	7991	N/A

HEALTH AND WELFARE

FACILITY/ACTIVITY	BLDG NO/LOC	PHONE	DAYS/COMMENTS
AF Family Svcs	222	7191	M-F
AF Relief	157	7303	M-F
Ambulance	151	116	24 hours daily
Central Appts	151	7495	M-F
CHAMPUS Office	157	7849	M-F
Chaplain	118	7864	M-F
Chapel	118	7577	M-F
Comm Drug/Alc Ctr	212	7727	M-F
Dental Clinic	151	7676	M-F
Medical Emergency	151	7703	24 hours daily
Mental Health	151	7666	M-F
Poison Control	151	7703	24 hours daily
Red Cross	222	7464/7031	M-F
Veterinary Svcs	31	6578	By appointment

REST AND RECREATION

FACILITY/ACTIVITY	BLDG NO/LOC	PHONE	DAYS/COMMENTS
Bowling Lanes	136	7569	Daily
Craftshops			
Automotive	146	7804	Tu-Su
Ceramics	201	7605	Tu-Sa
Wood	201	7719/7629	Tu-Su
Enlisted Club	201	7719	Call for hours.
Gymnasium	105	7530	Daily
	Racket and field sports, contact gymnasium.		
Info Tour & Travel	201	7571	N/A
Library	115	7895	Daily
NCO Club	201	7719	Call for hours.
O'Club	109	7611	Call for hours.
Racket Courts	105	7530	Daily
Recreation Center	201	7571	M-F
Rod and Gun Club	254	6106	W,Sa,Su
Special Services	105	7172	M-F
Theater	145	7624	Daily
	19	7429	Daily
Video Rental	105	7780	Call for hours.
Water Recreation	201	6422	Call for hours.
Youth Center	66	7687	M-Sa

GERMANY

SPANGDAHLEM AIR BASE (GE19R7)
APO New York 09126-5000

TELEPHONE INFORMATION: Main installation numbers: Civ: 49-06565-61-1110. ETS/ATVN: 452-1110. Civ prefix: 06565-____. ETS/ATVN prefix: 452-XXXX. Civ to Mil prefix: 06565-61-XXXX.

LOCATION: From the Koblenz-Trier Autobahn E-1 exit at Wittlich, to B-50 west toward Bitburg. The AB is near Binsfeld 24 km west of Wittlich. Signs mark the AB entrance. HE: p-39, F/1. NMC: Trier, 21 miles southeast.

GENERAL INSTALLATION INFORMATION: Spangdahlem Air Base is the only exclusively defense-suppression oriented or "wild weasel" wing outside the continental United States. The 52nd Tactical Fighter Wing based at Spangdahlem has three tactical fighter squadrons, the 23rd, the 81st and the 480th. All fly the F-4G and F-16 aircraft. The 52nd's mission is to provide tactical fighter support to NATO and U.S. Forces and to maintain a fully trained, combat-ready force capable of immediate response for defense-suppression operations.

GENERAL CITY/REGIONAL INFORMATION: The nearby city of Trier is Germany's oldest, founded in 16 B.C. by the Romans. Historical and archaeological sources indicate that it became a major cultural and political center in the Roman empire in the centuries that followed. The cityscape is like a textbook in the history of major European architectural styles and modes, with splendid examples of Romanesque, Gothic, Renaissance, Baroque, Rococo and Classical architecture in abundant evidence. Tours are available to the city's many cathedrals, monuments and museums. Trier is also Germany's oldest "wine city," where a number of famous vineyards that grow around 3,000,000 Riesling vines are located.

ADMINISTRATIVE SUPPORT

FACILITY/ACTIVITY	BLDG NO/LOC	PHONE	DAYS/COMMENTS
Customs/Duty	Transient Alert		24 hours daily
Duty Officer	19	6141	24 hours daily
Fire(Mil)	47	114	24 hours daily
Fire(Civ)	N/A	C-4117	24 hours daily
Housing	22	6560	M-F
Info(Insta)	N/A	113	24 hours daily
Inspector Gen'l	23	6378	M-F
Legal Assist	23	6796	M-F
Locator(Mil)	149	6308	M-F
	38	6504	After duty hours
Personnel Spt	107	6255	M-F
Police(Mil)	18	6665	24 hours daily
Police(Civ)	N/A	C-4444	24 hours daily
Public Affairs	T-77	6012	M-F
Tax Relief	124	6567	M-F

LOGISTICAL SUPPORT

FACILITY/ACTIVITY	BLDG NO/LOC	PHONE	DAYS/COMMENTS
Auto Drivers Testing	170	6620	M-F
Auto Parts(Exch)	31	6762	Tu-Sa

GERMANY
Spangdahlem Air Base, continued

Facility	Bldg	Phone	Days
Auto Repairs	31	6762	Tu-Sa
Bakery	454	6606	Tu-Sa
Bank	192	6879	M-Sa
Barber Shop(s)	125	6313	M-F
Beauty Shop(s)	421	C-4002	M-F
Bookstore	196	None	M-Sa
Bus	120	6110	M-F
Child Care/Dev Ctr	440	6697	M-Sa
Clothing Sales	187	6097	M-Sa
Commissary(Main)	454	6606/6241	Tu-Sa
Credit Union	148	6674	M-F
Dining Facility	147	6727	Daily
Dry Clean(Exch)	146	C-4114	M-F
Education Center	192	6063	M-F
Elec Repair(Gov)	36	6590	M-F
Exchange(Main)	123	6061/6851	Daily
Finance(Mil)	23	6730	M-F
Food(Snack/Fast)			
Burger King	124	None	Daily
Pizza Parlor	N/A	6810	Daily
Foodland	174	C-4489	Daily
Laundry(Self-Svc)	145	None	24 hours daily
Motor Pool	120	6645	M-F
Package Store	122	6254	Tu-Sa
Photo Laboratory	44	6639	M-F
Pick-up Point	146	None	M-Sa
Postal Svcs(Mil)	151	6768	M-Sa
Postal Svcs(Civ)	151	None	M-F
SATO-OS	120	C-4866	M-F
Space-A Air Ops	See Ramstein Air Base listing.		
Schools			
Elementary	433	N/A	M-F (K-6)
	Trier Elementary N/A		M-F (K-6)
High School	See Bitburg Community listing.		
Svc Stn(Insta)	31	C-4255	Daily
Tel Repair(Gov)	44	6696	M-F
Thrift Shop	403C	4514	Tu,W,F,1st Sa
TML			
Billeting	38	6504/6253	24 hours daily
Protocol Office	23	6057	M-F
TLF	38	6504	24 hours daily
DV/VIP	38	6253	24 hours daily

HEALTH AND WELFARE

FACILITY/ACTIVITY	BLDG NO/LOC	PHONE	DAYS/COMMENTS
AF Family Svcs	106	6143	M-F
AF Relief	107	6255	M-F
Ambulance	137	116/6116	24 hours daily
CHAMPUS Office	137	6527	M-F
Chaplain	137	6215	N/A
Chapel	135	6711	N/A
Comm Drug/Alc Ctr	148	6391	M-F
Dental Clinic	137	6864	M-F
Medical Emergency	137	6215	M-F
Mental Health	137	6610	N/A

GERMANY

Spangdahlem Air Base, continued

Poison Control	137	116/6116	24 hours daily
Red Cross	153	6330	M-F
Veterinary Svcs	See Bitburg Community listing.		

REST AND RECREATION

FACILITY/ACTIVITY	BLDG NO/LOC	PHONE	DAYS/COMMENTS
Aero/Flying Club	On Base	6613 C-4963	Daily
Bowling Lanes	300	6753	Daily
Enlisted Club	121	6510/6588	Daily
Golf Course	58	6821	Daily
Gymnasium	N/A	6251	Daily
Info Tour & Travel	N/A	6203	Daily
Library	149	6203	Daily
NCO Club	121	6510/6588	Daily
O'Club	42	6530/6810	Daily
Racket Courts	Same as gymnasium		
Recreation Center	124	6567	Daily
Special Services	152	6875	M-F
Sport Field	Same as gymnasium		
Theater	253	6650	Daily
Track	Same as gymnasium		
Video Rental	146	4114	M-F
Youth Center	427	6238	Tu-Su

STUTTGART COMMUNITY (GE20R7)
APO New York 09154-5000

TELEPHONE INFORMATION: Main installation numbers: Civ: 49-0711-819-113 (Robinson Barracks, Wallace Barracks, Grenadier Kaserne); 49-0711-5201-113 (Hospital in Bad Cannstatt); 49-0711-7292-113 (Kelley Barracks); 49-0711-680-113 (Patch Barracks). ETS: 420-113 (Robinson Barracks, Wallace Barracks, Grenadier Kaserne); 422-2113 (Hospital in Bad Cannstatt); 421-2113 (Kelley Barracks and Echterdingen Airfield); 430-113 (Patch Barracks). ATVN: 420-1110. Civ prefix: 0711-_____ (all locations). ETS prefix: 420-XXXX (Robinson Barracks, Wallace Barracks, Grenadier Kaserne); 422-2XXX (Hospital in Bad Cannstatt); 421-2XXX (Kelley Barracks and Echterdingen Airfield); 430-XXXX (Patch Barracks). Civ to mil prefix: 0711-819-XXXX (Robinson Barracks, Wallace Barracks, Grenadier Kaserne); 0711-5201-XXX (Hospital in Bad Cannstatt); 0711-7292-XXX (Kelley Barracks and Echterdingen Airfield); 0711-680-XXXX (Patch Barracks).

LOCATION: Stuttgart can be reached from both the E-11 and E-70 Autobahns. Look for signs to Grenadier Kaserne. HE: p-40, C/4. NMC: Stuttgart, in the city.

GENERAL INSTALLATION INFORMATION: The installation is composed of six sub-communities: Böblingen-Sindelfingen (Panzer Kaserne), Ludwigsburg-Kornwestheim (Pattonville), Nellingen-Esslingen, Möhringen-Degerloch (Kelley Barracks), Vaihingen (Patch Barracks) and Bad Cannstatt-Zuffenhausen (Robinson Barracks, Grenadier Kaserne, Wallace Barracks and 5th General Hospital). This listing will cover the last three sub-communities:

GERMANY
Stuttgart Community, continued

Möhringen-Degerloch, Vaihingen and Bad Cannstatt-Zuffenhausen. **Note: the following abbreviations are used in this listing only: BC (5th General Hospital in Bad Cannstatt); EA (Echterdingen Airfield); GK (Grenadier Kaserne); KB (Kelley Barracks); PB (Patch Barracks); RB (Robinson Barracks); Stgt (Stuttgart); WB (Wallace Barracks).**

GENERAL CITY/REGIONAL: Stuttgart is the political, economic and cultural capital of Baden-Württemberg. Situated among forests, vineyards, parks and gardens, the city is one of the greenest in Germany. The variety of sights in Stuttgart will keep a tourist busy for weeks. Some "must-see" places are the Old and New Castle, Schiller Square, Collegiate Church, Staatsgalerie (State Art Gallery), Wilhelma Zoo and Botanical Gardens, the indoor Farmers' Market, the Planetarium, the Porsche Museum and the Leuze Mineralbad, the second largest mineral bath facility in Europe. Shoppers can look for bargains in crystal, linens, ceramics and Christmas items.

ADMINISTRATIVE SUPPORT

FACILITY/ACTIVITY	BLDG NO/LOC	PHONE	DAYS/COMMENTS
Customs/Duty	110/RB	6604/6095	M-F
Duty Officer	BC	806/800	24 hours daily
	RB	6095	24 hours daily
Fire(Mil)	All locations	117	24 hours daily
Fire(Civ)	All locations	112	24 hours daily
Housing			
Family	106/RB	6017/7156	M-F
Unaccompanied	196/RB	7177	M-F
Referral	106/RB	6354	M-F
Info(Insta)	BC/PB/RB	113	24 hours daily
Inspector Gen'l	RB	2362	M-F
Legal Assist	3314/KB	636/855	M-F
	2301/PB	636/430	M-F
	110/RB	6020/6244	M-F
	4304/WB	6447	M-F
Locator(Civ)	111/RB	6293	M-F
Personnel Spt	106/RB	6036/6024	M-F
Police(Mil)	3306/KB	606/856	24 hours daily
	2307/PB	5261/2	24 hours daily
	112/RB	7307/7043	24 hours daily
Emergency	All locations	114	24 hours daily
Police(Civ)	All locations	C-110	24 hours daily
Public Affairs	KB	614	M-F
	RB	6373/6025	M-F
Tax Relief	RB	6387	M-F

LOGISTICAL SUPPORT

FACILITY/ACTIVITY	BLDG NO/LOC	PHONE	DAYS/COMMENTS
Audio/Photo Ctr	PB	7133 C-6877061	Tu-Su
Auto Drivers Testing	2307/PB	7206/5493	M-F
Auto Parts(Exch)	2326/PB	309 C-6877768/9 C-6877873	M-Sa
Auto Registration	2307/PB	7107	M-F

U.S. Forces Travel & Transfer Guide Europe — 215

GERMANY

Stuttgart Community, continued

	106/RB	7229	M-F
Auto Rental(Exch)	132/RB	C-852604	Daily
Auto Rent(Other)	Near EF	C-7979056	Daily
	Bernhauser St	C-79500103	Daily
Auto Repairs	PB	C-6877873/	M-F
		730873	
Auto Sales	RB	C-8566478	Chrysler. Dly.
	RB	C-859028	Ford. Daily
	RB	C-814115	GM. Daily.
	RB	C-854954	Harley. Daily.
	RB	C-8566819	Jeep. Daily.
	RB	C-850839	VW. Daily.
	Echterdingen	C-7545026	Saab. Daily.
	Echterdingen	C-796011	Volvo. Daily.
	Haupt St	C-6874274	Toyota. Daily.
	Haldenrain St	C-8402706	Mitsubishi. Dly.
	Rotweg	C-879775	Daily

==

Bank	4229/BC	710	M-W,F
	3312/KB	326	M,W,Th,F
		C-721342	
	2325/PB	8468	M-F
		C-687787	
	132/RB	7103/6474	M-SA
		C-814631	
Barber Shop(s)	Hospital/BC	None	M-F
	3312/KB	630	M-F
		C-727551	
	2301/PB	5674/5208	M-F
Beauty Shop(s)	3312/KB	630	M-F
		C-727551	
	2307/PB	5200/7355	M-Sa
		C-6877673	
	132/RB	C-858775	M-Sa

==

Bookstore	Hospital/BC	None	M-F
	T3252/EA	160	M-F
		C-793594	
	GK	C-814596	M-F
	3356/KB	2588	M-Sa
		C-721564	
	2332/PB	C-6877247	Daily
	PB	C-730247	
	S-132/RB	C-812882	Daily
	132/WB	7397/6212	M-F
		C-541739	
Bus	WB	7397/6121	Daily
Child Care/Dev Ctr	433/GK	6682/6346	M-F
		C-8701402	
	3352/KB	541/904	M-F
		C-7292541	
	2312/PB	5123/8506	M-F
	112/RB	6112/6287	M-F
Clothing Sales	RB	7065	Daily
		C-854239	
Commissary(Main)	3316/KB	366/779	Tu-Su
	2350/PB	8401/8455	M-Sa

GERMANY
Stuttgart Community, continued

	145/RB	7408	Tu-Su
Credit Union	132/RB	6102 C-813835	Tu-Sa
Dining Facility	BC	786/730	Daily
	KB	577	Daily
	RB	6084	Daily
Dry Clean(Gov)	2308/PB	5507	M-F
	132/RB	6308	M-Sa
Education Center	3250/EA	4244	M-F
	4257/BC	745	M-F
	3312/KB	793	M-F
	2320/PB	5345/7113	M-F
	108/RB	6123/7114	M-F
Learning Center	4257/BC	738	Daily
	3364/KB	718	Daily
	2320/PB	7256	Daily
	108/RB	6058	Daily

Elec Repair(Gov)	Stgt	6185/115	Daily
Elec Repair(Civ)	See Pick-up Points.		
Eng'r/Publ Works	404/GK	115/6153	Daily
	3320/KB	556	M-Th
Self Help Issue			
Points	3319/KB	556/586	M-F
	2342/PB	5675	M-F
	6365	6365	M-Th
Exchange(Main)	RB/132	C-814571	Daily
Exchange(Annex)	4235/BC	0711-528-	M-F
	3252/EA	C-791219 1522	M-Sa
	3312/KB	C-721309	M-Sa
	PB	5601 C-730578	M-Sa

Exchange(Concess)			
Bavarian Shop	132/RB	C-8566889	Daily
Boutique	132/RB	C-814031	Daily
Carpet Store	132/RB	C-813399	Daily
Computer Store	132/RB	C-8567300	Daily
Furniture	132/RB	C-814571	Daily
Furs	132/RB	C-8566890	Daily
Gift Shop	132/RB	C-8568076	Daily
Jewelry	132/RB	None	Daily
Keys & Engraving	132/RB	C-813315	Daily
Light Reflections	132/RB	C-855875	Daily
Moms & Babes	132/RB	C-814031	Daily
Noritake Shop	132/RB	C-8566153	Daily
Optical Shop	132/RB	C-855372	Daily
Rosenthal Store	132/RB	C-8566979	Daily
Shoe Store	132/RB	C-814571	Daily
Sight & Sound Ctr	132/RB	C-857322	Daily
Tapestry Shop	132/RB	C-8567300	Daily
Finance(Mil)	2325/PB	7103/8454	M-F
	106/RB	7051/6111	Tu-F
	WB	6111	Tu-F
Food(Caf/Rest)	PB	C-732449	Daily
Four Seasons	2333/PB	5285	Daily

GERMANY

Stuttgart Community, continued

Food(Snack/Fast)	4232/BC	C-5282561	Daily
	3252/EA	C-893594	Daily
	3312/KB	C-721316	Daily
	2301/PB	5329	Daily
	132/RB	C-859518	Daily
Baskin Robbins	132/RB	C-854362	Daily
Burger Bar	3312/KB	C-721316	Daily
Burger King	132/RB	C-8568989	Daily
CA Cookies	132/RB	C-8566963	Daily
Pizza Parlor	3312/KB	C-721316	Daily
Foodland	KB	C-721309	Daily
	RB	C-814571	Daily
Laundry(Self-Svc)	3312/KB	None	Daily
	2331/PB	5295	M-Sa
	2313/RB	None	Daily
Package Store	3312/KB	445	M-Sa
	2325/PB	7291	Tu-Sa
	99/RB	6490	Tu-Sa

==

Photo Laboratory	3307/KB	590/607	M,Tu,W,F
	2303/PB	5144/5177	M-F
Pick-up Point	4229/BC	C-567522	M-F
	4227/BC	None	M-Th
	3252/EA	C-791219	Daily
	3449/EA	289	Tu-F
	3312/KB	577/630	M-Sa
	2331/PB	5295	M-Sa
		C-6877874	
	132/RB	C-857372	Daily
Postal Svcs(Mil)	3311/KB	542/592	M-F
	2325/PB	5520/7226	M-F
	132/RB	6223	Tu-Sa
	Main/WB	7061	M-F
Postal Svcs(Civ)	132/RB	C-857373	M-F
	3312/KB	542	Tu,Th
		C-721317	
	2325/PB	C-6877562	M-W,F

==

Railroad/RTO	Stgt main stn	6086	M-F
	GK	7151	Daily
SATO-OS	2320/PB	C-6877121	M-F
	106/RB	C-8566787	M-F
Schools(DOD Dep)	4303/WB	6118	M-F. Supt.
Elementary	2387/PB	5200	M-F (K-6)
		C-6877225	
	148/RB	7363/6164	M-F (K-6)
Middle School	2388/PB	7191/5347	M-F (7-8)
	148/RB	7363/6164	M-F (7-8)
High School	2388/PB	7191/5347	M-F (9-12)
	PB	7191	M-F (7-12)
Svc Stn(Insta)	KB	339	M-Sa
	PB	5600	M-Sa
	RB	6288	M-Sa
		C-859347	
Space-A Air Ops	EA	385	Daily
Flights to:	German locations		
Tailor Shop	3312/KB	630	M-F

GERMANY
Stuttgart Community, continued

	2310/PB	5111	M-Sa
	132/RB	C-8567287	Tu-Sa
Taxi(Comm)	EA	C-795001	Daily
	Stgt	C-566061	Daily
Tel Repair(Gov)	All locations	119	24 hours daily
Tel Repair(Civ)	All locations	0	24 hours daily
Thrift Shop	3312/KB	644	Tu,W,Th
	2307/PB	5510	M,W,F
	113/RB	C-854242	Tu,Th-Sa
TML			
Billeting	169/RB	6209/7308	24 hours daily
		C-859522	
	106/RB (SDO)	6420	After hours
Guest House	169/RB	6209	Daily
Travel Agents	Haldenrain St	C-841066	M-Sa
	2332/PB	5601	Daily
		C-6872004	
	132/RB	C-8568077	Daily

HEALTH AND WELFARE

FACILITY/ACTIVITY	BLDG NO/LOC	PHONE	DAYS/COMMENTS
Ambulance	BC	116/816	24 hours daily
		C-110	
Army Comm Svcs	3317/KB	600/800	M-F
	2307/PB	5724/7270	M-F
	106/RB	6046/7110/6155	M-F
Army Emerg Relief	3317/KB	600/800	M-F
	2307/PB	7176/5674	M-F
	107/RB	6155/6123	M-F
Central Appts	BC	790	M-F. Info.
	BC	796	M-F
	BC	896	Admissions
CHAMPUS Office	4227/BC	845	M-F
	2347/PB	5227	M-F
Chaplain	110/RB	6461/7319	Daily
Chapel	4256/BC	819	Su-F
	3322/KB	501	Su-F
	2307/PB	5280	Su-F
	118/RB	6219	Su-F
Comm Drug/Alc Ctr	BC	777/851	Daily
	3317/KB	353/834	M-F
	2307/PB	5645/7245	M-F
	112/RB	6010	M-F
Dental Clinic	4247/BC	843/733	M-F
	3358/KB	725/317	M-F
	2347/PB	7140/7211	M-F
	135/RB	7069/6289	M-F
Eye Clinic	4247/BC	627/788	M-F
	4347/PB	7122	M-F
Medical Emergency	BC	816	24 hours daily
	Or see ambulance above.		
Mental Health	BC	709/809	M-F
Poison Control	BC	816/885	24 hours daily
Red Cross	Hospital/BC	218/742	M-F

GERMANY

Stuttgart Community, continued

	135/RB	6366/6060 0	M-F After hours
	Stgt	7039/6014 C-8566875	M-F
Veterinary Svcs	138/RB	6038	M,Tu,Th,F

REST AND RECREATION

FACILITY/ACTIVITY	BLDG NO/LOC	PHONE	DAYS/COMMENTS
Amer Forces Ntwk	151/RB	6434/6272	M-F
Amerika Haus	Stgt	C-229830	M-F
Bowling Lanes	3337/KB	559	Daily
	PB	5395	Daily
	RB	6254	Daily
Craftshops			
Automotive	EA	279	Sa-Th
	3320/KB	603	Sa-Th
	GK	6222	Sa-Th
	2322/PB	5258/7240	Sa-Th
Motorcycle	464/PB	C-83550	Tu-Su
Multi-crafts	3319/KB	519	Sa-Th
	2337/PB	5270	Sa-Th
Photography	GB	6222	Daily
	3350/KB	500	Daily
	2342/PB	7113 C-6877061	Daily
Enlisted Club	BC	782	M-F
	3253/EA	C-793541	M-F
	KB	315 C-721290	M-Sa
	RB	6377	M-Sa
Equip/Gear Locker	121/RB	6202/7221	M-Sa
Golf Course	PB	484 C-82750	Tu-Sa
Gymnasium	EA	207	Daily
	3326/KB	543	Daily
	2337/PB	7136/5386	Daily
	109/RB	6317	Daily
Info Tour & Travel	2325/PB	7189 C-6877756	M-F
	132/RB	6090 C-854034	Tu-Sa
Kontakt	3317/KB	353	M-F
	2302/PB	5581	M-F
Library	BC	737	M-F
	3312/KB	638	Sa-Th
	2307/PB	5232/7138	Sa-Th
	116/RB	6424/7385	Tu-Su
MARS	3317/KB	353/834	M-F
	2337/PB	5547	M-F
	110/RB	7195/6305	M-F
Music Center	735/WB	C-29244	W-Su
NCO Club	BC	782	M-Sa
	KB	315	M-Sa
	2345/PB	5473/8228	Daily
	RB	6377	M-Sa

GERMANY
Stuttgart Community, continued

O'Club	3300/KB	586/811 C-721343	Daily
	2505/PB RB	5527/8205 6129 C-854245	Tu-Sa Daily
Recreation Center	3350/KB	611 C-29244	Daily
	2307/PB RB	5559/8276 7082	Daily Daily
Rod and Gun Club	2359/PB	5293 C-6877253	Daily
Theater	4230/BC	785/739	Call for schedule.
	4232/BC	739	Call for schedule.
	3321/KB	629	Call for schedule.
	2339/PB	5310	Call for schedule.
	145/RB	6137/7164	Call for schedule.
Video Rental	3312/KB	None	M-Sa
	2343/PB	7133 C-6877061	Daily
	132/RB	C-854012	Daily
Youth Center	3369/KB	548/975	M-Sa
	2337/PB	7204/5378	M-Sa
	120/RB	6140/6016	M-Sa

===

TEMPELHOF CENTRAL AIRPORT (GE25R7)
APO New York 09611-5000

TELEPHONE INFORMATION: Main installation numbers: Civ: 49-303-819-112. ETS/ATVN: 332-1110. Civ prefix: 303-___. ETS/ATVN prefix: 332-XXXX. Civ to mil prefix: 303-819-XXXX.

LOCATION: In the center of West Berlin and at the corner of Columbia Damm and Tempelhofer Damm Streets. HE: city map 6, Berlin (West). NMC: Berlin, in the city.

GENERAL INSTALLATION INFORMATION: In 1909, Orville Wright demonstrated the first motor-powered flying machine on the Tempelhofer Field. In 1922, the field was converted to a full-time airport. The air terminal was laid out in its present form between 1934 and 1939 and today is one of the largest dimensional buildings in the world. During World War II, after a fierce battle with the Luftwaffe in May, 1945, the Russians took over the base. It came under control of the European Transport system in September of that year and in December, 1947, operation of the base was transferred to the United States Air Forces Europe.

Today the 7350th Air Base Group operates and maintains TCA as an aerial port of entry into West Berlin. Tenant units include the 690th Electronic Security Wing and the 1946th Communications Squadron. Most support facilities are provided by the Army.

GENERAL CITY/REGIONAL INFORMATION: Tempelhof Central Airport's district is one of six in the American Sector of Berlin. West Berlin, the only remaining occupied city from World War II, is divided into three sectors: American; British, with four districts; and French, with two districts. The

Tempelhof Central Airport, continued

GERMANY

eastern part of Berlin comprises the Soviet sector, which is divided from West Berlin by the 28-mile long Berlin Wall. Tempelhof, the alternate civil international airport in Berlin, is always available for civilian and military use. Today Tempelhof Airways U.S.A. is providing civil regional airline services and private charter services from Tempelhof.

Berlin is an exciting city and tourists and residents alike will have no trouble keeping busy there. The Dahlem Museum of Art, the new National Gallery and the Museum of Musical Instruments provide hours of enjoyment to visitors of all ages. The world famous Plotzeasee Memorial, which commemorates victims of the 3rd Reich, is another must-see attraction, as is the Kaiser Wilhelm Memorial Church. The Charlottenburg Palace, Bellevue Palace and a number of other castles are architecturally and culturally important. For a relaxing break, take a stroll through Viktoria Park or the Olympic Stadium, or enjoy some tasty bratwurst at the Market Area Sausage Stand. Finally, no one should miss visiting the Checkpoint Charlie Exhibit.

Evenings in Berlin can be spent at the opera, ballet or theater. Concerts featuring music from classical to jazz to folk to hard rock are held frequently, and the city's many discos, pubs and night clubs offer entertainment to suit everyone's taste.

ADMINISTRATIVE SUPPORT

FACILITY/ACTIVITY	BLDG NO/LOC	PHONE	DAYS/COMMENTS
Customs/Duty	923	6923	M-F
Duty Officer	A2	5300	M-F
Fire(Mil)	N/A	117	24 hours daily
Housing	See Berlin Community listing.		
Info(Insta)	N/A	113	24 hours daily
Inspector Gen'l	A2	5369	M-F
Legal Assist	A2	5032	M-F
Locator(Mil)	A2	5511	M-F
Personnel Spt	K2, Rm 1027/30	5180	M-F
Police(Mil)	K2	5314	24 hours daily
Police(Civ)	K2	5168 C-110	24 hours daily
Public Affairs	A2	5283	M-F
Tax Relief	See Berlin Community listing.		

LOGISTICAL SUPPORT

FACILITY/ACTIVITY	BLDG NO/LOC	PHONE	DAYS/COMMENTS
Audio/Photo Ctr	B-Halle	5209/5269	Tu-Sa
Auto Drivers Testing	D2, Rm 902/4	5548	M-F
Auto Parts(Exch)	South side	5263	Tu-Sa
Auto Registration	D2	5067	M-F
Auto Repairs	K2	5162	Sa-W
Auto Wash	N/A	5162	Sa-W
Bank	A2	5512	M-F
Barber Shop(s)	K2	5603	M-F
Bookstore	A2	6723	M-F
Bus	919	3140	M-F
		3431	After hours
Child Care/Dev Ctr	A2	5379	M-F

GERMANY
Tempelhof Central Airport, continued

Facility	Bldg No/Loc	Phone	Days/Comments
Clothing Sales	K2	5330	M-F
Credit Union	B-Halle	N/A	Tu,Th,Paydays
Dining Facility	TCA	5696	Daily
	Marienfelde	5581	Daily
Dry Clean(Exch)	K2	5255	M-F
Education Center	H2 Long	5847/5132	M-F
Eng'r/Publ Works	H2 Long	5554	M-F
Exchange(Annex)	K2	5211	M-Sa
Finance(Mil)	A2	5272	M-F
Food(Snack/Fast)	A2	5224	24 hours daily
	Ice Cream	5224	M-F
Foodland	K2	5211	Daily
Laundry(Exch)	K2	5255	M-F
Laundry(Self-Svc)	K2	5681	24 hours daily
Motor Pool	D2	5150	M-F
Package Store	K2	5506	M-F
Parking	H2	5314	24 hours daily
Photo Laboratory	A2	5244	M-F
Pick-up Point	K2	5211	M-F
Postal Svcs(Mil)	K2	5609/5535	M-F
Railroad/RTO	Lichterfelde W	6381	M-F
SATO-OS	A2	6523	M-F
Schools(DOD Dep)	See Berlin Community listing.		
Svc Stn(Insta)	Garage	6417	Daily
Space-A Air Ops	A2	5586/5514	M-F
Pax Lounges(Gen'l)	Tempelhof Central	5586	M-F
Flights to:	Charleston AFB/IAP SC; RAF Mildenhall UK; Nürnberg Arpt GE; Ramstein AB GE; Rhein-Main AB GE.		
Tailor Shop	K2	5774	M-Sa
Taxi(Comm)	N/A	785-6025	24 hours daily
Tel Booking Oper	N/A	112	24 hours daily
Tel Repair(Gov)	N/A	119	N/A
TML			
Billeting	K2	5574	24 hours daily
Guest House	C2, D2	5574	24 hours daily
Protocol Office	A2	5151	M-F

HEALTH AND WELFARE

FACILITY/ACTIVITY	BLDG NO/LOC	PHONE	DAYS/COMMENTS
AF Comm Svcs	A2	5191	M-F
AF Relief	A2	5036	M-F
Ambulance	N/A	116	24 hours daily
Central Appts	Berlin Hospital	4211	M-F
CHAMPUS Office	A2	5564	M-F
Chaplain	K2	5317/5314	M-F
Chapel	H2, K2	5317/5888	M-F
Comm Drug/Alc Ctr	1019	5671	M-F
Dental Clinic	Andrews Bks	3491	M-F
Medical Emergency	Berlin Hospital	116/4133	24 hours daily
Mental Health	Berlin Hospital	4190/4191	24 hours daily
Poison Control	Berlin Hospital	4130/4131	24 hours daily
Red Cross	Clay Housing	6459/6437	24 hours daily
Veterinary Svcs	Berlin Hospital	4242	M-F

U.S. Forces Travel & Transfer Guide Europe — 223

GERMANY

Tempelhof Central Airport, continued

REST AND RECREATION

FACILITY/ACTIVITY	BLDG NO/LOC	PHONE	DAYS/COMMENTS
Bowling Lanes	C2	5580	Daily
Craftshops			
Automotive	N/A	5162	Sa-W
Ceramics	H2	5123/5280	W-Su
Multi-crafts	H2	5280	W-Su
Enlisted Club	H2	5318	Daily
Equip/Gear Locker	C2	5188	M-F
Golf Course	Wannsee Lake	N/A	Daily. 18 hole.
Gymnasium	C2	5731	Daily
Info Tour & Travel	C2	5067	M-Sa
Library	C2	5059	Daily
MARS	Andrews Barracks	3567	Daily
NCO Club	C2	5318	Daily
O'Club	H2	5005	Daily
Picnic/Park Area	C2	5713	Daily
Recreation Center	C2	5167	Daily
Special Services	C2	5122	M-F
Theater	Columbia	5522	Daily
Youth Center	Clay Housing	6592/6249	Daily

VILSECK SUB-COMMUNITY (GE85R7)
APO New York 09112-5000

TELEPHONE INFORMATION: Main installation numbers: Civ: 49-09662-83-113. ATVN: 460-1110 (ask for Vilseck). ETS: 476-2113. Civ prefix: 09662-__. ETS prefix: 476-2XXX. Civ to mil prefix: 09662-83-XXX.

LOCATION: Vilseck is located on the south side of the 7th Army Training Area between GE-85 and GE-299. Take the Sigras exit east from GE-85 or the Freihung exit west from GE-299. HE: p-40, G/1-2. NMC: Nürnberg, 37 miles southwest.

GENERAL INSTALLATION INFORMATION: Vilseck is a 7th Army Training Command support community. The 547th General Dispensary is located at Vilseck.

GENERAL CITY/REGIONAL INFORMATION: Vilseck is a small village on the south side of the 7th Army Training Area. The area is wooded and mountainous, approximately 57,000 square acres in size and is near the Czech border.

ADMINISTRATIVE SUPPORT

FACILITY/ACTIVITY	BLDG NO/LOC	PHONE	DAYS/COMMENTS
Fire(Mil)	336	883/117	24 hours daily
Housing			
Referral	420	705/544	M-F
Info(Insta)	On Barracks	113	24 hours daily

GERMANY
Vilseck Sub-Community, continued

Legal Assist	355	518	M-F
Locator(Mil)	On Barracks	113	24 hours daily
Police(Mil)	336	490/890	24 hours daily
Emergency	336	114	24 hours daily
Public Affairs	305	701	M-F
Tax Relief	222	532	M-F

LOGISTICAL SUPPORT

FACILITY/ACTIVITY	BLDG NO/LOC	PHONE	DAYS/COMMENTS
Auto Parts(Exch)	205	C-9741	M-Sa
Auto Registration	336	490	M-F
Inspection	352	631	M,W,F
Auto Rental(Exch)	217	C-9327	N/A
Auto Repairs	205	C-9741	M-Sa
Bank	224	539	M-F
Barber Shop(s)	224	C-9789	M-Sa
Beauty Shop(s)	224	C-8043	Tu-Sa
Bookstore	229	609	Daily
Child Care/Dev Ctr	2234	651	Su-F
Clothing Sales	222	516	M-Sa
Commissary(Main)	333	896	M-Sa
Credit Union	224	C-9235	M-F
Dining Facility	CATC	816/716	Daily
	610	410	Daily
Dry Clean(Exch)	222	C-1015	M-Sa. Pick-up Point.
Education Center	234	653/753	M-F
Eng'r/Publ Works	116	577	M-F
Exchange(Main)	217	700	Daily
Food(Caf/Rest)	226	C-9760	Daily
Foodland	273	C-9363	Daily
Laundry(Exch)	269	660	M-F
Laundry(Self-Svc)	222	None	24 hours daily
Motor Pool	On Barracks	831	M-F
Package Store	224	529	Tu-Sa
Photo Laboratory	221	652	Tu-Sa
Pick-up Point	222	C-1015	M-Sa
Postal Svcs(Mil)	224	581	M-F
Postal Svcs(Civ)	221	C-593	M-F
Railroad/RTO	680	860	M-F
Schools(DOD Dep)			
Elementary	2232	673/812	M-F
High School	480	864	M-F
Svc Stn(Insta)	258	C-9785	Daily
Tailor Shop	222	None	M-Sa
Tel Booking Oper	305	801/601	M-F
Tel Repair(Gov)	On Barracks	119	M-F
Thrift Shop	131	649	Tu,Th
TML			
Billeting	275	555	Su-F
	SNCO	633	Su-F
	Officers	521	Su-F

Vilseck Sub-Community, continued

GERMANY

HEALTH AND WELFARE

FACILITY/ACTIVITY	BLDG NO/LOC	PHONE	DAYS/COMMENTS
Ambulance	On Barracks	116	24 hours daily
Army Comm Svcs	234	650/733	M-F
Army Emerg Relief	234	650/733	M-F
Central Appts	301	536	M-F
Chaplain	218	879	Su-F
Chapel	218	879	Su-F
Comm Drug/Alc Ctr	680	690/731	M-F
Dental Clinic	222	646	M-F
Medical Emergency	On Barracks	116	24 hours daily
Poison Control	See Nürnberg Community listing.		
Red Cross	234	458	M-F
Veterinary Svcs	See Nürnberg Community listing.		

REST AND RECREATION

FACILITY/ACTIVITY	BLDG NO/LOC	PHONE	DAYS/COMMENTS
Bowling Lanes	215	576	Daily
Consolidated Club	431	784	Su-F
Craftshops			
Automotive	264	521/510	Daily
Multi-crafts	221	652	Tu-Sa
Photography	221	652	Tu-Sa
Gymnasium	323	500	Daily
Info Tour & Travel	225	634	M-F
Library	221	635	Su-F
Outdoor Rec Ctr	228	563	M-F
Racket Courts	See Gymnasium.		
Railhead Club	113	561	Daily
Recreation Center	322	749	Daily
Theater	354	519	Daily
Video Rental	222	468	Daily
Youth Center	225	535	M-F

WERTHEIM SUB-COMMUNITY (GE52R7)
APO New York 09047-5000

TELEPHONE INFORMATION: Main installation numbers: Civ: 49-09342-75-113. ETS: 355-5113. ATVN: 350-1110 (ask for Wertheim). Civ prefix: 09342-___. ETS prefix: 355-5XXX. Civ to mil prefix: 09342-75-XXX.

LOCATION: Take the Marktheidenfeld-Wertheim exit from the Frankfurt-Nürnberg E-3 Autobahn. HE: p-40, D/1. NMC: Würzburg, 25 miles west.

GENERAL INSTALLATION INFORMATION: On July 1, 1952, Wertheim, a sub-community of Würzburg, became an American military post providing logistical support, and in 1953, Battery B, 29th Field Artillery, was stationed here. Battery B was redesignated Battery A, 25th Field Artillery, in April of 1984. The unit, a target acquisition battery, is known as the "eyes and ears of

GERMANY
Wertheim Sub-Community, continued

the Marne Division artillery." Peden Barracks in Wertheim is also headquarters for the 72nd Artillery Brigade and the VII Corps aviation unit. Note: the following abbreviations are used in this listing only: PB (Peden Barracks).

GENERAL CITY/REGIONAL INFORMATION: The old city of Wertheim lies on the "Romantic Straße" below an old castle between the Main and the Tauber Rivers. It has often been called "Little Heidelberg." The city is an amalgam of modern and ancient buildings and culture. The history of Wertheim dates back to the 8th century. Owing to its favorable location between two rivers, the settlers were chiefly fishermen and boatsmen.

During World War II the city suffered little damage and many displaced people from throughout the war-ravaged country came to settle here. The population has more than doubled since 1940 and a number of new industries have been introduced in recent years. In spite of all the new construction that has taken place, Wertheim still maintains the romantic air of an old city from centuries gone by.

Just a few of the fascinating sights in the city are the Burg, with ruins from one of the oldest and largest stone castles in South Germany; Spitzer Türm (pointed tower), erected in 1200; Neuplatz, where Wertheim Jewish families lived during the 18th and 19th centuries; the historical museum; the glass museum; and Engelsbrunnen (Angel's Well), built in 1574.

ADMINISTRATIVE SUPPORT

FACILITY/ACTIVITY	BLDG NO/LOC	PHONE	DAYS/COMMENTS
Customs/Duty	109	707	M,Tu,Th,F
Duty Officer	2	648/783	24 hours daily
Fire (Mil)	104	117	24 hours daily
Housing	109	789/855	M-F
Inspector Gen'l	10	679	M-F
Legal Assist	2	646	M-F
Police (Mil)	1/PB	818	24 hours daily
Emergency	1/PB	114	24 hours daily
Police (Civ)	1/PB	C-39405	24 hours daily
Public Affairs	2	746	M-F
Tax Relief	2	748	M-F

LOGISTICAL SUPPORT

FACILITY/ACTIVITY	BLDG NO/LOC	PHONE	DAYS/COMMENTS
Auto Drivers Testing	13	616	M-F
Auto Parts (Exch)	34	653	M-Sa
Auto Registration	PB	627	M-F
Bank	27/PB	872 C-7068	M-F
Barber Shop(s)	36/PB	C-6808	M-F
Beauty Shop(s)	36/PB	C-6808	By appointment
Bookstore	39/PB	687	M-Sa
Bus	132	785	M-Sa
Child Care/Dev Ctr	223/PB	608 C-38223	M-Sa
Clothing Sales	14/PB	605	M-F

GERMANY

Wertheim Sub-Community, continued

Commissary(Main)	111/PB	830	Tu-Sa
		C-38110	
Credit Union	See Würzburg Community listing.		
Dining Facility	Cons Mess	675	Daily
Dry Clean(Exch)	115/PB	730	M-F
Eng'r/Publ Works	106	739	M-F
Exchange(Main)	26/PB	C-38002	M-Sa
Finance(Mil)	2	888	M-F
Food(Snack/Fast)	26/PB	C-7130	Daily
Foodland	34/PB	C-7130	Daily
Laundry(Self-Svc)	38/PB	None	Daily
Motor Pool	132	681	Daily
Package Store	101/PB	683	Tu-Sa
Pick-up Point	14	C-3451	M-F
Postal Svcs(Mil)	13/PB	840	M-F
Schools(DOD Dep)			
Elementary	207	824	M-F (K-6)
Svc Stn(Insta)	34/PB	653	M-Sa
		C-4421	
Tailor Shop	36	C-3451	M-F
Taxi(Comm)	Wertheim	C-1294/92	24 hours daily
Thrift Shop	126T/PB	751	Tu,F
TML			
Billeting	6	689	Daily
TLQ	6	689	Daily
DV/VIP	Dep Comm Cmdr	724/800	

HEALTH AND WELFARE

FACILITY/ACTIVITY	BLDG NO/LOC	PHONE	DAYS/COMMENTS
Ambulance	On Barracks	116	24 hours daily
Army Comm Svcs	28/PB	667/834	M-F
Army Emerg Relief	28/PB	667	M-F
CHAMPUS Office	17/PB	766	M-F
Chapel	112	759/619	Daily
Comm Drug/Alc Ctr	28/PB	592	M-F
Dental Clinic	17/PB	675/767	M-F
Medical Emergency	17/PB	642/766	24 hours daily
Red Cross	28/PB	661	M-F
Veterinary Svcs	See Würzburg Community listing.		

REST AND RECREATION

FACILITY/ACTIVITY	BLDG NO/LOC	PHONE	DAYS/COMMENTS
Bowling Lanes	32/PB	677	M-Sa
Craftshops			
Automotive	105/PB	655	Daily
Multi-crafts	30	732	Tu-Su
Photography	28/PB	664	Tu-Su
Wood	28/PB	664	Tu-Su
Enlisted Club	See NCO Club.		
Gymnasium	113/PB	777	Daily
Info Tour & Travel	27/PB	784	M-Sa
Library	27/PB	693	Sa-Th
NCO Club	33/PB	688	Daily

GERMANY
Wertheim Sub-Community, continued

O'Club	6/PB	689	Daily
Outdoor Rec Ctr	115	678	M-F
Racket Courts	See gymnasium.		
Recreation Center	27/PB	784	M-F
Rod and Gun Club	28/PB	670 C-7000	M-Sa
Theater	PB	840	Daily
Video Rental	36	None	Daily
Youth Center	9/PB	751 C-7020	M-Sa

==

WIESBADEN COMMUNITY (GE27R7)
APO New York 09457-5000

TELEPHONE INFORMATION: Main installation numbers: Civ: 49-06121-78-113 (Wiesbaden Air Base); 49-06121-82-113 (Camp Pieri and Wiesbaden Regional Medical Center); 49-06134-604-113 (Mainz Kastel). ETS: 337-113 (Wiesbaden Air Base); 339-113 (Camp Pieri and Wiesbaden Regional Medical Center); 334-2113 (Mainz Kastel Storage Station). ATVN: 320-1110 (ask for Wiesbaden). Civ prefix: 06121-_____ (Wiesbaden Air Base, Camp Pieri, and Wiesbaden Regional Medical Center); 06134-_____ (Mainz Kastel Storage Station). ETS prefix: 337-XXXX (Wiesbaden Air Base); 339-XXXX (Camp Pieri and Wiesbaden Regional Medical Center); 334-2XXX (Mainz Kastel Storage Station). Civ to mil prefix: 06121-78-XXXX (Wiesbaden Air Base); 06121-82-XXXX (Camp Pieri and Wiesbaden Regional Medical Center); 06134-604-XXX (Mainz Kastel Storage Station). **Note: Civilian prefixes for Hainerberg Housing Area in Wiesbaden are always 06121; military prefixes vary, so the entire military number is provided in the listing below.**

LOCATION: Accessible from Autobahns E-3, E-5, E-61. Take exits marked Wiesbaden Air Base. HE: p-40, A/1. NMC: Wiesbaden, in the city.

GENERAL INSTALLATION INFORMATION: Wiesbaden Air Base is now the home of the U.S. Military Community Activity (USMCA), Wiesbaden, and the 4th Brigade, 4th Infantry Division (Mechanized). USMCA Wiesbaden is composed of approximately 120 U.S. Army personnel and 800 local Department of the Army civilians whose mission is to provide installation and personnel service support to assigned, attached, and tenant organizations within the Wiesbaden area. The community's population is approximately 17,000. **Note: the following abbreviations are used in this listing only: CP (Camp Pieri); HB (Hainerberg Housing in Wiesbaden); MK (Mainz Kastel Station Storage); RMC (Regional Medical Center); WAB (Wiesbaden Air Base).**

GENERAL CITY/REGIONAL: Wiesbaden is a beautiful city located between the Taunus Mountains and the Rhein River. While many of the cities along the Rhein are industrial, Wiesbaden has managed to survive, even thrive, without heavy industrial complexes.

Wiesbaden is a modern city with a population of slightly more than a quarter of a million people. Fountains grace the city's parks, squares and streets as symbols of the 26 thermal springs whose curative powers were prized even by the ancient Romans.

U.S. Forces Travel & Transfer Guide Europe — 229

GERMANY

Wiesbaden Community, continued

Among Wiesbaden's points of interest are its Kurhaus and casino; the Wilhelmstraße with its elegant shops and sidewalk cafes; the Hesse State Theater and Opera House; the Biebrich Palace, a gem of early 18th-century architecture; and the Neroberg, 804 feet high, which offers a breath-taking view both of the city and the Rhein River Valley. Not to be missed at the Neroberg is a ride on its unique rack railway and a visit to the Russian Chapel, built in 1855 in the Russian-Byzantine style.

ADMINISTRATIVE SUPPORT

FACILITY/ACTIVITY	BLDG NO/LOC	PHONE	DAYS/COMMENTS
Customs/Duty	WAB	5958	M-F
Duty Officer	N/A	5088	24 hours daily
Fire(Mil)	All locations	117	24 hours daily
Housing	1023W/WAB	5556/5157	M-F
Info(Insta)	All locations	113	24 hours daily
Legal Assist	1023M/WAB	3669	M-Th
Personnel Spt	WAB	5689	M-F
Police(Mil)	1006/WAB	5096/5097	24 hours daily
Emergency	All locations	114	24 hours daily
Public Affairs	WAB	5772/5972	M-F

LOGISTICAL SUPPORT

FACILITY/ACTIVITY	BLDG NO/LOC	PHONE	DAYS/COMMENTS
Audio/Photo Ctr	HB	C-719081	M-F
	MK	402	M-F
Auto Drivers Testing	1023W/WAB	5825	M,W,F
		C-5116	
Auto Registration	7513/MK	470	M-F
Auto Rental(Exch)	Amelia Earhart Hotel—WAB prefix	C-816026	M-Sa
Auto Sales	198/HB	C-72216	Amer Motors
	198/HB	C-761379	Chrysler
	198/HB	C-702752	Ford
	198/HB	C-78818	GM
Bank	14/CP	3613	M-F
	HB	337-3567	M-Sa
	RMC	3876	M-F
	WAB	5908	M-F
		C-702411	
Barber Shop(s)	HB	C-701869	M-Sa
	RMC	7397	M-Sa
	WAB	C-72395	M-F
Beauty Shop(s)	HB	C-701675	M-Sa
	WAB	C-701782	Tu-Sa
Bookstore	3102/CP	N/A	M-F
	77/HB	339-3526	Daily
	RMC	C-843665	M-F
Bus	WAB prefix	5659	M-F
Child Care/Dev Ctr	17/HB	C-74245	M-F
	1213/WAB	C-701488	M-F
Clothing Sales	WAB	5567	M-F
Commissary(Main)	7765/CP	6186	Daily
	WAB	5968/5828	Daily

GERMANY
Wiesbaden Community, continued

Credit Union	21/WAB	5748	M-F
Dining Facility	5/RMC	N/A	Daily
	43/WAB	N/A	Daily
Education Center	3102/CP	N/A	M-F
	1023W/WAB	5559/5412	M-F
Eng'r/Publ Works	All locations	115	Daily
Exchange(Main)	CP	C-420733	M,Tu,Th-Sa
	HB	C-719081	Tu-Su
	RMC	C-843665	Tu-Sa
	WAB	C-701889	Tu-Sa
Finance(Mil)	WAB	5563	M-F
Food(Caf/Rest)	HB	C-701596	Daily
Food(Snack/Fast)	CP	C-21696	Daily
	RMC	C-843665	Daily
	WAB	C-72396	Daily
Foodland	HB	C-701664	Daily
	WAB	C-701460	Daily
Laundry(Self-Svc)	HB	C-701314	Daily
Motor Pool	WAB prefix	5440	M-F
Package Store	HB	337-3472	Tu-Sa
	MK	4707	Tu-Sa
	WAB	5784	Tu-Sa
Pick-up Point	HB	C-701627	Daily
	WAB	C-72393	M-F
Postal Svcs(Mil)	CP	N/A	M-F
	HB	337-5125	Tu-Sa
	WAB	N/A	M-F
Postal Svcs(Civ)	21/WAB	5600	M-F
	Wiesbaden	C-8003348	M-F
Railroad/RTO	30/WAB	5510	M-F
Schools(DOD Dep)			
Elementary	Aukamm Housing	339-6387	M-F (K-8)
	(use CP prefix)	C-561518	
	HB	339-5160	M-F (K-8)
		C-72004	
Middle School	HB	339-6228	M-F (7-8)
High School	HB	339-3701	M-F (9-12)
Svc Stn(Insta)	WAB	5720	Daily
Space-A Air Ops	WAB	5662	Daily
Flights to:	German locations		
Tailor Shop	CP	C-420733	M-Sa
	HB	C-73624	M-Sa
	WAB	C-72395	M-Sa
Tel Repair(Gov)	WAB prefix	5950	Daily
TML			
Billeting	American Arms Hotel—WAB prefix	6525	24 hours daily
Guest House	Amelia Earhart Hotel—WAB prefix	3288	Daily
DV/VIP	Dep Comm Cmdr Wiesbaden	5693	M-F

HEALTH AND WELFARE

FACILITY/ACTIVITY	BLDG NO/LOC	PHONE	DAYS/COMMENTS
Ambulance	All locations	116	24 hours daily

GERMANY

Wiesbaden Community, continued

Army Comm Svcs	HB	5754	M-F
		C-789591	
	1023/WAB	5708	M-F
Army Emerg Relief	1023W/WAB	5615/5754	M-F
Central Appts	RMC	6106/3036	Daily
		C-801070/9	
Chaplain	WAB prefix	5176/5818	Daily
Chapel	CP	6642	Daily
	HB	3791	Daily
	WAB	5573	Daily
Dental Clinic	1040/WAB	5804	M-F
Medical Emergency	1/RMC	3801	24 hours daily
Red Cross	3/RMC	7220/6224	M-F
		113	After hours
Veterinary Svcs	2/RMC	6268	Call for hours.

REST AND RECREATION

FACILITY/ACTIVITY	BLDG NO/LOC	PHONE	DAYS/COMMENTS
Bowling Lanes	CP	3027	Daily
	WAB	5654/5867	Daily
Craftshops			
Automotive	CP	3394	W-Su
Multi-crafts	WAB	5449	Tu-Su
Photography	WAB	5536	Tu-Su
Wood	WAB	5449/5722	Tu-Sa
Enlisted Club	Amelia Earhart Hotel—Wiesbaden	3351	Daily
Golf Course	Rheinblick Golf Club—CP prefix	3889/6158	W-Su
Gymnasium	3110/CP	3024	Daily
	43/WAB	5943	Daily
Info Tour & Travel	HB	C-701968	N/A
Library	29/WAB	5951	Daily
MARS	WAB prefix	5133	Daily
NCO Club	Eagles Nest—WAB prefix	5877	Daily
	Hilltop—CP prefix	3421	Daily
O'Club	American Arms Hotel—WAB prefix	5111	Daily
	Bayrischer Garten—WAB prefix	4413	Daily
Outdoor Rec Ctr	67/WAB	5760	M-Sa
Recreation Center	1322/CP	6108	Daily
	29/WAB	5822	Daily
Rod and Gun Club	Rheinblick Small Ammo Range—CP prefix	4455 C-428649	Daily
Theater	HB	3530	Daily
	WAB	5774	Daily
Youth Center	07775/HB	6355	M-Sa
	07790/HB	6355	M-F

GERMANY

WILDFLECKEN COMMUNITY (GE86R7)
APO New York 09026-5000

TELEPHONE INFORMATION: Main installation numbers: Civ: 49-09745-35-113. ETS: 326-3113. Civ prefix: 09745-____. ETS prefix: 326-3XXX. Civ to mil prefix: 09745-35-XXX.

LOCATION: Take the Autobahn toward towards Kassel and Fulda (A-66). Exit at Fulda and follow signs to Coburg. After coming over the Schwedenschanze, follow signs to Wildflecken. Once in Wildflecken, follow signs to the U.S. Army Post. HE: p-36, F-G/6. NMC: Fulda, 25 miles north.

GENERAL INSTALLATION INFORMATION: The USMCA Wildflecken is one of three military training areas of the U.S. Army in Europe. Five major units are permanently stationed in Wildflecken.

GENERAL CITY/REGIONAL INFORMATION: Wildflecken is located in an area abounding in resorts and spas. One of the main attractions is the "Wasserkuppe," where gliding was born. A well known museum of gliding history is located there. The region also boasts a number of hiking trails and fine ski slopes. The fascinating cities of Fulda and Würzburg are both short drives from Wildflecken.

ADMINISTRATIVE SUPPORT

FACILITY/ACTIVITY	BLDG NO/LOC	PHONE	DAYS/COMMENTS
Customs/Duty	607	784	M-F
Duty Officer	71	418/824	N/A
Fire(Mil)	436	657	24 hours daily
Fire(Civ)	Downtown	112	24 hours daily
Housing			
Family	141	883	M-F
Referral	141	583	M-F
Info(Insta)	On Barracks	113	24 hours daily
Legal Assist	500	766	M-F
Locator(Mil)	8	471	M-F
Locator(Civ)	8	777	M-F
Personnel Spt	252	468/792	M-F
Police(Mil)	9	898	24 hours daily
Emergency	9	114	24 hours daily
Police(Civ)	N/A	774	24 hours daily
Public Affairs	7	863	M-F

LOGISTICAL SUPPORT

FACILITY/ACTIVITY	BLDG NO/LOC	PHONE	DAYS/COMMENTS
Auto Drivers Testing	607	609	M-F
Auto Parts(Exch)	362	C-3047	M-Sa
Auto Registration	9	610	M-F
Auto Rental(Exch)	31	C-1210	M-F
Auto Repairs	607	C-3047	W-Su
Auto Sales	252	C-2190	M-F
Auto Wash	604	479	W-Su
Bank	352	482 C-777	M-F

GERMANY

Wildflecken Community, continued

Facility	BLDG NO/LOC	PHONE	DAYS
Barber Shop(s)	1	563	M-F
	271	282	M-Sa
	233	573	M-F
Beauty Shop(s)	233	573	M-F
Bookstore	372	485	M-Sa
Bus	607	498	M-F
Child Care/Dev Ctr	45	584	M-F
		C-604	
Clothing Sales	420	564	M-F
Commissary(Main)	700	847/967	M-Sa
Commissary(Annex)	233	321	Tu-Su
Dry Clean(Exch)	271	326	M-F
Dry Clean(Gov)	270	420	M-F
Education Center	330	550/785	M-F
Elec Repair(Gov)	7	487	M-F
Eng'r/Publ Works	608	696	M-F
Exchange(Main)	371	C-3061/51	Daily
Finance(Mil)	141	873	M-F
Food(Snack/Fast)			
Burger Bar	Downtown	C-684	M-Sa
Burger King	31	472	Daily
Pizza Parlor	252	C-3062	Daily
Foodland	271	C-3261	Daily
Laundry(Self-Svc)	233	573	Daily
Motor Pool	607	786	Daily
Package Store	375	409	Tu-Sa
Photo Laboratory	31	656	W-Su
Pick-up Point	270	420	M-Sa
Postal Svcs(Mil)	8	471/750	M-Sa
Postal Svcs(Civ)	31	C-684	M-F
Railroad/RTO	607	653	M-F
SATO-OS	31	C-1210	M-F
Schools(DOD Dep)			
Elementary	N/A	426/864	M-F
Svc Stn(Insta)	N/A	C-3812	N/A
Tailor Shop	271	C-3106	N/A
Taxi(Comm)	Downtown	C-677	N/A
Tel Booking Oper	Gelnhausen	112	N/A
Tel Repair(Gov)	1	551	N/A
Thrift Shop	31	677	N/A
TML			
Billeting	32	553/964	M-F
	SDO	418/824	After hours
Guest House	32	553/964	Daily
VOQ	25	553/964	Daily
DV/VIP	50	553/964	Daily
Travel Agents	31	C-1210	M-F

HEALTH AND WELFARE

FACILITY/ACTIVITY	BLDG NO/LOC	PHONE	DAYS/COMMENTS
Ambulance	3	116	24 hours daily
Army Comm Svcs	143	939	M-F
Army Emerg Relief	143	712	M-F
Central Appts	N/A	735	M-F
CHAMPUS Office	3,4	756	M-F

GERMANY
Wildflecken Community, continued

Chaplain	177	631	M-F
Chapel	177	631	M-F
Comm Drug/Alc Ctr	143	490/940	M-F
Dental Clinic	4	650	M-F
Medical Emergency	3	470/662	24 hours daily
Red Cross	141	453/869	N/A

REST AND RECREATION

FACILITY/ACTIVITY	BLDG NO/LOC	PHONE	DAYS/COMMENTS
Bowling Lanes	460	659	Daily
Camping/RV Area	Kippelbach	876	Daily
Craftshops			
Automotive	607	C-3047	
Multi-crafts	31	656	W-Su
Photography	31	656	W-Su
Enlisted Club	N/A	603	Tu-Sa
Gymnasium	630	652	Daily
Info Tour & Travel	31	C-731	M-F
Library	31	816	W-Su
MARS	31	931	M-F
NCO Club	12	603	Tu-Sa
O'Club	50	443	N/A
Racket Courts	630	652	N/A
Recreation Center	31	472	N/A
Rod and Gun Club	373	665	M-Sa
Service Club	31	472	M-F
Special Services	143	815	M-F
Sport Field	630	652	Daily
Tennis Courts	630	652	Daily
Theater	16	647	Daily
	31	607	W-Su
Video Rental	470	430 C-3813	Daily
Youth Center	510	957	Tu-Sa

WORMS/NORTHPOINT/WEIERHOF COMMUNITY (GE31R7)
APO New York 09058-5000

TELEPHONE INFORMATION: Main installation numbers: Civ: 49-06241-48-113 (Worms); 49-06358-86-113 (Weierhof). ETS: 383-113 (Worms); 491-2113 (Weierhof). Civ prefix: 06241-____ (Worms); 06352-____ (Weierhof if dialing civ to civ). ETS prefix: 383-XXXX (Worms); 491-2XXX (Weierhof). Civ to mil prefix: 06241-48-XXXX (Worms); 06358-86-XXX (Weierhof).

LOCATION: Take the Worms exit from the Mannheim-Saarbrucken E-6 Autobahn and follow signs. HE: p-40, B/2. NMC: Worms, in the city.

GENERAL INSTALLATION INFORMATION: The mission of the installation is to provide support to the Worms Military Community, the 5th Signal Command, and all tenant units. **Note: the following abbreviations are used in this listing only: PB (de la Police Barracks); TB**

U.S. Forces Travel & Transfer Guide Europe — 235

Worms/Northpoint/Weierhof Community, continued   GERMANY

(Taukkunen Barracks); TJV (Thomas Jefferson Village). All three barracks are located in Worms.

GENERAL CITY/REGIONAL INFORMATION: Visitors coming to Worms today are greeted by a modern city of 75,000 inhabitants. The city lies on both sides of the Rhein River. The Worms Cathedral (Dom St. Peter) and the churches of St. Martin, St. Paul, St. Andrew, and the Church of Our Lady, situated in the famous vineyards, dominate the Worms skyline. The Dom was built on a site first used by the Romans as a Roman Forum. In the 4th century, the forum was replaced by a cathedral of the Diocese of Worms. The Dom's architecture is primarily from the 12th century. St. Martin's church was founded prior to 1000 A.D. and was reconstructed during the 13th century. St. Andrew's church, which was built during the same time period, now houses the city's museum. St. Paul's church is now used as a Dominican monastery. The Church of Our Lady was built during the 14th and 15th centuries.

The Worms City Museum contains displays and exhibits about the history of the area as far back as 5000 years ago. Art exhibits are always on display in the museum auditorium. Works of art by many of Europe's greatest artists from the 15th through the 19th century are on display at the Heylshof art collection near the Dom.

ADMINISTRATIVE SUPPORT

FACILITY/ACTIVITY	BLDG NO/LOC	PHONE	DAYS/COMMENTS
Customs/Duty	5824/TB	7807/7507	M-F
Duty Officer	5814/TB	7234/7384	24 hours daily
Fire(Mil)	All locations	117	24 hours daily
Fire(Civ)	All locations	112	24 hours daily
Housing			
Family	5834/TB	7200/7994	M-F
Referral	5834/TB	7292/7997	M-F
Info(Insta)	All locations	113	M-F
Inspector Gen'l	5824/TB	7890	M-F
Legal Assist	5822/TB	7782/8326	M-F
Locator(Mil)	5810/TB	7640/7448	M-F
Personnel Spt	5824/TB	7363/7891	M-F
Police(Mil)	5824/TB	7033	24 hours daily
Emergency		114	24 hours daily
Police(Civ)	Worms	110	24 hours daily
Public Affairs	5829/TB	7432/7103	M-F
Tax Relief	5824/TB	7458	M-F

LOGISTICAL SUPPORT

FACILITY/ACTIVITY	BLDG NO/LOC	PHONE	DAYS/COMMENTS
Audio/Photo Ctr			
Auto Drivers Testing	5824/TB	7989	M-F
Auto Parts(Exch)	5815/TB	7052	M-F
		C-43934	M-Sa
Auto Registration	5824/TB	7811/7793	M-F
Auto Rent(Other)	Worms	C-45767	M-Sa
Auto Repairs	5815/TB	7052	M-F
		C-43934	

GERMANY
Worms/Northpoint/Weierhof Community, continued

Auto Ship(Gov)	5834/TB	7337	M-F
Bank	5810/TJV	7490	M-F
Barber Shop(s)	5821/TB	C-44495	M-Sa
Beauty Shop(s)	5810/TJV	C-51932	Tu-Sa
Bookstore	5810/TJV	None	M-Sa
Child Care/Dev Ctr	5906/PB	7937	M-F (preschool)
	5810/TJV	7515	Daily
Commissary(Main)	5810/TJV	7901/7521	M-Sa
Dining Facility	5831/TB	7276/7758	Daily
Dry Clean(Exch)	5808/TJV	7256	M-F
Education Center	5815/TB	7895/7632	M-F
	5015/TJV	7980	M-F
Eng'r/Publ Works	5827/TB	7857	M-F
	Emergency	115	24 hours daily
Exchange(Main)	5810/TJV	7562/7563	M-Sa
		C-51933	
Exchange(Annex)	5825/TJV	7563	M-Sa
Finance(Mil)	5824/TB	7960/7984	M-F
Food(Caf/Rest)	5825/TB	C-43305	M-Sa
Food(Snack/Fast)	5825/TB	C-43305	M-Sa
Foodland	5810/TJV	7761	Daily
		C-51933	
Laundry(Self-Svc)	5011/TJV	None	Tu-Su
Motor Pool	5838/TB	7718	M-F
Package Store	5808/TB	7329	M-F
Photo Laboratory	5832/TB	7090/7990	M-F
Pick-up Point	5808/TB	7256	M-F
		C-44180	
Postal Svcs(Mil)	5810/TJV	7448/7640	M-F
Schools(DOD Dep)	In Worms:		
Elementary	5015/TJV	7980/7219	M-F (K-6)
Jr/Sr High School	See Mannheim Community listing.		
	In Weierhof:		
Elementary	Housing area		M-F (K-6)
Middle School	See Sembach Community listing.		
High School	See Kaiserslautern Community listing.		
Space-A Air Ops	See Rhein-Main Air Base listing.		
Tailor Shop	5825/TB	N/A	N/A
Taxi(Comm)	Worms	C-52033	24 hours daily
Tel Booking Oper	All locations	112	24 hours daily
Tel Repair(Gov)	All locations	119	N/A
Tel Repair(Civ)	Worms	C-011701	N/A
Thrift Shop	Worms	6028	Tu,Th
		C-592871	
TML			
Billeting	5032/TJV	7374/7763	M-F
	SDO/TB	7589	After hours
Guest House	5032/TJV	7374/7763	M-F
Protocol Office	Hq 5th Sig Cmd	7589	M-F
TLF	5032/TJV	7374/7763	Daily
Travel Agents	5810/TJV	N/A	M-F

HEALTH AND WELFARE

FACILITY/ACTIVITY	BLDG NO/LOC	PHONE	DAYS/COMMENTS
Ambulance	All locations	116/7747	24 hours daily

GERMANY

Worms/Northpoint/Weierhof Community, continued

Army Comm Svcs	5831/TB	7546/7339	M-F
	5010/TJV	7936	M-F
	Weierhof	830/801	M-F
Army Emerg Relief	5831/TB	7021/7790	M-F
Central Appts	5821/TB	7095/7747	M-F
CHAMPUS Office	Health Clinic/ Worms	7747	M-F
Chaplain	5819/TB	7619/7919	Su-F
Chapel	5819/TB	7619/7919	W,Sa,Su
	Weierhof	810	Su
Comm Drug/Alc Ctr	5838/TB	8307/7407	M-F
Dental Clinic	5921/TB	7831/7631	M-F
	Weierhof	835	M-F
Medical Emergency	All locations	116/7747	24 hours daily
Red Cross	Health Clinic/ Worms	7882	M-F
Veterinary Svcs	See the Heidelberg Community listing.		

==
REST AND RECREATION
==

FACILITY/ACTIVITY	BLDG NO/LOC	PHONE	DAYS/COMMENTS
Bowling Lanes	5837/TB	7165	Daily
Craftshops			
Automotive	5804/TB	7052	Daily
Ceramics	5804/TB	7876	W-Su
Multi-crafts	5804/TB	7876	W-Su
Photography	5804/TB	7876	W-Su
Wood	5804/TB	7876	W-Su
Enlisted Club	5836/TB	7689/7290	M-Sa
Gymnasium	5837/TB	7482	Daily
Info Tour & Travel	5010/TJV	7491 C-592302	M-F
Library	5831/TB	7210	Daily
NCO Club	5836/TB	7290	Daily
O'Club	5031/TJV	7420	M-F
Outdoor Rec Ctr	5011/TJV	7512/7754	Th-Tu
Picnic/Park Area	Site 53	7937	M-Sa
Racket Courts	Near 5837/TB	7482	Daily
Rod and Gun Club	5803/TB	7117 C-43136	Tu-Sa
Sport Field	Helipad Area	7482	Daily
Tennis Courts	See gymnasium.		
Theater	5826/TB	7550	As posted
Track	Helipad Area	None	Daily
Trails	Site 53	None	Daily
Video Rental	5010/TJV	None	Daily
Youth Center	5028/TJV	7855	Tu-Su

==

WÜRZBURG COMMUNITY (GE21R7)
APO New York 09801-5000

TELEPHONE INFORMATION: Main installation numbers: Civ: 49-0931-889-113. ETS: 350-5113 (Emery Barracks); 350-113 (Leighton Barracks,

GERMANY
Würzburg Community, continued

Faulenberg Kaserne, Hindenberg Barracks); 350-4113 (River Building); 350-3113 (Hospital). ATVN: 350-1110. Civ prefix: 0931-_____. ETS prefix: 350-XXXX (Leighton Barracks, Faulenberg Kaserne, Hindenberg Barracks); 350-5XXX (Emery Barracks); 350-4XXX (River Building); 350-3XXX (Hospital). Civ to mil prefix: 0931-889-XXX(X).

LOCATION: From west on Autobahn E-3 take Heidingsfield exit to Rottendorfer Straße north to Leighton Barracks. Take first right after Hq Building 6, proceed to Bldg 2. HE: p-40, D/1. NMC: Würzburg, 1 mile south.

GENERAL INSTALLATION INFORMATION: Würzburg is home to the 3rd Infantry Division's headquarters. The 3rd Infantry Division's mission is to maintain peace through a state of combat readiness. Würzburg is also home to Division Artillery and a host of support units including the 69th Air Defense Artillery Brigade, the 103rd Military Intelligence Battalion, the 631st TAC Air Squadron, the 6th Battalion/52nd ADA and the 11th Signal Battalion. As the Marneland base camp, thousands of soldiers and their families reside in and around Würzburg. Note: the following abbreviations are used in this listing only: EB (Emery Barracks); FK (Faulenberg Kaserne); HB (Hindenberg Barracks); LB (Leighton Barracks); RB (River Building).

GENERAL CITY/REGIONAL INFORMATION: Situated in the wide valley of the Main River, Würzburg is a picturesque city whose history dates back almost 3,000 years. Today, Würzburg is a bustling city of about 130,000. It boasts a major university and a great number of industries. Würzburg has more tourists per capita than any other German city, no doubt because of the number of sights worth seeing, including the Residency, a palace over 250 years old; St. Killian's Cathedral; the Main-Frankisches Museum in the Festing Marienberg Castle; the marktplatz; and the modern theater.

ADMINISTRATIVE SUPPORT

FACILITY/ACTIVITY	BLDG NO/LOC	PHONE	DAYS/COMMENTS
Fire(Mil)	All locations	117 C-25578	24 hours daily
Housing			
Family	FK	7229/6109	M-F
Referral	258/FK	6126/7104	M-F
Legal Assist	47A/LB	6255/7174	M-F
	Claims/LB	6321	M-F
Personnel Spt	LB	6323	M-F
Police(Mil)	LB	114	24 hours daily
Emergency	LB	114	24 hours daily
Public Affairs	7/LB	6408/6409 C-706478	M-F. 3rd Inf Div.
	45/LB	7142/6388	M-F. Information.
	3-15/RB	606/708 C-72096	M-F
Tax Relief	13/LB	7159	M-F

LOGISTICAL SUPPORT

FACILITY/ACTIVITY	BLDG NO/LOC	PHONE	DAYS/COMMENTS
Audio/Photo Ctr	LB	C-706685	M-F

Würzburg Community, continued

GERMANY

Auto Drivers Testing	56/LB	6325	M-F
Auto Parts(Exch)	9/LB	C-706676	M-Sa
Auto Registration	229/FK	None	Daily
Auto Rental(Exch)	LB	C-708475	M-Sa
Auto Repairs	9A/LB	C-706676	M-F
Auto Sales	Würzburg	C-707379	M-Sa. Ford.
	Würzburg	C-108422	M-Sa. VW.
	Würzburg	C-706680	M-Sa. AMC.
	Würzburg	C-700515	M-Sa. GM.
	Würzburg	C-706631	M-Sa. Chrysler.
Bank	328E/EB	729	M-F
	11/LB	6111	M-Sa
		C-11081	
Barber Shop(s)	307E/EB	N/A	M,Tu,Th,F
	286/HK	N/A	M,Tu,Th
	9/LB	C-706682	Tu-Sa
	Hospital	N/A	M
Beauty Shop(s)	9/LB	C-706682	Tu-Sa
Bookstore	307/EB	C-93239	M-F
	10/LB	6142	Daily
	345/Hospital	C-8893760	M-F
Child Care/Dev Ctr	45/LB	6175	M-F
		C-706684	
Clothing Sales	229/FK	C-283420	M-F
Commissary(Main)	10/LB	7190	M-Sa
		C-870247	
Credit Union	10/LB	6229	M-F
		C-709066	
Education Center			
Learning Center	EB	760	M-F
	HB	355	M-F
	15/LB	7181/6441	M-F
Eng'r/Publ Works	Würzburg	6313	Daily
Exchange(Main)	10/LB	7066	Daily
Exchange(Annex)	307/EB	C-96128	M-F
	277/HK	C-412440	M-F
Finance(Mil)	10/LB	7210/6348	M-F
Food(Snack/Fast)	307/EB	C-96239	Daily
	221/FB	C-285621	Daily
	277/HK	C-412533	F-W
	9/LB	C-706689	Daily
Burger King	183/LB	C-706294	Daily
Foodland	307/EB	C-96128	Daily
	965/LB	C-846350	Daily
Laundry(Self-Svc)	305/EB	None	Daily
Package Store	77/LB	6405	Tu-Sa
		C-708758	
Pick-up Point	302/EB	796	M-F
	286/HK	7164/6219	M-F
	9/LB	None	M-Sa
Postal Svcs(Mil)	304/EB	784	M,Tu,Th,F
	284/HK	6274	M,Tu,Th,F
	12/LB	7129	M-Sa
Postal Svcs(Civ)	10/LB	C-709021	N/A

GERMANY
Würzburg Community, continued

Schools(DOD Dep)

Elementary	100/LB	7169	M-F (K-6)
	Skyline Hsg	6158	M-F (K-6)
High School	134/Skyline Hsg	7176/6328	M-F (7-12)
Svc Stn(Insta)	12	C-70695	Daily
Space-A Air Ops	See Rhein-Main Air Base listing.		
Tailor Shop	LB	C-706678	M-Sa
Taxi(Comm)	Würzburg	C-50707	Daily
Thrift Shop	19/LB	C-700104	Tu,Th,F
TML			
Billeting	2/LB	6383	Daily
	6/LB (SDO)	6223	After hours
Guest House	2/LB	6383	Daily
Protocol Office	6/LB	8308/8306	Daily
DV/VIP	2/LB	8308/8306	Daily
Travel Agents		C-71083	

HEALTH AND WELFARE

FACILITY/ACTIVITY	BLDG NO/LOC	PHONE	DAYS/COMMENTS
Ambulance	Würzberg	116	24 hours daily
	Hospital	700/887	24 hours daily
Army Comm Svcs	26/LB	6231/7103 C-709758	M-F
Central Appts	RB	824	24 hours daily
Chapel	87/EB	770	Daily
Comm Drug/Alc Ctr	26/LB	7205	M-F
Dental Clinic	24/LB	6227/6125	M-F
Medical Emergency	Hospital	862	24 hours daily
Red Cross	26/LB	6113/7215	M-F
		113	After hours
Veterinary Svcs	248/FB	6132 C-284151	Tu,Th,F

REST AND RECREATION

FACILITY/ACTIVITY	BLDG NO/LOC	PHONE	DAYS/COMMENTS
Amer Forces Ntwk	45/LB	7142/6368	M-F
Bowling Lanes	14/LB	6364 C-900373	Daily
	320/EB	751	Daily
Craftshops			
Automotive	EB	752	Th-Sa
	HK	6345	Tu-Sa
Leather	HK	6345	Tu-Sa
Multi-crafts	EB	752	Tu-Sa
	HK	6345	Tu-Sa
Photography	EB	756	Tu-Sa
	LB	6442	Tu-Sa
Wood	HK	6345	Tu-Sa
Enlisted Club	280/HK	6238	Daily
	HK	6108	Daily
Gymnasium	320/EB	717	Daily
	295/HK	6303	Daily
	14/LB	6115/6245	Daily

GERMANY

Würzburg Community, continued

Info Tour & Travel	14/LB	6434/7161	M-F
MARS	11/LB	7114/6269	M-F
NCO Club	LB	6112	N/A
O'Club	5/LB	6305	Tu-Su. E7+.
Outdoor Rec Ctr	94/LB	6272	M-F
Recreation Center	88/LB	6127	Th-Tu
Theater	EB	72435 C-72345	Daily
Youth Center	153/LB	6141	M-Sa

WÜSCHHEIM AIR STATION (GE87R7)
APO New York 09122-5000

TELEPHONE INFORMATION: Main installation numbers: Civ: 49-06762-41-1110. ETS/ATVN: 451-1110. Civ prefix: 06762-____. ETS/ATVN prefix: 451-XXXX. Civ to mil prefix: 06762-41-XXXX.

LOCATION: From Frankfurt IAP, take Autobahn 3 towards Köln. Change to Autobahn 67 toward Mainz, then to Autobahn 60 toward Mainz/Bingen. At the end of Autobahn 60, change to Autobahn 61 toward Koblenz and get off at Rheinboellen exit. Take B-50 toward Simmern/Kirchberg, get on B-421 toward Zell/Kappel. At Kappel intersection, get on B-327 toward Koblenz. Take exit to Simmern/Hasselbach just before the town of Kastellaun. Wüschheim Air Station is very near the exit. HE: p-36, C/6. NMC: Koblenz, 24 miles northeast.

GENERAL INSTALLATION INFORMATION: The mission of the 38th Tactical Missile Wing at Wüschheim is to train personnel, maintain readiness, and be prepared to operate its Ground-Launched Cruise Missile system.

GENERAL CITY/REGIONAL INFORMATION: The Hunsrück area, which surrounds the air station, is a rural area with small farming towns and little industry.

ADMINISTRATIVE SUPPORT

FACILITY/ACTIVITY	BLDG NO/LOC	PHONE	DAYS/COMMENTS
Duty Officer	200	3272	Daily
Fire(Mil)	105	2063	24 hours daily
Housing	See Hahn Air Base listing.		
Legal Assist	200	N/A	M
Personnel Spt	200	2035	M-F
Police(Mil)	100	2248	Daily
Public Affairs	200	3397	M-F
Tax Relief	100	2195	M,W

LOGISTICAL SUPPORT

FACILITY/ACTIVITY	BLDG NO/LOC	PHONE	DAYS/COMMENTS
Bank	100	3282	M-F
Barber Shop(s)	100	3278	M-F
Dining Facility	100	2209	Daily

GERMANY
Wüschheim Air Station, continued

Exchange(Annex)	100	3233	M-F
Finance(Mil)	100	2751	M-F
Food(Snack/Fast)	100	2209	Daily
Burger King	Mobile	None	M-F
Pick-up Point	See Hahn Air Base listing.		
Postal Svcs(Mil)	100	3210	M-F
Schools(DOD Dep)	See Hahn Air Base listing.		

HEALTH AND WELFARE

FACILITY/ACTIVITY	BLDG NO/LOC	PHONE	DAYS/COMMENTS
Chaplain	200	7533	Th

REST AND RECREATION

FACILITY/ACTIVITY	BLDG NO/LOC	PHONE	DAYS/COMMENTS
Info Tour & Travel	200	2196	W

ZWEIBRÜCKEN AIR BASE (GE88R7)
APO New York 09860-5001

TELEPHONE INFORMATION: Main installation numbers: Civ: 49-06332-47-113. ETS: 498-113. Civ prefix: 06332-____. ETS prefix: 498-XXXX. Civ to mil prefix: 06332-47-XXXX.

LOCATION: Take Autobahn 6/E12 to Autobahn 8 exit southwest. Continue for approximately six miles to the air base exit. Turn right at the end of the exit road. The entrance road is 100 feet down the road on the right. HE: p-39, G/2. NMC: Frankfurt, 105 miles southwest.

GENERAL INSTALLATION INFORMATION: The 26th Tactical Reconnaissance Wing was established on Zweibrücken Air Base in 1973 when USAFE consolidated its two Germany-based reconnaissance squadrons into one wing. The unit performs tactical reconnaissance and military airlift functions. Assigned units include the 10th Military Airlift Squadron, the 38th Photographic Reconnaissance Squadron, the 7426th Tactical Reconnaissance Squadron, the 2143rd Communications Squadron and the 609th Contingency Hospital. Please be aware that many facilities, such as the commissary, are located nearby at the Zweibrücken Military Community.

GENERAL CITY/REGIONAL INFORMATION: Although many of Zweibrücken's structures have been destroyed during its long and rich history, the city still offers a number of fascinating sites. The Rosengarten abounds with the blooms of 70,000 rose bushes every spring. Alexanderkirche (Alexander's church) near the town market place, an ancient church that was destroyed during World War II, has been rebuilt by the townspeople. The ruins of a Celtic-Roman village can be found at Schwarzenacker, a small village four miles away. Spelunkers will want to explore the interesting caves at Homburg, around eight miles from Zweibrücken.

U.S. Forces Travel & Transfer Guide Europe — 243

GERMANY

Zweibrücken Air Base, continued

ADMINISTRATIVE SUPPORT

FACILITY/ACTIVITY	BLDG NO/LOC	PHONE	DAYS/COMMENTS
Advocate	59	2171	M-F
Fire(Mil)	391	2527	24 hours daily
Fire(Civ)	391	C-43021	24 hours daily
Housing			
Family	631	2934	M-F
Unaccompanied	37	2697	M-F
Referral	631	2907	M-F
Inspector Gen'l	40	2515	M-F
Legal Assist	59	2171	M-F
Locator(Mil)	50	2582	M-F
Police(Mil)	54	2386	24 hours daily
Public Affairs	40	2940/2540	M-F
Tax Relief	40	2204/2540	M-F

LOGISTICAL SUPPORT

FACILITY/ACTIVITY	BLDG NO/LOC	PHONE	DAYS/COMMENTS
Audio/Photo Ctr	54	2448	M-F
Auto Drivers Testing	24	2588	M-F
Auto Registration	38	2211	M-F
Auto Rental(Exch)	60	2921	M-F
Bakery	47	None	M-Sa
Bank	47	2843	M-F
Barber Shop(s)	49	2283	M-Sa
Beauty Shop(s)	49	2871	M-Sa
Bookstore	19	None	M-Sa
Bus	24	2167	Daily
Child Care/Dev Ctr	2	2623	M-F
Clothing Sales	45	2909	M-F
Credit Union	8	2589	M-F
Dining Facility	50	2107/2360	Daily
Dry Clean(Exch)	49	2377	M-Sa
Dry Clean(Gov)	4	None	M-F
Education Center	34	2365	M-F
Exchange(Main)	47	2641	Daily
Finance(Mil)	8	2393	M-F
Food(Snack/Fast)	48	2241	Daily
Baskin Robbins	48	2246	Daily
Foodland	41	2542	Daily
Laundry(Exch)	49	2377	M-Sa
Laundry(Self-Svc)	4	None	24 hours daily
Motor Pool	24	2167	N/A
Package Store	26	2263	M-Sa
Photo Laboratory	54	2448	M-F
Pick-up Point	47	2371	M-Sa
Postal Svcs(Mil)	50	2714	M-Sa
SATO-OS	38	2250	M-Sa
Schools(DOD Dep)			
Elementary	Housing area	2198/2889 C-43260	M-F (K-6)
	Kreuzberg	C-44626	M-F (K-6)

GERMANY
Zweibrücken Air Base, continued

High School	57	2807	M-Sa (7-12)
Svc Stn(Insta)	26	2413	M-Sa
Tailor Shop	47	2377	Tu-Sa
Thrift Shop	52	2363	M,W,F
TML			
Billeting	3	2181	24 hours daily
TLF	3,4	2404	Daily
VAQ	3	2404	Daily
DV/VIP	40	2601	Daily

HEALTH AND WELFARE

FACILITY/ACTIVITY	BLDG NO/LOC	PHONE	DAYS/COMMENTS
AF Family Svcs	54	2476	M-F
Ambulance	1	116	24 hours daily
Central Appts	1	2168/9	M-F
CHAMPUS Office	2160	2523/2809	M-F
Dental Clinic	1	2874	M-F
Medical Emergency	1	2532	24 hours daily
Mental Health	1	2765	M-F
Poison Control	1	2532	M-F
Red Cross	N/A	494-6000	M-F

REST AND RECREATION

FACILITY/ACTIVITY	BLDG NO/LOC	PHONE	DAYS/COMMENTS
Bowling Lanes	70	2668	Daily
Consolidated Club	2	2779	Daily
Craftshops			
Automotive	62	2851	Daily
Ceramics	62	2854	W-Su
Wood	52	None	W-Su
Gymnasium	39	2727	Daily
Info Tour & Travel	60	2921	M-F
Library	52	2327	Daily
Recreation Center	60	2921	Daily
Skating Rink	70	2420	Daily
Special Services	52	2996/2971	M-F
Theater	48	2983	Daily
Video Rental	60	2971	M-Sa
Youth Center	48	None	Daily

ZWEIBRÜCKEN COMMUNITY (GE29R7)
APO New York 09052-5000

TELEPHONE INFORMATION: Main installation numbers: Civ: 49-06332-86-113 (Kreuzberg Kaserne); 49-06372-842-113 (Miesau). ETS/ATVN: 494-113 (Kreuzberg Kaserne); 486-3113 (Miesau). Civ prefix: 06632-_____ (Kreuzberg Kaserne); 06372-_____ (Miesau). ETS/ATVN prefix: 494-XXXX (Kreuzberg Kaserne); 486-3XXX (Miesau). Civ to mil prefix: 06332-86-XXXX (Kreuzberg Kaserne); 06372-842-XXX (Miesau).

Zweibrücken Community, continued

GERMANY

LOCATION: Take the Neukirchen exit from the Mannheim-Saarbrucken E-6 Autobahn. Follow signs to the community. HE: p-39, G/2. NMC: Zweibrücken, in the city.

GENERAL INSTALLATION INFORMATION: The 200th TAMMC is a logistical support center subordinate to USAREUR. Tenant units include the Defense Subsistence Region—Europe, which oversees the commissary system; the Troop Support Agency; U.S. Army Information Systems Command—Europe; HQ, 60th Ordnance Group; 517th Maintenance Battalion; 327th Signal Battalion; 2/60th Air Defense Artillery; and several smaller support and liaison units.

All support facilities not available in the Zweibrücken Community are available at Zweibrücken Air Base. **Note: the following abbreviations are used in this listing only: KK (Kreuzberg Kaserne); MD (Miesau Depot).**

GENERAL CITY/REGIONAL INFORMATION: Zweibrücken is known as the city of roses and horses. The city's history dates from 1150 when it was founded on the ruins of a Roman fort. Many historic Baroque and Rococo buildings that were destroyed World War II have been rebuilt, including the Ducal Castle, the Barogue Houses of Herzogsvorstadt and the Alexanderkirche. Today's Zweibrücken is a charming city of lush gardens, comfortable homes and growing commerce spanning the Schwarzbach River. Its extensive indoor and outdoor swimming complex and attractive central pedestrian shopping zone stand in contrast to the surrounding, rolling green hills of forest and farmland.

Horse lovers won't want to miss a visit to the famous Zweibrücken Stud Farm, home of the famous Zweibrücken breed of horses. Everyone will enjoy a visit to the wonderful Rose Garden, one of the largest and most beautiful in the world, with more than 60,000 roses bushes in thousands of varieties.

Meisau Army Depot lies about 20 miles west of Kaiserslautern. Soldiers assigned there and their families live in the Vogelweh and Landstuhl areas around Kaiserslautern.

ADMINISTRATIVE SUPPORT

FACILITY/ACTIVITY	BLDG NO/LOC	PHONE	DAYS/COMMENTS
Customs/Duty	4003/KK	6668/8373	M-F
Duty Officer	4016/KK	7145	After hrs
Fire(Mil)	4005/KK	7127	24 hrs daily
	Emergency	117	24 hrs daily
Fire(Civ)	Zweibrücken	C-772	24 hrs daily
Housing			
Family	4004/KK	6636/7396	M-F
Referral	White Kaserne	C-43090	M-F
Info(Insta)	On Barracks	113	24 hrs daily
Inspector Gen'l	4016/KK	6205/8330	M-F
Legal Assist	4016/KK	6183	M-F
	1216/MD	841	M-F
Locator(Mil)	4007/KK	6493	M-F
	4000/KK	7202/6659	M-F
Locator(Civ)	4052/KK	6444/7286	M-F
	4052/KK	7145	After hrs

GERMANY
Zweibrücken Community, continued

Personnel Spt	4041/KK	6520/8266	M-F
Police(Mil)	4000/KK	6672/8257	24 hours daily
Emergency	4000/KK	114	24 hours daily
Police(Civ)	Zweibrücken	110	24 hours daily
Public Affairs	4000/KK	6627/7260	M-F
Tax Relief	4017/KK	6311	M-F

LOGISTICAL SUPPORT

FACILITY/ACTIVITY	BLDG NO/LOC	PHONE	DAYS/COMMENTS
Auto Drivers Testing	4041/KK	6512	M-F
	1236/MD	636	M-F
Auto Parts(Exch)	4014/KK	6172	Tu-Sa
Auto Registration	4037/KK	6690	M-F
Auto Rent(Other)	Zweibrücken	N/A	M-Sa. Budget.
Auto Repairs	4014/KK	6076	Tu-Sa
Auto Ship(Gov)	4010/KK	6651	M-F
Bakery	47/Air Base	None	Daily
Bank	4010/KK	6025	M-F
		C-17800	
	1315/MD	3565	M-F
Barber Shop(s)	4040/KK	6400	Tu-Sa
	1206/MD	N/A	M-F
Beauty Shop(s)	4034/KK	C-17700	Tu-Sa
Bookstore	4034/KK	6328	Tu-Su
Bus	4014/KK	6670/8344	M-F
Child Care/Dev Ctr	4007/KK	6030/7187	M-F
	1314/MD	774	M-F
Clothing Sales	See Zweibrücken Air Base listing.		
Commissary(Main)	4065/KK	6445/7219	Tu-Su
Credit Union	See Zweibrücken Air Base listing.		
Dining Facility	4036/KK	7288	Daily
Dry Clean(Exch)	4036/KK	C-14549	Tu-Sa
Dry Clean(Gov)	4613/Pirmasens	495-6254	M-F
Education Center			
Learning Center	4041/KK	6660/6064/	M-Sa
		6289	
	1222,1329/MD	863	M-F
Elec Repair(Gov)	Zweibrücken	6128	M-F
		7145	After hours
Eng'r/Publ Works	4080/KK	6105/8366	M-F
	Emergency	115	After hours
Exchange(Main)	4034/KK	6084	Daily
		C-2981	
	1206/MD	169	M-Sa
Exchange(Annex)	4036/KK	C-17200	Daily
Exchange(Concess)	4036/KK	C-18685	Daily
Finance(Mil)	4001/KK	6418/7330	M-F
Food(Caf/Rest)	4033/KK	C-2982	Daily
	1311/MD	C-1288	Daily
Food(Snack/Fast)			
Pizza Parlor	KK	6076	Daily
Foodland	4036/KK	C-17200	Daily
Laundry(Exch)	4036/KK	C-14549	Tu-Sa
	1206/MD	766	Tu-Sa
Laundry(Self-Svc)	4040/KK	None	24 hours daily

GERMANY

Zweibrücken Community, continued

	1312/MD	None	Daily
Motor Pool	4020/KK	6503/7123	M-F
	4025/KK	6595	M-F
Package Store	4010/KK	6580	Tu-Sa
Pick-up Point	4036/KK	C-14548	M-F
	1206/MD	None	M-F
Postal Svcs(Mil)	4007/KK	6215/8246	M-F
	1345/MD	635	M-F
Postal Svcs(Civ)	1 Post St	C-8071	M-Sa
Railroad/RTO	Zweibrücken	3492	24 hours daily
SATO-OS	See Zweibrücken Air Base listing.		
Schools(DOD Dep)			
Elementary	42/KK	7393/6561	M-F
High School	See Zweibrücken Air Base listing.		
Svc Stn(Insta)	4014/KK	C-3462	M-Sa
Space-A Air Ops	See Ramstein Air Base listing.		
Tailor Shop	4036/KK	None	Tu-Sa
	1206/MD	None	Tu-Sa
Taxi(Comm)	Zweibrücken	C-2223	24 hours daily
	Mil Dispatch	6595	24 hours daily
Tel Booking Oper	Zweibrücken	112	24 hours daily
Tel Repair(Gov)	4000/KK	119	24 hours daily
Tel Repair(Civ)	Zweibrücken	C-01171	M-Sa
Thrift Shop	4032/KK	6121	M,W,F
TML			
Billeting	4206/KK	7166/6566	M-F
Other Times (SDO)	4000/KK	7145	After hours
BOQ (All ranks)	4206/KK	7166/6566	M-F
DV/VIP (O6+)	Commander	6647	M-F
Travel Agents	4034/KK	6676	M-F
Watch Repair	4036/KK	C-14549	M-Sa

HEALTH AND WELFARE

FACILITY/ACTIVITY	BLDG NO/LOC	PHONE	DAYS/COMMENTS
Ambulance	Zweibrücken	116	24 hrs daily
	Zweibrücken	C-110	24 hrs daily
Army Comm Svcs	4011/KK	6586/7231	M-F
	1204/MD	877/683	M-F
Army Emerg Relief	4011	8330/7231	M-F
CHAMPUS Office	See Zweibrücken Air Base listing.		
Chaplain	4011/KK	6689/8216	M-F
	1363/KK	3846/3884	M-F
	1363/MD	884/646	M-F
Chapel	1363/MD	884/646	M-F
Comm Drug/Alc Ctr	4011/KK	6410/7272	M-F
	1218/MD	730/832	M-F
Dental Clinic	4010/KK	6683/8230	M-F
Medical Emergency	See Zweibrücken Air Base listing.		
Mental Health	See Landstuhl Community listing.		
Poison Control	See Landstuhl Community listing.		
Red Cross	4011/KK	6586/6000	M-F
	1204/MD	877/683	M-F
Veterinary Svcs	Obere Denis St	C-2912	M-F

GERMANY
Zweibrücken Community, continued

REST AND RECREATION

FACILITY/ACTIVITY	BLDG NO/LOC	PHONE	DAYS/COMMENTS
Amer Forces Ntwk	Zweibrücken	6128/7145	Daily
Bowling Lanes	4038/KK	6149	Daily
	1301/MD	667	Daily
Consolidated Club	4208/KK	7135	Daily
	1304/MD	777	Daily
Craftshops			
Automotive	4005/KK	6265	Sa-W
Multi-crafts	4019/KK	6481	Tu-Sa
	1312/MD		Tu-Th, 1&3 Sa
Photography	1312/MD	3600	Tu-Sa
Gymnasium	4039/KK	7253/6562	Daily
	1220/MD	653	Daily
Info Tour & Travel	4034/KK	6676	M-F
	MD	888	N/A
Library	4036/KK	6047	Daily
	1222/MD	728	Daily
MARS	See Zweibrücken Air Base listing.		
Outdoor Rec Ctr	4071/KK	7234	Daily
	1222/MD	782/888	M-F
Recreation Center	4006/KK	6466/7155	M-Sa
	1222/MD	567/741	M-F
Rod and Gun Club	4065/KK	6333/6483	M-Sa
Skating Rink	See Zweibrücken Air Base listing.		
Special Services	4017/KK	6431/8211	M-F
Sport Field	4039/KK	6562	Daily
Tennis Courts	4039/KK	6562	Daily
Theater	See Zweibrücken Air Base listing.		
Track	4039/KK	6562	Daily
Video Rental	4065/KK	6333	M-Sa
	1304/MD	N/A	N/A
Youth Center	4243/KK	6100/7319	M-Sa
	1300/MD	696	M-Sa

GREECE
Hellenic Republic
Athens

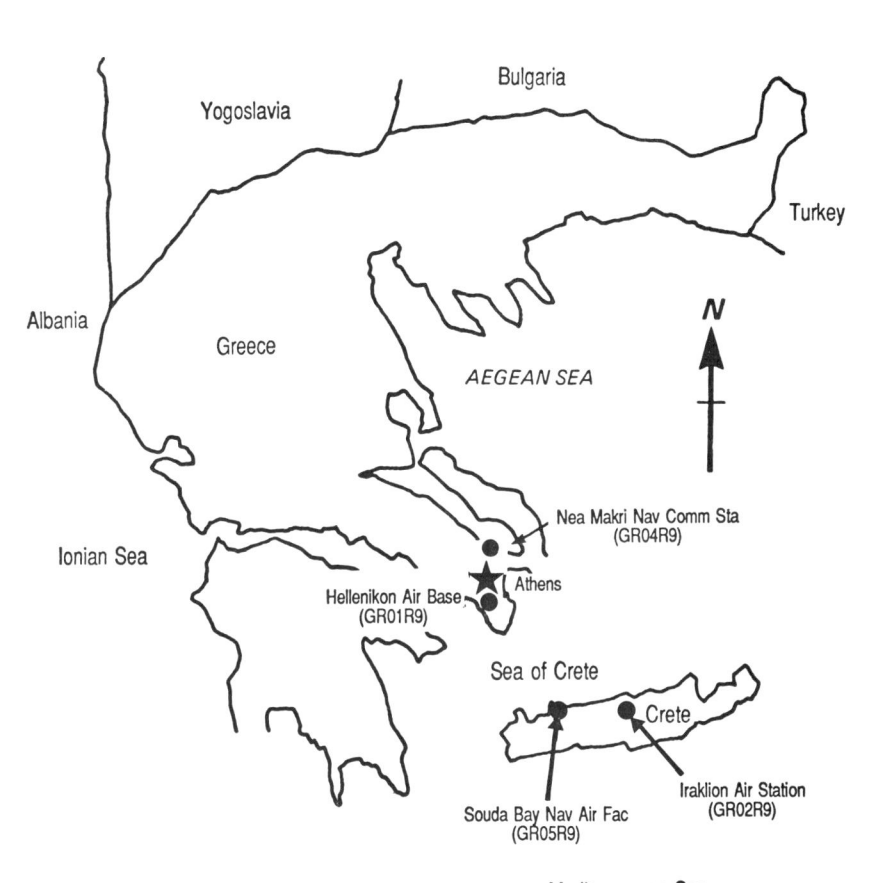

Approximately the size of Alabama, Greece is located in southeastern Europe on the southern tip of the Balkan Peninsula and is bounded by Bulgaria, Yugoslavia and Albania and the Ionian, Aegean and Mediterranean Seas. Ninety-eight percent of the population of 9.95 million people are Greek and the official language is Greek. Greece is a republic with universal suffrage over age 18. Natural resources include bauxite, lignite, magnesite and oil. Exports are textiles, metal products, pharmaceuticals and chemicals. Imports consist of petroleum, machinery, meat and animals. Greeks work in agriculture, industry and services. Half the labor force is self-employed. The currency is the *drachma*. There is an extensive rail network. An adequate, hard-surfaced street and highway system declines into rough, ungraded roads. Intercity and public transportation is inexpensive. Athens telephone service is satisfactory and calls to the U.S. are easily made. Greece is seven hours

GREECE

ahead of U.S. EST. Climate is moderate—lightweights May-September and woolens October-April. Tourism is a major factor in the Greek economy due to its natural beauty, climate and location, "the cradle of the world." Evidences of the Stone Age and many of the world's finest architectural and sculptural monuments are sightseeing highlights. Relations between Greece and the U.S. are based on a shared cultural heritage and common values. Both countries realize the importance of continued positive association.

ENTRY REQUIREMENTS: Passport—yes. Visa—not required for stay up to three months for business/pleasure. Check with the Embassy of Greece, Washington D.C., Tel: 202-667-3168. Immunizations—EUR.

HELLENIKON AIR BASE (GR01R9)
APO New York 09223-5000

TELEPHONE INFORMATION: Main installation numbers: Civ: 30-1-989-5513. ATVN: 662-5513. Civ prefix: varies; complete civilian numbers are listed below. ATVN prefix: 662-XXXX.

LOCATION: Located on Vouliagmenis Avenue approximately ten miles south of Athens. Follow airport signs to get to the base. Hellenikon Air Base is located two blocks before the international airport. HE: p-83, G/2. NMC: Athens, 10 miles northeast.

GENERAL INSTALLATION INFORMATION: The 7206th Air Base Group at Hellenikon provides support to associate units located at Hellenikon and 19 other locations throughout Greece. Hellenikon Air Base is located ten miles south of Athens and is co-located with the Athens State Airport. Associate units include the 922nd Strategic Squadron; the 6916th Electronic Security Squadron, Det. 3; the 625th Military Airlift Support Group; the 2140th Communications Group and its outlying detachments; Naval Security Group Activity; the 558th U.S. Army Artillery at Elefsis and its associated sites and the Military Traffic Management Command Transportation Terminal Unit located in Piraeus. Because of its strategic location, the 7206th ABG provides numerous support missions to the DOD and other U.S. government organizations located between Rota, Spain, and Riyadh, Saudi Arabia.

GENERAL CITY/REGIONAL INFORMATION: Greater Athens has a population of 4.5 million people and is a modern city with a charm all its own—a unique blend of ancient monuments, Byzantine churches, 19th-century houses and tall, contemporary buildings. Apart from the picturesque old quarter huddled at the base of the Acropolis, known as the Plaka, the rest of Athens is a city of broad avenues, attractive squares, busy shopping centers, parks and open-air cafés. Located on Acropolis is the famous Parthenon. Other monuments include the Temple of the Wingless Victory, the Propylaea and the Erechtheion, which date from the period between 488 and 400 B.C.

ADMINISTRATIVE SUPPORT

FACILITY/ACTIVITY	BLDG NO/LOC	PHONE	DAYS/COMMENTS
Advocate	301	5723	Daily
Customs/Duty	261	5655	Daily
Duty Officer	N/A	5613	Daily
Fire(Mil)	512	5777	Daily
Fire(Civ)	Off base	C-999	Daily

GERMANY

Hellenikon Air Base, continued

Housing
Referral	Cons Open Mess Bldg	C-895-1401 ext. 120	M-F
Info(Insta)	338	5556	Daily
Inspector Gen'l	332	5611	Daily
Legal Assist	301	5723	Daily
Locator(Mil)	331	5698	M-F
	406	5414	After hours
Locator(Civ)	Off base	5378/5322	M-F
Personnel Spt	124	5656	M-F
Police(Mil)	203	5676	Daily
Police(Civ)	Athens suburbs	C-109	Daily
Public Affairs	338	5698	Daily
Tax Relief	301	5723	Daily

LOGISTICAL SUPPORT

FACILITY/ACTIVITY	BLDG NO/LOC	PHONE	DAYS/COMMENTS
Auto Drivers Testing	431	5283	Call for schedule.
Auto Parts(Exch)	1301	C-961-9273	M-Sa
Auto Registration	124	5656	M-F
Auto Rent(Other)	505	5226	Daily
Auto Repairs	214	5583	Daily
Auto Sales	PB17	5638	M-Sa
Auto Ship(Civ)	Piraeus Port	C-462-8988	M-F
Auto Wash	214	5583	Daily
Bank	120	5631	M-Sa
Barber Shop(s)	108	C-981-1685	M-Sa
Beauty Shop(s)	Cons Club/Bltg	C-895-1401	Call for schedule.
Bookstore	215	C-894-0079	M-Sa
Bus	319	5262	Daily
Child Care/Dev Ctr	Off Base	C-922-4190	Tu-Sa
Clothing Sales	211	5336	M-F
Commissary(Main)	Off Base	C-922-4190	Tu-Sa
Commissary(Annex)	129	5770	M-Sa
Credit Union	120	C-894-0883	Call for schedule.
Dining Facility	Closed for renovation as of January 1989.		
Dry Clean(Exch)	PB15	C-981-1685	Tu-Sa
Dry Clean(Gov)	Cons Club/Bltg	C-895-1401	Call for schedule.
Education Center	265	5237	Daily
Elec Repair(Civ)	108/208	5312/5244	Call for schedule.
Exchange(Main)	108	5337	M-Sa
Exchange(Annex)	Cons Club/Bltg	C-895-1401	Call for schedule.
Finance(Mil)	120	5365	Daily
Food(Caf/Rest)	215	5665	Daily
Food(Snack/Fast)	505	5593	Daily
	Beside 109	None	M-Sa
Foodland	108	5312	Daily
Laundry(Exch)	PB15	C-981-1685	Tu-Sa
Laundry(Self-Svc)	132	5684	Daily
Motor Pool	319	5262	Daily
Package Store	110	None	M-Sa
Photo Laboratory	212	5582	M-F
Postal Svcs(Mil)	209	5234	M-Sa
Railroad/RTO	319	5262	Daily

GREECE
Hellenikon Air Base, continued

Schools(DOD Dep)			
Elementary	Glyfada	C-962-2471	M-F (K-2)
	Vari	C-895-8447	M-F (3-6)
High School	Athens Comm Sch in Halandri	C-639-3200	M-F (7-12)
	Tasis in Kifisia	C-808-1426	M-F (7-12)
Space-A Air Ops	505	5473	Call for schedule.
Pax Lounges(Gen'l)	500	5474	24 hours daily
Protocol Svc	339	5373	M-F
Flights to:	Akrotiri Arpt CY; Aviano AB IT; Ben Gurian IAP IS; Brindisi/Casale Arpt IT; Capodichino Arpt IT; Cigli TAFB TU; Esenboga Arpt TU; Incirlik Arpt TU; Iraklion Arpt GR; Lajes Fld PO; McGuire AFB NJ; Norfolk NAS VA; Philadelphia IAP PA; Ramstein AB GE; Rhein-Main AB GE; Sigonella Arpt IT; Souda Bay NAF GR; Torrejon AB SP.		
Tailor Shop	PB16	C-981-1685	Tu-Sa
Taxi(Comm)	Off base	C-321-4058	Daily
Tel Booking Oper		5513	Daily
Tel Repair(Gov)	122	5712	Daily
Tel Repair(Civ)	122	5712	Daily
Thrift Shop	263	5207	Tu-Th
TML			
Billeting	Apollon Hotel	C-895-1401	Daily
Protocol Office	332	5611	Daily
Travel Agents	208/Cons Club	5226 C-895-1401	Daily

HEALTH AND WELFARE

FACILITY/ACTIVITY	BLDG NO/LOC	PHONE	DAYS/COMMENTS
AF Family Svcs	262	5291	M-F
AF Relief	232	5437	Daily
	103	5676	After hours
Ambulance	216	116	Daily
Army Emerg Relief	103	5676	After hours
Central Appts	216	5424	M-F
CHAMPUS Office	216	5441	Daily
Chaplain	203	5676	After hours
Chapel	127	5294	Daily
Comm Drug/Alc Ctr	216	5546	M-F
Dental Clinic	218	5466	M-F
Medical Emergency	216	5413	Daily
Mental Health	216	5546	M-F
Poison Control	216	5413 C-981-2740	Daily
Red Cross	262/203	5417/5676	Daily
Veterinary Svcs	198	5205	M-F

REST AND RECREATION

FACILITY/ACTIVITY	BLDG NO/LOC	PHONE	DAYS/COMMENTS
Amer Forces Ntwk	239	5206	Daily
Beach(es)	Local area	None	Daily
Bowling Lanes	155	5534	Daily

GERMANY
Hellenikon Air Base, continued

Consolidated Club	Off base	C-895-1401	Daily
Craftshops			
Automotive	214	5583	Daily
Photography	211	5566	M-Sa
Wood	211	5583	Tu-Sa
Golf Course	Glyfada	N/A	Seasonal
Gymnasium	210	5535	Daily
Info Tour & Travel	505	5474	M-F
Library	212	5579	Daily
Marina	Access Cons Club	C-895-1401	Seasonal
MARS	105	5250	Daily
NCO Club	Off base	C-895-1401	Daily
O'Club	Off base	C-895-1401	Daily
Outdoor Rec Ctr	PB12	5590	M-F
Picnic/Park Area	On base	5637	Daily
Racket Courts	210	5535	Daily
Recreation Center	208	5637	Daily
Rod and Gun Club	227	5627	Daily
Special Services	PB12	5590	M-F
Sport Field	On base	5535	Daily
Swimming Pool	Youth Center	C-895-1401	F-Su
Tennis Courts	On base	5535	Daily
Theater	115	5638	Daily
Track	Behind 2140th	5535	Daily
Video Rental	57	5684	M-Sa
Water Recreation	See Marina		
Youth Center	137	5573	M-Sa

==

IRAKLION AIR STATION (GR02R9)
APO New York 09291-5000

TELEPHONE INFORMATION: Main installation numbers: Civ: 30-81-761-281/2/3. ATVN: 668-1110. To reach the extensions in this listing, dial the main installation numbers and then ask for the desired extension.

LOCATION: On the Greek island of Crete. From Iraklion Airport, turn right at the main entrance and go past the Greek military base. Take the next left and drive for 20 minutes to Gournes. The air station will be on the left. HE: p-85, B/3. NMC: Iraklion, 8 miles west.

GENERAL INSTALLATION INFORMATION: The 7276th Air Base Group assumed host unit responsibilities on October 1, 1978. Its primary mission is to provide administrative and logistical support to the 6931st ESS, the major tenant unit and an integral part of the worldwide communications network. The 6931st, an Electronic Security Command unit, provides rapid relay and secure communications for the defense of the U.S. and its allies. Additional functions of the 6931st include transmission security and research into electronic phenomena. The 2115th Communications Squadron, an Air Force Communications Command unit, maintains a tropospheric scatter terminal seven miles from the base atop Mt. Edheri.

GENERAL CITY/REGIONAL INFORMATION: The Greek island of Crete is the home of Europe's oldest recorded civilization. The Minoan civilization began here some 2,500 years before Christ and reached its peak about 1450

GREECE
Iraklion Air Station, continued

B.C. Since the Roman occupation in 66 B.C., the island's history has been one of nearly constant occupation. While most of the remains of the Roman period are in museums, the remains of the next period, the Byzantine, are scattered over the countryside in the many churches left on the island. The Byzantines were followed by the Arabs and then the Venetians. The Venetians held Crete from 1204 to 1666. The Venetian heritage includes the walls of Iraklion's harbor. Crete became part of Greece in 1913. In 1941, German soldiers took over the island as a strategic stronghold and held it until 1944.

ADMINISTRATIVE SUPPORT

FACILITY/ACTIVITY	BLDG NO/LOC	PHONE	DAYS/COMMENTS
Advocate	301	3506	M-F
Customs/Duty	509	3947/3803	M-F
Fire(Mil)	401	3414	24 hours daily
Housing	695	3842	M-F
Info(Insta)	N/A	113	N/A
Inspector Gen'l	207	3556	M-F
Legal Assist	301	3506	M-F
Locator(Mil)	301	2859	Daily
		3426	After hours
Personnel Spt	308	3406	Daily. Flag orders.
	301	3926	Daily
	301	3561	Daily
Police(Mil)	301	3426	24 hours daily
Public Affairs	207	3511	Daily
Tax Relief	See 1st Sergeant.		

LOGISTICAL SUPPORT

FACILITY/ACTIVITY	BLDG NO/LOC	PHONE	DAYS/COMMENTS
Auto Drivers Testing	301	3926	2nd Th of month
Auto Parts(Exch)	217	3207	Daily
Auto Registration	301	3926	Daily
Auto Repairs	152	3298	Daily
Auto Ship(Gov)	509	3947	Daily
Auto Wash	152	3298	24 hours daily
Bank	302	3301	Tu-Sa
Barber Shop(s)	301	3398	M-Sa
Beauty Shop(s)	301	3225	M-Sa
Bookstore	213	3364	M-Sa
Child Care/Dev Ctr	159	3219	Daily
Clothing Sales	217	3259	Daily
Commissary(Main)	556	3417	Tu-Sa
Credit Union	301	3875	M-Sa
Dining Facility	210	3320	Daily
Dry Clean(Exch)	108	3330	Tu-F
Education Center	301	3910	Daily
Eng'r/Publ Works	523	3439	Daily
Exchange(Main)	202	3828	Daily
Finance(Mil)	302	3972	Daily
Food(Caf/Rest)	220	3278	Daily
Food(Snack/Fast)	202	3215	Daily
Foodland	212	3214	Daily
Laundry(Self-Svc)	692	3224	Daily

GERMANY

Iraklion Air Station, continued

Motor Pool	505	3517	Daily
Package Store	216	3894	Tu-Sa
Photo Laboratory	411	3820	M-F
Postal Svcs(Mil)	219	3801	Daily
SATO-OS	509	3835	Daily
Schools(DOD Dep)			
Elementary/Jr High	J.R. Kearns	3548	M-F
Svc Stn(Insta)	555	None	M-Sa
Space-A Air Ops	509	3920	M-F
Flights to:	Athinai Arpt GR; Incirlik Arpt TU; Ramstein AB GE; Rhein-Main AB GE.		
Tailor Shop	217	N/A	Daily
Tel Booking Oper	430	3815	Daily
Tel Repair(Gov)	423	3868	Daily
Thrift Shop	116	3344	Tu,Th,Sa
TML			
Billeting	208	3942/3842	M-F
	MPs	3426	After hours
BEQ	302	3942/3842	M-F
TLQ	Evina Villas	3942/3842	M-F
VAQ	305	3942/3842	M-F
VOQ	208	3942/3842	M-F
DV/VIP	207	3556	M-F
Travel Agents	509	3303	Daily

HEALTH AND WELFARE

FACILITY/ACTIVITY	BLDG NO/LOC	PHONE	DAYS/COMMENTS
AF Family Svcs	302	3450/3561	M,W,F
AF Relief	301	3561	M-F
Ambulance	306	116	24 hours daily
Central Appts	306	3128/3528	Daily
CHAMPUS Office	306	None	M-F
Chaplain	154	3886/3887	Daily
Chapel	154	3887/3882	Daily
Comm Drug/Alc Ctr	301	3596	M-F
Dental Clinic	306	3286	Daily
Medical Emergency	306	116	24 hours daily
Mental Health	306	3503	Daily
Poison Control	306	117/114	M-F
Red Cross	302	3897	M
Veterinary Svcs	Visiting Vet	3509	Call for info.

REST AND RECREATION

FACILITY/ACTIVITY	BLDG NO/LOC	PHONE	DAYS/COMMENTS
Beach(es)	906	3396	June-September
Bowling Lanes	127	3916	Daily
Camping/RV Area	At marina	3296	June-September
	On beach	3296	Daily
Consolidated Club	210	3320	M-F
Craftshops			
Ceramics	203	3918	
Wood	152	3918/3876	Tu-F
Enlisted Club	Spartan Lounge	3318	Daily

GREECE
Iraklion Air Station, continued

Gymnasium	201	3884	Daily
Info Tour & Travel	N/A	3515	M-Sa
Library	310	3851	Daily
Marina	907	3296	June-September
MARS	On Base	3463	M-F
Picnic/Park Area	Near hospital	3378/3415	June-September
Racket Courts	201	3884	24 hours daily
Recreation Center	693	3929/3378	Daily
Special Services	693	3819	Daily
Tennis Courts	201	3884	24 hours daily
Theater	115	3297	Daily
Video Rental	217	3207	Daily
Youth Center	693	3328	Daily

GREECE

NEA MAKRI NAVAL COMMUNICATION STATION (GR04R9)
FPO New York 09525-5000

TELEPHONE INFORMATION: Main installation numbers: Civ: 30-1-882-7211/2/3/4/5. ATVN: 667-1110. Note: **to reach the extensions listed below, dial the main installation number and ask the operator for the desired extension.**

LOCATION: Follow the signs north from Athens to Marathon. The station is located on the north edge of Nea Makri, just before Marathon on Marathon Road. HE: p-83, G/2. NMC: Athens, 34 miles south.

GENERAL INSTALLATION INFORMATION: Nea Makri's mission is to provide communications support to units of the Navy's 6th Fleet. Tenant commands include a Navy Broadcasting Detachment, a Personnel Support Detachment, a Naval Investigative Unit and medical and dental facilties.

GENERAL CITY/REGIONAL INFORMATION: Warm, sunny weather and beautiful beaches await the visitor to Nea Makri. The crystal-clear water is perfect for swimming and snorkeling. The beautiful town of Marathon offers a number of historical attractions, as does nearby Athens with its cafés, tavernas, and its famous Acropolis and other 2000-year-old ruins.

ADMINISTRATIVE SUPPORT

FACILITY/ACTIVITY	BLDG NO/LOC	PHONE	DAYS/COMMENTS
Customs/Duty	62	322/315	24 hours daily
Duty Officer	62	322/315	24 hours daily
Fire(Mil)	6	408/432 333	24 hours daily Fire only
Housing	58	301	M-F
Info(Insta)	Dial main numbers listed above.		
Legal Assist	9	412/470	M-F
Locator(Mil)	9	332/345	M-F
Personnel Spt	62	322/315	24 hours daily
Police(Mil)	62	322/315	24 hours daily
Police(Civ)	Nea Makri	C-93333	24 hours daily
Public Affairs	9	412/470	M-F

LOGISTICAL SUPPORT

FACILITY/ACTIVITY	BLDG NO/LOC	PHONE	DAYS/COMMENTS
Auto Drivers Testing	42	467	M-F
Auto Repairs	52	404	M-F
Auto Ship(Gov)	62	378	M-F
Bank	38	471 C-91453	M-F
Barber Shop(s)	12	391	M,W,F
Beauty Shop(s)	12	377	M,W,F
Bookstore	12	483	M-F
Child Care/Dev Ctr	102	489	M-F
Clothing Sales	12	451/478	Tu-Sa
Commissary(Annex)	65	448	Tu-Sa
Credit Union	63	420	M-F

GREECE
Nea Makri Naval Communication Station, continued

Facility	Bldg	Phone	Days
Dining Facility	13	464/473	Daily
Education Center	46	347/407	M-F
Eng'r/Publ Works	6	317/410	M-F
Exchange(Main)	12	451/478	Tu-Sa
Food(Caf/Rest)	29	473	Daily
Laundry(Self-Svc)	58	327	24 hours daily
Motor Pool	42	513/467	M-F
Package Store	29	490	W,F,Sa
Photo Laboratory	11	435/485	M-F
Postal Svcs(Mil)	62	336	M-Sa
Postal Svcs(Civ)	62	336	M-Sa
SATO-OS	9	332/345	M-F
Svc Stn(Insta)	81	356	Tu-Sa
Space-A Air Ops	See Hellenikon Air Base listing.		
Taxi(Comm)	Nea Makri	C-91300	24 hours daily
Tel Repair(Gov)	5	325	M-F
Tel Repair(Civ)	Nea Makri	C-22121	M-F
Travel Agents	27	515/491	M-F

HEALTH AND WELFARE

FACILITY/ACTIVITY	BLDG NO/LOC	PHONE	DAYS/COMMENTS
Ambulance	9	416/481	M-F
Central Appts	9	416/481	M-F
CHAMPUS Office	9	416/481	M-F
Chaplain	44	349/510	Su-F
Chapel	44	349/510	Su-F
Comm Drug/Alc Ctr	Ask base operator for assistance.		
Dental Clinic	9	472	M-F
Medical Emergency	9	416/481	24 hours daily
Navy Fam Svcs	Ask base operator for assistance.		
Navy Relief	Ask base operator for assistance.		
Poison Control	9	416/481	M-F
Red Cross	44	349/510	M-F

REST AND RECREATION

FACILITY/ACTIVITY	BLDG NO/LOC	PHONE	DAYS/COMMENTS
Bowling Lanes	30	494	M,Tu,Th,F
Consolidated Club	29	473	Daily
Craftshops			
Automotive	52	404	Daily
Ceramics	52	406	Tu,Th
Enlisted Club	29	473	Daily
Equip/Gear Locker	45	466	M-F
Gymnasium	45	466/456	24 hours daily
Info Tour & Travel	27	515/491 C-91395	M-F
Library	44	337	M-F
O'Club	14	475	N/A
Picnic/Park Area	94	None	24 hours daily
Racket Courts	45	466/456	24 hours daily
Recreation Center	63	323	Call for schedule.
Special Services	63	346/323	M-F
Sport Field	Available	None	24 hours daily

GREECE

Nea Makri Naval Communication Station, continued

Swimming Pool	58	497	Tu-Su
Tennis Courts	25	None	24 hours daily
Theater	63	323	Call for schedule.
Track	Available	None	24 hours daily
Video Rental	75	452	M-Sa
Water Recreation	Marathon Bay, beaches		

SOUDA BAY NAVAL AIR FACILITY (CRETE) (GR05R9)
FPO New York 09528-5000

TELEPHONE INFORMATION: Main installation numbers: Civ: 30-76-1391. ATVN: 399-9489.

LOCATION: On the northwest end of the island of Crete in Souda Bay. The NATO Missile Firing Installation (NAMFI) is five miles north of Souda. HE: p-85-B/5. NMC: Chania, GR, 10 miles west.

GENERAL INSTALLATION INFORMATION: Naval Air Facility Support Activity at Souda Bay operates in support of all U.S. Forces on Crete. The NAF is co-located with Chania Airport. NOTE: the following abbreviations are used in this listing only: AFX (ask for extension); NAMFI (NATO Missile Firing Installation).

GENERAL CITY/REGIONAL INFORMATION: Crete is the largest of all the Greek Islands, and is considered by many to be its most beautiful. Greece's oldest civilization was born in Crete, so the landscape is naturally dotted with the ancient ruins of temples and other historic sites. Museums on the island contain fascinating relics from the island's history. Outdoors, the landscape is varied and beautiful, with mountains, forests and beaches to be explored and enjoyed.

ADMINISTRATIVE SUPPORT

FACILITY/ACTIVITY	BLDG NO/LOC	PHONE	DAYS/COMMENTS
Duty Officer	N/A	AFX	24 hours daily
Fire(Mil)	N/A	AFX	24 hours daily
Police(Mil)	N/A	AFX	24 hours daily

LOGISTICAL SUPPORT

FACILITY/ACTIVITY	BLDG NO/LOC	PHONE	DAYS/COMMENTS
Bus	NAMFI/Chania	N/A	Daily
Dining Facility	NAMFI	AFX	Daily
Exchange(Main)	NAMFI	AFX	Daily
Space-A Air Ops	Hangar 5	Ext. 228	Daily
Flights to:	Athinai Arpt GR; Aviano AB IT; Brindisi/Casale Arpt IT; Capodichino Arpt IT; Ramstein AB GE.		
Taxi(Comm)	Chania Term	N/A	24 hours daily
Travel Agents	NAMFI	AFX	M-Sa

GREECE
Souda Bay Naval Air Facility, continued

HEALTH AND WELFARE

FACILITY/ACTIVITY	BLDG NO/LOC	PHONE	DAYS/COMMENTS
Medical Emergency	NAMFI	AFX	24 hours daily

REST AND RECREATION

FACILITY/ACTIVITY	BLDG NO/LOC	PHONE	DAYS/COMMENTS
NCO Club	N/A	Ext. 268	Daily
O'Club	N/A	Ext. 268	Daily

ICELAND
Republic of Iceland
Reykjavik

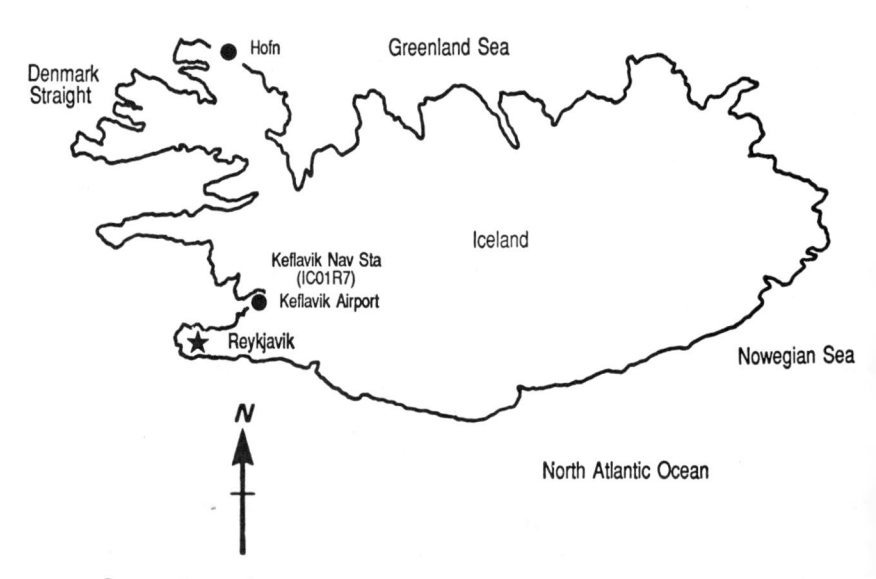

Copyright © 1989 Military Living Publications

Iceland, a North Atlantic island located east of Greenland and south of the Artic Circle, is slightly smaller in size than Kentucky. It is 2,600 miles from New York. Nearly 80 percent of its rugged terrain consists of glaciers, lakes, lava desert and wasteland. The 240,000 Icelanders are descendants of Norwegian and Celtic settlers, live mainly on the coast and speak a Nordic language relatively unchanged since the 12th century. Iceland has a constitutional republic government with universal suffrage over age 18. Fishing is the basis of the economy. Export markets include the U.S.,

ICELAND

the U.K., West Germany and the U.S.S.R. Imports include petroleum products, machinery and transportation equipment, fishing vessels, food and textiles. About half of the work force is employed in industry and commerce. Icelandic currency is the *kronur*. Telephone and telegraph service is available to all points on the island and to major overseas points. Air service connects the island to the U.S. and Europe. There is local taxi and bus service, but neither streetcar nor rail service. Roads out of Reykjavik are gravel and in fair condition. Iceland is five hours ahead of U.S. EST. Climate is similar to the U.S. northwest; warm clothing is worn year around. The major historical attraction is Thingvellir—site of the world's first parliamentary convention. Iceland and the U.S. maintain close, cooperative relations as NATO allies and economic partners. Iceland is the only NATO member with no military forces. **ENTRY REQUIREMENTS:** Passport—yes. Visa—not required for stay up to three months. Check with the Embassy of Iceland, Washington, D.C. 20008, Tel: 202-265-6653, for other requirements. Immunizations—EUR.

KEFLAVIK NAVAL STATION (IC01R7)
FPO New York 09571-5000

TELEPHONE INFORMATION: Main installation numbers: Civ: 354-25-0111. ATVN: 450-0111 (from USA); 228-0111 (from Europe).

LOCATION: From the Reykjavik seaport take Highway South and follow signs to Keflavik. The way is well marked. The naval station is four kilometers before you reach Keflavik. HE: p-1, A/2. NMC: Reykjavik, 35 miles north.

GENERAL INSTALLATION INFORMATION: In making military facilities available to NATO, Iceland has provided an effective base for anti-submarine warfare (ASW) patrol aircraft, for radar and communication facilities and for fighter/interceptor aircraft. Tenant units include the 57th Fighter/Interceptor Squadron; the 960th AWACS Squadron; and Detachment 14, 67th Aerospace Rescue and Recovery Squadron.

GENERAL CITY/REGIONAL INFORMATION: A 45-minute drive from Iceland's capital, Reykjavik, the U.S. Naval Air Station in Keflavik lies on a rocky, lava plateau, surrounded by beautiful countryside. Visitors will see erupting volcanoes; picturesque farms and fishing villages; beautiful streams, lakes, waterfalls, geysers and glaciers, all in an environment that is almost entirely free of pollution, primarily because Iceland is heated exclusively by geothermal heat.

ADMINISTRATIVE SUPPORT

FACILITY/ACTIVITY	BLDG NO/LOC	PHONE	DAYS/COMMENTS
Customs/Duty	980	2208	M-F
Duty Officer	752/NAS	2100	24 hours daily
	126/IDF Hq	4309	24 hours daily
Fire(Mil)	7587	17	24 hours daily
Housing			
Family	937	6123/4559	M-F
Unaccompanied	761	4333	24 hours daily
Referral	937	6123/4559	M-F
Legal Assist	752	7900/7901	M-F
Personnel Spt	T-170	7820/4394	M-F

ICELAND
Keflavik Naval Station, continued

Police(Mil)	810	2211	24 hours daily
Emergency	810	110	24 hours daily
Police(Civ)	980	4555	24 hours daily
Public Affairs	936	4552/7315	M-F

LOGISTICAL SUPPORT

FACILITY/ACTIVITY	BLDG NO/LOC	PHONE	DAYS/COMMENTS
Auto Parts(Exch)	520	7935	Daily
Auto Rent(Other)	771	4200/6180	M-F
Auto Repairs	520	7935	M-F
Auto Wash	501	7731	Daily
Bank	645	4625/4270	M-F
Barber Shop(s)	771	7932	M-Sa
	771	2277	M-F
Beauty Shop(s)	771	6211	M-Sa
Bookstore	750	7980	Daily
Child Care/Dev Ctr	774	7603	M-F
Clothing Sales	771	4569	M-Sa
Commissary(Main)	720	4107/7694	Tu-Sa
Credit Union	771	6441	M-F
Dining Facility	743	2220/4459	Daily
Dry Clean(Exch)	632	4163	M-F
Education Center	349	6226	M-F
Elec Repair(Gov)	839	4100	N/A
Eng'r/Publ Works	506	4100	24 hours daily
Exchange(Main)	869B	2141	Tu-Sa
Exchange(Annex)	771	4105	Daily
Food(Caf/Rest)	869B	6587	Tu-Sa
Food(Snack/Fast)			
Baskin Robbins	771	2149	Daily
Pizza Parlor	771	2149	Daily
Laundry(Exch)	632	4163	M-F
Package Store	632	6533	Tu-Sa
Photo Laboratory	773	7584	Daily
Postal Svcs(Civ)	773	2203/7961	Tu-Sa
Schools(DOD Dep)			
Elementary	624	7412	M-F
High School	910	7008	M-F
Svc Stn(Insta)	552	4470	Daily
Space-A Air Ops	782	6139/2218	24 hours daily
Flights To:		Andrews AFB MD; Bermuda NAS BM; McGuire AFB NJ; RAF Mildenhall UK; Norfolk NAS VA; Philadelphia IAP PA.	
Tailor Shop	632	4163	M-F
Taxi(Comm)	603,772	4141/2525	24 hours daily
Tel Booking Oper	839	4500/4501	M-F
Tel Repair(Gov)	839	4500/4501	M-F
Tel Repair(Civ)	839	4500/4501	M-F
Thrift Shop	861	7726	Th-Sa
TML			
Billeting	786/Navy Lodge	7594/2210	24 hours daily
BEQ/BOQ	761	4333	24 hours daily
Travel Agents	771	4200/4420	M-F

U.S. Forces Travel & Transfer Guide Europe — 263

Keflavik Naval Station, continued   ICELAND

HEALTH AND WELFARE

FACILITY/ACTIVITY	BLDG NO/LOC	PHONE	DAYS/COMMENTS
Ambulance	710	100	24 hours daily
CHAMPUS Office	710	3203/3216	M-F
Chapel	775	4111/4211	N/A
Comm Drug/Alc Ctr	782	7333/7688	M-F
Dental Clinic	862	4591/7425	M-F
Medical Emergency	710	3300/100	24 hours daily
Navy Fam Svcs	776	4357/4401	M-F
Navy Relief	776	4602	M-F
Red Cross	776	6210/6255	M-F

REST AND RECREATION

FACILITY/ACTIVITY	BLDG NO/LOC	PHONE	DAYS/COMMENTS
Aero/Flying Club	885	N/A	1st Su
Amer Forces Ntwk	T-44	4614	Daily
Bowling Lanes	771	6213/4323	Daily
Craftshops			
Automotive	520	7935	Daily
Ceramics	773	2184	Daily
Electronics	773	6191	Tu-Su
Multi-crafts	773	6191	Daily
Photography	773	7584	Daily
Wood	772	2298	Daily
Enlisted Club	749	6126	Daily
	920	4115	Th-Sa
	741	7083	Daily
Equip/Gear Locker	T-180	4554	M-Sa
Gymnasium	701	4588	Daily
Info Tour & Travel	771	4200/4420	M-F
Library	758	4510/7323	Daily
NCO Club	749	6126	Daily
	920	4115	Th-Sa
	741	7083	Daily
O'Club	691	7004	Daily
Rod and Gun Club	2306	4646	W-Su
Swimming Pool	701	6131	Daily
Theater	700	4511	Th-Tu
Video Rental	771	6504	Daily
Youth Center	179	7822/7508	Th-Sa

ITALY
Republic of Italy
Rome

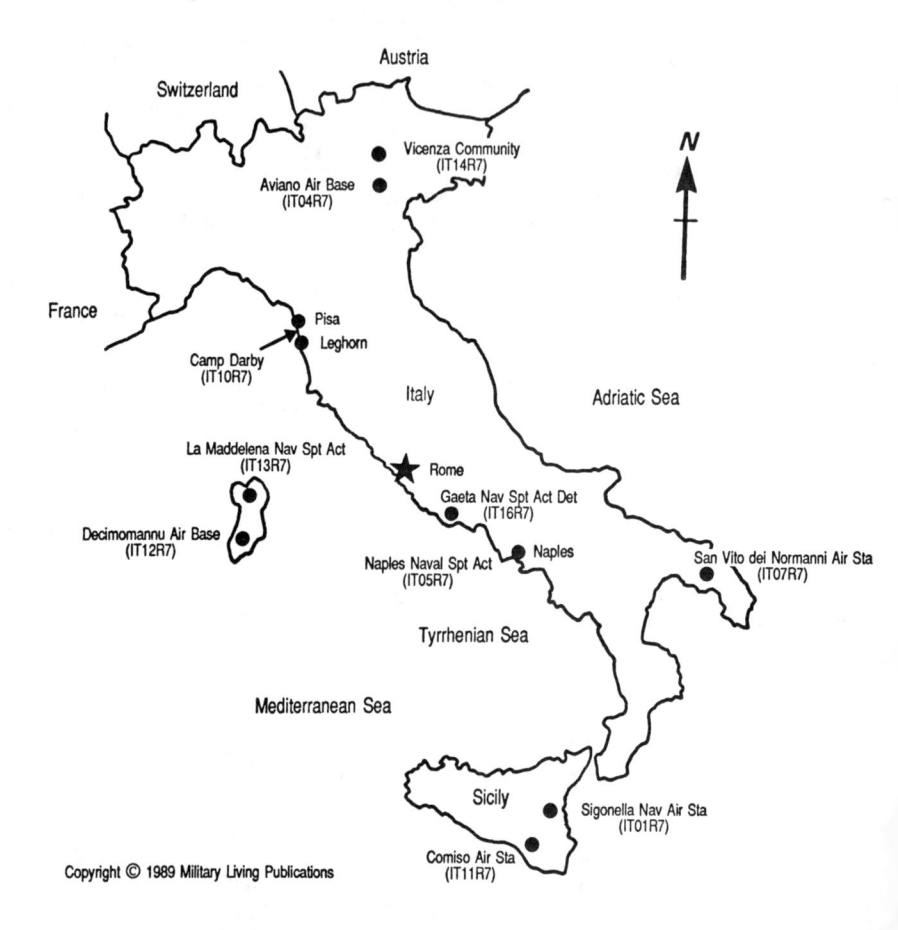

Map of Italy showing U.S. military installations:
- Aviano Air Base (IT04R7)
- Vicenza Community (IT14R7)
- Camp Darby (IT10R7)
- Pisa / Leghorn
- La Maddelena Nav Spt Act (IT13R7)
- Decimomannu Air Base (IT12R7)
- Rome
- Gaeta Nav Spt Act Det (IT16R7)
- Naples Naval Spt Act (IT05R7)
- San Vito dei Normanni Air Sta (IT07R7)
- Sigonella Nav Air Sta (IT01R7)
- Comiso Air Sta (IT11R7)

Copyright © 1989 Military Living Publications

Italy is a 700-mile long peninsula that extends from southern Europe into the Mediterranen Sea, bordered by the Tyrrhenian Sea on the west, the Adriatic Sea on the east and on the north by France, Switzerland and Austria. The population of 57.3 million is primarily Italian and the fifth largest in Europe. Sixty percent of the work force is employed in services, the remainder in industry and commerce (28 percent is unionized) and agriculture. Since 1946, when the monarchy was abolished by popular vote, Italy has been a republic with eight major political parties. Suffrage is universal over age 18. The official language is Italian and the currency is the *lire*. Italy's pre-World War II agrarian-based economy evolved after the war into one of the largest industrialized economies in Europe, largely through creation of state-owned industries. Italy's strength rests in the processing and manufacturing of goods such as automobiles, machinery, fashions and textiles. Machinery and transport equipment, foodstuffs and petroleum are imported.

ITALY

Import deficits are offset by tourism. Sixty percent of the workforce is employed in the service industry. Transportation services including international air, ferries to neighboring islands and Adriatic ports and domestic public, train and taxi services are excellent. Domestic and international communication facilites are reliable. Rome is six hours ahead of U.S. EST. The climate varies from mild Mediterranean in the south (like California) to a northern climate (like Colorado but with more humidity). Rome is the capital of western history and culture, fashion and opera. Italian food, based on simple ingredients, is probably most enjoyable when sampled at "trattorie," more homelike restaurants. Other specialities include fashion design, alabaster and marble figurines and sculptures and jewelry. Stores normally close between 1-4 p.m. and reopen until 8 p.m. Italy is a strong NATO ally with which we enjoy warm, friendly relations.

ENTRY REQUIREMENTS: Passport—yes. Visa—tourist visa not required for stay up to three months. Check with the Embassy of Italy, Washington, D.C. 20009, Tel: 202-328-5500, for further information. Immunizations—EUR.

AVIANO AIR BASE (IT04R7)
APO New York 09293-5000

TELEPHONE INFORMATION: Main installation numbers: Civ: 39-0434-651141/651144. ATVN: 632-1110.

LOCATION: From A-28 north exit at Pordenone to IT-159 north for eight miles to Aviano Air Base. HE: p-93, C/4. NMC: Udine, 30 miles east.

GENERAL INSTALLATION INFORMATION: In 1955, the U.S. Air Force moved to Aviano with Detachment 1, 17th Air Force. In December of 1955, the base was redesignated the 7227th Combat Support Group. In 1966, the 7227th was deactivated when the 40th Tactical Group was reactivated and assigned to the Air Base. The group assumed the 7227th's personnel and mission. Aviano is the only U.S. Air Force tactical air base in Italy. As such, it is vital to NATO's southern defense. Aviano Air Base is the support unit for the 7401st Munitions Support Squadron (MUNSS) at Rimini, 20 miles from the Republic of San Marino; the 7402nd MUNSS at Ghedi, in the Po Valley; and the 40th Munitions Maintenance Squadron at Camp Darby, north of Livorno.

GENERAL CITY/REGIONAL INFORMATION: Aviano, with a population of more than 8000, is located in the Friuli region of northeast Italy, near the Austrian and Yugoslav borders. With a history that spans more than 2000 years, the region is called the "Gateway to Italy." Although Aviano is an agricultural town with a nearly flat terrain to the south, parts of the base are nestled at the foot of the Italian pre-Alps. Mount Cavallo, the highest peak in the vicinity, looms 7000 feet above the town. The nearest major city, Udine, is located 30 miles to the east, while Venice, the legendary "Pearl of the Adriatic," is 50 miles southwest. Numerous historical sites are located within a short drive of Aviano. Among these are the Castello di Aviano and the Madonna del Monte church, also called the Chrome Dome because of its aluminum dome. Other places of interest include the Lago di Barcis, or Barcis Lake; Cortina, a winter resort area where the 1956 Winter Olympics were held; Grado, Lignano, Bibione, Caorle, and Jesolo beach resorts; and Trieste, a large seaport southeast of Aviano.

ITALY
Aviano Air Base, continued

ADMINISTRATIVE SUPPORT

FACILITY/ACTIVITY	BLDG NO/LOC	PHONE	DAYS/COMMENTS
Advocate	1360	2344	M-F
Customs/Duty	933	2353	M-F
Duty Officer	1360	2673	24 hours daily
Fire(Mil)	N/A	117	24 hours daily
Fire(Civ)	Aviano	C-222222	24 hours daily
Housing	Off base	2418	M-F
Info(Insta)	1360	2344	M-F
Inspector Gen'l	1360	2604	M-F
Legal Assist	600	2843	M-F
Locator(Mil)	N/A	2734	M-F
Locator(Civ)	N/A	2562	M-F
Personnel Spt	600	2216	M-F
Police(Mil)	1019	2200	24 hours daily
Emergency	Crime Stop	114	24 hours daily
Police(Civ)	602	2359	M-F
Public Affairs	1360	2344	M-F
Tax Relief	600	2843	M-F

LOGISTICAL SUPPORT

FACILITY/ACTIVITY	BLDG NO/LOC	PHONE	DAYS/COMMENTS
Auto Drivers Testing	904	2449	M-F
Auto Parts(Exch)	105	C-651305	M-Sa
Auto Registration	600	2769	M-F
Auto Rental(Exch)	106	2857	M-F
Auto Sales	Area 1	C-652635	Tu-F
Auto Ship(Gov)	See Camp Darby listing.		
Bank	140	2637	M-F
Barber Shop(s)	105	2737	M-Sa
Beauty Shop(s)	105	C-651303	Tu-Sa
Bookstore	102	2394	M-Sa
Bus	1004	2666	M-F
Child Care/Dev Ctr	174	2279	Su-F
Clothing Sales	105	2755	M-Sa
Commissary(Main)	141	2278	Tu-Sa
Credit Union	140	2288	M-F
Dining Facility	Area 2	2297	Daily
	Ital Din Fac	2463	M-F
Dry Clean(Exch)	105	C-651302	M-Sa
Dry Clean(Gov)	256	2781	M-F
Education Center	264	2365	M-F
Elec Repair(Civ)	105	C-651302	M-Sa
Eng'r/Publ Works	407	2529	M-F
Exchange(Main)	179	2571	M-Sa
Exchange(Concess)	179	N/A	M-Sa
Finance(Mil)	600	2409	M-F
Food(Snack/Fast)			
Baskin Robbins	179	2335	Daily
Burger King	Area 1	2840	Daily
Pizza Parlor	179	2335	Daily
Foodland	102	2897	Daily

ITALY

Aviano Air Base, continued

Laundry(Exch)	179	2737	M-Sa
Laundry(Self-Svc)	257	None	24 hours daily
Motor Pool	1004	2666	24 hours daily
Package Store	176A	2397	Tu-Sa
Photo Laboratory	1360	2846	M-F
Pick-up Point	179	2737	M-Sa
Postal Svcs(Mil)	142	2735	M-Sa
SATO-OS	933	2791	M-F
Schools(DOD Dep)			
Elementary	155/157	2283	M-F (K-6)
High School	168/186	2256	M-F (7-12)
Space-A Air Ops	933	2520	Daily
Flights to:	Athinai Arpt GR; Brindisi/Casale Arpt IT; Capodichino Arpt IT; Decimomannu ITAB IT; RAF Mildenhall UK; Philadelphia IAP PA; Pisa Arpt IT; Ramstein AB GE; Rhein-Main AB GE; Sigonella NAB IT; Torrejon AB SP.		
Tailor Shop	105	C-651304	M-Sa
Tel Booking Oper	N/A	0	24 hours daily
Tel Repair(Gov)	N/A	119	N/A
TML			
Billeting	256	2581 C-652306	24 hours daily
Protocol Office	1360	2605	M-F
DV/VIP	1360	2604	24 hours daily

HEALTH AND WELFARE

FACILITY/ACTIVITY	BLDG NO/LOC	PHONE	DAYS/COMMENTS
AF Family Svcs	150	2598	M-F
AF Relief	600	2216	M-F
Ambulance	N/A	116	24 hours daily
Central Appts	120	2656	M-F
CHAMPUS Office	120	2695	M-F
Chaplain	172	2211	M-F
Chapel	172	2211	M-F
Comm Drug/Alc Ctr	120	2703	M-F
Dental Clinic	117	2383	M-F
Medical Emergency	120	2692	24 hours daily
Mental Health	120	2719	M-F
Red Cross	150	2215	M-F
Veterinary Svcs	1369	2425	M-F

REST AND RECREATION

FACILITY/ACTIVITY	BLDG NO/LOC	PHONE	DAYS/COMMENTS
Bowling Lanes	176	2487	Daily
Camping/RV Area	Fam Camp	C-651141	Daily
Consolidated Club	147	2493	Daily
Craftshops			
Automotive	264	2892	Tu-Sa
Wood	262	2892	W,F,Sa
Golf Course	1399	2386	Daily
Gymnasium	240	2574	Daily
Info Tour & Travel	106	2479	M-F

ITALY
Aviano Air Base, continued

Library	145	2893	M-Th
Outdoor Rec Ctr	106	2633	M,Tu,Th-Sa
Recreation Center	106	2479	M-F
Service Club	147	2463	M-F
Swimming Pool	178	2841	May-October
Theater	136	2252	Call for schedule.
Video Rental	105	N/A	Tu-Sa
Youth Center	240	2575	M-Sa

COMISO AIR STATION (Sicily) (IT11R7)
APO New York 09694-5000

TELEPHONE INFORMATION: Main installation numbers: Civ: 39-932-73-1111. ATVN: 628-1110.

LOCATION: The air station is located 11 miles west of Ragusa in the southeast corner of the island of Sicily.

GENERAL INSTALLATION INFORMATION: The 487th Tactical Missile Wing at Comiso maintains and operates the BGM-109 ground-launched cruise missiles (GLCM) for the North Atlantic Treaty Organization. Subordinate units include the 487th Combat Support Group, the 487th Civil Engineering Squadron, the 302nd Tactical Missile Squadron, the 487th Missile Defense Squadron, and the 2189th Communications Squadron.

Comiso Air Station is an Italian Air Force Base and entrance to the base is restricted and controlled by Italian authorities. Any person wishing to visit Comiso should call the base Pass and Registration Office for current information (932-73-2313).

GENERAL CITY/REGIONAL INFORMATION: The largest island in the Mediterranean Sea, Sicily is located just off the toe of the boot of Italy. With 9,926 square miles of territory, it is approximately the same size as Maryland. The island is rugged and scenic with more preserved ruins than all of mainland Italy. Roman and Greek cultures first met and merged here at a time when much of the rest of the world was largely uncivilized.

The most active volcano in Europe is on Sicily—Mount Etna. Etna is 11,030 feet high and on its extensive slopes are many villages where a large number of Americans live who are assigned to Sigonella Naval Air Station.

ADMINISTRATIVE SUPPORT

FACILITY/ACTIVITY	BLDG NO/LOC	PHONE	DAYS/COMMENTS
Advocate	107, Rm 207	2342	24 hours daily
Customs/Duty	441	2470	M-F
Duty Officer	2047	2439	24 hours daily
Fire(Mil)	302	117	24 hours daily
Info(Insta)	107	0	24 hours daily
Inspector Gen'l	107, Rm 305	2626	M-F
Legal Assist	107	2216/2611	M-F
Locator(Mil)	107, Rm 101	2620/2354	24 hours daily
Locator(Civ)	107	2621	M-F

ITALY

Comiso Air Station, continued

Personnel Spt	107, Rm 214	2276	M-F
Police(Mil)	107, Rm 119	2313	24 hours daily
Police(Civ)	Comiso	C-996821	24 hours daily
Public Affairs	107, Rm 207	2530	M-F

LOGISTICAL SUPPORT

FACILITY/ACTIVITY	BLDG NO/LOC	PHONE	DAYS/COMMENTS
Auto Drivers Testing	351	2471	M-F
Auto Registration	107	2778	M-F
Auto Rental(Exch)	36	C-965870	Daily
Auto Sales	24	2678	Daily
Auto Ship(Gov)	351	2718	M-F
Barber Shop(s)	32	2482	M-Sa
Beauty Shop(s)	32	2203	M-Sa
Bookstore	222	2781	M-F
Bus	351	2405	M-F
Child Care/Dev Ctr	T-37	2576	M-F
Clothing Sales	T-44	2914	Tu-Sa
Commissary(Main)	135	2410	Tu-Sa
Credit Union	T-32	2819	M-F
Dry Clean(Exch)	32	2821	M-Sa
Dry Clean(Gov)	221	2639	M-F
Education Center	107	2487	M-F
Elec Repair(Gov)	401	2703	M-F
Elec Repair(Civ)	32	2272	M-Sa
Eng'r/Publ Works	107, 352	2628/2464	M-F
Exchange(Main)	32	2821	Tu-Sa
Exchange(Annex)	24	2678	Daily
Exchange(Concess)	24	2271	M-F
Finance(Mil)	107/302	2230	M-F
Food(Snack/Fast)			
Burger Bar	26	2580	Daily
Foodland	24	2678	Daily
Laundry(Exch)	32	2780	M-Sa
Laundry(Self-Svc)	32	N/A	Daily
Motor Pool	351	2718	M-F
Package Store	T-4	2503	Tu-Sa
Photo Laboratory	24	2540	M-F
Postal Svcs(Mil)	107	2709	M-Sa
SATO-OS	441	2912	M-F
Schools	1000	2636	M-F (K-12)
Space-A Air Ops	441	2461	M-F
Tailor Shop	T-19	2272	M-Sa
Tel Booking Oper	113	0	24 hours daily
Tel Repair(Gov)	On Station	2643	M-F
Thrift Shop	T-11	2460	M-F
TML			
Billeting	241	2560	Daily
TLQ	201	2560	Daily
Travel Agents	441	2268	M-F
Watch Repair	32	2460	M-Sa

ITALY
Comiso Air Station, continued

HEALTH AND WELFARE

FACILITY/ACTIVITY	BLDG NO/LOC	PHONE	DAYS/COMMENTS
AF Family Svcs	107	2768	M-F
AF Relief	107	2766	M-F
Ambulance	123	116	24 hours daily
Central Appts	123	2367	M-F
CHAMPUS Office	123	2729	M-F
Chaplain	16	2277/2756	Daily
Chapel	16	2729	Daily
Comm Drug/Alc Ctr	107	2657	M-F
Dental Clinic	123	2357	M-F
Medical Emergency	123	2516	24 hours daily
Mental Health	123	2289	M-F
Poison Control	123	2310	M-F
Red Cross	107	2766	M-F
Veterinary Svcs	123	2806	M-F

REST AND RECREATION

FACILITY/ACTIVITY	BLDG NO/LOC	PHONE	DAYS/COMMENTS
Amer Forces Ntwk	T-4	2707	Daily
Bowling Lanes	139	2296	Daily
Consolidated Club	139	2385	Daily
Consolidated Club	139	2607	Daily
Craftshops			
Photography	139	2252	Daily
Equip/Gear Locker	139	2591	Daily
Gymnasium	139	2591	Daily
Library	139	2343	Daily
Racket Courts	139	2591	Daily
Special Services	139	2252	Daily
Sport Field	139	2252	Daily
Swimming Pool	42	2408	W-M
Theater	36	2468	M,W,F,Sa,Su
Video Rental	24	None	M-Sa
Youth Center	T-9	2282	M-Sa

DECIMOMANNU AIR BASE (IT12R7)
APO New York 09161-5000

TELEPHONE INFORMATION: Main installation numbers: Civ: 39-70-668971 extension 670. ETS/ATVN: 621-9267/9589. Civ prefix: 070-____. ETS/ATVN prefix: 621-XXXX. Civ to mil prefix: 070-668971 extension 670.

LOCATION: Located on the southern coast of the island of Sardinia. Off IT-130 west. HE: p-54, B/5. NMC: Cagliari, 10 miles southeast.

GENERAL INSTALLATION INFORMATION: The Air Weapons Training Installation (AWTI) at Decimomannu Air Base is a NATO undertaking that operates under the terms of the Quadrinational Agreement signed between

ITALY
Decimomannu Air Base, continued

Italy, Germany, the United States and the United Kingdom. As host nation, Italy is responsible for all common user facilities such as airfield facilities, fire-fighting/crash rescue services, refueling, range maintenance, technical and on-base domestic accommodation, all main services and so on. Italian Air Force Base Decimomannu is commanded by an Italian Air Force colonel with German Air Force, Royal Air Force and U.S. Air Force officers commanding their own national forces.

The AWTI comprises the airfield at Decimomannu; the air-to-ground range at Capo Frasca, 40 miles northwest of Decimomannu; the Air Combat Maneuvering Instrumentation (ACMI) group and ACMI range off the west coast; the air-to-air range also off the west coast; a weapons storage area at Villasor (adjacent to the air base); and a radar site at Capo Frasca.

The 7555 TTS is responsible for the operating, maintaining and logistically supporting the USAFE ACMI. It provides base support for the various squadrons that deploy at the air base for training. The ACMI became operational in August 1979.

Note: Please be aware that if you enter the air base via Space-A air transportation but are not on official orders, once you leave the base you will find it difficult if not impossible to return without an on-base sponsor.

GENERAL CITY/REGIONAL INFORMATION: Decimomannu (pronounced DECHEE-MOW-MAH-NEW) is located in the southern part of Sardinia, one of the largest and most heavily populated islands in the Med. The air base is located close to Cagliari, the capital and main port of the island. Visitors here will want to see the National Archaeological Museum and the city's many galleries, churches and ancient towers, walls and ramparts. The Roman Amphitheater, the Villa di Tigellio, and the Grotta della Vipera are a few of the structures of historical importance nearby and are well worth a visit. Nature lovers and bird watchers will treasure excursions to the surrounding countryside, lagoons, beaches and mountains.

Winters in Sardinia are quite cold because of the high humidity and strong winds. Summers, on the other hand, are hot and dry. From April to mid-November, tourists flock to the beaches of this island resort.

ADMINISTRATIVE SUPPORT

FACILITY/ACTIVITY	BLDG NO/LOC	PHONE	DAYS/COMMENTS
Customs/Duty	153	2721	M-F
Duty Officer	150	2711/2569	24 hours daily
Fire(Mil)	153	2721	24 hours daily
Fire(Civ)	On Base	2333	24 hours daily
Referral	On base	N/A	M-F
Info(Insta)	150	2564	Daily
Inspector Gen'l	150	2711	M-F
Legal Assist	150	2711	M-F
Locator(Mil)	150	2569	Daily
Locator(Civ)	150	2564	Daily
Personnel Spt	150	2569	M-F
Police(Mil)	Hanger 62	2732	24 hours daily
Police(Civ)	Decimomannu	2326/2670	24 hours daily
Public Affairs	150	2564	M-F

ITALY
Decimomannu Air Base, continued

| Tax Relief | 150 | 2711 | M-F |

LOGISTICAL SUPPORT

FACILITY/ACTIVITY	BLDG NO/LOC	PHONE	DAYS/COMMENTS
Auto Drivers Testing	154	2568	M-F
Auto Registration	Hangar 61	2732	M-F
Auto Rent(Other)	On Base	2594	Daily
Auto Ship(Gov)	153	2289	M-F
Auto Ship(Civ)	Decimomannu	2594	M-F
Bank	Credito Italiano	2396	M-Sa
Barber Shop(s)	On Base	2495	M-Sa
Bus	154	2568	24 hours daily
Commissary(Main)	On Base	2570	Tu-Sa
Commissary(Annex)	On Base	2570	Tu-Sa
Dry Clean(Exch)	Tailer 2	2784	Tu-Sa
Dry Clean(Gov)	Trailer 2	2784	M-F
Education Center	Hangar 61	2678	M-F
Eng'r/Publ Works	153	2712	Daily
Exchange(Main)	Trailer 1	2530	M-F
Exchange(Annex)	Trailer 2	2530	Tu-Sa
Exchange(Concess)	Italian	2511	Tu-Sa
Finance(Mil)	150	2710	M-F
Food(Caf/Rest)	On Base	2729	Daily
Laundry(Self-Svc)	162	2726	24 hours daily
Motor Pool	154	2568	24 hours daily
Package Store	162	2730	N/A
Photo Laboratory	On Base	2336/2692	M-F
Postal Svcs(Mil)	Trailer 2	2714	M-Sa
Postal Svcs(Civ)	Decimomannu	2353/2524	M-Sa
Railroad/RTO	Decimomannu	2594	Daily
SATO-OS	153	2289	M-F
Schools(DOD Dep)			
Elementary	Located in Selarg N/A		M-F (K-8)
High School	Students attend London American HS as boarders.		
Space-A Air Ops	153	2289	Daily
Pax Lounges(Gen'l)	153	2289	Daily
Flights to:	Aviano AB IT; Bitburg AB GE; Capodichino Arpt IT; RAF Alconbury UK; Ramstein AB GE; Soesterberg AB NT; Torrejon AB SP		
Tailor Shop	On Base	2495	Tu-Sa
Tel Repair(Gov)	153	2787	24 hours daily
Thrift Shop	Villasor	C-6948512	Th
TML			
Billeting	162	9267/9589	24 hours daily Official duty only
Travel Agents	On Base	2594	M-F

HEALTH AND WELFARE

FACILITY/ACTIVITY	BLDG NO/LOC	PHONE	DAYS/COMMENTS
Ambulance	On Base	2778	24 hours daily
Chaplain	Hangar 61	3704/2704	Daily
Chapel	Hangar 61	3704/2704	Daily
Comm Drug/Alc Ctr	162	3780	M-F

U.S. Forces Travel & Transfer Guide Europe — 273

ITALY

Decimomannu Air Base, continued

Medical Emergency	On Base	2700	24 hours daily
Red Cross	In Naples	C-0813228692	24 hours daily

REST AND RECREATION

FACILITY/ACTIVITY	BLDG NO/LOC	PHONE	DAYS/COMMENTS
Beach(es)	Plentiful beach resort areas		
Enlisted Club	On Base	2730	Daily
Info Tour & Travel	On Base	2594	M-F
Library	162	2726	Daily
NCO Club	On Base	2730	Daily
O'Club	On Base	2508	Daily
Outdoor Rec Ctr	153	742	M-Sa
Racket Courts	On Base	742	24 hours daily
Recreation Center	163	2730	Daily
Tennis Courts	On Base	742	24 hours daily
Video Rental	162	2726	Daily

GAETA NAVAL SUPPORT ACTIVITY DETACHMENT (IT16R7)
FPO New York 09522-5000

TELEPHONE INFORMATION: Main installation numbers: Civ: 39-0771-465715/465842. ATVN: 625-4583/4/5.

LOCATION: Gaeta is located in approximately midway between Rome and Naples. NSA Naples is approximately one hour and twenty minutes away. HE: p-51, D/5. NMC: Naples, 60 miles south.

GENERAL INSTALLATION INFORMATION: The NSA Det Gaeta was established to provide and maintain facilities and services to support COMSIXTHFLT staff and Flagship personnel, along with their families stationed in the Gaeta area. The Det is under the overall command of U.S. NSA Naples and receives support from the NSA Naples.

GENERAL CITY/REGIONAL INFORMATION: Gaeta is historically famous in Virgil's Tales as the mythical burial place of Caieta, the nurse of Aeneas, who died on the shore while traveling with refugees from Troy. Historical sources dates Gaeta's founding many centuries B.C. Gaeta became famous as a vacation and resort area for Rome's emperors and other prominent citizens. Roman ruins still exist to some extent in the area. These and many other historical landmarks may be seen in "Old Gaeta," including ancient churches, a magnificent cathedral, a mighty fortress and quaint, winding, narrow streets leading up to Split Mountain, which overlooks the entire Bay of Gaeta.

ADMINISTRATIVE SUPPORT

FACILITY/ACTIVITY	BLDG NO/LOC	PHONE	DAYS/COMMENTS
Duty Officer	NSA Det	C-461261	24 hours daily
Fire (Mil)	N/A	C-460931	24 hours daily
Housing	NSA Det	C-465096	M-F
Personnel Spt	NSA Det	C-461624	M-F

ITALY
Gaeta Naval Support Activity Detachment, continued

Police(Mil)	NSA Det	C-465892	24 hours daily
Police(Civ)	Gaeta	C-460203	24 hours daily

LOGISTICAL SUPPORT

FACILITY/ACTIVITY	BLDG NO/LOC	PHONE	DAYS/COMMENTS
Bank	NSA Det	C-461624	M,W,F
Barber Shop	Seabreeze Center	N/A	Daily
Beauty Shop	Seabreeze Center	N/A	Daily
Child Care/Dev Ctr	Community Center	C-465715	M-F
Commissary(Main)	N/A	C-470562	M-Sa
Dining Facility	Snackbar at exchange		
Eng'r/Publ Works	N/A	C-740631	N/A
Exchange(Main)	N/A	C-470562	M-Sa
Food(Snack/Fast)	N/A	C-465345	N/A
Laundry(Self-Svc)	Seabreeze Center	N/A	Daily
Package Store	Exchange	N/A	M-Sa
Postal(Gov)	NSA Det	N/A	M-F
Schools(DOD Dep)	Community Center	C-463160	M-F
Space-A Air Ops	Sea Naples Naval Air Station listing.		

HEALTH AND WELFARE

FACILITY/ACTIVITY	BLDG NO/LOC	PHONE	DAYS/COMMENTS
Ambulance	NSA Det	C-460446	24 hours daily
Central Appts	N/A	C-460446	N/A
CHAMPUS Office	At Naples Hospital		
Chaplain	NSA Det	C-740520	N/A
Dental	NSA Det	C-460440	M-F
Medical Emergency	NSA Det	C-460440	24 hours daily
Navy Fam Svcs	Behind Public Works Building	C-740383	M-F
Red Cross	See Chaplain.		

REST AND RECREATION

FACILITY/ACTIVITY	BLDG NO/LOC	PHONE	DAYS/COMMENTS
Bowling Lanes	Community Center	C-463606	Daily
Gymnasium	Community Center	C-465345	Daily
Info Tour & Travel	On Base	C-461117	M-F
Library	Community Center	C-463606	Daily
O'Club	On Base	N/A	Daily
Recreation Center	Community Center	C-463606	Daily
Seabreeze Club	On Base	C-470562	Daily
Tennis Courts	Formia	N/A	Daily
Theater	Community Center	C-463606	W-Su

ITALY

LA MADDALENA NAVY SUPPORT OFFICE
(IT13R7)
FPO New York 09533-0051

TELEPHONE INFORMATION: Main installation numbers: Civ: 39-0789-790270. ATVN: 726-2701.

LOCATION: Located on the northern tip of the island of Sardinia. Take the main road (IT-125) north from Olbia to Palau, then take a 15 minute ferry ride to La Maddalena and follow signs to the installation. HE: p-54, C/1. NMC: Olbia, 45 kilometers southeast.

GENERAL INSTALLATION INFORMATION: The primary mission of the Navy Support Office in La Maddalena is to provide support to visiting ships of the operating forces and to the personnel, including dependents, of ships and embarked staffs homeported in the La Maddalena area. The Trinita Area and the Paradiso Complex are in the vicinity of La Maddalena. The Santo Stefano NATO Site is on the island of Santo Stefano. Additional recreational facilities exist in nearby Palau. **The following abbreviations are used in this listing only:** NSO (Naval Support Office); SS (Santo Stefano Island).

GENERAL CITY/REGIONAL INFORMATION: As a permanently inhabited island, La Maddalena is very young. It was known to the Romans as "Isola Ilva," while the entire archipelago was known as "Isole Cunicularie", or "island of the rabbits." In the middle ages the island was controlled by pirates who used it as a base of operations. In the mid-1600s, a group of Corsican shepherds established flocks of sheep on La Maddalena. But these early residents remained here for only a short time, frequently returning to Corsica. Thus the long history of contact between Corsica and La Maddalena began. When the Sardinians gained control of the island in 1767, they established a small Navy base here finally making the island a safe place to live.

With the establishment of the naval base, La Maddalena became a safe place to settle. By 1780 about 400 people were living on the island, most from Corsica or Pisa. Because of its location, La Maddalena has been and is of great military importance. More than 50 fortresses dot the island's landscape, all but one now used only by hikers and campers.

ADMINISTRATIVE SUPPORT

FACILITY/ACTIVITY	BLDG NO/LOC	PHONE	DAYS/COMMENTS
Advocate	NSO	C-790221 221/2	M-F
Customs/Duty	NSO	C-790227 227/242	M-F
Duty Officer	NSO	C-790244 244/5	24 hours daily
Housing			
Family	Trinita/Paradiso	C-790223/4/5	M-F
Unaccompanied	Paradiso	84+214	24 hours daily
	SS	216	24 hours daily
Info(Insta)	NSO	C-790270	M-F
Legal Assist	Judge	C-736302	M-F
Locator(Mil)	See Duty Officer.		
Locator(Civ)	See Duty Officer.		

ITALY
La Maddalena Navy Support Office, continued

Facility	Bldg No/Loc	Phone	Days/Comments
Personnel Spt	NSO	C-790285 285/6	M-F
Police(Mil)	See Duty Officer.		
Police(Civ)	La Maddalena	C-737004	24 hours daily
Public Affairs	NSO	C-790261 261/2	M-F

LOGISTICAL SUPPORT

FACILITY/ACTIVITY	BLDG NO/LOC	PHONE	DAYS/COMMENTS
Auto Drivers Testing	NSO	226/227	M-F
Auto Parts(Exch)	N/A	C-790271 271	Tu-Sa
Auto Registration	See Drivers Testing.		
Auto Rental(Exch)	NSO Supply	C-790242 242/3	M-F
Auto Ship(Gov)	See Drivers Testing.		
Auto Ship(Civ)	See Drivers Testing.		
Bookstore	See Exchange.		
Bus	Palau	C-738668	Daily
Child Care/Dev Ctr	Paradiso	C-722013	Daily
	Trinita	C-737621	Daily
Clothing Sales	See Exchange.		
Commissary(Main)	SS	C-736401 268	Tu-Sa
Credit Union	NSO	256	M-F
Education Center	NSO	261	M-F
	Univ of Maryland	C-738107 355	M-F
Eng'r/Publ Works	NSO	C-790211 211/2	M-F M-F
Exchange(Main)	N/A	C-790271 271	Tu-Sa
Exchange(Annex)	SS	C-790268 268	Tu-Sa
Finance(Mil)	See Personnel Support.		
Food(Caf/Rest)	Paradiso	C-722088 84+286	
Food(Snack/Fast)	NSO	253	M-Sa
Laundry(Exch)	See Exchange.		
Laundry(Self-Svc)	See Family Service Center		
Motor Pool	NSO	C-790260 260	M-F
Package Store	See Exchange.		
Parking	NSO	None	Daily
Postal Svcs(Mil)	NSO	230	M-F
Postal Svcs(Civ)	La Maddalena	None	M-F
SATO-OS	See Personnel Support.		
Schools(DOD Dep)			
Elementary	Trinita	C-739001	M-F
High School	None	236	
Space-A Air Ops	Olbia Arpt	C-69191	Tu,Th,Sa
Flights to:	Naples IT		
Tel Booking Oper	See Information.		
Tel Repair(Civ)	See Information		
Thrift Shop	Paradiso	C-790025	M-F

ITALY

La Maddalena Navy Support Office, continued

TML		205/6	
Billeting	Paradiso	C-722318	24 hours daily
BEQ		C-736638	Daily
Travel Agents	La Maddalena	C-738668	M-Sa

HEALTH AND WELFARE

FACILITY/ACTIVITY	BLDG NO/LOC	PHONE	DAYS/COMMENTS
Ambulance	Security	C-790244/5 244/5	24 hours daily
Central Appts	Medical	C-738415 275/6/7	M-F
CHAMPUS Office	Medical	C-738415 275	M-F
Chaplain	See Chapel.		
Chapel	Paradiso	C-790272 272/3	Daily
Comm Drug/Alc Ctr	See Family Services.		
Dental Clinic	Medical	C-736673 274	M-F
Medical Emergency	See Ambulance.		
Mental Health	See Family Services.		
Navy Fam Svcs	Paradiso	C-790205 205/6	M-F
Navy Relief	Paradiso	C-790205	M-F
Poison Control	Medical	C-738415 275/6/7	24 hours daily
Red Cross	See Family Services.		

REST AND RECREATION

FACILITY/ACTIVITY	BLDG NO/LOC	PHONE	DAYS/COMMENTS
Amer Forces Ntwk	SEB	C-790247 247	Daily
Bowling Lanes	SS	217	Daily
Consolidated Club	Paradiso	C-790286 84+286	Daily
	SS	255	Daily
Craftshops			
Automotive	NSO	280/1	Sa,Su
Multi-crafts	Paradiso	None	M-Sa
Gymnasium	SS	217	Daily
Nautilus	Paradiso	273	Daily
Info Tour & Travel	NSO	292	M-F
Library	Paradiso	C-790289	Sa-Th (closed F)
Racket Courts	NSO	292	Daily
Recreation Center	Paradiso	5-294	M-Sa
Tennis Courts	Paradiso	5-294	Daily
Theater	NSO	248	Daily
Video Rental	NSO	292	M-Sa
Youth Center	Trinita	N/A	Daily

278 — U.S. Forces Travel & Transfer Guide Europe

ITALY

LIVORNO (CAMP DARBY) COMMUNITY (IT10R7)
APO New York 09015-5000

TELEPHONE INFORMATION: Main installation numbers: Civ: 39-0586-94-7111. ETS: 633-7113. ATVN: 633-7225. Note: from civ exchanges in Italy dial prefix 94. From civ exchanges in Germany dial 00-39-586.

LOCATION: Located midway between Livorno and Pisa. From Autostrada E-1 take the Pisa south exit. Turn left and continue to end of road, turn left onto Via Aurelia, then right onto Cantiere Navale and follow Camp Darby signs. HE: p-50, A/3. NMC: Pisa, six miles north.

GENERAL INSTALLATION INFORMATION: Units at Camp Darby provide logistical support to the southern NATO bases. Units include HQ, 8th Support Group; and the 509th Signal Battalion. The local U.N. Supply Depot and the ocean terminal in Livorno are administered by Camp Darby personnel.

GENERAL CITY/REGIONAL INFORMATION: There are many historical sites to see in the Livorno/Camp Darby vicinity. The famous Leaning Tower of Pisa is six miles away; the walled city of Lucca, 20 miles away; and Florence, 75 miles away. Camp Darby is a short distance from the American Beach on the Tyrrhenian Sea where safe swimming is available at no charge.

ADMINISTRATIVE SUPPORT

FACILITY/ACTIVITY	BLDG NO/LOC	PHONE	DAYS/COMMENTS
Advocate	731	7084/7814	M-F
Customs/Duty	731	7542/7397	M-F
Duty Officer	302	7575/7083	24 hours daily
Fire(Mil)	302	95	24 hours daily
Fire(Civ)	302	94-7513	24 hours daily
Housing			
Family	302	7871	M-F
Unaccompanied	302	7303	M-F
Info(Insta)	302	92	24 hours daily
Inspector Gen'l	303	7763	M-F
Legal Assist	302	7227/7686	M-F
Locator(Mil)	302	92	24 hours daily
Locator(Civ)	302	92	24 hours daily
Police(Mil)	731	95/98	24 hours daily
Emergency	731	94/7510	24 hours daily
Police(Civ)	731	7310/7835	M-F
Public Affairs	302	8011/7245	M-F
Tax Relief	302	7818	M-F

LOGISTICAL SUPPORT

FACILITY/ACTIVITY	BLDG NO/LOC	PHONE	DAYS/COMMENTS
Auto Drivers Testing	702	7042	M-F
Auto Parts(Exch)	702	7467	Tu-Sa
Auto Sales	Shopping Center	C-444-500386	Chrysler

ITALY

Livorno (Camp Darby) Community, continued

Facility	Bldg	Phone	Days
	Shopping Center	C-444-500871	Ford
Bank	725	7678	M-F
Barber Shop(s)	725	7469	Tu-Sa
Beauty Shop(s)	725	7469	Tu-Sa
Bookstore	725	7577	Tu-Sa
Bus	TMP #1	7538/7640	Daily
Child Care/Dev Ctr	413	7459/7642	M-F
Clothing Sales	723	7666	Tu-Sa
Commissary(Main)	725	7672/7400	Tu-Sa
Credit Union	775	7436	M-F
Dining Facility	408	7498/7698	Daily
Dry Clean(Gov)	728	7669/7460	M-F
Education Center	423	7694	M-F
Learning Center	423	7073	M-F
Elec Repair(Civ)	724	7478	Tu-Sa
Exchange(Main)	725	7468/7655	Daily
Exchange(Concess)	723	7418	Tu-Sa
Finance(Mil)	303	7292	M-F
Food(Snack/Fast)			
Burger Bar	725	7464	Daily
Foodland	725	7468/7655	Daily
Laundry(Self-Svc)	724	7392	24 hours daily
Motor Pool	702	7247	M-F
Package Store	724	7456	Tu-Sa
Photo Laboratory	302	7279/7237	M-F
Pick-up Point	723	7418	Tu-Sa
Postal Svcs(Mil)	771	7035/7630	M-F
Schools(DOD Dep)			
Elementary	201	7588/7058	M-F
High School	501	7367	M-F
Svc Stn(Insta)	729	7396	M-Sa
Space-A Air Ops	San Guisto Arpt (Pisa)	C-586-94-3001 ext. 7773	Daily
Flights to:	Naples IT; Ramstein AB GE; Rhein-Main AB GE; Torrejon AB SP.		
Tailor Shop	723	7418	Tu-Sa
Taxi(Comm)	Livorno	94-401294	Daily
		94-21094	Daily
		94-24336	Daily
Tel Repair(Gov)	836	7225/7758	Daily
Tel Repair(Civ)	724	7478	Tu-Sa
Thrift Shop	206	7060	W,F
TML			
Billeting	303	7225/7303	24 hours daily (15 June-15 Sept)
		7575	After hours
Guest House	836	7225	Daily
DV/VIP	836	7758	Daily
Watch Repair	723	7418	Tu-F

HEALTH AND WELFARE

FACILITY/ACTIVITY	BLDG NO/LOC	PHONE	DAYS/COMMENTS
Ambulance	113	97/116	Daily

ITALY
Livorno (Camp Darby) Community, continued

Army Comm Svcs	730	7814/7584	M-F
Army Emerg Relief	730	7814/7584	M-F
Central Appts	113	7620	M-F
CHAMPUS Office	113	7883	M-F
Chaplain	301	7267/7257	Su-F
Chapel	301	7267	Su-F
Comm Drug/Alc Ctr	113	7077	M-F
Dental Clinic	113	7461/7881	M-F
Medical Emergency	113	7620	M-F
Red Cross	730	7584/7814	M-F
Veterinary Svcs	830	7297	M-F

REST AND RECREATION

FACILITY/ACTIVITY	BLDG NO/LOC	PHONE	DAYS/COMMENTS
Beach(es)	American Beach	7800	Daily
Bowling Lanes	305	7446/7458	Daily
Camping/RV Area	Off Base	C-0586-94-7111	Daily
Consolidated Club	204	7462/7463	Daily
Craftshops			
Automotive	778	7009	W-Su
Multi-crafts	778	7009	W-Su
Equip/Gear Locker	695	7775	M-Sa
Gymnasium	305	7440	Daily
Info Tour & Travel	775	7509	M-F
Library	703	7623/7000	Tu-Sa
Recreation Center	305	7771/7413	M-F
Rod and Gun Club	AE North Gate	7149	Daily
Theater	304	7417	Th-Su
	730	7453/7653	M-F
Youth Center	407	7624/7472	M-F

NAPLES NAVAL SUPPORT ACTIVITY (IT05R7)
FPO New York 09521-1000

TELEPHONE INFORMATION: Main installation numbers: Civ: 39-081-724-1110. ATVN: 625-1110. Note: **all 4XXX and 5XXX numbers take a 724 prefix; all 2XXX numbers take a 721 prefix.**

LOCATION: From Autostrada A2 take the tangenziale through the city of Naples. Take the Agnano/Terme exit. Pay the L.500 toll and make a left. Keep driving straight to the first traffic light then make a right. The NSA is located on the right side one kilometer ahead. HE: p-51, E/6. NMC: Naples, in the city.

GENERAL INSTALLATION INFORMATION: NSA Naples provides support to units of the U.S. Sixth Fleet and logistic support to U.S. Navy and NATO commands located in Naples. Note: **Admiral Carney Park Recreation Facility is located five miles from the NSA. Many recreational opportunities and facilities are available including TML in cabins and trailers.** Telephone: Civ: 39-081-867-4158, or ATVN: 625-1110 extension 4158.

U.S. Forces Travel & Transfer Guide Europe — 281

ITALY

Naples Naval Support Activity, continued

GENERAL CITY/REGIONAL INFORMATION: Founded by Greeks in approximately 500 B.C., Naples was invaded by Roman, Byzantine, and Gothic subjects before coming under the dominance of Swabian and Norman kings. After the liberation of Italy in 1860, the citizens of Naples voted to become a part of the newly formed country. Naples today is a major seaport in which modern industrial operations sit side by side with ancient castles and ruins.

ADMINISTRATIVE SUPPORT

FACILITY/ACTIVITY	BLDG NO/LOC	PHONE	DAYS/COMMENTS
Customs/Duty	Edilizia II	4536	M-F
Duty Officer	Admin Bldg	4546	24 hours daily
Fire(Mil)	N/A	4333	24 hours daily
Fire(Civ)	Naples	C-455555	24 hours daily
Legal Assist	Edilizia II	4508	M-F
Locator(Mil)	Admin Bldg	4556/4546	24 hours daily
Locator(Civ)	Edilizia II	4513	M-F
Personnel Spt	PSD Bldg	4151/4833	24 hours daily
Police(Mil)	Sec Bldg	4109/4686	24 hours daily
Public Affairs	62	4486/4487	M-F
Tax Relief	Edilizia	4508	M-F

LOGISTICAL SUPPORT

FACILITY/ACTIVITY	BLDG NO/LOC	PHONE	DAYS/COMMENTS
Auto Registration	Edilizia II	4639/4640	M-F
Auto Rent(Other)	Bldg L	2492	Daily
Auto Ship(Gov)	Edilizia II	4639/4640	M-F
Auto Ship(Civ)	Edilizia II	4639/4640	M-F
Bank	Bldg L	C-7244774	M-F
	Banca d'Italia	2278/4348	M-F
Barber Shop(s)	Bldg L	2949	Tu-Sa
Beauty Shop(s)	Exchange	2949	Tu-Sa
	Bldg L	2115	Tu-Sa
Child Care/Dev Ctr	Rainbow Junction		M-F
	Rainbow Center		M-F
Commissary(Main)	Beside Exchange	4730	Tu-Sa
Credit Union	Supply Bldg	4145/4481	M-F
Dry Clean(Exch)	Bldg L	2462	Tu-Sa
Education Center	Bldg E	2474	M-F
	High School	4350	M-F
Learning Center	Bldg E	2083	M-F
Exchange(Main)	Admin Bldg	4336	Daily
Finance(Mil)	PSD Bldg	4756	M-F
Food(Snack/Fast)	Admin Bldg	2910	M-F
Foodland	Admin Bldg	4336	Daily
Package Store	Near Exchange	4336	Tu-Sa
Postal Svcs(Mil)	Admin Bldg	4750	M-F
	Admin Bldg	4140	M-F
Postal Svcs(Civ)	AF South	2463	M-F
SATO-OS	PSD Bldg	4155/4253	M-F
Space-A Air Ops	Capodichino	724-5214/	M-Sa
	Arpt (Naples)	5283	
Flights to:	Brindisi/Casale Arpt IT; RAF Mildenhall UK;		

ITALY
Naples Naval Support Activity, continued

	Olbia/Costa Smeralda IT; Ramstein AB GE; Rhein-Main AB GE; Rota NAS SP; Sigonella Arpt IT; Souda Bay NAF GR.		
Tailor Shop	Bldg L	2228	Tu-Sa
Taxi(Comm)	Naples	C-364444	24 hours daily
Tel Booking Oper	Public Works	4236	24 hours daily
Tel Repair(Gov)	On Base	4235	M-F
Tel Repair(Civ)	Naples	4235	Daily
TML			
Billeting	71	4842/4567	Daily
BEQ	See Billeting		

HEALTH AND WELFARE

FACILITY/ACTIVITY	BLDG NO/LOC	PHONE	DAYS/COMMENTS
Ambulance	Naval Hospital	4110	24 hours daily
Chaplain	Chapel Bldg	4787	Duty hours
		4556	After hours
Chapel	Chapel Bldg	4787	Daily
Comm Drug/Alc Ctr	Chapel Bldg	4123	M-F
Dental Clinic	Naval Hospital	3300	24 hours daily
Medical Emergency	Naval Hospital	3333	24 hours daily
Mental Health	Edilizia II	4514	M-F
Navy Fam Svcs	Pelli Bldg	4808/4139	M-F
Navy Relief	NSA Chapel	4139	M-F
Poison Control	Near Exchange	4664	Daily
		C-313983	
Red Cross	Chapel Bldg	4789	Duty hours
		4546	After hours
Veterinary Svcs	Near Commissary	4755	M-F

REST AND RECREATION

FACILITY/ACTIVITY	BLDG NO/LOC	PHONE	DAYS/COMMENTS
Craftshops			
Automotive	On Base	4180	M-Sa
Enlisted Club	On Base	4673	M-Sa
Gymnasium	Bldg N	4821	Daily
Info Tour & Travel	On Base	4774	Tu-Sa
Library	On Base	4559	Daily
NCO Club	AF South	2240	Daily
O'Club	AF South	2801	Daily
Racket Courts	See Gymnasium.		
Special Services	On Base	4834	M-F
Video Rental	Beside barbershop	C-867-1579	Tu-Sa
Youth Center	On Base	4834	M-Sa

SAN VITO DEI NORMANNI AIR STATION (IT07R7
APO New York 09240-5000

TELEPHONE INFORMATION: Main installation numbers: Civ: 39-0831-42 1110. ATVN: 622-1110. Civ prefix: 0831-____. ATVN prefix: 622-XXXX. Civ to

San Vito dei Normanni Air Station, continued
ITALY

mil prefix: 0831-42-XXXX.

LOCATION: The air station is located on the heel of Italy's boot midway between the port cities of Brindisi and the town of San Vito dei Normanni. The air station services the area on the SS-379, four miles from the Adriatic shore. Follow the signs to "U.S. Base." HE: p-52, G/2. NMC: Brindisi, five miles south.

GENERAL INSTALLATION INFORMATION: The 7275th Air Base Group stationed at San Vito is the installation's host unit, with the 2113th Communications Squadron and the 6917th Electronic Security Group as tenant units.

GENERAL CITY/REGIONAL INFORMATION: "Sunny San Vito" is home to around 3500 American military service members and their families. The base is on the Adriatic Sea, around six miles from the port city of Brindisi.

ADMINISTRATIVE SUPPORT

FACILITY/ACTIVITY	BLDG NO/LOC	PHONE	DAYS/COMMENTS
Duty Officer	On Base	1110	24 hours daily
Fire(Mil)	On Base	1110	24 hours daily
Inspector Gen'l	312	3468	Daily
Legal Assist	On Base	3401	M-F
Locator(Mil)	On Base	3408	M-F
Police(Mil)			
Emergency	On Base	114	24 hours daily
Public Affairs	On Base	3344	M-F

LOGISTICAL SUPPORT

FACILITY/ACTIVITY	BLDG NO/LOC	PHONE	DAYS/COMMENTS
Auto Parts(Exch)	542	3632	M-Sa
Barber Shop	On Base	N/A	N/A
Bookstore	532	3632	Tu-Sa
Child Care/Dev Ctr	On Base	2596	M-Sa
Commissary(Main)	On Base	3524	M-Sa
Credit Union	On Base	N/A	M-F
Exchange(Main)	542	3632	M-Sa
Finance(Mil)	On Base	N/A	M-F
Food(Caf/Rest)	On Base	3640	Daily
Food(Snack/Fast)			
Pizza Parlor	On Base	3691	Daily
Foodland	542	3632	M-Sa
Laundry(Self-Svc)	On Base	3632	Daily
Package Store	On Base	3942	N/A
Postal Svcs(Mil)	On Base	N/A	M-Sa
SATO-OS	TMO Office	3612/3625	M-F
Schools(DOD Dep)			
Elementary	Brindisi	N/A	M-F
High School	Brindisi	N/A	M-F
Space-A Air Ops			
Pax Lounges(Gen'l)	733	3395	Daily
Flights to:	Athinai Arpt GR; Aviano AB IT; Capodichino Arpt IT; Reggio Calabria ITAF IT; Rhein-Main AB GE;		

ITALY
San Vito dei Normanni Air Station, continued

	Sigonella Arpt IT.		
Thrift Shop	472	N/A	M,W,F,1st Sa
TML			
Billeting	455	3906	Daily
BOQ	455	3906	Daily
TAQ	435	3906	Daily
TLF	435	3906	Daily
TLQ	603	3906	Daily
VOQ	601	3906	Daily
DV/VIP	602	3906	Daily

HEALTH AND WELFARE

FACILITY/ACTIVITY	BLDG NO/LOC	PHONE	DAYS/COMMENTS
AF Family Svcs	On Base	3362/3563	M-F
Ambulance	612	3511/117	24 hours daily
Central Appts	612	3566	Daily
CHAMPUS Office	612	3566	M-F
Chaplain	616	3404	Daily
Chapel	616	3301/3404	Daily
Comm Drug/Alc Ctr	434	3537	M-F
Dental Clinic	612	3529	M-F
Medical Emergency	612	3511/117	24 hours daily
Mental Health	612	3436	M-F
Poison Control	612	3511/117	24 hours daily
Red Cross	434	3411	M-F

REST AND RECREATION

FACILITY/ACTIVITY	BLDG NO/LOC	PHONE	DAYS/COMMENTS
Amer Forces Ntwk	606	3953	24 hours daily
Bowling Lanes	555	3551	Daily
Consolidated Club	525	3691	Daily
Craftshops			
Automotive	424	3577	Tu-Sa
Ceramics	558	3954	M-Sa
Electronics	558	2531	M-F
Multi-crafts	558	3954	M-Sa
Photography	558	3954	M-Sa
Enlisted Club	525	3691	M-Sa
Golf Course	400	3525	Daily
Gymnasium	556	3383	Daily
Info Tour & Travel	531	2296	M-F
Library	456	3574	M-F
NCO Club	525	3691	Daily
Picnic/Park Area	Three parks	3609	Seasonal
Racket Courts	556	3383	Daily
Recreation Center	531	3609/2717	Daily
Special Services	434	3360	M-F
Sport Field	Several	3483	Seasonal
Swimming Pool	440	3609	Seasonal
Tennis Courts	On Base	3609	Daily
Theater	620	3732	Daily
Youth Center	484	3524	M-Sa

U.S. Forces Travel & Transfer Guide Europe — 285

ITALY

SIGONELLA NAVAL AIR STATION (Sicily) (IT01R7)
FPO New York 09523-5000

TELEPHONE INFORMATION: Main installation numbers: Civ: 39-095-56-1110 (NAS I); 39-095-86-1110 (NAS II). ATVN: 624-1110. **Note: 56 and 86 are prefixes used to dial from civilian to military phones only.**

LOCATION: On the east coast of the island of Sicily. Accessible from A-19 or IT-417. HE: p-53, E/4. NMC: Catania, IT, 10 miles northeast.

GENERAL INSTALLATION INFORMATION: NAS Sigonella plays a crucial role in supporting American naval operations in the Mediterranean Sea. Although the NAS is a tenant command and, as such, occupies only a portion of the base, the NAS is landlord to over 40 U.S. commands and activities affecting the Mediterranean area.

GENERAL CITY/REGIONAL INFORMATION: NAS Sigonella is located in the rustic farmlands of Sicily, an island of six million people separated from the Italian mainland by the Straits of Messina. Although Sicily is located in the middle of the Med, it is an ideal jumping-off point for travelers bound for Europe or North Africa. The island itself offers visitors a great variety of sights and activities. Beyond the natural beauty of mountains, forests, citrus groves and sunny beaches, you can find many manifestations of a rich cultual heritage. Grecian temples, Roman amphitheaters, Byzantine chapels, Arab baths, Norman cathedrals and castles and Baroque churches are all evidence of Sicily's position at a cultural crossroads.

ADMINISTRATIVE SUPPORT

FACILITY/ACTIVITY	BLDG NO/LOC	PHONE	DAYS/COMMENTS
Duty Officer	NAS II	5253/5255	24 hours daily
Fire (Mil)	NAS I	4222	24 hours daily
	NAS II	5222	24 hours daily
Housing	NAS I	4311	M-F
Referral	NAS I	4313	M-F
Legal Assist	NAS II	5258	M-F
Police (Mil)	200/NAS I	4201	24 hours daily
Public Affairs	NAS II	5440/5330	M-F

LOGISTICAL SUPPORT

FACILITY/ACTIVITY	BLDG NO/LOC	PHONE	DAYS/COMMENTS
Auto Drivers Testing	NAS II	5430	M-F
Auto Registration	NAS I	N/A	M-F
Auto Rent (Other)	NAS I	4261	M-F
	436/NAS II	5468	M-F
Auto Repairs	NAS II	N/A	Tu-Sa
Auto Sales	NAS I	4324/4325	Tu-Sa
Bank	NAS I	4382	Tu-Sa
	436/NAS II	4308	Tu-Sa
Barber Shop(s)	NAS I	4346	Tu-Sa
	549/NAS II	5423/5424	M-Sa
Beauty Shop(s)	NAS I	4268	M-Sa
Bookstore	NAS I	N/A	Tu-Sa
	NAS II	N/A	Tu-Sa

ITALY
Sigonella Naval Air Station Station, continued

Bus	NAS I & II	None	Hourly
Child Care/Dev Ctr	NAS I	4226	M-Sa
	NAS I	4280	M-F
Commissary(Main)	NAS I	4303/4304	M-Sa
Credit Union	NAS II	5332	M-F
Dining Facility	NAS I	N/A	Daily
	NAS II	4321/2272	Daily
Dry Clean(Exch)	NAS I	4346	M-Sa
Eng'r/Publ Works	NAS I	4288	24 hours daily
Exchange(Main)	192/NAS I	4326/4330	Tu-Sa
	549/NAS II	5423/5424	M-Sa
Food(Caf/Rest)	436/NAS II	5469	24 hours daily
Food(Snack/Fast)			
Baskin Robbins	NAS I	4302	Tu-Sa
Laundry(Self-Svc)	NAS I	None	Daily
Package Store	NAS I	4497	Daily
Postal Svcs(Mil)	NAS I	4309	Tu-Sa
	NAS II	5242	Tu-Sa
SATO-OS	Air Term/NAS II	5248	Daily
Schools(DOD Dep)			
Elementary	NAS I	4281	M-F
Middle School	NAS I	4281	M-F
High School	NAS I	4281	M-F
Space-A Air Ops	436	5576	24 hours daily
Flights to:	\multicolumn{3}{l}{Athinai Arpt GR; Brindisi/Casale Arpt IT; Capodichino Arpt IT; Jomo Kenyatta Intl KE; Khartoum Arpt SU; King Abdullah AB JO; Norfolk NAS VA; Philadelphia IAP PA; Ramstein AB GE; Rhein-Main AB GE; Rota NAS SP; Shannon Arpt IR; Torrejon AB SP.}	
Taxi(Comm)	200/NAS I	4201/4202	24 hours daily
TML			
Billeting	NAS II	5575	24 hours daily
BEQ/BOQ	NAS II	2300/2301	24 hours daily
DV/VIP	545	5251/5252	24 hours daily

HEALTH AND WELFARE

FACILITY/ACTIVITY	BLDG NO/LOC	PHONE	DAYS/COMMENTS
Ambulance	NAS I	4333	24 hours daily
	NAS II	5333	24 hours daily
Central Appts	NAS II	5455	M-F
Chaplain	NAS I	4295/4296	M-F
		5225	After hours
	NAS II	5459/5460	24 hours daily
Chapel	NAS I	4295	24 hours daily
	NAS II	5459	24 hours daily
Comm Drug/Alc Ctr	NAS II	5439	M-F
Dental Clinic	NAS I	4205	M-F
	NAS II	5447	M-F
Navy Fam Svcs	NAS I	4291/4490	M-F
Navy Relief	NAS I	4382/4490	M,W,F
Red Cross	NAS II	5921	M-F

ITALY

Sigonella Naval Air Station, continued

REST AND RECREATION

FACILITY/ACTIVITY	BLDG NO/LOC	PHONE	DAYS/COMMENTS
Bowling Lanes	NAS I	4302	M-Sa
Craftshops			
Automotive	NAS II	5244	M-Sa
Multi-crafts	NAS I	4323	M-Sa
Wood	NAS II	5244	M-Sa
Enlisted Club	NAS I	4263	N/A
Equip/Gear Locker	NAS I	4348/5248	M-Sa
Gymnasium	NAS I	4348	Daily
	NAS II	5248	Daily
Info Tour & Travel	NAS I	4229/4396	M-F
Library	NAS I	4332	Daily
NCO Club	NAS II	5245	M-Sa
O'Club	NAS I	4335	M-F
	NAS II	5853	Daily
Recreation Center	NAS I	4229/4339	Daily
Swimming Pool	NAS I	4334	Seasonal
	NAS II	5335	Seasonal
Theater	NAS I	4297	Daily
Youth Center	NAS I	4301	M-Sa

VICENZA COMMUNITY (IT14R7)
APO New York 09168-5125

TELEPHONE INFORMATION: Main installation numbers: Civ: 39-444-51-XXXX. ATVN: 634-1110.

LOCATION: Take the Vicenza east exit from the No. 4 Autostrada, which runs from Trieste to Milano. Follow signs to Caserma Carlo Ederle or SETAF Hq. HE: p-91, H/6. NMC: Vicenza, in the city.

GENERAL INSTALLATION INFORMATION: The Southern European Task Force (SETAF) Hq is located at Vicenza, where full support facilities are available, including a hospital and dependent schools.

GENERAL CITY/REGIONAL INFORMATION: Vicenza is located in Northern Italy, 35 miles west of Venice in the heart of the Po Valley. This is an ancient city, first occupied by the Romans in 49 B.C. Today Vicenza is an industrial area with a population of 160,000.

ADMINISTRATIVE SUPPORT

FACILITY/ACTIVITY	BLDG NO/LOC	PHONE	DAYS/COMMENTS
Duty Officer	109	7711	24 hours daily
		C-517711	From off post
Fire(Mil)	113	7793	24 hours daily
		C-562222	From off post
Fire(Civ)	Off Post	C-507707	24 hours daily

ITALY
Vicenza Community, continued

Housing

Family	Off Post	7620	M-F
Unaccompanied	Off Post	7620	M-F
Referral	Off Post	7620	M-F
Inspector Gen'l	33	7595	M-F
Legal Assist	2	7041	M-F
Police(Mil)	4	7626/7233	24 hours daily
		C-501800	From off post
Emergency	Off Post	113	
Police(Civ)	Off Post	C-507717	24 hours daily
Public Affairs	34	7011/7866	M-F
Tax Relief	2	7041	M-F

LOGISTICAL SUPPORT

FACILITY/ACTIVITY	BLDG NO/LOC	PHONE	DAYS/COMMENTS
Audio/Photo Ctr	302	C-500354	M-Sa
Auto Drivers Testing	103	7601	M-F
Auto Registration	207	7363	M-Th
Auto Repairs	201	7368	M-Sa
Auto Sales	302A	C-500386	M-F
Auto Wash	215	7014	Daily
Bank	243	7221	M-F
Barber Shop(s)	302	7356	M-F
		C-500391	
Beauty Shop(s)	17	C-500536	Tu-Sa
Bookstore	302	7545	M-Sa
Child Care/Dev Ctr	308	7502/7958	Su-F
Clothing Sales	103	7504	M-F
Commissary(Main)	302	7494/7649	Tu-Sa
Credit Union	28A	7470	M-F
Dining Facility	10	7442	Daily
Dry Clean(Gov)	103	7653	M-F
Education Center	241	7698	M-F
Learning Center	305	7615	Daily
Eng'r/Publ Works	23	7491/7628	M-F
Exchange(Main)	302	7676	Daily
		C-515127	
Exchange(Annex)	243	7903	Tu-Su
Exchange(Concess)	302	C-500923	Tu-Sa
	243	7273	Tu-Su
Finance(Mil)	28	7612	M-Sa
Food(Caf/Rest)	302	C-500447	Daily
Food(Snack/Fast)			
Baskin Robbins	302	None	Daily 1130-1900
Burger Bar	112	None	Daily
Burger King	None	7529	Daily
Pizza Parlor	302	7023	M-Sa
Foodland	302	7561	M-Sa
Laundry(Self-Svc)	302	None	Daily
Motor Pool	28A	7792	M-F
Package Store	243	7317	Tu-Sa
Pick-up Point	103	C-500528	Tu-Sa
Postal Svcs(Mil)	227	7872	M-Sa
Schools(DOD Dep)	307	7391	M-F
Elementary	309	7710	M-F

ITALY

Vicenza Community, continued

High School	309	7656	M-F
Space-A Air Ops	See Aviano Air Base listing.		
Tailor Shop	308	7515	M-Sa
Tel Booking Oper	1	90	24 hours daily
Tel Repair(Gov)	1	96	M-F
Thrift Shop	110	7460	Tu,Th
TML			
Billeting	136	7301	Daily
		C-5190	
		7711	After hours
Guest House/DVQ	136	See bltg	Daily
Protocol Office	N/A	1110/7712	M-F
Watch Repair	302A	7676	Tu-Sa

HEALTH AND WELFARE

FACILITY/ACTIVITY	BLDG NO/LOC	PHONE	DAYS/COMMENTS
Ambulance	On Post	97	24 hours daily
	Off Post	113	24 hours daily
Army Comm Svcs	108	7500/7420	M-F
Army Emerg Relief	28	7473	M-F
CHAMPUS Office	113	7294	M-F
		C-517777	
Chaplain	29	7719/7519	Daily
Comm Drug/Alc Ctr	241	7554/7806	M-F
Dental Clinic	2	7059	M-F
Medical Emergency	113	7097	24 hours daily
		C-501700	Off post
Red Cross	28	7027	M-F
Veterinary Svcs	14	7786	M-F

REST AND RECREATION

FACILITY/ACTIVITY	BLDG NO/LOC	PHONE	DAYS/COMMENTS
Amer Forces Ntwk	10	7835	24 hours daily
Bowling Lanes	112	7013	Daily
Craftshops			
Automotive	361	7014	Tu-Su
Multi-crafts	306	7074	Tu-Su
Enlisted Club	300	7869/7685	Daily
Gymnasium	112	7616	M-F
Info Tour & Travel	108	7453/7617	M-Sa
Library	305	7615	Tu-Su
NCO Club	300	7869/7685	Daily
O'Club	311	7046/7886	Daily
Rod and Gun Club	Lake Marola	C-581058	Daily
Service Club	108	7076	Daily
Special Services	109	7073	M-F
Theater	11	7755	M-F
Track	301	7872	Daily
Video Rental	103	C-500575	M-Sa
Youth Center	308	7378	M-F

THE NETHERLANDS
Kingdom of the Netherlands
Amsterdam

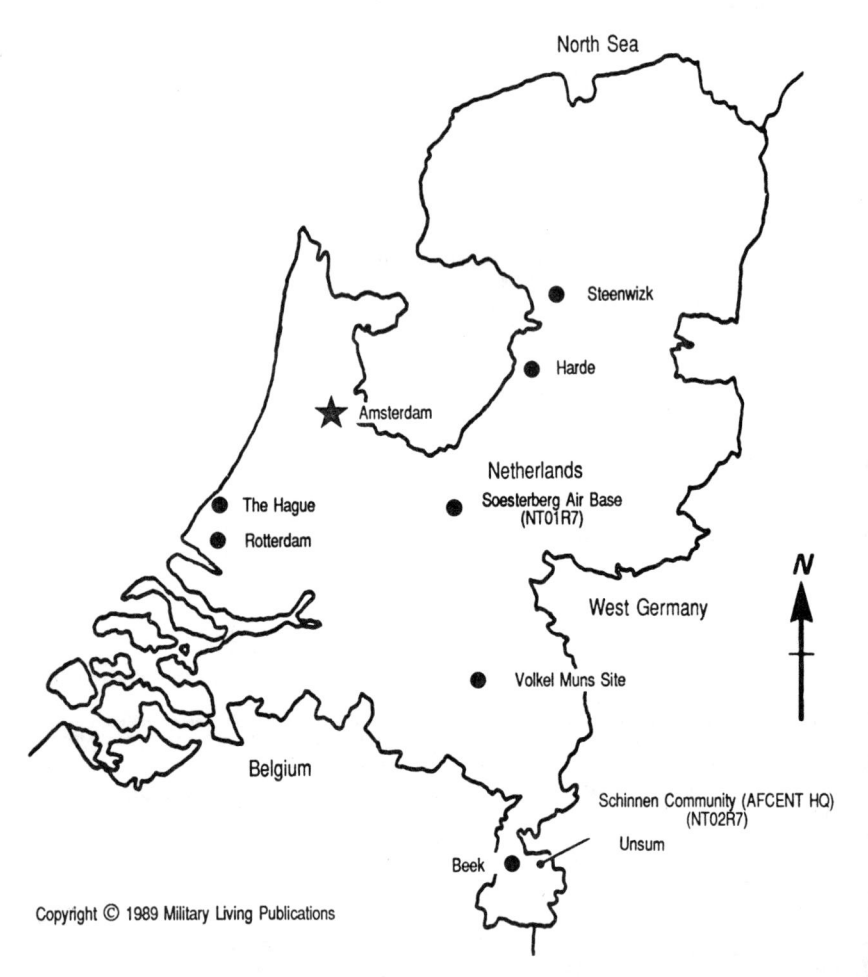

Map labels: North Sea, Steenwizk, Harde, Amsterdam, Netherlands, The Hague, Rotterdam, Soesterberg Air Base (NT01R7), West Germany, Volkel Muns Site, Belgium, Schinnen Community (AFCENT HQ) (NT02R7), Unsum, Beek

Copyright © 1989 Military Living Publications

    Bordered by the North Sea, Belgium and the Federal Republic of West Germany, The Netherlands is low and flat—one-third of it is below sea level, the result of an extensive sea reclamation effort. The Dutch population of 14.3 million is primarily of Germanic descent. The current government is a parliamentary democracy under a constitutional monarchy. Suffrage is universal over age 18. The Dutch empire once included Indonesia and Suriname, both of which are now independent. The official language is Dutch and the currency is the ***Dutch guilder***. The economy, based on private enterprise, is strongly regulated by the government. Exports and imports include mineral fuels, chemical products, foods, machinery and transportation equipment. The work force is divided between industrial, commercial, service-oriented, government and agricultural occupations. Rail transportation is

NETHERLANDS

frequent—there are about two dozen international trains. The Netherlands has excellent local bus and streetcar networks, two daily ferry crossings to the U.K. and an extensive bicycle path system. Amsterdam is six hours ahead of U.S. EST. Clothing needs are similar to those in Washington, D.C., but cooler in summer, warmer and rainier in winter. Premier attractions are the fishing villages of Marken and Volendam, cheese and flower farms, windmills, decorative tiles and Delft porcelain. Amsterdam is best seen by foot; canal trips also provide access to the city's more than 125 museums, galleries, concert halls and theaters. The Holland Leisure Card, available by application from the Netherlands Board of Tourism, provides discounts on hotel, airline, railroad, bus and subway travel-and-admission fees. The bulb blooming season begins the end of March (visit Keukenhof where 6-7 million bulbs have been planted), followed by other flowers throughout summer. After World War II, the Netherlands abandoned its traditional neutral political stance and actively supported the NATO alliance and participated in the United Nations. We enjoy excellent relations with The Netherlands, based on economic, mutual defense pact and cultural ties.

ENTRY REQUIREMENTS: Passport—yes. Visa—not required for business/pleasure up to 90 days. Check with the Embassy of The Netherlands, Washington, D.C., Tel: 202-244-5300, for other requirements. Immunizations—EUR.

SCHINNEN COMMUNITY (AFCENT HQ) (NT02R7)
(USMC The Netherlands)
APO New York 09011-5000

TELEPHONE INFORMATION: Main installation numbers: Civ: 31-04493-7-210/310 (Schinnen Kaserne); 31-045-26-113 (Hendrik Kaserne in Brunssum); 31-043-847-113 (Tapijn Kaserne in Maastrich). ATVN: 221-8656 (all locations). ETS: 360-7113 (Schinnen Kaserne); 360-3113 (Hendrik Kaserne); 360-4113 (Tapijn Kaserne). Civ prefix: 04493-_____ (Schinnen Kaserne); 045-_____ (Hendrik Kaserne); 043-_____ (Maastrich). ETS prefix: 360-7XXX (Schinnen Kaserne); 360-3XXX (Hendrik Kaserne); 360-4XXX (Tapijn Kaserne). Civ to mil prefix: 04493-7-XXX (Schinnen Kaserne); 045-26-XXX (Hendrik Kaserne); 043-847-XXX (Tapijn Kaserne).

LOCATION: Take Autobahn A-2, A-76, or E-9. Or take NE-39 and exit at Schinnen, cross the railroad tracks then turn left onto the base. HE: p-35, G/2, NMC: Maastricht, NT, 15 miles southwest.

GENERAL INSTALLATION INFORMATION: Units at Schinnen provide support to Headquarters, AFCENT (Hendrik Kaserne), Brunssum, Netherlands, three miles east. Some facilities are located at Tapijn Kaserne in Maastrich. **The following abbreviations are used in this listing only: HD (Hendrik Kaserne); SK (Schinnen Kaserne); TK (Tapijn Kaserne).**

GENERAL CITY/REGIONAL INFORMATION: Schinnen is located in the province of South Limburg, nestled between Germany and Belgium, both of which are only minutes away. The local climate is variable, but generally cool and wet. There are many historical sites to see in the vicinity.

ADMINISTRATIVE SUPPORT

FACILITY/ACTIVITY	BLDG NO/LOC	PHONE	DAYS/COMMENTS
Duty Officer	SK	425	24 hours daily

NETHERLANDS
Schinnen Community, continued

Housing
Family	SK	241	M-F
Referral	SK	416/345	M-F
Legal Assist	2/SK	319	M-F
Locator(Mil)	2/SK	299	M-F
Police(Mil)	2/SK	555/228	24 hours daily
Emergency	2/SK	114	24 hours daily
Public Affairs	T-18/SK	331	M-F

LOGISTICAL SUPPORT

FACILITY/ACTIVITY	BLDG NO/LOC	PHONE	DAYS/COMMENTS
Auto Drivers Testing	SK	433	M-F
Auto Registration	4/HK	N/A	M-F
Auto Repairs	Brunnsum	C-250787	N/A
Bank	HQ Bldg/HK	412	Tu-Th,Sa
Barber Shop(s)	23/HK	N/A	M-Sa
	G/TK	N/A	M-F
Beauty Shop(s)	SNCO Club/TK	N/A	N/A
Bookstore	5-13/SK	360-1524	M-Sa
	X/TK	360-2135	M-Sa
Child Care/Dev Ctr	HK	566	M-Sa
Clothing Sales	SK	446	N/A
Commissary(Main)	T-25/SK	441/442/443	Tu-Su
Credit Union	T/TK	N/A	M-F
Dining Facility	13/HK	N/A	Daily
Education Center	HK	C-270027	M-F
Learning Center	HK	C-270027	M-F
Exchange(Main)	10/SK	233	Daily
Exchange(Annex)	23/HK	N/A	Tu-Sa
Food(Caf/Rest)	SK	336	Daily
Foodland	A/TK	N/A	M-F
Laundry(Exch)	23/HK	N/A	Daily
Motor Pool	SK	200/317	N/A
Package Store	SK	318	N/A
Postal Svcs(Mil)	HK	111	M-F
Postal Svcs(Civ)	SK	432	M-F
Schools(DOD Dep)			
Elementary	HK	C-278250	M-F
High School	HK	C-298260	M-F
Tel Repair(Gov)	SK	241	M-F
TML			
Billeting	6/SK	C-2230	Daily
BEQ	42/HK	N/A	Daily
BOQ	58/HK	C-253302	Daily
DV/VIP	58/HK	C-253302	Daily

HEALTH AND WELFARE

FACILITY/ACTIVITY	BLDG NO/LOC	PHONE	DAYS/COMMENTS
Ambulance	All locations	116	24 hours daily
Army Comm Svcs	SK	231	M-F
Army Emerg Relief	SK	454	M-F
CHAMPUS Office	SK	219	M-F
Chaplain	11/HK	360-2307	Daily

NETHERLANDS

Schinnen Community, continued

Chapel	11/HK	360-2307	Daily
Dental Clinic	SK	219	M-F
Medical Emergency	HK	451	24 hours daily
Veterinary Svcs	HK	458	N/A

REST AND RECREATION

FACILITY/ACTIVITY	BLDG NO/LOC	PHONE	DAYS/COMMENTS
Amer Forces Ntwk	SK	218	N/A
Craftshops			
Automotive	54/SK	454	N/A
Photography	54/SK	454	N/A
Enlisted Club	13/HK	228	N/A
Gymnasium	HK	571	Daily
	A/TK	452	Daily
Info Tour & Travel	13/SK	413	N/A
Library	A/TK	269	M,W,F
NCO Club	B/TK	197	N/A
O'Club	58/HK	C-253302	N/A
	A Dutch Officers' Club, the "d'Alsace," is located one miles northwest of HK.		
Outdoor Rec Ctr	SK	414	N/A
Racket Courts	SK	418	N/A
Special Services	SK	236	N/A
Sport Field	HK	490	N/A
Theater	HK	360-2110	Call for schedule.
Youth Center	HK	508	N/A

SOESTERBERG AIR BASE (NT01R7)
APO New York 09292-5000

TELEPHONE INFORMATION: Main installation numbers: Civ: 31-03463-5-8199. ATVN: 363-8199. Civ Prefix: 03463-____. ATVN prefix: 363-XXXX. Civ to mil prefix: 03463-5-XXXX.

LOCATION: On Utrechtseweg between Utrecht and Amersfoort in Huis ter Heide. Take the turn to Den Dolder. HE: p-34, D-E/4. NMC: Utrecht, NT, eight miles southwest.

GENERAL INSTALLATION INFORMATION: The 32nd Tactical Fighter Squadron prepares for and conducts all-weather interception, identification and air-superiority operations in support of NATO. The 32nd is the only U.S. AF flying unit assigned to NATO's 2nd Allied Tactical Air Force. Note: the following abbreviations are used in this listing only: AB (Soesterberg Air Base); DS (Dutch Side); VZ (Camp Van Zeist); WS (W. S. Camp).

GENERAL CITY/REGIONAL INFORMATION: Soesterberg AB is located about 60 kilometers southeast of Amsterdam, halfway between Utrecht and Amersfoort. Amsterdam, Rotterdam, the Hague, the coast and lakes are all within a 40-minute drive. The base is surrounded by a heavily wooded area. Bicycle paths, horse trails, foot paths, cobblestone streets and modern highways wind through the countryside. Lovely flower gardens, windmills, castles and museums are but a few of the local sites.

NETHERLANDS
Soesterberg Air Base, continued

ADMINISTRATIVE SUPPORT

FACILITY/ACTIVITY	BLDG NO/LOC	PHONE	DAYS/COMMENTS
Advocate	101/AB	8941	M-F
Customs/Duty	35/DS	2483	M-F
Duty Officer	101/AB	8132	M-F
Fire(Mil)	84/AB	2499	24 hours daily
Fire(Civ)	84/AB	2499	24 hours daily
Housing	8/AB	8923	M-F
Unaccompanied	31/WS	8499	M-F
Referral	8/WB	8152	M-F
Info(Insta)	AB	113	24 hours daily
Inspector Gen'l	101/AB	8132	M-F
Legal Assist	101/AB	8941	M-F
Locator(Mil)	34/AB	8580	M-F
Locator(Civ)	6/AB	8599	M-F
Personnel Spt	6/AB	8249	M-F
Police(Mil)	7/AB	3012	24 hours daily
Police(Civ)	2/DS	2073	24 hours daily
Public Affairs	35/AB	8121	M-F
	35/AB	3155	After hours
Tax Relief	101/AB	8533	M-F

LOGISTICAL SUPPORT

FACILITY/ACTIVITY	BLDG NO/LOC	PHONE	DAYS/COMMENTS
Auto Drivers Testing	4/WS	8246	M-F
Auto Parts(Exch)	49/AB	8999	Daily
Auto Registration	7/AB	8996	M-F
Auto Repairs	49/AB	8999	Daily
Auto Ship(Gov)	10/AB	8113	M-F
Auto Ship(Civ)	10/AB	8113	M-F
Auto Wash	49/AB	8999	Daily
Bank	10/AB	8598	M-F
Barber Shop(s)	9/AB	8603	M-Sa
Beauty Shop(s)	9/AB	8508	M-Sa
Bookstore	87/AB	8269	Daily
Bus	4/WS	8248	M-F
Child Care/Dev Ctr	88/AB	8234	Su-F
Clothing Sales	10/AB	8175	M-F
Commissary(Main)	VZ	8549	Tu-Sa
Credit Union	10/AB	C-8504	M-F
Education Center	44/AB	8983	M-F
	4/WS	8983	M-F
Elec Repair(Civ)	15/WS	8181	F-W
Exchange(Main)	15/WS	8181	F-W
Exchange(Annex)	9/AB	8472	F-W
Finance(Mil)	5/AB	8173	M-F
Food(Caf/Rest)	4/AB	8590	Daily
Food(Snack/Fast)	6/WS	8955	Daily
Foodland	36/AB	8912	Daily
Laundry(Self-Svc)	AB	None	24 hours daily
Motor Pool	4/WS	8244	M-F
Package Store	86/AB	8907	Tu-Sa

NETHERLANDS

Soesterberg Air Base, continued

Photo Laboratory	34/AB	8576	M-F
Postal Svcs(Mil)	12/AB	8197	24 hours daily
Postal Svcs(Civ)	12/AB	8197	24 hours daily
SATO-OS	10,Rm 16/AB	C-2664	M-F
Schools(DOD Dep)			
Elementary	VZ	3527	M-F
High School	AB	2289	M-F
Tailor Shop	15/WS	8181	Daily
Taxi(Comm)	Zeist	03404-2511	24 hours daily
Tel Booking Oper	AB	112	24 hours daily
Tel Repair(Gov)	11/AB	8221	M-F
Thrift Shop	11/AB	None	W,F
TML			
Billeting	31/WS	8915	24 hours daily
Protocol Office	101/AB	8132	M-F
VAQ/VOQ	31/WS	8915	24 hours daily
Travel Agents	10/AB	C-2664	M-F

HEALTH AND WELFARE

FACILITY/ACTIVITY	BLDG NO/LOC	PHONE	DAYS/COMMENTS
Ambulance	3/WS	8679	M-F
	3/WS	2200	24 hours daily
Central Appts	3/AB	8540	M-F
CHAMPUS Office	3/AB	8523	M-F
Chaplain	63/AB	3155	After hours
Chapel	63/AB	8503	M-F
Comm Drug/Alc Ctr	101/AB	8456	M-F
Dental Clinic	2/AB	8990	M-F
Medical Emergency	3/AB	8540/41	M-F
Mental Health	61/AB	8956	M-F
Poison Control	3/AB	8540	M-F
Red Cross	6/AB	8249	M-F
Veterinary Svcs	36/AB	8386	Tu,Th

REST AND RECREATION

FACILITY/ACTIVITY	BLDG NO/LOC	PHONE	DAYS/COMMENTS
Amer Forces Ntwk	35/AB	8220	M-F
Bowling Lanes	89/AB	8497	Daily
Consolidated Club	4/AB	8590	Daily
Craftshops			
Automotive	49/AB	8999	By appointment
Electronics	77/AB	8238	Tu-Sa
Gymnasium	46/WS	8270	Daily
Library	12/AB	8949	Daily
O'Club	27/AB	8592	W,F
Special Services	16/WS	8177	M-F
Sport Field	AB	8870	Need reservations.
Tennis Courts	AB	8870	Need reservations.
Theater	WS	8271	Call for schedule.
Track	AB	8270	Need reservations.
Video Rental	9/AB	8181	Tu-Sa
Youth Center	89/AB	8397	M-Sa

NORWAY
Kingdom of Norway
Oslo

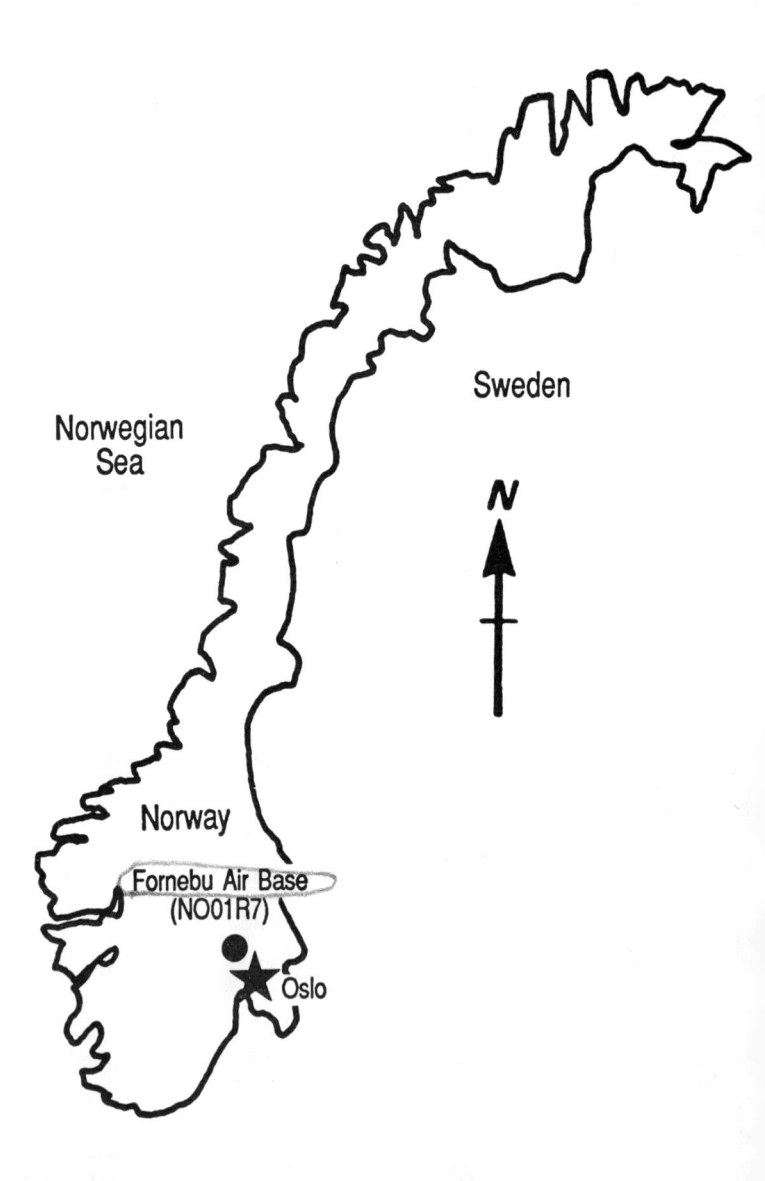

- Fornebu Air Base (NO01R7)
- Oslo

Norwegian Sea

Sweden

Norway

Copyright © 1989 Military Living Publications

NORWAY

Norway is located on the Scandanavian Peninsula in northwest Europe, has 2,125 miles of coastline on the North and Norwegian Seas and is bordered by Sweden on the East. It is approximately the size of New Mexico. There are about 4.1 million Norwegians, most of whom are Germanic with some Laplanders. Languages are Norwegian and Lappish. The government is a hereditary constitutional monarchy (which performs largely ceremonial functions), while the Council of Ministers exercises the most important executive powers. There is universal suffrage over age 18. About 65 percent of the population lives along the coast. Norway is one of the richest developed countries and a major oil and gas producer and exporter. Machinery, transportation equipment, foodstuffs, iron and steel, textiles and clothing are imported. Almost half of the work force is employed in the areas of industry and banking and commerce. The currency is the *Norwegian kroner*. Transportation services include daily flights to Europe and the U.S., passenger ships from Scandanavia, Europe and England and ferries from England, Denmark and Germany. Public transportation and domestic and international communications are excellent. Norway is six hours ahead of U.S. EST. Thanks to the Gulf Stream, Norway has a mild climate along the coast; the interior is much colder. Main attractions in Oslo are the Norwegian Folk Museum, comprised of 170 buildings reflecting national heritage, and the Viking Ship Museum which houses 1000-year-old longships in excellent condition. Norway is noted for "linie akevitt", a tasty cousin to vodka. After being overrun in World War II, Norway joined NATO and imposed defense restrictions upon itself in order not to threaten the Warsaw Pact.
ENTRY REQUIREMENTS: Passport—yes. Visa—not required for stay up to three months (begins when entering Scandanavian area of Finland, Denmark, Sweden and Iceland). Check with the Embassy of Norway, Washington, D.C., Tel: 202-333-6000, for further requirements. Immunizations—EUR.

OSLO (FORNEBU/GARDERMOEN) COMMUNITY (NO01R7)
APO New York 09085-5270

TELEPHONE INFORMATION: Main installation numbers: Civ: 47-2-24-30-30 + extension. ATVN: None.

LOCATION: From Oslo take 168 north for seven miles. HQ address is Østerndalen 13, Østeras. HE: p-25, D-E/3. NMC: Oslo, seven miles south.

GENERAL INSTALLATION INFORMATION: The 7240th ABS/LGTTR operates the MAC terminal at Østerndalen 13, Østeras. Fornebu is one mile north of Oslo in the Bærum Community. Gardermoen is adjacent to Jessheim. Note: only active duty personnel are allowed commissary and exchange privileges.

GENERAL CITY/REGIONAL INFORMATION: Located in the beautiful capital city of Oslo. Holmenkollen park, ski jumps and skiing opportunities are within easy driving distance.

ADMINISTRATIVE SUPPORT

FACILITY/ACTIVITY	BLDG NO/LOC	PHONE	DAYS/COMMENTS
Fire(Civ)	Local	Ext. 001	24 hours daily
Housing	None on base. On local economy.		
Police(Civ)	Local	Ext. 002/3	24 hours daily

NORWAY
Oslo Community, continued

LOGISTICAL SUPPORT

FACILITY/ACTIVITY	BLDG NO/LOC	PHONE	DAYS/COMMENTS
Commissary(Annex)	N/A	00422-170-814	M-Sa
Exchange(Main)	7240 ABS	00472-240-815	M-F
Food(Snack/Fast)	7240 ABS	N/A	Daily
Schools(DOD Dep)	N/A	Ext. 152	M-F
Space-A Air Ops	7240 ABS	Ext. 193/4	Daily
Flights to:	Ramstein AB GE.		

HEALTH AND WELFARE

FACILITY/ACTIVITY	BLDG NO/LOC	PHONE	DAYS/COMMENTS
Ambulance	Local	Ext. 002	24 hours daily
Chaplain	N/A	Ext. 153	M-F
Medical Emergency	N/A	Ext. 168	M-F

PORTUGAL
Republic of Portugal
Lisbon

Copyright © 1989 Military Living Publications

PORTUGAL

Portugal consists of the mainland, located on the west side of the Iberian Peninsula, and the Azores and Madeira Islands. The total area is the size of Indiana. The mainland is bordered by Spain on the east and the North Atlantic Ocean on the west, where the islands are located. Terceira, the third largest of the nine-island Açores archipelago and the location of Lajes Field, is located 900 miles west of Lisbon, Portugal, and is an important refueling stop for the U.S. The Portuguese population of 9.75 million is descended from a mixed stock of Germanic, Celtic, Roman, Arabic and African peoples who speak Portuguese. The government made a transition from an authoritarian rule to a parliamentary constitutional democracy in 1976. Suffrage is universal over age 18. The economy has recently recovered from a severe trade deficit and is largely nationalized. Exports include clothing, pulp, leather goods, wines and fish products. Non-electrical machinery and appliances, crude oil and petroleum products, sugar, wheat and chemicals are imported. Close to one-half of the Portuguese are employed by the government or work in commercial and service-oriented industries. The currency is the *escudo*. Daily flights to the U.S. and other worldwide locations, an extensive domestic railway network with connections to Spain and a good public transportation system in Lisbon are available. Good telephone and telegraph service to western Europe and most other points worldwide is available. Lisbon and Terceira are five hours ahead of U.S. EST. The climate is sunny and moderate from May through September; cool-weather clothing and rain gear is advised otherwise. Caldeirada, fish stew, is a specialty. "Pousadas," a network of state-owned and -operated hotels, consists of restored castles, palaces, monasteries, convents and other historic buildings. The national tourist office has reservation-and-rate information. Portugal and the U.S. share excellent diplomatic relations dating to 1791 and defense facility cooperation.
ENTRY REQUIREMENTS: Passport—yes. Visa—not required for up to 60 days, must be used within 120 days. Check with the Embassy of Portugal, Washington, D.C. 20008, Tel: 202-332-3007, for further requirements. Immunizations—EUR.

LAJES FIELD (AÇORES) (PO01R7)
APO New York 09406-5000

TELEPHONE INFORMATION: Main installation numbers: Civ: 351-95-52101 + extension. ATVN: 723-1410 (CONUS direct); 858-1110 (via Andrews AFB, MD); 236-1110 (via RAF Croughton, UK).

LOCATION: Lajes Field is located on Terceira Island, Açores, Portugal. The island is 20 miles long and 12 miles wide. Lajes Field is two miles west of Praia de Vitoria off Mason Highway. NMC: Lisbon, 850 miles east.

GENERAL INSTALLATION INFORMATION: Commander, U.S. Forces Açores and the 1605th Air Base Wing, a MAC unit, are located at Lajes Field, along with 1936th Communications Squadron support units. A Naval Air Facility, which operates in support of P-3 Orion aircraft; a Naval Security Group Activity; and a U.S. Army Transportation Terminal (Port) Unit are also based at Lajes. Personnel at Lajes provide area management and support for air and sea operations in the Atlantic.

GENERAL CITY/REGIONAL INFORMATION: The Açores are nine inhabited islands located 2,200 miles east of Boston and 850 miles west of Lisbon. Terceira is the third largest island in the chain. The island has old-

PORTUGAL
Lajes Field, continued

world charm because of its quaint villages, unspoiled countryside and beaches. Bull fights (in which the bull cannot be killed by law) are a popular local entertainment.

ADMINISTRATIVE SUPPORT

FACILITY/ACTIVITY	BLDG NO/LOC	PHONE	DAYS/COMMENTS
Duty Officer	T-100	113	24 hours daily
Fire(Mil)	T-100	117/5217	24 hours daily
Fire(Civ)	T-100	C-53000	24 hours daily
Housing			
Family	T-416	7107	M-F
Referral	T-416	7107	M-F
Info(Insta)	T-100	113	24 hours daily
Legal Assist	T-100	3154	M-F
Locator(Mil)	N/A	6201	Duty hours
		C-23222	After hours
Personnel Spt	T-500	6106	M-F
Police(Mil)	T-815	C-23222	24 hours daily

LOGISTICAL SUPPORT

FACILITY/ACTIVITY	BLDG NO/LOC	PHONE	DAYS/COMMENTS
Auto Repairs	T-584	C-23219	M-Sa
Barber Shop(s)	T-112	C-21211	M-Sa
Beauty Shop(s)	T-307	C-22166	M-Sa
Child Care/Dev Ctr	T-241	C-23188/23192	Daily
Commissary(Main)	T-204	6174	Tu-Sa
Dining Facility	T-415	4156	Daily
Dry Clean(Gov)	T-331	7230	M-Sa
Education Center	T-241	3155/5290	M-F
Eng'r/Publ Works	T-596	6273	M-F
Exchange(Main)	T-323	C-21290	M-Sa
Exchange(Annex)	T-627	C-23206	Tu-Su
Exchange(Concess)	T-330	C-23173	M-Sa
Finance(Mil)	T-100	3173	M-F
Food(Snack/Fast)	T-167	6169	M-Sa
	T-629	C-21114	M-Sa
	T-319	C-22211	Daily
	T-810	C-21219	M-Sa
	T-1203	C-23270	M-F
Foodland	T-330	C-23190	Daily
Motor Pool	Official taxi	C-23151	Daily
Package Store	T-627	C-21213	Daily
Postal Svcs(Mil)	T-324	3138	M-Sa
Schools(DOD Dep)			
Elementary	T-233	3291/6216	M-F (K-3)
	T-416	4151	M-F (4-6)
High School	T-234	4151	M-F
Svc Stn(Insta)	T-320	C-23293	M-Sa
Space-A Air Ops	T-612	C-23227/8	Daily
Pax Lounges(Gen'l)	T-612	C-23227/8	Daily
Protocol Svc	Base Ops	C-6201	24 hours daily
Flights to:	Andrews AFB MD; Athinai Arpt GR; Charleston

PORTUGAL

Lajes Field, continued

	AFB SC; Cigli TAB TU; Esenboga Arpt TU; Incirlik AB TU; Kinshasa N'Djili Arpt ZA; McGuire AFB NJ; Monrovia Roberts IAP LI; Rhein-Main AB GE; Sigonella Arpt IT; Torrejon AB SP.		
Tel Repair(Gov)	T-800	6251	M-F
Thrift Shop	T-263	7167	M,W,F
TML			
Billeting	T-166	5178/6176	24 hours daily
	Reservations	7283	Duty hours
	Reservations	4237	After hours

HEALTH AND WELFARE

FACILITY/ACTIVITY	BLDG NO/LOC	PHONE	DAYS/COMMENTS
AF Family Svcs	T-166	3117	M-F
Ambulance	T-241	C-23233	24 hours daily
Central Appts	T-241	4233	24 hours daily
		C-23261	
Chapel	T-305	3211/4211	M-F
Comm Drug/Alc Ctr	T-241	6111	M-F
Dental Clinic	T-238	C-23139	M-F
Medical Emergency	T-241	C-23233	24 hours daily
Red Cross	T-615	7116/3263	M-F
		4106	Sa,Su
Veterinary Svcs	T-264	3220	M-F

REST AND RECREATION

FACILITY/ACTIVITY	BLDG NO/LOC	PHONE	DAYS/COMMENTS
Bowling Lanes	T-167	6169	Daily
Consolidated Club	T-112	7138	Daily
Craftshops			
Automotive	T-424	7162	Tu-Su
Ceramics	T-308	7287	W-M
Multi-crafts	T-308	5220	Tu-Su
Photography	T-307	5190	Tu-Su
Wood	T-308	7233	W-M
Golf Course	Off base		
Gymnasium	T-333	7288	Daily
MARS	T-246	5252	Daily
NCO Club	T-112	C-23203	Daily
O'Club	T-121	7217	Daily
		C-23100	
Recreation Center	T-307	4235	Daily
Rod and Gun Club	T-153	C-23184	Tu-Sa
Skating Rink	T-629	C-62021/	Th-Su
		23138	
Special Services	T-629	4140	M-Sa
Swimming Pool	T-304	3163	Daily
Theater	T-300	C-23187	Daily
Youth Center	T-240	6263	Daily

SAUDI ARABIA
Kingdom of Saudi Arabia
Riyadh

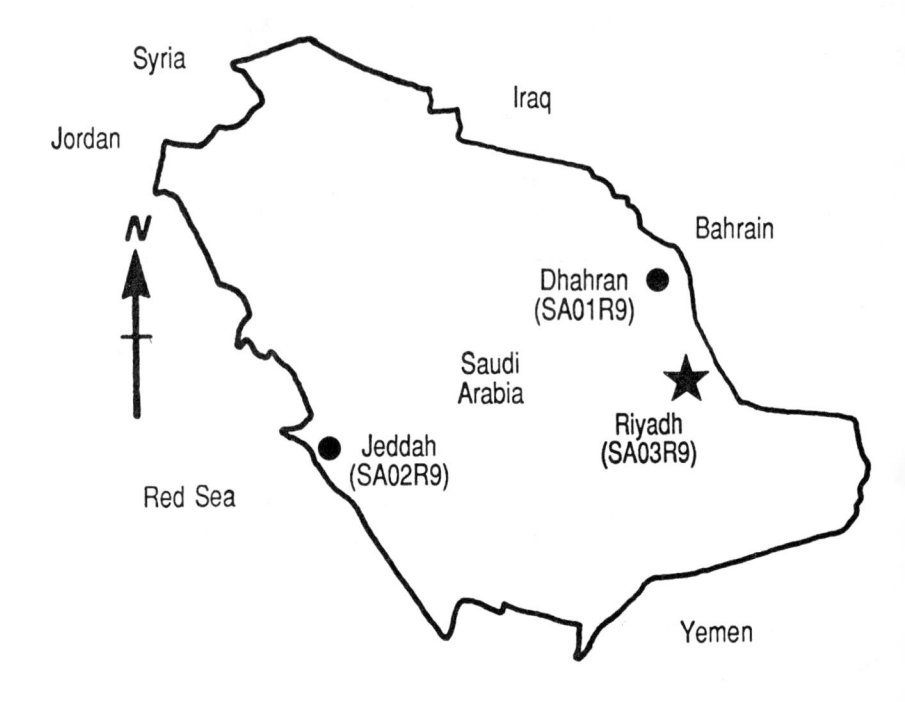

Map showing Saudi Arabia with neighboring countries (Syria, Jordan, Iraq, Bahrain, Yemen), the Red Sea, and cities Dhahran (SA01R9), Jeddah (SA02R9), and Riyadh (SA03R9).

Copyright © 1989 Military Living Publications

Saudi Arabia is located on the Arabian Peninsula, bordered on the west by the Red Sea, on the north by Jordan and Iraq, on the east by the Persian Gulf and on the south by several smaller Arab countries. It is approximately the size of the continental U.S. east of the Mississippi. About one-half of the Saudi population of roughly 9.6 million people consists of foreign residents. Saudis are ethnically Arab with a mixture of middle easterners, Indians and Indonesians. The official language is Arabic. Saudi government is a monarchy (royal family consensus) with authority based on Islamic law and is advised by a Council of Ministers. Thus, there are neither political parties nor suffrage. Saudi Arabia is the world's leading oil exporter and the economy revolves around the world's oil consumption. An oil glut in 1982 necessitated expanding the economic base; now, agriculture and industry account for a larger portion of the economic structure. Natural resources also include hydrocarbons, iron ore and precious metals. Imports have risen sharply since 1974 and include manufactured goods, food products, transportation equipment and construction material. Over half the work force is employed by the government or in commercial or service-oriented

SAUDI ARABIA

businesses. Saudi currency is the *Saudi riyal*. Daily domestic and foreign air travel is available, as are taxis and rental cars (in major cities). Domestic and foreign telephone and telegraph services are available and being expanded. Saudi Arabia is eight hours ahead of U.S. EST. The climate is hot—temperatures often exceed 120 F. in the shade and the coast is very humid. Saudi Arabia is the birthplace of Islam. Women are forbidden to drive and are normally not allowed to rent a hotel room if staying alone. Caution is advised concerning food and drink outside of major hotels and restaurants. U.S./Saudi relations center on international economic and development issues and are good.
ENTRY REQUIREMENTS: Passport and visa—yes. No tourist visa issued at this time. Check with Embassy of Saudi Arabia, Washington, D.C. 20037, Tel: 202-342-3800, for further restrictions. Immunizations—AF.

DHAHRAN COMMUNITY (SA01R9)
APO New York 09616-5000

TELEPHONE INFORMATION: Main installation numbers: Civ: 966-3-879-2281. ATVN: 550-1311. **Note: all telephone numbers below are civilian numbers.**

LOCATION: On the Persian Gulf near the island of Bahrain. The airport/air base is five miles west of the city. NMC: Dhahran, five miles east.

GENERAL INSTALLATION INFORMATION: Headquarters for the U.S. Military Training Mission to Saudi Arabia (USMTM) is located at Dhahran Air Base/International Airport. Its mission is to provide maximum assistance in the development of the Armed Forces of Saudi Arabia into an effective combat force capable of defending the Kingdom against potential enemies. The USMTM's Chief, its Chief of Support Activities and certain staff divisions are located at Dhahran. Other USMTM communities are located in Riyadh, Jeddah, Khamis-Mushayt, Taif, Jubail and Tabuk. **Note: the following abbreviations are used in this listing: AFX (ask for extension); USMTM (U.S. Military Training Mission Compound).**

GENERAL CITY/REGIONAL INFORMATION: Dhahran is located near the Persian Gulf in the northeastern part of the country. The weather is generally warm and dry, though cool days and cooler nights are the norm in January and February.

ADMINISTRATIVE SUPPORT

FACILITY/ACTIVITY	BLDG NO/LOC	PHONE	DAYS/COMMENTS
Fire(Civ)	Dhahran	998	24 hours daily
Housing	USMTM	AFX	M-F
Police(Mil)	USMTM	879-2281 ext. 7121	24 hours daily
Police(Civ)	Dhahran	999	24 hours daily

LOGISTICAL SUPPORT

FACILITY/ACTIVITY	BLDG NO/LOC	PHONE	DAYS/COMMENTS
Auto Rent(Other)	Abu Diyab	891-8403	N/A
	Avis	864-2384	N/A

SAUDI ARABIA
Dhahran Community, continued

	Budget	827-3045	N/A
Commissary(Main)	USMTM	879-2281 ext. 7110	Su-Th
Exchange(Main)	AAFES	879-2281 ext. 7280	Su-Th
Schools(DOD Dep)			
Elementary	Dhahran Academy	N/A	M-F (K-9)
Space-A Air Ops	Dhahran AB/IAP	879-2281 ext. 1337/8	Daily
Flights to:	Athinai Arpt GR; Jeddah Afld SA; Ramstein AB GE; Rhein-Main AB GE.		
Tel Repair(Civ)	Dhahran	904	N/A
TML			
Billeting	USMTM	879-2281 ext. 5136	Daily

HEALTH AND WELFARE

FACILITY/ACTIVITY	BLDG NO/LOC	PHONE	DAYS/COMMENTS
Ambulance	Hospital	997	24 hours daily
Dental Clinic	Hospital	826-2111	Daily
Medical Emergency	Hospital	891-0054	24 hours daily
Red Cross	USMTM	891-2281 ext. 7241	M-F

REST AND RECREATION

FACILITY/ACTIVITY	BLDG NO/LOC	PHONE	DAYS/COMMENTS
Consolidated Club	USMTM	AFX	N/A
Library	USMTM	AFX	Daily
Swimming Pool	USMTM	N/A	Seasonal

JEDDAH COMMUNITY (SA02R9)
APO New York 09697-5001

TELEPHONE INFORMATION: Main installation numbers: Civ: 966-02-682-0951/0942. ATVN: 550-1311. **Note: all telephone numbers below are civilian numbers.**

LOCATION: On the shores of the Red Sea. Mecca is 50 miles east. NMC: Jeddah, 5 miles west.

GENERAL INSTALLATION INFORMATION: The air defense advisor (Army) in Jeddah assists the Saudi Arabian Air Defense Command, the Air Defense Projects and Planning Section, the Air Forces Institute, the Central Maintenance Technical Site, the Air Defense Forces Operations Centers and all Tactical Batteries in providing the Saudi Government with effective air-defense capabilities. The Navy advisors in Jeddah assist the Royal Saudi Navy. **Note: the following abbreviations are used in this listing: AFX (ask for extension); USMTM (U.S. Military Training Mission Compound).**

Jeddah Community, continued

SAUDI ARABIA

GENERAL CITY/REGIONAL INFORMATION: Jeddah is one of the world's oldest inhabited places. It lies on a centuries-old route to Mecca for pilgrims throughout the Islamic world and has become one of the world's most cosmopolitan cities. With more than one million inhabitants, half of them foreigners, Jeddah is Saudi Arabia's largest city and its foremost commercial center.

ADMINISTRATIVE SUPPORT

FACILITY/ACTIVITY	BLDG NO/LOC	PHONE	DAYS/COMMENTS
Fire(Civ)	Jeddah	998	24 hours daily
Housing	USMTM	AFX	N/A
Police(Civ)	Jeddah	999	24 hours daily

LOGISTICAL SUPPORT

FACILITY/ACTIVITY	BLDG NO/LOC	PHONE	DAYS/COMMENTS
Auto Rent(Other)	Avis	651-1668	N/A
	Budget	651-6196	N/A
Bank	Natl Commercial Bank	644-6644	Sa-W
	Saudi American Bank	644-4111	Sa-W
Commissary(Annex)	Supplies provided through the Riyadh Commissary on a weekly basis.		
Exchange(Main)	AAFES	N/A	Su-Th
Postal Svcs(Mil)	USMTM	N/A	Sa-W
Space-A Air Ops	Jeddah Afld	644-7368	Daily
Tel Repair(Civ)	Jeddah	904	Sa-W

HEALTH AND WELFARE

FACILITY/ACTIVITY	BLDG NO/LOC	PHONE	DAYS/COMMENTS
Ambulance	Jeddah	997	24 hours daily
Medical Emergency	Bakhash Hospital	651-0555/0666	24 hours daily

REST AND RECREATION

FACILITY/ACTIVITY	BLDG NO/LOC	PHONE	DAYS/COMMENTS
Recreation	Numerous recreational facilities are available in Jeddah, including tennis, squash, swimming and weight-lifting facilities.		

RIYADH COMMUNITY (SA03R9)
APO New York 09038-7001

TELEPHONE INFORMATION: Main installation numbers: Civ: 966-1-478-1100/6841/6843. ATVN: None. **Note: all telephone numbers below are civilian numbers.**

SAUDI ARABIA
Riyadh Community, continued

LOCATION: Riyadh is located in the Province of Riyadh, 535 miles northeast of Jeddah and 235 miles southwest of Dammam. NMC: Riyadh, in the city.

GENERAL INSTALLATION INFORMATION: The Joint Section (JS) of the U.S. Military Training Mission (USMTM) to Saudi Arabia is located in Riyadh. The JS advises the Saudi Minister of Defense and Aviation. There are two tenant units in Riyadh: the postal service unit and a communications detachment. **Note: the following abbreviations are used in this listing: AFX (ask for extension); COE (Corps of Engineers Compound); IASA (Interagency Support Agreement); USMTM (U.S. Military Training Mission Compound).**

GENERAL CITY/REGIONAL INFORMATION: Riyadh, the capital of the Kingdom of Saudi Arabia, developed from an ancient walled city on the historical route between Iran and the Holy City of Mecca. The city was originally built near a water source, as were all cities in the Kingdom. The center of the city lies clustered around the original "wadi" where water was found. During the 20th century, the city has expanded in every direction with many constructions projects on-going throughout the year.

Sites of interest include the Riyadh Museum of Archaeology and Ethnography; Fort Masmak, the oldest structure in the city, which dates from 1865; Murabba Palace, built by King Abdul Aziz after Riyadh expanded outside its original walls; and The College of Arts Museum at King Saudi University's women's division.

ADMINISTRATIVE SUPPORT

FACILITY/ACTIVITY	BLDG NO/LOC	PHONE	DAYS/COMMENTS
Fire(Civ)	Riyadh	998	24 hours daily
Housing	USMTM	AFX	M-F
Personnel Spt	USMTM	478-1100 ext. 2336	M-F
Police(Civ)	Riyadh	999	24 hours daily

LOGISTICAL SUPPORT

FACILITY/ACTIVITY	BLDG NO/LOC	PHONE	DAYS/COMMENTS
Auto Rent(Other)	Avis	476-5751	N/A
	Budget	464-7116	N/A
Bank	Saudi American Bank	477-4770	N/A
	COE	491-3072 ext. 733474	Sa-Th
	USMTM	492-6822	Sa-Th
Barber Shop(s)	USMTM	492-6811	Sa-Th
	COE H-10	491-3072 ext. 73473	Sa-F
Beauty Shop(s)	USMTM	241-2800 ext. 1110	Varies
	USMTM	478-1100 ext. 2282	Su
Commissary(Main)	1000	491-2932/ 3188	Su-Th
Credit Union	COE	AFX	N/A

SAUDI ARABIA
Riyadh Community, continued

Facility	Location	Phone	Days/Comments
Dining Facility	USMTM	464-0433 ext. 245	Daily. AD only.
Exchange(Main)	AAFES	491-2420	Su-Th
Food(Caf/Rest)	COE H-9	491-3072 ext. 733282	Daily
	USMTM	478-1100 ext. 2227	Daily
Postal Svcs(Mil)	USMTM	478-1100 ext. 2224	Sa-Th
Schools(DOD Dep)			
Elementary	SA Intl School	491-4270	M-F
Tel Repair(Civ)	Riyadh	904	N/A
TML			
Billeting	USMTM	AFX	M-F

==
HEALTH AND WELFARE
==

FACILITY/ACTIVITY	BLDG NO/LOC	PHONE	DAYS/COMMENTS
Ambulance	Riyadh	997	24 hours daily
	IASA Clinic	491-9351	24 hours daily
Army Comm Svcs	USMTM	463-4007 464-1115	Sa-W
Central Appts	IASA Clinic	492-6567/8	M-F
	USMTM Clinic	478-1100 ext. 2500	Sa-W
Comm Drug/Alc Ctr	See Army Community Services.		
Dental Clinic	IASA Clinic	492-6569	M-F
	COE H-10B	491-6004 ext. 733569	Sa-Th
Medical Emergency	IASA Clinic	491-9351 492-6566	24 hours daily
Mental Health	See Army Community Services.		
Poison Control	King Khalid	467-1500	24 hours daily

==
REST AND RECREATION
==

FACILITY/ACTIVITY	BLDG NO/LOC	PHONE	DAYS/COMMENTS
Recreation	Contact the ACS Office for information about recreational activities in Riyadh.		

SPAIN
Spanish State
Madrid

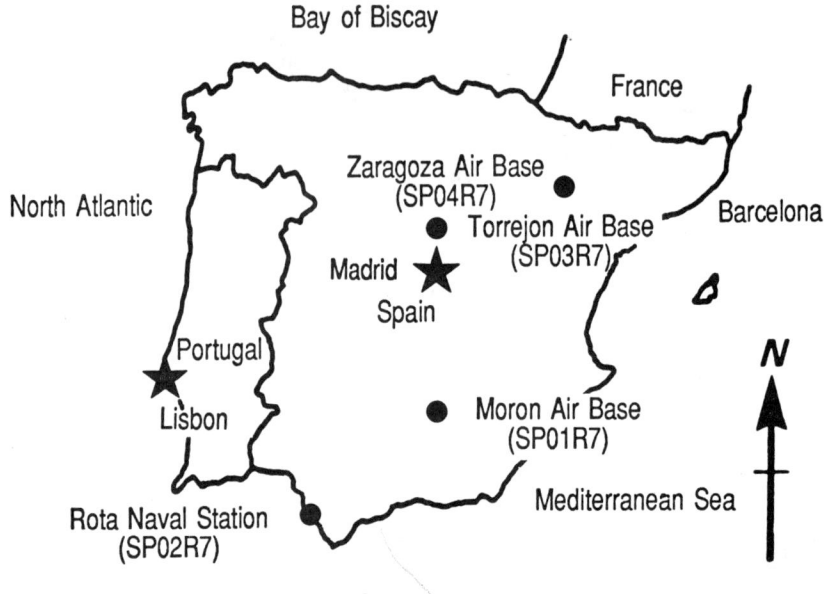

```
Bay of Biscay
                                    France
        Zaragoza Air Base
        (SP04R7)
                    Torrejon Air Base    Barcelona
                    (SP03R7)
        Madrid ★
North Atlantic      Spain
    Portugal
    ★                                    N ↑
    Lisbon
                    ● Moron Air Base
                      (SP01R7)
                              Mediterranean Sea
Rota Naval Station
(SP02R7)
        Strait of Gibraltar
```

Copyright © 1989 Military Living Publications

The Iberian Peninsula, consisting of Spain and Portugal, is surrounded from the north to southwest by the North Atlantic Ocean and by the Mediterranean Sea to the south and east. France borders Spain on the north. Spanish territory also includes the Balearic and Canary Islands and five sovereignties and is roughly the size of Arizona and Utah combined. The population of 38.2 million Spaniards are of Mediterranean and Germanic descent. Spanish is the official language. The government is a constitutional monarchy with 17 regional autonomous governments and suffrage is universal over age 18. Within the past ten years, Spain has developed a strong and diversified economy and is one of the world's leading tourist countries. Natural resources include coal, minerals and hydroelectric power. Spain exports fruits, automobiles, iron and steel products and textiles. Imports include grains, oil, chemicals, machinery and transportation equipment. Nearly one-half of the work force is employed in the services area. Spanish currency is the *peseta*. Public transportation and taxis are plentiful and reasonable. The domestic rail system, Renfe, is frequent with good international connections, including several luxury and express trains. Domestic and international air connections are good. Local and international telephone and telegraph service is available. Spain is six hours ahead of U.S. EST. Clothing needs are similar to Washington, D.C. Sightseeing highlights are the Alhambra Palace, the Costa del Sol (75 miles of coastline) and the

SPAIN

Basque country, known for fairs, festivals and folklore. Gasoline prices are among the highest in Europe. Women may wear slacks but not shorts in public. Spanish-U.S. relations are based on defense and security and are cooperative for developing education, culture, science and technology.
ENTRY REQUIREMENTS: Passport—required. Visa—not required for stay up to six months. Check with the Embassy of Spain, Washington, D.C. 20009, Tel: 202-265-0190, for other requirements. Immunizations—EUR.

MORON AIR BASE (SP01R7)
APO New York 09282-5000

TELEPHONE INFORMATION: Main installation numbers: Civ: 34-54-573-956 (if dialing civilian in-country dial 954-573-956). ATVN: 722-1110.

LOCATION: Drive southeast from Sevilla on E-334. Just beyond Alcala de Guadaira turn right onto C-342 to Moron de la Frontera. Moron AB is on the left about ten miles before the town of Moron. HE: p-61, D/4. NMC: Sevilla, 40 miles northwest.

GENERAL INSTALLATION INFORMATION: Moron AB'S stand-by mission is accomplished with approximately 275 personnel, which includes contract personnel. U.S. units at Moron include the 1989th, Det 8; the 2188th Communications Squadron; and a USN Radio Transmission Facility. The U.S. Air Force shares Moron with the 21st Tactical Wing of the Spanish Air Force.

GENERAL CITY/REGIONAL INFORMATION: Moron is located close to the foothills of the Sierra de Ronda mountain chain along the southern coast of Spain in Andalusia. Area attractions include the Tower of Gold (1220), the largest cathedral in Spain and the 3rd largest Christian church in the world.

ADMINISTRATIVE SUPPORT

FACILITY/ACTIVITY	BLDG NO/LOC	PHONE	DAYS/COMMENTS
Duty Officer	101	2401	24 hours daily
Fire(Civ)	1427	2068	24 hours daily
Housing			
Family	202	2156	M-F
Referral	202	2156	M-F
Inspector Gen'l	101	2285	M-F
Locator(Mil)	101	1110	24 hours daily
Personnel Spt	101	2410	M-F
Police(Mil)	110	2132	M-F
Emergency	110	2114	24 hours daily. Spanish language only.

LOGISTICAL SUPPORT

FACILITY/ACTIVITY	BLDG NO/LOC	PHONE	DAYS/COMMENTS
Auto Drivers Testing	By appointment with safety officer.		
Auto Parts(Exch)	534	2202	M,W,F
Auto Registration	110	2132	M-F
Bank	106	2787	M,W,F
Barber Shop(s)	106	None	W
Bookstore	107	2793	M-F

SPAIN
Moron Air Base, continued

Dining Facility	115	2249	Daily
Motor Pool	512	2063	M-F
Package Store	107	2445	M,W,F
Postal Svcs(Mil)	106	2267	M-F
Postal Svcs(Civ)	106	2267	M-F
Schools(DOD Dep)			
Elementary	314	2674	M-F (K-8)
High School	Located in London		
Svc Stn(Insta)	534	None	M-F
Space-A Air Ops	See Rota Naval Air Station listing.		
TML			
Billeting	303	2798	24 hours daily

HEALTH AND WELFARE

FACILITY/ACTIVITY	BLDG NO/LOC	PHONE	DAYS/COMMENTS
Ambulance	306	2069	M-F
	After hours call main Base number.		
Chapel	109	None	Su
Medical Emergency	306	2069	M-F
	After hours call main Base number.		

REST AND RECREATION

FACILITY/ACTIVITY	BLDG NO/LOC	PHONE	DAYS/COMMENTS
Bowling Lanes	311	2557	M-Sa
Consolidated Club	302	None	M-F
Gymnasium	312	2307	M-F
Library	312	2307	M-F
Swimming Pool	313	2308	May-Sept
Tennis Courts	312	None	Daily
Video Rental	106	2445	M-F

ROTA NAVAL STATION (SP02R7)
FPO New York 09540-3500

TELEPHONE INFORMATION: Main installation numbers: Civ: 34-56-862780. ATVN: 727-0111. Note: when dialing the base from within Spain, but outside the province of Cadiz, dial Civ: 956-862780. When dialing the base within Cadiz, dial Civ: 862780.

LOCATION: On Spain's South Atlantic coast. Accessible from E-25 south and SP-342 west. HE: p-61, C/5. NMC: Cadiz, 22 miles south.

GENERAL INSTALLATION INFORMATION: Rota's primary mission is to provide support to the U.S. Navy's 6th Fleet. Its port is one of the busiest in the Med, and its tenant commands keep fuel oil, ammunition and spare parts flowing to the operational forces. Tenant commands include the Antisubmarine Warfare Operations Center; Company F, Marine Support Battalion; the Naval Cryptologic Support Group, 6th Fleet; MAC Liaison Det 1, 625; the VR-22 Fleet Logistics Support Squadron; and many other units.

U.S. Forces Travel & Transfer Guide Europe — 311

SPAIN

Rota Naval Station, continued

GENERAL CITY/REGIONAL INFORMATION: A Spanish navy installation under the command of a Spanish rear admiral, Rota NS covers more than 6,000 acres. It is located in the region of Andalusia on the Bay of Cadiz in southwestern Spain between the towns of Rota and Puerto de Santa Maria.

The Atlantic fringe of Andalusia has been called La Costa de la Luz or the Coast of Light. This name accurately describes the sunny climate and the warmth of the local population. The area is well known for fine Andalusian cuisine—gazpacho, stews, mountain hams—as well as excellent seafood and local wines.

Festivals, dances and local celebrations occur year round. Rota itself has some wonderful fine-sand beaches and the remains of the Medieval Wall and the 13th-century Luna Castle. Puerto de Santa Maria offers lovely churches, an ancient monastery, San Marcos Castle, famous wine cellars and beautiful beaches.

ADMINISTRATIVE SUPPORT

FACILITY/ACTIVITY	BLDG NO/LOC	PHONE	DAYS/COMMENTS
Duty Officer	1	2222	24 hours daily
Fire(Mil)	58	333	24 hours daily
Housing	1610	4602	M-F
Legal Assist	521	2531	M-F
Police(Mil)	207	2000	24 hours daily
Emergency	36	2225	24 hours daily
Police(Civ)	N/A	C-91-10103	24 hours daily

LOGISTICAL SUPPORT

FACILITY/ACTIVITY	BLDG NO/LOC	PHONE	DAYS/COMMENTS
Auto Drivers Testing	230	2094	F during ICR class
Auto Registration	207	2547	M-F
Auto Rental(Exch)	2	2675	M-Sa
Auto Ship(Gov)	555	0 (ask for MTMC in Cadiz)	M-F
Bank	1	2913	M-F
Barber Shop(s)	39	2510	M-Sa
	40	2507	M-Sa
	134	4599	M-Sa
Beauty Shop(s)	134	4034	M-Sa
Bookstore	1626	2634	Tu-Su
Bus	197	2403	Daily
Child Care/Dev Ctr	42	2962	M-Sa
	204	2684	M-F
Clothing Sales	578	7175	Tu-Su
Commissary(Main)	40	2925	Tu-Sa
Credit Union	40	2986	M-F
Dining Facility	38	2317	Daily
Dry Clean(Exch)	41	2558	M-Sa
Education Center	1	2711	Daily
Exchange(Main)	40	2033	M-Sa
Food(Snack/Fast)			
Pizza Parlor	231	7213	Daily

SPAIN
Rota Naval Station, continued

Foodland	174	7143	Daily
Laundry(Self-Svc)	183	2275	Daily
Package Store	246	2132	M-Sa
Postal Svcs(Mil)	209	2518	M-F
SATO-OS	1	C-812050 ext. 2034	M-F
Schools(DOD Dep)			
Elementary	73	4185	M-F
High School	77	4181	M-F
Svc Stn(Insta)	178	2450	Daily
Space-A Air Ops	2	2803	24 hours daily
Pax Lounges(Gen'l)	2	2411	24 hours daily
Protocol Svc	1	2744	M-F
Flights to:	Bahrain IAP BA; Capodichino Arpt IT; Dover AFB DE; Norfolk NAS VA; Philadelphia IAP PA; Ramstein AB GE; Rhein-Main AB GE; Sigonella Arpt IT; Torrejon AB SP; Zaragoza AB SP.		
Tailor Shop	41	2558	M-Sa
Taxi(Comm)	Rota Gate	2929	24 hours daily
TML			
Billeting	1610	2567/2568	Daily
BEQ	37	2460	24 hours daily
BOQ	39	2510/2511	24 hours daily
Navy Lodge	1674	2643	24 hours daily
Travel Agents	2	2429	Call for hours.
Watch Repair	41	None	M-Sa

HEALTH AND WELFARE

FACILITY/ACTIVITY	BLDG NO/LOC	PHONE	DAYS/COMMENTS
Ambulance	Housing	4601/2225	24 hours daily
Central Appts	52	7146	M-F
Chaplain	42	2161	M-F
Chapel	42	2161	Daily
Comm Drug/Alc Ctr	35	2077	M-F
Dental Clinic	52	2324	M-F
Medical Emergency	36,52	2303	24 hours daily
Navy Fam Svcs	1743	7231	M-F
Navy Relief	268	2805	Daily
Red Cross	54	2333	M-F
USO	38	7105	M-F
Veterinary Svcs	168	4266	M-F

REST AND RECREATION

FACILITY/ACTIVITY	BLDG NO/LOC	PHONE	DAYS/COMMENTS
Bowling Lanes	228	2112	Daily
Camping/RV Area	On Base	C-862780 ext. 256314	Daily
Craftshops			
Automotive	4322	2268	Daily
Ceramics	97	2550	Daily
Multi-crafts	97	2550	M-Sa
Wood	557	2284	Call for hours.
Enlisted Club	1631	2317	Daily

Rota Naval Station, continued

SPAIN

Facility	Bldg	Phone	Days
Golf Course	231	2260	Daily
Gymnasium	44	2565	Daily
	289	2201	Daily
Info Tour & Travel	N/A	7101	M-F
Library	98	2418	Daily
Marina	523	2497	F-Su
NCO Club	49	2433	Daily
O'Club	50	2509/2617	Daily
Swimming Pool	593	5437	Daily
	45	2129	M-F
Theater	43	2328	Daily
	229	4205	Daily
Youth Center	160	4203	Daily

TORREJÓN AIR BASE (SP03R7)
APO New York 09283-5000

TELEPHONE INFORMATION: Main installation numbers: Civ: 34-1-665-7777. ATVN: 723-1110. Civ prefix: 665-____. ATVN prefix: 723-XXXX.

LOCATION: Take Highway N-11 toward Zaragoza, pass the IAP at Barajas on the left. The air base is on the left and clearly marked. HE: p-59, D/2. MNC: Madrid, 15 miles southwest.

GENERAL INSTALLATION INFORMATION: The host unit, the 401st Tactical Fighter Wing, maintains three mission-ready F-16 fighter squadrons with support personnel to meet mission objectives of the U.S. Air Force and NATO. Associate units include the 625th Military Airlift Support Group; the 1989th Communications Wing; the 2186th Communications Squadron, Field Training Detachment 926; and headquarters, 16th Air Force.

GENERAL CITY/REGIONAL INFORMATION: Torrejón Air Base is located 15 miles northeast of Madrid, the capital of Spain and its largest city. Madrid is the cultural, intellectual and political center of the country, and as such boasts many well-known parks, plazas, churches, palaces, museums and restaurants. The nearby cities of Toledo, Segovia and Sevilla also offer many attractions, including splendid palaces, castles and cathedrals. Spain's historical importance, sunny climate and fine cuisine make it a wonderful place to live or visit.

ADMINISTRATIVE SUPPORT

FACILITY/ACTIVITY	BLDG NO/LOC	PHONE	DAYS/COMMENTS
Customs/Duty	403	3267	24 hours daily
Duty Officer	105	5105	24 hours daily
Fire(Mil)	404	117	24 hours daily
Housing			
Family	123	3136	M-F
Referral	123	1840	M-F
Info(Insta)	105, Rm 236	5052	M-F
Inspector Gen'l	105, Rm 234	5060	M-F
Legal Assist	208	5306	M-F
Locator(Mil)	200	1841	M-F

SPAIN
Torrejón Air Base, continued

Locator(Civ)	206	3231	M-F
Personnel Spt	206	3231	M-F
Police(Mil)	290	5400	24 hours daily
Public Affairs	105, Rm 236	5051	M-F
Tax Relief	208	5306	M-F

LOGISTICAL SUPPORT

FACILITY/ACTIVITY	BLDG NO/LOC	PHONE	DAYS/COMMENTS
Audio/Photo Ctr	110	5912	Daily
Auto Drivers Testing	300, Hut 3	3393	M-F
Auto Parts(Exch)	109	5937	M-Sa
Auto Registration	206	1853	M-F
Auto Rental(Exch)	406	5930	Daily
Auto Repairs	109	5937	M-F
Auto Sales	139	5790	N/A
Auto Ship(Gov)	392	1849	M-F
Auto Wash	Behind 300	None	24 hours daily
Bank	300	5941	M-F
Barber Shop(s)	110	5936	M-Sa
	123	5898	M-F
Beauty Shop(s)	123	5927	M-Sa
Bookstore	125	5860	M-Sa
Bus	392	5419	24 hours daily
Child Care/Dev Ctr	134	5900	Daily
Clothing Sales	215	5565	M-Sa
Commissary(Main)	112	5158	Tu-Sa
Credit Union	300	3397	M-F
Dining Facility	205	3317	M-F
Dry Clean(Exch)	120	5940	Tu-Sa
Dry Clean(Gov)	270	3328	M-Sa
Education Center	206	5175	M-F
Elec Repair(Gov)	360	5889	Daily
Eng'r/Publ Works	500	5653	M-F
	500	5105	After hours
Exchange(Main)	110	5811	Daily
Finance(Mil)	206	5182	M-F
Food(Caf/Rest)	110	5810	M-F
Food(Snack/Fast)	403	3989	24 hours daily
Foodland	117	5846	Daily
Laundry(Exch)	120	5940	Tu-Sa
Laundry(Self-Svc)	330	5950	Daily
Motor Pool	392	5419	24 hours daily
Package Store	240	5345	Tu-Sa
Photo Laboratory	231	5364	Daily
Pick-up Point	360	N/A	N/A
Postal Svcs(Mil)	237	3851	M-Sa
SATO-OS	403	5437	M-F
Schools(DOD Dep)			
Elementary/Jr	101	7071	M-F (K-7)
	Royal Oaks Hsg	7071	M-F (K-7)
High School	263	7071	M-F (8-12)
Svc Stn(Insta)	133	5905	M-Sa
Space-A Air Ops	403	1854	24 hours daily
Pax Lounges(Gen'l)	403	1854	24 hours daily
Protocol Svc	105	7432	M-F

SPAIN
Torrejón Air Base, continued

Flights to: Athinai Arpt GR; Aviano AB IT; Charleston AFB SC; Cigli TAFB TU; Dhahran IAP SA; Dover AFB DE; Esenboga Arpt TU; Incirlik Arpt TU; Jomo Kenyatta IAP KE; Khartoum Arpt SD; King Abdul Aziz IAP SA; Lajes AB PO; McGuire AFB NJ; RAF Mildenhall UK; Norfolk NAS VA; Palma de Mallorca Arpt SP; Ramstein AB GE; Rhein-Main AB GE; Rota NAS SP; Sigonella Arpt IT; Zaragoza AB SP.

Facility	Bldg	Phone	Days
Tailor Shop	120	5844	Tu-Sa
Taxi(Comm)	406	5930	M-Sa
Tel Booking Oper	104	112	24 hours daily
Tel Repair(Gov)	201	5698	M-F
Thrift Shop	300	5736	Tu,Th
TML			
Billeting	121	3150	24 hours daily
BEQ	121	3150	24 hours daily
BOQ	121	3150	24 hours daily
Protocol Office	105	5098	24 hours daily
TLF	121	3150	24 hours daily
DV/VIP	121	3150	24 hours daily
Travel Agents	403	5710	M-Sa
Watch Repair	120	5940	Tu-Sa

HEALTH AND WELFARE

FACILITY/ACTIVITY	BLDG NO/LOC	PHONE	DAYS/COMMENTS
AF Family Svcs	300	5401	M-F
AF Relief	206	5204	M-F
Ambulance	108	116	24 hours daily
Central Appts	108	3787	M-F
CHAMPUS Office	108	5555	M-F
Chaplain	115	3174	M-F
Chapel	115	3174	M-F
Comm Drug/Alc Ctr	207	3194	M-F
Dental Clinic	108	1846	M-F
Medical Emergency	108	116	24 hours daily
Mental Health	108	5518	M-F
Poison Control	108	116	24 hours daily
Red Cross	300	1855	M-F
	300	5428	After hours
Veterinary Svcs	129	5125	M-F

REST AND RECREATION

FACILITY/ACTIVITY	BLDG NO/LOC	PHONE	DAYS/COMMENTS
Aero/Flying Club	437	5800	M-F
Amer Forces Ntwk	123	5135	24 hours daily
Bowling Lanes	237	3327	24 hours daily
Craftshops			
Automotive	439	3533	Daily
Ceramics	236	3341	Tu-Sa
Electronics	231	5364	Daily
Multi-crafts	236	3341	Tu-Sa
Enlisted Club	116	5165	N/A
Golf Course	Off base	None	Daily

SPAIN
Torrejón Air Base, continued

Gymnasium	251	3320	Daily
Info Tour & Travel	236	5808	M-F
Library	118	3177	Daily
NCO Club	116	5165/5105	Daily
O'Club	122	5912	Daily
Racket Courts	251	3320	Daily
Recreation Center	236	3853	Daily
Riding Club	236	3853	Daily
Rod and Gun Club	647	5932	Th-Su
Sport Field	251	3380	Daily
Swimming Pool	251	3380	Daily
Tennis Courts	251	3380	Call for appointment.
Theater	111	3133	Daily
Track	251	3380	Daily
Video Rental	231	5364	Daily
Youth Center	231	5453	M-F

ZARAGOZA AIR BASE (SP04R7)
APO New York 09286-5000

TELEPHONE INFORMATION: Main installation numbers: Civ: 34-76-326711 (from U.S.); 34-976-326711 (from Spain). ATVN: 724-1110.

LOCATION: From the French border crossing Gerona, take Autopista 2 and drive four hours to the base. From Madrid, take National Highway N-11 to the base. HE: p-56, H/5. NMC: Zaragoza, 12 miles northeast.

GENERAL INSTALLATION INFORMATION: The mission of the 406th Tactical Fighter Training Wing is to operate and maintain a U.S. Air Forces-in-Europe weapons training site for tactical aircraft stationed at various USAFE bases.

GENERAL CITY/REGIONAL INFORMATION: Zaragoza is the capital of the ancient kingdom of Aragon, which united with the kingdoms of Castilla and Navarra in the 15th century to form the foundation of modern Spain. Today Zaragoza is a modern, attractive city of over 650,000 and is the cultural, political, industrial, agricultural, military and educational center of an area extending beyond the boundaries of the province.

Zaragoza is known as the "Lady of Four Civilizations." The first was the early Iberian city of Salduba, where some of the first coins were minted. The era of Roman rule under Emperor Caesar Augustus was the second period. Caesar Augustus founded Zaragoza in 24. B.C. Well-preserved remnants of the city's Roman walls still remain in downtown Zaragoza. The third era was as the Moorish city of Saracosta, the home of a rich Arab culture. Last was the Christian city of Zaragoza, which came into being in 1118 as the capital of a prosperous medieval kingdom. Among the many historical sites to see in the area are the Basilica del Pilar, the Cathedral de la Seo, the 14th-century Church of San Pablo, the 11th-century Aljaferia Palace and the Fine Arts Museum.

Zaragoza Air Base, continued

SPAIN

ADMINISTRATIVE SUPPORT

FACILITY/ACTIVITY	BLDG NO/LOC	PHONE	DAYS/COMMENTS
Duty Officer	612	113/2000	24 hours daily
Fire(Mil)	602	17	24 hours daily
Housing	928	2255	M-F
Legal Assist	823	2318/2343	M,W,F
Locator(Mil)	646	2210	M-F
	646	2715	After hours
Police(Mil)	825	2178	24 hours daily
Emergency	825	2114	24 hours daily
Public Affairs	841	2491	M-F

LOGISTICAL SUPPORT

FACILITY/ACTIVITY	BLDG NO/LOC	PHONE	DAYS/COMMENTS
Audio/Photo Ctr	776	2688	M-Sa
Auto Rental(Exch)	1035	2793	M-Sa
Auto Sales	1033	2790	M-Sa
Barber Shop(s)	1033	2776	Tu-Sa
Beauty Shop(s)	1033	2792	Tu-Sa
Bookstore	1028	2712	Daily
Child Care/Dev Ctr	803	2020	Daily
Clothing Sales	711	2487	M-F
Commissary(Main)	1034	2321/2531	Tu-Su
Credit Union	1144	2706	M-F
Dining Facility	830	2310	Daily. Airmen.
	801	2347	Daily. NCOs.
	902	2763	M-F. Officers.
Education Center	775	2596/2597	M-F
Eng'r/Publ Works	642	2247	Daily
Exchange(Main)	1033	2790	M-Sa
Finance(Mil)	824	2256/2250	M-F
Food(Snack/Fast)	1003	2553	Daily
	837	2593	Daily
	1020	2970	Daily
Burger Bar	1033	2795	Daily
Pizza Parlor	1020	2841	Daily
Foodland	1039	2798	Daily
Four Seasons	719	2688	M-Sa
Laundry(Self-Svc)	1022	None	24 hours daily
Motor Pool	640	2408	Daily
Package Store	1026	2062	Tu-Sa
Pick-up Point	712	2684	M-F
Postal Svcs(Mil)	1031	2198	M-F
Schools(DOD Dep)			
Elem/High School	765	2446	M-F
Svc Stn(Insta)	1035	2796	M-Sa
Space-A Air Ops	686	2517	M-Sa
Pax Lounges(Gen'l)	686	2517	M-F
Flights to:	RAF Mildenhall UK; Ramstein AB GE; Rhein-Main AB GE; Rota NAS SP; Torrejon AB SP.		
Spanish Giftshop	812	2695	M-Sa
Taxi(Comm)	640	2070	Daily

SPAIN
Zaragoza Air Base, continued

TML

Billeting	900	2141/2715	24 hours daily
VAQ	827,829,831,833	2141/2715	24 hours daily
VOQ	900	2141/2715	24 hours daily
DV/VIP	829,900	2558	Daily
Travel Agents	686	2698	M-F

HEALTH AND WELFARE

FACILITY/ACTIVITY	BLDG NO/LOC	PHONE	DAYS/COMMENTS
AF Family Svcs	710	2955/2169	M-F
Ambulance	810	2116	24 hours daily
Central Appts	810	2035	M-F
Chaplain	1030	2122	M-F
	N/A	2060	After hours
Medical Emergency	810	2116	24 hours daily
Red Cross	810	2363	M-F
	N/A	2060	After hours

REST AND RECREATION

FACILITY/ACTIVITY	BLDG NO/LOC	PHONE	DAYS/COMMENTS
Amer Forces Ntwk	776/780	2503	Daily
Bowling Lanes	837	2705	Daily
Craftshops			
Automotive	811	2218	W-M
Multi-crafts	776	2968	Tu,Th-Sa
Equip/Gear Locker	812	2562	M-F
Golf Course	1003	2669	Daily
Gymnasium	802	2453	Daily
Library	1025	2046	Daily
NCO Club	801	N/A	Daily
O'Club	902	2763	M-F
Recreation Center	1020	2970/2829	Daily
Rob & Gun Club	On Base	2510	W,Sa,Su
Swimming Pool	806	2012	Seasonal
Theater	1032	2308	Call for schedule.
Youth Center	804	2964	M-F

TURKEY
Republic of Turkey
Ankara

Map locations:
- Bulgaria
- Black Sea
- Istanbul
- Istanbul Spt Group (TU09R9)
- Sinop
- Sinop Army Field Station (TU02R9)
- U.S.S.R.
- Ankara
- Agean Sea
- Izmir Air Station (TU04R9)
- Ankara Air Station (TU01R9)
- Turkey
- Pirinclik
- Diyarbakir Airport (TU06R9)
- Iran
- Incirlik Air Base (Adana) (TU03R9)
- Syria
- Iraq
- Mediterranean Sea
- N

Copyright © 1989 Military Living Publications

Located in the western Mediterranean, Turkey is one-tenth in Europe and nine-tenths in Asia. It is slightly larger than Texas. About half of the Turkish population of 51.8 million lives in urban areas. Turkish is the official language. In 1923, the 600-year-old Ottoman empire collapsed and the Republic of Turkey was founded. Suffrage is universal over age 21. Natural resources include coal, copper, boron and oil. Agriculture and natural resource processing operations account for the economic base, although it is being diversified. Tobacco, cotton, textiles, raisins, nuts, glass and ceramics are exported. Imports included petroleum, pharmaceuticals, plastics, rubber and leather. Fifty-eight percent of the workers are farmers. The currency is *Turkish lira*. More than 20 airlines serve Turkey and a state-wide rail system provides domestic service and international connections. Domestic and international telephone and telegraph service is dependable but often overloaded during peak periods. Local transportation service is provided by taxis and buses. Main roads are in good condition; secondary roads are usually adequate. Turkey is eight hours ahead of U.S. EST. The climate is similar to the eastern U.S. Istanbul has a large market with exotic handmade goods. Ottoman-period craft techniques are honored and practiced today, especially in architecture, ceramics and carpet weaving. Although U.S.-Turkish relations have recently been strained, they are currently friendly.
ENTRY REQUIREMENTS: Passport—yes. Visa not required for stay up to three months. Check with the Embassy of Turkey, Washington, D.C., Tel: 202-387-3200, for further requirements. Immunizations—EUR.

TURKEY

ANKARA AIR STATION (TU01R9)
APO New York 09254-5000

TELEPHONE INFORMATION: Main installation numbers: Civ: 90-4-133-7080. ATVN: 672-1110.

LOCATION: From Esenboga Airport take the bus or taxi to Balgat. NMC: Ankara, in the city.

GENERAL INSTALLATION INFORMATION: Ankara Air Station is headquarters for the U.S. Logistics Group in Turkey (TUSLOG). During peacetime, TUSLOG is responsible for logistical support to all DOD and U.S. federal agencies, operational control of in-country USAFE forces and aircraft, and in-country command and support of U.S. Air Force forces participating in NATO and JCS exercises. The 7217th Air Base Group at Ankara is responsible for daily support to U.S. agencies spread across 300,000 square miles.

GENERAL CITY/REGIONAL INFORMATION: Ankara, the capital of Turkey, is a delight for the shopper and the history buff. The bazaars, "Copper Alley," offer bargains in curios, antiques, and handicrafts. "Gold Alley" is famous for the best and largest concentration of gold, silver, and gemstone shops in the city. Carpets and leather goods are also good buys in Turkey.

Ankara abounds in famous and fascinating sights: the Citadel; the Hittite Museum; the Roman baths; the Roman Theatre; the Temple of Augustus and Roma; and the Haci Bayram Camii the Arslahane Camii, two ancient mosques; and the Railroad Museum, to name only a few.

ADMINISTRATIVE SUPPORT

FACILITY/ACTIVITY	BLDG NO/LOC	PHONE	DAYS/COMMENTS
Customs/Duty	2424	3182/3266	M-F
Duty Officer	2001	2241	24 hours daily
Fire(Mil)	2443	117	24 hours daily
Fire(Civ)	Ankara	C-000	24 hours daily
Housing			
Family	2001	3128	M-F
Info(Insta)	2018	2116	M-F
Inspector Gen'l	2018	2200	M-F
Legal Assist	2001	4112	M-F
Locator(Mil)	2018	4116	M-F
Locator(Civ)	Emek Bldg	2173	M-F
Personnel Spt	2018	4131	M-F
Police(Mil)	2001	2241	24 hours daily
		C-125-2329	
Police(Civ)	Ankara	C-055	24 hours daily
Public Affairs	2018	2116/2222	M-F
		2241	After duty hours

LOGISTICAL SUPPORT

FACILITY/ACTIVITY	BLDG NO/LOC	PHONE	DAYS/COMMENTS
Air Tickets	2424	2154	M-F

U.S. Forces Travel & Transfer Guide Europe — 321

TURKEY

Ankara Air Station, continued

Auto Drivers Testing	2426	3178	M-F
Auto Parts(Exch)	Exchange	3275	Daily
Auto Registration	2426	3178/295	M-F
Auto Sales	2051	3275/3196	Daily
Auto Ship(Gov)	2424	2154	M-F
Bakery	2051	3145	Tu-Sa
Barber Shop(s)	2051	300	M-Sa
Beauty Shop(s)	2051	300	M-Sa
Bookstore	2051	3154	M-Sa
Clothing Sales	2051	3196	Tu-Sa
Commissary(Main)	2051	3145	Tu-Sa
Credit Union	2422	None	M-F
Dry Clean(Exch)	2051	300	M-Sa
Education Center	2018	2163	M-F
Elec Repair(Gov)	2051	285	24 hours daily
Eng'r/Publ Works	2440	2113	M-F
Exchange(Main)	2051	3275	Daily
Finance(Mil)	2001	3188	M-F
Food(Caf/Rest)	2001	234	M-Sa
Food(Snack/Fast)			
Baskin Robbins	2606	251	Daily
Pizza Parlor	2606	251	Daily
Foodland	Kirkpinar Palas	2275	Daily
Laundry(Exch)	2051	300	M-Sa
Motor Pool	2088	255	Daily
Package Store	2420	2184	Tu-Sa
Parking	SP Desk	2241	24 hours daily
Photo Laboratory	2018	4111	M-F
Postal Svcs(Mil)	2421	3185	M-Sa
Schools(DOD Dep)	2026	4114	M-F (K-12)
Svc Stn(Insta)	2034	None	M-F
Space-A Air Ops	2018	2206	M-F
Flights to:	Athinai Arpt GR; Cigli TAFB TU; Eskishehir TUAF TU; Incirlik Arpt TU; Ramstein AB GE; Rhein-Main AB GE; Sigonella Arpt IT; Torrejon AB SP; Yesilkoy Arpt TU.		
Tailor Shop	2051	300	M-Sa
Taxi(Comm)	Stands throughout city	N/A	24 hours daily
Tel Booking Oper	354/Ankara	3200	M-F
		0	After duty hours
Tel Repair(Gov)	354/Ankara	2233	24 hours daily
Tel Repair(Civ)	354/Ankara	2233	24 hours daily
Thrift Shop	On Air Station	None	Tu,F
TML			
Billeting/TLF	135	C-138-9453 3128/3183	24 hours daily
Travel Agents	2438	4247	M-F

===
HEALTH AND WELFARE
===

FACILITY/ACTIVITY	BLDG NO/LOC	PHONE	DAYS/COMMENTS
AF Family Svcs	Kirkpinar Palas	C-138-9453 3163	Tu-Sa Ask for Fam Svc
AF Relief	Incirlik	676-6927	M-F
Ambulance	2001	C-125-2329	24 hours daily

TURKEY
Ankara Air Station, continued

Central Appts	2001	3224	Daily
CHAMPUS Office	2001	303	M-F
Chaplain	2001	2241	24 hours daily
Chapel	2001	2192	M-F
Dental Clinic	2001	2115	M-F
Medical Emergency	None at AS	3224	Call for list of hospitals
Red Cross	Incirlik	676-6927	24 hours daily

REST AND RECREATION

FACILITY/ACTIVITY	BLDG NO/LOC	PHONE	DAYS/COMMENTS
Bowling Lanes	2438	253	Daily
Craftshops			
Automotive	2054	249	W-Su
Ceramics	2054	249	W-Su
Wood	2054	249	W-Su
Equip/Gear Locker	2444	232	M-F
Gymnasium	2027	3176	Daily
Info Tour & Travel	2438	4247	M-F
Library	2018	3290	Daily
NCO Club	2029	3296	Daily
O'Club	Koroglu Cad, 123 Kankaya	N/A	Daily In Ankara
Picnic/Park Area	East Ankara	None	24 hours daily
Racket Courts	2027	3176	Daily
Recreation Center	2438	253/4247	Daily
Service Club	2438	253/4247	Daily
Special Services	2423	2127	M-F
Sport Field	Ankara AS	3176	Daily
Swimming Pool	2059	249	Call for hrs
Tennis Courts	Near 2001	3176	Daily
Theater	2001	249	F,Sa,Su
Track	2018	3176	Daily
Trails	Perimeter of AS	None	24 hours daily
Video Rental	2051	300	M-Sa

DIYARBAKIR AIRPORT (TU06R9)
(Pirinclik Air Station)
APO New York 09294-5000

TELEPHONE INFORMATION: Main installation numbers: Civ: 90-11913-1110. ATVN: 679-1110.

LOCATION: Diyarbakir Airport is located in southeast Turkey, 60 miles north of the Syrian border. NMC: Diyarbakir, 2 miles east.

GENERAL INSTALLATION INFORMATION: The 7022 ABS/LGT operates at Diyarbakir in support of TUSLOG detachments.

GENERAL CITY/REGIONAL INFORMATION: Located near the 2nd century capital of the Hittite Empire, Diyarbakir is surrounded by a fertile plain at the foot of the Anti-Taurus Mountains.

Diyarbakir Airport, continued

TURKEY

ADMINISTRATIVE SUPPORT

FACILITY/ACTIVITY	BLDG NO/LOC	PHONE	DAYS/COMMENTS
Duty Officer	On Base	1110	24 hours daily
Fire(Mil)	On Base	1110	24 hours daily
Police(Civ)	On Base	1110	24 hours daily

LOGISTICAL SUPPORT

FACILITY/ACTIVITY	BLDG NO/LOC	PHONE	DAYS/COMMENTS
Barber Shop(s)	On Base	N/A	M-Sa
Beauty Shop(s)	On Base	N/A	M-Sa
Exchange(Main)	On Base	N/A	M-Sa
Food(Snack/Fast)			
Baskin Robbins	On Base	N/A	Daily
Package Store	On Base	N/A	M-Sa
Space-A Air Ops	7022	1110	Daily

INCIRLIK AIR BASE (ADANA) (TU03R9)
APO New York 09289-5000

TELEPHONE INFORMATION: Main installation numbers: Civ: 90-71-119062//114228/110580/111285. ATVN: 676-1110. When dialing from a civilian phone, dial one of the main installation numbers listed above and ask the operator for the desired extension.

LOCATION: From Adana, located in southeast Turkey 30 miles north of the Mediterranean Sea, drive east on E-5 for three miles then turn left at the sign for Incirlik Air Base. NMC: Adana, 8 miles west.

GENERAL INSTALLATION INFORMATION: Incirlik (pronounced In-JUR-lik) is the largest American military center in Turkey and the only U.S. tactical air operation between Italy and the Far East. The 39th Tactical Group has been the senior American unit since 1958. The group is responsible for preparing and conducting air, support and tactical operations as directed by CINC/U.S. Air Forces—Europe. The air base maintains a peacetime commitment to air-crew training, war readiness and support to other NATO units within Turkey and the Middle East. Incirlik is a joint-user air base. The Turkish side of the base supports an air gunnery and bombardment support group and has a peacetime mission to direct Turkish fighter air-combat training operations.

The base boasts a number of new structures including a commissary, a gym, an elementary school and a consolidated support center.

GENERAL CITY/REGIONAL INFORMATION: Incirlik is located eight miles east of Adana, Turkey's fourth largest city, with a population of approximately 800,000. Adana, part of an old trade route, has been inhabited continuously for over 3,000 years. The city itself offers fine shopping on Attaturk Boulevard and in the Bazaar at Old Adana. Many famous historical sites are within a short distance of the base (fewer than 80 miles). These

TURKEY
Incirlik Air Base, continued

sites include the "Castle of Snakes" at Yilanikale, the mountain fortress at Karatepe and the medieval structures in Payas. Visitors to Tarsus, an hour west of the base, won't want to miss seeing St. Paul's Well, Cleopatra's Gate (where she and Marc Antony allegedly met), the Eski Cami (old mosque) and Uli Cami (grand mosque). Other popular attractions include the beach at Karatas 31 miles away; the major ports of Mersin and Iskenderun; and Antakaya, also known as the biblical city of Antioch, 120 miles away. The Mediterranean Sea is less than two hours away by car.

ADMINISTRATIVE SUPPORT

FACILITY/ACTIVITY	BLDG NO/LOC	PHONE	DAYS/COMMENTS
Advocate	966	6540	M-F
Customs/Duty	430	6295	M-F
	500	6726	M-F
Duty Officer	362	6376	24 hours daily
Fire(Mil)	370	6381	24 hours daily
Housing			
Family	952	5455/5207	M-F
Info(Insta)	475	113	24 hours daily
Inspector Gen'l	967	6347	M-F
Legal Assist	966	6540	M-F
Locator(Mil)	972	6289	M-F
		6516	After hours
Locator(Civ)	870	6578	M-F
	448 HNSI	3208	M-F
Personnel Spt	552	6876	M-F
Police(Mil)	1070	3200	24 hours daily
Police(Civ)	Adana (emerg)	C-055	24 hours daily
Public Affairs	3604	3217	M-F

LOGISTICAL SUPPORT

FACILITY/ACTIVITY	BLDG NO/LOC	PHONE	DAYS/COMMENTS
Auto Drivers Testing	433	3115	M-F
Auto Parts(Exch)	871	6655	W-Su
Auto Rent(Other)	Outside main gate		
Auto Sales	958	4355	M-Sa
Auto Ship(Gov)	430	6038	M-F
Auto Wash	871	6655	W-Su
Bakery	877	6588	M-Sa
Barber Shop(s)	958	6937	M-Sa
	952	6937	M-Sa
Beauty Shop(s)	957	6093	M-Sa
Bookstore	999	4155	Daily
Child Care/Dev Ctr	944	6553	Daily
Clothing Sales	912	6937	Daily
Commissary(Main)	877	6855/6937	Tu-Sa
Dry Clean(Gov)	484	6394	M-F
	883	6396	M-Sa
Education Center	870C	6046	M-F
Elec Repair(Gov)	1026	6849	Tu-Sa
Eng'r/Publ Works	967 TUSEG	3183	M-F
Exchange(Main)	912	6937	Daily
Food(Snack/Fast)	957	6053/6981	Daily

TURKEY

Incirlik Air Base, continued

Hot Dogs	Between 955/958	N/A	M-Sa
Pizza Parlor	5958	6993	Daily
Foodland	912	6053	Daily
Laundry(Self-Svc)	958	4355	24 hours daily
Package Store	955	6996	Tu-Sa
Photo Laboratory	311	6470	M-F
Postal Svcs(Mil)	870	6301	M-Sa
SATO	430	6763	M-F
Schools(DOD Dep)			
Elementary	870	6047	M-F (K-3)
Middle School	870	6047	M-F (4-6)
High School	870	6047	M-F (7-12)
Svc Stn(Insta)	487	None	Daily
Space-A Air Ops	500	6424	Daily
Pax Lounges(Gen'l)	500	6424	Daily
Protocol Svc	480	6347	M-F
Flights to:			Athinai Arpt GR; Balikesir Arpt TU; Cigli TAFB TU; Diyarbakir Arpt TU; Dover AFB DE; Esenboga Arpt TU; Eskisehir TUAF TU; Erhac TUAF TU; Erzurum Arpt TU; McGuire AFB NJ; RAF Mildenhall UK; Ramstein AB GE; Rhein-Main AB GE; Sigonella Arpt IT; Sinop AAF TU; Torrejon AB SP; Yesilkoy Arpt TU.
Tailor Shop	912	None	M-Sa
Taxi(Comm)	Outside main gate	6421	24 hours daily
Tel Booking Oper	475	0	24 hours daily
Tel Repair(Gov)	475	6312	24 hours daily
	Emergency repair	110	24 hours daily
Thrift Shop	870D	6247	M,W,F
TML			
Billeting	952/6th St	6709 C-119062	24 hours daily
TLF	1066	6709 C-119062	24 hours daily
VAQ/VOQ	7 buildings	6709 C-119062	24 hours daily
DV/VIP	1072	6709 C-119062	24 hours daily

HEALTH AND WELFARE

FACILITY/ACTIVITY	BLDG NO/LOC	PHONE	DAYS/COMMENTS
AF Family Svcs	1022	6178	M-F
AF Relief	1022	6178	M-F
Ambulance	3850	6666	24 hours daily
Central Appts	3850	6172	M-F
CHAMPUS Office	3850	6628	M-F
Chaplain	945	6441	M-F
		6376	After hours
Chapel	945	6441	Daily
Comm Drug/Alc Ctr	3850	6452	M-F
Dental Clinic	3850	6435	M-F
	Emergency	6666	After hours
Medical Emergency	3850	6666	24 hours daily
Mental Health	3850	3452	M-F

TURKEY
Incirlik Air Base, continued

Facility	BLDG	PHONE	Days/Comments
Poison Control	N/A	6666	24 hours daily
Red Cross	872	6927	M-F
		6376	After hours
Veterinary Svcs	590	3119	M-F

REST AND RECREATION

FACILITY/ACTIVITY	BLDG NO/LOC	PHONE	DAYS/COMMENTS
Amer Forces Ntwk	900	6421	24 hours daily
Bowling Lanes	914	6789	Daily
Craftshops			
Automotive	871	6655	W-Su
Ceramics	946	6051	W-Su
Multi-crafts	946	6051	W-Su
Enlisted Club	846	6010/6376	Daily
Equip/Gear Locker	970	6966	Daily
Golf Course	6	6249	Tu-Sa
Gymnasium	973	6966	Daily
Info Tour & Travel	970	6049	Tu-Sa
Library	968	6759	Daily
MARS	See Hellenikon Air Base listing.		
NCO Club	846	6010	Daily
	950	6967	Top three
O'Club	950	6967	Daily
Racket Courts	973	N/A	Daily
Recreation Center	970	6966	Daily
Riding Club	190	6595	Daily
Rod and Gun Club	866	6898	Daily
Special Services	854	6795	Daily
Swimming Pool	925	6598	Daily
Tennis Courts	Several on base		
Theater	954	6986	Call for schedule.
Video Rental	916	6953	Daily
	970	6966	Daily
Youth Center	3975	3546	Daily

ISTANBUL SUPPORT GROUP (TU09R9)
(Çakmakli Army Post)
(528th U.S. Army Artillery Group)
APO New York 09380-5000

TELEPHONE INFORMATION: Main installation numbers: Civ: 90-1-836-1448; ATVN: 672-1110 (Support Group), 671-9888 (Çakmakli AP). **Note:** for all facilities listed below, dial main numbers above and ask for facility.

LOCATION: Located in the city of Istanbul, Yesilkoy Airport is on the European side of the Bosphorus and the Mamarac Denizi some nine miles from Istanbul. HE: p-80, H/6. NMC: Istanbul, in the city.

GENERAL INSTALLATION INFORMATION: The 528th USAAG, OL-B/LGTT and the 7217th ABG provide support services to the Istanbul Military Community. A large construction project was completed early in 1989 and virtually all post facilities are new. **Note:** All Instanbul Support Group

U.S. Forces Travel & Transfer Guide Europe — 327

TURKEY

Istanbul Support Group, continued

facilities, except for the PX, commissary, S&S Bookstore and the consolidated club, are for the sole use of personnel assigned to the 528th. Access to the Post is very limited because of extreme security precautions taken by the Turkish Army Battalion that controls access to the Post. A military I.D. card may not be enough to get you on Post. Personnel on leave status and retirees should go to the 528th only in cases of emergency. **Note: the following abbreviation is used in this listing: AFX (ask for extension).**

GENERAL CITY/REGIONAL INFORMATION: Previously known as Constantinople, Istanbul is an ancient city located on the east and west banks of the Bosphorus River, the only ship passage between the Black Sea and the Mediterranean Sea.

ADMINISTRATIVE SUPPORT

FACILITY/ACTIVITY	BLDG NO/LOC	PHONE	DAYS/COMMENTS
Housing			Available only to assigned personnel. All tours are unaccompanied.
Legal Assist			One JAG lawyer and legal clerk on Post
Police(Mil)			Security provided by Turkish Army Battalion

LOGISTICAL SUPPORT

FACILITY/ACTIVITY	BLDG NO/LOC	PHONE	DAYS/COMMENTS
Barber Shop(s)	At Pick-up Point	AFX	Tu-Sa
Bookstore	On Post	AFX	Tu-Sa
Clothing Sales	In Exchange	AFX	Tu-Sa
Commissary(Main)	In Exchange	AFX	Tu-Sa
Dining Facility	On Post	AFX	Daily
Dry Clean(Exch)	At Pick-up Point	AFX	Tu-Sa
Education Center	On Post	AFX	M-F
Elec Repair(Civ)	On Post	AFX	Tu-Sa
Exchange(Main)	On Post	AFX	Tu-Sa
Finance(Mil)	On Post	AFX	Tu-Sa
Food(Snack/Fast)			
Baskin Robbins	In Bowling Alley	AFX	Daily
Burger Bar	At Consolidated Club	AFX	Daily
Pizza Parlor	In Bowling Alley	AFX	Daily
Foodland	In Exchange	AFX	Tu-Sa
Laundry(Exch)	At Pick-up Point	AFX	Tu-Sa
Package Store	In Exchange	AFX	Tu-Sa
Pick-up Point	On Post	AFX	Tu-Sa
Postal Svcs(Mil)	On Post	AFX	M-Sa
Space-A Air Ops	Yesilkoy Airport	C-573-9435	Daily
Flights to:	Incirlik TU.		
Tailor Shop	At Pick-up Point	AFX	Tu-Sa
Taxi(Comm)	Yesilkoy Airport	C-573-2315	Daily
Travel Agents	On Post	AFX	M,W

HEALTH AND WELFARE

FACILITY/ACTIVITY	BLDG NO/LOC	PHONE	DAYS/COMMENTS
Army Emerg Relief	On Post. Handled by S1/Adjutant.		

TURKEY
Istanbul Support Group, continued

Chaplain	On Post	AFX	Daily
Chapel	On Post	AFX	Daily
Medical Emergency	Troop Medical Center in Çakmakli for assigned personnel		
Red Cross	See Incirlik Air Base listing.		

REST AND RECREATION

FACILITY/ACTIVITY	BLDG NO/LOC	PHONE	DAYS/COMMENTS
Beach(es)	Thirty minutes away on the Sea of Marmara		
Bowling Lanes	On Post	AFX	Daily
Camping/RV Area	Civilian campground nearby		
Consolidated Club	On Post	AFX	Daily
Equip/Gear Locker	On Post	AFX	Daily
Gymnasium	On Post	AFX	Daily
Library	On Post	AFX	Daily
Racket Courts	On Post	AFX	Daily
Recreation Center	On Post	AFX	Daily
Sport Field	On Post	AFX	Daily
Swimming Pool	On Post	AFX	Daily
Tennis Courts	On Post	AFX	Daily
Theater	On Post	AFX	Daily
Track	On Post	AFX	Daily
Video Rental	At Exchange and Library		

IZMIR AIR STATION (TU04R9)
APO New York 09224-5000

TELEPHONE INFORMATION: Main installation numbers: Civ: 90-51-145360. ATVN: 675-1110. When calling Izmir from a civilian or a military phone, dial the main installation numbers listed above and ask for the desired extension.

LOCATION: In the center of the port city of Izmir on the central west coast of Turkey. HE: p-82, G/6. NMC: Izmir, in the city.

GENERAL INSTALLATION INFORMATION: The 7241st Air Base Group, a unit of the U.S. Air Force in Europe, is the host organization in Izmir. It operates within the civilian community rather than on a base and has two major NATO units—the 6th Allied Tactical Air Force (SIXATAF) and the Allied Land Forces Southeastern Europe (LSE).

In peacetime, SIXATAF has the primary mission of planning for the full-time air defense of Turkey, conducting technical evaluations of Turkish units and maintaining Turkish and external NATO forces at a high state of readiness. Its wartime mission is to conduct counter-air operations in defense of Turkey's land mass and to provide tactical air support to NATO land forces.

LSE, a NATO principal subordinate command, is responsible for conducting and coordinating military operations for three Turkish armies during wartime. LSE is also responsible for the preparation of operational plans for NATO exercises during peacetime.

U.S. Forces Travel & Transfer Guide Europe — 329

TURKEY

Izmir Air Station, continued

GENERAL CITY/REGIONAL INFORMATION: The third largest city in Turkey, Izmir is located on the west coast of the country, approximately 200 miles across the Aegean from Athens. The 2000 members of the American military community live and work among the 2,000,000 friendly Turkish residents of the city. The area around Izmir has a long and fascinating history. Within a short drive are a number of famous archaeological sites, such as the ancient cities of Ephesus, Pergamon, Priene, Miletos Didyma and Aphrodisias. Snow skiers will enjoy the mountain resort of Uludag. Sun and sea lovers will want to spend time at the beautiful beaches nearby.

ADMINISTRATIVE SUPPORT

FACILITY/ACTIVITY	BLDG NO/LOC	PHONE	DAYS/COMMENTS
Customs/Duty	48	3405	M-F
Duty Officer	48	3222	N/A
Fire(Mil)	48	117	24 hours daily
Info(Insta)	N/A	C-145360	N/A
Legal Assist	51	3345	M-F
Locator(Mil)	N/A	3431	M-F
Personnel Spt	48	3283/3306	M-F
Police(Mil)	51	3434	24 hours daily
Police(Civ)	Izmir	C-140990	24 hours daily
Public Affairs	48	3332	M-F

LOGISTICAL SUPPORT

FACILITY/ACTIVITY	BLDG NO/LOC	PHONE	DAYS/COMMENTS
Auto Registration	48	3210	M-F
Auto Sales	2	3368	Daily
Auto Wash	Bayrakli Park	5551	W-Su
Bakery	2	3204	Tu-Sa
Barber Shop(s)	Kordon Hotel	3379	M-Sa
	2	3318	M-Sa
Beauty Shop(s)	2	3318	M-Sa
Bookstore	47	3232	M-F
Child Care/Dev Ctr	14	3470	Su-F
Clothing Sales	2	3368	Tu-Su
Commissary(Main)	2	3398	Tu-Sa
Dining Facility	Kordon Hotel	N/A	24 hours daily
	Sultan Inn	N/A	Daily
Exchange(Main)	2	3368	Daily
Finance(Mil)	48	3225	M-F
Food(Snack/Fast)	14	3432	Daily
Baskin Robbins	2	3368	Daily
Pizza Parlor	2	3368	Daily
Foodland	2	3430	Daily
Laundry(Exch)	2	3368	Daily
Package Store	47	3303	Tu-Sa
Postal Svcs(Mil)	46	3409	M-Sa. Beside HS.
Schools(DOD Dep)			
Elementary	3	3478	M-F
High School	46	3209	M-F
Space-A Air Ops	Cigli TAB	C-3-9690 ext. 3442	Daily
Flights to:	Athinai Arpt GR; Balikesir Arpt TU; Esenboga Arpt		

TURKEY
Izmir Air Station, continued

TU; Eskisehir TUAF TU; Incirlik Arpt TU; Ramstein AB GE; Rhein-Main AB GE; Sigonella Arpt IT; Yesilkoy Arpt TU.

TML
Billeting	Kordon Hotel 190 Attaturk Caddesi	3379	24 hours daily
Travel Agents	N/A	3432	M-F

HEALTH AND WELFARE

FACILITY/ACTIVITY	BLDG NO/LOC	PHONE	DAYS/COMMENTS
AF Family Svcs	47	3249	M-F
Ambulance	5	3251	24 hours daily
Central Appts	5	3483	M-F
CHAMPUS Office	5	3843	M-F
Chaplain	48	3264	M-F
Chapel	Across from APO		
Dental Clinic	51	3308	M-F
Medical Emergency	5	3251	24 hours daily
Mental Health	5	3274	M-F
Poison Control	5	3251	24 hours daily
Red Cross	5	3251	Ask for rep.
Veterinary Svcs	51	3260	N/A

REST AND RECREATION

FACILITY/ACTIVITY	BLDG NO/LOC	PHONE	DAYS/COMMENTS
Bowling Lanes	6	3444	Daily
Consolidated Club	Kordon Hotel	3482	M-F
Craftshops			
Automotive	Bayrakli Park	5551	W-Su
Ceramics	14	3472	Daily
Multi-crafts	14	3472	Daily
Photography	14	3472	Daily
Wood	Bayrakli Park	5559	W-Su
Enlisted Club	Kordon Hotel	3482	F-Sa
Gymnasium	Bayrakli Park	N/A	Daily
Info Tour & Travel	Community Center	3432	M-F
Library	14	3440	Daily
NCO Club	Kordon Hotel	3482	Daily
O'Club	Kordon Hotel	3482	Daily
Outdoor Rec Ctr	Bayrakli Park	N/A	N/A
Recreation Center	14	3432	Daily
Skating Rink	Bayrakli Park	5558	F-Su
Sport Field	Bayrakli Park	None	Daily
Swimming Pool	Bayrakli Park	None	Daily
Theater	91	3240	Daily
Video Rental	2	3368	Daily
	14	3364	M-F
Youth Center	14	3387	M-Sa

U.S. Forces Travel & Transfer Guide Europe — 331

TURKEY

SINOP ARMY FIELD STATION (TU02R9)
APO New York 09133-5000

TELEPHONE INFORMATION: Main installation numbers: Civ: 90-3761-5431/5432. ATVN: 672-1110 (ask for Sinop).

LOCATION: Take the coastal highway west from Samsun until you reach Sinop. There are no major highways that connect Sinop to the rest of Turkey. There is daily bus service to Samsun (three hours), and Istanbul (12 hours). There is a community airport in Samsun. NMC: Samsun, 100 miles east.

GENERAL INSTALLATION INFORMATION: Sinop is an intelligence and security station.

GENERAL CITY/REGIONAL INFORMATION: Sinop is a small fishing village of 18,000 people on the south shore of the Black Sea. Founded in 1200 B.C., its museums contain artifacts from the Greek, Roman, Byzantine and Ottoman periods in Turkish history.

ADMINISTRATIVE SUPPORT

FACILITY/ACTIVITY	BLDG NO/LOC	PHONE	DAYS/COMMENTS
Duty Officer	On Station	0	24 hours daily
Info(Insta)	On Station	0	Daily
Inspector Gen'l	On Station	Ext. 349	Daily
Legal Assist	On Station	Ext. 349	Daily
Police(Mil)	On Station	Ext. 222	24 hours daily
Public Affairs	On Station	Ext. 209/334	M-F

LOGISTICAL SUPPORT

FACILITY/ACTIVITY	BLDG NO/LOC	PHONE	DAYS/COMMENTS
Bookstore	5-515	C-3761-1856 ext. 264	Tu-Sa
Exchange(Main)	On Station	Ext. 360	Tu-Sa
Food(Caf/Rest)	On Station	Ext. 267	Daily
Food(Snack/Fast)			
Baskin Robbins	On Station	Ext. 276	Daily
Foodland	On Station	Ext. 360	Daily
Space-A Air Ops	Army Air Field	C-90-3761-5431/32	Daily
Flights to:	Local Near East areas		
TML			
Billeting	S-512	EX-213	M-F
	DEH	EX-345	After hours
Guest House	Hotel Melia Kasim	EX-213	Daily

HEALTH AND WELFARE

FACILITY/ACTIVITY	BLDG NO/LOC	PHONE	DAYS/COMMENTS
Chaplain	On Station	Ext. 278/280	Daily
Medical Emergency	On Station	Ext. 331	24 hours daily

TURKEY
Sinop Army Field Station, continued

==
                         REST AND RECREATION
==
FACILITY/ACTIVITY	BLDG NO/LOC	PHONE	DAYS/COMMENTS
NCO Club	On Station	Ext. 363	Daily
O'Club	On Station	Ext. 223	Daily
Theater	On Station	Ext. 332	Daily
==

UNITED KINGDOM
United Kingdom of Great Britain and Northern Ireland
London

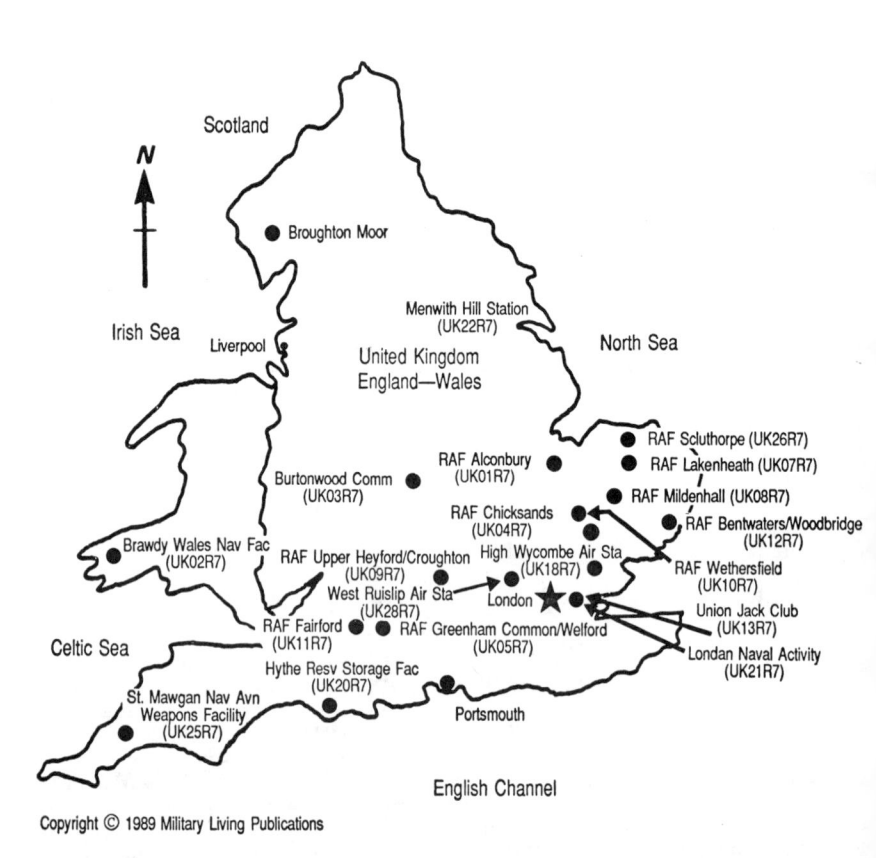

- Broughton Moor
- Menwith Hill Station (UK22R7)
- Liverpool
- United Kingdom England—Wales
- RAF Sculthorpe (UK26R7)
- RAF Lakenheath (UK07R7)
- RAF Alconbury (UK01R7)
- RAF Mildenhall (UK08R7)
- Burtonwood Comm (UK03R7)
- RAF Chicksands (UK04R7)
- RAF Bentwaters/Woodbridge (UK12R7)
- Brawdy Wales Nav Fac (UK02R7)
- RAF Upper Heyford/Croughton (UK09R7)
- High Wycombe Air Sta (UK18R7)
- RAF Wethersfield (UK10R7)
- West Ruislip Air Sta (UK28R7)
- London
- Union Jack Club (UK13R7)
- RAF Fairford (UK11R7)
- RAF Greenham Common/Welford (UK05R7)
- London Naval Activity (UK21R7)
- Hythe Resv Storage Fac (UK20R7)
- St. Mawgan Nav Avn Weapons Facility (UK25R7)
- Portsmouth

Irish Sea — North Sea — Celtic Sea — English Channel — Scotland

Copyright © 1989 Military Living Publications

UNITED KINGDOM

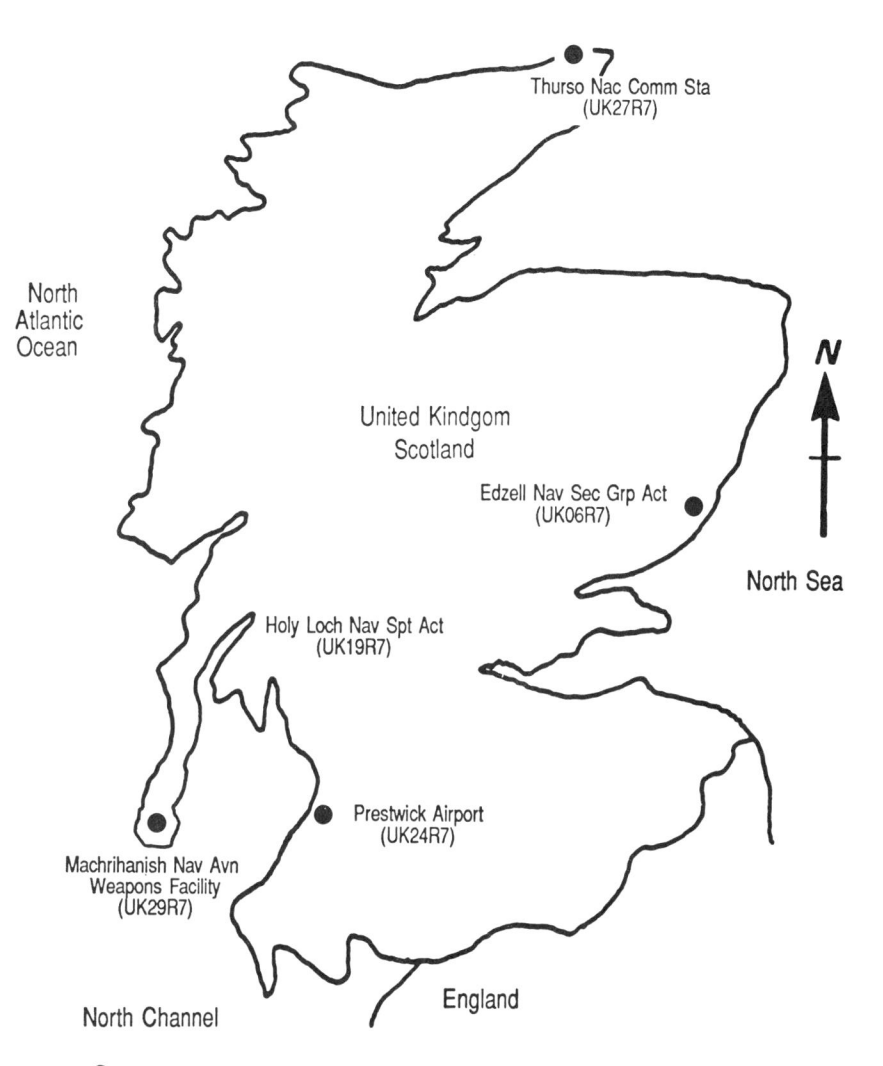

Map of Scotland showing:
- Thurso Nac Comm Sta (UK27R7)
- Edzell Nav Sec Grp Act (UK06R7)
- Holy Loch Nav Spt Act (UK19R7)
- Prestwick Airport (UK24R7)
- Machrihanish Nav Avn Weapons Facility (UK29R7)

Labels: North Atlantic Ocean, United Kindgom Scotland, North Sea, England, North Channel

Copyright © 1989 Military Living Publications

The U.K., consisting of England, Scotland, Wales and Northern Ireland, lies off the northwest coast of Europe. Its land mass is slightly smaller than Oregon. With 56.6 million people, it is one of the most densely populated countries in the world and is predominantely urban and suburban.

334 — *U.S. Forces Travel & Transfer Guide Europe*

UNITED KINGDOM

Languages are English, Welsh and Gaelic. The British government is a constitutional monarchy with suffrage for subjects and Irish Republican U.K. residents over age 18. The U.K. is energy rich with coal and significant North Sea oil and gas reserves. It is one of the world's great trading powers and its capital, London is an unmatched international finance center. A highly industrialized country, the U.K. both exports and imports machinery and transportation equipment, petroleum and services. Over 60 percent of the work force is employed in the services area. The currency is the *U.K. pound*. Since the U.K. is a maritime nation, it is totally accessible by sea. It is a major air and shipping crossroads to points worldwide. Rail and bus transportation is frequent with connections to Europe via ferry. Nearly all the U.K. has direct dial telephones for domestic and foreign calling. It is five hours ahead of U.S. EST. Climate is temperate, averaging 40° F. in winter, 60° F. in summer. Specialities include cashmere sweaters, china, linens, raincoats, soaps and antique silver. U.S.-U.K. relations are very close and friendly. TRAFFIC MOVES ON THE LEFT, PASSES ON THE RIGHT. The "London Planner," a monthly listing of theatrical, artistic and cultural events, is available from the British Tourist Authority.
ENTRY REQUIREMENTS: Passport—yes. Visa—not required for stay up to six months. Check with the Embassy of the United Kingdom, Washington, D.C. 20008, Tel: 202-462-1340. Immunizations—EUR.

RAF ALCONBURY (UK01R7)
APO New York 09238-5000

TELEPHONE INFORMATION: Main installation numbers: Civ: 44-0480-82-3000 (Huntingdon); 44-0733-83-3000 (Peterborough). ATVN: 223-3000. Civ prefix: 0480-____ (Huntingdon); 0733-____ (Peterborough). ATVN prefix: 223-XXXX. Civ to mil prefix: 0480-82-XXXX (Huntingdon); 0733-83-XXXX (Peterborough).

LOCATION: From London, take A-1 north to A-604 and the exit marked RAF Alconbury and follow signs. Located approximately 65 miles north of London. HE: p-13, D/3. NMC: Huntingdon, 4 miles east.

GENERAL INSTALLATION INFORMATION: The 10th Tactical Fighter Wing at RAF Alconbury is made up of two squadrons of A-10 aircraft that arrived from RAF Bentwaters in the summer of 1988. RAF Alconbury is also home to the 17th Reconnaissance Wing, which flies TR-1 high altitude surveillance/reconnaissance aircraft.

RAF Molesworth is located 20 miles north of Cambridge in Huntingdon. All support facilities for Molesworth are provided by RAF Alconbury. Main installation numbers for Molesworth are Civ: 44-0480-84-3000; ATVN: 268-3000.

GENERAL CITY/REGIONAL INFORMATION: RAF Alconbury is located in East Anglia, a large stretch of land that extends out into the North Sea on the east coast of the country just north of London. The area's name is derived from that of the Northern European people who invaded the area many centuries ago, the Angles, as is the name England itself, which evolved from the expression "Angle Land."

The countryside around RAF Alconbury is remarkably flat, affording views of spectacular sunrises and sunsets. Two small villages lie on opposite sides of the base, Great Stukeley and Little Stukeley. Great Stukeley consists of

U.S. Forces Travel & Transfer Guide Europe — 335

UNITED KINGDOM

RAF Alconbury, continued

Church End, which was the original settlement, Green End and Owl End. The church at Little Stukeley has a number of interesting wood carvings and its entrance is the tomb of the Reverend Joshua Waterhouse, who was murdered by his houseboy in 1827.

ADMINISTRATIVE SUPPORT

FACILITY/ACTIVITY	BLDG NO/LOC	PHONE	DAYS/COMMENTS
Fire(Mil)	88	2218	24 hours daily
Emergency		117	24 hours daily
Housing	659	3518/3519	M-F
Info(Insta)	N/A	113	24 hours daily
Inspector Gen'l	645	2212	M-F
Legal Assist	582	2535	M-F
Locator(Mil)	582	2565	24 hours daily
Personnel Spt	646	2808	M-F
Police(Mil)	511	2188/2815	24 hours daily
Emergency	On base	114	24 hours daily
	Off base	999	24 hours daily
Public Affairs	645	2174/2125	M-F

LOGISTICAL SUPPORT

FACILITY/ACTIVITY	BLDG NO/LOC	PHONE	DAYS/COMMENTS
Auto Drivers Testing	618	2878	M-F
Auto Repairs	596	3435	M-Sa
Auto Sales	Huntingdon	C-411824	M-F. AMC.
	Huntingdon	C-57630	M-F. Chrysler.
	Huntingdon	C-54140	M-F. Ford.
	Huntindon	C-50298	M-F. GM.
Auto Ship(Gov)	638	3641	M-F. Outbound.
	638	3357	M-F. Inbound.
Bank	582	2160	M-Sa
Barber Shop(s)	2	4236	M-Sa
Beauty Shop(s)	2	4236	M-Sa
Bookstore	699	2872	Daily
Child Care/Dev Ctr	700	3795	Daily
Clothing Sales	593	2272	M-Sa
Commissary(Main)	620	3639	Tu-Sa
Dining Facility	674	3610	Daily
Dry Clean(Exch)	651	2515	M-F
Education Center	507	2301/2525	M-F
Exchange(Main)	584	3432	Daily
Finance(Mil)	562	3783/3640	M-F
Food(Caf/Rest)	593	3246	M-Sa
Food(Snack/Fast)			
Burger King	585	3426	Daily
Pizza Parlor	678	3411	Daily
Foodland	585	3427	Daily
Package Store	660	2604	M-Sa
Photo Laboratory	591	2380	M-F
Postal Svcs(Mil)	502	2539	M-Sa
SATO-OS	638	HC-56426	M-F
Schools			
Elementary	693	3621	M-F

UNITED KINGDOM
RAF Alconbury, continued

Elementary	34 Upwood	4212	M-F
High School	691	3769	M-F
Svc Stn(Insta)	502	2539	M-Sa
Tailor Shop	584	HC-51046	Daily
Taxi(Comm)	N/A	2556 C-52131	24 hours daily
Thrift Shop	659	2700	N/A
TML			
Billeting	639	3670	24 hours daily
TLQ	628	3670	24 hours daily
DV/VIP	645	2111	Daily

HEALTH AND WELFARE

FACILITY/ACTIVITY	BLDG NO/LOC	PHONE	DAYS/COMMENTS
AF Family Svcs	633	2139	M-F
AF Relief	646	2808/2529	M-F
Ambulance	N/A	116	24 hours daily
Central Appts	AF Clinic	4507/4510	M-F
Chaplain	592	3343	M-F
	49	2203	After hours
Chapel	592	3343/2145	M-F
Comm Drug/Alc Ctr	647	2273	M-F
Comm Rel Advisor	W/Hq	2123	M-F
Dental Clinic	RAF Upwood	4850	M-F
Medical Emergency	RAF Upwood	4996	24 hours daily
Mental Health	RAF Upwood	4613	M-F
Poison Control	For American products, call and ask for the hospital. For HC-56131.		C-0638-52-2901/2226 British products, call 24 hours daily
Red Cross	573	2179/2189	M-F
	N/A	2121	After hours

REST AND RECREATION

FACILITY/ACTIVITY	BLDG NO/LOC	PHONE	DAYS/COMMENTS
Bowling Lanes	616	3682/2197	Daily
Craftshops			
Automotive	626	2701	Tu-Su
Multi-crafts	686	3734	Daily
Gymnasium	586	2744	Daily
Info Tour & Travel	678	3704	M-Sa
Library	678	2687	Daily
NCO Club	685	2353	Daily
O'Club	637	3382/2421	M-Sa
Recreation Center	678	3743	24 hours daily
Youth Center	679	2184/3604	Daily

UNITED KINGDOM

RAF BENTWATERS/WOODBRIDGE (UK12R7)
APO New York 09755-5000

TELEPHONE INFORMATION: Main installation numbers: Civ: 44-0394-43-3000. ATVN: 225-1110.

LOCATION: Take A-12 north from Ipswich to exit signs east on B-1069 to Melton to the twin bases of RAF Bentwaters/Woodbridge. HE: p-13, F.1. NMC: Ipswich, 15 miles southeast.

GENERAL INSTALLATION INFORMATION: Units at RAF Bentwaters/Woodbridge include in 81st Tactical Fighter Wing, the 39th Special Operations Wing—Woodbridge, the 527th Aggressor Squadron and the 2164th Communications Squadron. The mission of the 81st TFW is to support USAFE and NATO with A-10 attack aircraft. All facilities listed below are located at RAF Bentwaters unless otherwise noted. **Note: the following abbreviations are used in this listing only: BW (Bentwaters); WB (Woodbridge).**

GENERAL CITY/REGIONAL INFORMATION: The twin bases of RAF Bentwaters/Woodbridge are located in the county of Suffolk in East Anglia. The surrounding countryside is mainly agricultural. Nearby towns, such as Kersey and Lavenham, have remained relatively unchanged during the last five centuries. The ruins of castles at Oxford and Framlingham and the fully restored windmill at Saxstead Green are a short drive from the bases and are open to the public.

The larger cities of Colchester, Norwich and Cambridge are all less than two hours by car from the bases. Colchester is the oldest town in England and has many relics from its Roman history. Cambridge is home to the famous university. Norwich offers good shopping, a castle museum, a cathedral and an open air market.

ADMINISTRATIVE SUPPORT

FACILITY/ACTIVITY	BLDG NO/LOC	PHONE	DAYS/COMMENTS
Customs/Duty	62	2608	M-F
Fire (Mil)	557	117 C-420217	24 hours daily
Fire (Civ)	N/A	999	24 hours daily
Housing	160	2652	M-F
Info (Insta)	On Base	113	24 hours daily
Inspector Gen'l	89	3941	M-F
Legal Assist	33	2181	M-F
Locator (Civ)	164	2553	M-F
Personnel Spt	53	2635	M-F
Police (Mil)	679	C-420214	24 hours daily
Emergency	679	114	24 hours daily
Public Affairs	128	2381	M-F

LOGISTICAL SUPPORT

FACILITY/ACTIVITY	BLDG NO/LOC	PHONE	DAYS/COMMENTS
Auto Drivers Testing	32	2378	M-F

UNITED KINGDOM
RAF Bentwaters/Woodbridge, continued

Auto Parts(Exch)	233	C-420354	M-F
Auto Registration	53	2345	M-F
Auto Rental(Exch)	343	2968	M-F
Auto Sales	514	C-420356	M-F
Auto Ship(Gov)	529	2668/2669	M-F
Bank	222	2662	M-Sa
Barber Shop(s)	BW	2786	M-F
	722	6570	M-F
	162	2862	M-F
Beauty Shop(s)	162	2680	M-Sa
Bookstore	241	2938	N/A
	730	6657	N/A
Child Care/Dev Ctr	161	2548	M-F
Clothing Sales	456	2338	Daily
Commissary(Main)	521	2269	Tu-Sa
Credit Union	762	2737	M-F
Dry Clean(Exch)	141	C-420210	Daily
Education Center	452	2566	M-F
	579	6409	M-F
Elec Repair(Civ)	N/A	C-0206-564254	24 hours daily
Exchange(Main)	515	2867	Daily
Finance(Mil)	111	2149	M-F
Food(Snack/Fast)	776	C-420223	Daily
	747	2798	24 hours daily
Foodland	776	C-420306	Daily
	720/WB	C-461263	Daily
Laundry(Exch)	141	C-420210	Daily
Laundry(Self-Svc)	150	C-420365	Daily
Motor Pool	593	2725	M-F
Package Store	150	2257	Daily
	110/WB	6472	Daily
Photo Laboratory	544	2612	M-F
Postal Svcs(Mil)	59	2959	M-F
	22/WB	6458	M-F
SATO-OS	529	2962 C-420136	M-F
Schools(DOD Dep)	579	6409	M-F
Elementary	738	6655	M-F
High School	579	6665	M-F
Svc Stn(Insta)	775	2675	M-Sa
Space-A Air Ops	60	2328/2663	Daily
Flights to:	Ahlhorn GAFB GE; Leipheim GAFB GE; RAF Mildenhall UK; Norvenich GAFB GE; Sembach AB GE.		
Taxi(Comm)	140	2909 C-420232	24 hours daily
Tel Booking Oper	N/A	112	24 hours daily
Tel Repair(Gov)	128	118	M-F
Thrift Shop	163	2772	M-Sa
TML			
Billeting	629	2281/2837	24 hours daily
BOQ	629	2281/2837	24 hours daily
TLF	Quonset Huts	2281/2837	24 hours daily
VAQ	759	2281/2837	24 hours daily

U.S. Forces Travel & Transfer Guide Europe — 339

UNITED KINGDOM
RAF Bentwaters/Woodbridge, continued

Travel Agents 341 2642 M-F

HEALTH AND WELFARE

FACILITY/ACTIVITY	BLDG NO/LOC	PHONE	DAYS/COMMENTS
AF Family Svcs	240	2216	M-F
AF Relief	53	2141	M-F
Ambulance	N/A	116	24 hours daily
Central Appts	523	2756	M-F
CHAMPUS Office	523	2147	M-F
Chapel	153	2710	M-F
Comm Drug/Alc Ctr	529	2707	M-F
Dental Clinic	523	2712 C-420435	M-F
Medical Emergency	523	2574 C-420418	24 hours daily
Mental Health	523	2225	M-F
Red Cross	529,30	2120/2204	24 hours daily

REST AND RECREATION

FACILITY/ACTIVITY	BLDG NO/LOC	PHONE	DAYS/COMMENTS
Bowling Lanes	747	2798	24 hours daily
	581/WB	6675	24 hours daily
Craftshops			
Automotive	518	2220	M-Sa
Electronics	582	2775	M-F
Multi-crafts	500	6190	M-F
Wood	105	6434	M-Sa
Enlisted Club	194	2659	M-Sa
Gymnasium	766	2385	M-Sa
Info Tour & Travel	See Recreation Center.		
Library	210	2691	Daily
NCO Club	453	2659	Daily
O'Club	172	2979	Daily
Recreation Center	145	2999	Daily
Rod and Gun Club	597	2371	Daily
Special Services	525	2767	M-F
Theater	745	2871	Call for schedule.
Video Rental	517	2653	M-Sa
Youth Center	576	6115	M-F

BRAWDY WALES NAVAL FACILITY (UK02R7)
(Wales)
FPO New York 09519-5000

TELEPHONE INFORMATION: Main installation numbers: Civ: 44-0437-720654. ATVN: 391-4356 (from USA); 236-7540 (from Europe). Note: all calls to Brawdy Wales are routed through the central switchboard.

LOCATION: From Haverford West take UK A-487 for about ten miles northwest. Follow signs for RAF Brawdy. The naval facility is located adjacent

UNITED KINGDOM
Brawdy Wales Naval Facility, continued

to the RAF Base. HE: p-12, C/2. NMC: Swansea, 60 miles southeast.

GENERAL INSTALLATION INFORMATION: Brawdy Wales is a small naval shore facility operating primarily in support of oceanographic research.

GENERAL CITY/REGIONAL INFORMATION: Brawdy Wales is located acorss the Irish Sea from Ireland in the green Welsh countryside amidst ancient castles and manor houses. Large sheep and dairy farms lie to the north of the facility.

ADMINISTRATIVE SUPPORT

FACILITY/ACTIVITY	BLDG NO/LOC	PHONE	DAYS/COMMENTS
Customs/Duty	On Base	C-720654	M-F
Duty Officer	On Base	C-720654	24 hours daily
Fire(Mil)	RAF Base	C-764571	24 hours daily
Fire(Civ)	Off Base	C-0437-3355	24 hours daily
Housing	On Base	C-720654	M-F
Legal Assist	On Base	C-720654	M-F
Locator(Mil)	On Base	C-720654	24 hours daily
Personnel Spt	On Base	C-720654	M-F
Police(Mil)	RAF Base	C-764571	24 hours daily
Emergency	RAF Base	C-764571	24 hours daily
Police(Civ)	Off Base	C-0437-3355	24 hours daily
Public Affairs	On Base	C-720654	M-F

LOGISTICAL SUPPORT

FACILITY/ACTIVITY	BLDG NO/LOC	PHONE	DAYS/COMMENTS
Audio/Photo Ctr	On Base	C-720654	Tu-Sa
Bank	PSD Bldg	C-720654	M,Tu,Th,F
Barber Shop(s)	On Base	C-720654	M,Tu,Th
Clothing Sales	On Base	C-720654	N/A
Commissary(Annex)	On Base	C-720654	N/A
Credit Union	On Base	C-720654	N/A
Dining Facility	RAF Base	C-720654	N/A
Eng'r/Publ Works	On Base	C-720654	N/A. Seabee Det.
Exchange(Annex)	RAF Base	C-720654	N/A
Finance(Mil)	On Base	C-720654	N/A
Food(Snack/Fast)	On Base	C-720654	N/A
Burger Bar	On Base	C-720654	N/A
Pizza Parlor	On Base	C-720654	N/A
Package Store	On Base	C-720654	N/A
Parking	Limited on Base		
Pick-up Point	On Base	None	N/A
Postal Svcs(Mil)	On Base	C-720654	M-F
Postal Svcs(Civ)	On Base	C-720654	M-F
Railroad/RTO	Ten miles east in Haverfordwest		
Svc Stn(Insta)	On Base	C-720654	Tu-Sa
TML			
BEQ	RAF Base	C-720654	Singles only
BOQ	RAF Base	C-720654	Singles only
Travel Agents	On Base	C-720858	N/A

Brawdy Wales Naval Facility, continued

HEALTH AND WELFARE

FACILITY/ACTIVITY	BLDG NO/LOC	PHONE	DAYS/COMMENTS
Ambulance	RAF Base	C-764571	24 hours daily
Chaplain	On Base	C-720654	M-F
Chapel	RAF Base	C-720654	Su
Dental Clinic	RAF Base	C-720654	M-F
Medical Emergency	RAF Base	C-764571	24 hours daily
Navy Relief	On Base	C-720654	N/A
Poison Control	RAF Base	C-764571	24 hours daily

REST AND RECREATION

FACILITY/ACTIVITY	BLDG NO/LOC	PHONE	DAYS/COMMENTS
Beach(es)	Two miles from facility		
Bowling Lanes	On Base	C-720654	Daily
Craftshops			
Automotive	RAF Base	C-720654	N/A
Ceramics	RAF Base	C-720654	N/A
Enlisted Club	RAF Base	C-720654	N/A
Equip/Gear Locker	On Base	C-720654	N/A
Gymnasium	On Base	C-720654	N/A
Info Tour & Travel	On Base	C-720654	N/A
Library	RAF Base	C-720654	N/A
NCO Club	RAF Base	C-720654	N/A
O'Club	RAF Base	C-720654	N/A
Racket Courts	RAF Base	C-720654	N/A
Riding Club	In Haverfordwest		
Sport Field	RAF Base	C-720654	Daily
Tennis Courts	RAF Base	C-720654	Daily
Theater	RAF Base	C-720654	N/A
Video Rental	RAF Base	C-720654	N/A
Water Recreation	Beaches nearby		

BURTONWOOD COMMUNITY (UK03R7)
APO New York 09075-5000

TELEPHONE INFORMATION: Main installation numbers: Civ: 44-0925-36611 (Burtonwood); 44-291-420235 (RSAC); 44-421-43252 (RSAH). ATVN: 243-1110 (Burtonwood; ask for RSAC or RSAH).

LOCATION: Near Warrington, Cheshire. Exit Motorway 62 at the Burtonwood Service Area. NMC: Liverpool, 17 mi W. HE: p-11, B/4.

GENERAL INSTALLATION INFORMATION: Burtonwood is the headquarters for the 47th Area Support Group. The mission of the Group is to receive, inspect, classify, store, maintain, issue and rotate supplies. **NOTE: the following abbreviations are used in this listing: AFX (ask for extension);** RSAC (Reserve Storage Activity Caerwent); RSAH (Reserve Storage Activity Hythe).

UNITED KINGDOM
Burtonwood Community, continued

A Reserve Storage Activity is located at RSA Caerwent (RSAC), 163 miles from the Burtonwood Military Community. Caerwent is located in South Wales, 11 miles est of Newport and five miles east of Chepstow.

Reserve Storage Activity Hythe (RSAH) is the depot activity for the USAREUR Marine Fleet and Activity Fleet. Hythe is west of Southampton in New Forest accessible by sea or the B-3053 road. It is 89 miles south of London and 236 miles southeast of the Burtonwood Military Community.

GENERAL CITY/REGIONAL INFORMATION: USMCA Burtonwood is located 2 miles from the town of Warrington (pop. 65,000) in an area known for its heavy industry, particularly wire manufacturing. Although Warrington can provide for your immediate shopping needs, the cities of Chester, Manchester and Liverpool, all within 20 miles, offer a much greater variety of shopping and entertainment facilities. In addition, North Wales and the Lake District of England are both within a two-hour drive. Northwest beaches are only an hour away and Scotland is a pleasant and picturesque 10-hour drive from Burtonwood. Temperatures average 70° during the summer and 40° during the winter. Be prepared for wet weather in the fall and winter.

ADMINISTRATIVE SUPPORT

FACILITY/ACTIVITY	BLDG NO/LOC	PHONE	DAYS/COMMENTS
Duty Officer	Main Bldg	1110	24 hours daily
Public Affairs	Main Bldg	Ext. 310	M-F

LOGISTICAL SUPPORT

FACILITY/ACTIVITY	BLDG NO/LOC	PHONE	DAYS/COMMENTS
Child Care/Dev Ctr	500 A&B	Ext. 357	M-F
Exchange(Main)	On Base	AFX	M-Sa
Package Store	On Base	AFX	M-Sa
Pick-up Point	On Base	AFX	M-Sa
Postal Svcs(Mil)	On Base	AFX	M-Sa
Schools(DOD Dep)			
Elementary	Local schools		
High School	Local schools		
Svc Stn(Insta)	On Base	AFX	M-Sa
	RSAC	AFX	M-F
TML			
Billeting	Header House	Ext. 320/319	M-F
	SDNCO at Gate 12	N/A	After hours
BEQ/BOQ	RSAC	AFX	Daily
VOQ	505A	Ext. 320/319	M-F
DV/VIP	PAO	Ext. 310	M-F

HEALTH AND WELFARE

FACILITY/ACTIVITY	BLDG NO/LOC	PHONE	DAYS/COMMENTS
Ambulance	On Base	Ext. 999	24 hours daily
Army Comm Svcs	On Base	Ext. 299	M-F
Chapel	On Base	AFX	Daily
Dental Clinic	Upper Heyford		

UNITED KINGDOM

Burtonwood Community, continued

Medical Emergency   Local hospital

REST AND RECREATION

FACILITY/ACTIVITY	BLDG NO/LOC	PHONE	DAYS/COMMENTS
Bowling Lanes	On Base	AFX	Daily
Craftshops			
Automotive	244	Ext. 357	Tu,Th
Multi-craft	244	Ext. 357	Tu,Th
Gymnasium	Main Bldg	Ext. 217	Daily
Library	523A	Ext. 244	Evenings
Tennis	On Base	AFX	Daily
Theater	On Base	AFX	Call for schedule.
Youth Center	501A&B	Ext. 313	M-F

RAF CHICKSANDS (UK04R7)
APO New York 09193-5000

TELEPHONE INFORMATION: Main installation numbers: Civ: 44-0462-812571 extension 400. ATVN: 234-1110. Note: civilian numbers listed below are extensions of the main base civilian number.

LOCATION: From London take M-1 north to Luton, A-6 north to A-507 or A-600 to Shefford. Both A-507 and A-600 pass one of the RAF Checksands gates: HE: p-13, D/1. NMC: Bedford, 10 miles northwest.

GENERAL INSTALLATION INFORMATION: Host unit at RAF Chicksands is the 7247th Air Base Group. Other units at Chicksands include 6950th Electronic Security Group, the 2112th Communications Squadron and the 7025th Air Postal Squadron. NOTE: the following abbreviations are used in this listing only: AFX (ask for extension).

GENERAL CITY/REGIONAL INFORMATION: In 1086 the Norman-French conqueror of England, William I, ordered a systematic survey of lands and properties in all of England. Chicksands appears in the document that resulted, the Domesday Book, consisting at that time of two manors. One was given to the nuns and canons of the Gilbertine Order in 1150. In 1538, when King Henry VIII broke with the Catholic Church and declared himself head of the new Church of England, he abolished the monasteries and seized control of many church properties, including those at Chicksands. The king then granted the estate to the Osborne family, in whose possession it remained until a few years before World War II when it again became government property. In 1939 RAF Chicksands was activated.

The base is only 45 miles from London and ten miles from Bedford. A number of mid-sized and small towns lie within a ten mile radius of the base, all in a rural setting with a landscape dotted by farms and fields.

ADMINISTRATIVE SUPPORT

FACILITY/ACTIVITY	BLDG NO/LOC	PHONE	DAYS/COMMENTS
Duty Officer	250	C-285/291	24 hours daily

UNITED KINGDOM
RAF Chicksands, continued

Fire(Mil)	250	C-555	24 hours daily
Housing			
Family	400	AFX	M-F
Legal Assist	250	C-528	M-F
Public Affairs	250	C-374	M-F

LOGISTICAL SUPPORT

FACILITY/ACTIVITY	BLDG NO/LOC	PHONE	DAYS/COMMENTS
Auto Rental(Exch)	Beside exchange	AFX	M-Sa
Auto Sales	Beside exchange	AFX	M-Sa
Barber Shop(s)	Beside exchange	AFX	By appointment
Beauty Shop(s)	Beside exchange	AFX	By appointment
Bus	From Dining Facility to Bldg 600		
Child Care/Dev Ctr	795	AFX	Daily
Commissary(Annex)	354	AFX	N/A
Credit Union	121	C-486	M-F
Dining Facility	414	AFX	Daily
Dry Clean(Exch)	Beside exchange	AFX	M-Sa
Education Center	232	AFX	M-F
Eng'r/Publ Works	250	C-310	Daily
Exchange(Main)	357	AFX	M-Sa
Exchange(Annex)	301	AFX	M-Sa
Finance(Mil)	250	C-425	M-F
Food(Snack/Fast)	407	AFX	Daily
Burger Bar	407	AFX	Daily
Foodland	Beside exchange	AFX	M-Sa
Laundry(Exch)	Beside exchange	AFX	M-Sa
Laundry(Self-Svc)	Beside exchange	AFX	M-Sa
Motor Pool	N/A	C-223/361	Daily
Package Store	359	AFX	M-Sa
Postal Svcs(Mil)	125	C-350	M-Sa
Schools(DOD Dep)			
Elementary	On Base	AFX	M-F
Svc Stn(Insta)	135	AFX	M-Sa
TML			
Billeting	400	2400	M-F
		C-403	
		C-429	After hours
Guest House	403	C-400/476	Daily

HEALTH AND WELFARE

FACILITY/ACTIVITY	BLDG NO/LOC	PHONE	DAYS/COMMENTS
AF Family Svcs	251	C-571	M-F
AF Relief	250	AFX	M-F
Central Appts	100	C-317	M-F
Chapel	360	C-338	Daily
Comm Rel Advisor	250	AFX	M-F
Dental Clinic	106	C-216	M-F
Medical Emergency	100	C-999	24 hours daily
Red Cross	See RAF Alconbury listing.		

RAF Chicksands, continued

UNITED KINGDOM

REST AND RECREATION

FACILITY/ACTIVITY	BLDG NO/LOC	PHONE	DAYS/COMMENTS
Bowling Lanes	408	AFX	Daily
Craftshops			
Automotive	138	AFX	Daily
Gymnasium	340	267	Daily
Library	325	267	Daily
O'Club	431	170	M-F
Recreation Center	380	267	Daily
Rod and Gun Club	429	267	Call for hours.
Theater	330	267	Daily
Video Rental	Beside exchange	AFX	Daily
Youth Center	On Base	AFX	M-Sa

EDZELL NAVAL SECURITY GROUP ACTIVITY (UK06R7)
(Scotland)
FPO New York 09518-5000

TELEPHONE INFORMATION: Main installation numbers: Civ: 44-356-4431. ATVN: 229-1110.

LOCATION: From Aberdeen, take A-92 to A-94 south, follow Perth-Dundee signs. Last town before Edzell is Lawrencekirk. Look for RAF Edzell signs to base. HE: p-6, G/6. NMC: Aberdeen, 40 miles north.

GENERAL INSTALLATION INFORMATION: Edzell U.S. Naval Security Group Activity is located at RAF Edzell in the northeastern part of Scotland. The mission of the command is High Frequency Direction Finding and provision of communications support including communications relay, communications security and communications manpower assistance to Navy and other Department of Defense elements within the area. **NOTE: the following abbreviation is used in this listing: AFX (ask for extension).**

GENERAL CITY/REGIONAL: Because of Edzell's proximity to the sea and the mountains, temperatures average in the mid 50's and rarely exceed 70°. The city's main special attraction is Edzell Castle, built in the 16th century and renowned for its beautiful gardens. The surrounding region offers visitors a wealth of interesting sights, including museums, art galleries, churches, castles, parks, gardens and nature trails.

ADMINISTRATIVE SUPPORT

FACILITY/ACTIVITY	BLDG NO/LOC	PHONE	DAYS/COMMENTS
Duty Officer	1	232	24 hours daily
Fire (Mil)	1	222	24 hours daily
Legal Assist	6	236	M-F
Locator (Mil)	1	336/351	M-F
Personnel Spt	1	240	M-F
Police (Mil)	1	208	24 hours daily

UNITED KINGDOM
Edzell Naval Security Group Activity, continued

Police(Civ)	Edzell	208	24 hours daily
Public Affairs	22	337	M-F

LOGISTICAL SUPPORT

FACILITY/ACTIVITY	BLDG NO/LOC	PHONE	DAYS/COMMENTS
Bank(of Scotland)	32	472	Sub-branch
Barber Shop(s)	25	268	M-Sa
Beauty Shop(s)	25	268	M-Sa
Bookstore	80	297	Tu-Sa
Child Care/Dev Ctr	6	262	M-F
Commissary(Main)	25	301	Tu-Sa(base-assigned personnel only)
Credit Union	Navy Federal	AFX	M-F
Dining Facility	94	AFX	M-F
Education Center	77	AFX	M-F
Eng'r/Publ Works	69	AFX	Daily
Exchange(Main)	25	271/372	Tu-Sa
Exchange(Annex)	97	271	Tu-Sa
Finance(Mil)	77	209	M-F
Food(Caf/Rest)	N/A	253	Daily
Food(Snack/Fast)	25	270	Daily
Foodland	97	329	Daily
Laundry(Self-Svc)	Nr Navy Lodge	AFX	Daily
Motor Pool	62	AFX	Daily
Package Store	25	AFX	Tu-Sa
Postal Svcs(Mil)	76	AFX	M-Sa
Schools(DOD Dep)			
Elementary	Halsey Amer	AFX	M-F
High School	Aberdeen Amer	AFX	M-F
Svc Stn(Insta)	132	273	Daily
TML			
Billeting	Campbell Hall	218	24 hours daily
BEQ	333	218	24 hours daily
BOQ	Off Open Mess	218	24 hours daily
Guest House	Navy Lodge	251	M-Sa
DV/VIP	22(PAO)	337	M-F

HEALTH AND WELFARE

FACILITY/ACTIVITY	BLDG NO/LOC	PHONE	DAYS/COMMENTS
Central Appts	93	265	24 hours daily
CHAMPUS Office	93	264	M-F
Chaplain	3	201/275	Daily
Dental Clinic	93	267	M-F
Medical Emergency	93	266	24 hours daily
Navy Fam Svcs	N/A	350	M-F

REST AND RECREATION

FACILITY/ACTIVITY	BLDG NO/LOC	PHONE	DAYS/COMMENTS
Bowling Lanes	N/A	274	Daily
Consolidated Club	113	237	Daily

Edzell Naval Security Group Activity, continued

UNITED KINGDOM

Craftshops			
Automotive	88	328	M-Sa
Ceramics	88	278	M-Sa
Enlisted Club(E1-E6)	96	298/252	Daily
Golf Course	Driving range		
Gymnasium	25	AFX	Daily
Info Tour & Travel	97	338/9	M-F
Library	77	309	M-F
Outdoor Rec Ctr	97	338/9	Daily
Recreation Center	N/A	379	Daily
Rod and Gun Club	19	AFX	Daily
Tennis Courts	88	AFX	Daily
Theater	25	274	F-W
Youth Center	111	AFX	M-Sa

===

RAF FAIRFORD (UK11R7)
APO New York 09125-5000

TELEPHONE INFORMATION: Main installation numbers: Civ: 44-0285-71-4110. ATVN: 247-1110. Civ prefix: 0285-XXXX. ATVN prefix: 247-XXXX. Civ to mil prefix: 0638-71-XXXX.

LOCATION: Take A419 north out of Swindon to A417, turn right onto A417 and continue into the village of Fairford. Turn right on the road marked Welford in town. The base is one half mile up Welford Road. HE: p-13, B/12. NMC: Oxford, 18 miles east.

GENERAL INSTALLATION INFORMATION: Since 1979, the 7020th Air Base Group has been the host unit at RAF Fairford. The Group's mission is to provide for the operation and support of the 11th Strategic Group flying missions and to provide support for other associate units. Four squadrons come under the Group: the 7020th Headquarters Squadron; the 7020th Civil Engineering Squadron; the 7020th Security Police Squadron; and the 7020th Supply Squadron. The 66th Contingency Hospital at RAF Little Rissington, 25 miles north, also comes under the Group.

GENERAL CITY/REGIONAL INFORMATION: The ruins of the Chedworth Roman Villa near Fairford indicate that, as far back as 300 A.D., its occupants enjoyed such comforts as under-floor heating, beautiful mosaic floors and elaborate systems of hot, warm and cold baths. The village of Fairford, one half mile north, is a charming old market town. The magnificent stained-glass windows of the town's church are said to be the finest of their period in all of England.

Cirencester, 10 miles west, boasts a variety of shops and its Cornium Museum houses one of the country's more impressive collections of Roman relics. Railroad buffs will want to visit the Great Western Railroad Museum in Swindon, 13 miles south. Swindon also has an excellent shopping center, theater, cinema and leisure center. On the sporting side, Swindon has professional football and basketball, a municipal golf course and greyhound and speedway racing.
===

UNITED KINGDOM
RAF Fairford, continued

ADMINISTRATIVE SUPPORT

FACILITY/ACTIVITY	BLDG NO/LOC	PHONE	DAYS/COMMENTS
Advocate	2	4256	M-F
Customs/Duty	29	4259/4999	As needed
Fire(Mil)	31	4191	24 hours daily
Fire(Civ)	Off Base	C-999	24 hours daily
Housing	13	4224/4228	M-F
Info(Insta)	On Base	1110	M-F
Inspector Gen'l	2	4200	M-F
Legal Assist	2	4256	M-F
Locator(Mil)	2	4248	M-F
Personnel Spt	1	4222	M-F
Police(Mil)	491	4226	24 hours daily
Emergency	491	114	24 hours daily
Police(Civ)	Fairford	C-999	24 hours daily
Public Affairs	2	4822	M-F

LOGISTICAL SUPPORT

FACILITY/ACTIVITY	BLDG NO/LOC	PHONE	DAYS/COMMENTS
Auto Drivers Testing	25	4210	Call on Tu.
Auto Parts(Exch)	Auto Hobby Shop	None	Sa
Auto Registration	1	4220	M-F
Auto Rental(Exch)	Chapel parking lot	4375	M-Sa
Auto Rent(Other)	Swindon	C-38833	24 hours daily
Auto Repairs	80	4967	M-Sa
Bank	157	4913	M-Sa
Barber Shop(s)	490	4102	M-Sa
Beauty Shop(s)	490	4166	M-Sa
Bookstore	157	2511	M-Sa
Bus	84	4210	Call for schedule.
Child Care/Dev Ctr	163	4971	Daily
Clothing Sales	21	4926	M-F
Commissary(Main)	669	4924	Tu-Sa
Credit Union	159	2747 ext. 323	M-F
Dining Facility	581	4218	Daily
Dry Clean(Exch)	490	3594	M-Sa
Dry Clean(Gov)	581	4962	M-F
Education Center	181	4919	M-F
Eng'r/Publ Works	15	4974	M-F
Exchange(Main)	156	4911/4114	Daily
Exchange(Concess)	Black Knight	3214	M-Sa
Finance(Mil)	2	4976/4237	M-F
Food(Caf/Rest)	581	4218	Daily
Food(Snack/Fast)	490	4367	Daily
Baskin Robbins	490	4367	Daily
McFairford's	490	4367	Daily
Pizza Parlor	179	4293	M-F
Foodland	490	4115	Daily
	RAF Little Rissington	C-77331	Daily

UNITED KINGDOM

RAF Fairford, continued

Laundry(Self-Svc)	Between Sky-tanker Lanes & the Sterling Hs	N/A	24 hours daily
Motor Pool	84	4210	Call for schedule.
Package Store	153	4923	Tu-Sa
Postal Svcs(Mil)	66	4910	M-F
SATO-OS	29	4383	N/A
Schools(DOD Dep)	In Fairford:		
Elementary	625	4104	M-F (K-8)
High School	See RAF Greenham Commom listing.		
	In Little Rissington:		
Elementary		C-77278	M-F (K-8)
High School	See RAF Upper Heyford/Croughton listing.		
Svc Stn(Insta)	80	4967	Daily
Space-A Air Ops	29	4864	M-F and during flight processing
Pax Lounges(Gen'l)	29	4864	M-F. Limited.
	Note: retirees are not allowed Space-A privileges into or out of RAF Fairford.		
Flights to:	Pease AFB NH; Lajes AB PO. Unscheduled flights to major SAC bases in CONUS.		
Taxi(Comm)	662	C-714015	24 hours daily
Tel Booking Oper	See RAF Upper Heyford/Croughton listing.		
Tel Repair(Gov)	1202	4155	
Thrift Shop	147	N/A	M,W,F
TML			
Billeting	551	2784/4272	24 hours daily
TLF	551/552/593	4886	24 hours daily
DV/VIP	2	4200	M-F
Travel Agents	157	4358	M-F

HEALTH AND WELFARE

FACILITY/ACTIVITY	BLDG NO/LOC	PHONE	DAYS/COMMENTS
AF Family Svcs	476	4965	M-F
AF Relief	1	4222	M-F
Ambulance	N/A	116	24 hours daily
Central Appts	540/546	4179/4180	M-F
CHAMPUS Office	546	4131	M-F
Chapel	662	4833/4216	M-F
	43/Little Rissington	N/A	Sa,Su
Comm Rel Advisor	On Base	4256	M-F
Dental Clinic	540/546	4933	M-F
Medical Emergency	540/546	116	M-F
	After hours go to RAF Upper Heyford or to a British medical facility.		
Mental Health	540/546	4139	M-F
Red Cross	157	4188	M-F

REST AND RECREATION

FACILITY/ACTIVITY	BLDG NO/LOC	PHONE	DAYS/COMMENTS
Bowling Lanes	590	4444	Daily
Consolidated Club	179	4930	M-Sa

UNITED KINGDOM
RAF Fairford, continued

	43/Little Rissington	N/A	N/A
Craftshops			
Automotive	804	4130	W-Su
Ceramics	803	4912	Tu,Th,Sa
Multi-crafts	8030	4912	Tu,Th,Sa
	34/Little Rissington	N/A	N/A
Wood	808	4912	Sa
Equip/Gear Locker	157	4279	M-F
Golf Course	Swindon	N/A	Daily
Gymnasium	187	4929/4202	24 hours daily
Info Tour & Travel	157	4279/4358	M-Sa
Library	157	4938	M-Su
NCO Club	179	4930/4203	M-Sa
O'Club	179	4495	N/A
Picnic/Park Area	Base lake	None	Seasonal
Recreation Center	157	4279/4850	Daily
	43/Little Rissington	7360	M-Sa
Rod and Gun Club	See RAF Upper Heyford/Croughton listing.		
Special Services	157	4278	M-F
Sport Field	Inquire at Recreation Center.		
Tennis Courts	Inquire at Recreation Center.		
Theater	79	4276/4476	F-Su
Video Rental	490	N/A	M-Sa
Youth Center	181	4932	Su-F

==

RAF GREENHAM COMMON/WELFORD (UK05R7)
APO New York 09150-5000

TELEPHONE INFORMATION: Main installation numbers: 44-0635-51-2000. ATVN: 266-1110.

LOCATION: To reach Greenham Common from London, take M-4 west and exit at Newbury. Take A-34 through Newbury, then A-339 towards Basingstoke. Main gate is on the left. RAF Welford is seven miles north of Newbury. HE: p-13, B/3. NMC: London 40 miles east.

GENERAL INSTALLATION INFORMATION: The 501st Tactical Missile Wing was activated at RAF Greenham Common on July 1, 1982. The mission of the wing is to operate and maintain ground-launched cruise missiles. Another equally important mission is performed by the 850th Munitions Maintenance Squadron (Theater) at Welford. Welford's mission is to maintain a stock of conventional munitions required to support USAFE operations. **The following abbreviations are used in this listing only: GK (Greenham Common); WF (Welford).** If no abbreviation follows the building number, then the facility is at Greenham Common.

GENERAL CITY/REGIONAL INFORMATION: The area surrounding Greenham Common/Welford has been dubbed the "Silicon Valley" of the United Kingdom because of its many electronics firms. The racecourse at Newbury, the nearest town, is one of the major courses in the country. The town of Newbury also has a thriving market. To the north of Newbury are

U.S. Forces Travel & Transfer Guide Europe — 351

UNITED KINGDOM
RAF Greenham Common/Welford, continued

the lovely Cotswold Hills and the university city of Oxford—the City of Dreaming Spires. To the north, the Thames winds its way through peaceful and picturesque countryside and attractive towns. The high rolling downland north and west of the town is famous as the training ground for race horses. The cathedral city of Salisbury, near Stonehenge, lies to the southwest. South of Newbury is the original capital of England, Winchester.

ADMINISTRATIVE SUPPORT

FACILITY/ACTIVITY	BLDG NO/LOC	PHONE	DAYS/COMMENTS
Fire(Mil)	86, 147	2117	24 hours daily
Fire(Civ)		C-999	24 hours daily
Housing			
Referral	57	2244/1/8	M-F
Info(Insta)	N/A	0	24 hours daily
Inspector Gen'l	274	2424	M-F
Legal Assist	107	2429	M-F
Locator(Mil)	139	2222	N/A
Locator(Civ)	92	2232	N/A
Personnel Spt	42	2674	M-F
Police(Mil)	77	2200	24 hours daily
Police(Civ)	N/A	C-999	24 hours daily
Public Affairs	274	2124	M-F

LOGISTICAL SUPPORT

FACILITY/ACTIVITY	BLDG NO/LOC	PHONE	DAYS/COMMENTS
Auto Drivers Testing	55	2220	M-F
Auto Parts(Exch)	186	2228	M-Sa
Auto Registration	48	2450	M-F
Auto Repairs	186	2228	M-Sa
Auto Ship(Gov)	48	2450	M-F
Auto Ship(Civ)	48	2450	M-F
Bank	195/GK	2172	M-Sa
	18/WF	7363	M-F
Barber Shop(s)	64/GK	2230	M-Sa
	25/WF	N/A	M,W,F
Beauty Shop(s)	64	2262	M-Sa
Bookstore	56/GK	2203/3209	M-Sa
	144/WF	7396	M-F
Bus	88	2123	Call for schedule.
Child Care/Dev Ctr	106	2304	M-Sa
Clothing Sales	61	2330	M-Sa
Commissary(Main)	163	3293	M-Sa
Credit Union	56	2266	M-F
Dry Clean(Exch)	83	2876	M-Sa
Dry Clean(Gov)	118	2583	N/A
Education Center	47	2660	M-F
Exchange(Main)	80	2229	Su-F
Exchange(Annex)	129	2654	N/A
Finance(Mil)	105	2044	M-F
Food(Caf/Rest)	82	2208	Daily
Food(Snack/Fast)			
Baskin Robbins	82	2208	Daily
Burger Bar	82	2208	Daily

UNITED KINGDOM
RAF Greenham Common/Welford, continued

Pizza Parlor	82	2208	Daily
Foodland	129	2654	N/A
Laundry(Self-Svc)	64	None	24 hours daily
Motor Pool	88	2123	N/A
Package Store	83	3231	Tu-Sa
Postal Svcs(Mil)	84/GK	2317	M-Sa
	133/WF	7394	M-F
SATO-OS	137	2739	M-F
Schools(DOD Dep)			
Elementary	N/A	3501	M-F
High School	N/A	3521	M-F
Svc Stn(Insta)	192/GK	2896	Daily
	198/WF	7365	M-F
Space-A Air Ops	See RAF Fairford listing.		
Tailor Shop	61	2718	M-Sa
Taxi(Comm)	Main gate	None	Daily
Tel Repair(Gov)	103	2112	N/A
Thrift Shop	85	2132	Tu,Th
TML			
Billeting	24	2363	24 hours daily
TLF	221	2363	Daily
VAQ	24	2443	24 hours daily
VOQ	228	2761	Daily
Travel Agents	113	2237	M-F

HEALTH AND WELFARE

FACILITY/ACTIVITY	BLDG NO/LOC	PHONE	DAYS/COMMENTS
AF Family Svcs	115	2120	M-F
AF Relief	42	3205	M-F
Ambulance	GK	2116	Daily
	WF	8-2116	Daily
	British	C-999	After hours
Central Appts	184	2400	M-F
CHAMPUS Office	184	2522	M-F
Chaplain	Available 24 hours daily through operator		
Chapel	188	2249	Su-F
Comm Drug/Alc Ctr	46	2483	N/A
Comm Rel Advisor	274	2152/3152	M-F
Dental Clinic	183	2322	M-F
	183	2535	After hours
Medical Emergency	GK	2116	Daily
	WF	8-2116	Daily
	British	C-999	After hours
Mental Health	60	3272	M-F
Poison Control	184	2245	24 hours daily
Red Cross	57	3205/2708	M-F

REST AND RECREATION

FACILITY/ACTIVITY	BLDG NO/LOC	PHONE	DAYS/COMMENTS
Bowling Lanes	130/GK	2214	Daily
	68/WF	7370	Su-W
Consolidated Club	112	2213	N/A

RAF Greenham Common/Welford, continued

UNITED KINGDOM

Facility	Bldg	Phone	Days
Craftshops			
Automotive	12/WF	7380	Tu-Su
Enlisted Club	112	2213	N/A
Gymnasium	187/GK	2219	Daily
	144/WF	7381	M-F
Info Tour & Travel	113	2902	N/A
Library	81/GK	2988	M-F
	32/WF	7353	M-F
NCO Club	112	2213	M-Sa
O'Club	228	2858	Daily
Outdoor Rec Ctr	130	2901	M-F
Racket Courts	187	2219	Daily
Recreation Center	113	2902	M-Sa
Special Services	49	2391	N/A
Sport Field	Mello Field	2902	Seasonal
Tennis Courts	On base	None	Seasonal
Theater	104	2218	W,F-Su
Video Rental	61	2718	M-Sa
Youth Center	109	2224	M-F
	100/Teen Center	N/A	M-Sa

HIGH WYCOMBE AIR STATION (UK18R7)
APO New York 09241-5360

TELEPHONE INFORMATION: Main installation numbers: Civ: 44-0494-21242. ATVN: 232-1110.

LOCATION: Take UK-40 northwest from London. Exit to UK-404 north and drive two miles to the air station. HE: p-13, C/2. NMC: London, 30 miles southeast.

GENERAL INSTALLATION INFORMATION: The 7520th Air Base Squadron at High Wycombe provides limited administrative and logistical support to Air Force personnel in the London area.

GENERAL CITY/REGIONAL INFORMATION: High Wycombe is located outside the London beltway in the Buckinghamshire District on the main route to Oxford. The River Thames and all of London's many sites are nearby.

ADMINISTRATIVE SUPPORT

FACILITY/ACTIVITY	BLDG NO/LOC	PHONE	DAYS/COMMENTS
Duty Officer	Hq	5321	24 hours daily
Fire(Mil)	402	5355	M-F
Emergency	402	5117	24 hours daily
Housing	323	5227	M-F
Personnel Spt	201	5139	M-F
Police(Mil)	205	5151	24 hours daily
Emergency	205	5200	24 hours daily
Police(Civ)	High Wycombe	C-23131	24 hours daily

UNITED KINGDOM
High Wycombe Air Station, continued

LOGISTICAL SUPPORT

FACILITY/ACTIVITY	BLDG NO/LOC	PHONE	DAYS/COMMENTS
Auto Registration	202	5203	M-F
Bank	522	C-445639	M-F
Barber Shop(s)	On Base	5225	N/A
Beauty Shop(s)	On Base	5225	N/A
Child Care/Dev Ctr	104	5294	M-F. Preschool.
Dry Clean(Exch)	On Base	5220	M-F
Education Center	503	5228	Tu-F
Exchange(Main)	217	5208	Daily
Foodland	217	5208	Daily
Motor Pool	323	5173	M-F
Postal Svcs(Mil)	510	5183	M-F
SATO-OS	323	5351	M-F
Schools(DOD Dep)			
Middle School	13	5259	M-F
High School	902	5188	M-F
Tailor Shop	On Base	5220	M-F
Tel Repair(Gov)	Oxbridge	3-3211	N/A
Tel Repair(Civ)	High Wycombe	C-151	N/A
TML			
Billeting	On Base	238-5227	N/A
TLF	8A/B/C,9B/C	5274	N/A
Travel Agents	406	5332	M-F

HEALTH AND WELFARE

FACILITY/ACTIVITY	BLDG NO/LOC	PHONE	DAYS/COMMENTS
AF Family Svcs	504	5227	M,Th,F
Ambulance	N/A	999	24 hours daily
Chaplain	412	5315	Su-F
Chapel	412	5315	Su-F
Medical Emergency	205	5300	Duty hours
	205	5200	After hours

REST AND RECREATION

FACILITY/ACTIVITY	BLDG NO/LOC	PHONE	DAYS/COMMENTS
Bowling Lanes	413	5218	Daily
Consolidated Club	206	5243	Daily
Gymnasium	500	N/A	Daily
Info Tour & Travel	406	5332	M-F
Library	512	N/A	Tu-Th
Video Rental	On Base	5208	M-Sa
Youth Center	603	5217	Daily

U.S. Forces Travel & Transfer Guide Europe — 355

UNITED KINGDOM

HOLY LOCH NAVAL SUPPORT ACTIVITY
(UK19R7)
(Scotland)
FPO New York 09514-1008

TELEPHONE INFORMATION: Main installation numbers: Civ: 44-0369-XXXX. ATVN: 221-8634.

LOCATION: Holy Loch is actually a body of water adjacent to the Cowal Peninsula and River Clyde, 30 miles west of Glasgow, Scotland. Holy Loch is not usually marked on maps. The nearest landmark is the town of Dunoon. HE: p-8, C/3. NMC: Glasgow, 30 miles east.

GENERAL INSTALLATION INFORMATION: Holy Loch is home to Commander, Submarine Squadron 14, a submarine tender, floating drydock, Naval Support Activity and associated tenant activities. The Navy community in Holy Loch is smaller than many U.S. Navy communities. There are 1800 military personnel assigned to the afloat units and shore commands. NSA and tenant commands and activities are located in the towns of Sandbank and Dunoon. An enclosed base, as such, does not exist. Note: **the following abbreviations are used in this listing only:** AR (Argyle Road); Ard (Ardnadam); AS (Ardenslate Road); FSC (Family Support Center on High Road); GN (Greenock); HR (High Road); MSt (Montgomery Street); PE (Pier Esplanade); QSt (Queen Street); RB (Rankin Building); USS (USS *Simon Lake*).

GENERAL CITY/REGIONAL INFORMATION: Within a few miles of the Holy Loch area are beautiful mountains, steep fluted cliffs, rock-bound coasts, farms, gardens, waterfalls, tumbling streams and, of course, the lochs. These provide a natural setting for outdoor recreation, including golfing, mountain climbing, bicycling, hill walking, skiing, hunting and fishing. Nature study and photography are hobbies that can be pursued here year round.

The River Clyde is the most famous of Scottish rivers. The southern shore of the Clyde is dotted with many industrial towns where shipbuilding is still an important industry. Many resort towns are located on the shores of the Clyde as well; Dunoon is one of the more popular.

ADMINISTRATIVE SUPPORT

FACILITY/ACTIVITY	BLDG NO/LOC	PHONE	DAYS/COMMENTS
Advocate	HR	6811	M-F
Customs/Duty	RB	5773	M-F
Duty Officer	Ard	5522	24 hours daily
Housing	Ard	4585	M-F
Referral	Ard	4585/5371	M-F
Legal Assist	FSC	6824	Tu,F. By appoint.
Locator(Civ)	Ard	5635	M-F
Personnel Spt	RB	5686/5661	M-F
Police(Mil)	Ard	4967	24 hours daily

LOGISTICAL SUPPORT

FACILITY/ACTIVITY	BLDG NO/LOC	PHONE	DAYS/COMMENTS
Bank	MSt	2140	Tu-Sa

UNITED KINGDOM
Holy Loch Naval Support Activity, continued

Child Care/Dev Ctr	QSt	2309	M-F
Clothing Sales	QSt	5681	Tu-Sa
Commissary(Main)	QSt	3993	Tu-Sa
Commissary(Annex)	31	3993	Tu-Sa
Credit Union	QSt	4133	M-F
Dry Clean(Exch)	QSt	5681	Tu-Su
Education Center	Ard	5036	M-F
Eng'r/Publ Works	RB	5555	M-F
		4976	After hours
Exchange(Main)	QSt	3247	Tu-Sa
Exchange(Annex)	MSt	2930	Daily
Finance(Mil)	RB	5873	M-F
Food(Caf/Rest)	Ard	5766	Daily
Food(Snack/Fast)			
Baskin Robbins	QSt	6016	M-Sa
Foodland	MSt	2930	Daily
Laundry(Self-Svc)	QSt	None	Daily
Postal Svcs(Mil)	QSt	4017	M-F
SATO-OS	RB	5886	M-F
Schools(DOD Dep)			
Elementary	HR	3748	M-F
Svc Stn(Insta)	MSt	2930	Daily
Tailor Shop	QSt	5681	Tu-Su
Taxi(Comm)	Local area	4331/5990/	Daily
		2088	
Thrift Shop	QSt	None	Tu,F,Sa after payday

HEALTH AND WELFARE

FACILITY/ACTIVITY	BLDG NO/LOC	PHONE	DAYS/COMMENTS
Central Appts	HR	6811	M-F
CHAMPUS Office	HR	6811	M-F
Chaplain	Ard	5871	Su-F
Chapel	Ard	5871	Su-F
Comm Drug/Alc Ctr	On Base	4992	M-F
Comm Rel Advisor	MSt	5530	M-F
Dental Clinic	HR	6907	M-F
Navy Fam Svcs	HR	6824	M-F
Navy Relief	Ard	3833	M,W,F
Red Cross	USS	5566	M-F
		4976	After hours
Veterinary Svcs	Local economy or RAF Lakenheath.		

REST AND RECREATION

FACILITY/ACTIVITY	BLDG NO/LOC	PHONE	DAYS/COMMENTS
Bowling Lanes	Ard	5896	Daily
Craftshops			
Automotive	MSt	5509	Tu-Su
Multi-crafts	Ard	5996	Th-Sa
Enlisted Club	Ard	5791	F-W
Equip/Gear Locker	Ard	5598	Daily
Golf Course	Ard	6851	Daily
Gymnasium	Ard	5598	Daily
Info Tour & Travel	Ard	3651	M-Sa

U.S. Forces Travel & Transfer Guide Europe — 357

UNITED KINGDOM
Holy Loch Naval Support Activity, continued

NCO Club	Ard	5573	Daily
O'Club	Ard	5548	Daily
Recreation Center	Ard	5996	M-F
Special Services	Ard	3593/5996	M-F
Theater	Ard	5982	Tu,Th-Su
Youth Center	OSt	3330	Daily

==

RAF LAKENHEATH (UK07R7)
APO New 09179-5000

TELEPHONE INFORMATION: Main installation numbers: Civ: 44-0638-52-1110. ATVN: 226-1110.

LOCATION: Take the M11 north to the A11. Take the A11 to the Five-ways Roundabout. Change to the A1065 to RAF Lakenheath. Follow the road signs. HE: p-13, E-1. NMC: Cambridge, 25 miles southwest.

GENERAL INSTALLATION INFORMATION: Since 1960, the 48th Tactical Fighter Wing has been the host tactical air operations in support of NATO. Four flying squadrons are assigned here: the 492nd, the 493rd, and 494th Tactical Fighter Squadrons are fully operational and mission ready; the 495th Tactical Fighter Squadron is a replacement training unit. Whereas most facilities are located at RAF Lakenheath, some are located around 10 miles away at RAF Feltwell. RAF Lakenheath boasts the largest U.S. military hospital and exchange in the United Kingdom and the largest elementary school in Europe.

GENERAL CITY/REGIONAL INFORMATION: RAF Lakenheath is located in East Anglia, the easternmost region of central England. This region was a wealthy and populous center of trade with Europe during the Middle Ages. The churches, castles and abbey ruins that remain from that time attest to that prosperity. Later, however, as England turned its attention away from Europe and concentrated on colonizing America, East Anglia declined to a less important rural area. East Anglia now boasts quiet, picturesque towns and villages, farms, forests and many historical points of interest. For example, the cathedral at Ely is considered by many to be the most beautiful in the country and the old section of Bury St. Edmunds, 16 miles southeast, abounds with tiny old shops reminiscent of the Victorian era.

==
ADMINISTRATIVE SUPPORT

FACILITY/ACTIVITY	BLDG NO/LOC	PHONE	DAYS/COMMENTS
Customs/Duty	1084	2233	24 hours daily
Fire(Mil)	1200	2205	24 hours daily
Housing	965	2453	M-F
Info(Insta)	N/A	1110	24 hours daily
Inspector Gen'l	1156	3502	M-F
Legal Assist	On Base	3553	M-F
Locator(Mil)	1037	3770	M-F
Personnel Spt	971	2525	M-F
Police(Mil)	1047	3631	24 hours daily
Police(Civ)	1047	3784	24 hours daily
Public Affairs	1150	3638	M-F

UNITED KINGDOM
RAF Lakenheath, continued

LOGISTICAL SUPPORT

FACILITY/ACTIVITY	BLDG NO/LOC	PHONE	DAYS/COMMENTS
Auto Drivers Testing	1004A	2134	M-F
Auto Parts(Exch)	1030	2279	Daily
Auto Registration	972	2169	M-F
Auto Repairs	1030	2279	M-F
Bakery	650	3515	Daily
Bank	989	3750	M-F
Barber Shop(s)	998	2488	M-Sa
	683	2319	M-F. NCOs.
	982	2166	M-F. Officers.
	1212	3205	M-F. Flightline.
Beauty Shop(s)	998	2927	M-Sa
Bookstore	665	2310	Daily
Child Care/Dev Ctr	659	3285	M-F
	657	3829	M-F
	640	2263	M-F
	Feltwell/37	C-828101	M,W,F. Preschool.
Clothing Sales	995	2996	M-Sa
Commissary(Main)	650	3515	Tu-Su
Credit Union	987	2115	M-F
Dining Facility	934	2177	Daily
Dry Clean(Exch)	996	2996	M-Sa
Education Center	991	3851	M-F
Exchange(Main)	998	2996	Daily
Finance(Mil)	1092	2466	M-F
Food(Snack/Fast)	N/A	2540	Daily
Baskin Robbins	998	2996	M-Sa
Burger Bar	998	2996	M-Sa
Pizza Parlor	670	2497	Daily
Foodland	641	C-2573	Daily
Laundry(Self-Svc)	419	None	Daily
Motor Pool	1010	2297	24 hours daily
Package Store	658	3708	Tu-Sa
Photo Laboratory	1063	2285	M-F
Postal Svcs(Mil)	426	3548/2370	M-F
SATO-OS	644	2568	M-F
Schools(DOD Dep)			
Elementary	Phase III Hsg	3674/3721	M-F (K-5)
	RAF Feltwell	C-828504	M-F (K-5)
Middle School	RAF Feltwell	C-828245	M-F (6-8)
High School	RAF Lakenheath	C-2575	M-F (9-12)
Space-A Air Ops	See RAF Mildenhall listing.		
Taxi(Comm)	N/A	2306	24 hours daily
Tel Booking Oper	N/A	112	24 hours daily
Thrift Shop	255/261	2987	M,W,F
TML			
Billeting	956	3770	24 hours daily
Protocol Office	Hq Building	3500	M-F
TLQ	980	3770	24 hours daily
DV/VIP	956	3500	M-F
Travel Agents	681	C-2415	M-F

UNITED KINGDOM
RAF Lakenheath, continued

HEALTH AND WELFARE

FACILITY/ACTIVITY	BLDG NO/LOC	PHONE	DAYS/COMMENTS
AF Family Svcs	692	3134	M-F
Ambulance	932	116	24 hours daily
CHAMPUS Office	971	2525	M-F
Chaplain	990	2233	M-F
Chapel	990	2389	M-Sa
Comm Drug/Alc Ctr	692	3229	M-F
Comm Rel Advisor	On Base	3145	M-F
Dental Clinic	942	2950	M-F
Medical Emergency	932	2226	24 hours daily
Mental Health	914	2409	M-F
Poison Control	932	2394	M-F
Red Cross	692	2271	M-F
Veterinary Svcs	984	2235	M,F

REST AND RECREATION

FACILITY/ACTIVITY	BLDG NO/LOC	PHONE	DAYS/COMMENTS
Aero/Flying Club	1393	3152	Daily
Bowling Lanes	657	2108	24 hours daily
Consolidated Club	682	3869/2489	Daily
Craftshops			
Automotive	Feltwell/24	C-827661	Tu-Su
Multi-crafts	640	2194	Su-Th
Photography	909	2291	M-Sa
Enlisted Club	682	3869/2489	Daily
Equip/Gear Locker	430	2411	Daily
Golf Course	1298	2223	Tu-Su
Gymnasium	900	3607	Daily
Info Tour & Travel	981	C-2415	M-F
Library	907	3713	M-F
NCO Club	670	2206	Daily
O'Club	958	2535	Daily
Racket Courts	900	3607	24 hours daily
Recreation Center	642	3245	24 hours daily
	Feltwell/94	C-828366	Daily
Rod and Gun Club	777	2368	Daily
Special Services	958	3690/2414	M-F
Sport Field	N/A	3690	24 hours daily
Swimming Pool	908	2437	Daily
Tennis Courts	N/A	3690	Daily
Theater	694	2139	Daily
Video Rental	909	2291	M-Sa
Youth Center	249	3180	Daily

UNITED KINGDOM

LONDON NAVAL ACTIVITY (UK21R7)
7 North Audley Street, London W1, UK
FPO New York 09510-1000

TELEPHONE INFORMATION: Main installation numbers: Civ: 44-01-629-9222. ATVN: 235-0111.

LOCATION: Across from the American Embassy, the Navy Headquarters at 7 North Audley Street (Grosvenor Square) in the heart of London's West End represents a long history of American military presence in Europe. The Navy HQ was the SHAPE HQ used by General Eisenhower during the Second World War and is currently HQ for U.S. Naval Forces Europe.

GENERAL INSTALLATION INFORMATION: The U.S. Navy Personnel Support Activity in London provides facilities and exercises area coordination responsibilities for Naval shore activities located in the UK and in Northern Europe. It also functions as a Naval Station for Navy commands in the greater London area. Note: the following abbreviation is used in this listing: AFX (ask for extension).

GENERAL CITY/REGIONAL INFORMATION: As one of the largest and most historically important cities in Europe, London offers a wealth of historical sites to see and many recreational opportunities.

ADMINISTRATIVE SUPPORT

FACILITY/ACTIVITY	BLDG NO/LOC	PHONE	DAYS/COMMENTS
Duty Officer	Hq	C-9222	24 hours daily
Fire(Civ)	London	C-999	24 hours daily
Info(Insta)	Hq	C-142	London
		C-192	Rest of UK
Legal Assist	Hq	AFX	M-F
Personnel Spt	Hq	235-4464	M-F

LOGISTICAL SUPPORT

FACILITY/ACTIVITY	BLDG NO/LOC	PHONE	DAYS/COMMENTS
Bank	Hq/Ground Floor	AFX	M-F
Child Care/Dev Ctr	Childminders	C-249-8299	M-F
Education Center	Hq	C-485-5101	M-F
		C-486-1098	M-F
Exchange(Main)	Hq	C-409-4255	M-F
Finance(Mil)	Hq	C-409-4558	M-F
		235-4558	M-F
Postal Svcs(Mil)	Hq	AFX	M-F
SATO-OS	Hq	235-4538	M-F
Svc Stn(Insta)	Hamilton Motors	C-723-0022	Daily
Space-A Air Ops	See RAF Mildenhall listing.		
Taxi(Comm)	London	C-237-3030	24 hours daily
	London	C-263-9496	24 hours daily
TML	Non-government TML is available in London at the following facilities: The Union Jack Club, Sandell Street, Waterloo, London SE1 8UJ (Civ: 44-01-928-6401); The Columbia Hotel 95-99 Lancaster Gate, London W2 3NS (Civ: 44-01-402-0021); and The		

London Naval Activity, continued

UNITED KINGDOM

Travel Agents	Victory Services Club, 63/79 Seymour Street, London W2 2HF (Civ: 44-01-723-4474).		
	Hq	235-4177	M-F

HEALTH AND WELFARE

FACILITY/ACTIVITY	BLDG NO/LOC	PHONE	DAYS/COMMENTS
Ambulance	London	C-999	24 hours daily
Chaplain	Hq		Daily
Dental Clinic	Hq	C-409-4121	M-F
Medical Emergency	U.S. Embassy	C-409-4540	24 hours daily
	Emergency	C-409-4500	24 hours daily

REST AND RECREATION

FACILITY/ACTIVITY	BLDG NO/LOC	PHONE	DAYS/COMMENTS
Consolidated Club	Hq	C-629-4562/ 4544	Daily
Gymnasium	Hq	AFX	Daily
Library	Central London	C-930-3274	Daily
Recreation Center	Hq	C-629-4134	Daily
Special Services	Hq	C-629-4150	Daily

RAF MACHRIHANISH (UK29R7)
(Scotland)
FPO New York 09515-5000

TELEPHONE INFORMATION: Main installation numbers: Civ: 44-0423-770421. ATVN: 392-8578.

LOCATION: Located on the Kintyre Peninsula approximately 130 miles from Glasgow. From Glasgow take UK-83 northwest to the peninsula where the road turn south to Machrihanish, five miles west of Campbeltown. HE: p-8, B/4. NMC: Glasgow, 130 miles northeast.

GENERAL INSTALLATION INFORMATION: RAF Machrihanish supports four U.S. Naval units: a Naval Weapons Facility Detachment (NWFD); a Naval Telecommunications Center; a Mobile Mine Assembly Group; and a Naval Special Warfare unit. **Note: the following abbreviation is used in this listing: AFX (ask for extension).**

GENERAL CITY/REGIONAL INFORMATION: Located across the North Channel from Ireland, RAF Machrihanish is surrounded by a sea-coast environment.

ADMINISTRATIVE SUPPORT

FACILITY/ACTIVITY	BLDG NO/LOC	PHONE	DAYS/COMMENTS
Duty Officer	On Base(NWFD)	C-54010	24 hours daily
	On Base(RAF)	C-53021	24 hours daily
Housing	On Base	AFX	M-F

UNITED KINGDOM
RAF Machrihanish, continued

LOGISTICAL SUPPORT

FACILITY/ACTIVITY	BLDG NO/LOC	PHONE	DAYS/COMMENTS
Child Care/Dev Ctr	On Base(RAF)	AFX	Daily
Commissary(Main)	On Base	AFX	Tu-Sa
Exchange(Main)	On Base	C-586-54238	Tu-Sa
Laundry(Self-Svc)	On Base	AFX	24 hours daily
Postal Svcs(Mil)	On Base	AFX	M-F
Schools(DOD Dep)			
Elementary	Local	N/A	M-F
High School	See RAF Lakenheath listing.		
Svc Stn(Insta)	On Base	AFX	Tu-Sa
TML			
BEQ/BOQ	On Base	AFX	Daily

HEALTH AND WELFARE

FACILITY/ACTIVITY	BLDG NO/LOC	PHONE	DAYS/COMMENTS
Ambulance	Local civilian ambulance service.		
Central Appts	See the Holy Loch NSA listing.		
Dental Clinic	See the Holy Loch NSA listing.		

REST AND RECREATION

FACILITY/ACTIVITY	BLDG NO/LOC	PHONE	DAYS/COMMENTS
Beach(es)	Many in area		
Bowling Lanes	In gymnasium	AFX	Daily
Consolidated Club	On Base	AFX	Daily
Gymnasium	On Base	AFX	Daily
Library	On Base	AFX	Daily
NCO Club	On Base(RAF)	AFX	Daily
Swimming Pool	On Base(RAF)	AFX	Daily
Tennis Courts	On Base(RAF)	AFX	Daily

MENWITH HILL STATION (UK22R7)
APO New York 09210-5000

TELEPHONE INFORMATION: Main installation numbers: Civ: 44-0423-770421. ATVN: 262-1110.

LOCATION: From Leeds, take UK-61 north to Harrogate then UK-59 west toward Skipton for seven miles and watch for signs to the station. HE: p-11, C/3. NMC: Leeds, 20 miles southeast.

GENERAL INSTALLATION INFORMATION: Menwith Hill is a joint services installation.

GENERAL CITY/REGIONAL INFORMATION: Menwith Hill Station is located in open country north of the Liverpool/Manchester/Sheffield/Leeds industrial complex.

U.S. Forces Travel & Transfer Guide Europe — 363

Menwith Hill Station, continued   UNITED KINGDOM

ADMINISTRATIVE SUPPORT

FACILITY/ACTIVITY	BLDG NO/LOC	PHONE	DAYS/COMMENTS
Duty Officer	On Station	1110	24 hours daily
Fire (Mil)	24	7861	24 hours daily
Housing	12-G	7886	M-F
Personnel Spt	29	7879	M-F
Police (Mil)	On Base	7884	24 hours daily
Emergency	On Base	7777	24 hours daily

LOGISTICAL SUPPORT

FACILITY/ACTIVITY	BLDG NO/LOC	PHONE	DAYS/COMMENTS
Auto Registration	12	7885	M-F
Bank	40	C-770447	M-F
Commissary (Main)	14	7759	M-Sa
Dining Facility	18	7895	M-Sa
Exchange (Main)	17	7894	M-Sa
Schools (DOD Dep)	21	7778/9	M-F
Svc Stn (Insta)	Harrogate	C-770984	M-W,F,Sa
Space-A Air Ops	See RAF Mildenhall listing.		

HEALTH AND WELFARE

FACILITY/ACTIVITY	BLDG NO/LOC	PHONE	DAYS/COMMENTS
Ambulance	26	7885	24 hours daily
Dental Clinic	On Base	7777	M-F

REST AND RECREATION

FACILITY/ACTIVITY	BLDG NO/LOC	PHONE	DAYS/COMMENTS
Consolidated Club	18	7895	M-Su
Youth Center	34	7799	M-Sa

RAF MILDENHALL (UK08R7)
APO New York 09167-5000

TELEPHONE INFORMATION: Main installation numbers: Civ: 44-638-513000. ATVN: 238-1110.

LOCATION: Twenty-seven miles from Cambridge in the eastern United Kingdom. Follow the A-11(M) to Newmarket, then to Barton Mills. Take the A-1101 for 2.5 miles through Mildenhall Town to Beck Row Village to RAF Mildenhall. HE: p-13, E/1. NMC: Cambridge 24 miles southwest.

GENERAL INSTALLATION INFORMATION: Since 1972, the 3rd Air Force at Mildenhall has served as the single point of contact representing U.S. Air Forces in negotiating financial and technical arrangements with the British government. The 513th Tactical Airlift Wing is the host unit at the

UNITED KINGDOM
RAF Mildenhall, continued

base. As such, it is responsible for the operation of the base and the provision of mission-ready EC-135 aircraft and flight crews for the 10th Airborne Command Control Squadron and for the U.S. EUCOM's airborne command and control operation. Thirty associate organizations are provided logistical, administrative, and maintenance support.

GENERAL CITY/REGIONAL INFORMATION: Mildenhall is in the western part of the County of Suffolk in a region known as East Anglia. The area has been crossroads of migration, warfare, and trade with the continent since pre-historic times. Ruins of medieval castles, churches, abbeys, and towns attest to the wealth of this region during the Middle Ages. Today East Anglia is known for its quiet towns and villages, farms and forests. It also boasts many historic places of interest such as Cambridge, home of the famous university; Newmarket, a thoroughbred racing center; and Thetford, the birthplace of Thomas Paine. In addition to visiting these and other local attractions, popular activities include fishing, boating, biking, horseback riding, brass-rubbing, and pub-hopping. RAF Lakenheath, just five miles away, provides many facilities such as a commissary, full-service hospital, an exchange, a golf course, and an indoor pool.

ADMINISTRATIVE SUPPORT

FACILITY/ACTIVITY	BLDG NO/LOC	PHONE	DAYS/COMMENTS
Customs/Duty	598/MAC Term	2849	As required
Duty Officer	591	2121	24 hours daily
Fire(Mil)	661	2408	24 hours daily
Fire(Civ)	Local	C-999	24 hours daily
Housing	See RAF Lakenheath listing.		
Info(Insta)	On Base	113	24 hours daily
Inspector Gen'l	562	2212	M-F
Legal Assist	566	2028	M-F
Locator(Mil)	436	2669	M-F
Locator(Civ)	436	2669	M-F
Personnel Spt	436	2770/2084	M-F
Police(Mil)	645	2667	24 hours daily
Police(Civ)	Mildenhall	C-712222	24 hours daily
Public Affairs	562	2653	M-F

LOGISTICAL SUPPORT

FACILITY/ACTIVITY	BLDG NO/LOC	PHONE	DAYS/COMMENTS
Auto Drivers Testing	442	2153	M-F
Auto Parts(Exch)	511	2774	M-Sa
Auto Registration	436	2702	M-F
Auto Repairs	530	2774	Daily
Auto Sales	Behind theater	N/A	M-F
Auto Ship(Gov)	560	2386	M-F
Auto Wash	529	None	24 hours daily
Bank	436	2850	M-F
Barber Shop(s)	442	2676	M-Sa
Beauty Shop(s)	442	2977	M-Sa
Bookstore	196	2599	Daily
Bus	611	2845	Daily
Child Care/Dev Ctr	99	2235	Daily
	116	2405	M-F

U.S. Forces Travel & Transfer Guide Europe — 365

UNITED KINGDOM

RAF Mildenhall, continued

Clothing Sales	See RAF Lakenheath listing.		
Commissary(Main)	See RAF Lakenheath listing.		
Commissary(Annex)	131	2475	M-F
Credit Union	220	2686	M-F
Dining Facility	436/619	AFX	Daily
Dry Clean(Exch)	Behind Theater	C-717906	M-Sa
Education Center	123	2350	M-F
Eng'r/Publ Works	443	2532	Daily
Exchange(Main)	See RAF Lakenheath listing.		
Exchange(Annex)	127	2961	M-F
Finance(Mil)	504	2928	M-F
Food(Snack/Fast)			
Baskin Robbins	423	2961	Daily
Burger Bar	423	2488	Daily
Pizza Parlor	433	2795	Daily
Foodland	131	2475	Daily
Laundry(Self-Svc)	128	None	24 hours daily
Motor Pool	611	2845	Daily
Package Store	129	2808	Tu-Sa
Photo Laboratory	292	2469	M-F
Postal Svcs(Mil)	442	2949	M-Sa
Railroad/RTO	British Rail		
SATO-OS	598	2766/2968	M-F
Schools(DOD Dep)	See RAF Lakenheath listing.		
Svc Stn(Insta)	530	2774	Daily
	Beck Row	C-713032	M-Sa
Space-A Air Ops	598	2526	Daily
Pax Lounges(Gen'l)	598	2248	24 hours daily
Protocol Svc	239	2132	M-F
Flights to:	Aviano AB IT; RAF Bentwaters UK; Capodichino Arpt IT; Charleston AFB/IAP SC; Decimomannu AB IT; Dover AFB DE; Goose Bay AB CN; Leipheim GAFB GE; Norvenich GAFB GE; Philadelphia IAP PA; Ramstein AB GE; Rhein-Main AB GE; Sembach AB GE; Tinker AFB OK; Torrejon AB SP; Travis AFB CA; Zaragoza AB SP.		
	Note: Space-A flights also originate at the Naval Air Facility at Mildenhall. Check with the Air Force/Mac counter.		
Tailor Shop	127	C-712816	M-Sa
Taxi(Comm)	461	2984	24 hours daily
Tel Booking Oper	On Base	112	24 hours daily
Tel Repair(Gov)	On Base	2525	24 hours daily
Tel Repair(Civ)	Local	119	Daily
Thrift Shop	432	2303	M-F
TML			
Billeting	459	2407	24 hours daily
TAQ	100	2407	24 hours daily
TLF	104	2989	24 hours daily
DV/VIP	239	2132	24 hours daily

==
HEALTH AND WELFARE
==

FACILITY/ACTIVITY	BLDG NO/LOC	PHONE	DAYS/COMMENTS
AF Family Svcs	442	2032	M-F
AF Relief	436	2084	M-F

UNITED KINGDOM
RAF Mildenhall, continued

Ambulance	444	2765	24 hours daily
Central Appts	Clinic	2657	Daily
CHAMPUS Office	See RAF Lakenheath listing.		
Chaplain	On Base	2667	24 hours daily
Chapel	474	2822	M-F
Comm Drug/Alc Ctr	460	2468	M-F
Dental Clinic	446	2537	M-F
Medical Emergency	See RAF Lakenheath listing.		
Mental Health	See RAF Lakenheath listing.		
Poison Control	444	2657	24 hours daily
Red Cross	598	2113	M-F
Veterinary Svcs	See RAF Lakenheath listing.		

REST AND RECREATION

FACILITY/ACTIVITY	BLDG NO/LOC	PHONE	DAYS/COMMENTS
Aero/Flying Club	See RAF Lakenheath listing.		
Bowling Lanes	400	2348	Daily
Craftshops			
Automotive	240	2480	W-Sa
Ceramics	292	2469	W-Sa
Photography	292	2469	W-Sa
Wood	292	2469	W-Sa
Enlisted Club	449	2683 C-713564	Daily
Gymnasium	463	2349	Daily
Info Tour & Travel	404	2630	M-F
Library	425	2352	Daily
NCO Club	291	2323	Daily
O'Club	464	2615	Daily
Picnic/Park Area	Woodland Pavilion		
Racket Courts	463	2349	Daily
Recreation Center	404	2579	Daily
Rod and Gun Club	See RAF Lakenheath listing.		
Special Services	On Base	2851	M-F
Swimming Pool	See RAF Lakenheath listing.		
Theater	243	2351	M-F
Video Rental	442	2644	M-F
Youth Center	287	2831	Daily

PRESTWICK AIRPORT (UK24R7)
(Scotland)
OL-P, 313 APS/MAC
APO New York 09049-5364

TELEPHONE INFORMATION: Main installation numbers: Civ: 44-292 78966. ATVN: 238-1110 (ask for Prestwick).

LOCATION: On the west coast of Scotland. Take A-77 south from Glasgow, exit at Ayr and drive north to the airport. HE: p-8, C/4. NMC: Glasgow, 30 miles northeast.

GENERAL INSTALLATION INFORMATION: Prestwick Airport's OL-P

UNITED KINGDOM
Prestwick Airport, continued

313 APS/MAC serves U.S. bases in Scotland. Major stations served are Holy Loch Naval Activity, Edzell Naval Facility, Thurso Naval Communications Station, Greenock Naval Facility and RAF Machrihanish. Many U.S. support facilities are available at the airport. Note: **the following abbreviation is used in this listing: AFX (ask for extension).**

GENERAL CITY/REGIONAL INFORMATION: Prestwick Airport is located on the west coast of Scotland off the north channel of Ireland, surrrounded by a green and lovely land of farms and castles. Glasgow is only 30 miles northeast by good roads or rail.

ADMINISTRATIVE SUPPORT

FACILITY/ACTIVITY	BLDG NO/LOC	PHONE	DAYS/COMMENTS
Customs/Duty	Main concourse	AFX	Varies

LOGISTICAL SUPPORT

FACILITY/ACTIVITY	BLDG NO/LOC	PHONE	DAYS/COMMENTS
Auto Rental(Exch)	Main concourse	C-77218	Daily. Avis.
		C-70566	Daily. Eurocar.
		C-79822	Daily. Hertz.
		C-76517	Daily. Swan Natl.
Bank	Main concourse	C-79822 ext. 2049	N/A
Bus	Navy to Dunoon	8689	M-F
Exchange(Main)	Skyshop	C-78681	Daily
Food(Caf/Rest)	Mezzanine	C-79822/ 78326 ext. 3082	Daily
Food(Snack/Fast)	Rooftop	See above.	Daily
Postal Svcs(Mil)	Main concourse	C-79822	M-Sa
SATO-OS	Main concourse	C-79822 ext. 2013	Daily
Space-A Air Ops	Main concourse	C-79866	Daily
Pax Lounges(Gen'l)	Main concourse	C-79822	24 hours daily
Flights to:	Bradley IAP CT; Charleston AFB SC; Goose Bay AB CN; RAF Mildenhall UK.		
Taxi(Comm)	Information desk	C-79822 ext. 2013	Daily

RAF ST. MAWGAN (UK25R7)
FPO New York 09511-5000

TELEPHONE INFORMATION: Main installation numbers: Civ: 44-06373-2201/2775. ATVN: 231-4612.

LOCATION: Take UK-38 west from Plymouth to UK-30 south to UK-392 west to Newquay. Follow signs to RAF St. Mawgan, four miles northwest. HE: p-12, C/5. NMC: Plymouth, 48 miles east.

GENERAL INSTALLATION INFORMATION: U.S. units located at RAF

UNITED KINGDOM
RAF St. Mawgan, continued

St. Mawgan include the Naval Aviation Weapons Facility, the Naval Communications Center, the Explosive Ordnance Group and the Marine Corps Security Force Company. Note: the following abbreviation is used in this listing: AFX (ask for extension); NAAFI (Navy, Army, Air Force Institute).

GENERAL CITY/REGIONAL INFORMATION: RAF St. Mawgan is located on the northern coast of Cornwall, surrounded by hilly terrain with beautiful beaches and cliffs nearby.

ADMINISTRATIVE SUPPORT

FACILITY/ACTIVITY	BLDG NO/LOC	PHONE	DAYS/COMMENTS
Duty Officer	On Base	AFX	24 hours daily
Fire(Mil)	On Base(RAF)	AFX	24 hours daily
Housing	On Base(RAF)	AFX	M-F
Police(Mil)	On Base(RAF)	AFX	24 hours daily

LOGISTICAL SUPPORT

FACILITY/ACTIVITY	BLDG NO/LOC	PHONE	DAYS/COMMENTS
Barber Shop(s)	On Base(RAF)	AFX	M-Sa
Exchange(Main)	On Base(NAAFI)	AFX	M-Sa
Schools(DOD Dep)			
Elementary	Local schools		
High School	See RAF High Wycombe listing.		
Svc Stn(Insta)	On Base	AFX	M-Sa
TML			
BEQ/BOQ	On Base(RAF)	AFX	Daily

HEALTH AND WELFARE

FACILITY/ACTIVITY	BLDG NO/LOC	PHONE	DAYS/COMMENTS
Central Appts	AD only dispensary. Ask for extension.		
Chaplain	On Base	AFX	Daily
Dental Clinic	AD only dispensary. Ask for extension.		

REST AND RECREATION

FACILITY/ACTIVITY	BLDG NO/LOC	PHONE	DAYS/COMMENTS
Craftshops			
Automotive	On Base(RAF)	AFX	Tu-Sa
Ceramics	On Base(RAF)	AFX	Tu-Sa
Wood	On Base(RAF)	AFX	Tu-Su
Enlisted Club	On Base(RAF)	AFX	Daily
Gymnasium	On Base(RAF)	AFX	Daily
Library	On Base(RAF)	AFX	Daily
NCO Club	On Base(RAF)	AFX	Daily
Racket Courts	On Base(RAF)	AFX	Daily
Tennis Courts	On Base(RAF)	AFX	Daily
Youth Center	On Base(RAF)	AFX	M-Sa

UNITED KINGDOM

RAF SCULTHORPE (UK26R7)
APO New York 09048-5000

TELEPHONE INFORMATION: Main installation numbers: Civ: 44-0328-3121. ATVN: 227-1110.

LOCATION: Take UK-47 west from Norwich to UK-1065 north to Fakenham. Watch for RAF Sculthorpe signs in Fakenham. HE: p-11, F-G/5. NMC: Norwich, 25 miles southeast.

GENERAL INSTALLATION INFORMATION: Units at RAF Sculthorpe include Det 1, 48th Tactical Fighter Wing, which operates in support of RAF Air Operations. Note: the following abbreviation is used in this listing: AFX (ask for extension).

GENERAL CITY/REGIONAL INFORMATION: RAF Sculthorpe is located near Fakenham, Norfolk, about 150 miles north of London near the North Sea.

ADMINISTRATIVE SUPPORT

FACILITY/ACTIVITY	BLDG NO/LOC	PHONE	DAYS/COMMENTS
Duty Officer	On Base	1110	24 hours daily
Housing	On Base	AFX	M-F

LOGISTICAL SUPPORT

FACILITY/ACTIVITY	BLDG NO/LOC	PHONE	DAYS/COMMENTS
Bank	On Base	AFX	Bi-weekly
Commissary(Main)	On Base	263-4428	Tu-Sa
Exchange(Annex)	On Base	AFX	Tu-Sa
Foodland	On Base	AFX	Daily
Laundry(Exch)	On Base	AFX	Tu-Sa
Postal Svcs(Mil)	On Base	AFX	M-Sa
Schools(DOD Dep)			
Elementary	On Base	AFX	M-F
High School	See RAF Lakenheath listing.		
Space-A Air Ops	See RAF Mildenhall listing.		

HEALTH AND WELFARE

FACILITY/ACTIVITY	BLDG NO/LOC	PHONE	DAYS/COMMENTS
Ambulance	On Base	AFX	24 hours daily
Central Appts	On Base	AFX	Daily
Chapel	On Base	AFX	Daily

REST AND RECREATION

FACILITY/ACTIVITY	BLDG NO/LOC	PHONE	DAYS/COMMENTS
Craftshops			
Automotive	On Base	AFX	Daily

370 — U.S. Forces Travel & Transfer Guide Europe

UNITED KINGDOM

THURSO NAVAL COMMUNICATION STATION (UK27R7)
(Scotland)
FPO New York 09516-5000

TELEPHONE INFORMATION: Main installation numbers: Comm: 44-0847-86271. ATVN: 231-4101.

LOCATION: From Inverness, take National Road 9 north to Wick; L on National Road 882 to Thurso. Follow signs to USN Communication Station. HE: p-6, F/2. NMC: Wick, 13 mi SE.

GENERAL INSTALLATION INFORMATION: The Naval Communication Station is located just outside of Thurso, a small town at the extreme northeastern tip of Scotland. **Note: the following abbreviation is used in this listing: AFX (ask for extension).**

GENERAL CITY/REGIONAL: Thurso is located 700 miles due north of London. The area is cool and windy throughout the year, although average year-round temperatures are milder than one would expect: 55-65° in the summer and 30-50° in the winter. The region provides excellent opportunities for hunting and fishing. In nearby Wick, visitors can see the unique ancient stonebuilt town, some lovely old castles, and a number of fine craft workshops.

ADMINISTRATIVE SUPPORT

FACILITY/ACTIVITY	BLDG NO/LOC	PHONE	DAYS/COMMENTS
Advocate	On Station	AFX	M-F
Duty Officer	On Station	AFX	24 hours daily
Fire(Mil)	On Station	AFX	24 hours daily
Legal Assist	On Station	AFX	Twice per year.
Police(Mil)	On Station	AFX	24 hours daily

LOGISTICAL SUPPORT

FACILITY/ACTIVITY	BLDG NO/LOC	PHONE	DAYS/COMMENTS
Commissary(Main)	On Station	AFX	M-Sa
Credit Union	On Station	AFX	M-Sa
Education Center	On Station	AFX	M-F
Exchange(Main)	On Station	AFX	M-Sa
Postal Svcs(Mil)	On Station	AFX	N/A
Schools(DOD Dep)			
Elementary	Local schools		
High School	See High Wycombe Air Station listing.		
Svc Stn(Insta)	On Station	AFX	Daily

HEALTH AND WELFARE

FACILITY/ACTIVITY	BLDG NO/LOC	PHONE	DAYS/COMMENTS
Ambulance	Medical Fac	AFX	24 hours daily
Central Appts	Medical Fac	AFX	Daily (1 wk per qtr)
CHAMPUS Office	Medical Fac	AFX	Daily

Thurso Naval Communication Station, continued
UNITED KINGDOM

Chaplain	Local and auxiliary chaplains. Navy chaplain once per quarter.
Dental Clinic	Dental Fac	AFX	M-F
Veterinary Svcs	See RAF Lakenheath listing.

REST AND RECREATION

FACILITY/ACTIVITY	BLDG NO/LOC	PHONE	DAYS/COMMENTS
Bowling Lanes	On Station	AFX	Daily
Craftshops			
Ceramics	On Station	AFX	Tu-Su
Photography	On Station	AFX	Tu-Su
Gymnasium	On Station	AFX	Daily
Library	On Station	AFX	24 hours daily
Racket Courts	On Station	AFX	Daily
Rod and Gun Club	On Station	AFX	Daily
Swimming Pool	On Station	AFX	Daily

RAF UPPER HEYFORD/CROUGHTON (UK09R7)
APO New York 09194-5000

TELEPHONE INFORMATION: Main installation numbers: Civ: 44-086982-2331. ATVN: 263-1110. Civ prefix: 086982-XXXX. ATVN prefix: 263-XXXX. Note: when dialing extensions for Croughton, all of which begin with a 7, dial the 7, wait for a dail tone, then dial the remaining three digits.

LOCATION: From London, take M-40 to Oxford, then take either A-423 (Oxford-Banbury) or A-43 (Oxford-Northhampton), signs to base. HE: p-13, C/2. NMC: Oxford, 12 miles south.

GENERAL INSTALLATION INFORMATION: RAF Upper Heyford is the main operating base for the 20th Tactical Fighter Wing, the second largest tactical fighter wing in the United Kingdom. The mission of the 20th is to provide long-range, all-weather tactical fighter and electronic combat sorties for NATO. RAF Croughton, located eight miles northeast of RAF Upper Heyford, is the home of the 2130th Communications Squadron, the 2168th Communications Squadron, and Det 40/2nd Weather Wing. **Note: the following abbreviation is used in this listing: AFX (ask for extension).**

GENERAL CITY/REGIONAL INFORMATION: RAF Upper Heyford is about 60 miles northwest of London and 15 miles north of Oxford. Around 500 villages and towns dot the countryside in a 25 miles radius around the base. Local places of interest include Blenheim Palace, which boasts a rich heritage and lovely landscaped gardens; and the internationally famous Ashmoleum Museum in Oxford. Warwick, 45 miles away, has the oldest inhabited medieval castle in England, a doll museum, St. Mary's church, and Madame Tussaud's waxworks exhibit.

UNITED KINGDOM
RAF Upper Heyford/Croughton, continued

ADMINISTRATIVE SUPPORT

FACILITY/ACTIVITY	BLDG NO/LOC	PHONE	DAYS/COMMENTS
Duty Officer	52	4816	24 hours daily
Fire(Mil)	On Base	117	24 hours daily
Fire(Civ)	Local	2888	24 hours daily
Housing	401	AFX	M-F
Info(Insta)	125	4038	24 hours daily
Inspector Gen'l	125	4332	M-F
Legal Assist	52	4119	M-F
Locator(Mil)	52	4401	M-F
Personnel Spt	52	4881	M-F
Police(Mil)	100	4337	24 hours daily
Public Affairs	125	4338	M-F

LOGISTICAL SUPPORT

FACILITY/ACTIVITY	BLDG NO/LOC	PHONE	DAYS/COMMENTS
Audio/Photo Ctr	581	2851	Daily
Auto Drivers Testing	80	4297/4494	W,F
Auto Parts(Exch)	103	4230	M-Sa
	Croughton	7373	M-Sa
Auto Registration	80	AFX	M-F
Auto Rent(Other)	Upper Heyford	2029	M-Sa
Auto Repairs	103	4230	M-F
	Croughton	7355	M-F
Auto Sales	Upper Heyford	2666	M-F
	Leys Garage	2220/2048	M-F
	Europacar Intl	2807	M-F
	Auto Hotline	2681/2686	M-Sa
Auto Ship(Gov)	Upper Heyford	2666	M-Sa
Bakery	581	4165	M-F
Bank	404	4175	M-Sa
	38/Croughton	7397	M-F
Barber Shop(s)	581	4562	M-Sa
	Flightline	4584	M-F
	NCO Qtrs	4325	M-F
	Croughton	N/A	M-F. By appoint.
Beauty Shop(s)	581	4581	M-Sa
Bookstore	469	4661	M-Sa
	Croughton	7420	Daily
Child Care/Dev Ctr	442	4527	Daily
	Croughton	7420	Daily
Clothing Sales	581	4136/4645	M-Sa
Commissary(Main)	581	4165	Tu-Su
Credit Union	546	4438	M-Sa
Dining Facility	Croughton	7376	M-F
	Lamplighter Inn	4321	M-F
Dry Clean(Exch)	581	4544	M-Sa
	Croughton	C-810060	M-F
	Upper Heyford	2017	M-Sa
Education Center	488	4321	M-F
Elec Repair(Civ)	Bichester	C-0869-246460	M-Sa

UNITED KINGDOM

RAF Upper Heyford/Croughton, continued

Exchange(Main)	581	4641/2851	Daily
Finance(Mil)	400	4191	M-F
Food(Caf/Rest)	N/A	4582	Daily
Food(Snack/Fast)	Croughton	7357	M-Sa
Burger Bar	457	4027	Daily
Hot Dog House	457	4582	Daily
Pizza Parlor	457	4600	Daily
Foodland	463	4362	Daily
Laundry(Exch)	581	4544	M-Sa
Laundry(Self-Svc)	402	None	24 hours daily
Package Store	588	4586	Tu-Su
Photo Laboratory	455	N/A	M-F
Postal Svcs(Mil)	106	N/A	M-Sa
SATO-OS	172	4676	M-F
Schools(DOD Dep)	46	4260/1	M-F
Svc Stn(Insta)	462	4071	Daily
	Croughton	7373	M-Sa
Tailor Shop	581	4561	M-Sa
	Upper Heyford	2407	M-Sa
Taxi(Comm)	Fritwell Cab	C-08696-520	24 hours daily
	Sids Taxis	C-244610	24 hours daily
TML			
Billeting	73, 401	4905	24 hours daily
TLQ	78	4557	Daily
VOQ	74	4905	Daily
DV/VIP	73	4557	Daily
Travel Agents	409	2458/4368	24 hours daily
	Croughton	7401	Tu-Th

HEALTH AND WELFARE

FACILITY/ACTIVITY	BLDG NO/LOC	PHONE	DAYS/COMMENTS
AF Family Svcs	133	4875	M-F
AF Relief	133	4881	M-F
Ambulance	582	C-086982-2900	24 hours daily
Central Appts	582	6225	Daily
CHAMPUS Office	582	6295	M-F
Chapel	572	4471	Daily
Comm Drug/Alc Ctr	582	4285	M-F
Dental Clinic	582	6217	M-F
Medical Emergency	582	6225	24 hours daily
Mental Health	582	6336	M-F
Poison Control	582	6225	24 hours daily
Red Cross	582	4603/4940	M-F
		113	After hours
Veterinary Svcs	See RAF Lakenheath listing.		

REST AND RECREATION

FACILITY/ACTIVITY	BLDG NO/LOC	PHONE	DAYS/COMMENTS
Bowling Lanes	576	4280	Daily
	Croughton	7320	Daily

UNITED KINGDOM
RAF Upper Heyford/Croughton, continued

Craftshops			
Automotive	575	4286	Daily
Ceramics	575	4249	Daily
Photography	575	4519	Daily
Enlisted Club	Croughton	7476	Daily
Gymnasium	583	4662	24 hours daily
	Croughton	7449	Daily
Info Tour & Travel	On Base	4874	M-F
Library	529	4963	Daily
	Croughton	7365	Su-Th
NCO Club	472	4284	Daily
O'Club	74	4424	Daily
Racket Courts	583	4662	Daily
Recreation Center	472B Skyline	4433	24 hours daily
Special Services	575	4226	M-F
Sport Field	583	4662	Daily
Theater	130	4239	Daily
Video Rental	529	4519	Daily
Youth Center	On Base	4202	M-Sa

WEST RUISLIP AIR STATION (UK28R7)
APO New York 09128-5000

TELEPHONE INFORMATION: Main installation numbers: Civ: 44-08956-31733. ATVN: 235-1110.

LOCATION: Located off UK-B466 northwest from London. Or take the Central Underground to West Ruislip. It's a mile walk to the air station. HE: p-13, D/2. NMC: London, 17 miles southeast

GENERAL INSTALLATION INFORMATION: The support base for U.S. Naval Forces Europe, including those based at West Ruislip, is at North Audley Street in London. A complete range of logistical and recreational support services are provided. **Note: the following abbreviation is used in this listing: AFX (ask for extension).**

GENERAL CITY/REGIONAL INFORMATION: West Ruislip is located in the northwestern suburbs of London and is accessible via the Central Underground.

ADMINISTRATIVE SUPPORT

FACILITY/ACTIVITY	BLDG NO/LOC	PHONE	DAYS/COMMENTS
Duty Officer	K	1110	24 hours daily
Housing	K	4278	M-F
Unaccompanied	K	4274	M-F
Personnel Spt	V	AFX	M-F

LOGISTICAL SUPPORT

FACILITY/ACTIVITY	BLDG NO/LOC	PHONE	DAYS/COMMENTS
Bookstore	60	AFX	W-Su

West Ruislip Air Station, continued

UNITED KINGDOM

Child Care/Dev Ctr	F	AFX	Daily
Dining Facility	J	AFX	Daily
Education Center	15	AFX	M-F
Exchange(Main)	1	AFX	M-F
Motor Pool	T	AFX	Daily
Postal Svcs(Mil)	U	AFX	M-Sa
Svc Stn(Insta)	X	AFX	Daily
Thrift Shop	15	AFX	M-F

HEALTH AND WELFARE

FACILITY/ACTIVITY	BLDG NO/LOC	PHONE	DAYS/COMMENTS
Chaplain	A	AFX	Daily
Navy Fam Svcs	G	AFX	M-F

REST AND RECREATION

FACILITY/ACTIVITY	BLDG NO/LOC	PHONE	DAYS/COMMENTS
Bowling Lanes	Q	AFX	Daily
Craftshops			
Automotive	R	C-31995	Daily
Enlisted Club	39	AFX	Daily
Equip/Gear Locker	15	C-31950	M-F
Gymnasium	B	C-31950	Tu-Su
Library	P	AFX	Daily
NCO Club	39	AFX	Daily
Service Club	E	AFX	Daily
Special Services	N	C-31950	Daily
Swimming Pool	C	AFX	Daily
Theater	M	AFX	Daily
Youth Center	H	AFX	Daily

RAF WETHERSFIELD (UK10R7)
APO New York 09120-5000

TELEPHONE INFORMATION: Main installation numbers: Civ: 44-0371-850317. ATVN: 244-1110.

LOCATION: From London take UK-12 north to UK-120 west, watch for signs in Braintree for RAF Wethersfield. HE: p-13, E-F/2NMC: London, 50 miles northeast.

GENERAL INSTALLATION INFORMATION: Wethersfield is a standby base. Assigned units include the 819th "Red Horse" Civil Engineering Squadron, the 7119th Air Base Flight Squadron and the 2166th Communications Squadron.

GENERAL CITY/REGIONAL INFORMATION: Wethersfield is located in Essex County north of London near the northern English Channel, an easy drive from Cambridge to the northwest. The base is surrounded by a beautiful rural countryside that is dominated by a 14th-century castle known as Hedingham.

UNITED KINGDOM
RAF Wethersfield, continued

ADMINISTRATIVE SUPPORT

FACILITY/ACTIVITY	BLDG NO/LOC	PHONE	DAYS/COMMENTS
Duty Officer	On Base	1110	24 hours daily
Fire(Mil)	59	117	24 hours daily
Housing	1070	2241	M-F
Personnel Spt	1070	2486	M-F
Police(Mil)	345	2417	24 hours daily

LOGISTICAL SUPPORT

FACILITY/ACTIVITY	BLDG NO/LOC	PHONE	DAYS/COMMENTS
Bank	390	2279	Tu-Sa
Bookstore	389	C-2463	M-Sa
Commissary(Main)	342	2367	Tu-Sa
Dining Facility	1072	2268	Daily
Education Center	1070	2287	M-F
Exchange(Main)	364	2349	Th-Tu
SATO-OS	1070	C-851072 ext. 2345	N/A
Schools(DOD Dep)	401	2274	M-F
Svc Stn	Braintree	C-850317	Daily
Space-A Air Ops	See RAF Mildenhall listing.		
TML			
Billeting	1032	2298/2520	Daily
		2334	After hours
TLQ	301, 1032	2298/2520	Daily

HEALTH AND WELFARE

FACILITY/ACTIVITY	BLDG NO/LOC	PHONE	DAYS/COMMENTS
AF Family Svcs	1020	2245	M-F
Ambulance	1073	C-850-018	24 hours daily
Central Appts	1073	2308	M-F
Medical Emergency	1073	C-850-018	24 hours daily

REST AND RECREATION

FACILITY/ACTIVITY	BLDG NO/LOC	PHONE	DAYS/COMMENTS
Bowling Lanes	9	2571	Daily
Consolidated Club	300	2236	N/A
Craftshops			
Automotive	382	2497	N/A
Gymnasium	9	2562	Daily
Youth Center	1007	2577	M-Sa

APPENDIX A

BEFORE YOU GO...*Travel Aids*

PASSPORTS

Passports are needed to depart or enter the United States and to enter most foreign countries. Apply at the post office, to the clerk of court at your local courthouse or at regional passport agencies. Contact the Office of Passport Services, The State Department, 1425 K Street NW, Washington, D.C. 20006, Tel: 202-647-0518 for detailed information. Allow three weeks' processing time to get a passport. Customs and duty restriction notices are also available and should be reviewed prior to your journey.

CUSTOMS AND DUTY EXEMPTIONS

In clearing U.S. Customs, a traveler is considered either a "returning resident of the U.S." or a "nonresident." Generally speaking, if you leave the U.S. for purposes of traveling, working or studying abroad and return to resume residency in the U.S., you are considered a returning resident by Customs. As a returning resident, you are allowed a $400 duty-free exemption based on the fair value of each item in the country where acquired, subject to the limitations on liquors, cigarettes and cigars, if:

    a. Articles were acquired as an incident of your trip for your personal or household use.

    b. You bring the articles with you at the time of your return to the U.S. and they are properly declared to Customs. Articles purchased and left for alterations or other purposes cannot be applied to your $400 exemption when shipped to follow later. Duty is assessed when received.

    c. You are returning from a stay abroad of at least 48 hours.

    d. You have not used this $400 exemption, or any part of it, within the preceding 30 days. Also, your exemption is not cumulative. If you use your exemption on entering the U.S., then you must wait for 30 days before you are entitled to another exemption other than for $25.

    e. Articles are not prohibited or restricted.

VISAS AND TOURIST CARDS are endorsements or stamps in your passport, issued by a foreign government, which permit your entry into that foreign country. **VERIFY THESE REQUIREMENTS WELL IN ADVANCE.** Normally they must be obtained from the appropriate embassy or consulate before you leave the U.S.

TRAVEL WARNINGS AND ADVISORIES—Check with the State Department concerning travel warnings and advisories if you are traveling to an unsettled area. Tel: 202-647-5225.

ENTRY (PASSPORT AND VISAS) AND IMMUNIZATION REQUIREMENTS are noted in each country section of this book. Immunization codes **EUR** and **AF** requirements are:

EUR/Europe—Immunizations required (voluntary for non-military personnel) for travel to the European area: DPT, polio (oral) and influenza. Smallpox immunization required for all active duty and reserve personnel but not for DOD civilians (including dependents).

AF/Africa and Southwest Asia—DOD personnel traveling to this area require the following immunizations: DPT, polio (oral) and influenza

Appendix A, continued

(voluntary for non-military personnel). Yellow fever is also required for travel to or through yellow fever endemic or receptive areas. Smallpox is required for all active duty and reserve military personnel but not for DOD civilians (including dependents). **CARRY YOUR UP-TO-DATE IMMUNIZATION RECORDS AND PASSPORT WITH YOU AT ALL TIMES.** If you've been to an infected area, you may be required to have cholera and yellow fever immunizations.

ELECTRICAL SYSTEMS ABROAD

Currents vary throughout Europe and you will need adaptors for the different types of plugs. Refer to the appendix about electrical systems.

TRAVEL PUBLICATIONS

The Government Printing Office (GPO) publishes many helpful pamphlets. A selection published by the U.S. State Department, pamphlet numbers and ordering information is listed below. You may order any of the above by mail or telephone from: The U.S. Government Printing Office, Washington, D.C. 20402, Tel: 202-783-3238. Most of the pamphlets cost $1; exceptions are noted.
—Health Information for International Travelers (no #), $4.95.
—Passports, #9458
—Tips for Travelers to Eastern Europe and Yugoslavia, #9329
—Tips for Travelers to the Middle East and North Africa, #9629
—Tips for Travelers to Saudi Arabia, #9369
—Travel Tips for Senior Citizens, #8970

Also available from the GPO are:
—Travelers Tips—Food, Plants and Animal Products, #1083, Dept. of Agriculture, Tel: 301-436-8645
—Pets, Wildlife, #509, Dept. of Treasury/Customs, Tel: 404-329-2574
—U.S. Customs/Importing a Car, #520, Dept. of Treasury
—Your Trip Abroad, #8969

Pocket Guides to the following countries, published by American Forces Information Service (AFIS) are available through your command or your service publication distribution center: Arab Peninsula (DODPG1, 1981); Benelux (DODPG9A, 1987); Germany (DODPG3B, 1987); Greece (#DODPG5C, 1987); Iceland (DODPG13, 1983); Italy (DODPG6B, 1987); Portugal (DODPG20, 1962); Spain (PG16C, 1987); Turkey (PG18A, 1981); United Kingdom (DODPG4C, 1987); You and the Law Overseas (DODGEN37B, 1986). Also available are: Assignment Italy DA Pamphlet 608-13, 1974; Coming to the Army in Europe, USAREUR Pamphlet 608-10, 1987.

RENTING A CAR

Rental cars are available throughout Europe and some Middle Eastern countries; however, reservations should be made and confirmed before you arrive at the foreign rental office. Extra insurance can be purchased when making the reservation and also with your personal insurance agent. Many American rental car companies have offices in major foreign cities and airports. Some AAFES and most Canadian Forces exchanges (CANEX) have rental cars. See each base/community listing for details.

Appendix A, continued

TRAIN TRAVEL IN EUROPE

There is an extensive rail system throughout Europe which provides a frequent, safe and punctual mode of transportation. *Eurailpass* provides unlimited first-class travel in 16 countries for 15 days to three months. The regional *Scandinavian Rail Pass* and the *Benelux Tourrail Pass*, as well as individual country rail passes, are available. Check with ITT tourist offices or a travel agent for further information.

INSURANCE AND HEALTH TIPS

1. Check with your personal health insurance agent for initial or extra international medical/travel coverage.

2. International Association for Medical Assistance to Travelers (IAMAT)—members are guaranteed qualified medical assistance 24 hours a day from an English-speaking physician. For information, write or call: IAMAT, 417 Center Street, Lewiston, NY 14092-1796, Tel: 716-754-4883.

3. Take a doctor's certificate if traveling with narcotic medicine.

4. Take extra medicine in originally labeled containers.

5. Legal drugs in U.S. may not be legal in foreign countries. Check with pertinent embassy or consulate.

6. ALLERGIES—if you have an allergy, wear a medical alert bracelet and list the allergies in your immunization records.

7. IF ILL OR INJURED, the U.S. Embassy or Consulate will help find medical assistance and communicate for you if necessary. The U.S. government will not pay for civilian evacuation out of foreign countries. Active duty and retired personnel and their dependents may be evacuated through U.S. military hospitals out of foreign countries. It's best to have extra medical insurance.

8. MARRIAGES—performed in accordance with local laws, often with residence requirement. Consult the local U.S. embassy.

9. BIRTHS—a child born in a foreign country to a U.S. citizen can acquire U.S. citizenship, but must be naturalized. Contact the nearest embassy for documentation.

10. DEATHS—Active duty military personnel stationed overseas and their dependents are entitled to have remains returned to the U.S. at government expense. Retired military, their dependents and civilians must pay to have remains returned stateside. Deaths are reported by the U.S. Consulate to the next of kin for instructions and funds needed to return the body to the U.S. or to provide for local interment.

A WORD ABOUT TERRORISM

The likelihood of you or your family being victims of terrorism is small; however, the threat is real, more so in some areas. The following are some common-sense guidelines: Stay alert. Be observant. Follow your instincts if you feel uncomfortable. Keep a low profile. Don't look or act flashy and don't flash money around. Vary your routine. Report any unusual activity that

Appendix A, continued

might be related to security to the appropriate on-base or post authorities.

APPENDIX B
UNITED STATES EMBASSIES (E) AND CONSULATES (C) IN SELECTED COUNTRIES

AUSTRIA (AS)
(E) Boltzmanngasse 16
A-1091 Vienna, Austria
APO NY 09108-5000
Tel: 43-222-31-55-11
Telex: 114634
Pub. Hrs: 0830-1700, M-F

(C) Giselakai 51
A 5020 Salzburg, Austria
Tel: 43-662-28-6-01
Telex: 6-33164
Pub. Hrs: 0830-1700, M-F

BAHRAIN (BA)
(E) Shaikh Isa Road,
Manama, Bahrain
P.O. Box 26431, Bahrain
APO NY 09526-5000
Tel: 973-714151
Telex: 9398 USATOBN
Pub. Hrs: 0700-1500, Sa-W

BELGIUM (BE)
(E) 27 Boulevard du Regent
B-1000 Brussels, Belgium
APO NY 09662-5000
Tel: 32-2-513-3830
Telex: 846-21336
Pub. Hrs: 0830-1730, M-F

(C) Rubens Center
Nationalestraat 5
V-2000 Antwerp, Belgium
Tel: 32-3-232-1800
Telex: 31966
Pub. Hrs: 0830-1730, M-F

CYPRUS (CY)
(E) Dositheos & Therissos St.
Nicosia, Cyprus
FPO NY 09530-5000
Tel: 357-21-465151
Telex: 4160 AME CY
Pub. Hrs: 0800-1700, M-F

DENMARK (DN)
(E) Dag Hammarskjolds Alle 24
2100 Copenhagen 0, Denmark
APO NY 09170-5000
Tel: 45-1-42-31-44
Telex: 22216
Pub. Hrs: 0800-1700, M-F

EGYPT (EG)
(E) 5 Sharia Latin America

Egypt (continued)
Garden City, Cairo, Egypt
FPO NY 09527-5000
Tel: 20-2-355-7371
Telex: 93773
Pub. Hrs: 0800-1630, Su-Th

FINLAND (FI)
(E) Itainen Puistotie 14A, SF-00140
Helsinki, Finland
APO NY 09664-5000
Tel: 358-0-171931
Telex: 121644 USEMB SF
Pub. Hrs: 0830-1700, M-F

FRANCE (FR)
(E) 2 Avenue Gabriel
75382 Paris Cedex 08, France
APO NY 09777-5000
Tel: 33-1-42-96-12-02
Telex: 650221
Pub. Hrs: 0900-1800, M-F

(C) 22 Cours du Marechal Foch
33080 Bordeaux Cedex, France
APO NY 09777-5000
Tel: 33-56-52-65-95
Telex: 540918
Pub. Hrs: 0900-1800, M-F

(C) 7 Qual General Sarrail
69454 Lyon Cedex 3, France
Tel: 33-78-246-849
Telex: USCSUL 380597F
Pub. Hrs: 0900-1800, M-F

(C) 12 Boulevard Paul Peytral
13286 Marseille Cedex, France
APO NY 09777-5000
Tel: 33-91-549-200
Telex: 430597
Pub. Hrs: 0900-1800, M-F

(C) 1 Rue du Marechal Joffre
06000 Nice, France
Tel: 33-93-88-89-55
Telex: 970469F
Pub. Hrs: 0900-1800, M-F

(C) 15 Avenue D'Alsace
67082 Strasbourg Cedex, France
APO NY 09777-5000
Tel: 33-88-35-31-04
Telex: 870907
Pub. Hrs: 0900-1800, M-F

Appendix B, continued

WEST GERMANY (GE)
(E) Deichmannsaue 29
5300 Bonn 2, FRG
APO NY 09080-5000
Tel: 49-228-3391
Telex: 885-452
Pub. Hrs: 0830-1730, M-F

(C) Clayallee 170
D-1000 Berlin 33, (Dahlem), FRG
APO NY 09742-5000
Tel: 49-30-8324087
Telex: 183-701 USBER-D
Pub. Hrs: 0830-1730, M-F

(C) Cecillanallee 5
4000 Dusseldorf 30, FRG
Tel: 49-211-490081
Telex: 8584246
Pub. Hrs: 0830-1730, M-F

(C) Siesmayerstraße 21
6000 Frankfurt, FRG
APO NY 09213-5000
Tel: 49-69-75305-0
Telex: 412589 USCON-D
Pub. Hrs: 0830-1730, M-F

(C) Alsterufer 27/28
2000 Hamburg 36, FRG
APO 09215-0012
Tel: 49-40-44171-0
Telex: 213777
Pub. Hrs: 0830-1730, M-F

(C) Königinstraße 5
8000 Munchen 22, FRG
APO NY 09108-5000
Tel: 49-89-23011
Telex: 5-22697 ACGMD
Pub. Hrs: 0830-1730, M-F

(C) Urbanstraße 7
7000 Stuttgart, FRG
APO NY 09154-5000
Tel: 49-711-21-02-21
Telex: 07-22945
Pub. Hrs: 0830-1730, M-F

(C) President Kennedy Platz
2800 Bremen 1, FRG
Tel: 49-24-321609
Telex: 244901 ACNBD D
Pub. Hrs: 0830-1730, M-F

GREECE (GR)
(E) 91 Vasilissis Blvd.
10160 Athens, Greece
APO NY 09255-0006
Tel: 30-1-721-2951
Telex: 21-5548
Pub. Hrs: 0830-1700, M-F

ICELAND (IC)
(E) Laufasvegur 21
Reykjavik, Iceland

ICELAND (continued)
FPO NY 09571-5000
Tel: 354-1-29100
Telex: USEMB IS3044
Pub. Hrs: 0830-1230/1330-1730, M-F

IRELAND (IR)
(E) 42 Elgin Road
Ballsbridge, Dublin, Ireland
Tel: 353-1-688777
Telex: 93684
Pub. Hrs: 0830-1700, M-F

ITALY (IT)
(E) Via Veneto 119/A
00187 Rome, Italy
APO NY 09794-5000
Tel: 39-6-46741
Telex: 622322 AMBRMA
Pub. Hrs: 0830-1730, M-F

(C) Banca D'America d'Italia Bldg.
Piazza Portello
6-16124 Genoa, Italy
Tel: 39-10-282-741/5
Telex: 270324 AMCOGE 1
Pub. Hrs: 0830-1730, M-F

(C) Via Principe Amedeo 2/10,
20121 Milano, Italy
US Embassy, Box M,
APO NY 09794-0007
Tel: 39-2-652-841/5
Telex: 330208
Pub. Hrs: 0830-1730, M-F

(C) Piazza della Repubblica
80122 Naples, Italy
Box 18, FPO NY 09521-5000
Tel: 39-81-660966
Telex: ICA NAPLES, 720442, ICANA
Pub. Hrs: 0830-1730, M-F

(C) Via Vaccarini 1
90143 Palermo, Italy
APO NY 09794-0007
Tel: 39-91-343-532
Telex: 910313 USACON 1
Pub. Hrs: 0830-1730, M-F

(C) Lungarno Amerigo Vespucci 38,
Florence, Italy. Tel: 39-55-298-276
Telex: 570577 ANCOFI 1
Pub. Hrs: 0830-1730, M-F

(C) Via Roma 9 (4th fl.)
Trieste, Italy
Tel: 39-40-68728/29
Telex: 460354 AMCOTS 1
Pub. Hrs: 0830-1730, M-F

(C) Via Pomba 23 (2nd fl.)
10123 Turin, Italy
APO NY 09794-0007
Tel: 39-11-517-437
Telex: 224102 AMCOTO 1

Appendix B, continued

ITALY (continued)
Pub. Hrs: 0830-1730, M-F

LUXEMBOURG (LU)
(E) 22 Boulevard Emmanuel-Servais
2535 Luxembourg, Luxembourg
APO NY 09132-5000
Tel: 352-460123
Telex: 461401
Pub. Hrs: 0830-1230/1330-1730, M-F

NETHERLANDS (NT)
(E) Lange Voorhoout 102
The Hague, Netherlands
APO NY 09159-5000
Tel: 31-70-62-49-11
Telex: 044-31016
Pub. Hrs: 0830-1715, M-F

(C) Museumplein 19
Amsterdam, Netherlands
APO NY 09159-5000
Tel: 31-20-64-56-61
Telex: 044-16176 CGUSA NL
Pub. Hrs: 0830-1715, M-F

NORWAY (NO)
(E) Drammensveien 18
Oslo 2, Norway
APO NY 09159-5000
Tel: 47-2-44-85-50
Telex: 78470 AEOSL N
Pub. Hrs: 0830-1700, M-F

PORTUGAL (PO)
(E) Avenida das Forcas Armadas
1600 Lisbon, Portugal
APO NY 09678-0002
Tel: 351-1-726-6600
Telex: 12528 AMEMB
Pub. Hrs: 0830-1730, M-F

(E) Avenida D. Henrique
Ponta Delgada, Sao Miguel,
Azores, Portugal
APO NY 09406-0002
Tel: 351-96-22216
Telex: 82126 AMCNPD P
Pub. Hrs: 0830-1730, M-F

(C) Rua Julio Dinis 826, 3d floor
4000 Oporto
Lisbon, Portugal
Tel: 351-2-63094
Telex: None
Pub. Hrs: 0830-1730, M-F

SAUDI ARABIA (SA)
(E) Collector Road M
Riyadh Diplomatic Quarter
APO Box 9041, Riyadh 11143,
Saudi Arabia
APO NY 09038-5000
Tel: 966-1-488-3800
Telex: 406866
Pub. Hrs: 0800-1700, Sa-W

SPAIN (SP)
(E) Serrano 75, Madrid, Spain
APO NY 09285-5000
Tel: 34-1-276-3400
Telex: 27763
Pub. Hrs: 0900-1800, M-F

(C) Via Layetana 33
Barcelona, Spain
APO NY 09286-5000
Tel: 34-3-319-9550
Telex: 32589
Pub. Hrs: 0900-1800, M-F

(C) Avenida del Ejercito, 11-3
48014 Bilbao
APO NY 09285-5000
Tel: 34-4-435-8300
Telex: 32589
Pub. Hrs: 0900-1800, M-F

SWEDEN (SW)
(E) Strandvagen 101
S-11527 Stockholm, Sweden
Tel: 46-8-7835300
Telex: 12060 AMEMBS
Pub. Hrs: 0800-1630, M-F

(C) Sodra Hamngatan 2
Goteborg, Sweden
Tel: 46-8-63-05-20
Tel: 21165 AMCONSUL S
Pub. Hrs: 0800-1630, M-F

SWITZERLAND (CH)
(E) Jubilaumstraße 93
3005 Bern, Switzerland
Tel: 41-31-437011
Telex: 845-912603
Pub. Hrs: 0830-1230/1400-1800, M-F

(C) 11, Route de Pregny,
1292 Chambesy/Geneva, Switzerland
Tel: 41-22-335537
Telex: 22103 USMIO CH
Pub. Hrs: 0830-1230/1400-1800, M-F

TURKEY (TU)
(E) 110 Ataturk Boulevard
Ankara, Turkey
APO 09254-0001
Tel: 90-4-126-54-70
Telex: 43144 USIA TR
Pub. Hrs: 0830-1730

UNITED KINGDOM (UK)
(E) 24/31 Grosvenor Square
W.1A 1AE London, England
FPO NY 09509-5000
Tel: 44-1-499-9000
Telex: 266777
Pub. Hrs: 0900-1800, M-F

(C) Queen's House, 14 Queen St.
BT16EQ, Belfast, Northern Ireland
Tel: 44-232-328239

Appendix B, continued

UNITED KINDOM (continued)
Telex: 747512
Pub. Hrs: 0900-1800, M-F

(C) 3 Regent Ter, EH 75BW
Edinburgh, Scotland
Tel: 44-31-556-8315
Telex: 727303
Pub. Hrs: 0900-1800, M-F

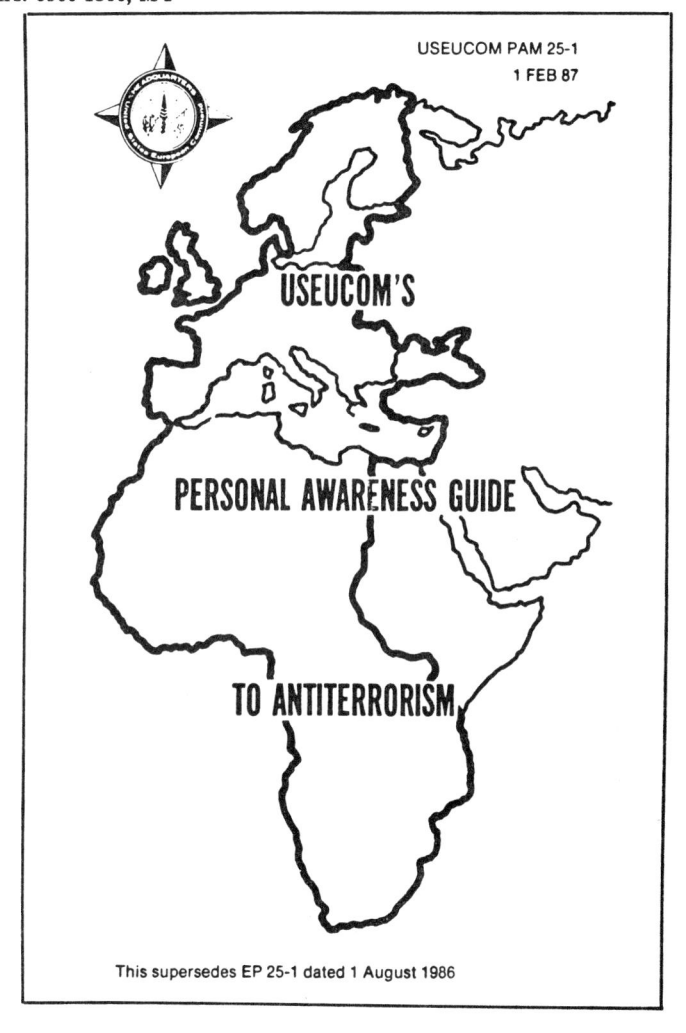

```
                               USEUCOM PAM 25-1
                                    1 FEB 87

              USEUCOM'S

       PERSONAL AWARENESS GUIDE

          TO ANTITERRORISM

       This supersedes EP 25-1 dated 1 August 1986
```

You may order this book through your unit personnel office in Europe or from Hq, USEUCOM, J-1, Directorate of Personnel/Administration, Adjutant General's Division, APO New York 09128-5000. ETS: 430-8236.

APPENDIX C

UNITED SERVICES ORGANIZATION (USO) EUROPE AND NEAR EAST AREA LOCATIONS

FRANCE

Paris USO
Pershing Hall
49 Rue Pierre Charron
75008 Paris, France
Civ. Tel: (011) 33-1-47237180
Fax: (011) 33-14-561-1498
Mailing address:
Paris USO
c/o General Delivery
APO NY 09777-5000

GERMANY

**USO Council of Germany
Administrative Offices (c)**
Oberstraße 19
6000 Frankfurt am Main 61
West Germany
Civ. Tel: (011) 49-69-419021
ETS/Mil. Tel: 320-7513
Fax: (011) 49-69-419022
Mailing address:
Box 10, FMC
APO NY 09710-5000

Baumholder USO
Hauptquartier
6587 Baumholder
Bldg. 8125, 2nd floor
West Germany
Civ. Tel: (011) 49-67-834694
ETS/Mil. Tel: 485-6155/7248
Mailing address:
Baumholder USO
HHD, USMCA
APO NY 09034-5000
Additional locations:
Kaserne Neubrücke
Strasbourg

Frankfurt USO
Eschersheimer Landstraße 166
Bldg. 1580-PX
6000 Frankfurt am Main 1
West Germany
Civ. Tel: (011) 49-69-567322
ETS/Mil. Tel: 320-7490/5472
Mailing address:
Frankfurt USO
Frankfurt Military Community, Box 74
APO NY 09710-5000

GERMANY (continued)

**USO/US Forces
Airport Lounge (a)**
Frankfurt Int'l Airport
Charter Section, Arrivals
Level 1, Flugplatz
Civ. Tel: (011) 49-69-691581
ETS/Mil. Tel: 320-8195/6364

USO Family Lounge (a)
Rhein Main Air Base
MAC Terminal
Frankfurt, West Germany
ETS/Mil. Tel: 330-6424
Mailing address for USOs at
Rhein-Main AB and Frankfurt
Int'l Airport: c/o Frankfurt USO

Fulda USO
Downs Barracks
Kettelerstraße, 6400 Fulda
West Germany
Civ. Tel: (011) 49-661-21805
ETS/Mil. Tel: 321-3607
Mailing address:
Fulda USO
USMCAM
Downs Barracks
APO NY 09146-5000
Additional location:
Bad Hersfeld

Hanau USO
Pioneer Kaserne, Bldg. 24
6450 Hanau-Wolfgang
West Germany
Civ. Tel: (011) 49-6181-56189
ETS/Mil. Tel: 322-8275/8042
Mailing address:
Hanau USO
Hanau Military Community
APO NY 09165-5000

Kaiserslautern USO
Bldg. #1003, VHA
6750 Kaiserslautern
Vogelweh Housing Area
West Germany
Civ. Tel: (011) 49-631-56091
ETS/Mil. Tel: 489-7275

Appendix C, continued

GERMANY (continued)

Mailing address:
Kaiserslautern USO
Bldg. 1003, VHA
APO NY 09094-5000
Additional locations:
Kleber Kaserne
Ramstein Air Force Base

Mannheim USO
Fürther Platz 1
6800 Mannheim 31
West Germany
Civ. Tel: (011) 49-621-721832
ETS/Mil. Tel: 380-7668
Mailing address:
Mannheim USO
U.S. Military Community Activity
APO NY 09086-5000

Stuttgart USO
Robinson Barracks
Aürbachstrasse 120
7000 Stuttgart 50
West Germany
Civ. Tel: (011) 49-711-8566875
ETS/Mil. Tel: 420-6261
Mailing Address:
Stuttgart USO, Bldg, 120
Robinson Barracks
APO NY 09457-5000
Additional locations:
Robinson Barracks PX Lobby

USO Wiesbaden/Mainz
Washington Str. 18
6200 Wiesbaden
West Germany
Civ. Tel: (011) 49-6121-72010
ETS/Mil. Tel: 337-5591
Mailing Address:
USO Wiesbaden, USMCA
Box 63, APO NY 09457-5000
Additional locations:
LASCOM Lobby Booth
Lee Barracks
Mainz-Finthen Army Airfield
Regional Medical Center Booth
The Source
Wiesbaden Air Base Lounge

ICELAND
USO Keflavik
NAS Keflavik, FPO NY 09751-5000
Civ. Tel: (011) 354-25-6113
Fax: (011) 354-25-2836

ITALY

Rome USO
Via Della Conciliazione 2
00193 Rome, Italy
Civ. Tel: (011) 39-6-6864272
Mailing address:
Rome USO
APO NY 09794-0007
Cable address:
USO CLUB, Roma (Italia)

USO Mediterranean Fleet Operations Admin. Offices (b/c)
Via E. Scarfoglio
NSA Agnano
80125 Naples Italy
Civil. Tel: (011) 39-81-7609076
Mil. Tel: 625-1110, ext. 4664
Fax: (011) 39-81-7244489
Telex: CITNAP 710156
Mailing address:
USO Mediterranean
Fleet Operations
NSA, Box 34
FPO NY 09521-5000

USO French Riviera (Cannes) Center (b/c)
53 Rue Felix Faure
06400 Cannes, France
Civ. Tel: (011) 33-93-385626
Mailing Address:
Cannes USO Fleet Center
c/o USO Consulate Marseille
APO NY 09777-5000

USO Naples Fleet Center (b)
Calata San Marco 10
80133 Naples, Italy
Civ. Tel: (011) 39-81-5513983
Mailing Address:
c/o USO Med Fleet Operations
NOTES:
(a) = USO Airport center
(b) = USO Fleet center
(c) = Administrative office <u>only</u>

Civilian telephone numbers indicate direct dialing from the USA. For calls in-country Europe, drop the overseas and country codes, dial "0" in front of the city code.

Appendix C, continued

MEDITERRANEAN AND ATLANTIC FLEET OPERATIONS

Corsica—Bastia.

Egypt—Alexandria, Port Said.

France—Brest, Cannes, Cavalaire, Cherbourg, Dunkerque, Golfe Juan, Le Harve, Marseille, Menton, Nice, St. Maxime, St. Raphael, St. Topez, Sète, Thèoule, Toulon, Villefranche.

Greece—Athens, Corfu.

Israel—Ashdod, Haifa.

Italy—Bari, Brindisi, Catania, Genoa, La Spezia, Livorno, Messina, Naples, Palermo, Rapallo, San Remo,

Italy (continued) Siracusa, Taranto, Taomina, Trieste, Venice.

Monaco—Monte Carlo.

Morroco—Tangiers.

Spain—Alicante, Algeciaras, Barcelona, Benidorm, Cartagena, Malaga/Torremolinos, Palma de Mallorca, Rota, Valencia.

Tunisia—Tunis.

Turkey—Istanbul, Antalya.

APPENDIX D

SUPPORT AUTHORIZED U.S. MILITARY ACTIVE DUTY PERSONNEL AND THEIR FAMILIES

Active duty personnel stationed in or on temporary duty to Belgium, West Germany, Greece, Italy, the Netherlands, Norway, Spain, Turkey and the United Kingdom have full commissary and exchange privileges in these countries. Active duty members from outside the NATO area on TDY for less than 30 days must have their TDY orders stamped by the local billeting office to enter commissaries and exchange facilities and to purchase rationed items. Those on TDY for more than 30 days must obtain a ration card to enter facilities in Greece, Turkey, the Netherlands and the United Kingdom, and to purchase rationed items in all countries. Members of the reserve components must be on active duty for training (ADT) status to enter facilities, according to authorities.

Active duty U.S. military on leave to Belgium, the Netherlands, Norway, Spain, Turkey and the United Kingdom do not have commissary and exchange shopping privileges at base facilities in these countries. Those on leave in West Germany who are stationed in Europe and North Africa may shop in commissary and exchange facilities in West Germany. Only personnel stationed in the NATO area have shopping privileges in Greece, except for the purchase of controlled items such as electronic merchandise. Members stationed in the NATO area on leave in Italy have shopping privileges, including the purchase of rationed items, from commissaries and exchanges in Italy. Those stationed outside the area may not purchase rationed items.

APPENDIX E
SUPPORT AUTHORIZED U.S. MILITARY RETIRED PERSONNEL AND THEIR FAMILIES

To our knowledge, only the following facilities/services are available in the following countries:

BAHRAIN: enlisted, NCO and officers' clubs; Fleet Post Office (FPO); legal assistance; medical/dental; Morale, Welfare and Recreation (MWR); mortuary; Space-A air opportunities (Space-A).

BELGIUM: enlisted, NCO and officers' clubs; legal assistance; local U.S. government transportation; medical/dental; mortuary, MWR; Temporary Military Lodging (TML); Space-A. Commissary and exchange privileges may be granted on a case-by-case basis.

CYPRUS: legal assistance; medical/dental; mortuary; Space-A.

EGYPT: Army Post Office (APO); banks/credit unions; Class VI; commissary; enlisted, and officers' clubs; legal assistance, medical/dental; mortuary; MWR; Space-A.

GERMANY: adult education; APO/FPO (one pound limit); banks/credit unions; enlisted, NCO and officers' clubs; legal assistance, local U.S. government transportation; medical/dental; mortuary; MWR; quartermaster laundry/dry cleaning; Space-A; TML. **NOTE:** Retired personnel, their accompanying family members and survivors of deceased retirees who are visiting for less than 30 days are considered tourists by the German government. After 30 days' residence, they may apply for and be granted resident alien status and can then access the commissary, exchange and Class VI facilities as well as the ARMED FORCES RECREATION CENTERS, provided they have registered with the 42nd Military Police Group (customs) ETS: 380-76101/6847, ask for Customer Service Information Sheet #8— and the local German customs authorities to obtain a German Customs Certificate. All purchases are subject to a monthly payment of 15 percent tax (subject to change). PURCHASE OF RATIONED ITEMS (COFFEE, TEA, HARD LIQUOR, TOBACCO AND PETROLEUM) IS NOT AUTHORIZED.

GREECE: APO/FPO; banks/credit unions; enlisted, NCO and officers' clubs; legal assistance; local U.S. government transportation; medical/dental; mortuary; MWR; Space-A; TML. **NOTE:** Limited support (i.e. commissary and exchange) is extended to retired U.S. military personnel, 100% disabled veterans and their family members who are residents of Greece. Rationed items may not be purchased. Tourists staying only a few months are not eligible.

ICELAND: banks/credit unions; enlisted, NCO and officers' clubs; legal assistance; local U.S. government transportation; medical/dental; mortuary; MWR; Space-A; TML.

ITALY: adult education; APO/FPO (one pound limit); banks/credit unions; Class VI (see note); commissary, enlisted, NCO and officers' clubs; exchange, legal assistance; local U.S. government transportation; medical/dental; mortuary; MWR; quartermaster laundry/dry cleaning; Space-A; TML. **NOTE:** PURCHASE OF RATIONED ITEMS (COFFEE, TEA, HARD LIQUOR, TOBACCO PRODUCTS AND PETROLEUM) IS NOT AUTHORIZED.

Appendix E, continued

NETHERLANDS: adult education, banks/credit unions; enlisted, NCO and officers' clubs; legal assistance; local U.S. government transportation; medical/dental; mortuary; MWR; quartermaster laundry/dry cleaning; Space-A; TML.

NORWAY: enlisted, NCO and officers' clubs; legal assistance; local U.S. government transportation; medical/dental; mortuary; MWR; Space-A. Retirees who are residents of Norway may obtain commissary and exchange privileges for the purchase of non-rationed items by paying a fixed 20 percent tax to Norwegian customs authorities.

PORTUGAL—LAJES FIELD ONLY: adult education; APO; banks/credit unions; Class VI; enlisted, NCO and officers' clubs; exchange; gasoline; legal assistance; local U.S. government transportation; medical/dental; mortuary; MWR; Space-A; TML. **NOTE:** Access to Lajes Field must be obtained from Portuguese Air Force authorities.

SAUDI ARABIA: APO; adult education; banks/credit unions; enlisted, NCO and officers' clubs; legal assistance; local U.S. government transportation; medical/dental; mortuary; MWR; Space-A.

SPAIN: adult education; APO/FPO; banks/credit unions; enlisted, NCO and officers' clubs; legal assistance; local U.S. government transportation; medical/dental; mortuary; MWR; Space-A; TML. **NOTE:** Retirees are required to obtain a Spanish Pass for access to each base. The pass is issued by the Spanish Forces at the base in question. This may be accomplished at the entrance to the base or, if arriving via MAC flight, at the MAC terminal upon arrival in Spain.

TURKEY: adult education; APO/FPO; banks/credit unions; enlisted, NCO and officers' clubs; legal assistance; local U.S. government transportation; medical/dental; mortuary; MWR; Space-A; TML.

UNITED KINGDOM: adult education; banks/credit unions; legal assistance; local U.S. government transportation; medical/dental; mortuary; Space-A; TML. **NOTE:** Currently, privileges extended to military retirees and their family members are limited. Transient retirees are not authorized to use the exchange or commissary facilities. Use of MWR and facilities is subject to local command approval. If transient retirees are employed by the Department of the Army Civilian (DAC) or if they are also DOD civilian employees, they are entitled to fuel, tobacco and alcoholic spirits. All purchases made by retirees who are residents of the U.K. are subject to a prepaid 15 percent tax levied by British customs authorities.

APPENDIX F
APO/FPO AND MAIL INFORMATION

While stationed overseas, you can receive letters, magazines, packages and newspapers through the Army Post Office (APO)/Fleet Post Office (FPO) mail systems if you have access to APO/FPO facilities. Your sponsor can get you an APO/FPO box before you arrive. Mail takes about a week between the U.S. and Germany and costs are computed from New York City for points beyond in the U.S. For postal costs, you can use cash and traveler's checks (you must spend at least 50 percent of the face value for each traveler's check used) and write personal checks. The APO-FPO system also provides money orders;

Appendix F, continued

travelers checks cannot be used to purchase money orders.
All items 12 ounces or less, when going to other European APOs, can be mailed free of charge (there are some restrictions). Also, packages weighing up to 70 pounds may now be mailed free from overseas military post offices to other APOs within the same theater, with the exception of certified, insured or registered packages. Check with your local APO facility for size restrictions on free package mailings.

There are restrictions on items mailed from Europe, including articles that may kill or injure a person, damage mail or other property, or for other reasons have been declared non-mailable by law or regulations. Examples of non-mailable matter are: intoxicating liquors and liquor-filled candies; contraband (knives, etc.); narcotic drugs; all USAREUR rationed items (coffee, tea, tobacco); poisonous animals (snakes); explosive and flammable material; concealable firearms; radioactive matter and poison or poisonous items. The restriction of mailing rationed items applies only to certain APOs.

The "Verification of Retired Status" and German Customs Certificates will be issued to retired U.S. military personnel residing or visiting in Germany for a period of <u>at least one month</u>. In order for you to obtain APO privileges, you must make arrangements with the local APO to receive your mail through "Box R" (General Delivery Mail Section). All your mail must be addressed to "Box R" of the APO concerned, and must include the word "retired" (i.e. U.S. Army Ret"). You must pick up your mail at the APO concerned. Check with your local APO for other regulations and assistance or call Mannheim Military ETS: 380-7610/6847.

When using a local German return address, you must use German postage.

==

Call the U.S.A. Direct from Europe

From	Dial
Belgium	11-0010
Denmark	0430-0010
Finland	9800-100-10
France	19*-0011
Germany (West)	**0130-0010
The Netherlands	06*-022-9111
Sweden	020-795-611
United Kingdom	0800-89-0011

* = Wait for second dial tone.
** = Available on a trial basis only; excludes the Frankfurt area.

Note: After dialing the numbers above, you will be connected with an AT&T operator in the U.S.A. You must have an AT&T card or call collect. There are many special U.S.A.-direct phones in airports, hotel lobbies, on military bases and at seaports.

APPENDIX G

UNITED STATES MILITARY CEMETERIES IN EUROPE

World War I Cemeteries

Aisne Marne—Belleau, France
Brookwood—Brookwood, England
Flanders Field—Waregam, Belgium
Meuse-Argonne—Romagne, France
Oise-Aisne—Fere-en-Tardenais, France
St. Mihiel—Thiacourt, France
Somme—Bony, France
Suresnes—Paris, France

U.S. European Command military forces provide ceremonies and honors at these locations as appropriate.

World War II Cemeteries

Ardennes—Ardennes, Belgium
Brittany—St. James, France
Cambridge—Cambridge, England
Epinal—Epinal, France
Florence—Florence, Italy
Henri-Chapelle—Henri-Chappelle, Belgium
Lorraine—St. Avold, France
Luxembourg—Luxembourg City, Luxembourg
Netherlands—Margraten, Holland
Normandy—St. Laurent, France
North Africa—Cartharge, Tunisia
Rhone—Draguignan, France
Sicily-Rome—Nettuno, Italy

NOTE: For more information on the above-listed cemeteries, write to: American Battle Monuments Commission, European Office, American Embassy, Paris, APO New York 09777-5000.

APPENDIX H

DRIVING IN EUROPE AND THE NEAR EAST

AUTOMOBILE CLUBS IN SELECTED EUROPEAN/NEAR EAST COUNTRIES

AUSTRIA (A)
Police: 133, Medical: 144,
Osterreichischer Automobil,
Motorrad und Touring-Club
  (OAMTCO)
  Schubertring 1-3,
  1010 Vienna, Austria
OAMTCO Tel: 43-222-7-29-90
  Breakdown Service, OAMTCO,
  Tel: 120
ADAC Tel: 43-222-73-65-11-18

BELGIUM (B)
Police: 906 Cities, 901 other areas
Medical: 900
Touring Club Royal de Belgique (TCB)

BELGIUM (continued)
  Touring-Secours, 44 rue de la Loi,
  1040 Brussels, Belgium
  TCB Tel: 32-2-233-2211
  Breakdown Service TCB
  Tel: (2)-233-2211, ask oper.
  in each city
Royal Automobile Club de Belgique
  (RACB)
  53 rue d'Arlon,
  1040 Brussels, Belgium
RACB Tel: 32-2-230-0810
ADAC Tel: 32-2-770-5830

Appendix H, continued

CYPRUS (CY)
Police and medical: Ask operator
Cyprus Automobile Association
 (CAA)
 12 Chr Mylonas Street
 Nicosia 141, Cyprus
 CAA Tel: 357-2-31-32-33
 Breakdown Service CAA
 Tel: (2)-31-32-33
 ADAC Tel: 357-2-44-43-62-4

DENMARK (DK)
Police and Medical: 000 toll-free
Forenede Danske Motorejere (FDM)
 Blegdamsvdj 124
 2100 Copenhagen, Denmark
 FDM: Tel: 45-1-38-21-12
 Breakdown Service (FDM); contact
 Falck, Copenhagen (1) 31-21-44 +
 ask oper in each city
 ADAC Tel: 45-1-26-16-22

FINLAND (SF)
Police: 000, Medical: 002
Automobile and Touring Club of
 Finland (Autoliitto)
 Kansakoulukatu 10
 00100 Helsinki, Finland
 Autoliito Tel: 358-0-6-94-00-22
 Breakdown Service (Autoliito)
 Tel: (90)-694-0496
 ADAC Tel: 358-0-6-94-33-55

FRANCE (F)
Police and Medical: 17
Association Francaise de
 Automobilistes (AFA)
 9 rue Anatole-de-la-Forge
 75017 Paris, France
 AFA Tel: 33-1-42-27-82-00/
 43-80-21-70
 Automobile Club de France (ACF)
 6-8 Place de la Concorde
 75008 Paris, France
 ACF Tel: 33-1-42-65-34-70
 Automobile Club De L'Ouest (ACO)
 31 Ave Friedland
 75008 Paris, France
 ACO Tel: 33-1-45-63-68-62
 ADAC Tel: 33-1-43-59-33-51
 Breakdown Service Paris
 Tel: (161)-4500-4295 + ask oper. in
 each city

GERMANY (WEST) (D)
Police and medical: 110
Allgemeiner Deutscher Automobile-
 Club (ADAC)

GERMANY (WEST) (continued)
 Am Westpark 8
 8000 Munchen 70, West Germany
 ADAC Tel: 49-89-76-76-0
 Breakdown Service: Dial the city
 code + 19211 for Germ. & emerg.
 ctrs outside Germ., 24 hrs.;
 22-22-22

GREECE (GR)
Police: Athens 171; others, 100
Medical: Athens 150, others, 166
Automobil und Touring Club
 von Griechenland (ELPA)
 Rue Messogion 2-4
 Athens 11527, Greece
 ELPA Tel: 30-1-7-79-16-15
 Breakdown Service: Athens,
 Tel: (01)-104, 24 hrs, + ask oper.
 in each city; hrs: 0700-2200.
 ADAC Tel: 30-1-3-69-41

IRELAND (IRL)
Police and Medical: 999, toll-free
The Automobile Association (AA)
 23 Suffolk Street, Dublin, Ireland
 AA Tel: 353-1-7794-81
 Breakdown Service: Dublin
 (1) 77-9481; + ask
 oper. in each city hrs: 0800-0100
 ADAC Tel: 353-1-69-30-11

ITALY (I)
Police and Medical: 113
Automobile-Club d'Italia (ACI)
 Via Marsala 8, Rome 00185, Italy
 ACI Tel: 39-6-4-99-81
 Breakdown Service Tel: 116
 ADAC Tel: 39-6-86-03-41/86-93-41
 Breakdown Service: ADAC Rome
 (06) 495-4730 + ask oper. in each
 city

LUXEMBOURG (L)
Police and Medical: 012
Automobile Club du Grand-Duché
 de Luxembourg (ACL)
 13 route de Longwy,
 Helfenterbruck, Luxembourg
 ACL Tel: 352-31-10-31
 Breakdown Service Tel: 31-10-31
 ADAC Tel: 352-2-67-91/92

NETHERLANDS (NL)
Police: 22-22-22 (Amst.) + varies,
 call oper.
Koninklijke Nederlandse
 Töristenbond (ANWB)

Appendix H, continued

NETHERLANDS (continued)
Wassenaarseweg 220
2596 E C Den Haag, Netherlands
ANWB Tel: 31-70-26-44-26
  Breakdown Service Amsterdam
  Tel: (020) 26-8251
  Breakdown Service Den Haag
  Tel: (070) 63-69-68, + ask oper. in
  each city
Koninklijke Nederlandse Automobile
  Club (KNAC)
  Westvlietweg 118
  2267 Leidschendam, Netherlands
KNAC Tel: 31-70-46-92-80
ADAC Tel: 31-70-46-92-06

NORWAY (N)
Police: 002 Oslo; others, oper.
Medical: 003 Oslo; others, oper.
Norges Automobil-Forbund (NAF)
  Storgaten 2, Oslo, Norway
NAF Tel: 47-2-42-94-00
  Breakdown Service Oslo: 24 hrs
  (02) 42-9400; other cities,
  hrs: 0600-2400 ask oper.
Kongelig Norsk Automobil-Klub
  (KNA)
  Parkveien 68, Oslo 2, Norway
KNA Tel: 47-2-44-69-70
ADAC Tel: 47-2-55-20-10

PORTUGAL (P)
Police and Medical: 115
Automovel Club de Portugal (ACP)
  Rua Rosa Arujo 24-26
  1200 Lisboa, Portugal
ACP Tel: 351-1-56-39-31
  Breakdown Service
  Tel: 01-775402/775475 and
  02-29271/2/3
ADAC Tel: 351-1-56-39-61/56-30-50

SPAIN (E)
Police and Medical: Varies, call oper.
Real Automovil Club de España
  (RACE)
  Jose Abascal 10
  28003 Madrid, Spain
RACE Tel: 3491-4-47-32-00
  Breakdown Service Madrid (91)
  441-22-22 + ask oper. in each city
ADAC Tel: 34-91-4-19-91-00

SWEDEN (S)
Police and Medical: 90000
Motormannens Riksforbund (MF)
  Sturegatan 32

SWEDEN (continued)
  10248 Stockholm, Sweden
MF Tel: 46-8-7-82-38-00
  Breakdown Service Stockholm
  (08)-13-10-00 + ask oper. in each
  city
ADAC Tel: 46-8-63-13-80

SWITZERLAND (CH)
Police: 117; Medical; 144
Touring Club der Schweiz (TCS)
  9 rue Pierre-Fatio
  1211 Geneva 3, Switzerland
TCS Tel: 41-22-35-80-00
Automobil Club der Schweiz (ACS)
  Wasserwerkgasse 39
  3000 Bern 13, Switzerland
ACS Tel: 41-31-22-47-22
  Breakdown Service: Tel: 140
ADAC Tel: 41-31-44-08-31-35

TURKEY (TR)
Police: Istanbul 5-28-53-69; other varies
Medical: varies, call oper.
Turkiye Turing ve Otomobil Kurumu
  (TTOK)
  Sisli Meydani 364, Istanbul,
  Turkey
TTOK Tel: 90-1-31-46-31
  Breakdown Service Ankara
  Tel: 31-76-48/49 + ask oper. in
  each city
ADAC Tel: 90-1-62-10-00/62-07-10

UNITED KINGDOM (UK)
Police and Medical: 999 toll-free
The Automobile Association (AA)
  Fanum House
  Basingstoke/Hampshire, UK
AA Tel: 44-02-56-2-01-23
  Breakdown Service
  Tel: (01) 954-73-73 + ask oper. in
  each city
ADAC Tel: 44-1-2-35-50-33

NOTE: Automobile decal symbols follow country names.

Appendix H, continued

INTERNATIONAL DRIVING PERMITS (IDPs)

NOTE: IDPs ARE NOT VALID IN THE COUNTRY IN WHICH THEY ARE ISSUED. YOU MUST HAVE YOUR VALID U.S. OR TERRITORIAL LICENSE WITH YOU WHEN USING YOUR IDP. The IDP is not valid in the U.S.

Many servicemembers unknowingly illegally operate their privately owned vehicles on a USAREUR Operators License when the country they're visiting may actually require an International Driving Permit (IDP), see column B below. Additionally, some countries have other unique requirements concerning proof of insurance, etc. See column A and footnotes below.

TO OBTAIN AN INTERNATIONAL DRIVING PERMIT, FOLLOW THESE STEPS:

PHOTO: Obtain a 1/2" wide x 2" long vertical photograph which must be taken in civilian clothes. Get several; often, more than one is needed.

APPLICATION:

1) You may obtain an international driving permit from your local American Automobile Association (AAA) travel office prior to departure. You do not have to be a member to take advantage of this service. Issuance is restricted to persons 18 years or over who hold a valid U.S. or Territorial License. IDPs cost $5, are valid for one year and are not renewable. Or, (2) purchase an IDP in a foreign country after you arrive, or (3) after arriving in Germany, you may obtain an application from the local Landratsmat (county courthouse) in the town or city where you live or from a local German Auto Club (ADAC). In Germany, application for the license must be made in the town or city where the applicant is stationed (local military police can provide the exact location of the Landratsmat). The following is necessary:
1. An application (forms in English are available at issuing agency).
2. A valid USAREUR POV operator's license (AE Form 206).
3. Vertical photograph (in civilian clothes) 1/2"w x 2"l inches. Some cities may require two photos.
4. U.S. passport (only DA/DAF civilians and dependents).
5. Expect to pay a fee of DM 10.
Submit the application, photo and other items with the fee to the Landrasmat. Normally, the license will be processed the same day.

INTERNATIONAL INSURANCE CARD (IIC) (GREEN CARD)

The IIC is referred to as the "green card" and can be obtained from your insurance company at no cost.

394 — U.S. Forces Travel & Transfer Guide Europe

INTERNATIONAL TRAFFIC SIGNS

SLIPPERY ROAD	CHILDREN	CONSTRUCTION SITE	DRAWBRIDGE AHEAD	WILD ANIMAL CROSSING	DOMESTIC ANIMAL CROSSING	SIDE WIND	FALLING STONES	PASSING ONLY FROM BROKEN LINE SIDE
QUAY OR RIVER BANK	LOW FLYING AIRCRAFT	PEDESTRIAN CROSSWALK AHEAD	PEDESTRIAN CROSSWALK	SINGLE CURVE	DOUBLE CURVE	ROAD NARROWS	ROAD NARROWS	MANDATORY DIRECTION OF TRAVEL
BICYCLE CROSSING	DANGEROUS DOWNGRADE	DANGEROUS UPGRADE	ROUGH ROAD	DANGER	STRASSENBAHN DANGER	ONCOMING TRAFFIC	CROSSROADS	AUSFAHRT AUTOBAHN EXIT / EINFAHRT AUTOBAHN ENTRANCE
MAXIMUM HEIGHT ALLOWED	MAXIMUM WIDTH ALLOWED	MAXIMUM WEIGHT ALLOWED	NO VEHICLES CARRYING MORE THAN 3000 LITERS OF POLLUTANTS	VEHICLES ABOVE A SPECIFIC AXLE WEIGHT PROHIBITED	MOTOR VEHICLES PROHIBITED	TRACTORS AND TRUCKS WITH AN AUTHORIZED LOADED WEIGHT OF MORE THAN 2.8 TONS (3 OR US TONS) PROHIBITED	MAXIMUM LENGTH ALLOWED	U 22 AUTOBAHN DETOUR
DISTANCE TO UNGUARDED RAILROAD CROSSING	RAILROAD CROSSING SIGNAL LIGHTS	RAILROAD CROSSING	GUARDED RAILROAD CROSSING	UNGUARDED RAILROAD CROSSING	MAXIMUM SPEED LIMIT	END OF SPEED LIMIT	MAXIMUM SPEED LIMIT WHEN WET	DIRECTION OF TRAVEL
NO PASSING FOR TRUCKS IN EXCESS OF 2.8 TONS AUTHORIZED WEIGHT	END OF NO PASSING ZONE	LIMITED PARKING PLACE CLOCK CARD IN WINDSHIELD	END OF LIMITED PARKING ZONE	END OF RESTRICTION	RIGHT OF WAY	ZOLL DOUANE CUSTOMS CONTROL	ONCOMING TRAFFIC HAS RIGHT OF WAY	STREETCAR STOP / BUS STOP
PRIORITY ROAD AHEAD	TAXI PARKING ONLY	ONE WAY STREET IN DIRECTION OF ARROW	DEAD END	ONE WAY STREET	ONCOMING TRAFFIC MUST WAIT	COMPULSORY MINIMUM SPEED	END OF COMPULSORY MINIMUM SPEED ZONE	DIRECTION ARROWS USE CORRECT LANE
SIGNAL LIGHTS AHEAD	STOP	YIELD RIGHT OF WAY	PRIORITY ROAD	PRIORITY ROAD	END OF PRIORITY ROAD	BEGINNING OF A PEDESTRIAN PRIORITY AREA	END OF A PEDESTRIAN PRIORITY AREA	MANDATORY DIRECTION OF TRAVEL
CHILDREN PLAYING	TEMPORARY "GO" SIGN	PROHIBITED FOR ALL VEHICLES	ENTRY PROHIBITED	DISTANCE TO GUARDED RAILROAD CROSSING	NO STOPPING ON SHOULDER	SOFT SHOULDER	BUILT UP AREA REVERSE REVISION	DIRECTION TO AUTOBAHN
RESTRICTED NO STOPPING	NO STOPPING	NO PASSING	END OF NO PASSING ZONE	SNOW CHAIN MANDATORY	HORSEMEN ONLY	PEDESTRIAN ONLY	BICYCLES ONLY	DETOUR ROUTE SIGN
MANDATORY DIRECTION OF TRAVEL	MANDATORY DIRECTION OF TRAVEL	MANDATORY DIRECTION OF TRAVEL	MANDATORY DIRECTION OF TRAVEL	POLICE	RECOMMENDED MINIMUM AND MAXIMUM SPEED	PARKING ON CURB PERMITTED	PARKING AREA	DIRECTIONAL SIGN
AUTOBAHN	AUTOBAHN ENDS	MOTOR VEHICLES ONLY	END OF MOTOR VEHICLES ONLY	CHANGE OF TRAFFIC LANES	DIRECTION SIGN	BYPASS ROUTING	UMLEITUNG DETOUR	E 36 EUROPEAN HIGHWAY
PEDESTRIAN CROSSWALK	NO PARKING	FIRST AID STATION	TELEPHONE	BUILT UP AREA (FRONT)	BUILT UP AREA (REVERSE)	AUTOBAHN DIRECTION SIGN	DIRECTION TO AUTOBAHN	233 FEDERAL HIGHWAY NUMBER

Appendix H, continued

BORDER, INSURANCE AND LICENSE REQUIREMENTS

Listed below, with numbered exceptions, are the border crossing, insurance, and license requirements for privately owned, passenger-carrying vehicles and those bearing USAREUR license plates. Auto decal codes are in parentheses.

Y: YES
N: NO

	International Insurance "Green" Card (IIC)	International Driving Permit (IDP)
Austria (A)	Y	Y
Belgium (B)	Y	N
Denmark (DK)	Y	N(Y)(1)
Egypt (EG)	N(5)	Y
Finland (SF)	Y	N
France (F)	Y	N
Great Britain (GB)	Y(2)	N(4)
Greece (GR)	Y(3)	Y
Ireland (IRL)	Y	Y
Italy (I)	Y(5)	N
Luxembourg (L)	Y	N
Netherlands (NL)	N	N(4)
Norway (N)	Y	N
Portugal (P)	Y	N
Spain (E)	Y	Y
Sweden (S)	Y	N
Switzerland (CH)	Y	N
Turkey (TR)	Y(6)	Y

Key to exceptions:
1. National driver's license has to bear a photograph. (Note: there is no photo on USAREUR license.)
2. A customs notice is issued at point of entry for temporary import.
3. IIC "green" card must be specifically validated for Greece.
4. International driving permit is required for dependents of U.S. Forces pesonnel driving a USAREUR-registered vehicle.
5. The IIC "green" card is not valid, but a certificate of carnet de passage and adequate insurance must be bought before or at the border.
6. For travel in Turkey, insurance must be purchased at the Turkish border if IIC "green" card is not specifically validated for Turkey.

NOTE: ALL WESTERN EUROPEAN COUNTRIES REQUIRE THAT THE OVAL "USA" DECALS BE AFFIXED TO THE REAR OF U.S. FORCES-LICENSED POVs, WITH THE EXCEPTION OF U.S. FORCES STATIONED IN ITALY WHO WILL HAVE "AFI" LICENSE PLATES AND WHO ARE REQUIRED TO HAVE THE OVAL "I" DECAL INSTEAD OF THE "USA" DECAL.

U. S. FORCES GAS COUPON SALES

Belgium/Great Britain—Only military and DOD personnel stationed here or on TDY can buy reduced-rate coupons.

Germany—Available at AAFES POL (petroleum) sales points located at each

Appendix H, continued

military community AAFES post or base exchange customer service area. Note: Unleaded normal/super POL coupons available.

Greece—Available at AAFES stations at Hellenikon AB, Nea Makri Naval Communication Station and Iraklion Air Station on the island of Crete. Note: no unleaded gasoline.

Italy—Available at exchanges on base such as Aviano, Vicenza, Camp Darby and Brindisi. No unleaded POL coupons.

The Netherlands—Available at major AAFES POL sales points in Europe. Note: Unleaded normal/super POL coupons available.

Spain—Travelers must first obtain a CAMPSA decal from their local security police/provost marshall's office. No unleaded CAMPSA coupons available.
NOTE: GAS COUPON ALLOWANCES ARE ESTABLISHED BY LOCAL COMMANDS. CHECK WITH EACH CONCERNING REGULATIONS.

GASOLINE COUPONS ON THE AUTOBAHN

On the Autobahn, coupons for diesel fuel, regular and premium gas are valid at 53 ESSO, BP, and FANAL stations. Off the Autobahn, coupons are accepted only at all AAFES service stations and all ESSO retail stations. If you're buying gas at an unfamiliar station, ask first if they accept AAFES-Europe gas coupons.

ALLGEMEINER DEUTSCHER AUTOMOBILE-CLUB (ADAC)

Similar to the American Automobile Association (AAA) in the U.S., ADAC's service includes over 1,000 road patrols who render assistance on Autobahns and major roads. The mechanics provide free labor, parts at cost, and one free towing service per year to members. ADAC also provides road information service, medical rescue facilities and a vehicle check-up service.

FIRST AID KIT ADDITION

German law requires drivers to have two pairs of disposable gloves in their emergency first aid kits in order to reduce the possibility of exposure to the AIDS virus when providing emergency medical care to an accident victim.

WHO CAN DRIVE YOUR VEHICLE?

Only parents, brothers, sisters, sons, daughters or in-laws of USAREUR personnel may drive vehicles with USAREUR license plates. Vehicle owners must ensure the vehicle insurance covers other drivers in addition to immediate family members. Relatives visiting personnel in USAREUR should get an international driving permit before coming to Europe. Also, before your visiting relative drives your vehicle, you must complete AE Form 3533-R (request for exception to policy), available from the community 42nd MP Group field office. Completed copies should be mailed to the Commander, 42nd MP Gp, ATTN: AEUMP-CS, APO 09086-5374.

Appendix H, continued

TUNNELS AND TOLL ROADS

There are numerous tunnels and toll roads in Austria, France, Germany, Italy, Spain and Switzerland. Books with maps, regulations and fees are readily available. Also, please refer to the Tunnel Routes to Southern Europe map near the end of this appendix.

AUTOMOBILE TERMS FOR TRAVELERS

English	German	French	Italian
Attention	Achtung	Attention	Attencione
Brake	Bremse	Frein	Freno
Broken	Kaputt	Casse	Spedachinio
Bumper	Stoßange	Pare Choc	Paracolpo
Carburetor	Vergaser	Carbarateur	Carburatore
Central	Zentral	Central	Centrale
Clutch	Kuppelung	Embrayage	Frizione
Chassis	Fahrgestell	Chassis	Autotelaio
Crankshaft	Kurbelwelle	Vilebrequin	Albero motore
Cylinders	Zylinder	Cylindres	Cilindri
Disc brake	Scheibenbremse	Frein a disques	Freno a disco
Distributor	Verteiler	Distributeur	Distributore
Door	Türe	Porte	Porta
Dry	Trocken	Seche	Secco
Empty	Unbelastet	A vide	A vuoto
Engine	Motor	Moteur	Macchina
Fan belt	Ventilatorriemen	Courroie de ventilateur	Cinghia del ventilatore
Front	Vorn	AV	Anteriore
Fuel pump	Benzin pumpe	Pompe a essence	Pompa d'alimentazione
Gas	Benzin	Essence	Benzina
Gears	Zahn Räder	Pignons	Ingranaggi
Ignition	Zündung	Allumage	Accensione
Injection	Einspritzung	Injection	Iniezione
Muffler	Schall dämpfer	Silencieux	Silenziatore
Oil	Öl	Huile	Olio
Oil filter	Ölfilter	Filter a huile	Filtro dell'olio
Power steering	Servolenkung	Servo-direction	Servosterzo
Premium gas	Superbenzin	Supercarburant	Benzina super
Puncture	Refendefekt	Crevasion de pneu	Scopio di pneumatico
Radiator	Kühler	Radiator	Radiatore
Road speed	Geschwindigkeit	Vitesse	Velocita
Spark plug	Zündkerze	Bougie	Candela
Steering	Lenkung	Direction	Sterzo
Tires	Reifen	Pneus	Pneumatici
Transmission	Kraftübertragung	Transmission	Transmissione
Wet	Naß	Humide	Umido
Window	Fenster	Fenetre (glace)	Finestra
Windshield	Frontscheibe	Pare-brise	Parabrezza

Appendix H, continued

EUROPEAN TRAFFIC AND SAFETY REGULATIONS

Kilometers per hour (KPH)

Country	KPH in town/city	KPH out of town/city	KPH on expressway	Mandatory seatbelts	Children in rear seats
Austria	50	100	130	Yes	Yes
Belgium	60	90 b	120	Yes	Yes
Denmark	60	80	100	Yes	No
Finland	50	80	120	Yes	No
France	60	90 c,d	130 d,g	Yes	Yes
Germany	50	100	a	Yes	Yes
Greece	50	80	100	Yes	Yes
Great Britain	48	96 e	112	Yes	Yes
Ireland	48	88	-	Yes	Yes
Italy	50	f	f	No	No
Luxembourg	60	90	120	Yes	Yes
Netherlands	50	80	100	Yes	Yes
Norway	50	80	90	Yes	No
Portugal	70	90	120 d	Yes	No
Spain	60	90 i	120	Yes, j	Yes
Sweden	50	70 h	110 h	Yes	No
Switzerland	50	100	130	Yes	Yes
Turkey	60	80 h	120	Yes	Yes

Key:
a. recommended speed —130 KPH.
b. on roads with at least two lanes in both directions—120 KPH.
c. on roads with two lanes in each direction, with medians—110 KPH.
d. drivers having held their licenses for less than one year may not exceed 90 KPH.
e. on roads with at least two lanes in both directions—112 KPH.
f. passenger cars with a cylinder
  capacity of: | normal roads | motorways
  up to 599 cc | 80 KPH | 80 KPH
  600-900 cc | 90 KPH | 110 KPH
  901-1300 cc | 100 KPH | 130 KPH
  over 1300 cc | 110 KPH | 140 KPH
g. 110 KPH when wet
h. also on highways—110 KPH.
i. on roads with at least two lanes in each direction—100 KPH.
j. outside of towns.

INFORMATION COURTESY OF ADAC.

U.S. Forces Travel & Transfer Guide Europe — 399

aafes GARAGES NEAR THE AUTOBAHNS IN GERMANY

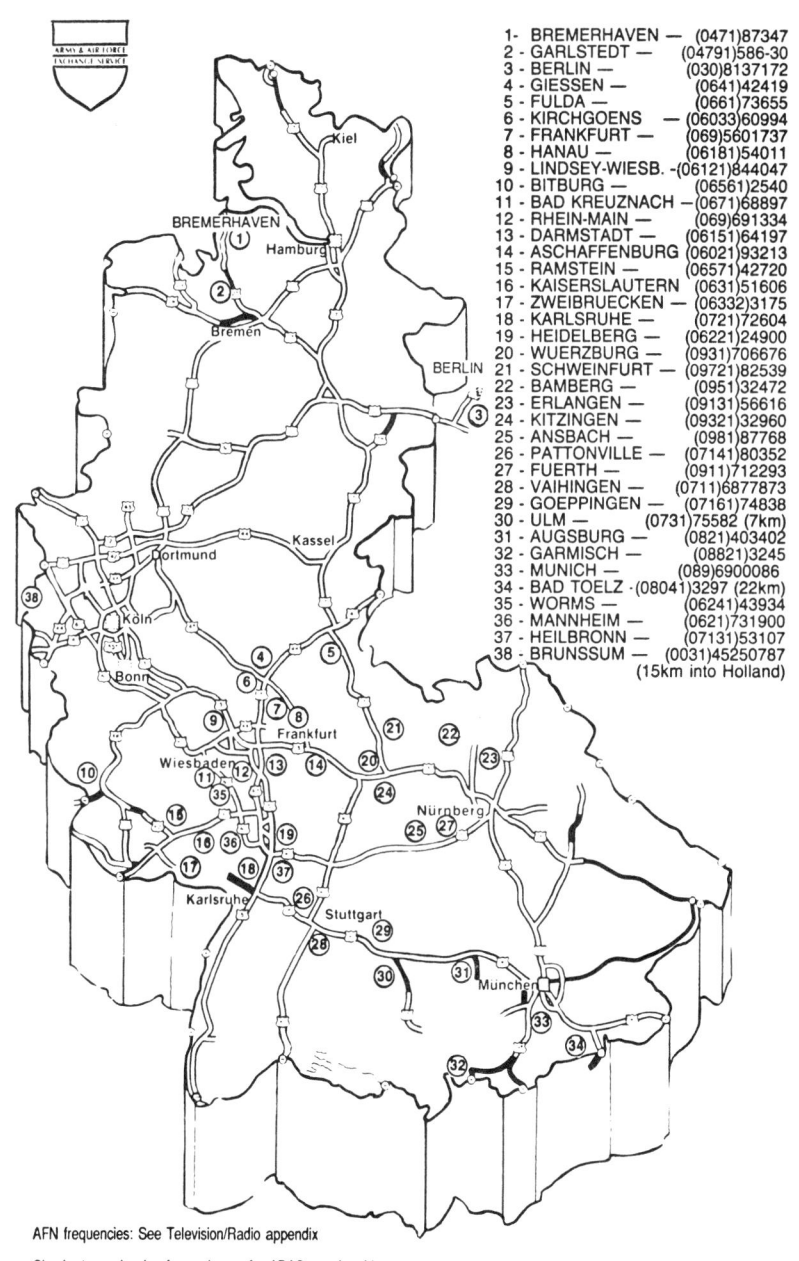

1- BREMERHAVEN — (0471)87347
2 - GARLSTEDT — (04791)586-30
3 - BERLIN — (030)8137172
4 - GIESSEN — (0641)42419
5 - FULDA — (0661)73655
6 - KIRCHGOENS — (06033)60994
7 - FRANKFURT — (069)5601737
8 - HANAU — (06181)54011
9 - LINDSEY-WIESB. -(06121)844047
10 - BITBURG — (06561)2540
11 - BAD KREUZNACH —(0671)68897
12 - RHEIN-MAIN — (069)691334
13 - DARMSTADT — (06151)64197
14 - ASCHAFFENBURG (06021)93213
15 - RAMSTEIN — (06571)42720
16 - KAISERSLAUTERN (0631)51606
17 - ZWEIBRUECKEN — (06332)3175
18 - KARLSRUHE — (0721)72604
19 - HEIDELBERG — (06221)24900
20 - WUERZBURG — (0931)706676
21 - SCHWEINFURT — (09721)82539
22 - BAMBERG — (0951)32472
23 - ERLANGEN — (09131)56616
24 - KITZINGEN — (09321)32960
25 - ANSBACH — (0981)87768
26 - PATTONVILLE — (07141)80352
27 - FUERTH — (0911)712293
28 - VAIHINGEN — (0711)6877873
29 - GOEPPINGEN — (07161)74838
30 - ULM — (0731)75582 (7km)
31 - AUGSBURG — (0821)403402
32 - GARMISCH — (08821)3245
33 - MUNICH — (089)6900086
34 - BAD TOELZ ·(08041)3297 (22km)
35 - WORMS — (06241)43934
36 - MANNHEIM — (0621)731900
37 - HEILBRONN — (07131)53107
38 - BRUNSSUM — (0031)45250787
(15km into Holland)

AFN frequencies: See Television/Radio appendix

Check at your local aafes exchange for ADAC memberships.

When needing to use Autobahn emergency phone:
Locate nearest one by following the black arrows along the highway; pick up receiver and state your name and location by autobahn number, direction of travel and what's wrong.

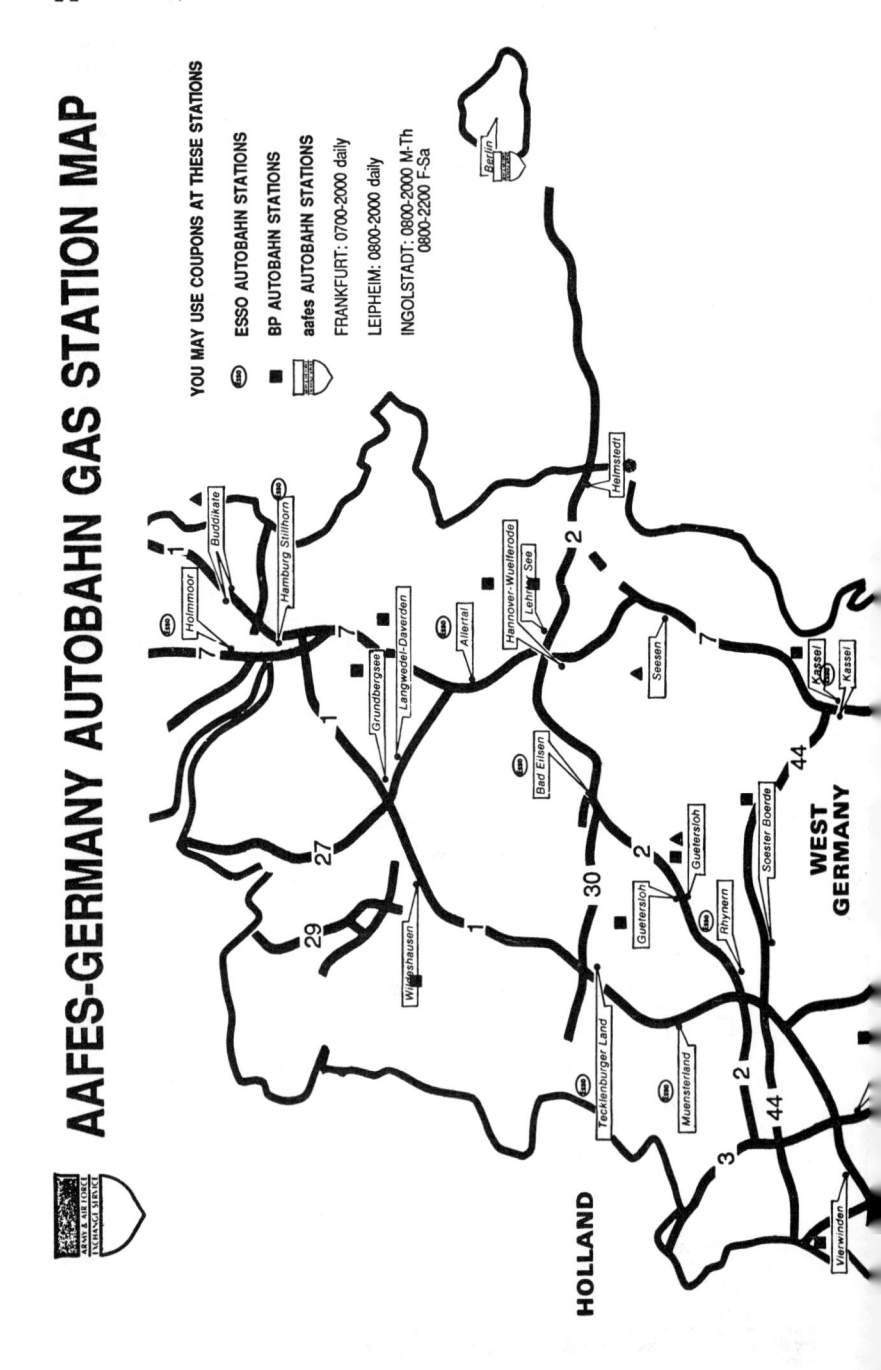

Appendix H, continued

AAFES-GERMANY AUTOBAHN GAS STATION MAP

YOU MAY USE COUPONS AT THESE STATIONS
- ESSO AUTOBAHN STATIONS
- BP AUTOBAHN STATIONS
- aafes AUTOBAHN STATIONS

FRANKFURT: 0700-2000 daily
LEIPHEIM: 0800-2000 daily
INGOLSTADT: 0800-2000 M-Th
0800-2200 F-Sa

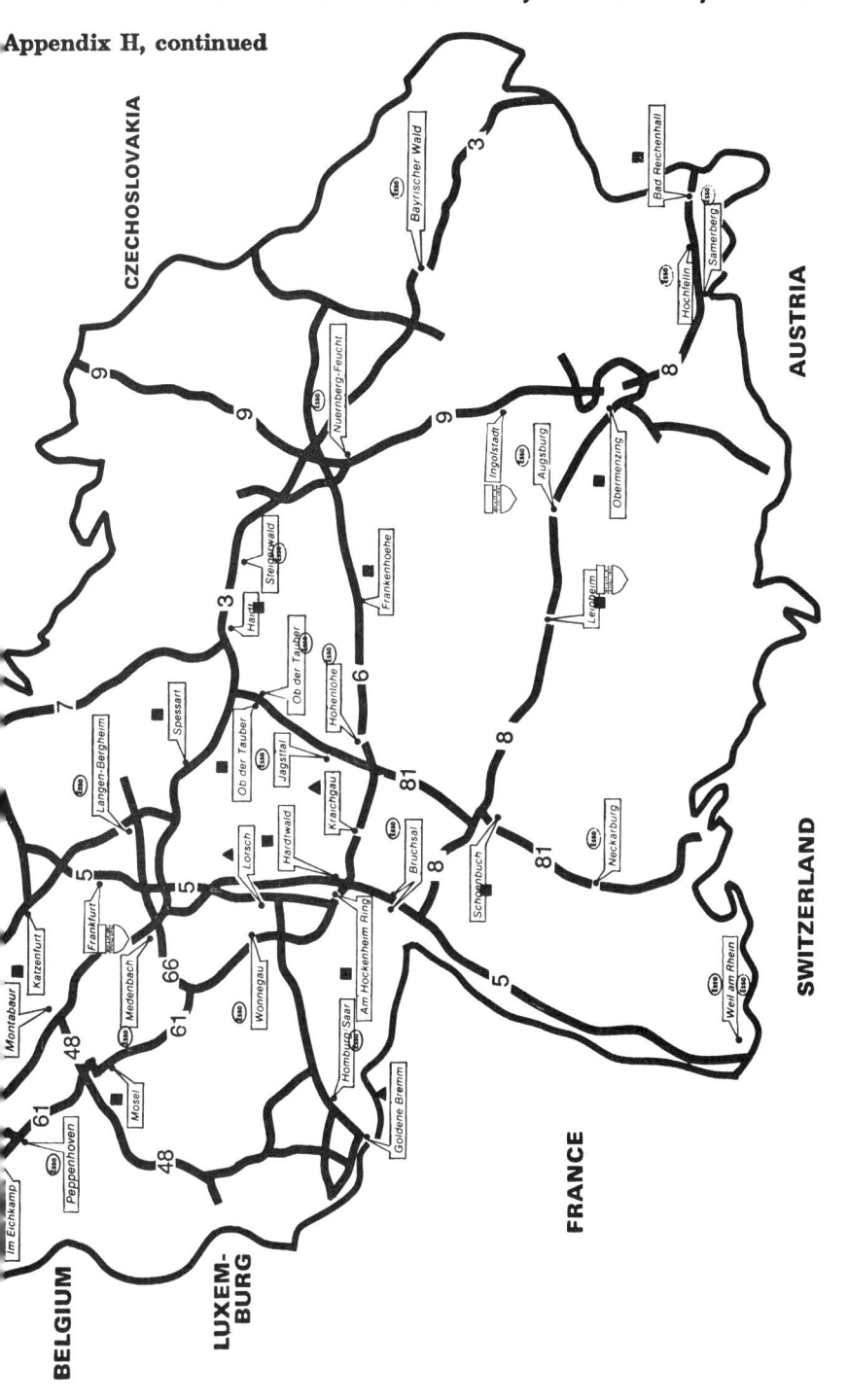

U.S. Forces Travel & Transfer Guide Europe — 401

Appendix H, continued

Appendix H, continued

ITALY GAS STATION MAP

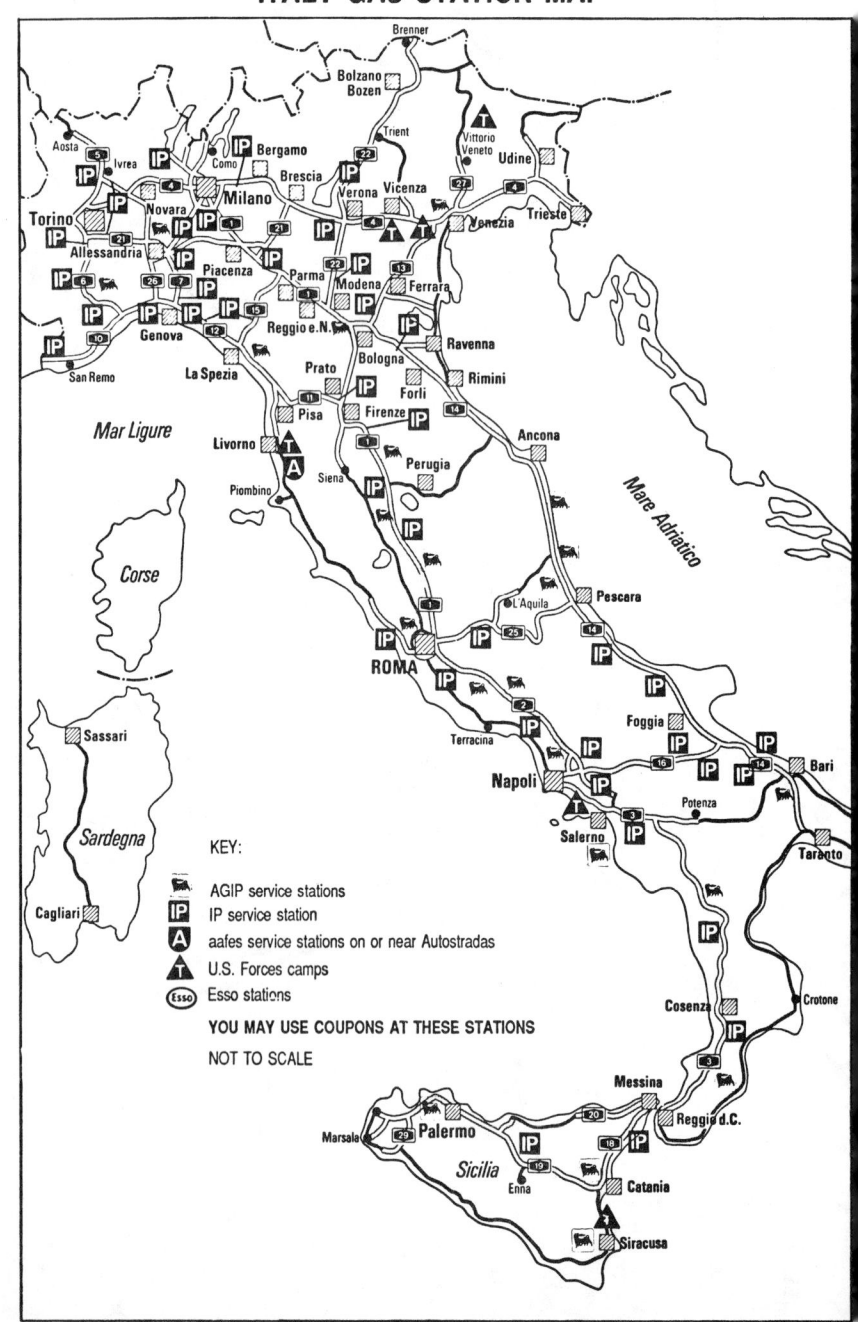

KEY:
- AGIP service stations
- IP service station
- aafes service stations on or near Autostradas
- U.S. Forces camps
- Esso stations

YOU MAY USE COUPONS AT THESE STATIONS

NOT TO SCALE

U.S. Forces Travel & Transfer Guide Europe — 403

Appendix H, continued

THE NETHERLANDS GAS STATION MAP

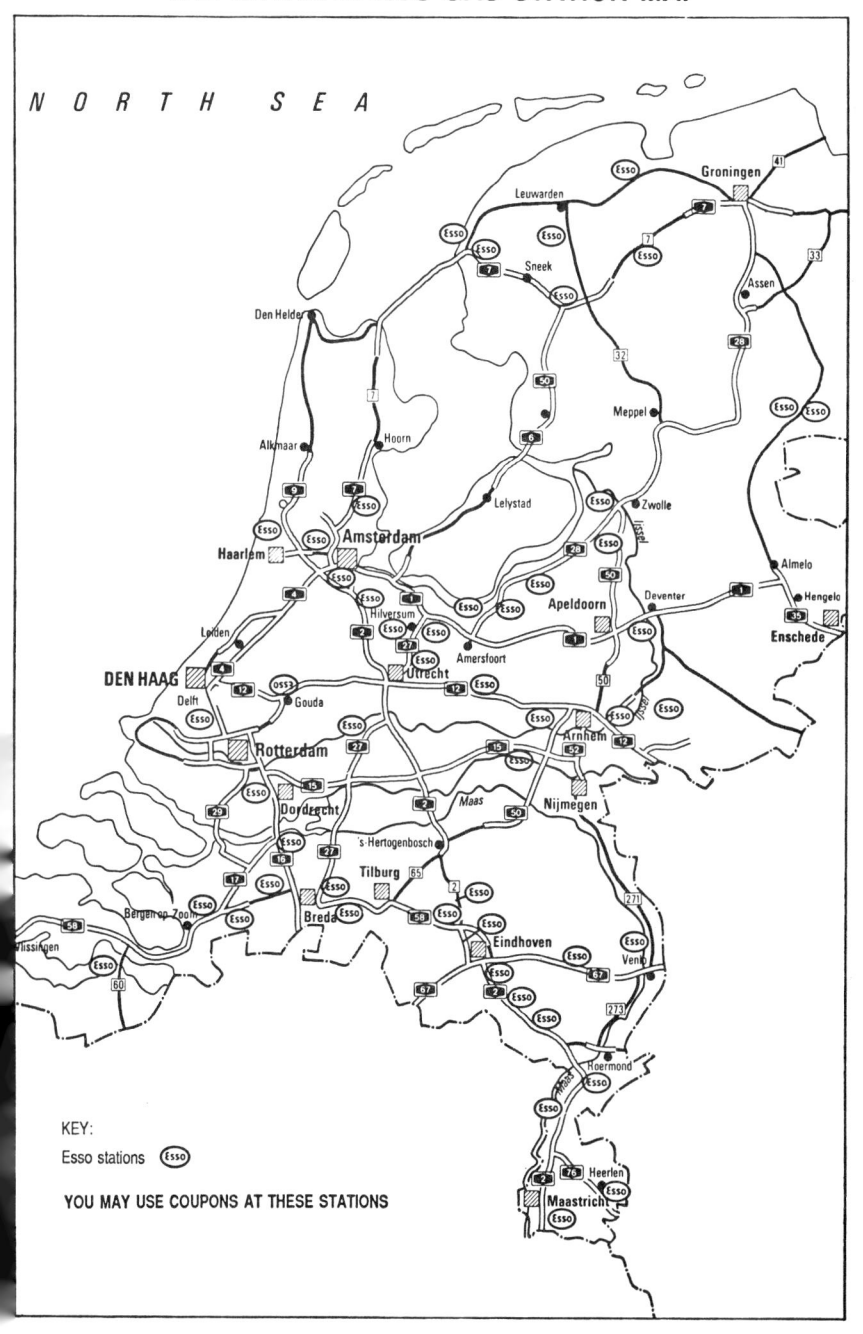

KEY:
Esso stations (Esso)

YOU MAY USE COUPONS AT THESE STATIONS

Appendix H, continued

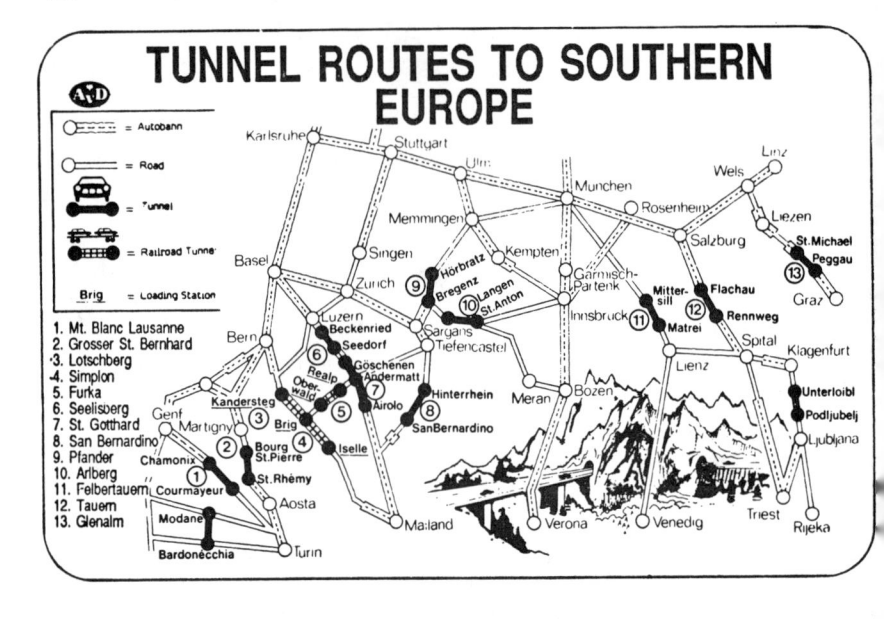

TUNNEL ROUTES TO SOUTHERN EUROPE

○━━ = Autobahn
○━ = Road
🚗 = Tunnel
🚂 = Railroad Tunnel
Brig = Loading Station

1. Mt. Blanc Lausanne
2. Grosser St. Bernhard
3. Lotschberg
4. Simplon
5. Furka
6. Seelisberg
7. St. Gotthard
8. San Bernardino
9. Pfander
10. Arlberg
11. Felbertauern
12. Tauern
13. Glenalm

TAX-FREE GAS COUPONS

While traveling in Germany, AAFES-Europe customers can purchase tax-free petroleum-oils-lubricants coupons for their civilian-rented motor vehicles.

Soldiers and Department of Defense civilian employees stationed in Germany and their family members are eligible to purchase coupons. Also eligible are authorized contract representatives and service members stationed in Europe who take leave in Germany.

Individuals purchasing coupons must have a driver's license, identification card and letter of authorization in German and English issued by the headquarters providing logistical support for the person. The letter must contain a description of the vehicle, the registration number, rental contract, identification of the driver and the quantity of POL coupons authorized.

The letter of authorization must be shown before pumping gas. (AAFES News Release)

U.S. Forces Travel & Transfer Guide Europe — 405

Appendix H, continued

MAIN FERRY ROUTES CROSSING THE CHANNEL

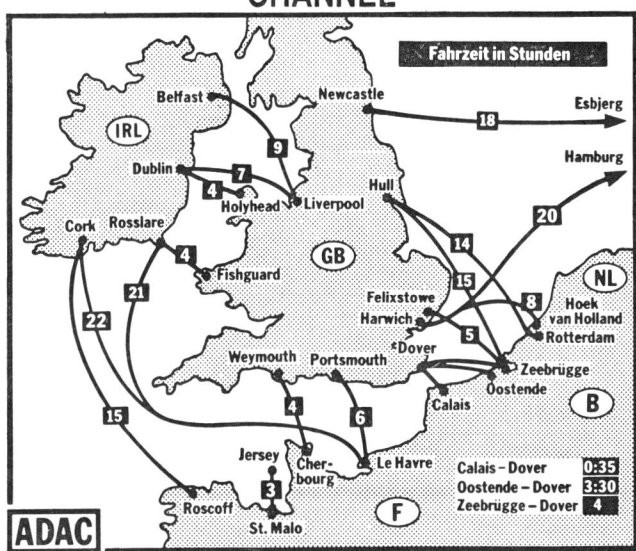

MAIN FERRY ROUTES TO THE NORTH

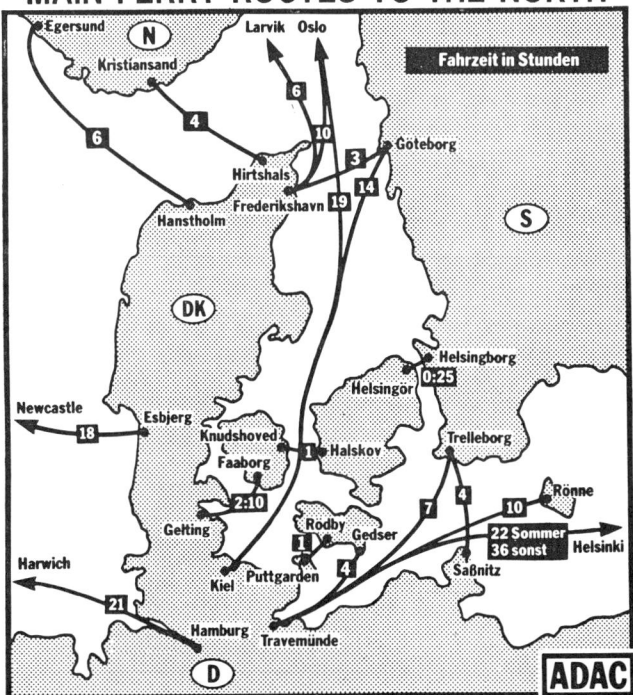

406 — U.S. Forces Travel & Transfer Guide Europe

Appendix H, continued

MAIN FERRY ROUTES CROSSING THE EASTERN MEDITERRANEAN

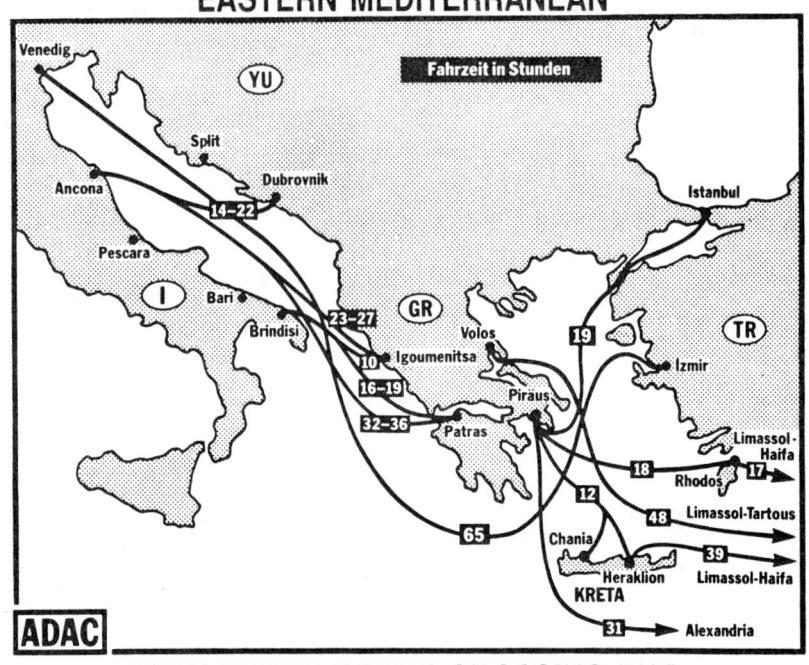

MAIN FERRY ROUTE CROSSING THE WESTERN MEDITERRANEAN

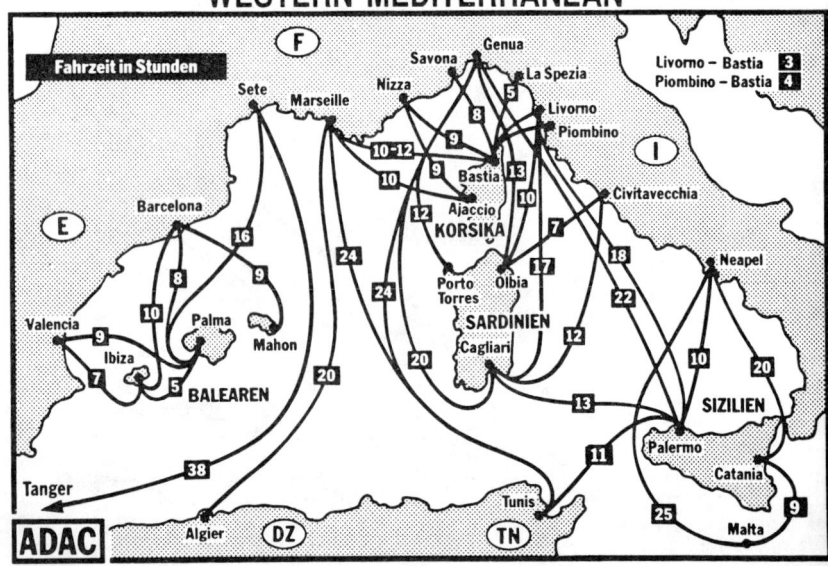

APPENDIX I
GERMANY
ACCESS TO BERLIN

By air: Commercial flights are available seven days a week. U.S. Forces may fly on U.S. and other commercial airlines; Berlin Movement Orders (Flag Orders) are not required for air travel. Check with a travel agent for weekend specials. Check Space-A to Templehof Central Airport (THF) Berlin, from RAF Mildenhall (MHZ), Ramstein AB (RMS) and Rhein Main AB (FRF).

By automobile: Active duty U.S. military personnel and their accompanying family members may travel in a USAREUR-registered vehicle to West Berlin via the Helmstedt-Berlin Autobahn (Autobahn E30), with flag orders, ID card, and leave orders. They must process through Allied Checkpoint Alpha at Helmstedt before entering East Germany and through Allied Checkpoint Bravo in Berlin before entering West Berlin. Drivers of USAREUR-registered vehicles must have a valid drivers license and vehicle registration, and should verify with their insurance agents that their coverage extends to a communist-controlled territory. Occupants must have an I.D. card or passport. Retired military who drive to Berlin in other than a USAREUR-registered vehicle which is in compliance with USAREUR access regulations do not enjoy the protection of the Four Power Berlin access agreement. This travel will result in a DDR (East German) entry stamp in your passport. You must get a waiver of this stamp in order to ride any of the Duty Trains. This is part of the Four Power agreement now being enforced by the U.S.S.R. Forces.

By train: There are British, French, and U.S. military duty trains. Travel for military members and DOD civilians is free. Children under age 16 must be accompanied by a parent or other responsible adult. Duty train travel is restricted to ID cardholders, to persons who are performing functions supporting the USAREUR mission, or to those who meet all the following prerequisites: they are members of the sponsor's or spouse's immediate family; they are U.S., British or French citizens with a valid passport; they are accompanied by the sponsor or an adult member of the sponsor's family.
Berlin:
   British Duty Train—Br. Mil: 13-4147
   French Duty Train—ETS: 332-6957
   U.S. Duty Train Reservations and Information—ETS: 332-6381
Braunschweig: British afternoon duty train to Berlin—Tel: Civ: 0531-72562
Bremerhaven Rail Transportation Office (RTO): Free U.S. duty train—ETS: 342-7869.
Frankfurt Duty Train: Free U.S. duty train. Rail Transportation Office (RTO): M-Sa. 0800-1700; Su. 1300-1700, ETS: 320-5182/5755. Reservations M-Sa 0800-1700, Su 1300-1700, ETS: 320-5159.
Strasbourg: French duty train, small charge. Call Berlin rail transportation office (RTO): ETS-332-6957.

HOW TO OBTAIN FLAG ORDERS

In Berlin: United States Military Community Activity (USMCA). HQ U.S. Commander, Berlin Adjutant General, Military Personnel Branch, Gen. Lucius D. Clay Headquarters, Bldg. 1-3. Flag Orders ETS: 332-6526. APO New York 09942-5000.
In Bremerhaven: Rail Transportation Office (RTO), Military Personnel. HQ USMCA Bremerhaven ETS: 342-7869. APO New York 09069-5000.
In Frankfurt: USMCA. Rail Transportation Office (RTO), 2nd floor, Main Train Station. ETS: 320-5159, Berlin Booking. APO New York 09710-5000.

Appendix I, continued

DOD civilians with ID cards, who are TDY to Berlin or who want to holiday, with or without their sponsors, can use the military trains on a space available basis, and flag orders are required. Reservations must be made exactly 42 days in advance. Check in one hour ahead of departure for a mandatory briefing. In Frankfurt, occasionally, "no-shows" free up a seat. Check in early and wait. Uniformed personnel must have I.D. card, Berlin Movement Orders (flag orders), and Leave/TDY orders. Details in USAFE Reg. 30-28 and USAREUR Reg. 550-180. Civilians must have passports, and Berlin Movement Orders.

THE FOLLOWING ARE BANNED ON DUTY TRAINS:
Alcohol; taking photographs between Berlin and Helmstedt; talking with or trading items with East German or Soviet guards; extending items out of windows; pulling the fire alarm unless in case of fire. **LISTEN TO THE TRAIN CONDUCTOR OR COMMANDER.**

Travel to Berlin by private, non-USAREUR auto, tour bus or civilian trains is forbidden to U.S. Forces, their dependents, retired military and DOD civilians and their dependents. See retired military under **By automobile:** above. **NOTE: RETIRED MILITARY CAN ONLY TRAVEL TO WEST BERLIN BY COMMERCIAL OR MILITARY AIR, BY MILITARY DUTY TRAIN OR USAREUR-PLATED AUTO.**

Berlin Tourist Information: Verkehrsamt Berlin, Europa Center, 1000 Berlin 30, West Germany.

BREMERHAVEN—GETTING THERE AND PICKING UP YOUR CAR

A daily chartered roundtrip bus from Frankfurt Hauptbahnhof RTO to Carl Schurz Kaserne in Bremerhaven is provided for military personnel to pick up their automobiles shipped from the U.S. Also check military bulletin boards for rides to and from Bremerhaven. Travel via the Deutsche Bundesbahn (rail) is also available. Onpost lodging at the U.S. Hospital Center is limited; call the Harbor House at ETS 342-7604 for reservations. There are numerous off-post German hotels and restaurants available as well. See Bremerhaven listing for full TML information.

Be sure to have the following when you arrive to pick up your car: two copies of AE Form 1598; double white insurance card; DD Form 788 (bill of lading—you got this when you dropped your car off); spare set of car keys; $10 cash, check or money order for car registration; ID card; permanent or temporary USAREUR POV license; warning triangle; German standard first aid kit; USA sticker (from your insurance company or AAFES) and one Phillips and one standard screwdriver for affixing license plate.

RAIL TRAVEL IN GERMANY

Rail travel in Germany on the Deutsche Bundesbahn (DB) is easy, fast and punctual. There are a variety of discounted individual, family and group rail passes which can be combined with city tours, vacation packages and bus and cruise tours. There are special fares for youths, couples, families with children under 18, large (3-8 members) families, one-month tramper passes, and student passes. Check with the local military recreation office travel facility, often called ITT or ITR.

Appendix I, continued

UPDATE ON GERMAN TRAFFIC LAWS

Listed below are recent changes:
—Passing is not allowed at pedestrian crosswalks even if there are no pedestrians in sight.
—Bicyclists passing a bus stop where passengers are entering or exiting a bus must slow down, and be prepared to stop.
—Bikers and motorcyclists may pass slowly on the right of vehicles stopped in the right traffic lane. Previous bicyclist passing regulations remain unchanged.
—On autobahn exit lanes, drivers in the right lane may drive faster than those in the left when in the block-marked lane separation area.
—Bicyclists up to three-years-old may use the sidewalk if no bicycle path is available but must get off their bikes and push them when crossing the road.
—In a parking lot, the first vehicle to reach a vacant space has priority for that space.
—Motorcyclists must drive on the road. They may drive on bicycle paths only when a sign expressly allows such.
—Stopping is allowed in "no stopping" zones for loading or unloading passengers or material, but only for three minutes. An exception to the time limit, however, is when someone is moving household goods.
—If the parking meter is broken where you park, leave a note indicating arrival time on the meter and do not park longer than the allowable meter time.
—Truck and bus drivers must maintain a minimum distance of 50 meters (about 150') behind any vehicle on an autobahn.

CANADIAN, FRENCH AND UNITED KINGDOM EXCHANGES

Canadian Forces Exchanges, PO Box 536, Canadian Forces Post Office 5056. Civ. tel: (49)07229-6030. Holders of U.S. ID cards may use these facilities. The Canadian Exchanges (CANEX) in Germany offer stock assortments similar to U.S. exchanges (AAFES) plus English and French items in their gourmet groceterias (similar to commissaries). Their assortment of French and English pottery and ceramics is excellent. Facilities which U.S. personnel may use include car rentals, cinemas, coffee shops, convenience stores, new car sales, restaurants and video centers. All sales are in U.S. dollars and German marks or you may write a check in U.S. dollars for the exact amount if you have a German/U.S. dollars bank account. MasterCard and Visa are also accepted.

Canadian Forces Base Baden-Söllingen Exchange: CFB Baden Exchange, PO Box 536, CFPO 5056, CFB Baden Söllingen, 7570 Baden-Baden. Located 30 minutes from Karlsruhe. Take A-5 Autobahn south toward Basel, CH; exit at Baden-Baden, right to first light, left to B-36, continue through village of Hugelsheim to base on left. Tel: BBC-07229-6030. Exchange and groceteria hrs: Mon.—only groceteria open; Tue. & Fri.—10 a.m.-6 p.m.; Wed. & Thurs.—10 a.m.- 9 p.m.; Sat.—9 a.m.-4 p.m. Sun.—CLOSED.

Canadian Forces Base Lahr Exchange: Postfach 2040, 7630 Lahr-Schwarzwald. Take A-5 Autobahn south toward Basel, CH, exit at Lahr, left to B-36 and continue through Lahr. Watch for sign with large Canadian flag, turn right at flag, proceed one block, turn left into base. Tel: LC 07821-2740. Exchange hours are the same as Baden-Söllingen. A NATEX combined exchange and foodland is also located at Geilenkirchen (NATO) AB. Please see the Geilenkirchen AB listing in this book.

Appendix I, continued

French Forces Economats: Economats, combined French commissaries and exchanges, are located in Baden-Baden, Berlin, Kaiserslautern and Speyer. They stock the famous bread, cheeses, meats, spices and wines. They also have bicycles, clothing, clocks, cookware, and novelty items. Many economats have a good selection of gifts, perfume and jewelry. Payment is in French francs, German marks, and Visa card. U.S. ID card holders granted access.

Baden-Baden Economat: "Paris" store (commissary type): Schwarzwald Str. 97. Civ. tel: (49)07221-69-7840. Take A-5 Autobahn south toward Basel, CH, exit toward Baden-Baden, look for "Cite Normandise" sign which directs you to French Forces Base. Hrs: Mon., Wed., & Thurs.—7:30 a.m.-noon; Tues.—7:30 a.m.-1 p.m. and 5-7 p.m.; Sat.—9 a.m.-1:30 p.m. Also "Normandie" store: Ortenau Str. 4; Civ. Tel: 07221-69-7837 and "Tirache" store: Briegel Acker Str. 40; Civ. Tel: 07221-69-7846.

Berlin Economat: "Foch" store: Avenue Charles de Gaulle, main French base; Civ. Tel. 030-418-8037. Smaller economats at Guynemer Base, Civ. Tel: 030-418-1044 and Pasture Base, Civ. Tel: 030-418-1146.

Kaiserslautern Economat: Mainzerstraße, Civ. Tel: 0631-45001-298/206.

Speyer Economat: Carolingerstraße, Civ. Tel: 06232-74021-222. Foodland (small commissary-type) facility. Take A-6 toward Saarbrucken, exit at Speyer Hockenheim. Cross Rhein River, exit at Speyer, go two blocks, facility is on right. Hrs: Mon. & Wed.—9 a.m.-1230 p.m; Tues., Thurs., and Fri.—9 a.m.-1230 p.m. and 4-7 p.m.; Sat.—9 a.m.-1 p.m.

There are also French Economats located at Landau, Tübingen, Trier and Wittlich, Germany. The Navy, Army, Air Force Institute located in the ACS Shopping Center below Hendrick Mine Complex, Brunssum, NE, is similar to AAFES and U.S. commissaries. It is located next to the AFCENT swimming pool. An AFCENT I.D. is required.

—NOTES—

APPENDIX J
RADIO AND TELEVISION SERVICE

DOD operates the American Forces Radio and Television Service (AFRTS) throughout Europe with live and taped programs from the three major American networks. In some areas, British Forces TV is available. German TV is accessible on black and white TV sets with a converter. Exchanges sell some TV sets which can receive German color broadcasts.

American Forces Network (AFN) provides radio services in Germany 24 hours a day. AFN broadcasts in both AM and FM and provides live hourly satellite news and live sports and special events. The British Forces Network and the Canadian Forces Network are widely received and Voice of America (VOA) and British Broadcasting Company (BBC) can be received on AM and shortwave frequencies.

AMERICAN FORCES NETWORK (AFN) LOCATIONS AND RADIO FREQUENCIES

AM LOCATION		FM LOCATION	
GERMANY	**FREQUENCY**	**BELGIUM**	**FREQUENCY**
Ansbach	1485	Brussels	101.7
Augsburg	1485	Florennes	107.7
Bad Hersfeld	1143	Kleine Brogel	106.2
Bad Kissingen	1143	SHAPE	104.2
Bamberg	1143		106.5
Berchtesgaden	1485		
Berlin	1107	**GERMANY**	
Bitburg	1143	Augsburg	100.0
Bremerhaven	1143	Berlin	87.9
Crailsheim	1485	Bonn	107.6
Frankfurt	873	Frankfurt	98.7
Fulda	1143	Garlstedt	92.9
Garmisch	1485	Heidelberg	104.6
Giessen	1143	Illesheim	101.0
Göppingen	1143	Kaiserslautern	100.2
Grafenwöhr	1107	Mannheim	101.9
Heidelberg	1143	Pirmasens	103.0
Hof	1143	Stuttgart	102.4
Hohenfels	1485	Ulm	102.6
Kaiserslautern	1143		
Karlsruhe	1143	**NETHERLANDS**	
Mönchen-		Soesterberg AB	98.0
Gladbach	1143	Maastricht	93.4
Munich	1107	Volkel AB	93.6
Nürnberg	1107	Schinnen	89.2
Regensburg	1485		
Schweinfurt	1143	**AFN FM Stereo Broadcasts:** Separate broadcasts are available in: Berlin (1107 AM mono); Kaiserslautern (100.2); SHAPE (103.3); and Stuttgart (102.3).	
Stuttgart	1143		
Wertheim	1143		
Wildflecken	1143		
Würzburg	1143		

Appendix J, continued

AFN RADIO TROUBLE NUMBERS

Use the following telephone numbers to report American Forces Europe (AFN) radio transmitter failures. All numbers are European Telephone System (ETS) except for Brussels and after hours Wönsdrecht AB (NL), which are civilian numbers. Florennes AB and Kleine Brogel AB are Autovon (A) numbers.

Stn./Community	Duty Hrs.	After Hrs.
BELGIUM (BE)/NETHERLANDS (NL)		
AFN SHAPE		
Brunssum (NL)	360-7555	same
Brussels (BE)	02-7209015	same
Florennes AB (BE)	791-3255 EX-430	same
Geilenkirchen AB (GE)	360-7555	same
Kleine Brogel AB (BE)	452-1110 EX-3275	same
Maastricht (NL)	360-7555	same
Schinnen (NL)	•	•
SHAPE (BE)	423-4012	361-5301
Volkel AB (NL)	450-1110 EX-2814	same
Wönsdrecht AB (NL)	364-7467	01640-66271
AFN SOESTERBERG (NL)		
Soesterberg AB (NL)	363-8187	same
GERMANY (GE)		
AFN BERLIN	332-6864	same
AFN BREMERHAVEN		
Bremerhaven	891-8212	891-8515
Carl Schurz Ksrn.	342-8212	342-8515
Clay Kaserne	•	•
Flensburg	•	•
Hessich-Oldendorf	•	•
Kellinghusen	•	•
Osterholz-Scharmbk	891-8212	891-8515
Schleswig	342-8212	342-8515
Sögel	•	•
AFN FRANKFURT		
Bad Hersfeld	320-6101 EX-212	same
Frankfurt	•	•
Fulda	•	•
Giessen	•	•
Mönchen-Gladbach	360-7555	same
Wiesbaden	320-6101 EX-212	same
Wildflecken	•	•

Stn./Community	Duty Hrs.	After Hrs.
(GE) cont.		
AFN KAISERSLAUTERN		
Baumholder	480-6535	same
Bitburg AB	453-7133	same
Pirmasens	495-6295	same
Prüm	453-7133	same
Ramstein AB	480-6535	same
Sembach AB	•	•
Spangdahlem	453-7133	same
Vogelweh	480-6535	same
Worms	•	•
Zweibrücken	495-6295	same
AFN MUNICH		
Augsburg	440-6497	434-6611
Bad Tölz	•	441-4800
Bertchesgaden	•	441-5826
Garmisch	•	440-2801
Munich	•	440-6244
AFN NÜRNBERG		
Amberg	460-7409	same
Ansbach	•	•
Bamberg	•	•
Bindlach	•	•
Crailsheim	•	•
Fürth	•	•
Grafenwöhr	•	•
Hof	•	•
Hohenfels	•	•
Illesheim	•	•
Nürnberg	•	•
Regensburg	•	•
AFN STUTTGART		
Göppingen	420-6434	425-3479
Heidelberg	•	370-8857
Karlsruhe	•	376-6433
Mannheim	•	380-8168
Neu-Ulm	•	427-6413
Schwäbisch-Gmünd	•	427-5722
Stuttgart	•	420-7301
AFN WÜRZBURG		
Bad Kissingen	350-7142	354-2727
Schweinfurt	350-6368	354-6673
Wertheim	350-7142	355-5648
Würzburg	•	350-6308

NOTE: The AFN radio trouble numbers are not identical with the television trouble reception numbers.

U.S. Forces Travel & Transfer Guide Europe — 413

Appendix J, continued

AFN TV NETWORK CHANNEL INFORMATION

Location	U.S. Channel	Local Country Channel	H&V Polar- ization	Location	U.S. Channel	Local Country Channel	H&V Polar- ization
BELGIUM				**GERMANY** cont.			
SHAPE(Casteau)	31-32	34	Vertical	Illesheim	56-57	53	Horizontal
ENGLAND				Kaiserslautern	26	30	Horizontal
All locations	11	-	Cable only	Karlsruhe	38	39	Horizontal
				Katterbach	54	51	Horizontal
GERMANY				Kirchgöns	56-57	53	Horizontal
Amberg	50	48	Horizontal	Kitzingen	63-64	58	Vertical
Ansbach	15	22	Horizontal	Landstuhl	27-28	31	Vertical
Aschaffenburg	22	27	Horizontal	Landau	35-36	37	Vertical
Augsburg	54	51	Horizontal	Mannheim			
Babenhausen	28-29	32	Horizontal	(Kaefertal)	60-61	56	Vertical
Bad Hersfeld	56-57	53	Horizontal	(Sandhofen)	15-16	22	Vertical
Bad Kissingen	62	57	Horizontal	Miseau	24-25	29	Horizontal
Bad Kreuznach	19-20	25	Horizontal	Möhringen	40-41	41	Horizontal
Bad Nauheim	40-41	41	Horizontal	Müchweller	18	24	Horizontal
Bad Tölz	63-64	58	Horizontal	Münster	22	27	Horizontal
Bamberg	38	39	Vertical	Munich	22	27	Horizontal
Baumholder	55-56	52	Horizontal	Neckarsulm	28-29	32	Vertical
	48-49	47	Horizontal	Nellingen	62	57	Vertical
Berlin	24-25	29	Horizontal	Neubrücke	38	39	Vertical
Bindlach	22	27	Vertical	Neu-Ulm	42	42	Horizontal
Birkenfeld	15-16	22	Horizontal	Nürnberg			
Bitburg Air Base	54	51	Vertical	(Merrell)	62	57	Horizontal
Böblingen	47-48	46	Vertical	(Pastorius)	44-45	44	Horizontal
Bremerhaven	20-21	26	Horizontal	Oberursel	15-16	22	Horizontal
Büdingen	62	57	Horizontal	Pirmasens	19-20	25	Vertical
Butzbach	14	21	Horizontal	Prüm	15-16	22	Horizontal
Crailsheim	14	21	Horizontal	Regensburg	46	45	Horizontal
Darmstadt	19-20	25	Horizontal	Rhein Main			
Dexheim	20-21	26	Vertical	(Air Base)	26	30	Vertical
Erlangen	22	27	Horizontal	(GatewayGdns.)	23-24	28	Vertical
Effingen	39-40	40	Horizontal	Schwabach	44-45	44	Horizontal
Frankfurt				Schwäbisch			
(Eschersheim)	27-28	31	Horizontal	Gmünd	15-16	22	Vertical
(Höchst)	16-17	23	Horizontal	Schwäbisch Hall	14	21	Vertical
Friedberg	28-29	32	Horizontal	Schweinfurt	64-65	59	Horizontal
Fürth				Schwetzingen	42	42	Vertical
(Darby)	26	30	Horizontal	Stuttgart			
(Monteith)	56-57	53	Horizontal	(Fürbach)	59-60	55	Vertical
Fulda	63-64	58	Vertical	(Vaihingen)	50	48	Horizontal
Garlstedt	32-33	35	Horizontal	Vilseck	46	45	Horizontal
Gelnhausen	47-48	46	Horizontal	Vogelweh	26	30	Horizontal
Giessen	36-37	38	Horizontal	Vertheim	58	54	Vertical
Göppingen	26	30	Horizontal	Wiesbaden	15-16	22	Horizontal
Grafenwöhr	27-28	31	Horizontal	Wildflecken	50	48	Horizontal
Hahn Air Base	52-53	50	Horizontal	Worms	50	48	Vertical
Hanau	50	48	Horizontal	Würzburg			
Heidelberg				(Hindenberg)	64-65	59	Horizontal
(PHV)	32-33	35	Vertical	(Leighton)	48-49	47	Horizontal
(Shopping Ctr.)	26	30	Vertical	Zirndorf	55-56	52	Horizontal
Heilbronn				Zweibrücken	59-60	55	Vertical
(Badnerhof)	54	51	Horizontal				
(J.F.Kennedy)	59-60	55	Vertical	**NETHERLANDS**			
Herzongenaurach	23-24	28	Horizontal	Soesterburg AB	80	-	Horizontal
Hohenfels	60-61	28	Horizontal				
Idar-Oberstein	44-45	44	Horizontal				

Appendix J, continued

AFN TELEVISION TROUBLE NUMBERS

If you have trouble receiving AFN Europe television, check with your neighbors and try to determine th following: (1) Is it only your set? (2) Is it only in your stairwell or building? (3) Is it the entire area? Once you'v determined the extent of the problem, call the area number listed below. **NOTE:** Brussels numbers are civilian (C Florennes are Autovon (A); SHAPE duty hrs. number is European Telephone System (ETS) and after duty hr; number is (A). All numbers in England are (C). All numbers in Germany and Netherlands are ETS.

Location	Duty Hours	After Duty Hours	Location	Duty Hours	After Duty Hours
BELGIUM			**GERMANY, cont.**		
Brussels	02-7209015	same			
Florennes	791-3255, EX-430	same	Heidelberg	370-8857	same
SHAPE	423-4102	361-5301	Heilbronn	426-2888	same
			Herzo	465-3821	465-3650
ENGLAND			Hohenfels	466-2838	same
			Hontheim	485-7533	same
RAF Alconbury	Eriswell 3943	same	Illesheim	467-4813	same
RAF Bentwaters	"	same	Kaiserslautern	480-6535	same
RAF Croughton	Croughton 810947	same	Kalkar	454-8735	(C)02842-16119
RAF Fairford	"	same	Karlsruhe	376-7381	same
RAF Greenham C.	"	same	Kirchgöns	343-6306	343-7140
RAF Lakenheath	Eriswell 3943	same	Kirchheim-Bol.	383-7234	same
RAF Mildenhall	"	same	Kitzingen	355-8620	same
RAF Upper Heyfrd	Croughton 810947	same	Landau	376-7381	same
RAF Wethersfield	Eriswell 3943	same	Landstuhl	480-6535	same
High Wycombe AS	Croughton 810947	same	Mainz	334-7752	334-8200
			Mannheim	380-7462	same
GERMANY			Miesau	480-6535	same
			Möhringen	421-2614	same
Amberg	476-5801	same	Münster	348-4831	348-4801
Ansbach	468-8807	same	Munich	440-6888	(C)6229-6888
Aschaffenberg	323-8800	same	Neckarsulm	426-5739	same
Augsburg	434-6679	(C)448-6679	Nellingen	421-6810	same
Babenhausen	348-3621	348-3701	Nürnberg	460-7407	same
Bad Hersfeld	321-5806	321-5818	Neu-Ulm	427-6286	same
Bad Kissingen	354-2688	354-2727	Oberursel	325-2740	325-2733
Bad Kreuznach	490-6303	490-7105	Osterholz	342-6351	342-6525
Bad Tölz	441-4845	441-4800	Pforzheim	376-7381	same
Bamberg	469-8650	469-8727	Pirmasens	495-7133	same
Baumholder	485-7533	same	Prüm	455-3710	same
Berlin	332-6864	same	Ramstein AB	480-6535	same
Bindlach	462-3801	same	Regensburg	471-3820	471-3818
Bitburg AB	453-7556	same	Rheindahlen (RAF)	(C)02161-47-5391	(C)02161-55-7936
Böblingen	431-6205	431-6206	Rhein Main AB	330-7678	same
Bremerhaven	342-8515	same	Schwäbisch Gmnd	427-5810	same
Büdingen	322-8372	322-8708	Schwäbisch Hall	426-4593	426-4525
Butzbach	343-6306	343-7140	Schweinfurt	354-6201	354-6708
Crailsheim	420-3527	same	Spangdahlem AB	453-7556	same
Darmstadt	348-8410	348-3527	Stuttgart	420-6095	420-6600
Dexheim	383-7300	383-7234	Vaihingen	430-5406	430-5606
Erlangen	464-3708	464-3843	Vilseck	476-2601	475-2805
Ettlingen	376-7381	same	Vogelweh	480-6535	same
Frankfurt	320-5166	320-8352	Welschbillig	485-7533	same
Friedberg	343-6306	343-7140	Vertheim	355-5612	same
Fulda	321-8303	321-3511	Wierhof	383-7234	same
Garlstedt	342-6351	342-6525	Wiesbaden	337-5101	same
Geinsheim	376-7381	same	Wildflecken	326-3800	326-3478
Geinhausen	321-2724	321-2801	Worms	383-7234	same
Giebelstadt	352-7408	352-7441	Würzburg	350-6308	350-6421
Geissen	343-6306	343-7140	Zirndorf	460-7407	same
Göppingen	425-3450	425-3475	Zweibrücken AB	498-2847	same
Grafenwöhr	475-8302	same	Zweibrücken Army	494-6128	same
Hahn AB	450-7788	same			
Hanau	322-8372	322-8708	**NETHERLANDS**		
			Soesterberg AB	363-8145	363-8187

U.S. Forces Travel & Transfer Guide Europe — 415

Appendix J,

SOUTHERN EUROPEAN BROADCASTING SERVICE IN ITALY

FM/FM STEREO LOCATIONS IN ITALY AND TELEVISION BROADCAST CHANNELS

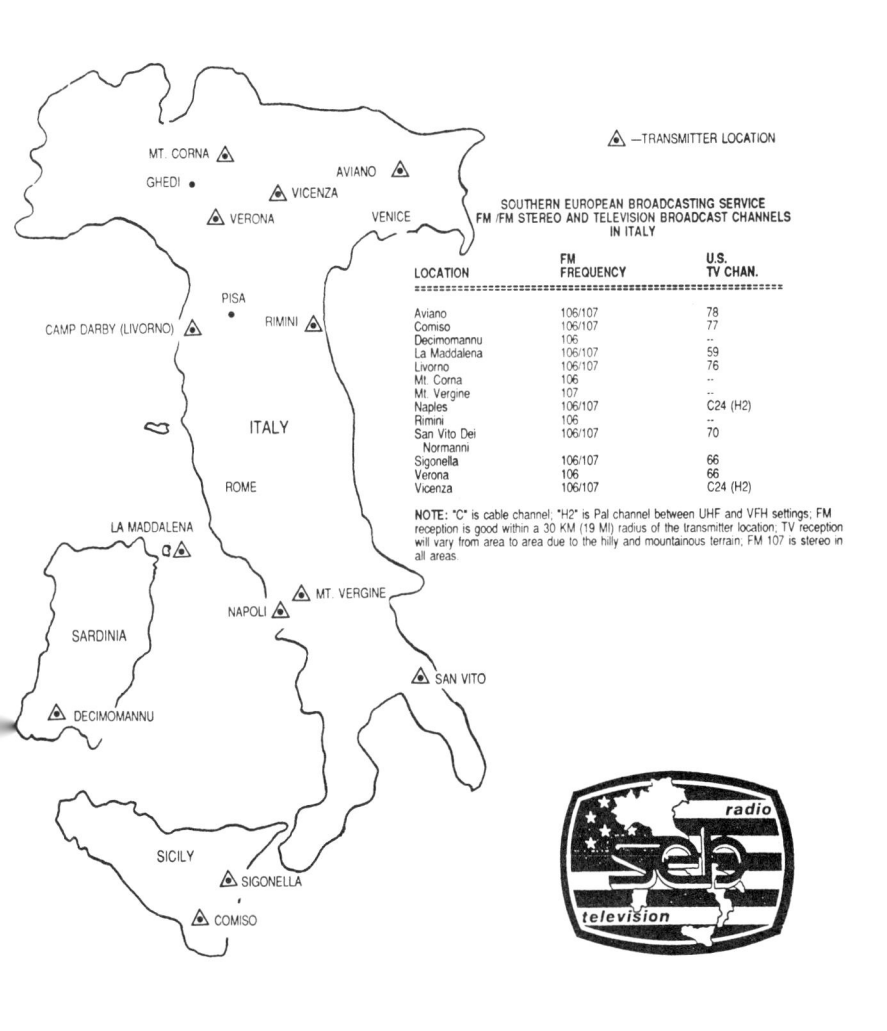

△ —TRANSMITTER LOCATION

SOUTHERN EUROPEAN BROADCASTING SERVICE
FM/FM STEREO AND TELEVISION BROADCAST CHANNELS
IN ITALY

LOCATION	FM FREQUENCY	U.S. TV CHAN.
Aviano	106/107	78
Comiso	106/107	77
Decimomannu	106	--
La Maddalena	106/107	59
Livorno	106/107	76
Mt. Corna	106	--
Mt. Vergine	107	--
Naples	106/107	C24 (H2)
Rimini	106	--
San Vito Dei Normanni	106/107	70
Sigonella	106/107	66
Verona	106	66
Vicenza	106/107	C24 (H2)

NOTE: "C" is cable channel; "H2" is Pal channel between UHF and VFH settings; FM reception is good within a 30 KM (19 MI) radius of the transmitter location; TV reception will vary from area to area due to the hilly and mountainous terrain; FM 107 is stereo in all areas.

APPENDIX K

CONVERSIONS OF WEIGHTS, MEASURES, TEMPERATURES AND CLOTHING SIZES

WEIGHT

For an approximate quick conversion of kilos into pounds, multiply kilos by 2.2.

FOR EXAMPLE:
5 kilos = 11.0 lbs
10 kilos = 22.0 lbs

For an approximate quick conversion of pounds into kilos, divide pounds by 2.2.

FOR EXAMPLE:
5 lbs = 2.27 kilos
10 lbs = 4.55 kilos

DISTANCE

For an approximate quick conversion of kilometers into miles, divide kilometers by 8, then multiply by 5.

FOR EXAMPLE:
10 km = 6.25 mi
50 km = 31.25 mi
100 km = 62.50 mi

For an approximate quick conversion of miles into kilometers, multiply miles by 1.6.

FOR EXAMPLE:
10 mi = 16 km
50 mi = 80 km
100 mi = 160 km

When you know the measure on the left, multiply by the number to find the measure on the right.

inches	2.5	centimeters
cent	.4	inches
feet	30	centimeters
meters	3.3	feet
yards	0.9	meters
meters	1.1	yards
miles	1.6	kilometers
km	0.6	miles

LITERS/GALLONS

3.785 liters = 1 gallon
5 liters = 1.32 gal
10 liters = 2.64 gal
25 liters = 6.60 gal
40 liters = 10.56 gal
50 liters = 13.21 gal

MASS AND VOLUME

When you know the quantity on the left, multiply by the number to convert to the quantity on the right.

ounces	28	grams
grams	0.035	ounces
pounds	0.45	kilograms
kilograms	2.2	pounds
fluid ozs	30	milliliters
milliliters	0.03	fluid ozs
cups	0.24	liters
liters	4	cups
pints	0.47	liters
liters	2.1	pints
quarts	0.095	liters
liters	1.06	quarts
gallons	3.8	liters
liters	0.26	gallons

TEMPERATURE

Formulas for approximate temperatures.

Celsius = 5/9 (F. - 32)
Ex. 5/9 = .56 C. = .56(70F.-32)
  C. = .56(38 F.)
  C. = 21 degrees

Fahrenheit = (9/5 x C.) + 32
Ex. 9/5 = 1.8 F. = (1.8 x 21C.) + 32
  F. = (37.80 C.) + 32
  F. = 70 degrees

Fahrenheit	Celsius
-20	-28
0	-18
10	-12

Appendix K, continued

Fahrenheit	Celsius	Fahrenheit	Celsius
15	-9	70	21
20	-7	80	26
32	0	90	32
40	5	100	38
50	10	120	49
60	16		

CLOTHING CONVERSIONS

Men—suits, overcoats, sweaters
Women—Dresses, coats, suits

U.S./U.K.	34	36	38	40	42	44	46
European	44	48	51	54	57	60	63
U.S./U.K	8	10	12	14	16	18	20
European	36	38	40	42	44	46	48

Men—shirts (neck size)
Women—Blouses, sweaters

U.S./U.K.	14.5	15	15.5	16	16.5	17	17.5
European	37	38	39	41	42	43	44
U.S.	10	12	14	16	18	20	22
U.K.	32	34	36	38	40	42	44
European	38	40	42	44	46	48	50

Men—shoes
Women—shoes

U.S.	7	8	9	10	11	12	13
U.K.	6	7	8	9	10	11	12
European	39.5	41	42	43	44.5	46	47
U.S.	5.5	6	6.5	7	7.5	8	8.5
U.K.	4	4.5	5	5.5	6	6.5	7
European	36	37	37	38	38	39	39

NOTE: Glove sizes are standard in the U.S., U.K., and Europe.

—NOTES—

APPENDIX L

ELECTRIC CURRENT AND SERVICE

Foreign Country	Service Plugs(1)	Adapters Available(2)	Type/Freq. of Current	# of Phases	Nominal Voltage
Austria	F	No	AC 50	1,3	220/380
Bahrain	D,G	Yes	AC 50	1,3	230/400
Belgium	C,E	No	AC 50	1,3	220/380
Cyprus	G	Yes	AC 50	1,3	240/415
Denmark	C	No	AC 50	1,3	220/380
Egypt	C	No	AC 50	1,3	220/380
France	C,E,F,G	Yes	AC 50	1,3	115/230
Finland	C,F	No	AC 50	1,3	220/380
Germany	F	No	AC 50	1,3	220/380
Greece	C,D,F	No	AC 50	1,3	220/380
Iceland	C,F	Yes	AC 50	1,3	220/380
Ireland	F,G	No	AC 50	1,3	220/380
Italy	C,F	Yes	AC 50	1,3	220/380
Luxembourg	C,F	Yes	AC 50	1,3	220/380
Netherlands	C,F	No	AC 50	1,3	220/380
Norway	C,F	No	AC 50	1,3	230
Portugal(Azores)	C,D	No	AC 50	1,3	220/380
Saudi Arabia	A,B,C,D,E,F,G,H,I,J	Yes	AC 50	1,3	127/220
Spain	C,E	Yes	AC 50	1,3	220/380
Sweden	C,F	No	AC 50	1,3	220/380
Switzerland	C,F	No	AC 50	1,3	220/380
Turkey	C,E,F	No	AC 50	1,3	220/380
United Kingdom	C,G	Yes	AC 50	1 3	240/480 240/405

1. See pictoral description.
2. Many hotels and lodging facilities have special circuits providing approximately 120 volts.
3. A "yes" indicates that the frequency is stable enough for electric clocks.

Appendix L, continued

CONNECTIONS IN SELECTED COUNTRIES

# of Wires	Frequency Stability(3)
2,4	Yes
2,3,4	Yes
2,3	Yes
2,4	Yes
2,3,4	Yes
2,3,4	No
2,4	Yes
2,4	Yes
2,4	Yes
2,4	Yes
2,3,4	Yes
2,4	Yes
2,4	Yes
3,4,5	Yes
2,4	Yes
2,3	Yes
2,3,4	Yes
2,4	No
2,3,4	Yes
2,3,4	Yes
2,3,4	Yes
2,3,4	Yes
2,3	Yes
4	

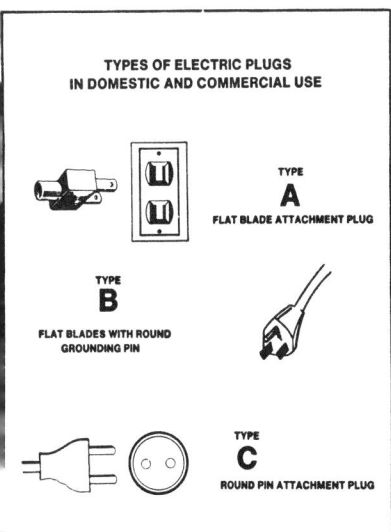

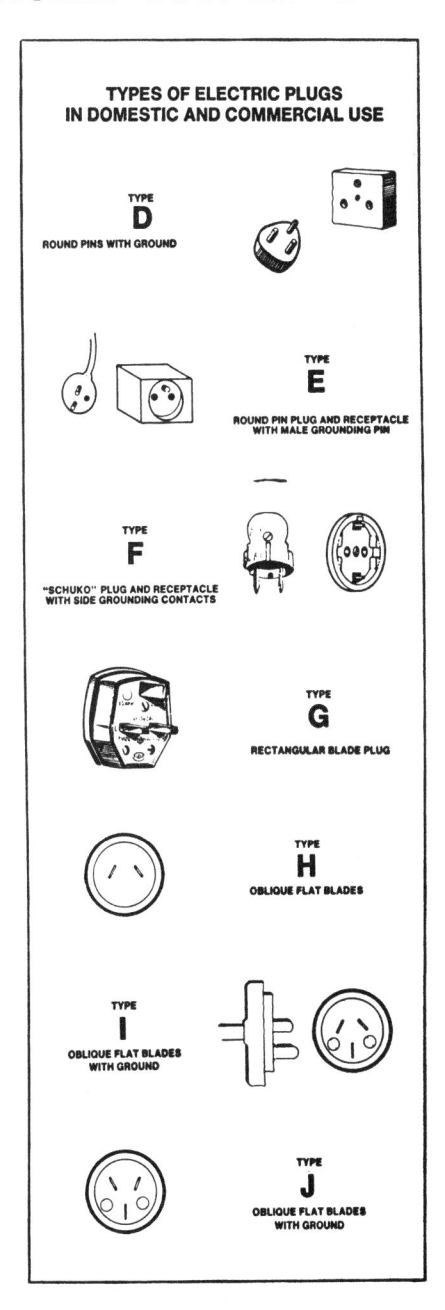

TYPES OF ELECTRIC PLUGS IN DOMESTIC AND COMMERCIAL USE

TYPE D — ROUND PINS WITH GROUND

TYPE E — ROUND PIN PLUG AND RECEPTACLE WITH MALE GROUNDING PIN

TYPE F — "SCHUKO" PLUG AND RECEPTACLE WITH SIDE GROUNDING CONTACTS

TYPE G — RECTANGULAR BLADE PLUG

TYPE H — OBLIQUE FLAT BLADES

TYPE I — OBLIQUE FLAT BLADES WITH GROUND

TYPE J — OBLIQUE FLAT BLADES WITH GROUND

TYPES OF ELECTRIC PLUGS IN DOMESTIC AND COMMERCIAL USE

TYPE A — FLAT BLADE ATTACHMENT PLUG

TYPE B — FLAT BLADES WITH ROUND GROUNDING PIN

TYPE C — ROUND PIN ATTACHMENT PLUG

APPENDIX M

STATE, COUNTRY AND GENERAL ABBREVIATIONS

State Abbreviations

AK-Alaska
AL-Alabama
AR-Arkansas
AZ-Arizona
CA-California
CO-Colorado
CT-Connecticut
DC-District of Columbia
DE-Delaware
FL-Florida
GA-Georgia
HI-Hawaii
IA-Iowa
ID-Idaho
IL-Illinois
IN-Indiana
KS-Kansas

KY-Kentucky
LA-Louisiana
MA-Massachusetts
MD-Maryland
ME-Maine
MI-Michigan
MN-Minnesota
MO-Missouri
MS-Mississippi
MT-Montana
NE-Nebraska
NC-North Carolina
ND-North Dakota
NH-New Hampshire
NJ-New Jersey
NM-New Mexico
NV-Nevada

NY-New York
OH-Ohio
OK-Oklahoma
OR-Oregon
PA-Pennsylvania
RI-Rhode Island
SC-South Carolina
SD-South Dakota
TN-Tennessee
TX-Texas
UT-Utah
VA-Virginia
VT-Vermont
WA-Washington
WI-Wisconsin
WV-West Virginia
WY-Wyoming

Country Abbreviations

AG-Argentina
AN-Antigua
AS-Ascension Island
AU-Australia
BA-Bahrain
BB-Barbados
BD-Barbuda
BE-Belgium
BH-Bahamas
BM-Bermuda
BO-Bolivia
BR-Brazil
BZ-Belize
CH-Chad
CH-Chili
CL-Columbia
CN-Canada
CR-Crete*
CS-Costa Rica
CU-Cuba
CY-Cyprus
DN-Denmark
DR-Dominican Republic
EC-Ecuador
EG-Arab Republic of Egypt
ES-El Salvador

GE-West Germany
GL-Greenland*
GR-Greece
GT-Guatemala
GU-Guam**
HA-Haiti
HO-Honduras
HK-Hong Kong
IC-Iceland
IE-Indonesia
IO-Indian Ocean
IR-Ireland
IS-Israel
IT-Italy
JA-Japan
JM-Jamaica
JO-Johnston**
JR-Jordan
KE-Kenya
LI-Liberia
MR-Mariana**
MW-Midway Island
NI-Nicaragua
NO-Norway
NT-Netherlands
NZ-New Zealand

OM-Oman
PE-Peru
PG-Paraguay
PN-Republic of Panama
PO-Portugal (Açores)
PR-Puerto Rico**
RK-Republic of Korea
RP-Philippines
SA-Saudi Arabia
SF-South Africa
SG-Singapore
SM-Somalia
SP-Spain
SU-Sudan
TH-Thailand
TT-US Trust Territories
TU-Turkey
UG-Uruguay
UK-United Kingdom
US-United States
VE-Venezuela
VI-Virgin Islands**
WC-West Caroline Is.
WK-Wake Island
ZA-Zaire

* = Not a separate country. ** = U.S. Territory or Protectorate.

Appendix M, continued

General Abbreviations

This appendix contains abbreviations used throughout this book. Commonly understood abbreviations, i.e. M-F for Monday through Friday, have not been included.

A
AAF-Army Airfield
AAFES-Army/Air Force Exchange System
AB-Air Base
ACS-Army Community Services
AD-Active Duty
AF-Air Force
AFB-Air Force Base
Afld-Airfield
AFN-American Forces Network
AFRC-Armed Forces Recreation Center
AFS-Air Force Station
AMC-Army Medical Center
Amer-American
APO-Army Post Office
Appoint-Appointment
Appts-Appointments
Arpt-Airport
AS-Air Station
ATVN-Automatic Voice Network (Autovon)

B
BEQ-Bachelor Enlisted Quarters
Bldg-Building
Bltg-Billeting
BOQ-Bachelor Officers' Quarters

C
Caf-Cafeteria
CHAMPUS-Civilian Health and Medical Program of the Uniformed Services
Civ-Civilian
Cmdr-Commander
Comm-Commercial
Comm-Communication
Comm-Community
Comm Drug/Alc Ctr-Community Drug and Alcohol Center
Comm Rel Advisor-Community Relations Advisor

D
Dep-Dependent
Dev Ctr-Development Center
Dly-Daily
DV/VIP-Distinguished Visitor/Very Important Person

E
E-East
Emerg-Emergency
Equip-Equipment
EST-European Telephone System
Exch-Exchange
Ext-Extension

F
Fac-Facility
Fam Svcs-Family Services
Fld-Field
FPO-Fleet Post Office

G
GAFB-German Air Force Base
Gen'l-General
Gov-Government

H
HE-Hallwag Road Atlas
Hol-Holiday
Hq (HQ)-Headquarters

I
IAP-International Airport
Insta-Installation
Intl-International
ITT-Information, Tour and Travel

J
JAG-Judge Advocate General

K
K-Kindergarten

L
Loc-Location

M
MAC-Military Airlift Command
MARS-Military Affiliated Radio Station
Mi-Miles
Mil-Military

N
N-North
N/A-Not Available (Unknown)
NAF-Naval Air Facility
NAS-Naval Air Station
Nav-Navy (Naval)

Appendix M, continued

N (continued)
NB-Naval Base
NCO-Noncommissioned Officer
NMC-Nearest Major City
No-Number
Ntwk-Network
NSA-Naval Support Activity

O
O'Club-Officers' Club
Oper-Operator
Ops-Operations

P
P-Page
Pax-Passengers
PCS-Permanent Change of Station
POC-Proof of Citizenship
POV-Privately Owned Vehicle

Q
Qtrs-Quarters

R
RAF-Royal Air Force
Rec-Recreation
Rest-Restaurant
Ret-Retired
RV-Recreational Vehicle

S
S-South
S&S-Stars and Stripes
SATO-OS-Scheduled Airlines Traffic Office-Overseas
SDO-Staff Duty Officer
Self-Svc-Self Service
Spon'd-Sponsored
Spt-Support
Svc-Service
Svc Stn-Service Station
Svcs-Services

T
TAD-Temporary Attached Duty
TAQ-Temporary Airmen's Quarters
TDY-Temporary Duty
Term-Terminal
TLF-Temporary Living Facility
TLQ-Temporary Living Quarters
TML-Temporary Military Lodging
TUAB-Turkish Air Base
TUAF-Turkish Air Force

U
US-United States
USA-United States Army

U (continued)
USAF-United States Air Force
USMC-United States Marine Corps
USN-United States Navy
USO-United Services Organization

V
VAQ-Visiting Airmen's Quarters
VOQ-Visiting Officers' Quarters

W
W-West

X/Y/Z
None

APPENDIX N

ARTICLES FROM MILITARY LIVING'S *R&R SPACE-A REPORT*

Paris and Rome are two of Europe's most visited cities. Though neither city has U.S. military facilities, both have USOs. The abridged articles below contain information that should prove useful to active duty and retired personnel in Paris and Rome.

A Letter From Paris
by Phil Gaffin
(Abridged from Report #94, May/June 1987)

...One very helpful source is the **Paris USO, located just off the famous Champs-Élysées**, and open every day of the year from 10 a.m. to 6 p.m. They can be contacted by writing: **Paris USO, c/o General Delivery, APO New York 09777**, for brochures, maps, and even hotel reservations. Paris is known for filling its hotels during the prime spring and summer months, so write three months before if possible. **The French Tourist Office, 610 Fifth Avenue, New York, New York 10022 (212-757-1125)**, can also provide an array of materials to help you plan your trip.

...My first stop on visiting Paris would be the **USO, located at 49 rue Pierre Charron (telephone 4723-7180)**, close to the Franklin Roosevelt Subway (called Metro in Paris) stop. It's one block off the Champs-Élysées on the ground floor of the Pershing Hall Building. The Paris USO entrance is next to the blue awning with a small sign in the window. Once you're there, you'll be helped by the bilingual USO staff.

...If you've called ahead or written, your hotel reservations will have been made, but if you didn't, the staff will check their various contacts for space that fits your needs. Hotels in Paris aren't cheap, but some are smaller, family run establishments with rates that match the needs of the strapped traveller. But the USO can also book the more expensive hotels if you're interested. I usually stay near the Arc de Triomphe on an open air market street. Most hotel rates include a small breakfast (petit dejeuner) of croissants and coffee. Depending on price range and needs, your hotel will cost $20 to $45 per person in a medium range. Rather than carry all your money and traveller's checks, put the extra ones in the hotel safe.

...The USO can also book a wide variety of city and regional tours. While USO does not sponsor its own tours because of French regulations, it does work closely with France Tourisme to sell discount tickets for tours operated by Paris Vision Company. The tours typically are three hours and are perfect for an orientation to the city...A half day city tour costs $23.00 per person, and is done in English.

Appendix N, continued

Bella Roma!
by Phil Gaffin
(Abridged from Report #95, July/August 1987)

...The Rome USO...has been helping U.S. military and their families since 1944. Located at **2 Via della Conciliazione**, the USO is in a perfect location. As you stand at its front door, the Vatican is to the right and the Castel Sant Angelo to the left. It's open from 9:00 am to 6:00 pm Monday through Saturday...The USO can assist you with hotel reservations at a discount. It's important to write ahead though, as much as two and a half months if you plan to visit Rome in the busy summer or Christmas seasons. Once you've got a place to rest your weary head, the USO will make sure you're truly exhausted when you finally get to bed. They offer a range of tours that will take you to the Sistine Chapel, the Trevi Fountain, the Catacombs, the Pantheon and more. There are four basic USO tours offered, and I would take them all. It's the cheapest way and best way to see Rome.

...Anyone visiting Rome wants to attend a Papal audience or mass even if they are not Catholic. I've been to both, and it was enthralling. The USO can help there, too. It can provide tickets for masses, especially during the very busy Christmas and Easter masses. I once attended Christmas Day mass, and was amazed. After passing by rows of security guards, there I was in St. Peters. I picked a seat near a center aisle, and shortly thereafter there he was...the Pope, coming down that aisle. He shook hands with many, waved at even more. People hopped up on chairs to see, flash bulbs lit the room. But once he reached the altar, a totally different tone took over. The crowd quieted and with thousands in the basilica that Christmas Day, I could still hear every word the Pope said. After the mass, the crowd inside joined the thousands more outside for the Papal blessing. As I exited the cathedral, thousands of people were there, stretching to all corners of the Piazza. Banners waved in the wind. I couldn't believe it was all happening and that I was there. And you won't either.

So plan ahead to enjoy Roma at its most "bella." To write the USO ahead of time, just get a letter off to: **USO Rome, APO New York 09794. A self-addressed stamped envelope with your APO or U.S. address is appreciated. The phone number is 6564.232 or 66564.272.** Another helpful address is the **Italian Tourist Bureau, 630 Fifth Avenue, New York, N.Y. 10111, telephone 212-245-4822.** They'll send you helpful information on Rome and all of Italy.

Subscribe to Military Living's **R&R Space-A Report** travel newsletter and be "in the know" before most everyone else is! Please see the coupons on pages 425, 429 and 431.

CENTRAL ORDER COUPON
Military Living Publications
P.O. Box 2347, Falls Church, VA 22042-0347, Telephone: (703) 237-0203

Publications	Qty.	Publications	Qty.
Military Space-A Air Opportunities Around the World*. *The one everyone is talking about!* $15.45.		Assignment Washington: A Guide to Washington Area Military Installations. *A "must" book for every Capital area military family!* $8.45.	
Temporary Military Lodging Around the World*. *Our all-time best seller!* $11.45.		U.S. Forces Travel & Transfer Guide Europe & Near East Areas*. *The complete military guide to Europe!* $16.45.	
Military RV, Camping & Rec Areas Around the World*. *You can have fun with this book!* $9.45.		U.S. Military Museums, Historic Sites & Exhibits*. *A great, practical book. Wonderful gift!* $26.45 (hardcover).	
U.S. Forces Travel & Transfer Guide U.S.A. & Caribbean Areas*. *This book should be in every car!* $10.45.		U.S. Military Museums, Historic Sites & Exhibits*. *The only all-military museum book!* $16.45.	
Military Living's R&R Space-A Report. *The world-wide travel newsletter.* 5 yrs.—$42.00 2 yrs.—$20.00 3 yrs.—$27.00 1 yr.—$12.00 (6 issues)		Military Living. *Local Washington area magazine.* 3 yrs.—$16.00 1 yr.—$7.00 2 yrs.—$12.00 (12 issues)	

* If you are an R&R Space-A Report Subscriber, you may deduct $1.00 per book. (No discount on the R&R Report itself.)

Total: $_____

VA addressees add 4.5 % sales tax: $_____
(Books only)

For 1st Class Mail, add $1.00 per book.
Mail Order Price are for the U.S., APO & FPO addresses. Please consult Publisher for International Mail Price. Sorry, no billing. GREAT FUND RAISERS! Please write for wholesale rates.

Total Amount Enclosed: $_____

We're as close as your telephone...by using our Telephone Ordering Service. We honor American Express, Mastercard and VISA. Call us at (703) 237-0203 or FAX—(703) 237-2233 and order today!. Sorry, no collect calls. Or...fill out the the mail-order coupon below.

Name: _____

Street: _____

City/State/ZIP: _____

Phone: (____) _____

Signature: _____

Rank: _____ or Rank of Sponsor: _____

Branch of Service: _____

Active Duty: ___   Retired: ___   Widower: ___   100% Disabled Veteran: ___   Guard: ___

Reservist: ___   Other: ___

Card No.: _____   Card Expiration Date: _____
Mail check/money order to: **Military Living Publications, PO Box 2347, Falls Church, VA 22042-0347.**

426 — U.S. Forces Travel & Transfer Guide Europe

MILITARY Living's
Family of Publications

Coming summer 1989. *U.S. Military Museums, Historic Sites & Exhibits!*

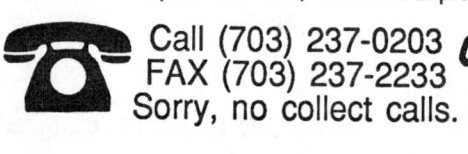

Phone orders are accepted with Visa, American Express and Mastercard.

Call (703) 237-0203
FAX (703) 237-2233
Sorry, no collect calls.

U.S. Forces Travel & Transfer Guide Europe — 427

TRANSFERRING TO WASHINGTON, D.C. AREA?

MOVING TO WASHINGTON COUPON

"One Shot" Help

MOVING TO WASHINGTON? Make one call or send this coupon & help will be on its way. As a military wife, one of my chief goals is to boost military family morale... so mail this coupon today & help will be on its way.
Hope to hear from you soon.

Ann Crawford, Publisher
Military Living Magazine

TO: Mrs Ann Crawford, Publisher, Military Living
P.O. Box 2347, Falls Church, VA 22042-0347
Phone: (703) 237-0203, FAX (703) 237-2233

Our Family Is:
- [ ] Army
- [ ] Navy
- [ ] Air Force
- [ ] Marine
- [ ] Coast Guard
- [ ] P.H.S.
- [ ] NOAA
- [ ] Other
- [ ] Active
- [ ] Retired
- [ ] 100% DAV

Military member's name/rank: _____
Spouses Name: _____
Address: _____
City/State/Zip: _____
Tel: _____
Total number in family: _____
Number of children: _____

Area assigned to: _____
We expect to arrive: _____

We would like info, if possible, on the following:
- [ ] House [ ] Apt. [ ] Condo
- [ ] Renting [ ] Buying
- [ ] Car
- [ ] Furniture
- [ ] Major Appliances
- [ ] Short Term Housing
- [ ] Military Lodging
- [ ] Hotel/Motel [ ] B & B
- [ ] Short Term Apt.

Type of job: _____

- [ ] Banking/Checking Accounts
- [ ] Employment Opportunities for spouse
- [ ] Real Estate Career Opportunities
- [ ] Legal Services/Settlement Atty.
- [ ] College Opportunities
- [ ] Investment Opportunities
- [ ] Travel in nearby areas
- [ ] Back Issues of **Military Living**
- [ ] Window Treatments
- [ ] Dentist [ ] Doctor

All New! Available Now!

Military Living's

U.S. Forces Travel & Transfer Guide U.S.A. and Caribbean Areas

by

Roy and Ann Crawford

The only travel guide you will need to visit U.S. Military Installations in CONUS, OCONUS and nearby foreign countries.

"Travel on less per day...the military way."

You can save thousands of dollars on your travels with this book! Look for it at military exchanges around the world. If not available, you may order by mail at P. O. Box 2347, Falls Church, Virginia 22042-0347, or by phone (703) 237-0203 with VISA/MC/American Express. See the central order coupons at the back of this book.

Military Living Publications
P. O. Box 2347
Falls Church, Virginia 22042-0347
(703) 237-0203
FAX (703) 237-2233

CENTRAL ORDER COUPON
Military Living Publications
P.O. Box 2347, Falls Church, VA 22042-0347, Telephone: (703) 237-0203

Publications	Qty.	Publications	Qty.
Military Space-A Air Opportunities Around the World*. *The one everyone is talking about!* **$15.45.**		Assignment Washington: A Guide to Washington Area Military Installations. *A "must" book for every Capital area military family!* **$8.45.**	
Temporary Military Lodging Around the World*. *Our all-time best seller!* **$11.45.**		U.S. Forces Travel & Transfer Guide Europe & Near East Areas*. *The complete military guide to Europe!* **$16.45.**	
Military RV, Camping & Rec Areas Around the World*. *You can have fun with this book!* **$9.45.**		U.S. Military Museums, Historic Sites & Exhibits*. *A great, practical book. Wonderful gift!* **$26.45 (hardcover).**	
U.S. Forces Travel & Transfer Guide U.S.A. & Caribbean Areas*. *This book should be in every car!* **$10.45.**		U.S. Military Museums, Historic Sites & Exhibits*. *The only all-military museum book!* **$16.45.**	
Military Living's R&R Space-A Report. *The world-wide travel newsletter.* 5 yrs.—$42.00 2 yrs.—$20.00 3 yrs.—$27.00 1 yr. —$12.00 (6 issues)		Military Living. *Local Washington area magazine.* 3 yrs.—$16.00 1 yr.—$7.00 2 yrs.—$12.00 (12 issues)	

* If you are an R&R Space-A Report Subscriber, you may deduct $1.00   Total: $_____
per book. (No discount on the R&R Report itself.)
 VA addressees add 4.5 % sales tax: $_____
 (Books only)

For 1st Class Mail, add $1.00 per book.
Mail Order Price are for the U.S., APO & FPO addresses. Please consult Publisher for International Mail Price. Sorry, no billing. GREAT FUND RAISERS! Please write for wholesale rates.   Total Amount Enclosed: $_____

We're as close as your telephone...by using our Telephone Ordering Service. We honor American Express, Mastercard and VISA. Call us at **(703) 237-0203 or FAX—(703) 237-2233** and order today!. Sorry, no collect calls. Or...fill out the the mail-order coupon below.

Name: _____

Street: _____

City/State/ZIP: _____

Phone: (____) _____

Signature: _____

Rank: _____ or Rank of Sponsor: _____

Branch of Service: _____

Active Duty: ____ Retired: ____ Widower: ____ 100% Disabled Veteran: ____ Guard: ____

Reservist: ____ Other: ____

Card No.: _____ Card Expiration Date: _____
Mail check/money order to: **Military Living Publications, PO Box 2347, Falls Church VA 22042-0347.**

Coming Late Spring 1989

Military Living's

U.S. Military Museums Historic Sites & Exhibits

by

Bryce D. Thompson

A guide to Army, Navy, Air Force, Marine Corps and Coast Guard museums in the U.S. and overseas. Also includes other military museums, relevant aviation and maritime museums, sites associated with history of all military powers in the U.S. and its territories and historic warships and submarines. Hundreds of places for the family to explore our nation's military history.

Look for this book at your U.S. military exchanges and Stars & Stripes newsstands overseas. If not available, you may order by mail at P. O. Box 2347, Falls Church, Virginia 22042-0347, or by phone (703) 237-0203 with VISA/MC/American Express. See the central order coupons at the back of this book.

Military Living Publications
P. O. Box 2347
Falls Church, Virginia 22042-0347
(703) 237-0203
FAX (703) 237-2233

CENTRAL ORDER COUPON
Military Living Publications
P.O. Box 2347, Falls Church, VA 22042-0347, Telephone: (703) 237-0203

Publications	Qty.	Publications	Qty.
Military Space-A Air Opportunities Around the World*. *The one everyone is talking about!* **$15.45.**		Assignment Washington: A Guide to Washington Area Military Installations. *A "must" book for every Capital area military family!* **$8.45.**	
Temporary Military Lodging Around the World*. *Our all-time best seller!* **$11.45.**		U.S. Forces Travel & Transfer Guide Europe & Near East Areas*. *The complete military guide to Europe!* **$16.45.**	
Military RV, Camping & Rec Areas Around the World*. *You can have fun with this book!* **$9.45.**		U.S. Military Museums, Historic Sites & Exhibits*. *A great, practical book. Wonderful gift!* **$26.45 (hardcover).**	
U.S. Forces Travel & Transfer Guide U.S.A. & Caribbean Areas*. *This book should be in every car!* **$10.45.**		U.S. Military Museums, Historic Sites & Exhibits*. *The only all-military museum book!* **$16.45.**	
Military Living's R&R Space-A Report. *The world-wide travel newsletter.* 5 yrs.—$42.00 2 yrs.—$20.00 3 yrs.—$27.00 1 yr. —$12.00 (6 issues)		Military Living. *Local Washington area magazine.* 3 yrs.—$16.00 1 yr.—$7.00 2 yrs.—$12.00 (12 issues)	

* If you are an R&R Space-A Report Subscriber, you may deduct $1.00 per book. (No discount on the R&R Report itself.)

Total: $_____

VA addressees add 4.5 % sales tax: $_____
(Books only)

For 1st Class Mail, add $1.00 per book.
Mail Order Price are for the U.S., APO & FPO addresses. Please consult Publisher for International Mail Price. Sorry, no billing. GREAT FUND RAISERS! Please write for wholesale rates.

Total Amount Enclosed: $_____

We're as close as your telephone...by using our Telephone Ordering Service. We honor American Express, Mastercard and VISA. Call us at **(703) 237-0203 or FAX—(703) 237-2233** and order today!. Sorry, no collect calls. Or...fill out the the mail-order coupon below.

Name: _____

Street: _____

City/State/ZIP: _____

Phone: (___)_____

Signature: _____

Rank: _____ or Rank of Sponsor: _____

Branch of Service: _____

Active Duty: ___   Retired: ___   Widower: ___   100% Disabled Veteran: ___   Guard: ___

Reservist: ___   Other: ___

Card No.: _____   Card Expiration Date: _____
Mail check/money order to: **Military Living Publications, PO Box 2347, Falls Church, VA 22042-0347.**

Space-A Travel Newsletter

(Space-A Air ... Space-A RV & Camping ... Space-A Temporary Military Lodging)

FREE COPIES FOR PURCHASERS of THIS BOOK

"TRAVEL ON LESS PER DAY.... THE MILITARY WAY"

We'ed like to acquaint you with our travel newsletter, Military Living's R&R Space-A Report. It gives late breaking info on Space-A air travel, new info on military camping and rec areas, and temporary military lodging plus informative and helpful reader trip reports.

We'll send you two back issues (a $4.00 value) if you will send $1.00 to cover the cost of postage and handling.

To get your copies, send your name and address and $1.00 to:

Military Living R&R (Dept. SA)
Box 2347
Falls Church, Virginia 22042-0347

Note: We regret that this must be a one-time offer and may not be used to extend a current R&R Space-A Report subscription or combined with any other discount.

U.S. Forces Travel & Transfer Guide Europe — 433

MILITARY Living's™

Family of Publications

U.S. Forces Travel and Transfer Guide Europe and Near East Areas

Military RV, Camping & Rec Areas Around the World

U.S. Forces Travel and Transfer Guide U.S.A and Caribbean Areas
- This book should be in every military family's car!
- Bigger and better than ever!
- NEW– Civilian travel & transfer directory

Military Space-A Air Opportunities Around the World

A Guide to Washington Area Military Installations

Temporary Military Lodging Around the World
Travel on Less per Day...
The Military Way
- Officer or Enlisted Active or Retired You can save $$$ with this book
- Completely Revised – Semi-chart format
- New Civilian Hotel/Motel Directory

Military Living R&R — Rest Recreation Travel — Serving Military Families Worldwide
P.O. Box 2347
Falls Church VA 22042

Coming summer 1989. *U.S. Military Museums, Historic Sites & Exhibits!*

Phone orders are accepted with Visa, American Express and Mastercard.

Call (703) 237-0203
FAX (703) 237-2233
Sorry, no collect calls.

US Forces Travel & Transfer Guide Europe

DID WE MISS ANYTHING?

US Forces Travel Guide Europe was first published in 1971 and was a runaway best seller. At that time, Ann Crawford, the Founder of Military Living, lived in Europe and produced the first book of its kind for military and their families. This is the first all new Military Living edition since that time. To reflect serving not only leave travelers but also those transferring on PCS, the title has been changed to: **US Forces Travel And Transfer Guide Europe and Near East Areas.**

This all new edition is a result of over two year's work with many changes in format and additions of helpful material. In order to make this book even better, we ask for **your** assistance. By helping us on a volunteer basis, you join a network of military and their families helping each other through this central clearing house of information. Your thanks will come not only from us, but from the thousands of your fellow military and their families who will benefit. By your sharing information with others, they, too, will be encouraged to share with you!

Please inform us if any military community has been omitted. Also, as this book has literally hundreds of thousands of data points, changes will be occurring. Please notify us if you are aware of any changes which affect the accuracy of this book. If you know of a new facility or camping area opening, we'd also appreciate hearing about it.

We are also looking for "handouts," those handy "everything you need to know about......," sheets of info or pamphlets which are often available at local military installations. These are usually very accurate and help us complete the listing for a particular installation we send to local community officials for an accuracy check before publishing it in our books.

On a more permanent arrangement, Military Living is also seeking correspondents and/or "stringers" in Europe to help us keep up-to-date with changing situations in their home locale. While this is primarily a volunteer function, we pay small honorariums for this service for our regular staff correspondents or stringers. If you are interested in becoming a part of our staff network which helps military and their families, please contact us. Note: House spouses, teenagers and seniors are welcome, too!! If you get around in your community, you can help us help others. Thank you!

FOR MORE INFO, WRITE:

Military Living Publications
PO Box 2347
Falls Church, VA 22042-0347
Phone: (703) 237-0203   FAX (703) 237-2233